Red Fortress

CATHERINE MERRIDALE

Red Fortress

The Secret Heart of Russia's History

ALLEN LANE
an imprint of
PENGUIN BOOKS

ALLEN LANE

Published by the Penguin Group
Penguin Books Ltd, 80 Strand, London WC2R ORL, England
Penguin Group (USA) Inc., 375 Hudson Street, New York, New York 10014, USA
Penguin Group (Canada), 90 Eglinton Avenue East, Suite 700, Toronto, Ontario, Canada M4P 2Y3
(a division of Pearson Penguin Canada Inc.)
Penguin Ireland, 25 St Stephen's Green, Dublin 2, Ireland (a division of Penguin Books Ltd)
Penguin Group (Australia), 707 Collins Street, Melbourne, Victoria 3008, Australia
(a division of Pearson Australia Group Pty Ltd)
Penguin Books India Pvt Ltd, 11 Community Centre, Panchsheel Park, New Delhi – 110 017, India
Penguin Group (NZ), 67 Apollo Drive, Rosedale, Auckland 0632, New Zealand
(a division of Pearson New Zealand Ltd)
Penguin Books (South Africa) (Pty) Ltd, Block D, Rosebank Office Park,
181 Jan Smuts Avenue, Parktown North, Gauteng 2193, South Africa

Penguin Books Ltd, Registered Offices: 80 Strand, London WC2R ORL, England

www.penguin.com

First published 2013
001

Set in 10.2/13.87pt Sabon LT Std
Typeset by Jouve (UK), Milton Keynes
Printed in Great Britain by Clays Ltd, St Ives plc

ISBN: 978-1-846-14037-2

947.
31

www.greenpenguin.co.uk

To Frank

Contents

List of Illustrations

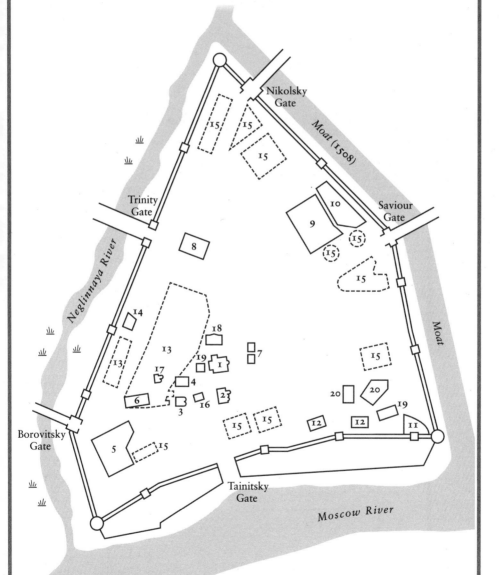

1 Dormition Cathedral
2 Archangel Cathedral
3 Annunciation Cathedral
4 Faceted Palace
5 Grand Prince's residence
6 Residence of Sofiya Palaeologa
7 Churches (soon to be completed with bell tower of Ivan the Great)
8 Moscow residence of the Trinity-St Sergius Monastery
9 Chudov Monastery
10 Ascension Women's Monastery
11 Prison (on the former Beklemishev estate)
12 Residences for the use of religious houses outside Moscow
13 Palace buildings, including living quarters and service buildings
14 Residence for 'Anton Fryazin'
15 Boyars' residences
16 Treasury (with connection to Annunciation Cathedral)
17 Cathedral of the Saviour in the Forest
18 Metropolitan's residence
19 Cemeteries
20 Residences for brothers of Ivan III

1. The Kremlin in the Reign of Vasily III, 1505–33

White S

K A R E L I A

Lake O

Vyborg•

Revel
•

Narva
•

Ivangorod
•

Neva

Lake Ladoga

Beloozero •

L I V O N I A

Dorpat (Yurev)
•

Novgorod
•

Volo

Pskov
•

Lake Ilmen

Riga
•

Baltic Sea

Yarosl

Uglich •

Velikie Luki
•

Toropets
•

Tver
•

Rostov

W. Dvina

Trinity-St Sergius Monastery •

Su

Polotsk•

Moscow *Klyaz*

• Vlad

Smolensk
•

Viazma•

Mozhaisk
•

Serpukhov •

Kolo

Dnieper

Ryaz

L I T H U A N I A

Briansk•

P O L A N D

Novgorod-
• Seversk

Chernigov •

Putivl
•

Kiev •

Dniester

Dnieper

C R I M E A N

K H A N A T E

A
(T

Sea of Azov

CIRCASSIA

Danube

Sudak •
• Caffa

Black Sea

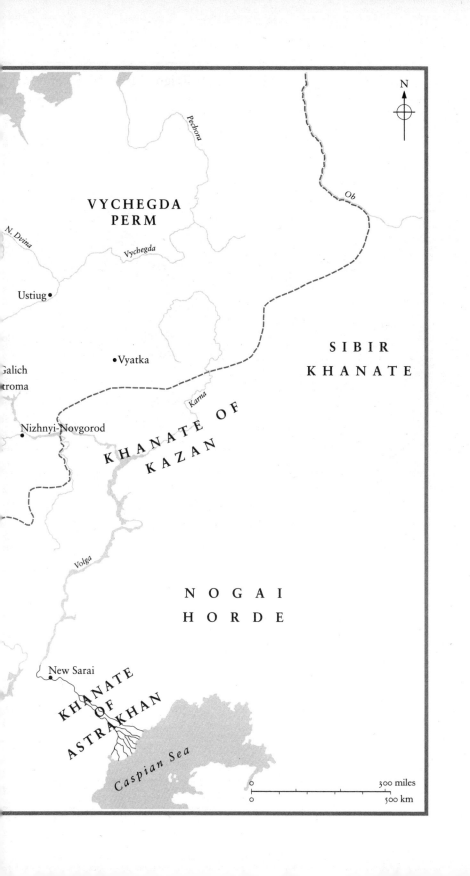

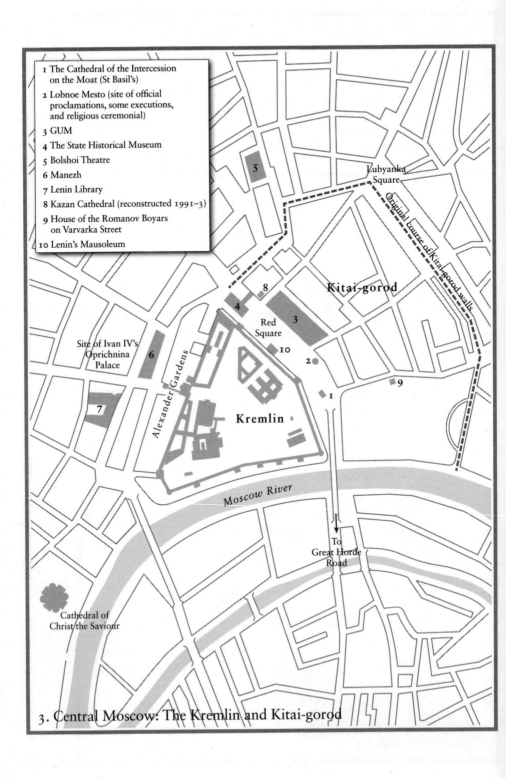

1 The Cathedral of the Intercession on the Moat (St Basil's)

2 Lobnoe Mesto (site of official proclamations, some executions, and religious ceremonial)

3 GUM

4 The State Historical Museum

5 Bolshoi Theatre

6 Manezh

7 Lenin Library

8 Kazan Cathedral (reconstructed 1991–3)

9 House of the Romanov Boyars on Varvarka Street

10 Lenin's Mausoleum

Lubyanka Square

Original course of Kitai-gorod walls

Kitai-gorod

8

4

Red Square

3

Site of Ivan IV's Oprichnina Palace

6

Alexander Gardens

10

2

7

1

9

Kremlin

Moscow River

To Great Horde Road

Cathedral of Christ the Saviour

3. Central Moscow: The Kremlin and Kitai-gorod

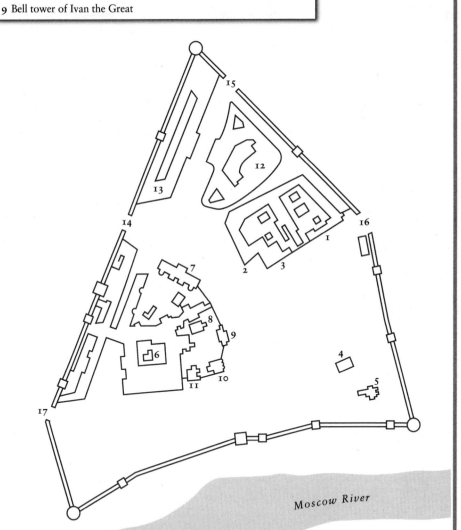

1 Ascension Women's Monastery
2 Chudov Monastery
3 Small Nicholas Palace
4 Monument to Alexander II
5 Church of Constantine and Elena
6 Cathedral of the Saviour in the Forest
7 Egotov's Armoury Chamber
8 Dormition Cathedral
9 Bell tower of Ivan the Great
10 Archangel Cathedral
11 Annunciation Cathedral
12 Senate
13 Arsenal
14 Trinity Gate
15 Nikolsky Gate
16 Saviour Gate
17 Borovitsky gate

Moscow River

4. Plan of the Kremlin in 1903 including buildings destined for demolition after 1917

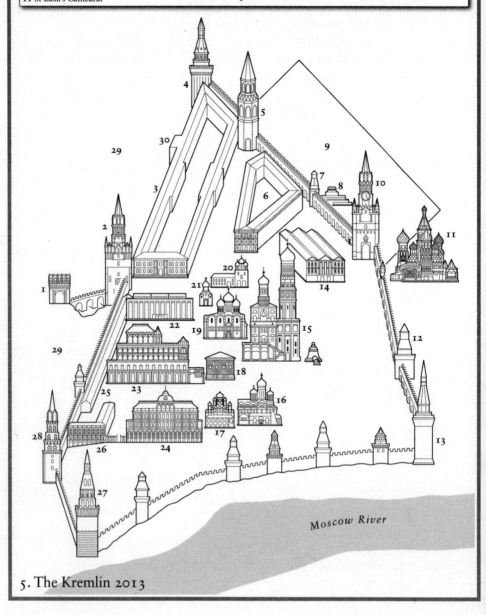

1 Kutafia Tower and Gatehouse
2 Trinity Tower and Gatehouse
3 Arsenal
4 Corner Arsenal Tower
5 Nikolsky Tower and Gatehouse
6 Senate (President's Building)
7 Senate Tower
8 Lenin's Mausoleum
9 Red Square
10 Saviour Tower and Gatehouse
11 St Basil's Cathedral
12 Constantine and Elena Tower
13 Beklemishev Tower
14 Administrative Block 14
15 Bell tower of Ivan the Great
16 Archangel Cathedral
17 Annunciation Cathedral
18 Faceted Palace
19 Dormition Cathedral
20 Patriarch's Palace and Cathedral
   of the Twelve Apostles
21 Church of the Deposition of the Robe
22 Palace of Congresses
23 Terem Palace and Red Stair
24 Grand Kremlin Palace
25 Remains of 'Communist Street'
   and Potenshnyi Palace
26 Armoury Chamber Museum
27 Vodovzvodnaya Tower
28 Borovitsky Tower and Gatehouse
29 Alexander Gardens
30 Tomb of the Unknown Soldier
   and Eternal Flame

Moscow River

5. The Kremlin 2013

A Note on the Text

No one has yet found a universally accepted system for rendering Russia's Cyrillic into clear Latin script. Academics tend to use precise but rather ugly systems, while everyone else gets by with an easier but more chaotic approach. In my text, I have used the simplest and most familiar-looking version I could find (which is why I have ended up with Trotsky rather than Trotskii or Trockij), but the endnotes follow the precepts of the Library of Congress, which is the best way to track Russian material through online catalogues.

Introduction

The Kremlin is one of the most famous structures in the world. If states have trademarks, Russia's could well be this fortress, viewed across Red Square. Everyone who comes to Moscow wants to see it, and everyone who visits seems to take a different view. 'The only guarantee of a correct response is to choose your position before you come,' wrote the German philosopher Walter Benjamin. 'In Russia, you can only see if you have already decided.' In 1927, his decision was to be enthralled.[1] A hundred years before, however, a Frenchman called the marquis de Custine had opted for a scandalized tirade. To him, the Kremlin was 'a prop of tyrants', a 'satanic monument', 'a habitation that would suit some of the personages of the Apocalypse'. 'Like the bones of certain gigantic animals,' he concluded, 'the Kremlin proves to us the history of a world of which we might doubt until after seeing the remains.'[2]

The site still mesmerizes foreign visitors. As the newspaper correspondent Mark Frankland once lamented, 'there can be few other cities in the world where the feeling is so strong of being carried towards the centre whether one wants it or not.'[3] 'Do not forget that people went into some of those buildings and came out blinded,' a British government interpreter reminded me.[4] When it comes to falling for the magic of the place, however, no outsider competes with the Russians themselves. The Kremlin is the symbol of their nationhood.[5] Its walls may not have managed to withstand invading hordes of Mongol horsemen, and they were later breached by Poles and even Frenchmen, but like Russia itself, the citadel endured. Most Russians know that it was here, outside the Kremlin gates, that Stalin reviewed the fresh Red Army troops as they marched off to fight and die in 1941. Less than four years later, in steady early summer rain, the same iconic walls and towers looked down on rank upon rank of marching men. As Marshal Zhukov struggled to control a tetchy thoroughbred horse, the banners of two hundred vanquished Nazi regiments were hurled on to the gleaming stones beside the steps of Lenin's mausoleum. The country's second capital, St Petersburg, may be an architectural miracle, but the Kremlin is Russia's wailing wall.

The structure is not democratic. Built from specially hardened bricks, the walls of this red fortress were designed for war. Although they are so elegant that the fact is disguised, they are also exceptionally thick – honeycombed by a warren of stairs and corridors that feels like a city in itself – and in places they rise more than sixty feet above the surrounding land. The four main gates are made of ancient Russian oak, but their venerable iron locks have long been superseded by the pitiless systems of a digital age. Even now, the Kremlin is a military compound, managed by a person called the commandant, and its subterranean maze of tunnels and control-rooms is designed to survive a nuclear strike. There is no public access to the north-east quarter where the president's building stands. On Thursdays, in a tradition that dates from the era of the Communist Politburo, the entire site is closed, and it is also sealed, these days, at the first whiff of public disorder. But beauty of the most transcendent kind has flourished in this atmosphere of menace. The Kremlin's spired silhouette is crowned by its religious buildings, and the most entrancing of these are clustered like so many jewel-boxes round a single square. From almost any point on this historic ground, the eye will be drawn upwards from the white stones to an effulgence of coloured tile and on to the cascades of gilded domes that lead yet higher, up among the wheeling Moscow crows, to a dazzling procession of three-barred Orthodox crosses. The tallest towers are visible for miles around, standing white and gold above the city. Magnificent and lethal, holy and yet secretive, the fortress is indeed an incarnation of the legendary Russian state.

Its spell depends on an apparent timelessness. History is everywhere. The Dormition Cathedral, which is the oldest and most famous sacred building on the site, has witnessed every coronation since the days of Ivan the Terrible. Across the square, in the Cathedral of the Archangel Michael, most visitors can barely squeeze between the waist-high caskets that hold the remains of almost every Moscow prince from the fourteenth to the seventeenth centuries. In the reign of the last tsar, a nationalist court administration had forty-six of the carved stone coffins covered in uniform bronze casings, row upon sombre row, reinforcing the impression of unbroken lineage. By then the shifting of the capital to St Petersburg had long put an end to royal Kremlin burials, but the coronations continued until 1896, and each was followed by a banquet. The fifteenth-century Faceted Palace, where the royal diners gathered in a blaze of diamonds and gold, still graces the western margin of Cathedral Square. Towering behind it, the vast Grand Palace is a nineteenth-century pastiche, but anyone who ventures past the armed police will come upon the curving stair, mutely guarded by stone lions, that leads up to the older royal quarters and the churches that were carefully preserved within. Like Jerusalem, Rome, or Istanbul, the Kremlin is a place where history is concentrated, and every stone seems to embody several pasts. The effect is hypnotic.

It is also deliberately contrived. There is nothing accidental about the Kremlin's current appearance, from the chaos of its golden roofline to the overwhelming mass of palaces and ancient walls. Someone designed these shapes to celebrate the special character of Russian culture, and someone else approved the plans to go on building in a style that would suggest historically rooted power. The ubiquitous gold, in Orthodox iconography, may be a reminder of eternity, but for the rest of us it is also an impressive reflection of earthly wealth. From the churches and forbidding gates to the familiar spires that are its emblem, the Kremlin is not merely home to Russia's rulers. It is also a theatre and a text, a gallery that displays and embodies the current governing idea. That – and the incongruity of its survival in the heart of modern Moscow – has long been the secret of its magnetism.

I have been fascinated by the place since I first saw it three decades ago, and its story has seemed to acquire an ever-deeper resonance. A turning point came in 2007, towards the end of Vladimir Putin's second four-year term as president, a time when the question of his future was beginning to preoccupy the Russian press. In true arch-nationalist style, his supporters had begun to justify an unconstitutional third term by drawing on the supposed lessons of the past. They argued that the Russian nation had endured because it followed special rules. The people suffered most when there was weakness at the heart of power. The national genius took a unique creative form, they said, and it could flourish only when it was protected by a strong and centralizing state. Obliging textbook-writers duly came up with historical proof. From

Peter the Great to Stalin, and from the bigoted Alexander III to Putin himself, the past showed just why Russia still needed a firm governing hand. Even doubters were aware that the alternative was risky. Weak government was something every Russian knew about, for the most recent case had been Boris Yeltsin's presidency in the 1990s, a time of national humiliation and desperate human misery. The statist message therefore fell on willing ears. In a poll to find the greatest name in Russian history, organized by the *Rossiya* television channel in 2008, the implacably reactionary Nicholas I took an early lead, and Stalin followed close behind in second place.[6]

The result came as no surprise to Russia-watchers in the west. If anything, there was a depressing inevitability about it, as if the country were indeed eternally marked out for tyranny. Outsiders had been saying as much for centuries. 'The prince alone controls everything,' a Jesuit envoy decided in the 1580s. 'The deference accorded the Prince is something the mind can scarcely comprehend.'[7] A succession of Englishmen who reported on Moscow in the reigns of Elizabeth and James I agreed.[8] More than three hundred years later, when the Bolshevik revolution of 1917 turned into a dictatorship, expert onlookers were ready with a range of theories based on Russia's special path.[9] It was the same when the reforms of *perestroika* faltered under Gorbachev. As one political scientist put it at the time: 'too much freedom makes many Russians feel uncomfortable.'[10] This sort of commentary flatters western prejudice, which is why it has persisted through so many complete changes of regime. In the end, however, the idea that Russia has a special destiny has survived because it suits the government of Russia itself. As a recent book on the subject neatly stated, 'the statist interpretation of Russian history is a justification for unaccountability and an absolution of past crimes'.[11] By using history, in the words of another writer, even the current government can 'integrate itself with the traditions of the past', casting the state itself as 'a focus of social and private life, in a way an ultimate justification for the life of the individual'.[12]

The Kremlin is an ideal site from which to think about all this. It is a place where myths are born, the stage on which the Russian state parades its power and its pedigree. But the fortress is also a character in its own right. I set out to explore its past because I wanted to know more about the present day, but in the end I found myself absorbed in its biography. It is a tale where show and fable often triumph over substance, but it is also very much about real things. In writing it, I have had to think about the stories rulers tell about themselves, and I have also had to master subjects ranging from the ideology behind the coronation ritual to the intricacies of Orthodox Christian theology. At the same time, however, I have found myself reading about clock-mechanisms, cannon-foundries and the technicalities of restoring old plaster. The story covers many cultures and at least two continents. In tracing it, I have looked to the grasslands of the east to follow the evolution of armies that began life on the Asian steppe, and I have also tried to picture the ride across forest and marsh that brought so many European craftsmen to Moscow's solemn, chilly, ritual-bound court. Each time the Kremlin was destroyed (it was not as eternal as it seemed), I have tried to discover how its masters saw the task of rebuilding and repossessing it. The French historian of places, Pierre Nora, would certainly have called the citadel a 'site of memory', but it has also been a place of action and change, a theatre where the dramas have been about the present even when they were disguised as evocations of the past.

I soon confirmed that the idea of predestined continuity was very old. I also came to understand how the familiar stories were conceived. From monks to court scribes and from Soviet propagandists to Putin's favourite textbook-writers, there is nothing unusual in the idea that Russian courtiers should edit entire chapters of the past. They have usually done it in a calculated attempt to secure the authority of history in the name of a specific person, for the Russian state, far from enjoying stable and continuous leadership, has in fact suffered frequent crises at the heart of power. From princes and tsars to general secretaries and unelected presidents, many of its rulers have had only the slenderest of claims. To fend off chaos or potential civil war, therefore, their courts have worked to create a more or less convincing series of succession myths. Some appealed to religion, others invoked the people's will, but history has been the basis of almost everyone's tale. Ivan the Terrible's advisors were among the most assiduous when it came to rewriting the old records – he was accorded divine authority as well as a fabulous pedigree – and their successors in the seventeenth century did the same job for the first Romanov tsars. The Bolsheviks, despite their modernizing rhetoric, called on the blessing of a pantheon of dead heroes; they also made full use of the symbolic possibilities of the Kremlin itself. Through crisis after crisis, the immediate circumstances were so troubled that the people, for their part, were prepared to welcome even an implausible pretender if they believed that he conformed to a nostalgic, almost fairytale, ideal. Life was so hard, and every future so precarious, that even the most ordinary peasant craved the certainties of vanished times. 'The highest good in Muscovy was not knowledge but memory,' James Billington decided half a century ago. 'There was no higher appeal in a dispute than the "important good and firm memory" of the oldest available authority.'[13]

But memory, as we all know, is mutable. The Kremlin itself is a record of the past. It is also a sacred place, and its buildings once marked Moscow's holiest sites. The rituals that formed round them, from celebrations of divine liturgy to coronations and royal funerals, were originally designed to embody the truth of a religious timelessness. Even in the age of saints, however, the ceremonial changed and mutated. From generation to generation, the meaning of the same words and the same processions evolved into radically new shapes. The buildings also did not stand unaltered, and they could be the most treacherous witnesses of all. If a wall was repainted, or a palace knocked down and rebuilt, it was as if its previous incarnation had never been. The cycle of familiar prayers returned, with lines of icon-bearing priests and courtiers in golden robes, but the setting had been modified so completely that it encouraged entirely new ideas, and (for want of a better term) false memories. With buildings, which are so concrete, the only past is what is there right now. It was a lesson that the Bolsheviks put to dramatic use when they destroyed the Kremlin's ancient monasteries in 1929. As I would find, few people, even Muscovites, can now say where the buildings stood. Some even doubt that they existed, scratching their heads over the old photographs that prove the case.

This book, then, is about the Kremlin over centuries of time, but it is also very much about the Kremlin now. As I began to work on it, I quickly discovered the benefits of an association – even an unreciprocated one – with Russia's ultimate elite. Although the Kremlin's research staff work in conditions that are worse, if anything, than those of any university historian outside the walls, the general environment is spectacular. As I waved my hard-won cardboard pass at the armed guards at the Borovitsky Gate and swept past queues of early-bird tourists, I tasted the superiority that fellows of Oxford and Cambridge colleges surely enjoy every working day. I left the Moscow smog and traffic noise behind. Inside the walls, before the tour-groups really start, there is a pleasant quiet, and even now, in that land of diesel and cigarettes, the breeze carries a subtle perfume of incense. The library that I was heading for was high up, too, in an annex to the bell tower of Ivan the Great, which leaves the team who runs it without an inch of free space but means the crowds stay very far away.

Any sense of membership is relative, however, for this is not a normal research site. In the Kremlin, a visitor will see what she is meant to see. Locked doors are waiting even for the most persistent guest. To write this book, I had to travel well beyond that tower reading-room. The trail has taken me to Italy (home of the architects who designed the renaissance fort) and to libraries in the United States and Great Britain. When written records would not do, I have tracked down expert witnesses. Among the first people I interviewed were some of the politicians and diplomats who have known the Kremlin as a place of work. On one surreal evening, hours north of Stockholm, I met six of Sweden's former ambassadors to Moscow at a single sitting ('you will have concluded that every adult Swedish male is required to serve his nation in this way,' the last one quipped when I expressed surprise). I have also talked to some of the architects and restorers who know the buildings inside out. Art historians have helped me to appreciate the icons and frescoes. Specialists in unfamiliar periods of history have answered questions and suggested new types of source. Tacking to and from the Moscow fortress over several years, I have even had a chance to admire the elusive falcons that are kept to kill the Kremlin crows.

One story seems to capture the excitement of the chase, however, and for me it was a kind of introduction in itself. Among my ambitions as a researcher, one of the hardest to achieve was any glimpse behind the obvious displays. As every archaeologist knows, you can learn a great deal about a culture, and especially a secretive one, by looking at the things it throws away. The Kremlin is not an obvious place to look for junk, but there was one occasion when I managed to visit the local equivalent of an attic. The chance came as an unexpected bonus when a busy woman who directs one of the Kremlin's specialist research departments kindly offered to escort me round the palace on a private tour. The idea was to look at all the extant churches, and there are lots of them.

I arrived early on the appointed morning, for I loved to spend a moment in the empty fortress, watching subtle autumn light play on the old limestone. My guide, whose office was located in an annex of the Annunciation Cathedral, had not quite finished collecting her things, so we chatted as she made her thoughtful selection from a box of keys. I marvelled at each one as they were lined up on her desk, for keys like these should really have been forged from meteorites and guarded by a dragon. Some were long and heavy, others intricate, and most were so ornate that they were hard to balance in one hand. I had no time to test them all, however, before the curator had finished rummaging in her cupboard and produced a pair of pliers. It turned out that their purpose was to break the heavy seals that safeguard the contents of the palace's numerous hidden chambers.

The first such seal awaited us at the top of a flight of polished marble steps. On the far side of an internal atrium, across a lake of gleaming parquet, we came upon a sealed pair of exquisitely wrought and gilded gates and beyond these, also locked and sealed, a pair of solid wooden doors. The prospect looked forbidding, but the pliers soon pulled off the wax, the long key turned with satisfying ease, and the wooden doors swung open to admit us to a seventeenth-century church with icons by the master Simon Ushakov. The first surprise was just how dim and even clammy the room seemed after the blazing chandeliers outside. We found the switch for the electric bulb, and by its unforgiving light I saw why the initial gloom had struck me with such force. Russian churches are meant to glint and shine, but this one had no gold or silver any-where; the precious icons themselves were displayed in a crude-looking wooden iconostasis. It turned out that the antique silver with which the screen had once been finished, a work of fine art in its own right, had been stripped and melted down in Lenin's time, ostensibly to buy bread for the people but in fact to keep the government afloat. As our tour took in more churches, more forlorn iconostases, and chambers unlit and uncanny in their emptiness, I discovered that the same fate had befallen treasures elsewhere in the palace. But there was still plenty to see, and for some hours we wove back and forth, pausing at one point to peer into the winter-garden that had once been Stalin's cinema.

My new friend was generous with both time and expertise, but she hesitated before we descended the final set of stairs. 'Don't tell the fire department,' she muttered. The corridor was narrowing; the carpets had not been replaced in a long time. We were on our way down to a fourteenth-century church that had been thought lost until it was rediscovered during building-work in the reign of Tsar Nicholas I. After more than six hundred years (so many wars, so many fires, so many redevelopment projects) there is not much left of the church itself (the walls are whitewashed), but there was a good deal else to see. Along the corridor and down the stairs were ladders, tins of paint, and broken chairs in awkward-looking stacks. There was a red flag rolled against a wall, a gilded table quarantined from some themed exhibition-space, dust sheets spattered with whitewash, a chunky radio. The expedition down through Nicholas's palace, and Mikhail Romanov's, Ivan the Terrible's, and the renaissance foundations of far older chambers was not only an experience of going back in time, which is what journeys into undercrofts are all supposed to be. I felt more as if a selection of discarded versions of the Kremlin's past had been assembled in a time-capsule, collapsing decade upon decade into one surreal space.

Russian history is full of destruction and rebuilding; the country has seen more than its fair share of change. For complex reasons, not always the same ones, the state, in a succession of different forms, has almost always managed to achieve priority at the expense of popular rights. At every moment of crisis, a set of choices has been made, often in the Kremlin, and always by specific people with a range of short-term interests to defend. There is nothing inevitable about this, and the discarded options testify to the fragmented nature of the tale. When today's Russian leaders talk about the mighty state, the so-called traditions that they have dubbed 'sovereign democracy', they are making yet another choice. History has nothing to do with it, for precedent, as that red flag and those old chairs attest so well, is something that can be thrown out like last week's flowers. There have been many Russian pasts. Once its sealed doors have been unlocked, the Kremlin need no longer seem the prop of tyrants that Custine reviled. In a culture that seeks to control history itself, it is an awkward survivor, a magnificent, spellbinding, but ultimately incorruptible witness to the hidden heart of the Russian state.

I

Foundation Stones

It feels like good poetic justice to begin the tale of an iconic fortress with a real icon. Generations of artists have worked in the Kremlin, so there are plenty of potential images from which to choose. Many of the finest were originally painted for the Kremlin's own cathedrals and monasteries, including works by masters like Theophanes the Greek and his brilliant fifteenth-century disciple, Andrei Rublev. Serene, eternal, contextless, the saintly faces still gaze out at our frenetic world from an infinity of gold. In the age when they were made, time itself belonged to God, and sinful men (at least if they believed the message of the icon-painters' art) could find salvation only if they shaped their brief years in the world to the pattern of heaven. But meditation and repentance have never been the Kremlin's real point. A better image for its founding story, in a very different style, is Simon Ushakov's masterpiece of 1668, *The Tree of the State of Muscovy*. It was and is a sacred work of art, but it is also a text about history.

Today, the icon's message is so resonant that the original has been given pride of place in the Tretyakov Gallery in Moscow. Although it is modest in size, the painting has a whole wall to itself, and careful lighting on the gold creates an air of special reverence. You know before you even look that this is treasure, but the design comes as a surprise. At first glance the icon seems like a conventional tree of life, a motif that is more familiar from oriental rugs than Russian painting.[1] Closer inspection indeed reveals the stylized curling tree, but the fruit (or the blossom, for this is a magic plant) consists of cameos, including a large image of the Virgin and smaller ones of some of Moscow's ruling princes, tsars and holy men. They are arranged in a succession, adorning branches that rise up towards the gates of heaven. As the Tretyakov's own guidebook helpfully points out, Ushakov drew his inspiration from traditional representations of the genealogy of Jesus Christ.[2]

The picture gets even more interesting as you follow the tree to its root, for here imagined space gives way to real buildings. Like a frame within a frame, the fortified walls and towers of the Moscow Kremlin run along the painting's base, and it is here that the icon's principal historical characters are also to be found. In one corner, like an impresario presenting a particularly successful show, you see the immediately recognizable figure of Aleksei Mikhailovich Romanov (ruled 1645–76), the tsar of Ushakov's time. But at the centre of it all, bending tenderly over their work, are the two men who have planted the tree. On the left, holding the medieval equivalent of a watering can, is a priest, and painted letters tell us that he is Peter, the leader of the early fourteenth-century Russian church. On the right, in charge of the plant itself, is a prince, Ivan I, who ruled Moscow for sixteen years from 1325 until his death in 1341.

You need to know some history to understand what Ushakov was trying to explain. Among other things, his painting is a political manifesto on behalf of his tsar. Like the tree, the picture is saying, Aleksei and his heirs have roots in Moscow's past; like the pious tsars of former times – like the founder in the foreground, indeed – they are part of a continuous line whose work has always been to nurture and develop Russia's soil. The case was worth arguing in Aleksei's time because he was only the second member of his family to take the throne. In the early 1600s, during a prolonged civil war, Russia had almost disintegrated. When peace eventually returned in 1613, a council of citizens had been forced to scour the land for a new tsar. The accession of Aleksei's father, Mikhail Romanov, was not quite the organic progress that the icon's imagery suggests, in other words, and the semi-derelict Kremlin that he inherited was a far cry from the pristine red fortress that the painting shows. As his artist's brush erased the memory of turmoil and murder, Ushakov was urging a new generation to believe that Moscow's story was specially blessed. His Kremlin was no ordinary place. It had become the link between Russia and heaven, a space protected by the Mother of God herself.

But there is a further message in the founding scene, and it is represented by the planting of that tree. What the head of the Orthodox Church in Russia, Peter, and the newly appointed prince of Moscow,

Ivan I, actually did, in 1326, was to lay the first stone of a new cathedral. It features in the icon as a soaring building with exquisite golden domes, but the accuracy of the detail was less important than the symbolism of an act that marked the moment when Moscow, with the Kremlin at its heart, had staked a claim to be the religious and political capital of the Russian world. At the time, the Kremlin was neither magnificent nor serene; its walls were a patchwork of mud and timber and its defences included stretches of noxious swamp. The world around it was at war, and its prince was not even the undisputed sovereign of Russia's people. But some trees thrive in poor and even thirsty soils. When Ushakov wanted to find a root for his symbolic plant, he was not wrong to choose the ceremony of 1326. Ironically, moreover, the prince he painted, Ivan I, had been invoking history himself as he laid that first portentous stone. The Kremlin's story, like that of Russia as a whole, is fragmented, and much has been lost. In the midst of the fires, revolutions and palace coups, however, the single genuinely continuous thread is the determination of successive Russian rulers to rewrite the past so that the present, whatever it turns out to be, will seem as deeply rooted and organic as Ushakov's tree.

There is no reliable record of the Kremlin's beginnings. The chronicles that form the most important written source for the period mention a princes' residence in Moscow in 1147 and again in 1156, but no-one really knows who first built something fort-like on the hill above the Moscow and Neglinnaya rivers. The dates are contested, though the existence of a twelfth-century wall turns out to be a fact.[3] Archaeologists digging in the 1950s found its remnants at a depth that corresponds to the correct decades, and though the finds are incomplete, and also disrupted by a lot of later construction, they are consistent with an earth and timber rampart, and a most impressive one. The giant logs alone would have been immovable. The structure enclosed a much smaller area than the current Kremlin, but it would have been impossible to breach. The wooden rampart was not the first building on the wedge-shaped hill, however, as further digging soon revealed. Beneath the earthworks, deeper layers hold bones. There are the ribs and limbs of pigs and cattle, scraps from centuries of meals, and the remains of horses and dogs. There are also the bones of game and fur-bearing animals, including elk, hare, beaver and wild boar. A spindle-whorl made of pink slate, the work of a craftsman in Kiev, testifies to trade links with the Dnieper valley, as do glass beads and metal bracelets in the coldest seams of earth.[4] Deeper still there is silence.

The hill on which the Kremlin stands would always have had a lot of potential as a fort. It was easily defensible and well-supplied with workable timber, but in its early years it was remote even by Russian standards. While other regions in the north developed thriving ports and markets, this site stayed huddled in the forest, swamped by brambles and the fungal winter fog. The tapestry of oak and birch that stretched away on every side was so dense that it could easily swallow a whole army. Exactly that was said to have happened in 1176, when two rival princes and their retinues managed to clink past each other, the thud and jangle of their beasts dying to nothing in the web of leaves.[5] The rivers were easier landmarks to follow, but even they were treacherous, and local hunters often cut a path through drier parts of the forest when they set out in search of elk and wild boar. Important routes could be kept open for a time by surfacing them with logs, an ancient technique that was still in use a thousand years later when Soviet troops laid their famous 'corduroy roads', but many early tracks into these woods were reclaimed in a season by the nettles, scrub and mud. Even if a traveller could find it for a second time, the chilly ground above the river-bend was not an obvious candidate for capital-city status.

The first people to settle here, hunters perhaps, were probably Finns, but no-one can be sure, for though successive rulers came and went, there was no state to count or name the tribes, and no obvious border. Unlike the Christians of the west or the Jews and Muslims to the south and east, the locals here cremated their dead, so there are no graves to excavate, and since they had no alphabet they left almost no words. But their traces survive in the names that these first people gave to the rivers and the wooded swamps; by most accounts (though Slavic patriots dispute the fact) Moscow itself is one.[6] The name, derived from the Finnish, was almost certainly established before the first Slavs arrived, probably at the beginning of the 800s.

The newcomers belonged to a tribe called the Viatichi.[7] Even in this bloody age they had a reputation for ferocity. They may, indeed, have held back the region's development, since peaceful travellers would have hesitated before crossing their land. But their world was not entirely sealed off. The Moscow river that flowed through their territory

carried wooden boats; it was one of several possible trade routes connecting the Volga with the west and north, and archaeologists now
think that at least two important land-based routes also converged near
the site of today's Kremlin.[8] Increasing traffic – boats, horses, even
camels – had started to venture across the north-eastern European plain
by this time. The little town beside the Moscow river was not on a main
trade route, but nonetheless someone who passed through at this time
managed to drop two silver coins, Islamic dirhams, one of them minted
far away in Merv.[9] Elsewhere in Russia more substantial quantities of
silver, real hoards, have come to light, mostly of Muslim origin and
mostly bearing tenth-century dates, a certain indication of the volume
and the value of the region's trade with the sophisticated civilizations of
Asia and the Mediterranean.

The merchants must have come with lavish expectations. The cara-
vans that headed south and east to Khwarezm, a market-centre deep in
Central Asia, were loaded with the forest's riches. 'Sables, miniver,
ermines, and the fur of the steppe foxes,' an Arab geographer gloated.
'Martens, foxes, beavers, spotted hares, and goats; also wax, arrows,
birch-bark, high fur caps, fish glue, fish teeth [i.e. walrus tusks] . . .
Slavonic slaves, sheep and cattle.'[10] Accounts like this are reminiscent of
much later European writings about Africa, and it turns out that the
north-eastern European forest zone was indeed the dark continent of
the ninth and tenth centuries. Like Africa in later times, it seemed to be
a dangerous, exotic place, where fortunes waited for adventurers.
Human slaves were one source of profit, for while Muslims and Christians were forbidden to enslave each other, the pagan Slavs were fair
game.[11] The appetite for fur, meanwhile, seemed to be inexhaustible,
and it was purchased by everyone from the Arabs and Turks of Asia to
the Franks and Anglo-Saxons of Europe's Atlantic fringe. The northern
birchwoods and the taiga beyond them produced the best. If the goods
could be brought to market – in Constantinople, maybe, or Bolghar, the
great city on the Volga route towards the east – serious money, silver,
was on hand to pay for them.

The profits on offer, and the many opportunities to set up customs posts
and levy taxes on the precious freight, meant that the trade routes were
worth fortunes, but the local Slavs were neither organized nor swift enough
to take control of them. Instead, the prize fell to some bands of Vikings
from Scandinavia, soon known to Greeks and Arabs as *Rhōs*. This used to

be another controversial issue (Russian nationalists resented the suggestion that their founding princes might have come from somewhere else[12]), but the archaeological evidence around the Baltic is conclusive. By protecting some convoys, raiding others, and seizing any promising tribute, the rough freebooters became formidable regional players. From their first permanent settlement on Lake Ilmen, on navigable water near modern Novgorod, they had extended their network along the Dnieper and the Upper Volga by the middle of the ninth century. Like their relatives, the Vikings who raided Alfred the Great's Wessex in the same decades, they were ambitious, warlike and incorrigibly mobile. In 860, they even managed to attack Constantinople, the heir of Rome, by closing on the great walled city from the sea. Before long, they had wrested the Dnieper capital of Kiev from the people known as the Khazars and mounted a succession of campaigns against Slav settlements as far east as the middle Volga. In a world where hundreds of miles separated the main ports and markets, and a good average speed for overland travel was no more than thirty miles a day, it was no easy matter to complete a long journey with a fleet of loaded craft. The evolution of the region's intercontinental trade was an epic of endurance, skill and simple human greed.

It was also the first act of the Russian drama, the founding moment that begins all subsequent histories and myths. The Primary Chronicle, the first official record of the era, relates the story of a semi-mythical figure called Riurik, from whom the princes who ruled Russia's cities would eventually derive their dynastic title, Riurikids. This man and his two brothers were said to have settled the territory round Lake Ilmen by invitation; the story goes that the perpetually warring local tribes of Slavs, Balts and Finns viewed strong outside authority as their one hope of peace.[13] Invited or not, however, these Vikings – referred to now by most historians as the Rus – were not above consorting with the region's older tribes. They also learned from their steppe neighbours, buying wooden hulls from Slav craftsmen and using local networks to procure the furs, wax, honey, hides and slaves with which to load them. Over time the Rus and native Slavs began to merge and even intermarry, sharing a landscape and its local gods and inventing new stories, in a common language, to make sense of their world. They were not yet a single people, but the foundations of a culture had certainly been laid.

It was always crucial for the warlike Rus to persuade their various neighbours to trade with them. Unfortunately, the wealthiest of these, the citizens of Constantinople, were horrified by stories of the Vikings to the north. The very harshness of their world, to say nothing of that recent sea-attack, made this particular group of pagans seem especially uncouth. Although Constantinople's imperial government hired Vikings of its own to serve as mercenaries (they were the most resourceful sailors, after all, and staunch fighters to boot), undomesticated ones, whatever they called themselves, were regarded as barbarians, and at first the Rus were not permitted to enter the imperial capital at all. Instead, they had to trade through the Black Sea ports of Cherson and Tmutorokan, which meant sharing their profits with a swarm of middle-men.[14] They finally secured a trade treaty with Constantinople in 911, but its terms made clear that Rus merchants were permitted to enter the city only if they kept to their own designated gate. They were also forbidden to arrive in groups of more than fifty at a time.[15]

The turning point came in the late tenth century. Dazzled by Constantinople's gold and fascinated by its power, the pagan Rus adopted the Christianity of the patriarchs. It was a choice, and there were other options, not least the chance of allegiance to Rome. At the time, the gulf that lay between the two main Christian churches was not deep, but the Rus' decision to align themselves with Constantinople's version of the faith would shape their people's future for centuries. The cultural impact was incalculable. It was the splendour and the beauty of eastern monotheism, apparently, that captivated Russia's Norsemen. After a visit to Constantinople's magnificent Church of the Holy Wisdom, a party of Rus emissaries was struck with awe. The building was a miracle, the liturgy spectacular. 'We knew not', one of them reported to his prince, Vladimir of Kiev, 'whether we were in heaven or on earth.'[16] Around 988 (no date can be entirely fixed), Prince Vladimir accepted baptism for himself, and extended the same boon to his subjects by ordering their mass immersion in the Dnieper. Just to make sure, he also had the pagan idols flogged and dragged about the streets before condemning them to death.[17]

Christianity brought the lands of the Rus into the orbit of a commonwealth. Constantinople was its centre, but the culture of Christian Kiev also inherited something from the religious traditions of Alexandria, Asia Minor and the Balkans. A veritable black-robed tide swept into Kiev after its official conversion, and the foreign monks brought much more than the principles of faith. Their other legacies included a new alphabet, a new set of ideas about the state, and a Christian calendar.[18] Some were talented artists, and icon-painters, many of them Greeks, were soon producing images of saints. Christ and the Holy Virgin were universal, but the Greek church also favoured St John of the Ladder, St Anthony the Great, and St Andrew the First-Called, the apostle whom legend held to have foreseen the Christian glories that awaited Kiev. The Holy Wisdom, the divine spirit of the Word behind the Incarnation, was at the heart of all, for both Kiev and its wealthy rival, Novgorod, followed Constantinople in dedicating their most important cathedrals to it. The conversion of the Rus was not quite a revolution, for there had been little in the way of authentic culture to overturn, but it was certainly a stunning change, and Kiev's princely government, with its imported faith and its veneer of Greek precepts, became a model for the eastern Slavic world.

None of these developments implied a future glory for the outpost on the Moscow river, however. The rulers of Muscovy were keen, much later, to find a precedent for their own court in eleventh-century Kiev, but at its best their case was flimsy. The prince in Simon Ushakov's icon, Ivan I, was almost certainly descended from Vladimir, but the line was hardly direct. He had a claim to the Riurikid dynastic title, but he was only one of countless princes of that royal blood, many of whom ruled flourishing cities of their own.[19] Ivan and Vladimir were separated by three hundred years, and though human affairs, when viewed from the twenty-first century, may appear to have moved slowly in the medieval world, three centuries was always a long time. It is roughly the same interval, for comparison, that separates today's England from the one that sent the Duke of Marlborough to fight at Blenheim, and an even shorter gap divides our generation from the last to witness British rule in the American colonies.

The passage of time was not the only fact that separated Kiev and Moscow, either, for their geography, economies, political systems and even their diplomatic orientations were worlds apart, with Kiev looking southwards to the Black Sea and Moscow trading on the forest and its links to distant cultures on the Volga and beyond. But there was one important sense in which Moscow was truly Kiev's heir. The Dnieper city had been the region's first spiritual capital, a status that Constantinople confirmed when it chose Kiev's Holy Wisdom to be queen of every Christian church in the vast territory. Byzantine clerics also proposed an ecclesiastical hierarchy to manage the Rus congregation. As a barbarian frontier, and a wild one at that, the princes' world did not merit the creation of a separate patriarchate (there were only five of those on the planet[20]), but the Rus did get a metropolitan (the next rank down), a man who acted as the link between the Slavic north and civilization as Constantinople defined it. The newly created job involved a lot of travel, for churches were being built at almost every prosperous princely court from the Baltic to the middle Volga, but the metropolitan's official residence was Kiev, and on his death each one was laid to rest in or around the great cathedral there. The region's spiritual geography shifted decisively, then, when the man in Ushakov's icon, Metropolitan Peter, broke with convention by stipulating that his body should instead be buried in the cathedral that he and Ivan had founded in Moscow, nearly five hundred miles to the north-east.

The journey that ended with that moment did not lead directly from Kiev but paused, for well over a hundred years, at Vladimir, a fortress-city even further to the east on the River Klyazma. The route was complex, and there is no easy way to understand it without making a detour into the elaborate world of inheritance law. Primogeniture, the system that kept property and titles in convenient straight lines in other kingdoms and in later times, was alien to the Rus princely clan. Their world was one of constant movement, and the heads of every major family could hope to claim a territory somewhere, ruling from its local capital with a small court and a retinue of warriors. But the clan insisted on dynastic hierarchies, including a convention that gave primacy, in political terms, to the princes of the most important cities of the time. In the Rus lands, as an expert on the region has observed, the royal family was viewed 'as a corporate entity, and, as such, all had a claim on its constituent parts'.[21] If it was a system of collective wealth-management, however, it was also subject to an expanding list of partners and sporadic violent take-over bids.

The kindest thing that could be said about the system of inheritance itself was that it guaranteed a healthy pool of male heirs. Instead of betting on a single son, custom (in a land where life-expectancy was short) put a prince's brothers in line for his throne, so that an adult male (the younger brother of the senior prince) was likely to inherit ahead of second-generation royal infants. If a member of the older generation did not live to inherit a princely seat, however, his heirs might be barred, in perpetuity, from doing so. These rules were seldom absolute because there were so many opportunities to do away with rivals. To complicate inheritance still more, a title and associated lands and wealth were not necessarily conferred for life. The princely estates, or appanages, were arranged along a scale of notional desirability, and increasing seniority within the clan allowed each prince to move up, maybe several times, from a lesser to a greater one. Claimants with ambition could compete for the best lands of all, moving from city to city or facing their cousins in battle in a murderous game of musical chairs as death and promotion created vacancies. For more than a century, the mother-city of Kiev remained the prize that all desired, but though the contest for that throne was particularly fierce, the entire system could have been designed to generate feuds.[22]

Until his death in 1015, Prince Vladimir of Kiev had kept the family in order, but his successors soon looked set to dissipate his legacy in fratricide. Steppe tribesmen, notably the energetic Polovtsy, were quick to take advantage, mounting increasingly damaging raids on any treasure that looked vulnerable (they sacked Kiev in 1061), and for a time it seemed as if the Rus might disappear like every other clan that had once ruled the Dnieper grasslands and the woods beyond. In 1097, the princes finally convened to shape a truce under the stern gaze of a magnate called Vladimir Monomakh.[23] In future, most of the lesser appanages would be attached to named, specific members of the clan. There was a distinction between the inner circle of senior princes and their humbler cousins, but most could now begin to build a stable, even heritable, estate. The changed conditions also encouraged the development of a new pole within the Slavic world. Though Kiev remained glorious, and fortunes could be made in the markets of Novgorod, the lands held by Vladimir Monomakh emerged as the most powerful of all.

Monomakh's territory lay beyond the Moscow forest in a range of gently rolling hills whose rivers drained not south, to the familiar Black Sea, but eastwards to the Volga and the markets of the Asian plateau. The region may have seemed remote, but at a time when wealthy cities to the west had become vulnerable to nomad raids, its location was appealingly secure. The land was lightly settled in the days of Monomakh, but it also turned out to be reasonably fertile, and in trading terms it made a useful entrepôt between the Volga and the Dnieper.

Here, then, on the banks of the rivers Nerl and Klyazma, a succession of powerful princes developed their own centre, first at Suzdal and then at a new fortress, Vladimir, possibly founded by Monomakh himself. The region grew prosperous and even opulent within decades, but Monomakh still opted to rule in Kiev when the chance arose, as did at least three of his sons. It fell to his grandson to change the geographical balance for good. Andrei Bogoliubsky followed the family example when he accepted the throne of Kiev in 1169 (thereby asserting his own primacy within the clan), but instead of settling there he chose to move his capital to Vladimir. In a system where no prince was equal, the Prince of Vladimir, not Kiev, would henceforth stand as lord above them all, and eventually the title would itself inflate. In years to come, a series of powerful and already wealthy men would willingly risk their lives to gain the right to call themselves Grand Prince of Vladimir.

Andrei's next task was to create a city to eclipse Kiev. Power and glory came from God, so the prince's scribes gave him the attributes of an Old Testament king. He was, they said, a Solomon in wisdom and a David in his virtue and his strength.[24] The most conspicuous demonstration of his kingship, however, was achieved through a massive programme of building. For years, the thin north-eastern light was to play on piles of earth and scaffolding as masons and craftsmen from all over twelfth-century Europe hastened to meet this ruler's deadlines.[25] Because Andrei had resolved to outshine the metropolitan seat of Kiev, his cathedral in Vladimir had to be higher, at 106 feet, than the 93 feet of Kiev's famous Holy Wisdom.[26] The finished building blazed with jewel colours. Sheets of gilded copper covered the cupola, while the white limestone itself was patterned with raised designs in red, blue and green as well as gold and gemstones. The pulpit inside glinted with more gold and silver, and sunlight coming through the vault scattered and pooled on many smooth-cut precious stones. When it came to exterior detail, Andrei favoured intricate carving, and other churches in his realm were decorated with menageries: lions and panthers, dogs, hares, deer and mythical creatures like the griffin and the sirin-bird.[27] The building programme continued with a walled palace and several ominous triumphal gates. In a landscape dotted with thatch and mud, the structures made the kind of statement that no-one, let alone a rival prince, could miss.

The confidence and swagger of it all hint at Andrei's true qualities. God's loyal servant was also a ruthless, vengeful and imperious man.

No other kind, perhaps, could have constructed a city on this scale, and curt, decisive government was needed in an age of constant war. But Andrei's cruelties added daily to the list of his enemies. In the summer of 1174, a rumour began to circulate that he was planning to get rid of certain discontented noblemen, and in particular the sons of a land-owner from Moscow whom Andrei's family had murdered and whose property had recently been seized. Another version, more appealing to later Muscovite chroniclers, held that the murdered landlord's sons (avenging Muscovite heroes) took the initiative themselves. Either way, the conspirators agreed that Andrei had to die, and on the eve of 29 June a group of twenty of them broke into his bedchamber and hacked him to pieces.[28] The tyrant's buildings did not fare well in the years to come. The great cathedral in Vladimir was damaged in a fire soon after his death, and his palace was eventually looted for treasure and, later, for stone. Only an arch and one tower still stand. A short distance away, the elegant church that Andrei commissioned to commemorate one of his most resounding victories, a building that once rose from a tiered white stone platform, has subsided into the riverside grass as if to cut the prince's glory down to size.[29]

Buildings, however, were not the only legacy that Andrei left. In their determination to prove the city's special destiny, his advisors also created a new cult of the Mother of God. The festival of the Protection of the Veil, sponsored by Andrei himself, was meant to celebrate the Virgin's special care for all Rus lands, but the prince's men made sure that it was the new capital at Vladimir that topped the list.[30] In the same spirit, Andrei's cathedral was not named for the Holy Wisdom, but for the Dormition of the Virgin, the death and miraculous resurrection of his city's holy protectress. The prince endowed his building with numerous icons, many of which were painted to order, but he brought its centrepiece to Vladimir from Kiev. According to legend, this likeness of the Virgin and Child had originally been painted by St Luke, though in reality Andrei's icon was probably less than a century old.[31] Whatever its pre-history, however, it had a special place in the religious practice of the region, and its arrival in Vladimir marked an epoch. Even later, when it had been moved to Moscow and its story had been woven into legends like that of Ushakov's tree, the miracle-working icon was still known as the Virgin of Vladimir.

*

In Andrei's lifetime, Moscow did not even rate a palace, though the cruel ruler seems to have commissioned a new set of walls. The settlement remained a military outpost and a centre for collecting tithes and taxes; successive princes of Vladimir hardly wasted an hour's prayer on it. Most Orthodox believers were more concerned about the fate of distant, iconic Constantinople, which was sacked by the pope's own men, the soldiers of the Fourth Crusade, in 1204. Rome's insult to the eastern faith was widely felt.[32] But no-one could have predicted how quickly that particular drama was to be forgotten. A storm was about to break directly on the Rus. The princes were preoccupied as usual with quarrels of their own, but traders on the old silk routes knew all about the powerful new force. An enemy that Europeans had not seen before crossed the Caucasus mountains from Persia in the summer of 1223. Its forces were composed of horsemen, many of them lightly armed, and they moved rapidly, too fast for the princes' defending armies, whom they engaged and defeated in battle on the River Kalka before vanishing almost as swiftly as they had appeared. Nervous military experts in Kiev and the border city of Ryazan attempted to dismiss the skirmish as another steppe-based tribal raid, the sort of thing their cities had endured and overcome for centuries. In fact, it was a mission of reconnaissance.

The battle on the Kalka was followed, somewhere in the heart of Asia, by a period of detailed preparation and training. For the horsemen, such drill and planning had become routine. By the early 1220s, they had already humiliated Khwarezm and sacked Merv, Bukhara and Samarkand; they had crossed the Gobi desert and defeated the hosts of the Jin; and they had ridden westward from the Oxus to the edge of the Crimean steppe. The territory they controlled was four times larger than the Roman empire at its greatest extent, and most of it had been subdued in one lifetime. For such a host, the Dnieper region would have seemed like easy meat, but their plans received a setback in 1227 with the sudden death of their revered leader, Chinghis (or Genghis) Khan. The interval was relatively brief, however. In 1234, a council of the clans of the Mongol Horde, meeting in their capital at Karakorum twelve weeks' fast ride east of the Volga, agreed to a sustained strike deep into the European plain. As ever, the planning was thorough. The Mongol army began by neutralizing the steppe people of the east and south, removing all potential allies of the Rus. In the winter of 1237, their troops, led by Batu-khan, a grandson of Chinghis, sprang their attack on towns and villages in the Russian north-east. The first to fall was Ryazan, which was overrun after a siege in late December. Batu's horsemen then headed for Vladimir, which surrendered after bitter fighting in February 1238. Almost in passing, they sacked and burned Moscow, killing its governor and plundering its meagre treasure.[33] The wooden settlement and its fortress burned like a torch.

Away to the south-west, Kiev and its immediate neighbours remained untouched for two more years, but at the end of 1240 the great army returned, perhaps 140,000-strong, this time heading for the Dnieper.[34] By now the Mongols' methods were familiar. They relied on good preparation, including excellent advance intelligence, and they launched surprise attacks with overwhelming force. They were expert in field and siege tactics, consummate archers, masters of Greek fire. They also knew the value of terror; the importance of visible, disproportionate and unforgettable brutality. Kiev and nearby Pereyaslavl and Chernigov fell that same winter, and in 1241 Batu moved west to Galich and onwards into Hungary. His army seemed invincible, and might have reached the Rhine or further if the death, in Karakorum, of the Great Khan, Ugudey, the third son of Chinghis, had not summoned the commander back to settle the succession. The territories of west-central Europe were spared, but the scattered and internally divided lands of the Rus princes would spend the next two centuries in subjugation to Mongol rule.

Eye-witness accounts of the first shock are understandably scarce. If they survived, most city-dwellers tried to flee, dispersing through the woods to escape the hoofbeats that presaged capture or death. Some found refuge in monasteries – the conquerors respected local religion almost everywhere – but even if these people had the strength to tell their tales it would have needed a monk with an unusually cool head to find a pen and take a note. As a result, there is almost no reliable picture of conditions in the princes' lands in the decade of the Mongol raids. The brunt of suffering, as always, was borne by the civilian poor, whose future (if they had not been slaughtered in the first terrible assault) often involved forced deportation and imprisonment as hostages or slaves. To evade that, many melted northwards to the taiga and the Arctic Sea. The rest ended up paying tribute (and providing board) to any armed stranger who hammered on their door. The nobility, however, found itself in a different kind of trap. Some, like their subjects, were killed in the bloodbaths of the first months, but the survivors became the vassals of a new empire.

It did not matter whether or not a city had burned. Novgorod, for instance, had escaped the first round of attacks (thanks to an early spring flood that blocked the horsemen's route), but it was ordered nevertheless to pay tribute to the conquerors, a yearly tax in silver, gold and furs, in grain, and also soldiers for the khan's army.[35] There were short-lived rebellions in several cities when the taxmen came, but these merely called down greater ruin. Fire seemed to be the princes' destiny. In the 1250s, their cities and surviving farms faced further raids from neighbours on their other flanks, including the Teutonic knights and Swedes in the north, the Polovtsy in the south, and Lithuanian tribesmen from the west. The Rus elite also persisted in fighting each other, and few stopped short of treachery, deceit, or even the murder of brother-princes. Every city and its leaders had to calculate where to build friendships and whom to fight. But ultimate authority no longer rested in the princes' clan. The Mongol khan came to be seen as something like an emperor (the Rus sometimes referred to their new suzerain's power as *tsarstvo*, from the word *tsar* – or caesar), and each prince owed his sceptre, in the end, to him.

The case for appeasement was overwhelming, but in the confusion and carnage it took an imaginative prince to strike a lasting deal. Though many of the Rus eventually negotiated with the khan's men, the most consistent and trusted in these early years was Alexander Nevsky. His frequent visits to the khan's headquarters suggest that he was willing to work with Mongol overlords, and even that he acted as a sort of local advisor on Rus affairs.[36] The khan could count on his new vassal to suppress rebellion at home (Nevsky made short work of an uprising in Novgorod), and also to ensure that tribute from the new empire was collected and paid. Alexander's reward was an endorsement of his title to the throne of Vladimir. In years to come, even as Vladimir itself declined, the charter to rule this crumbling city would continue to confer pre-eminence upon its holder, regardless of where he was physically based, and the quest to obtain it became the focus of complex diplomacy between the Rus world and the Mongol court. As peoples of the medieval steppe, the Mongols honoured royal blood. They did not lightly overturn the Riurikid system of governance. But since the princes were their vassals, they expected homage just as any feudal lord in

Europe might, and anyone who sought advantage in their Rus empire had henceforth to negotiate with them.

Life had never been tranquil in the northern woods, but now it was precarious for everyone. Ironically, these were exactly the conditions that would favour Moscow, not least because the place appeared remote and insignificant. In part because its forests were so uninviting, refugees from richer cities like Vladimir were drawn to look for shelter there. The township's population soon recovered and began to grow. Ten years after Batu's onslaught, in 1247 or 1248, the fortress even acquired a prince of its own, Mikhail the Brave, though this man's ambitions and his (short) future turned out to lie elsewhere. In 1262, however, Moscow and its associated lands were awarded to Alexander Nevsky's two-year-old son, Daniil, and the town's continuous history as a princely seat – a real city – began. Once he became an adult (somewhere between the ages of nine and twelve), Daniil took up permanent residence in a wooden palace in the walled compound on the city's main hill. A Mongol army sacked the place a decade later, but the wooden buildings were rebuilt as usual – a church could be completed in a day – and business limped back to life.

Daniil had been a younger son, which explained why he received this town, the meanest and least glamorous of his father's estates. Although he built new churches and expanded the appanage lands, and though his successors, the Daniilovichi, amassed increasing wealth over the years, this sub-branch of the Riurikids had little prospect of wide influence or continental power. Moscow did not even rate its own bishop, and it remained an outpost in a diocese whose centre was two hundred miles away in Rostov.[37] But Mongol rule distorted all realities. In the early fourteenth century, the princes of a better-placed and larger city, Tver, seemed destined to inherit the coveted throne of Vladimir, but their ambition made them suspect in the khans' eyes. The Mongols needed someone more compliant, easier to push around. Because each prince was required to apply in person to the khan, too, the next act in the Muscovite foundation drama was played out far from its chill northern forests at the fabulous Mongol court.

Most early Russian chronicles are a little prim about their leaders' dealings with the Horde. Their authors (usually court clerics of later times) mention that princes and leading figures in the church 'visited the

Horde', but they tend not to spell out what that meant in practice. It is an awkward fact, the sort that does not fit the epic template, and medieval scribes must have struggled with it much as modern patriots still do. There is no consensus about the cultural impact on Russia of its Mongol centuries, which is why some prefer to focus on the icons and the purely Russian saints. In fact, however, most Rus political figures, including leaders of the church, spent substantial amounts of time at the courts of various successive khans. At first, that meant an arduous pilgrimage beyond the Ural mountains to Karakorum, a journey of such rigour that more than one exhausted rider perished on the way. But Batu, the man who had led the sack of Eastern Europe, founded a capital for his own khanate, often known as the Golden Horde, at Sarai, in splendid landscape near the mouth of the Volga, and before long this was the destination for embassies from the conquered Russian lands.

The Golden Horde evokes a memorable set of legends. It is easy to imagine a forest of tents, rough men tearing at lumps of meat, perhaps a desiccated scalp or two. It is easy to imagine gold, too, but history has painted its barbaric owners in the guise of shiftless thieves; the oriental menace echoes still in the name of the road that leads south from the Kremlin: Bolshaya Ordinka, Great Horde Road. In fact, however, the 'Horde' was simply the khan's imperial base; the Turkic word had nothing to do with its later connotations of a warlike rabble, and deserves to be translated as 'the ruler's pavilion'.[38] In the weeks that it took to cross the steppe, petitioners would have been well advised to banish every other prejudice along these lines. As they discovered when the glint of the first roof emerged out of the khaki haze, the Mongols lived like the emperors that they had become.[39] Batu's original capital had certainly been made of tents, but his successors built on a truly luxurious scale.[40]

Sarai was a real city, not a camp. The khans still used their tents for hunting expeditions – and for military campaigns – but in its heyday the capital of the Golden Horde was a permanent centre of commerce and cultural exchange. Building-labour was no problem, for the khan owned slaves from two continents, including craftsmen from the old Slav lands. Gold, gems, silver and porcelain from the entire known world were used to adorn his palaces. The result was stupendous. The city, according to an Arab visitor of 1333, was an 'extraordinary size, filled to overflowing with people, handsome markets, and broad streets'. Slavs, Germans and Hungarians rubbed shoulders in the market-place with

Mongols, Chinese and Sogdian silk traders. The value of the goods in Sarai's merchant quarter represented so vast a sum that the district had to be specially fortified.[41] The khan's pavilions themselves were topped with such a quantity of gold that even a visitor from Egypt was startled.[42] The city was also rich in culture, and its leaders subtle in their management of diverse populations. By the fourteenth century, Sarai even had a bishop of its own. In all, it was remarkable for its open aspect, and that, too, was a deliberate choice. Fortifications, in Mongol tradition, were regarded as a sign of cowardice. Battles were lost and won at speed, so walls were simply barriers to be breached or burned.[43] How any prince of the Russian lands, arriving at last after many weeks' trek, and having set out from a wooden citadel, would have been struck by all of this can only be imagined.

They came with any tribute they were bidden to deliver, but they also carried gifts and bribes. Intricate rings, finely matched furs, hunting falcons from the steppe and jewelled drinking-cups were all welcomed by members of the khan's extended family. The princes' aim was to secure support in a complex struggle for supremacy at home. By the 1300s the major players on the Russian side were the principalities of Moscow and Tver. The latter city was the stronger in both military and strategic terms; it even boasted its own kremlin, a citadel with timber walls on a commanding promontory site. But Moscow's relative weakness was no bar to its ambition, and the city sent frequent embassies south-east to Sarai. First came Daniil's son, Yury of Moscow, who not only married the khan's sister but engineered the murder of a fellow-prince: Mikhail of Tver was kicked to death, with the khan's approval, in 1318. By these and other unsavoury means, including the conquest of several valuable Rus cities, Yury became the first of Moscow's rulers to acquire the title and the rights of Grand Prince of Vladimir. But his own murder (like Mikhail's, it took place at Sarai) brought his reign to a premature end in 1325. When it came to the turn of his younger brother, Ivan I, the groundwork was better laid. The youth had taken the road south in 1320, remaining at the Horde for eighteen months. It was a long stay, almost an apprenticeship, and Ivan used it to acquaint himself with the basic principles of Mongol law, the workings of the court, and a good deal else that influenced his later policy towards the continental superpower.

On his brother's death, Ivan inherited the throne of Moscow but not the honoured title of Grand Prince of Vladimir. That passed back to Tver, but only for a brief, unnerving year. In 1327, the khan, Uzbek, sent his cousin to subdue the city, whose growing power was becoming wearisome. On that occasion, Tver's walled fortress withstood the attack so successfully that even the Mongols gave up, though both sides sustained heavy losses. Ivan set off for Sarai again within months. His mission was to promise troops and support in a fresh campaign to capture Tver, and he probably took a supply of sable-pelts to underline his point. Uzbek, predictably, was charmed. In 1328 an army that included Mongols and soldiers from Moscow sacked Tver and forced its reigning prince, Alexander, to flee. The victorious troops loaded carts and saddlebags with plunder, and Ivan's accession to the title of Grand Prince was sealed. In 1339, after a brief trial, the deposed prince Alexander of Tver was executed at Sarai. At the same time, on Grand Prince Ivan's orders, the city bell of Tver was brought in triumph to the Moscow Kremlin and hung in its palace cathedral of the Saviour.[44]

The medieval Russian chronicles tend to give Ivan I the benefit of a rose-tinted hindsight. 'There came a great peace for forty years,' wrote one source on his impact as grand prince. 'The Christians found relief and appeasement away from the great troubles, the many oppressions, and from Tatar [i.e. Mongol] violence, and there was great peace in all the land.'[45] Even by medieval standards, this is largely hogwash. Ivan, after all, was the Mongols' ally against Christian Tver; he may also have been Uzbek's political apprentice. He was even noted for oppressions of his own, since one of his major selling-points, from the Mongol point of view, was the efficiency with which he collected the tribute that they were owed. He was, in fact, a tax-farmer, and he used force to guarantee prompt and generous payment. By squeezing silver from his fellow-princes, he made sure of Uzbek's portion and kept the surplus to build up his army and to make his city rich. Anything that was left (and he was not the kind to tolerate a loss) was salted away for his own use, or at least that of his throne and court. It was a talent that earned him the nickname 'Kalita', or 'Moneybags', and though there have been some attempts to hint at his financial saintliness (the moneybags could, after all, have been used to distribute pennies to the poor), the title was not originally meant to flatter.

Moscow's prosperity was self-reinforcing. When Tver's prince was defeated, his boyars, the nobility who served him both in battle and at court, began to gravitate to Moscow, and each defector brought a levy of valuable troops and land. The balance between Tver and Moscow shifted permanently, in turn attracting more resources to the upstart court.[46] Ivan Kalita's role as grand prince also offered far more than prestige. As the Mongols' senior intermediary, he had a share of the profits made in Novgorod.[47] This was a valuable prize, for the northern city had continued to trade with the Baltic, and its merchants were among the wealthiest in the region. Novgorod was sophisticated, proud and ancient, but it could not resist the military pressure that Ivan applied, repeatedly, under the guise of collecting Mongol tribute. The worldly prince offered it protection, in the mafia understanding of the term, against potential threats from other regional armies. His boyars profited proportionately, and Moscow turned into the kind of place where anyone who had ambition simply had to live.[48]

At last Moscow began to shed its backwoods feel. It was still a small place, no more than a mile across at its widest. Trees grew everywhere, despite the recent building-boom, and there was uncleared forest stretching off to both the west and south. A thriving trading district nestled to the south of the Kremlin hill, on the opposite bank of the river, and there were artisans' quarters to the north and east, but the most striking civic landmarks were the massive walls, patched, pitted and scarred from successive fires, that defined Ivan's fortress on the central hill. Since almost everything was made of timber (including Ivan's palace), those fires were probably the city's greatest enemy. The wooden fortress walls were smeared with clay, which reduced the risk of combustion, but other parts of Moscow burned repeatedly. Chronicles of the period (which are incomplete) record four major fires in fifteen years, including the catastrophes of 1337 ('eighteen churches burned'), and 1343 ('twenty-eight churches burned').

The word 'Kremlin', which first appeared in Moscow at about this time, was not the city's monopoly. It may have been coined for the stronghold of Novgorod's vulnerable neighbour, Pskov, and it came to Moscow (and its rival, Tver) when craftsmen with experience from older towns were hired to build the fourteenth-century princes' wooden walls.[49] Russian fortresses were nothing like the castles of the European west, let alone the familiar (usually gloomy-looking) Norman keep.[50] A fourteenth-century Austrian castle typically occupied 1,800 square yards; the Moscow Kremlin of Ivan Kalita's time, which covered about 47 acres, was more than a hundred times larger.[51] The design followed the natural contours of the land, taking advantage of the river and the steepest banks, but a compound of this size was difficult to maintain. Almost invariably there was a corner somewhere that looked derelict, a gate that opened through a sea of mud. It was a measure of Ivan Kalita's good relationship with Uzbek that he was able to secure permission to repair (and in effect, to replace) the ruins of the Kremlin walls in 1339. The defences that he ordered, twenty-foot beams of incorruptible new oak, were not quite the token barrier that the Mongols had originally envisaged.

The gates – also of oak – were equally imposing, and the fortress projected a regal atmosphere from a distance. But anyone who managed to enter it would have noticed a bucolic informality around the timber palaces inside. The Moscow Kremlin was laid out like a small town; in Ivan Kalita's time it was usually known simply as the 'city' (*grad*). Apart from the prince and his family, its most important residents were the boyars, whose rank was second only to the prince, and their extended families, whose pedigree often reached back as far as Ivan's own.[52] A few wealthier merchants also had their homes inside the walls – there were already more than twenty principal houses on the hill – but though the compound was beginning to feel crowded by the expansive standards of the age, each wooden mansion stood in separate substantial grounds, allowing space for kitchens, store-rooms, stables, vegetable gardens, orchards and small livestock in their pens.[53] In later iconography, the Kremlin was imagined as an ante-room of heaven, but in Ivan Kalita's day it would have reeked of mildewed fur and mould and long-fermented sweat.

But there must have been at least some trace of resinous incense, for the Kremlin was Moscow's central religious site. It was already established as a focus of pilgrimage in 1262, when it was granted to Prince Daniil. The first recorded Kremlin monastery, dedicated to the Saviour, was located near the spot that the prince eventually chose for his palace, and an early church (probably attached to it) became the burial-place of Moscow's original Daniilovich rulers.[54] Daniil himself may well have added the even more prestigious one that stood, at the beginning of Ivan Kalita's reign, on the slightly higher ground beyond. This building seems to have been made of stone, and Ivan would have had to demolish it in

1326 to make way for his new cathedral.[55] The purpose of such projects was not merely to engage in a display of wealth. The fear of judgement and damnation was pervasive; it was already common, if death did not strike him too suddenly, for a prince to prepare for the next world by having himself tonsured under a new name, thereby distancing himself from any sin that he had perpetrated under the old one. The merit gained by founding any sacred building was incalculable. The time has come to introduce the final actor in this early drama, and he is a monk.

Metropolitan Peter played a decisive part in the Kremlin's story. Officially, he had responsibility for all the Russian lands. His own birthplace was in the south, so theoretically he could have focused his mission on the old Rus heartland around the Dnieper. But Kiev had become a frontier-town, harried by constant steppe-based raids, and Peter's predecessor had already moved the metropolitan's main residence to the relative safety of Vladimir.[56] It was Peter, however, who shifted the focus of religious loyalty to Moscow. His motives for aligning himself with Ivan Kalita are lost in time, but the main one may have been antipathy to Tver. At the time of Peter's appointment in 1308, Grand Prince Mikhail of Tver had an alternative candidate in mind, and he attempted to overturn the patriarch's choice of Peter for the post of metropolitan by accusing the new man of simony, the medieval church's version of corruption. The threat of prison was enough to prejudice Peter against Tver's prince for life, and the priest, who evaded the charge, turned out to be at least as skilled a politician as his enemy.[57]

Peter's dislike of Tver made him Moscow's natural ally, but it was only when Ivan came to the throne that he could forge a lasting alliance with the city's ruler.[58] Before that, he had worked to build relations with Uzbek, visiting the Horde several times and consolidating a relationship of mutual respect and mutual political advantage.[59] Over the years, and almost always with the khan's blessing, the shrewd metropolitan steadily replaced the church's key appointments in the Russian lands with sympathizers of his own. At one point, he even frustrated one of Tver's military campaigns by withholding his blessing from its troops as they awaited orders near Vladimir.[60] But he and Ivan also seem to have become good friends. Later chronicles insist that the pair liked to sit and talk alone.[61] Peter certainly acquired a residence (*podvor'e*) in the Kremlin in 1322, and spent increasing amounts of time there. When Ivan's older brother Yury was murdered in 1325, it was Peter who conducted the burial, and as the metropolitan began to think of his own grave, the idea of Ivan's Kremlin was not ruled out.[62] For the newly created prince, the honour was unprecedented, for his upstart city lacked a native saint, and as yet it had no pretensions to the charisma of Vladimir.

The scene that Ushakov would later paint unfolded on 4 August 1326. There was a special solemnity as the young prince Ivan and the ailing priest gathered with their entire court beside a new hole in the ground. Around them were supplies of rock and the oak for deep foundation piles. Their task was to lay the first stone of a church with an ambitious dome, the daughter and successor of the Cathedral of the Dormition in Vladimir. Some said that they were also marking the site of the metropolitan's future grave, though Peter probably took a few months more to decide. In the end, however, his stone shrine was indeed built into the heart of the new cathedral. Ivan was at the Horde when the old man died that December, but he hurried back to attend a service on the half-completed site. The Kremlin had acquired its sacred centre and the sort of religious gravitas that only Kiev among the Russian cities had ever equalled. Moscow's leaders lost no time establishing Peter's credentials as a 'wonder-worker', and in 1339 he was officially declared to be the Kremlin's first true saint.[63] Future historians of Moscow would now have something holy to put in the place of taxes and extortion when they needed a foundation myth.

Ivan's Dormition Cathedral was not his last stone building on the Kremlin hill. In the next few years, his growing wealth enabled him to commission several more, including the Church of St John of the Ladder (1329) and the Cathedral of the Archangel Michael (1333). He also rebuilt (some say he founded) the Cathedral of the Saviour of the Forest (1330), replacing the Saviour Monastery's existing wooden building with a fine stone structure that he could admire from his palace windows.[64] In all, it was a considered building programme, each element of which played a part in the Kremlin's ritual life, and it had the welcome result that Moscow could now boast more stone churches than Tver.[65] But though the new foundations were to form the cardinal points of Moscow's religious geography for centuries to come, their first incarnations (with the possible exception of the Dormition Cathedral dome) were relatively modest.[66] None has survived. The skills that had created Andrei Bogoliubsky's soaring roofs were not available to Kalita, for

Mongol rule had cut the Russian north-east off from European crafts-men, and the khan had drafted its native master-stonemasons to work at Sarai. Dilapidated though Vladimir's great cathedral had become by 1326, it would be many more decades before an architect in Moscow could better it.

But church scribes wrote the history of Muscovy, so everything was made to point towards a blessed end, and the Kremlin buildings, how-ever modest in their time, were retrospectively endowed with majesty. Ivan's Dormition Cathedral was the most sacred of these, but the Chu-dov (Miracles) Monastery, whose first stones were laid in the reign of Ivan Kalita's grandson, Dmitry Donskoi (ruled 1359–89), became another holy and auspicious place, and the metropolitan who founded it, Aleksii, later joined Peter in the pantheon of Moscow saints. In 1407, it was followed by the first stone church of a woman's monastery, named for the Ascension, whose patron may have been Donskoi's widow, Evdokiya.[67] Neither of the new religious houses was splendid at first, but ultimately both became magnificent, and so their stories have acquired a sort of vigorous inevitability. But this is a deliberate illusion, however tempting it may be to see all later Moscows in Ivan Kalita's Kremlin. True, Metropolitan Aleksii continued Peter's work of bracing Moscow against Tver, building relations with the khan, and fighting off regional threats to the city's security. And unlike Peter's, Aleksii's parti-ality for Moscow was overt (he was Ivan Kalita's godson), but even he did not preside over the sublime capital of much later myths.

Like its church buildings, the fourteenth-century Kremlin had a long way to go before it looked much like the centre of an empire. Kalita's walls fell prey to fire and general decay; in 1365 the city burned disas-trously once again. At Metropolitan Aleksii's urging, Dmitry Donskoi and his boyars donated the funds to replace the wooden Kremlin walls with stone. In the winter of 1366–7, lines of sledges from the villages of Domodedovo, Syanovo and Podolsk converged upon the ice-bound fortress bearing piles of freshly quarried white limestone.[68] An army of peasant labourers followed them into the city, spitting and cursing as they worked to complete the entire structure in a single summer. This was an epic project, far more ambitious than Ivan Kalita's stone church, and the investment paid off for some years.[69] Moscow withstood attacks from several quarters, and its prince, a war-hero as well as a successful politician, greatly increased its regional prestige.[70] But in August 1382, the Mongol leader, Tokhtamysh, led a punitive attack against Dmitry's capital, and what happened next was not the stuff of patriotic icon-painting.

As Tokhtamysh approached, Dmitry fled, and so did Moscow's metropolitan.[71] The Kremlin nonetheless withstood several days of siege, answering the Mongols' arquebuses with stones, boiling water and arrows. Conceding that he could not batter his way into the fortress, Tokhtamysh sent a delegation to the city authorities. His messenger announced that the Mongols' quarrel was with the prince alone, and since the prince was not at home he asked, no doubt with a disarming bow, if his lord might admire the Muscovites' fine new walls from the inside. Proudly, and in some relief, Moscow opened its gates (there is a version of the tale that also mentions Mongol scaling-ladders). The city's temporary ruler, Ostei, was the first person the Mongols slaughtered. Then the invaders sacked the Kremlin, splattering the new white stone with its defenders' blood and torching any building that would burn.[72] It was a human and an economic tragedy, and it was followed by another eighty years of Russian civil war. If the Golden Horde had not been attacked from the east, by Tamerlane, or if luck had been with some of Moscow's rivals or its enemies, the famous limestone Kremlin might have sunk into the same picturesque provincial ruin as its wooden namesake in Tver. Even the Black Death had a salutary role to play, for it ravaged the region several times, and in the process wiped out so many younger members of the royal line that there were fewer wasteful fratricidal property disputes.[73]

All that uncertainty is missing from Ushakov's founding scene. Peter and Ivan plant their tree, the Virgin extends her protective cloak, and Moscow rises from the gleaming rock, the heir of Kiev and Vladimir and of golden, transcendent Byzantium. The succession of rulers also runs unbroken, featuring generation after generation of saintly warriors and wise, divinely ordained Russian tsars. The fact that almost every element in the icon is fantasy is almost incidental. The myth itself, not the confused and murky truth, was to become the cornerstone of Kremlin politics.

2

Renaissance

The brick structure in Ushakov's icon, the Kremlin that is still a short-hand for the state of Russia now, was built in the last two decades of the fifteenth century. 'Once a building is up,' writes the architectural historian Spiro Kostof, 'it becomes a live presence.'[1] All but the blandest also have their personalities, and few have been as continuously distinctive, for five hundred years, as Moscow's red fortress. Today, it looks so solid and coherent that it is difficult to imagine how the site could ever have been different. By the time that Dmitry Donskoi's descendant, Ivan III (ruled 1462–1505), commissioned the present structure, however, there had already been a limestone citadel, a white fort, on the Kremlin hill for more than a century. The fact that any prince was prepared to undertake the risky and expensive tasks of demolition and rebuilding speaks volumes for Moscow's development in the years that followed Donskoi's death. The fifteenth century saw the city almost constantly at war. Its princes' armies were largely successful in the field, but as their stronghold's wealth increased, the dangers that it faced grew ever more complex. When Ivan III ordered his builders to use brick, he was not merely indulging a whim. The decision was practical. Limestone was becoming obsolete, for as Russian troops were starting to discover, the soft rock shattered under cannon-fire.[2]

The raising of Ivan III's Kremlin was so closely linked to Moscow's own consolidation that it became a chapter in many later Russian narratives of nationhood. The nineteenth-century historian Nikolai Karamzin spoke for many when he described the citadel as 'the home of great historical memories' and the cradle of an 'autocratic power that was created not for the personal benefit of the autocrat himself, but for the people's common good'.[3] Inspired by lyrical prose of that sort, it is tempting to imagine the tale as a classic opera. The music, probably composed by Borodin, would need to have an oriental theme, for the story is supposed to open in the final days of Mongol rule.[4] It is set in a palace in the old Kremlin, the year is 1471, and the curtain rises on an all-male court with scores of characters in gorgeous golden robes. They have gathered to discuss the tribute that their prince has long been forced to pay, and the high point (which was immortalized in several nineteenth-century paintings[5]) comes when Ivan III finally leaps from his throne, towering above the khan's envoy. As the unfortunate messenger cringes at his feet, the prince (cue the lead Russian bass) declares that Moscow will no longer be the Mongols' vassal. Ivan becomes a sovereign ruler, and a glorious chapter in the annals of Russia, a moment that the new Kremlin itself will soon immortalize, begins.

This Kremlin is a hymn to Russian genius, combining palaces and cathedrals of daring beauty with walls that will be proof against assault. It is unique, iconic, like a pure expression of the nation's soul. But that mystique, although it has nurtured some of them for generations, owes a great deal to the imaginations of Russian nationalists. When Ivan III built his fortress, he was still a prince of the steppes and trade routes, and far from blazing some new cultural trail, his building itself followed European trends. In the age of the renaissance, magnificent buildings topped the list for any ruler seeking to make his mark in an expanding world. 'The palace of a king should stand in the heart of a city,' wrote the brilliant Genoese architect Leon Battista Alberti in 1452. 'It should be easy of access, beautifully-adorned, and delicate and polite rather than proud or stately.'[6] Ivan III was never going to win a prize for delicacy, but he did know something about power. By the time the Kremlin's first new layers of brick were being laid, he had expanded Moscow's territory more than three-fold, incorporating some of Russia's oldest cities, including Tver and Novgorod. But he still needed to get himself noticed, to join the international diplomatic game. He also needed to defend his winnings against a sea of rivals, including some alarmingly sophisticated ones.

Because the pride of Russia is at stake, facts such as these have often been obscured. In 1950, under Stalin's ageing xenophobic eye, a Soviet academic called P. V. Sytin felt obliged to insist that the Kremlin's 'planning ... followed purely Russian architectural principles'.[7] If that man could have travelled, a tour of northern Italy might well have prompted him to find a different phrase. He would have been surrounded by the inspirations for the Moscow Kremlin everywhere, from the swallow-tail battlements above Verona's city gates to Milan's Castello Sforzesco and, in the case of Bologna, the very bricks in the town walls. The history of the Kremlin in its era of rebirth involves a great deal more than noble princes and hard-working native craftsmen. It leads from Moscow to the Black Sea coast and onwards to Europe, it offers glimpses of a rough-edged court still half-embedded in the woods, and at its centre is a set of buildings: mortar, scaffolding and brick.

The Muscovites did not defeat the Golden Horde in a decisive battle. The Mongol empire collapsed under the pressure of internal conflict. Sarai was sacked by Tamerlane in the 1390s, and though it was rebuilt, the city never really recovered. Ivan III's father, Vasily II (ruled 1425–62), was the last prince in the Kremlin to hold his titles even theoretically by grace of the Horde. The empire of the grasslands fragmented in the 1420s, leaving at least four contenders for its legacy: the khanate of Sibir, the khanates of Kazan and Astrakhan on the Volga, and the khanate of the Crimea. The fifth heir, arguably, was the state of Moscow (also known as Muscovy) itself. Like any gaggle of legatees, these five successors spent years contesting their collective heritage. Ivan III's most consistent ally was Mengli-Girey, the leader of the Crimean khanate, and with his help the prince (who sometimes used the word khan to describe himself[8]) extended Moscow's influence along the Volga to Kazan. But the whole southern border was unstable. For decades to come, the frontier with the steppe was to be a constant drain on Moscow's armies and its men.

Disunity and civil war were not Mongol monopolies, however. Moscow also came close to disintegration during Ivan's childhood; the prince took part in his first battle in 1452, at the age of twelve. As usual, the issue was the succession. A civil war began in 1433, when Vasily II was challenged for the grand princely throne by members of his uncle's family in a last-gasp revival of the tradition that brothers might inherit in the place of sons. The subsequent hostilities dragged on for fourteen years, and both sides resorted to extreme tactics, including kidnap, murder and the breaking of oaths. In a move reminiscent of Constantinople at its nastiest, Vasily II ordered the blinding of one of his rivals. Ten years later, during the brief ascendancy of the opposing side, a captive

Vasily was brought to the Kremlin and forcibly blinded in revenge. The sightless prince was left alive, however, and managed to assemble a fresh military coalition to defeat his tormentors. By the spring of 1447 his victory – and the right to bequeath his lands and titles to his eldest son – was secure.

Moscow now claimed the Grand Principality of Vladimir in perpetuity, and from 1447 its prince also began to call himself the 'Lord of all the Rus'. But the neighbours along his western borders – Lithuania, Poland and Livonia – were in a good position to challenge that ambition. Fifteenth-century Lithuania was the most obvious rival. Unlike its present-day successor, this grand duchy was one of the largest states in Europe, and as the Mongol grip had loosened, it had come to dominate the Dnieper lands, including Chernigov and Smolensk as well as the ancient capital of Kiev. In that respect, it was a real pretender to the Rus heritage, and it also enjoyed strong links with Catholic Europe, including dynastic connections to Cracow and Buda. After generations of stubborn paganism, its rulers now vacillated between Orthodoxy and Catholicism, alternately vying with Moscow for control of Russia's metropolitan (whose seat, despite recent changes, was still officially meant to be Kiev) or courting the support of Rome. Cultured, wealthy and intellectually diverse, Lithuania was more open than Moscow, and almost every traveller who ended up in its capital, Vilno, found the place more congenial than its neighbour.[9] There was more than one potential future for the Russian people, in other words, and the possibilities did not all point to autocracy.

But Moscow was determined to secure its own trade routes and hinterland, and its expansion was prodigious. The scale of its growth as a regional power testifies to the skill and flexibility of three princes – Vasily II, Ivan III, and Ivan's son, Vasily III – but it speaks volumes, too, about their ruthlessness. The Kremlin became the centre of a military regime. The old appanage system, where each prince ruled his own ancestral territory from a recognized seat, was reduced to a shadow. By using diplomacy, military pressure, and even marriage, Moscow's princes absorbed the cities of the Oka, Klyazma and Upper Volga valleys one by one. The displaced clans from the provincial capitals were usually obliged to move to Moscow permanently, and soon the opportunity disappeared to make an independent fortune anywhere else. As a result, politics in the Kremlin grew tenser, circling ever more tightly around the grand prince himself.[10] Where Ivan Kalita's fortress had been run by a company of buccaneers, this one was full of whispers and the muffled footfalls of conspiracy. Everything depended on personal contact.

For a time, however, the one prize that eluded Moscow was the ancient northern city, Novgorod. Although the net was sweeping close, the old trading capital seemed to thrive despite the pressure from its upstart neighbour to the south. It paid tribute to Moscow (and through it, for decades, to the Golden Horde), but Novgorod preserved a distinctive culture and a most unautocratic pattern of civic government. The city had a cosmopolitan air. Wealthy, proud and free to build links of its own with foreigners, Novgorod took an active part in northern Europe's Hanseatic League.[11] With such connections, it was hardly surprising that a faction among its ruling class resented the Muscovite grand princes' endless financial demands. It did not help, either, that businesses were suffering from Muscovite competition on fur-trading routes that Novgorod regarded as its own. This city would not buckle easily. When Vasily II and two of his younger sons paid a visit in 1460, there were rumours of a plot to murder all of them. Some members of Novgorod's ruling council even advocated an alliance with Lithuania, hoping to find a diplomatic (or even a military) route out of their subjection to Moscow.[12] In 1470, when Ivan III learned that Novgorod's dissidents had made a fresh approach to Vilno, he seized the excuse to raise an army and ride north.

Novgorod could field more men, but Ivan's troops were better led, and on 14 July 1471 the defenders were routed. The battle was one of the most decisive of Ivan's career, and Novgorod's absorption into Muscovy began. Like a python with an antelope, the smaller state set about consuming its enormous prize, but (just as in the python's case) the process took considerable time. First, Novgorod was forced to sever diplomatic ties with Lithuania; in future the city would follow Moscow's line in international affairs. Its leaders also paid a hefty fine, although at this stage they could still afford the 15,000 rubles that Ivan required. What seemed a fair and even magnanimous treaty in other ways, however, in fact allowed Ivan to regroup for the next round. In 1477 the Muscovite army mobilized for a second time, again on the pretext of treachery in Novgorod, and in December of that year the city was forced to accept far more humiliating terms. Its independent council was dissolved. The bell that had been used to summon it, the symbol of established civic pride, was taken down and carried off to Moscow, where it took its place among the others in Ivan's Kremlin. More carts – three hundred of them – trundled south with Novgorod's treasury of pearls, gold, silver and gems, adding enormously to the wealth that blazed round Ivan's throne.[13] And finally, the authoritarian political style of Moscow's court was forced upon the older city. 'We shall prosecute our sovereign rule,' Ivan decreed, 'as in the lower lands.'[14]

Disgrace was followed by dismemberment. In 1478, Ivan seized about a million hectares (roughly 3,860 square miles) of territory from the city-state. To make sure there would be no revolt, he deported the residents on a mass scale, and redistributed their land to his own retainers. Novgorod itself faced new restrictions. In 1493, the offices of the Hanseatic trading league in the city were closed on Ivan's orders, cutting off Novgorod's European links and forcing it more closely into Moscow's orbit. Meanwhile, Novgorod's archbishop, Feofil, who spoke against Ivan's tyranny, was arrested and imprisoned in the Kremlin's Chudov Monastery.[15] Two decades after the first fatal blow, the python had finished with its most spectacular prey. The victory brought Ivan's Moscow unprecedented riches. By issuing the northern land grants on a loan-for-service basis, the grand prince also laid the foundations for an expanded army that was almost self-financing, for in return for their estates, the settlers (*pomeshchiki*) were required to serve as cavalrymen and even to provide their own equipment, including their horses and attendants. By the end of the fifteenth century, the army at Ivan's disposal was roughly four times the size of anything that Moscow had ever fielded before.[16] The old Rus south-west, Galicia and what is now western Ukraine, remained in Lithuanian control, but Ivan could now call himself the sovereign and protector of the wealthy Russian north.

That wealth was not the only source of Moscow's lustre, however, and military force was not the only glue that held its far-flung territories together. Religious institutions were as crucial in the age of Moscow's expansion as they had been to Ivan Kalita. The relationship was one of mutual benefit. The Kremlin's charisma derived at least as much from the metropolitan's presence as from the prince and his throne room. The two, in fact, were parts of the same whole, and in the reigns of Vasily II and Ivan III their relationship was reinforced by events beyond

Moscow's borders. For centuries, the Russian church had existed on the remote margins of the dazzling and sophisticated Byzantine commonwealth. Its spiritual capital had been Constantinople, and its metropolitans had owed their jobs to politicians and religious leaders there. Though their subjection to the Mongols had long masked the fact, this adherence to Constantinople was a major obstacle to any close alliance between Moscow and Europe's numerous Catholic states. In the 1450s, however, a series of crises around the Mediterranean tested the strength of many ancient religious loyalties. Moscow resisted the temptations of Rome, and the Kremlin was launched on its path to leadership in the Orthodox world.

The first of these crises was triggered by the rapid expansion of the Ottoman Turkish empire in the 1400s. Though Constantinople had been in decline for some time, the rise of a well-organized Turkish military force on the Mediterranean coast marked its ultimate death knell. By the early fifteenth century, the spiritual capital of the Orthodox faith was no more than a fortified island in a Muslim landscape that stretched from Eastern Anatolia to the Aegean and northwards round the Black Sea into present-day Bulgaria. The trap was closing, too, and its desperate need for armed support led Constantinople's rulers to consider a theological rapprochement with Rome. But there were so many hatchets to be buried first that the Bosphorus itself might have flowed red with rust. The desecrations wrought during the Fourth Crusade in 1204 were just the start; the leaders of the Eastern Church also had a vast stock of theological grievances against the schismatics in Rome. Many church leaders in the eastern world believed that any compromise with the Papists, however small, would lead them all to damnation and hell.

In the short term, however, some Orthodox clerics took a more diplomatic view, and a few even believed in Christian unity for its own sake. This was a prospect welcomed by some parties on the other side – Europe itself had troubled borders with the Turk, and the embattled pope of the time, Eugene IV, may also have hoped that unity with the old east would heal his own flock's bitter internal feuds – so ecumenical talks were organized. These opened in 1438 as the Council of Ferrara. The discussions were intense and prolonged. In 1439, the entire meeting moved to Florence to escape an outbreak of plague, whereupon the arguments resumed, sticking (as always) on such thorny issues as the nature of the Trinity, the wording of the Creed, and the inclusion of yeast in the Communion bread, to say nothing of the overall spiritual primacy of the pope. The metropolitan that Constantinople had recently appointed to take care of the Russian lands, a Greek called Isidor, argued consistently for Christian reconciliation.[17] At one point, thanks to his enthusiasm, the Russian church was even poised to recognize the existence of Purgatory (another stubborn sticking-point). To their surprise, almost every Orthodox delegate at the Council also accepted the overall authority of the Latin Pope. Isidor himself left Florence with the new title of cardinal.[18] But what had been agreed under the friendly Tuscan sun looked scandalous to many who had not attended the meeting for themselves. Back in Anatolia, the archbishop of Ephesus was so horrified by the alien advances of the Catholics that he refused to sign the Council's final papers. Even further to the east, in Moscow, the treachery at 'Frolents' was the pretext for a coup.

Vasily and the Russian church refused to recognize Isidor. On his arrival in Moscow, the cardinal-metropolitan was thrown into a cell in the Kremlin's Chudov Monastery. The charge was heresy, and the penalty (on this occasion, just for once, Moscow's authorities did not carry it out) could have been public burning. Clearly, Isidor had no chance at the Kremlin court, and it also turned out that while he had been at Florence, the prince had found a candidate of his own, a Russian called Yona, for the metropolitan's seat. This step was a veritable declaration of spiritual independence, though a flurry of correspondence between the Kremlin and Patriarch Mitrofan of Constantinople attempted to cloak the decision in the language of grievance. In 1441, rejecting Isidor decisively, Vasily's priests requested Mitrofan to send a replacement metropolitan of his own choice. The Orthodox Church in Russia was neither Roman nor Jewish, they wrote. Instead, it was the disciple of the blessed Constantine, the faithful child of Kiev's St Vladimir, and after generations of such piety, its servants should not be forced into Latin heresies.[19] Moscow's appeal for a substitute metropolitan was unsuccessful, and in 1448, its prince finally informed the patriarch that he had acted unilaterally, replacing Isidor with Yona for himself.[20]

The new man, as Vasily stressed, would serve as metropolitan of Kiev and all Rus. For centuries, after all, that had been the title that had been conferred, more or less without controversy, on each of his predecessors. But in 1448, the move was doubly inflammatory, for Vasily was not merely wresting control of the metropolitanate from Constantinople's hands; he was also laying claim (on behalf of the Kremlin's religious candidate) to primacy in the Lithuanian-controlled cities of the Dnieper, including Kiev. The coup caused indignation in a range of foreign courts.[21] For nervous observers beyond his borders, Vasily's letter hinted that Moscow's political reach might one day extend into what is now Ukraine.

For the present, however, the real revolution was that Moscow had acted without the sanction of Constantinople. For the first time, a new metropolitan owed his job directly to Moscow's grand prince, and not surprisingly the Russian church became an even closer ally of the Kremlin. The asset it brought to the partnership was its theocratic ideology. For years to come, while princes did the fighting and sat on their golden thrones, it was the church that crafted the rituals, edited the hagiographical chronicle-histories, and designed the iconography of charismatic government. It also offered commentaries on the events of the day. When the city of Constantinople finally fell to the Ottomans in 1453, the Russian church was ready with context. The catastrophe, as it explained, was a judgement for the heresy of Florence. Vasily's unilateral move, in appointing Yona in place of a doomed apostate, turned out to have been doubly blessed, and so was the grand prince himself.

But close associations have a price, and in this case the princes paid with scrupulous public piety. They were not free to test the waters of ecumenism. Their priests, too, often blocked the path to cultural diplomacy in the form of overtures to Europe. When Ivan III agreed to betroth his daughter, Elena, to the Catholic prince Alexander of Lithuania in 1494, he made it a condition that she had to retain her Orthodox faith. There were political reasons for this (the marriage was a power game on Ivan's part), but an Orthodox priest from Moscow called Foma took the letter of religion to an unacceptable extreme. He nearly wrecked the wedding ceremony in Vilno by intoning his own prayers above the Catholic service, and at one point, when the bride and groom had just shared a ritual cup of wine, he grabbed the vessel from their hands and smashed it on the church flagstones.[22] The marriage was never a happy one.

The princes themselves were not exempt from the church's wrath. The notion of Moscow as the Third Rome, which emerged in the 1520s, began life as a warning to the government. Rather than praising

Moscow, it was intended to remind its rulers what could happen when a great empire deserted the paths of virtue. Sinful leaders, the church scribes pointed out, had proved the ruin of Rome and Constantinople, both of which had once appeared so blessed. If Moscow – the Third Rome – should also stray as they had done, its doom was sealed.[23] The range of errors that provoked that warning in the years to come was comprehensive, but none was more serious than the thought that any prince might build too close a link with the perfidious Catholics.

More usually, however, the church reserved the torments of hell for those who had displeased the Kremlin. In that respect, it proved to be a resolute supporter of Muscovite government. The religious leaders at Ivan III's court were happy to accuse Novgorod's Bishop Feofil of flirtation with the Latin Poles, for instance, and they also attacked the citizens of Pskov, whose independent culture bordered, for a time, on heresy.[24] The Grand Prince of Moscow was now defender of the Russian faith in all but name.[25] If any city disobeyed him, its punishment was certain. Ivan Kalita had depended on the khan – and on his genes – for sovereignty. By the reign of Ivan III, the prince's right to rule was beginning to look as if it came – with conditions – from heaven.

The Kremlin's enhanced religious status was also a spur to rebuilding, and in particular to efforts by the new metropolitan, Yona. At the time of his appointment in 1448, the Kremlin was not in the greatest of repair. It had been sacked several times during the recent civil war, it had suffered what chroniclers insisted was an earthquake, and much of it had burned in the great fire of 1445.[26] It is hard to imagine how the buildings looked, or how the overall landscape, which must have been littered with builders' clutter, related to the art and treasure that both church and palace had begun to gather. It was no accident that many churches and monastic buildings doubled as strongrooms.[27] Their limestone crypts were used to hide the city's valuables; in times of danger everyone tried to move their treasure to the safety of the Kremlin walls. But some things were harder to carry than others. The Kremlin Cathedral of the Annunciation, built some time in the 1360s, was adorned with an iconostasis created by the master-artists Theophanes the Greek and Andrei Rublev.[28] There were beautiful wall-paintings and more icons in the Archangel Cathedral and the Church of the Nativity of the Virgin. Among the other wonders was a gilded clock, the work of an early fifteenth-century Serb master, which struck the hours in a way that locals regarded as miraculous.[29] Some of the icons have survived, but that clock, and much of the great art of the fourteenth and early fifteenth centuries, was destroyed within decades of its creation. Vasily II was prince over a timber-yard.

The whole place seemed to need repair, but under Yona there was also pressure to imbue it with a godly splendour. In 1450, the metropolitan commissioned a stone palace for himself – the first such building in the citadel – and though its use was ceremonial (the metropolitan lived, like almost everyone else, in cosily built wooden chambers), the residence was a landmark in the Kremlin's architectural development. Adjoining it, Yona added a new church, dedicated to the Deposition of the Robe, in honour of Moscow's allegedly miraculous preservation from the Mongols.[30] The building-work was supervised by Vladimir Khovrin, a wealthy businessman of Greek extraction whose family had moved to Moscow from the Crimea only a generation earlier. Khovrin became one of the age's most prolific master-builders, a man so influential that, despite his status as a mere merchant, he was permitted to build a church of his own in the Kremlin. Though long gone now, it once stood in his opulent palace compound behind the Frolov (Saviour) gates, and it was notable because it was probably the first religious structure in Moscow to combine the traditional limestone with brick.[31]

The other Kremlin builder of this time was an entrepreneur called Vasily Ermolin. Like Khovrin, he had long-standing connections to the culture of the Black Sea region, and his masons had worked in a string of provincial Russian cities. He was often in demand for large projects, including a new cathedral for the Kremlin's Ascension Convent, but the shabby Kremlin walls were his most urgent concern, and in 1462 he began to renovate them in the name of the new prince, Ivan III. He personally commissioned a giant bas-relief to face the city from the Frolov gates. Its subject was not the Virgin and Child, but a mounted St George spearing a dragon in a crude but eye-catchingly three-dimensional style. A second sculpture, on the inward-facing side, honoured Dmitry Solunsky, the saint most closely linked to Dmitry Donskoi.[32]

These innovations hinted that the Kremlin might be set to change, but the real turning-point came with the rebuilding of Ivan Kalita's Dormition Cathedral. The catalyst was yet another fire. In August 1470, much of the Kremlin was destroyed by flames that blew across the compound from the south and east. Some accounts claim that only three households escaped, and at least one stone cathedral was certainly gutted.[33] Moscow's metropolitan was now a deeply pious man called Filipp, and he saw the destruction as an opportunity to rebuild the Kremlin's holiest shrine on a magnificent scale. By this stage, only scaffolding and prayer were keeping Ivan Kalita's church upright; the fire was providential (and Filipp certainly saw it as an act of God), but rebuilding was already overdue.[34] The metropolitan began by trying to raise funds – extorting silver from his bishops, taxing the monasteries, and skimming off the coins the faithful offered to their local saints. He also tried to recruit the grand prince to his cause by hinting that the cathedral would be a true memorial to Moscow's military victories. But Ivan never saw the need to contribute, and even after the fall of Novgorod (and Moscow's 15,000-ruble windfall) Filipp was left to raise the cash alone. It was an epic labour worthy of the sort of man who wore iron chains under his robes to remind himself of the mortality of flesh.[35]

The team Filipp assembled was a Russian one. His builders were Ivan Krivtsov and Myshkin, whose main distinction, historically speaking, is probably the fact that we know their names at all.[36] Working with them was an army of slaves, some drawn from the church's own reserve of captive manpower (slave-labour was ubiquitous in Russia at this time) and others purchased from the Tatars of the steppe.[37] Many were already skilled, and some of these looked on the work as a chance to bargain for their freedom. Because its Greek-derived design was said to have been laid down, in the earliest days of Christianity, by God himself, the pious Filipp's principal goal was to build a cathedral in the exact style of Vladimir's. This was a real challenge, for the great building had originally owed much to the skills of the foreign masons who had worked at Andrei Bogoliubsky's court. Impressive enough at the time of its construction, too, the cathedral had been enlarged after a serious fire, and now boasted five breathtaking cupolas at the top of its improbably high walls.

Nothing daunted, in the winter of 1471–2, Filipp sent his master-builders to the older city to draw and measure the twelfth-century prototype, not least to ensure that Moscow's version would be yet more splendid, more beautiful, and larger.[38] As the early snow began to fall, Filipp watched as carters started unloading his fresh limestone from Moscow's frozen wharf (transport was always easier in winter). They were still working at Christmas, and again at Epiphany, when comets of exceptional brilliance appeared above the Kremlin, surely portents of a prodigy to come.[39] The following April, as the ground started to thaw, the metropolitan's men were ready to dig foundations and to start laying the drains. To the clanging of the Kremlin bells, a thankful company of priests joined Filipp and the icons in a procession around the site, accompanied by Ivan III and his entire court.

Filipp's new building was to stand over the outline of Ivan Kalita's, but though the old walls had to go, there were important rituals to complete first. By this stage, the tomb of Metropolitan Peter the Wonder-Worker was not the only shrine in the Dormition Cathedral. Filipp's builders had to down tools several times between May and early July, each time to allow prayers and processions and the discreet relocation of bones. Those of Yona, who had died in 1461, were said to smell so sweet that the whole site was perfumed by them. When Peter's coffin was opened, a white dove flew into the air, vanishing only when the lid was resealed. Clearly, these remains were not mere corpses. Orthodoxy took things literally (it still does), which meant that the saints were truly present in their dust. Their bones were holy relics, miraculous, and a wooden chapel was constructed to protect them. For eighteen months, it was here that services continued while the old building was knocked away and the new walls went up.[40]

But Filipp was never to see his cathedral. In April 1473, another fire swept through the Kremlin. The shock, following months of strain, proved too much for the metropolitan, and he died of a stroke. His greatest work continued without him, and by the summer of 1474 the vaults of the enormous structure were almost complete. As promised, it was grander than its ancestor in Vladimir, and seemed set to become the citadel's most awe-inspiring sight. The shell, as it was being built, became an attraction for the locals, who scrambled up the wooden scaffolding to marvel at the view, so it was fortunate that when the next disaster struck, in May, it was already evening. The last mason had bustled home at sunset, and even the most determined sightseers had climbed down from the rafters as the light began to fade. Only one lad remained, and he was nimble enough to escape. Some say there was another earthquake, others that the massive building was doomed from the start. Either way, that evening the north wall suddenly collapsed, crushing the wooden church inside and leaving the whole project in ruins.[41]

Recriminations started instantly. Ivan III consulted masters from Pskov, a city that had preserved its long-standing Baltic links and where the local stone-masons still talked occasionally with passing experts from north German towns. The Pskovians prudently refused to rebuild Filipp's church, but suggested that the problem lay with the poor quality of the lime that had been used in the builders' mortar. The question now was what to do about the ruin. It had been centuries since any mason in the Russian world had attempted to out-build the masters of pre-Mongol Vladimir, and some claimed that the skills had been entirely lost. But Ermolin (who acted as a consultant for Filipp's church) and the Khovrins (the old man had a son who continued the family interest in architecture) might well have succeeded with the project once the lessons had been learned. It was not so unusual, after all, for large structures to collapse in the medieval and renaissance world. The Cathedral of St Pierre at Beauvais was so disaster-prone that at one point the only person who dared to attempt its rescue was a condemned criminal, who accepted the job in order to escape the hangman's rope.[42] The Muscovites were still a long way from desperation of that order.

What no-one in Ivan's Moscow could do, however, was to match the skills that were now taking European courts by storm. The Russians knew how to cut stone, and the Khovrins had experience with brick, but none had mastered the new precision, the passion for exact proportion and persistent measurement. In Italy by the 1470s, however, there were builders who could manage veritable miracles. Their fame had spread so widely that even the Turkish sultan was interested. Some Russian bishops would have seen the cathedral dome in Brunelleschi's Florence for themselves (the lantern was still under construction at the time of the ecumenical council in 1439), and there were rumours of a plan for the wholesale transformation of the Papal capital at Rome. Further east, on the Danube, the king of Hungary had employed Italians to build a range of walls that had proved so fearsome that he was already said to be after more. What finally persuaded Ivan to hire an Italian engineer, however, was probably the influence of his new wife. Misogynists in the historical profession used to claim that she nagged him twice a week.[43]

The princess in this story was the niece of the last emperor of Christian Constantinople, Constantine XI Palaeologus. Her parents called her Zoe, and she spent her infancy in the Byzantine province of the Morea (today's Peloponnese). When that fell to the Turks in 1460, seven years after the capture of Constantinople, her family fled to Italy, taking as much as they could carry from the last imperial court, including books and icons, jewels and chestfuls of holy relics. Her father used some of the treasure to secure his children's future. In Zoe's case, a casket containing the head of the Apostle Andrew eased the negotiations to make her a ward of the pope, Paul II. Zoe grew up at his court among the most sophisticated thinkers of the age, maturing into an accomplished, ambitious and self-confident woman. She was raised as a Catholic (naturally), but as the heir of Constantinople she was also open to more ecumenical ideas.[44] When her immediate guardian, Cardinal Bessarion of Nicea, proposed a marriage to the grand prince of Orthodox Muscovy, the plan had a certain poetry.

Bessarion had already tried and failed several times to find his protégée a royal husband. Moscow was not the ideal choice – it was too far, too dangerous and too cold – but rumours of its growing wealth were beginning to spark Europe's interest. The evidence, in the shape of magnificent diplomatic gifts of sable, was starting to spill out of packing-crates more frequently as Moscow's isolation from the Catholic world drew to an end. The Papal court was also keen to forge a closer link with Ivan III for strategic reasons, as optimists still nursed a hope that the prince might be induced to support the European struggle against the Turks. As an incentive, Zoe's dowry was the Morea itself, which, the negotiators promised, would be Ivan's as soon as Mehmet II could be driven out. In the event, the Turks held on to Greece for another three hundred and fifty years.

It turned out that the bait that really worked with Ivan was the promise of European prestige. It was Zoe's name, and not her charm (or the Morea), that counted at the diplomatic stage. The Italians provided a portrait for Ivan's approval, but negotiators back in Moscow were so unaccustomed to drawings from life that they mistook the picture for an icon (it has since been lost). Zoe's Catholic religion was a problem, too, since Moscow had become the stronghold of the very Orthodoxy that her family had failed to protect. Ivan's marriage plans stalled for some months while the theological dangers were debated; Metropolitan Filipp, predictably, was the most sceptical of all. It was only in January 1472 that Ivan's envoy (and sometime mint-master), Gian-Battista della Volpe, finally embarked on the five-month journey back to Rome. By the time he got there at the end of May, Paul II had died. Nimbly, Volpe altered the pope's name on the documents he was carrying and created a cheerful gloss for the withering commentary on Catholicism that Filipp had inserted into the contract. On 1 June 1472, Zoe, now named Sofiya in honour of her new allegiance to Moscow, was symbolically married to an absent Ivan III. The Italian poet Luigi Pulci left a description of the princess at the time of her wedding. 'A mountain of fat,' he pronounced after an evening audience. 'All I could dream about all night were mountains of butter and grease. . .'[45] It was not the kindest of assessments, but Sofiya's future husband, as she may have known, was in turn reputed to be so terrifying that his glance alone made women faint.[46]

Three weeks after the ceremony, and following a farewell interview with the new pope, Sixtus IV (of Sistine Chapel fame), Sofiya set out for Moscow. Her caravan included a handful of homeward-bound Russians as well as a selection of fellow-Greeks, among whom was a close associate of her father's, Yury Trakhaniot, soon to become one of Ivan III's most effective diplomats. Sixtus insisted that the delegation should be greeted everywhere as if the pope himself were at its head. He even sent a special representative, Cardinal Bonumbre of Ajaccio, to lead the company, which must have made a most impressive sight. At least a hundred horses were needed to carry the people and their ziggurats of freight, which included Sofiya's belongings (and her person), gifts, and a selection of treasures from Rome and Constantinople. Relays of servants laboured with the baggage as the troupe progressed from city to city, for every stop seemed to involve more wedding gifts and more exchanges of jewels and relics. There was a lot of feasting, too.

But the journey also provided the princess and her entourage with a tour of Europe's finest buildings and most gracious courts. From Rome they travelled to Siena (a city to which Sofiya's father, the dispenser of sacred body parts, had once presented the embalmed hand of John the Baptist), where a reception costing 200 lire (five times the sum recently allocated for a dinner in honour of Lorenzo di Medici) was held for her in the famous black-and-white cathedral. Sofiya continued through Florence and Bologna (where people 'fought to have the honour of leading her horse'), to Vicenza (della Volpe's own home city) and the outskirts of Venice. Her party crossed the Alps via Innsbruck and Augsburg and arrived in Nuremberg – one of the finest walled cities in

Europe – in early August. The sun on her back would still have been warm as she headed north, more or less in a straight line, via Greussen, Nordhausen, Braunschweig, Celle, Lüneburg and Mölln to the Baltic port of Lübeck, jewel of the north, where she arrived on 1 September.

The contrast between the prosperous charms of northern Europe and the grey world to the east must have been chilling. By the time Sofiya's party reached Kolyvan (Tallinn), they had endured a stormy eleven-day voyage across the Baltic. Ahead lay two more months of wearying travel, much of it through dense autumnal forest. The crowds now seemed more alien, their curiosity less kind. In Pskov, observers stared at the Italians as if they were some species of fiend. Even the educated ones took exception to the scarlet-clad cardinal, Bonumbre, whose interpretation of his role as papal representative included an undiplomatic devotion to the Catholic cross and a socially disastrous contempt for icons.[47] Sofiya was getting a pungent taste of Russian cultural difference. As her retinue finally entered Moscow on 12 November, the light and warmth of Italy must have seemed very far away. As usual, too, it was snowing.[48]

What must have struck Sofiya most, when she had toured the Kremlin palaces at last, was the gap between what she could see and the splendour that her new husband so clearly thought to be his due. Even if it had been finished, Filipp's vaunted and expensive building was clearly no match for the Florentine dome. Her own quarters were somewhere in the jumble of wooden buildings below its building-site, and the view was sepia and grey. Ivan was not a great one for apologies, and he would never openly accept that anything he had commissioned was effectively a compromise. In terms of what Russians could do, his builders were already working at full stretch, and the size of his labour-force dwarfed anything that an Italian could raise. In the weeks to come, however, while the delegation wintered in Moscow, the conversation must have turned to what might really be achieved. Sofiya, as a student of Bessarion, was committed to the idea that Moscow could be Europe's valued ally in the struggle to regain Constantinople. There may have been discussions, too, about the nature of statehood; by 1472, Italy was experimenting with the proposition that government involved far more than feasting, churches and coercive force. The large pool of interpreters worked hard: Filipp, apparently, spent almost every waking hour in theological debate with Bonumbre.[49] But the conversation certainly turned to buildings, and from them to Europe's miraculous new architects. Whatever else, the arrival in the Kremlin of a well-placed and well-educated group from Italy's most wealthy courts would have dispelled any lingering fear that hiring builders from outside might be a leap into the unknown.

There really was only one place to go in fifteenth-century Europe if you were after an impressive master-builder. You did not have to be a Muscovite with a new and determined wife. When any prince wanted something gracious, something prestigious, and something that could be expected to stay up, he imported an expert from Italy.[50] Filipp might have resisted foreign (Catholic) help, but by the time his great project collapsed he was already dead. The next round was the grand prince's affair. Just three years after Ivan and Sofiya's wedding, in 1475, Aristotele Fioravanti, native of Bologna, arrived in Moscow at Ivan's invitation to offer his services as architect, mint-master, military engineer, deviser of instruments and all-purpose magician.[51] The choice suited everyone. Sofiya's guardian, Bessarion, had known Fioravanti personally for years. When Ivan's agent, Semen Tolbuzin, travelled to Venice in 1474 to hire a master-builder for the Russian court, he was already primed to recognize the name. Fioravanti's work was widely celebrated, too, though Tolbuzin's assumption that he had built the Cathedral of St Mark was overcredulous. His real forte was rescuing monuments and city walls; he had also moved an entire building, the eighty-two-foot tower of Santa Maria Maggiore in Bologna, without damage to the structure. An early commission in Rome had won him the approval of Pope Paul II, and his international fame increased still further in 1467, when he had carried out a project to strengthen Europe's defences against the Turk on behalf of Hungary's Italian-educated ruler, Matthias Corvinus.

In 1473, he was invited back to Rome, this time by Sixtus IV, but he was obliged to flee soon after in fear of his life, for he had been accused of forging money, the penalty for which would have involved swallowing molten lead.[52] Ivan's Moscow may well have seemed a better prospect, although the master-builder's ultimate insurance-policy was an invitation to build a seraglio for the Turkish sultan, Mehmet II. He did not really need to travel far, however. Bologna, or even Venice, would have sheltered him, for engineers of his ability were rare, and the Venetians made sure that Tolbuzin appreciated that as he prepared to lure this one from his homeland. The building task that Tolbuzin out-lined must have fascinated the Bolognese master, and the promise of a salary of ten rubles a month was exceptionally generous. As an extra privilege, and a rare one, the architect's household was offered lodgings in the Kremlin itself.[53]

Fioravanti was probably about sixty years old when he set off for Moscow with 'his son, named Andrey, and a boy called Petrushka'.[54] Unlike Sofiya, he took the shortest route, a three-month dash across the plains, skirting the frozen Pripet marshes and catching his first glimpse of Ivan's chilly capital in late March 1475. It was the sort of journey that a man might make in pursuit of a last fast buck, a final commission before retirement. Fioravanti, after all, had come to repair and complete Filipp's cathedral. He planned to go home a rich man. Instead, when he attempted to leave Russia several years later, he found himself facing a new threat of imprisonment or death. His skills as builder, cannon-founder and military advisor belonged to Moscow for the rest of his life.

That first spring, however, was brisk and professional. Fioravanti inspected the wreck of Filipp's church and confirmed the Pskov masons' diagnosis about the mortar. He also insisted, with a healthy Bolognese disdain for Russian workmanship, that the ambitious project could not be achieved unless the soft local limestone were supplemented by copi-ous quantities of brick. By this time, almost everyone in Moscow was observing him, and when he declared that Filipp's ruined structure would have to go completely, large crowds gathered to watch. Such jobs usually dragged on through a whole season, for Russian builders worked by hand, but the Italian had a machine, a metal-capped oak ram of his own design. The effect could only be compared to Joshua at Jericho. 'It was miraculous to see', the chronicle recorded, 'how it was that some-thing that took three years to build could be entirely demolished by him in a single week, or even less.' The walls came down so fast that the labourers who had to load the rubble on to clumsy horse-drawn carts scarcely had time to scratch their fleas.[55]

The next thing was to take a look at Vladimir, for its cathedral, as Ivan and his churchmen insisted, was still to be the model for the Mos-cow site. To his surprise, on arriving outside the older cathedral, Fioravanti found himself examining a fine – and substantial – building. 'It must have been the work of our masters,' he muttered, ever-loyal to his native roots. Despite the contempt implied by that remark, however, he went on to make an extended tour that summer (partly to secure the falcons he had promised to a patron back at home), visiting Novgorod and the remote White Sea monasteries and taking in a landscape that few European travellers had seen since the days of the Vikings. When he returned to Moscow, armed with those falcons and some ermines for himself, he was better informed about the local architecture and ready to start making bricks. But his tour had not entirely changed his view of Russian craftsmanship. He spent his first winter in Moscow setting up his own brickworks, where trainees could be taught to follow his exacting rules. As they discovered, he wanted thousands of flattish, heavy bricks of uniform hardness and uniform size. Even by modern standards, they look huge.

The brick factory at Kalitnikovo was a triumph, and it heralded a series of technical innovations that confirmed the Italian's reputation as a magician. First, he wanted foundations that could have swallowed a full-grown elephant. The men kept digging till they were fourteen feet deep, and then they packed the trenches with oak stakes. While some laboured with the new bricks, others were taught to make a marvellous mortar, far thicker than the formula that they had used before; the Italian issued them with metal spades to work it with, another innovation. His walls were to be built of pale cream stone, but this was cut and laid without the usual rubble-filling. The building seemed finer and lighter-looking as a result, and the magic bricks were so strong and precise that the arches and cupolas appeared to float above it. The architect showed his builders how to brace the structure with metal rods, rather than chunks of oak, and as the walls grew higher he installed a pulley-system for raising the heavy trays of materials.[56] His insistence on measurement was remarked on by everyone. In what was sorcery indeed, the locals observed that 'everything is done by the ruler and compass'. The delicacy of it all, the lightness, seemed miraculous. The finished building was so perfect that it seemed to have been cut out of a single block.

Though the internal decoration would take much longer to complete, Fioravanti's Dormition Cathedral was formally consecrated by Metropolitan Geronty on 12 August 1479. The Italian had fulfilled his commission in a little less than five years, but he had not quite kept to his original brief, for the church was neither an exact replica of Filipp's nor of its sacred prototype in Vladimir. It had the same five domes, but they appeared weightless, the same sequence of bays and piers, but executed with unprecedented regularity and precision. Meanwhile, instead of being square, Fioravanti's building was elongated, and where most Russian cathedrals would have included a choir gallery, this one remained uncluttered, light. The interior space was probably the largest that the Muscovites had ever seen. The effect was definitely Russian, but it had a distinctly European twist.[57] For years to come, the fact that Moscow's most sacred cathedral had been built by a fellow-countryman continued to make Italian visitors to the city feel proud.[58]

The plan was now to rebuild the whole Kremlin in impressive style. By the time of Fioravanti's death in 1486, Ivan had the resources to hire the finest specialists, and – thanks to his new links with Europe – the necessary local knowledge. A fresh detachment of Italians duly appeared in Moscow, including cannon-founders, silver-smiths and apprentices from Rome and Venice. The most important member of the group was another builder, Pietro Antonio Solari, a Milanese who was expected to continue the late Fioravanti's work.[59] Experienced and confident, this man soon started to describe himself as the grand prince's chief architect, but (though distinguished) he was not the only Italian in town. Two others, whom the Russians knew as Marco and Onton Fryazin (Fryazin was not an Italian surname but the generic name that Russians gave to Europeans – 'Franks'), were already at work when he arrived in 1490, their task to raise a new system of walls and towers round Ivan's fortress-court.[60] In 1493, another Italian, the Lombard Alevisio de Carcano, was hired by Ivan's hard-working agents, and in 1504 the Crimean khan, Mengli-Girey, sent his fellow-prince a gift in the shape of the master-builder who had just completed a commission for his own palace at Bakhchisarai. The gift was a Venetian, Alevisio Lamberti da Montagnana, and even he was not the last Italian on Ivan's site.[61]

With German cannon-founders (they had proved to be the best), Persian smiths, assorted master-builders from Italy and a physician from Venice who called himself Leon the Jew, the Kremlin must have been a multi-ethnic, multi-lingual cauldron. Despite the presence of so many foreigners, however, a few natives of Russia were still working on royal building plans. Their influence was particularly visible around the irregular square that was now dominated by Fioravanti's cathedral.

A team from Pskov replaced Yona's little Church of the Deposition of the Robe in 1485. Their next commission was the palace Cathedral of the Annunciation. Despite the loss of priceless frescoes, the dilapidated fourteenth-century original was demolished, and for the next five years a modest new brick structure slowly rose on its foundations. But soon the Russians' building was upstaged. Facing their work across the sacred square, the Cathedral of the Archangel Michael had long served as the burial place of Moscow's princes, and Ivan III commissioned a replacement in expectation of his own approaching death. The prince never saw the result (he died in 1505, three years before it was finished), but the final building, by Alevisio Lamberti da Montagnana, was spectacular. When it was new, its red brick and white stone facing must have looked almost garish, and some of the imported details – especially the Venetian scallop-shells under the domes – were shocking in the Moscow light. It might be Russia's royal mausoleum, but this was certainly no patriotic replica. It was beautiful, however, and gracious, and any honest visitor could see it as a synthesis of the cultures that had converged in Ivan III's Kremlin: Moscow, Vladimir and Pskov on the one hand; Milan, Venice and Constantinople on the other.

The busy quarter at the Kremlin's heart contained a lot of smaller buildings of all kinds, and these contributed to the eclectic, sometimes confusing, geography of Ivan's court. There were monks' cells behind the metropolitan's stone palace, steps and walkways to avoid the sea of mud, and a brick-built treasury in the square itself, another of Ivan III's innovations, whose warren of underground chambers connected to the Annunciation Cathedral's limestone crypt.[62] But one final masonry building was needed to complete the central religious ensemble. Ivan Kalita had commissioned a bell tower for his own cathedral complex, and generations later it still stood beside the little Church of Ivan Lestvichnik, or St John of the Ladder, 'Under the Bell'. In the early 1500s Kalita's tower was demolished to make way for the now iconic bell tower that came to be known as Ivan the Great (after the church rather than any prince). The upper tiers of this, and the famous cupola, were added later, but even in its original form the new structure, completed in 1508 by an Italian whose only surviving name is Bon Fryazin, was theatrical.[63] It was also extraordinarily robust. Like Fioravanti, Bon Fryazin liked to dig foundations deep, and the walls of his tower, which rose nearly two hundred feet above the Kremlin's central square, were so thick and solid that when Napoleon's sappers mined them in October 1812 they managed to achieve no more than a slight list.[64]

Ivan III's palaces turned out to be more fragile. By shifting the entire Saviour Monastery to new premises beyond the Kremlin walls, the prince's men cleared an extensive site close to the existing royal quarters. Ivan himself moved out in 1492, leaving his master-builder, Solari, free to work. The Milanese created a group of elegant structures in brick and stone, probably a series of distinct blocks arranged around central reception-rooms and antechambers. No-one can say what they looked like for certain, however, for the complex was destroyed by a fire almost at once. The next version, also of Italian design, was on a grander scale, again incorporating separate buildings. The foundations of some are still there, but the rest disappeared in a succession of fires and radical changes of fashion. The one survivor is the beautiful Faceted Palace, finished in 1491.

This building, by Solari and Marco Fryazin, was planned as a reception hall. Inside, it consists of a single arched room of roughly seventy feet by seventy-seven, its roof supported by a central pier. This design was as Russian in essence, if not in every detail, as Ivan might have wished; Vasily Ermolin had recently finished something of the same kind for the monks of the wealthy Trinity-St Sergius Monastery forty miles outside Moscow.[65] But Solari's building was also an Italian palace in classic renaissance taste. The exterior walls are still decorated with the diamond-shaped blocks (rustications) that give it the almost jewelled appearance that was all the rage in fifteenth-century Venice. This kind of decoration was soon to seem as Russian as the new passion for brick.[66] The local genius was one of adaptation, rapid learning followed by new variations on a theme. Even the Italians' own term, *palazzo*, was promptly adopted by their hosts (as *palata*), to mean any high-end stone-built mansion for the rich.[67]

More Russian yet, at least for every later generation, were the brick walls and towers that were built to surround it all. Even now, these remain the ultimate symbol of the Muscovite age. In Ivan's day, when the outcome of an entire continental war could be determined by a single siege, the specifications were demanding. The Kremlin's old defensive towers had been designed for archers and for townsmen armed with cauldrons and stones; the new ones would have to accommodate massed rows of cannon and the men to service them. It was also important to create an early-warning system, to the point of building underground listening-posts that would amplify the sounds of any sapper who might try to tunnel in. Sieges could drag on for years, and a supply of drinking water would be needed to support a population of thousands. There would also have to be somewhere to store large quantities of grain and salt. Finally, if an attack should ever breach the walls, the city's treasure – and the prince's own considerable reserve – had to be kept hidden and secure. Ivan's new team of architects was instructed to develop the old cathedral crypts, and as they worked they created a network of chambers and tunnels whose extent still remains unknown.[68]

The work began in 1485 along the Moscow riverbank. Onton and Marco Fryazin began by clearing the old walls and digging deep into the mud to establish the foundations for a brick fortification, starting with a massive tower in the centre of the embankment. Their design included a hidden passage down to the river for raising water into the Kremlin in time of siege, and for that reason the tower and the entrance gates beneath it were called 'Tainitskie': 'secret'. Like all the other Kremlin towers of Ivan's time, this one was a solid-looking block with interior stairways and tiered parapets, purposeful and elegant rather than fanciful. The decorative tent-shaped roofs on today's Kremlin (the things that look like follies, several of which support red stars) were added later (and at different times); for now, this was a structure that meant business. Above the wooden huddle of the city, it would have been visible for miles.

The side above the Moscow riverbank, the side that faced invaders from the south, was considered to be the most vulnerable part of the Kremlin, and work continued rapidly here once the old walls had been knocked down. As soon as the central entrance gate was completed, the architects turned to the two end-points, and by 1489 two further towers were finished: the Beklemishev, at the Kremlin's south-eastern tip (named for the nearby estate of Nikita and Semen Beklemishev), and the Sviblova (now usually called the Vodovzvodnaya, after the hydraulic systems that were eventually installed), in the south-western corner. These were both round (to give the defenders the widest possible line of sight), and each was large enough to house the coveted new cannon. In all, seven towers were constructed to defend the Kremlin's south bank, each conceived as an independent fortress but standing close enough for the defenders to maintain a clear view of each other as they delivered a storm of impassable cross-fire into their enemies' path.

This was the point that had been reached when Pietro Antonio Solari arrived from Milan in 1490, bringing the style and technology of the Sforza princes to Ivan's fortress. Under his direction, two impressive gate-towers, one to the south-west (the Borovitskaya) and one beside a little church dedicated to the Christian emperor Constantine and Elena (Helena) his mother, were completed in 1490. The following year, the Kremlin's most important sets of towers and entrance gates, the Frolov (or Saviour) and Nikolsky, were built to face the trading quarter on the edge of what is now Red Square. In constructing these, Solari had to move the bas-relief of St George, and though it was briefly replaced on his gatehouse it was soon upstaged by a new clock, whose hands were visible across the city and whose marvellous mechanical system may even have played music.[69] But Solari had no time to pause and listen. His Moscow must have reeked of baking clay and fresh-cut logs. Tens of thousands of bricks were needed for the next phase of the job, which was to complete the main line of walls. The river would have vanished under a permanent film of builders' dust as these began to snake around the south and east sides of the hill, seldom less than fourteen feet thick and in places more than fifty feet high.[70] Milan had come to Moscow, so the entire perimeter was topped by seven-foot-high swallow-tail battlements in the best contemporary style. On their inner side, however, the elegance gave way to firing platforms and a walkway that was always wide enough to accommodate several ranks of archers at a time.

Solari, who was also working simultaneously on the Faceted Palace, now turned his attention to the steep bank leading down to the Neglinnaya river. He began with a round tower, the Sobakin (later Corner Arsenal) Tower, commanding the north-western point of the Kremlin's triangular defences. Its foundations included another reservoir, this time fed by a seemingly inexhaustible underground spring. There may have been a set of strongrooms, too, each sealed behind an iron door for which the smiths designed a lock so massive and so intricate that none could open it without the subtle key. Beyond, the legend goes, the rooms themselves were lined with giant storage-chests, again secured with fiendish locks.[71] This tale dates from the 1720s, when the vaults were rediscovered during building-work for a new arsenal, and though the details are impossible to verify, much later excavation did find a deep chamber, flooded after centuries of neglect.[72] The Neglinnaya was always the sort of river that pools and oozes rather than flows; in Ivan's time its chills did for the unfortunate master-mason as well as his secret rooms. Solari died in 1493, leaving the last section of the Kremlin's defences to be completed by his successors.

There was a lot of landscaping involved. So much timber was consumed in the building-work – as fuel, as scaffolding, as props – that by 1500 the Moscow forest had all but disappeared.[73] Using only hand tools, a vast crowd of workers dug and hacked at the Kremlin soil, carting and tipping the sullen heaps until the land itself had been reshaped. If the fortress still looks natural today, as if moulded to fit its site, it is because the hill beneath was rearranged when these great walls were built. Ivan III also altered the setting around it. The fire of 1493 had alerted everyone to the potential threat to brand new walls, so Ivan ordered that a 780-foot-wide fire-break should be cleared around his fort. Red Square began life in this way (at this stage it was called the *pozhar*, or fire), but clearance could be controversial. On the Neglinnaya side, Ivan's project involved razing large numbers of wooden residential buildings and at least one church. The people were, as always, pushed aside, but Archbishop Gennady of Novgorod, a former archimandrite (the equivalent of a senior abbot) of the Chudov Monastery, condemned the prince for sacrilege when the church disappeared, for dogs and cattle had begun to wander on what should have been consecrated ground.[74] The space stayed clear, however, for another hundred years.[75]

Ivan continued with his plans. In 1500, the Kremlin acquired its first internal road, which cut its way through the jumble of boyar palaces and wooden chapels from the Saviour and Nikolsky gates to the brand new Cathedral Square.[76] At the same time, Alevisio de Carcano set about transforming the entire hill from a promontory into an island. Ivan did not live to see this work done, but his successor, Vasily III (ruled 1505–33), encouraged efforts to complete and develop his father's plans. Further reservoirs were built beside the Kremlin walls, and in 1508, Alevisio created a brick-lined moat to join the Moskva and Neglinnaya rivers along the edge of the recently cleared territory below the Saviour Tower. The work involved was prodigious even by the standards that Ivan had set; the moat was over forty feet deep and a hundred and thirty feet wide, protected by low walls and spanned by drawbridges beside the two main gates.[77] Its width was intended to rule out the possibility that besiegers might set up camp under the walls. It also prevented an army of determined foes from tunnelling underneath and streaming into the Kremlin like a plague of moles.[78] No-one ever did. When the moat, which lapped straight down the edge of what is now Red Square, was filled with water, the Kremlin was cut off from the land around, and for a few decades at least it was impregnable.

Ivan III was the first Russian sovereign to be described as 'the Great', and in his lifetime he was also known in Russia, justifiably, as *groznyi*, or terrible, the epithet that later seemed far better-suited to his grandson, Ivan IV. Under the influence of Sofiya, his Italian-educated wife, the Grand Prince of Muscovy began to call himself a tsar, or emperor, and he adopted a very European-looking double-headed eagle as an emblem for the Muscovite throne.[79] His renaissance palaces were meant to impress outsiders as much as his own people with the extent of his power and culture. Beyond the Slav world, however, people still knew very little of Moscow. The Italians of course had some notion of Russia's wealth (even before Ivan's marriage to Sofiya, Milan's ruler, Francesco Sforza, had made an effort to inform himself about the realm of the distant 'White Emperor'), but further north, Emperor Frederick III assumed that Moscow's prince was merely a vassal of the Lithuanian king.[80]

In 1487, a German visitor, Nikolaus Poppel, visited the Kremlin and seems to have been amazed by its wealth and splendour. On his return, Poppel's excited report was so convincing that Frederick decided to woo the barbarian, and in 1489 the German adventurer was sent back to Moscow to arrange a match between Ivan's daughter and the margrave of Baden. One sweetener, which Poppel may have added on his own account, was the offer of a crown for Ivan from Frederick himself, for only the Holy Roman Emperor, Poppel explained, had powers to confer kingship. Ivan's reply was magisterial. 'By God's grace,' he told the unfortunate visitor, 'we have been sovereigns in our own land since the beginning . . . Our appointment comes from God, as did that of our ancestors . . . We do not desire to be appointed by any one.' As for the marriage, only Frederick's own son would do. Yury Trakhaniot, now in the role of Ivan's envoy, conveyed the message to the emperor in person. There was no chance, he affirmed, that a sovereign as great as Ivan would give his daughter in marriage to some mean 'Makraby'.[81]

His wealth made visitors think twice, but Ivan did not rule a secure or peaceful land. All those impressive fortress walls were built to hold real enemies at bay. The need for defence did not end at the Moscow river. Ironically, Novgorod was actually the first place Ivan fortified (beginning a year before Moscow, in 1484), though the point here was probably to make sure that his governors could escape from angry crowds of local citizens if the need arose. After Ivan III's death, relations with the Crimean khanate deteriorated, and the new prince, Vasily III, presided over fresh defensive work. Italian expertise was brought to bear again, and a string of strategic towns along the southern frontier began to sprout new fortresses in a range of Lombard designs. These included Tula, Kolomna, Nizhnyi-Novgorod and Zaraysk, each of which still treasures fragments of its old brick walls and battlements.[82] The citadels were soon needed, for the frontier suffered repeated raids, and even if they remained safe in their new forts, the defenders were powerless to stop the devastation of surrounding lands. When a combined army of horsemen from the khanates of Crimea and Kazan reached Moscow in 1521, the city was attacked and burned. The Kremlin itself remained unscathed, but the large business quarter to the east was not so fortunate. One set of walls, the court agreed, was not enough to keep the city's treasure safe.

A team led by another Italian, Pietro Annibale, began to dig the first earthworks for a second line of walls and towers in 1535.[83] At first, the structure was staked out in wood, although it was protected by a cruel ditch and also by the Moscow and Neglinnaya rivers. By 1538, however, the engineers had replaced the wooden palisade with two miles of brick wall, pierced in seven places by gates and defended by thirteen new towers. The design was an advance on that of the Kremlin to the extent that the new fortification was as thick as it was high, a refinement intended to defeat a new generation of artillery. The local nickname for the site derived from the wooden bundles of stakes (*kity*) that the builders used in the initial phase, however, and the new enclosure was soon called Kitai-gorod. Enclosing Moscow's old commercial district (*posad*), its fortifications ran in an elongated loop north and eastwards from the Kremlin's Corner Arsenal Tower and back south to the Moscow river near the Beklemishev Tower. The Kremlin remained separate, looming behind its own brick walls and Alevisio's moat, to say nothing of the wide space that had been cleared since the great fire of 1493. But from a distance the two parts of the city-centre could easily be mistaken for one fortress.[84] Some called the Kremlin the 'old' city to distinguish it from the new one.

The centre of Moscow was now a maze of walls, forbidding as a mythic dragon's lair. Its court was so protective of the new security that the entire set of fortifications was treated as a state secret (notwithstanding the fact that almost all had been designed by foreigners), and later visitors sometimes reported that they were blindfolded, crowded about with guards, or forced to travel in closed carriages as they entered the Kremlin itself, especially if renovations were in hand.[85] Kitai-gorod was more accessible, and it became the city's main commercial hub, not least because Ivan III had banned foreign merchants from the Kremlin, but even this walled district had the feeling of a citadel. Its military character was emphasized by the presence of prisons, torture-chambers and a massive arsenal.[86] As any merchant counting silver in the shadow of Kitai-gorod's new walls could see, Moscow's rulers viewed the entire city as a fortified stronghold. In building it, they had imported the best engineering advice that money could buy. It was ironic, then, that the technological revolution that had driven fifteenth-century Italian fort-design should have continued without them once the building-work was done.

From artillery to muskets and drilled, disciplined, full-time infantry, Europe's armies and the thinking that went into them rapidly surpassed the level that had been the benchmark for Fioravanti and Solari in the 1480s and 1490s. Even siegecraft changed, and within decades of its completion, the Kremlin looked old-fashioned when compared to the more sophisticated star-shaped forts for which some European cities had begun to bankrupt themselves. Since Moscow chose to rely on imported inventions, rather than nurturing home-grown masters of the new science, it remained permanently one step behind. The problem was not confined to the battlefield, either, and extended to technologies such as printing as well as a whole range of arts. Only geographical accident – a matter of distance and cold – preserved the illusion of Moscow's impregnability. For as long as its main enemies were steppe Tatars, the balance was even at least. From the middle of the sixteenth century, however, a new kind of unease began to cloud the Russian court. Somehow, it seemed, the European heretics had stolen a march. Centuries later, experts in Russia and elsewhere would start to call the problem backwardness.[87]

Aloof even compared with walled Kitai-gorod, meanwhile, the Kremlin stood above the confusion of real life, cut off from its messy hubbub; defended, certainly, but also locked in. It was a metaphor for a good deal of Russia's subsequent history, and several of the country's later revolutions amounted to a struggle to escape. But none entirely overcame the barrier. 'A wall', writes Ryszard Kapuscinski (who had no time at all for Russian patriots), 'is simultaneously a shield and a trap, a veil and a cage.' Solid defensive walls, he continues, 'produce a mental attitude that sees a wall running through everything, imagines the world as being divided into an evil and inferior part, on the outside, and a good and superior part, on the inside.'[88]

3

The Golden Palace

Ambrogio Contarini, an envoy from Catholic Venice, passed through Ivan III's Moscow in the 1470s. His notes record a memorable scene:

> By the end of October the [Moscow] river is frozen over, and shops and bazaars for the sale of all sorts of things are erected on it, scarcely anything being sold in the town. They do this, as the river . . . is less cold than anywhere else. On this frozen river may be seen, daily, numbers of cows and pigs, great quantities of corn, wood, hay, and every other necessity, nor does the supply fail during the whole winter. At the end of November, all those who have cows or pigs, kill and bring them, from time to time, to the city market. They are frozen whole, and it is curious to see so many skinned cows standing upright on their feet . . . The meat that you eat has sometimes been killed three months or more. Fish, fowls, and all other provisions are treated in the same way. Horses run on this river when it is frozen, and a good deal of amusement takes place.[1]

Nearly a century later, in 1558, an Englishman called Anthony Jenkinson observed the same 'great market' on the frozen river, but he was also witness to an even stranger spectacle. It took place at Epiphany, and it involved the entire court, 'all most richly apparelled with gold, pearles, pretious stones, & costly furres'. The day's events had begun with a religious service in the Dormition Cathedral, but after that the company made its stately way towards a pre-cut hole in the frozen surface of the Moscow river. There, the metropolitan took his seat on a throne in the place of honour, but the sovereign remained standing, as did the rest of the assembled court. The apparent reversal in the hierarchy of church and state was unexpected, but so was the ceremony that followed, for once the leader of the Russian church had blessed the river underneath the ice, handfuls of water were scooped up and 'cast' over the sovereign and his noblemen. 'That done,' Jenkinson went on,

> the people with great thronging filled pots of the said water . . . and divers children were throwen in, and sicke people, and plucked out quickly again, and divers Tartars christened: all of which the Emperour beheld. Also there were brought the Emperours best horses, to drink at the said hallowed water. All this being ended, he returned to his pallace again.[2]

These separate episodes involved a similar stretch of river, but in other respects the contrast between them could scarcely have been greater. The first was part of red-blooded commercial life, a market whose abundance would astonish foreigners for centuries.[3] It was a festival in its own right, and that could make proceedings riotous. The church preached a staid, sober and self-denying life, but Russian popular culture was a colourful affair involving lewdness and cross-dressing, buffoonery, and large quantities of alcoholic drink. At Christmas and Epiphany, the celebrations bordered on debauchery, for it was widely feared that evil spirits stalked the land and had to be appeased or exorcized with swearing and satanic games. But the annual appearance on the ice of the entire court, a ritual that was probably adopted in Moscow in the early sixteenth century, was neither spontaneous nor wild. Even today, no-one has really managed to explain it all.[4] The most convincing account views the scene as a tableau, a living icon stepping from its frame. The sovereign plays the role of Christ and the metropolitan that of John the Baptist. The chilly Moscow river is a Jordan, and behind it, looming in the winter light, the Kremlin has become the Holy City, a Jerusalem.

If this interpretation of the ritual is correct, the participants themselves must have had a peculiar relationship with time, and especially with history. From the solemn blessing of the waters at Epiphany to the daily reverence for holy images, the court's religious practices speak of a world where centuries could be compressed, where saints still walked, and long-dead princes could exert an influence that few of the living would ever match. As for the future, that was overshadowed by the vivid expectation of the end of days. The Orthodox calendar had placed the date of the world's end in its own year 7000, which coincided with Catholic Europe's 1492.[5] Even when that fateful date had come and gone, icons showing the apocalypse were prominent in every recently completed cathedral, including all three of the famous Kremlin ones.

A Protestant like Jenkinson might not have grasped these details, but for the wealthy few who gathered on the winter ice, the threat of everlasting fire was as familiar as the pearls on the trim of their own fur gloves.

Theological niceties mattered most to priests, of course, but in the sixteenth century it was they who largely shaped the theory and the outward form of Russian kingship, the principles by which the Kremlin's inner world was run. They made abundant use of Christian metaphor, encouraging their flock with promises of glory for the faithful on the Day of Judgement. But ecclesiastics at the Kremlin court also harnessed the potential of history. Their prince, Ivan the Terrible (Ivan IV, ruled 1533–84), turned out to be an apt and even a creative pupil. What started as court theatre, a series of experiments with sovereign power, was to end in the blood and gristle of his torture-chambers. It was appropriate, indeed, that Ivan had such an affinity with icons. Christ-like at first, the evidence suggests that in his later life he came to see himself in an apocalyptic role that would have challenged any iconographer, even the most inventive.

Two generations previously, in the 1440s, it had taken a civil war to make sure that Ivan III would inherit his father's throne. To extinguish any further claims by his uncles and cousins, he promptly ordered the arrests of several of his male relatives. It was a strategy that guaranteed the crown for his sons, and Ivan fathered quite a few of these, not least because he married twice. The short-lived wife of his youth, Mariya of Tver, produced the undisputed heir, who was also given the name Ivan, and before the lad reached thirteen years of age, Ivan III had named him as his successor. Disaster struck in 1489, however, when the younger man fell ill with gout. His father went to every length to find a cure, and deliverance seemed to have come at last when the Venetian doctor, Leon the Jew, arrived in the Kremlin in 1490, but the regime that the physician ordered resulted in the younger Ivan's slow and painful death. Leon was duly beheaded, but the grand prince was still left with a dilemma.[6] His remaining sons were children of his second wife, Sofiya. The eldest of these, Vasily, was an obvious heir, but the picture was complicated by the fact that the late prince Ivan had fathered a son of his own, Dmitry Ivanovich, who had been born in 1483. Ivan III showed a special fondness for this grandchild and also for the infant's mother,

Elena Stepanovna of Moldavia, a distant kinswoman whose family was crucial to Moscow's delicate diplomatic network in Europe.[7]

Whatever the court might have said in other times, Ivan III considered that he had a real choice about the succession. For some generations, as their surviving wills attest, the Muscovite rulers' idea of power had been synonymous with ownership. They viewed the city as a vast estate; each dying prince bequeathed the throne in much the same way as he also left his jewels and his honey-farms. While he considered which potential heir to favour, Ivan III treated the candidates more or less even-handedly, but in 1497, when Vasily was eighteen years old and Dmitry just thirteen, the ageing prince announced his choice of the latter, his grandson, as heir. The rival camp immediately launched a rebellion, including a plot to assassinate Dmitry himself, but no-one could gainsay Ivan III. Six of the conspirators were executed and both Sofiya and her son were disgraced.[8] All hope for Vasily seemed lost, and to underline the point, Ivan took the unprecedented step of crowning his grandson as co-regent.

The ceremony, which was staged in February 1498, was the first of its kind to be held in Russia, and it took place, like every coronation after it, in the Kremlin's Dormition Cathedral. There was no precedent in Moscow's past, so Ivan's priests consulted various Byzantine texts before deciding on the wording of the prayers and the order of the ceremonial. Thrones were made ready on a raised dais, and the entire court prepared to attend in full costume.[9] The gold robes that the nobles had to wear were so expensive that most of them borrowed their outfits from the Treasury for the day, but the spectacle left a memory that later churchmen would never forget. Within four years, however, the old grand prince had changed his mind about the heir himself. In April 1502, Dmitry and his mother Elena were arrested, and soon after Vasily was proclaimed the 'Autocrat of all Russia'. Conveniently enough, and probably not accidentally, Dmitry died in prison just a few years later.[10] On Ivan's death in 1505, it was Vasily who succeeded him.

Vasily III was never crowned, but that, if anything, was a mark of his evident legitimacy. There was no need for theatricality. Although he was successful in the role of leader and grand prince, however, fatherhood eluded him. His first wife, Solomoniya Saburova, failed to produce a male heir, and in 1523 the prince sought a divorce. It was a move that split the court, and some church leaders disapproved of it on moral grounds. But

Vasily eventually secured his wish, and Solomoniya (now accused of witchcraft) was packed off to a remote convent. Barely two months later, in January 1526, Vasily and his second bride, the fifteen-year-old Elena Glinskaya, were married. On this occasion, the need to silence court intrigue prompted the prince to opt for a dramatic ceremony.[11]

The wedding of 1526, then, like the coronation of February 1498, was invented to convey a decisive message at an uncertain moment, and also like the coronation it created an enduring precedent.[12] The central sacrament was celebrated in the Dormition Cathedral, and candles from it were then used to illuminate the couple – and their troupe of attendants – in the coming nights. Every detail of the pageant was invested with significance, from the choice of bedchamber icons (depicting mother-hood) to the scattering of earth (to call mortality to mind), and the lavish use of ancient fertility symbols such as honey and grain. In August 1530 a first son, Ivan Vasilevich, was born. That night, according to legend, an unseasonal wind of such ferocity swept through Moscow that the bells of the Kremlin's Saviour Cathedral began to toll of their own accord.[13]

The succession seemed secure at last, especially after the prompt birth of a second boy, Yury. Vasily presented the crown prince, Ivan, with a tiny helmet at about this time, a symbol of both majesty and future leadership.[14] An object of this kind was not a toy, but Ivan had no chance to play in any case. He was still barely a toddler in the winter of 1533 when his father became gravely ill. Vasily had been out on one of his beloved hunting expeditions when he was stricken with a noxious sore and raging fever. The doctors despaired, and Vasily returned to the snow-bound Kremlin on an invalid's litter. As he lay dying, he told a hastily summoned council that he intended to leave his title and estates to his eldest son. He also drew up a new will, the aim of which, in part, was to establish a regency under the leadership of trusted aides. His last wish, like that of generations of his forefathers, was to become a monk, taking the holy name Varlaam. Over the protests of his weeping wife and of his brother, Andrei, the prince's head was tonsured by the metro-politan himself, and at midnight, after watching his two surviving adult brothers kiss the cross in fealty to the three-year-old Ivan, Vasily died.[15]

The regents were an unattractive group. Prominent among them was Ivan Vasilevich Shuisky, a representative of one of the most powerful families in Moscow and an inevitable choice for the regency council as the dying Vasily dictated his will. On her husband's death, Elena Glinskaya took the first opportunity to add Ivan Ovchina Telepnev-Obolensky, a nobleman assumed by some to have been her lover. It was he whom later writers largely blamed for the murders of Vasily's brothers, the royal uncles, a move intended to secure the regents' undisputed power.[16] In 1534, the older one was thrown into a Kremlin dungeon. In 1537, it was his younger brother's turn. In both cases, since there were still taboos about spilling the blood of princes, the victims were starved to death; the younger brother, reputedly, behind a sort of iron gag. Mikhail Glinsky, the veteran council-member and uncle of the dowager princess, whom the dying Vasily had named as his sons' main personal guardian, was also seized and imprisoned in 1534, perhaps in part because he criticized the other regents' murderous plans.[17] He too was then deliberately starved to death.[18] Young Ivan and his brother Yury, a child who had been born deaf and was never taught to speak, were now as good as helpless in some very questionable hands.

If the regents ever planned to isolate the infant princes and remain in power for good, however, circumstances did not favour them. Elena died suddenly in 1538. She was not even thirty years old, and there were rumours that she had been poisoned.[19] A group of archaeologists recently claimed to have found proof of this when they discovered toxic chemical salts in the remains of her corpse, but the compounds involved were widely used as a purgative in the sixteenth century, and even for arcane cosmetic purposes, so the cause of her last illness, or at least its author, still remains unclear. On her death, Prince Ivan Ovchina Telepnev-Obolensky was thrown into the prison where he was to die.[20] That left two principal groups of contenders: the members of the Shuisky clan and their rivals, the Belskys. In the struggles to come, several members of each family were imprisoned and murdered. As each enjoyed brief seasons of ascendancy, two metropolitans in succession, Daniil and Yoasaf, were also forced from office.[21] A government of the boyars had the potential to evolve, and aristocratic rule, perhaps with a monarch as figurehead, need not have been disastrous in the proper hands. But sixteenth-century Muscovite politics were simply not designed this way.

A letter attributed to Ivan himself describes the world he and his brother faced after their mother's death.[22] 'When thus our subjects had achieved their desire,' he wrote, 'namely to have the kingdom without a ruler, they did not deem us, their sovereigns, worthy of any loving care, but themselves ran after wealth and glory . . . How many boyars and well-wishers of our father . . . did they massacre?'[23] The tone is plaintive, a note that Ivan would continually strike in later life, but the facts of his youth suggest a more complicated story. The records of the Kremlin court read as if the boy were exercising sovereign rule almost from the beginning. Even the most ambitious magnate would have been wary of him, not least because the lad soon learned to play the Kremlin's games himself. In 1543, at the age of thirteen, he almost certainly approved the murder of Andrei Mikhailovich Shuisky, who was thrown into the court kennels and ripped to pieces.[24] The prince's belief that his childhood was a time of culpable neglect may well explain some of his later conduct, but contemporary evidence suggests that he was no mere victim. Whatever the truth, however, one thing the internecine struggles of the prince's long minority certainly damaged was the Kremlin's international standing. As the future Ivan the Terrible approached adulthood, his prospects were so uncertain that no European princess could be found who was willing to marry him.[25]

The court – and the whole country – could well have been poised for yet another civil war. As boyars in the Kremlin weighed their chances, the only figure with the power to prevent disaster was the peevish, rather sickly prince; somehow this heir had to begin inspiring real awe. Just as it had in 1498, a coronation ceremony, combining sacred elements with plenty of old-fashioned pomp, seemed to promise a solution, and the recently appointed metropolitan, Makary, began to look for a suitable prototype. The rituals that had been created for Europe's high renaissance kings offered a range of possible alternatives, but Orthodoxy could not borrow quite so openly from Papists and heretics. Makary turned instead to sixth-century Constantinople, whose empire's government had been modelled (the priests said) on heaven itself. [26] The plans were finally approved in detail at a joint meeting of the boyar and church councils in December 1546. With so much to be settled and financed, the Kremlin's entire inner circle must have taken part, but Makary, who was also the young prince's mentor and spiritual guardian, was the chief architect and impresario.

Ostensibly, the metropolitan's aim was to install a prince who would unite his people. But the church leader also framed his argument in spiritual terms. Since the fall of Constantinople, he reminded the court, Orthodox believers had lost their first empire on earth, but this time Moscow had been spared. In consequence, its faithful people and their prince had special responsibilities in a world that was awaiting imminent apocalypse. No longer merely a grand prince, Ivan would be crowned an emperor on the model of Constantinople itself; he would be an absolute sovereign, or (in the noble, ancient, Russian word) a tsar. Numerous texts would guide his steps. 'The Emperor in body be like all other,' the sixth-century theorist Agapetus had explained, 'yet in power of his office he is like God.'[27] The Catholics might have their charters and their Roman law, but Russia's master was to rule like a latter-day Solomon, and, in theory, he would answer to God alone. Whatever the reality of court life then or later, the only human voice that had divine permission to restrain him would be Makary's own.[28] Agapetus had insisted, after all, that the church remained a moral arbiter: 'For though [the Emperor] be like God in face, yet for all that he is but dust.'[29]

The power of visual images, as Makary would have appreciated, is so vivid that it is hard to imagine the coronation today without remembering Sergei Eisenstein's wonderfully theatrical staging of it, filmed in the early 1940s. In this version, an actor playing the young prince (and wearing startling false eyelashes) stands before a venerable metropolitan, the latter lean and bearded, ascetic but politically lightweight. From this old man the youth receives the sceptre and the cross, the jewelled collar and the fur-trimmed crown. Slowly, then, and with portentous majesty, the new tsar turns to face his people, and this is the cue for his first major speech. The actor's script, with its call to national unity and greatness, would have struck chords with Russian audiences in Stalin's time, but like much of the scene it is a 1940s propaganda fantasy. In January 1547, it was the metropolitan, and not Ivan, who made the most important speech, and much of it concerned biblical kings.[30] The point was to make sure Ivan could wield his power at all, to neutralize the factions who remembered a weak boy. Significantly, too, since Eisenstein put several of them in his film, there were no foreigners inside the church. The entire coronation seemed so incidental to most Europeans at the time that it took two years for the news that Ivan had even been crowned a tsar to get as far as Poland.[31]

Ivan himself could not have missed a single message in the ritual that day. Even the date was loaded with significance, for 16 January coincided, in the Orthodox calendar, with the beginning of Christ's ministry.[32] It also recalled Vladimir's original conversion of the Rus, and Ivan was to be crowned as Vladimir's heir. Indeed, his line had been traced back, by the church scribes, to the mythic Riurikids and also (to make sure of a strong Christian and imperial lineage) to the emperors Constantine and Augustus of Rome. The story of Moscow's royal family, the Daniilovichi, was spelled out in pedantic detail, and the combination of record and fable had the effect of placing Ivan at the end of an indisputably prestigious line.[33] The legends were embodied in his very crown, the so-called Cap of Monomakh, a sable-edged and jewelled piece that had probably originated somewhere in Central Asia. In defiance of that awkward fact, the church pronounced that it was Byzantine. This sort of trick – a way of claiming all the rights and honours that could be accorded to new rulers anywhere – showed no more disregard for history than was the norm elsewhere in Europe at the time, but older Muscovites could still remember when their state had been a Mongol fief. At Ivan's coronation, among other things, it was asserting its young ruler's right to be treated, inside his realm and beyond it, as an established sovereign lord.

Those were the hopes, at least, that January day. It was a season when no sunlight could have reached the Kremlin's inner palace rooms, but all the same the fortress was transformed into a blaze of candlelight and gold. Even beyond its walls, the thin air must have carried overtones of hot beeswax and incense, and the spell-bound city, where winter snow could muffle less deliberate sounds, fell silent as the first of many bells began to clang, heaved into motion by a team of men.[34] Meanwhile, Makary and a battery of priests stood ready in their full splendour. After the procession into the Dormition Cathedral from the palace steps, the court watched as the prince and cleric took their places in the hallowed space. 'King of Kings and Lord of Lords,' Makary prayed, his hand on Ivan's lowered head, 'who by thy servant Samuel the prophet didst choose David and anoint him to be king over thy people Israel . . . look down from Thy sanctuary upon Thy faithful servant, Ivan.'[35] If the new tsar had looked up, however, his eyes would have encountered those of a painted Creator, an image made by court artists, impassively declining to participate in any human schemes.

Ivan stepped into daylight as unnumbered bells renewed their peal. Meanwhile, in a gesture that would have raised eyebrows in old Constantinople (where coins were thrown out to the crowd), the new tsar was showered with silver by his younger brother Yury. Ivan then led his entourage to the Archangel Cathedral to pray at the graves of his ancestors. His route, which was carpeted in cloth of scarlet and gold, became another stretch of holy ground. At the banquet that followed in the Faceted Palace, the tsar held court for his nobles and the highest officers of the church. Seated alone, for none was worthy to join him that day, Ivan began his life as a crowned head of state by pouring wine, breaking bread, and tasting the muddy flesh of a swan. But Makary, also sitting in the hall, must have picked at his fish with secret pride. His ceremony had achieved its goal. The wily cleric had secured the future glory of his church.[36] By giving Moscow the attributes of an empire, he hoped to become a patriarch in all but name. The tsar could be as splendid as he wished (and Ivan took the opportunity to have his title confirmed by the real patriarch, in Constantinople, as soon as he could[37]), but now there always had to be a place beside the throne for thinner, older men who could read Greek.

The coronation was followed, on 3 February, by a royal wedding. This, too, was a slightly desperate affair, for Ivan's bride was not the daughter of a European monarch but Anastasia Romanovna Yureva-Zakharina, the niece of a boyar from the days of Vasily III. But the couple were well matched and clearly happy. It may have seemed, as spring approached in 1547, as if the glamour of a youthful court would dazzle Moscow into amiable warmth. And the season did turn out to be unusually mild. As a result, the city's wooden buildings dried out fast, and by April the first of several fires had burned part of Kitai-gorod. A disaster of far greater proportions struck in June. On Midsummer's Day, a fire that had started somewhere in the city's wooden jumble swept up to the Kremlin walls. Twenty-four hours later, the flames had grown so fierce that they ignited the gunpowder stores in several of the defensive towers.

There was no hope for the buildings in this fire's path. The flames consumed the churches in the palace precinct and the porch and strong-rooms that led to the Annunciation Cathedral. They tore through heavy storage chests and destroyed a range of ancient treasures in the palace undercroft. The fire also gutted the Annunciation Cathedral itself. Works of art, including a priceless iconostasis, were lost, and then the flames swept through the Treasury, engulfing irreplaceable court documents.[38] The palaces that were not razed were scorched and scarred, their wooden detailing and gilt reduced to ash. Senior members of the court fled for their lives. The sixty-five-year-old Makary, who had stayed to rescue an icon painted by his miracle-working predecessor, the fourteenth-century metropolitan Peter, was lowered down the Kremlin walls at the end of a rope; the injuries he suffered in the process never fully healed.[39] Beyond the citadel, the destruction was more terrible still. Shocked citizens eventually scraped more than 3,700 corpses from the ash, while many thousands – a majority of Muscovites – had been made homeless.

Even in a city used to fire, it was a catastrophe. With so many people on the streets, there was bound to be unrest, but the public response betrayed a level of political disquiet that no fire could have kindled by itself. As the flames cooled and the tsar himself called for a hunt for arsonists, Muscovites began to mutter that the disaster had been the work of a witch. Their fury – fuelled, no doubt, by the Glinskys' enemies at court – settled on Anna Glinskaya, the mother of the late and still unpopular Elena.[40] This sorceress, the people said, had torn the hearts out of human corpses and soaked them in water. She had bottled the resulting brew and, flying through the brief summer night, had sprinkled it over the wooden buildings of the capital; it was a well-known trick, the rumour went, that witches often used to summon flames.[41] A mob gathered below the city walls, and eventually its leaders surged into the Kremlin and onwards to Cathedral Square, thrusting their way into the Dormition Cathedral during a celebration of matins and baying for Glinsky blood. Rough hands seized the tsar's uncle, who had entered the building in search of sanctuary. Before the startled gaze of Makary himself, the citizens proceeded to stone their captive to death.

The tsar had taken refuge at his hunting lodge at Vorob'evo, on hills overlooking Moscow from the south-west, and from there, he had watched his city turn to ash. That experience was harrowing enough, but soon a human tide began to close in from the ruined streets, demanding that the court hand over Anna and the other infernal Glinskys, whom they believed to have brought ruin on them all. Ivan refused to sacrifice his grandmother, but in the days to come a number of less distinguished suspects were tortured, beheaded, impaled or thrown into the dying flames.[42] The Moscow uprising had been brief, but Ivan had witnessed its fury with his own eyes, and, as he later said, this was a moment when 'fear entered into my soul and trembling into my bones'.[43] If the young man had ever liked Moscow, the events of his coronation year seemed calculated to change his mind.

The fire also forced the Kremlin to the top of Ivan's political agenda. The damage was so extensive that rebuilding and redecoration had to start at once. Moscow had nurtured a pool of talented artists in the decades of the Kremlin's reconstruction under Ivan III and Vasily III, but there could never be enough skilled men to deal with repairs on this scale. Masons, gilders and artists from as far away as Pskov and Novgorod were summoned to the capital. To save time and money, the tsar also ordered finished icons to be sent from Novgorod, Smolensk, Dmitrov and Zvenigorod. As the packages were opened in the Kremlin stores, the icon-painters, themselves from places far and wide, gathered to admire and compare the styles of several distinctive cultures. It was the inspiration for a kind of national art, and the Kremlin became its gallery and principal patron. From Ivan's time, a set of buildings in its western corner, beyond the palace, was given over permanently to the insalubrious and often noisy work of carving and fine metalwork, gilding, and mixing paint. In time, new studios opened in the shadow of the Annunciation Cathedral. There was even a special chamber where artists could study the icons in the tsar's collection that were not currently in use.[44]

The group that seized most eagerly upon the opportunities created by the fire was not composed of artists, however, but consisted of the ideologues of Muscovite state power. When they had recovered from their shock (and, in Makary's case, from injuries), these people grabbed their chance to recreate the damaged parts of the Kremlin as visual sermons on topics such as divine kingship, Christ-like government, and Moscow's unbroken royal succession. The work was managed by a group at court that included a hitherto unknown priest from the Annunciation Cathedral, the monk Sylvester, who had come to Ivan's notice at the time of the great fire. A team of gifted painters and craftsmen played its part, for this particular history-lesson called for art that was both eye-catching and sumptuous. But the guiding hand in the endeavour, as in so many others during Ivan's first years on the throne, was Makary's.

Under the metropolitan's creative gaze, and no doubt also with Ivan's blessing, the Kremlin was subjected to a comprehensive renovation programme that included murals, icons and carvings in wood and ivory.[45] Particular attention was paid to the palace Cathedral of the Annunciation, where a new iconostasis was furnished with images that echoed the divine aspects of Ivan's own destiny. An icon of his patron-saint, John the Forerunner (the Baptist), was particularly haunting, and showed the ascetic in profile as a gaunt, tormented figure, the ruined flesh contrasting with a burning spiritual energy. This image stood directly opposite the tsar's own seat, reflecting his prayers back at him, and near it, other icons seemed to emphasize his part in defending the one true faith.[46] An even greater masterpiece was the throne designed for Ivan's place in the Dormition Cathedral, which told the story of the heirs of Monomakh, and of their close association with a noble court, in twelve carved bas-reliefs.[47]

Similar combinations of themes inspired the frescoes in Ivan's main throne room, the Middle Golden Palace. Although these were subsequently lost when the palace was demolished, a record made in 1672 by Simon Ushakov has survived; as he contemplated the painted shapes, indeed, the Romanov court artist may himself have been inspired by them. His drawings show an anteroom that was decorated with figures such as David, Solomon and Jehosaphat, and a throne room that boasted a magnificent display of angels. Real figures also occupied important spaces, however, so Ivan held court in a hall where Andrei Bogoliubsky and Alexander Nevsky, his ancestors, were represented beside biblical scenes in a masterpiece of allegorical time-compression. Though princes from Moscow's more humble days (including Daniil and Ivan Kalita) were not given the same prominence, Ivan's father, Vasily III, who had been dead for less than twenty years, was represented in the same series of portraits as the holy Vladimir of Kiev, who had ruled, over five centuries before, in an entirely different place and culture. As if to emphasize the holiness of Kremlin government, the space was crowned by a majestic Christ.[48] No foreign visitor remarked on the paintings – their eyes would have been fixed on living hosts – but the murals certainly drew comments from Russians. In the mid-sixteenth century, the worldliness of some of them seemed revolutionary. There were so many unfamiliar themes, in fact, that at least one prominent courtier, Ivan Viskovatyi, claimed that the paintings were blasphemous.[49] A church council solemnly overturned his arguments in 1554.

In future, no-one would object if icons served the needs of an ambitious Russian state.

The throne room of Ivan the Terrible no longer stands, but there are several descriptions of his Kremlin in its heyday. One of the most vivid was written by an Englishman. In 1553, an adventurer called Richard Chancellor was forced to seek shelter in a harbour on the White Sea when his ship, part of an expedition to find a north-east passage to China, ran into a storm. By a stroke of good fortune, the company survived, helped by astonished locals, and the English party was arrested and escorted under guard along the Dvina river and southwards to Moscow. Chancellor had 'discovered' the port of St Nicholas, near today's Archangel, and he had also found a route that connected it to Ivan's capital. Within a year, the English, true to form, were attempting to establish a monopoly on Russian trade, and regular delegations from the newly founded Muscovy Company in London began to beat a path to the Kremlin.

It was the start of a long and troubled relationship. To ease the process, the queen of England sent Ivan a pair of lions, whose enclosure was set up by the Kremlin moat (the site became a menagerie when an elephant arrived in the capital a few years later).[50] The human migrants of the time included several fortification engineers, who travelled from London in 1567 during an amiable period in diplomatic relations.[51] But everything began with Chancellor's first formal meeting with the tsar. It was an audience that took twelve days to organize. In that time, almost certainly, the Englishmen were watched and studied, for foreigners were always treated with suspicion; four years later, when Anthony Jenkinson arrived, his company was forced to suffer the same kind of wait. In both cases, the visitors soon felt that they had kicked their heels for long enough. As Chancellor remarked, his men had seen their fill of Ivan's 'very faire Castle, strong, and furnished with artillerie' from the outside; they were more than ready to venture in.

On the appointed day, they were woken early, for it was assumed that they would need time to prepare.[52] Armed guards in coloured livery awaited them, and every move they made was watched. Their path probably took them through the Kremlin's most prestigious entrance, the Frolov (later Saviour) gates. From there, on foot, the English party would have crossed Cathedral Square and mounted one of three sets of canopied steps to an upper terrace that served as the entrance to the recently repainted royal audience hall. Before them, on the far side of an antechamber thronged with courtiers, waited the tsar himself. 'Our men began to wonder at the Majestie of the Emperor,' Chancellor wrote.

> His seat was aloft, in a very royall throne, having on his head a diademe, or Crowne of golde, apparelled with a robe all of Goldsmiths worke, and in his hand hee held a Scepter garnished, and beset with precious stones: and besides all . . . there was a Majestie in his countenance proportionable with the excellencie of his estate: on one side of him stood his chiefe Secretarie, on the other side, the great Commander of silence, both of them arrayed also in cloth of gold: and then there sate the Counsel of one hundred and fiftie in number, all in like sort arrayed, and of great state.

'So great a Majestie of Emperour, and of the place,' he added, getting right to the point, 'might well have amazed our men, and have dasht them out of countenance.'[53]

This meeting was not quite the sum of Chancellor's exposure to the court. After a formal conversation with the tsar, the English group presented its papers to Ivan's 'chiefe Secretarie' and were ushered out to wait for two more hours. They understood why when they were escorted into another splendid room for dinner. 'In the middes of the roome stood a mightie Cupboord upon a square foote,' Chancellor marvelled.

> Upon this Cupboord was placed the Emperours plate, which was so much, that the very Cupboord it selfe was scant able to sustain the weight of it: the better part of all the vessels, and goblets, was made of very fine gold: and amongst the rest, there were four pots of very great bignesse, which did adorne the rest of the plate in great measure: for they were so high that [we] thought them at least five feet long.

The dinner that followed was a protracted meal involving many toasts; a Danish visitor in similar circumstances claimed to have drunk sixty-five of them, though wine may well have ruined his arithmetic.[54] A feast, with fleets of servants and theatrically dressed roast swans, was as much about political display as any formal audience, and in Chancellor's case, at least, the show was a success. The court, the ritual, the sheer length of it all were impressive enough, and then there was the unmistakable charisma of wealth. The country outside was not unusually

rich, but the Kremlin's hoard of diplomatic gifts, of spoils from plundered Novgorod, and even of the treasure it could claim from taxing all
those trading routes, was astounding. 'This is true,' concluded Chancellor, 'that all the furniture of dishes, and drinking vessels, which were
then for the use of a hundred ghests, was all of pure golde, and the
tables were so laden with vesels of gold, that there was no roome for
some to stand upon them.'

All this was a far cry from the reception that had greeted Sofiya's bri-
dal entourage in 1472. The palaces Chancellor saw combined the
elegance of Italy with Russia's passion for hierarchies defined by
space. The Englishman described them as 'not of the neatest ... and of
lowe building', but they were extensive, and occupied a large area to the
north-west of Cathedral Square leading down to the Borovitsky gates.[55]
The main complex, consisting of a range of discreet but tightly packed
buildings, was roughly U-shaped. The longer arm was where the royal
women lived, screened from all uninvited male eyes. Across the line of
palace roofs, just visible above the Kremlin walls, the other arm of the
U was the Riverside Palace, whose picturesque name belied the fact that
it contained the dungeon in which Ivan's uncles had been starved to
death not twenty years before. Near that was an impressive building
mainly used for formal meetings and negotiations with foreign envoys.
To the rear, behind the Cathedral of the Saviour in the Forest, were
lodgings intended for privileged foreigners such as Fioravanti (and,
briefly, the Venetian envoy Contarini), and the mansions that had once
housed magnates such as the Khovrins. Here too lay several clutches of
service buildings, including studios and workshops. The appearance of
these had become so scruffy during the building work of the 1490s that
a wall had been constructed to screen the whole lot from royal eyes.[56]

The grandest chambers occupied the central portion of the U-shaped
complex. Jutting forward into Cathedral Square, the largest of these
was Pietro Solari's 1491 masterpiece, the Faceted Palace, which was
probably where Chancellor saw all the plate.[57] Beyond it, the main line
of buildings was punctuated by several sets of canopied steps leading up
to the royal terraces (the ground floors were used for storage and
included some workshops). These steps were major elements in their
own right, and each had a distinct ceremonial role (one was kept for the
use of infidels, for instance). The fact that they rose in grades turned out
to be irresistibly expressive. It was a sign of favour to be able to place

a foot on their lowest tread; only the highest-ranked climbed to the top. Once there, however, delegations such as Chancellor's could expect to step into the Middle Golden Palace and a chamber that blazed with images of Moscow's saints and heroic rulers. There were other reception halls – including one inside the Treasury – but Ivan received his most important foreign guests against a backdrop that insisted on his unique and God-given power.[58] His sovereignty was supposed to be as timeless and as dazzling as the golden surface of an icon. And there was certainly a lot of gold; the splendour was so extravagant that it bordered on vulgarity.[59]

The Kremlin was not just a ceremonial space, however, and the stiff formality of its throne rooms was powerless to smother the constant restless jostling for advantage that went on almost everywhere else. At the very top, and especially among the boyars, government was based on personal contacts (Chancellor was struck by the fact that Ivan seemed to know each of his courtiers by name), but the fortress was a state in microcosm, and in Ivan's time its social structure was evolving fast. The lowest tiers continued to be occupied by slaves and menials of various kinds. There were hundreds of palace staff: the cooks and carters and the lads in uniform who served at feasts. There were numerous professional interpreters, and usually at least one foreigner who claimed to have medical expertise. But a new figure had entered the scene: the embryonic civil servant.[60] Custom was often as influential as the written law, and in some parts of the realm there was no law of any kind. By the 1550s, however, despite the icons and the endless prayers, government was getting organized, records amassed, and that meant that the Kremlin had to find space for officials with the skills to manage it all.[61]

By the time of Ivan's coronation, top-ranking bureaucrats were almost as respected as boyars. Most feature in the historical records by name. Called *d'yaki* (the root is similar to the English deacon)[62] they were important enough to attend royal audiences; the one who advised Ivan during Chancellor's audience, 'arrayed also in cloth of gold', was probably the diplomatic expert (and critic of the palace frescoes), Ivan Viskovatyi.[63] But the growing number of chancelleries – most of which were known in Russian as *prikazy* – also needed whole armies of ordinary clerks. Depending on the level of responsibility involved, the job offered a reasonable salary, and there were often opportunities for supplementing that with bribes. By the end of Ivan's reign, the ancient system of administration, which had been based on literate slaves, had been replaced by the beginnings of a professional service.[64]

Converging daily through the Nikolsky gates, the gowned, whey-faced officials at the bottom of the administrative heap worked in conditions that would horrify their modern counterparts. The rooms in which they laboured were barely furnished and poorly lit. If there were windows, they were small, and any light that entered would have had to pass through a film of mica or fish-bladders rather than glass. Meanwhile, the stoves and tallow candles that burned almost all the time would have made the atmosphere permanently sooty.[65] In this unpromising environment, the clerks' main tasks were to copy text and enter numbers, and if one account of their working-conditions is really true, that feat alone demanded physical contortions. Only the chief clerks had the luxury of desks or chairs; the rest spent long days squatting on the office floor. 'All the underclerks held their inkpots, quills and paper in their left hands,' a German adventurer called Heinrich von Staden, who spent three years in Ivan's Russia, recalled in the 1570s. They had to copy documents by resting paper on their laps. The equipment used in the accounts department seemed even more primitive: 'All affairs large and small were written in books once a year,' von Staden remembered, 'and in every chancellery plum or cherry stones were used for counting.'[66] The system was surprisingly effective. Anyone who has watched a Russian cashier with an abacus, for instance, will understand how briskly the most complex calculations could be done.

There was, of course, a hierarchy among the offices themselves. The most important were the Treasury and the *Razryadnyi Prikaz*, the Office of Military Affairs, set up in the 1550s to deal with all aspects of the army, from provisioning to service rosters and appointments.[67] Then came the Chancellery for Foreign Affairs (*Posol'skii Prikaz*), whose best-known head in this era was Viskovatyi himself. Between them, these institutions employed scores of staff, and that is before such institutions as the Horse Chancellery, the Brigandage and the Post Chancelleries, and (later) the chancelleries for several newly conquered territories were added to the government roll. In the seventeenth century, there was even a *prikaz* to manage the affairs of the *prikazy*.[68]

The Treasury remained apart, but by the 1560s most of the remaining chancelleries sprawled across a series of lowish wooden buildings that extended further down the south side of what became known as Ivanov Square, the space beyond the bell tower called Ivan the Great.[69] It was a noisy, bustling place, where townsmen with petitions to their ruler rubbed shoulders with the gowned officials and the palace guards. Like many administrative centres in sixteenth-century Europe (think of an etching by Pieter Bruegel the Elder), the site was also used for public torture. Debtors, appropriately enough, were punished right outside the Treasury, a plum stone's toss beneath the clerks' window. The usual punishment for debt was *pravezh*, repeated beating on the shins with clubs: the victims' screams would have jolted the steadiest of quills.[70] For other crimes, justice amounted to a public flogging. If this was a theatre of torment, then routine government business was transacted in the dress circle.

The real heart of power, however, stood aloof. Exclusive, secretive, inbred, the members of the privy council chose to gather deep within the complex of the palaces themselves, well out of earshot of the busy square.[71] In theory, the tsar could select his own advisors, but choice was guided by unspoken rules, and the most important of these related to honour and official rank. *D'yaki* might be influential (and some served in the privy council by this time), but they were not to be confused with noblemen. The court at Moscow had developed round a small group of clans, and any that endured and had escaped disgrace still featured in its upper ranks. Whenever a high office needed to be filled, the ancient families expected to receive their call. And these jobs mattered, for though genealogy had an obvious role to play, it was service at the privy council level that paved the way to real power and a seat beside those marvellous displays of gold.

The rank of boyar was the most coveted of all, traditionally limited to about a dozen individuals at a time, and for these few, court life was a ballet designed to make sure that they and their clans remained unchallenged at the pinnacle of power. Some managed to reside within the Kremlin walls, others in mansions on the streets nearby, but it was vital to be present at the heart of government and to be seen to be there. After that, all advantage was relative, but it was essential not to lose status or to allow another clan to become disproportionately strong. In extreme cases, courtiers whose ambition exceeded reasonable limits could find themselves forced into exile by a jealous coalition of their peers.[72] The most infamous case of that kind had involved the boyar

Ivan Yurevich Patrikeyev, first cousin to Ivan III and probably the most powerful man in the fifteenth-century Kremlin after Ivan himself. His very success was his downfall. In January 1499, Patrikeyev was arrested on suspicion of a plot against the crown. Among the other accused were two of his sons and his son-in-law, Semen Ivanovich Ryapolovsky. All four were sentenced to death; Ryapolovsky was publicly beheaded on the Moscow river ice.

More usually, court politics was designed to prevent bloodshed, although the system also limited the sovereign's freedom to make appointments on the basis of mere talent. Though everyone was obliged to serve the grand prince, each role at court was ranked, and senior members of the leading families demanded to be given the most important ones. Ambitions could be shattered if a man accepted any office that was lower than his due, but since it was impossible for everyone involved to determine (or even to remember) the finer details of the hierarchy, especially at the humbler end, the system generated numerous disputes. Even the positions allocated to the diners at state banquets involved precise distinctions; if a courtier had been careless enough to accept the wrong seat at the dinner for Chancellor, for instance, he would have woken to a demotion that could drag on for years. The mistake could also taint the prospects of his heirs, for status ran along bloodlines, and a family that lost serious rank might struggle ever to regain it. Among the system's more sinister implications was the watchfulness it fostered within families, for since the dishonour of one affected every member of a clan, black sheep had to be penned – or sacrificed – at home.[73]

Newcomers were a regular irritant. Their rank was based (like everybody's) on the type of service that the prince had called them to perform. Since leading members of a rival court were best neutralized by bringing them to Moscow, providing them with lodgings and entrusting them with prominent roles, this meant that even refugee boyars from Lithuania had been known to jump straight to the top of the Kremlin hierarchy. As Moscow expanded, and more and more such outsiders arrived, resident families of longer standing began to insist that the details of each courtier's precise place on the seniority ladder should be entered in a permanent, binding record. There could still be movement – people died – but any accidental or capricious variation had to be forestalled before the dishonour became indelible. In its developed form, emerging in the sixteenth century, this system, with its ledgers and its crossings-out, was called *mestnichestvo*, from the Russian word for place. What started as a way of managing an expanding multi-cultural court was soon inscribed in leather-bound volumes, and it would remain a feature of Kremlin life for a century to come.

A politics based on families is also a politics of sex and motherhood, so Kremlin women generally led secluded lives. A careless marriage could disrupt the best-laid plans, for daughters were valuable only if they could be married to high-status heirs. Each time a royal boy needed a wife, therefore, there was an ugly contest and potentially a feud. The rivalry was so divisive that Moscow's rulers were eventually obliged to bypass the unmarried daughters of their own court clans and look beyond the capital. Ivan the Terrible, who married more wives than Henry VIII, was a case in point. By the time he was looking for his third (and in the absence of a willing European princess) the practice of sending agents to the provinces to select a collection of healthy but obscure young women had more or less become the norm. The girls were brought to the palace, where they were questioned, examined and probably frightened half to death. One by one, they were then paraded before the tsar in a so-called bride show. The point was that whichever girl the sovereign chose, there was a chance of healthy heirs, and at the same time it was unlikely that any boyar family would gain disproportionately from the marriage.[74]

The system left many noblewomen unmarried and prospectless. The tsar's own daughters, as well as his sisters and maiden aunts, were certainly too important for any ordinary marriage-market. No clan could be allowed to monopolize them. Some opted for the convent and a relatively comfortable religious life (there were several places where such women lived in discreet luxury), but many grew old in the Kremlin's own women's quarters. There, behind the pierced and gilded screens, they were meant to spend their time in prayer and fancy needlework. Some mixed a toxic range of white face-creams, and others seem to have experimented with poetry and letters.[75] Whatever their diversions, however, their spinsterhood was one convenient control on the production of possible pretenders to the throne.[76] Another was the devotion with which successive Muscovite rulers exiled their married male relatives to the provinces, ostensibly to give them valuable tasks and lands but more practically to keep their wretched sons out of the Kremlin.

At the centre of the entire costume dance, enthroned in his new palace, sat the tsar himself. His boyars and advisors clearly had important roles in the evolving government; some even managed complex *prikazy*. But the monarchy depended on its sovereign. This truth was clear to every visitor, and by the time of Richard Chancellor's visit it was an article of faith at court. The tsar of the 1550s was like the sun amid the circling planets. His Kremlin had been redesigned to paint him as the heir to an imperial line. But sovereignty had not been viewed like this for very long, and the message required a good deal of reinforcement. For courtiers, the pictures in the Golden Palace were one kind of text. Since few could read, the images were visible parables, filling the role that propaganda was to play in a much later age.[77] And Metropolitan Makary did not confine his efforts on the tsar's behalf to art. Between 1547 and 1549, he and his bishops also more than doubled the roll-call of Moscow's saints. Their selection was guided mainly by religious considerations, but the addition of princes like Alexander Nevsky and Mikhail of Tver showed clearly that the heavens loved a pious and God-chosen prince, especially if he happened to rule the lands of Rus.[78]

For those who could read – or who listened while their priests intoned to them – the other medium for conveying the new philosophy involved a series of written texts. Makary's most significant legacy may well have been the collection, editing and re-inscribing of the old Russian chronicles, the records of the past that had been kept and copied by armies of monks across the Russian lands for centuries. It was the Kremlin's first systematic attempt to rewrite history, and it was a dazzling success, placing Moscow at the summit of a progression from Kievan Rus to heaven-blessed empire. Through this project, Makary also encouraged a new bias against Islam, and notably against the Mongols and their successors, the Tatars. This was a tricky stance to take, for there were Tatar princes in the tsar's service, and the tradition of intermarriage on the steppes was so deep-rooted that few nobles could lay claim to purely Christian blood. But what Makary wanted was a new crusade – or the Orthodox equivalent of one. As Moscow learned to celebrate the Russian lands and Russian princely deeds, the leaders of its church were busily transforming the Tatars of Kazan and the Crimean steppe from cousins, neighbours and potential allies into the fatherless tribes of Hagar.

Makary gave his blessing to Ivan's first military plans. What might have been a routine Muscovite land-grab ended up being celebrated as a holy war. In 1550, the tsar created a new military force, the *streltsy*, a fledgling standing army composed of trained musketeers (who served for life). With their help, and some well-placed casks of gunpowder, his troops were able to besiege and capture the Tatar fortress of Kazan in 1552. When Ivan rode home after that triumph, Makary himself stood at the city's boundary to greet him. The tsar dismounted in the middle of a sea of banners and walked into his Kremlin as if it were indeed Jerusalem and he an image of Christ. Four years later, the Muscovites took Astrakhan, on the Caspian Sea, giving the Kremlin control of the Volga's entire length and raising a Christian (and Orthodox) standard over huge areas of territory that had hitherto lived under the rule of Islamic princes. In celebration, a prominent new icon, the Blessed Host of the Heavenly Tsar, was painted for the Dormition Cathedral. Though angels circle round a saintly procession, the icon may also have represented Ivan and his victorious army, their deeds reflected in a template that had been designed for heaven.[79] Orthodox Russia had found a mission in expansion and empire. To add to the celebratory mood, Ivan's first heir, a son, was born in 1553, and though he died in infancy, a second son, Ivan, looked set to grow up a survivor.

In the spring of 1553, Ivan unveiled the plans for a monument to his triumph at Kazan. The building, originally dedicated to the Trinity, started life as a brick church on the banks of the moat beneath the Kremlin walls. After the fall of Astrakhan, however, the prime site seemed to call for something more ambitious, and soon the Cathedral of the Intercession on the Moat was born.[80] It was conceived as a series of individual churches gathered round a central tower, but that description hardly captures the exuberance of St Basil's. Its architecture was another text about Ivan's God-given destiny. Much of it recalled the specific dates of his recent victories (the Festival of the Intercession, for instance, coincided with the start of the final assault on Kazan).[81] Among the other chapels, one was dedicated to St Varlaam, whose name Ivan's father, Vasily III, had taken when he became a monk on the eve of his death.[82] The exception, the wild card, was the smallest chapel, which Muscovites themselves began to associate with a holy man called Basil the Blessed. Basil, who had died in 1552, was a Holy Fool, famous for walking Moscow's icy streets barefoot and often naked underneath his dirt. But he was loved and revered as a truth-teller, a fool in Christ.[83] When it was finished, Ivan's fantastic cathedral was the tallest building in the city, but it was the spirit of the Holy Fool, the shaman, half in darkness, half in light, that came, eventually, to monopolize it all.

In Ivan's time, however, a different chapel in the same building seems to have played the really colourful role. This one was dedicated to Christ's Entry into Jerusalem. The name was a reference, not even thinly veiled, to Ivan's own return to Moscow from Kazan, but it was also the cue for another of the court rituals that seemed designed to mystify outsiders.

'On Palme Sunday,' Anthony Jenkinson recalled, 'they have a very solemne procession . . . First, they have a tree of good bignesse which is made fast upon two sleds, as though it were growing there, and it is hanged with apples, raisins, figs and dates, and with many other fruits abundantly.' The sight of brightly coloured food, in the lean days of early spring, may well have been miraculous in its own right, but the procession that came next was even more remarkable. 'First,' Jenkinson continued, 'there is a horse covered with white linnen cloth down to the ground, his eares being made long with the same cloth like to an asses eares. Upon this horse the Metropolitan sitteth sidelong like a woman.' Leading the horse, in the middle of the huge procession, was the tsar himself, on foot, a palm frond in the hand that did not hold the reins. Tsar and metropolitan were preceded by a wooden cross, and youths spread cloth on the ground to make way for the ritual 'asse'. Here was another living icon, and the route, from the Kremlin to the Chapel of Christ's Entry into Jerusalem, emphasized Moscow's status as the earthly image of God's chosen city.

The tsar's role in the tableau remains a puzzle. Some experts take the scene at face value, and argue that it shows Ivan deferring to his spiritual leader in an act of ritual submission.[84] Like some views of the dominant role of the boyars, this one runs counter to the popular image of the Russian ruler as an autocrat, and so it fascinates historians of Ivan's court. The mystery is never likely to be solved, but what is clear is that submission – in this world, at least – was never Ivan's strongest suit. By 1558, when Jenkinson observed him, the tsar was already earning a name for cruelty, and in later years his deference to metropolitans did not prevent him from having one of Makary's successors murdered. An alternative explanation for the ritual sees the scene as another assertion of Ivan's Christ-like role, and this seems more convincing in terms of iconography and even general context.[85] Like the ceremony on the ice each January, the Palm Sunday parade quickly became a favourite with Muscovites. In that respect, it was also a useful tool in the church's continuing battle against paganism and natural magic. As he approached middle age, that struggle made such a deep impression on Ivan himself that he seemed almost to embody it.

The tsar's long reign had been inaugurated with church bells, but by the 1560s there were rumours, fostered by his enemies, that Ivan's court was promiscuous, drunk and bawdy, his palace filled with louts and jesters, its candles burning late into the night as the shadows of minstrels and drunks capered and loomed. The persistent fable that there were two Ivans, a benevolent, reforming youth and an ailing, vindictive old man, is unconvincing, but there is evidence that the tsar's mental health, always fragile, began to collapse as he aged, and he certainly suffered from a painful, and occasionally excruciating, spinal deformity.[86] He was also beset by growing fears about the succession, for though he now had two male heirs, Ivan and Fedor, the boys were young, and in 1560 their mother, Tsaritsa Anastasia, had died. As he considered his children's futures, gruesome memories of his own childhood made Ivan suspicious of the clans who continued to figure so centrally at court. His faith in these was further tested by their resistance to his plan for an extended war against Moscow's neighbours on the Baltic coast. [87] Ivan became more and more volatile, and by the time of Makary's death in 1563, his conduct bore little evidence of the respectful piety that his mentor had marked out for him.

The most portentous change came in December 1564. The feast of St Nicholas fell on 6 December, and Ivan intended to celebrate it with his family in the fortress city of Kolomna, seventy miles south-east of Moscow. Such journeys, often involving a large part of the court, were common everywhere in Europe at the time; an annual round of pilgrimages and even hunting expeditions gave sovereigns an opportunity to assert their rule over the provinces directly, and afforded far-flung subjects a much-valued chance to glimpse a splendid prince with their own eyes. This time, however, Ivan packed to leave the Kremlin as if escaping from a threatened siege. He gathered up a huge weight of gold and jewels, and he also requisitioned icons, crosses, gold and sacred treasures from churches and monasteries beyond the Kremlin walls.[88] The line of sledges stretched over the snow like a small army on campaign, and like an army it eventually made camp. Ivan led the royal progress from Kolomna to the Trinity-St Sergius Monastery, and finally established himself some miles deeper still into the hills to the north-east, at his late father's fortified country estate of Alexandrovskaya sloboda. Again, such pilgrimages were not rare – the death of his beloved Anastasia was probably hastened by the incessant travelling on which Ivan insisted – but this time the tsar's journey was unscheduled. More puzzling still was Ivan's curt summons to a picked list of boyars, demanding that they leave Moscow and join him at the palace in the fields.

The land of Russia had been orphaned. No prayers and no appeals to the memory of Moscow's holy saints looked likely to bring Ivan back. And a court without a prince, as Muscovites were cruelly aware, was rudderless. In January 1565, nobles and church leaders struggled with the prospect of chaos. What they learned, through a series of terrifying embassies between the tsar's fortress and the metropolitan's residence in the Kremlin, was that Ivan was threatening to abdicate. The idea was unthinkable – it was a blasphemy, a betrayal, it would have made the country ungovernable – so Moscow's lords, chaired by the new metropolitan (Afanasy) and backed by a chorus of citizens, begged Ivan to resume his crown at any price.[89] The message given to the snow-bound palace was that his people would endow their tsar with any kind of power, pass any law, confess to every treachery. No-one dared call Ivan's apparent bluff, for he was neither mad nor dying. In effect, he was testing loyalties and making sure of personal support, but it was the strangest, and most chilling, atmosphere in which to shape his new programme for sovereignty.

As he considered his courtiers' entreaties, Ivan himself may not have known what terms he would eventually demand.[90] His immediate condition was that he should be permitted to dispose of certain enemies without further interference from the church, the bureaucrats or the boyars. The first victims, beheaded in the shadow of the Kremlin walls, were senior members of the ancient Shuisky clan.[91] Though he showed no pity for the condemned, Ivan paid for expiatory prayers to be said after the event; as tsar, he always saw his actions as service to God.[92] One of the more vivid explanations for his violence, indeed, sees it as a way of putting his own kingship to the test before the courts of heaven, casting Ivan more in the role of Lucifer than of Christ.[93]

But Ivan's plans were not limited to assassination. More far-reaching was his scheme to split his empire and create a separate kingdom within it where no plot or whisper (and certainly no pressure from a council of boyars) could challenge his personal writ. According to this programme, part of the Muscovite realm would continue more or less as it had done before, with a government in the Kremlin that involved the principal boyars and with *prikazy* to manage most routine administration. This territory, whose ruler in the first instance was to be a boyar called Ivan Mstislavsky, would soon be known as the *zemshchina*, from the Russian word for land. The other part, however, which included almost all the wealthiest towns, was the portion that Ivan intended to rule, alone and without interference, from his effective capital at Alexandrovskaya sloboda. In practice, Ivan never quit the Kremlin for all time, just as his threats to abdicate were never really implemented, but the uncertainty he generated was oppressive. Muscovites began to whisper a new term, *oprichnina*, the word (derived from the Russian for separate, apart) that Ivan had chosen to describe the unfortunate estates that he proposed to control for himself. In time, the same term would also become a byword for the terror that his tyranny unleashed.

To run the new *oprichnina*, Ivan shipped wagon-loads of clerks and trusted officials from Moscow to his out-of-town stronghold; his next requirement was an army to enforce his orders and make sure of his lands. The corps he recruited, the extortionists and bullies who became infamous as the *oprichniki*, was swathed in black, a nightmare vision of apocalypse. The symbols on their bridles were a dog's head and a broom, for their mission was to savage the tsar's enemies and drive them from the realm. Initially about a thousand in number, their ranks grew in the next five years and ultimately comprised about six thousand mounted men, drawn from all classes and united by a common greed.[94]

The appearance of these horsemen in a district almost always spelled misery. Not only adult males – the clansmen Ivan might justly have feared, the councillors who had queried a policy or chafed under a tax – but entire families including children were tortured and killed. Villages were burned and the houses of former boyars left to the wind and snow. Some of this property was supposed to go to the *oprichniki*, and many profited significantly from their work, but at the time the land seemed merely ruined.[95] Heinrich von Staden, the German who had visited the *prikazy* and described the conditions of the clerks, was also a hired mercenary with the *oprichniki*, and he left a chilling account of their impact. 'The villages were burned with their churches, and everything that was in them, icons and church ornaments,' he wrote. 'Women and girls were stripped naked and forced in that state to catch chickens in the fields.'[96]

As Ivan and his minions came and went, Moscow's sacred fort witnessed more than its share of executions. In 1568, the tsar's spies reported a new plot to remove him from power. The chief conspirator, Prince Ivan Petrovich Cheliadnin-Fedorov, was summoned to the Kremlin and stabbed in the heart by Ivan himself. His body was dragged several times around the fortress walls before being dumped in the main commercial square.[97] Cheliadnin-Fedorov's estates fell to the *oprichniki*. 'He did not spare them,' a contemporary source related, explaining how Ivan's men killed over a hundred of the prince's noble servitors. No-one was pardoned, not even 'their wives, nor their little children sucking at their mothers' breasts; and they say that he even ordered that not a single animal be left alive.'[98] But the tsar's wrath was not assuaged, and the land around Moscow's fortress continued to be stained with blood. The dead – impaled, beheaded, quartered or strangled – were left in piles under the Kremlin walls, and bodies choked the fetid ditch along the Neglinnaya river.[99]

The following year, the *oprichnina* claimed its most illustrious victim when Ivan's thirty-six-year-old cousin, Vladimir of Staritsa, was forced to swallow poison at the hands of the infamous *oprichnik* Malyuta Skuratov, at Alexandrovskaya sloboda. His children were murdered beside him. The pretext was a rumour (improbable) that Vladimir was plotting to seize the crown, but there did not have to be a reason for specific killings at this time. The terror had a logic of its own. No-one could feel safe, not even leaders of the church. In 1568, the new metropolitan, Filipp II, who had dared to speak against the tsar's cruelty, was seized by Ivan's men during a public service, forcibly unfrocked, and bundled off to a monastery in Tver. Months later, still protesting against unnecessary bloodshed, he was smothered there by Skuratov.[100] Ivan himself remained tormentedly devout despite this outrage, and he frequently ordered his torturers to suspend their activities, wherever he was, while he engaged in extended prostrations and prayers. 'Dying for the tsar,' the historian Sergei Bogatyrev explains, 'was represented as being akin to dying for Christ ... [Ivan] subjected his counsellors to disgrace and execution in the belief that he would thereby purify himself and his subjects on the eve of judgement day.'[101]

Apart from any plot to drive him from the throne, the treachery Ivan feared most was collaboration with neighbouring powers, and notably with the recently united state of Poland-Lithuania.[102] At stake, perhaps, was his chance of establishing a port for Russia on the Baltic Sea, to gain which he seemed determined to fight a coalition of regional rivals, including Sweden. One problem with this plan was that the preparations drained Ivan's exchequer, and more cash would be needed by the day if he unleashed the northern war. As townsmen and peasants struggled with grievous rates of tax, no attention was given to the vulnerable border to the south, and the risk to this increased considerably when the Crimean khan, Devlet-Girey, began to build an alliance of his own with the Ottoman sultan. The country was in mortal danger from a combination of internal misery, economic ruin and military threat. As if to aggravate these problems, Ivan's public life was also coloured by personal tragedy. In 1569, his second wife, Mariya, died, and her loss seems to have tipped him into even deeper hell.

The impact of his rage, whatever its source, was shattering. That winter, Ivan and his black-clad host made a progress north through Tver and Torzhok towards Novgorod. In Tver, which was accused of negotiating with the Lithuanians (and which had also given shelter in the past to the metropolitan, Filipp), Ivan's *oprichniki* ran riot, torturing and killing hundreds of citizens and throwing the mutilated bodies into the Volga. Among the torments that Tverites endured were prolonged sessions of *pravezh*, the painful and humiliating beating on the shins, or a further horrifying refinement that involved hacking the victim's legs off at the knee. *Pravezh* had always been a punishment for debt, and this savage version was designed to symbolize a profound indebtedness, material and in terms of loyalty to Ivan, on the part of the entire city.[103]

Novgorod's fate was even more extreme. Despite the pleas of its loyal archbishop, Pimen, the city was sacked, its coffers and stores were looted and several thousand of its people were put to death, sometimes after the kinds of torture – physical mutilation, scalding, simulated drowning, impalement – in which Ivan took such delight. 'Every day,' noted von Staden, 'the Grand Prince could be found in the torture-chamber in person.'[104] The miserable survivors, a fraction of the city's former strength, were abandoned to midwinter ice, disputing scraps of carrion and rags.[105] Novgorod's wealth, rebuilt in the decades since Ivan III had plundered it, now disappeared south a second time; even the altar-doors of its eleventh-century Cathedral of the Holy Wisdom were dragged away to adorn one of the two churches that Ivan was building at Alexandrovskaya sloboda 'in expiation for his sins'.[106]

The tsar's attention then turned back to the capital. In July 1570, several hundred former nobles and court servants were brought to the gallows in Moscow, many of them accused of collaboration with Archbishop Pimen. The spectacle was organized on a piece of ground beyond the city walls where public executions had been held for centuries; perhaps the idea was to draw the largest possible crowd.[107] Attendance was not really optional, however, and Ivan urged the people to draw close and watch. He even asked the crowd whether some traitors should be killed, goading them to collude as if he were a dictator from a much later age. The people, gripped by panic, naturally urged him on. As the knives glinted and the entrails spilled, the scene was like another icon, though this time the subject was the Last Judgement. Among the victims were the heads of several *prikazy*, including Ivan Viskovatyi. The official who had managed Ivan's diplomacy was strung up on one of the temporary scaffolds and hacked to pieces, dying only when an *oprichnik* cut off his genitals.[108] The families, as ever, were deemed to share a traitor's guilt. Over the next two or three weeks, the wives and children of the most distinguished of them were publicly drowned in the Moscow river.[109]

Ivan's most bloodthirsty campaigns were launched from Alexandrovskaya sloboda. The palace there suited the tsar; it was old, it was solid, and its ghosts were all of his own making. In 1571, a bride show was organized in it for him to select his third wife (she died soon after the wedding). Ivan even received some foreign diplomats at the provincial court. But Moscow's fortress was too valuable to abandon, and certainly too important to leave for others to annex. The Kremlin's grand spaces were practical: when Ivan needed to summon an assembly of his notable subjects (*zemskii sobor*) in 1566, a strategem to gain support for his intended northern war, for instance, there was no other place in Moscow with the room to host it.[110] The splendid Golden Palace was still the best venue in which to receive foreign embassies, too, and Ivan needed to impress potential friends abroad. The Kremlin as a whole was a sacred site, the only place where sovereignty was linked to God as well as to dynastic history. In 1575 Ivan used it to install a new ruler for the *zemshchina*, a Tatar prince from the dynasty of Chinghis

Khan called Simeon Bekhbulatovich. According to at least one witness, this nobleman's brief reign (Ivan demoted him in 1576) began with a desultory coronation in the Dormition Cathedral.[111]

Useful though the Kremlin was, however, the tsar vacillated over the question of establishing a residence for himself inside the fort. He had to weigh the need to keep control of its labyrinthine palaces against his horror of historic ghosts and real conspirators. At one point, he lived in a modest four-room wooden building on the site of his first wife's lodging near the Cathedral of the Saviour in the Forest.[112] But he also toyed with several possibilities in Moscow itself, and his most extravagant venture involved an entirely new palace. It stood at the notional boundary of his divided state, on land that he claimed for the *oprichnina*. But it was close to the Kremlin – a 'gunshot's distance' in Heinrich von Staden's words – and in its brief heyday it must have dominated the marshy bank of the Neglinnaya.

Ivan requisitioned the site in 1566, evicting the existing owners and taking advantage of another fire, which conveniently cleared much of the land. In January 1567, he moved in, accompanied by his aides, his spies, minstrels, doctors, astrologers and the entire *oprichnina* court. The new headquarters was defended by walls of stone and brick, and its gates, covered with lead and carved with two stone lions with mirrors for eyes, could be sealed at any time with two massive oak logs. A double-headed eagle, fashioned from wood and painted black, spread sinister wings above this gate, and there were more on the roofs of the palace buildings. Every entrance and passageway was watched, but Ivan's personal lodgings were designed so that he could not be observed. There were three regal buildings inside the walls, but Ivan's own preference was for an austere 'cottage' in a corner of the compound. His luxuries were few, although he did have a personal scaffold from which to mount and dismount his horse. It was a sensible concession to the pain that wracked his spine, as was the thick white sand that was spread over every courtyard, probably to counteract the damp.[113] In the 1930s, when teams of engineers were digging the first tunnels of Moscow's underground metro near the Lenin Library, this sand, like a flaxen thread within the claggy soil of the Mokhovaya, was the only trace they could find of Ivan's once-infamous palace.[114]

The end came in the spring of 1571. Russia's division, its people's suffering, and the decimation of its military class all pointed to catastrophe.

To add to the misery, a series of poor harvests led to famine in the winter of 1569–70, and hunger left the people without strength. The ravaged Novgorod region, where decomposing bodies still blocked the rivers, had already suffered from outbreaks of plague, but in 1570 the scourge spread southwards, and mass deaths occurred in at least twenty-eight cities.[115] According to Heinrich von Staden, a special pit had to be dug outside Moscow to hold its piles of dead.[116] Russia was sinking, and the following spring, in May 1571, the Crimean khan, Devlet-Girey, seized the chance to attack. Many of the Russian troops who were supposed to block his way deserted to the Tatars, and Ivan himself fled to safety (by this time he had begun to explore the possibility of permanent asylum in England), leaving the khan's route open to Moscow.

The citizens armed for battle, but in place of the expected siege they faced a more familiar enemy. For the second time in Ivan's reign, the capital was engulfed in flames, this time deliberately kindled by Devlet-Girey's army. Heinrich von Staden reported that it took just six hours to reduce Moscow to ash, while 'not three hundred persons capable of bearing arms remained alive'. Even the massive bells that hung in Ivan's *oprichnina* palace melted and cracked, and falling masonry killed many who had managed to escape the fire. As the flames swept on, Ivan's English lions were burned alive in their enclosure, and at least twenty-five human Englishmen, builders and craftsmen in the tsar's service, perished with them in the blaze. Many Kremlin buildings, including almost all the wooden offices, were swallowed up. 'In a word,' von Staden concluded, 'there is not a man in Moscow who can imagine Moscow's misery at this time.'[117] Although the Kremlin walls endured, the ruins of Ivan's *oprichnina* palace were abandoned to the wild dogs.

As he crossed the Oka river for a second time in July 1572, Devlet-Girey must have expected easy victory. But Russia, almost perversely, refused to abandon its tsar. An army composed largely of regular troops (incompetently backed by the *oprichniki*), pushed the Crimean horsemen back, and Moscow was spared new calamity. This miracle was Ivan's cue to change direction once again. He dissolved the *oprichnina* in the late summer of 1572, accompanying the reform with the usual round of executions. Several days' ride to the south of Moscow, meanwhile, a hard-pressed band of engineers began to fortify the borderlands that had just given such easy passage to the Tatar host.

*

The Kremlin still provided Ivan with a dazzling throne. Behind the safety of its walls, the tsar's treasury continued to amaze (he had a weakness for rubies and sapphires), his splendour to impress. According to a German visitor of 1576, Ivan's crown and mantle were more sumptuous than the regalia of any rival European prince, and outshone treasures he had seen in the Spain of Philip II and Italy's Medici courts. Ivan also wielded a jewelled staff, a cruel-looking object reputedly fashioned from the horn of a unicorn.[118] Like the crown itself, this was a symbol of the royal authority of which the tsar remained so jealous. 'The deference universally accorded the Prince is something the mind can scarcely comprehend,' commented a Jesuit envoy called Antonio Possevino. 'Even if the Muscovites do not really believe it, they incessantly declare that they owe their lives, their health, and all their worldly possessions to him . . . Even when beaten to the point of death they will sometimes say the Prince has done them a favour by chastising them.'[119]

At least the nation had a tsar. Indeed, it also had a healthy heir, which mattered because Ivan had worked as hard as any of his recent ancestors to score the hard black line of primogeniture into the Muscovite rule-books. The succession that descended from Daniil, Moscow's first prince, had been singled out, at least in Moscow, as the true and sacred continuation of the Riurikids of Kiev, and some at least of Ivan's cruelty arose from his obsession with protecting its future. After the death of his first son, he had shown a conspicuous concern for the second, his namesake. As his father, Vasily III, had done for him, he had even commissioned a miniature ceremonial helmet for the boy in token of his ruling destiny.[120] Another son, Fedor, was born in 1557, but Ivan was careful to ensure that the lad (who was in any case slow-witted and physically fragile) made no claim to his elder brother's crown.

With the succession guaranteed, Ivan's search for wives in his mature years had nothing to do with producing sons. Like Henry VIII, however, he remained unlucky when it came to marriage, and also like the English king he forced the leaders of his church to bless a long succession of new brides. His luck in that respect ran out in 1572, for though he had managed to get his third marriage annulled on the grounds that it had not (allegedly) been consummated, the Orthodox Church would not condone a fourth union. The last three of Ivan's numerous marriages were never recognized in canon law, which meant, in theory, that any children would be illegitimate. For years the issue was a legal nicety, however, and few would have dared to speak of it. There were no new male offspring in any case, or not at least until the very end. In 1582, and in a new set of dynastic circumstances, Ivan's final wife, Mariya Nagaya, produced a son. As a bastard, the child, Dmitry, was not eligible to succeed, but he was robust and sharp-witted, a worthy royal heir.

Just before Dmitry's birth, however, the story of the sacred house of the Daniilovich princes took an unexpected turn. Antonio Possevino, who visited Moscow at the beginning of 1582, heard his account from local witnesses, including one of the interpreters who worked at court. The background was Ivan's alleged impatience with his eldest son, Tsarevich Ivan, now twenty-seven years old and keen to make an impact of his own. Among the young man's many grievances (so the story went) was the tsar's repeated interference in his married life.[121] A first wife, Alexandra Saburova, chosen at a bride show in 1570, had failed to produce children, and the tsarevich was encouraged (or forced) to abandon her. A second princess, Praskovya Petrovna-Solovaya, followed her into the Pokrovsky Convent soon after.[122] In 1581, however, the young prince Ivan and his third bride, Elena Sheremeteva, at last conceived a child. Like pregnant women anywhere, Elena found the infant's bulk uncomfortable, and though it was November she did not always wear the three layers of robes that were required for women of her rank. This might not have been a problem, but the couple were staying with Ivan at Alexandrovskaya sloboda. 'It chanced,' Possevino reported, 'that the Grand Prince [i.e. the tsar] came upon her resting on a bench. She immediately rose, but he flew into a rage, boxed her ears, and hit her with the staff he was carrying. The following night she was delivered of a still-born child.'

As Possevino's informant affirmed, the tsarevich was furious. It will always be unclear exactly what happened, but Ivan must have raised the fateful staff a second time, for he managed to deal his son an even more savage, and fatal, blow. As blood poured from the young man's temple, the tsar struggled to grasp what he had done. A few short seconds of real time had stopped the course of Moscow's destiny; no helmet would protect this precious skull again. Five days later, young Ivan was dead. The body was laid out at Alexandrovskaya sloboda, but only Moscow and its Kremlin were worthy to be the prince's resting-place. At the funeral, Ivan the Terrible followed his son's bier into the Kremlin's Archangel Cathedral on foot, tearing his clothes and forsaking, for that day and many after, his jewels, rings and crown. He remained in the Kremlin palace throughout the months to come. 'Each night,' according to Possevino's informant, 'grief (or madness) would drive the Prince from his bed, to scratch the walls of his chamber with his nails and utter piercing sighs.'[123] Two years later, as Ivan lay on his deathbed, stinking acridly and covered in maggots, he prepared to face the Judgement that he had been tempting all his life. This tsar had reinforced the Muscovite royal line as no predecessor had ever done. Now he had destroyed it.

4

Kremlenagrad

The Muscovites may well have learned the art of drawing maps in the fifteenth century, when all those self-assured Italians were in the Kremlin.[1] The case is difficult to prove, especially since all the evidence has burned. But there are several maps of Moscow from the 1600s, and one of the most beautiful is called *Kremlenagrad*.[2] The copy that exists today, drawn by the Dutch East India Company's cartographer Joan Blaeu, was published in Amsterdam after 1662, but it is based on a much older drawing, and shows the Kremlin as it was around 1604. Blaeu's version has west, not north, at the top, but otherwise it is a model of clarity. As you unfold the Lilliputian panorama, you are drawn in and involved at once. The buildings are represented by little pictures, and every roof looks as if it would be warm and watertight.[3] The walls – and there are lots of them – trace reassuringly retentive lines with never an impaled head in view. This is the Kremlin at its flawless best; there must be children somewhere who could build it with a kit.

A map can say a lot about its creator's idea of the world. Joan Blaeu was very good at making sense of places he had never seen. He also took great pains, with his town maps, to make sure that he got the buildings right. When he began to draw the Kremlin, he called on plenty of the tricks he had already learned in forty years of map-making. The walls are presented accurately, but they also look very like the ones that snake around his lovely map of Delft, a masterpiece he had completed just three years before. In both maps, too, the rivers are the same contented blue. Despite that wishful Dutch precision, however, Blaeu's map has a great deal to teach us. The original he copied must have been unusually good. Clearly, someone with a trained eye and a sharp pencil had been working in the Kremlin at the turn of the seventeenth century, for the placing of the buildings that Blaeu copied is almost always accurate, as are the basic architectural details. The result is so faithful to its source that even now, scholars who spend their lives among the Kremlin archives can use it when (as they nearly always do) they draw a blank among the more authentic papers there.

To read the map beside the written history, moreover, is to turn it from a snapshot into commentary. One thing it shows is that the Kremlin had been changing at breathtaking pace in the years – not even twenty – since Tsar Ivan's death. There has been plenty of rebuilding and repair since the last fire, but all the same there are now fewer mansions for boyars. The names of the Belskys, Mstislavskys, Sitskys and Sheremetevs are mentioned in the key that Blaeu provides, and their walled palaces seem like small kremlins of their own, but the Patrikeyevs and Khovrins have disappeared along with half a dozen others. Instead, one name is mentioned several times: there are at least three mansions for the Godunovs. This is not a casual mistake, for the leader of this clan, the great lord Boris Godunov, has clearly added buildings everywhere. He has extended the tsar's palace, for instance, and he has made the bell tower of Ivan the Great into a serious landmark, adding new tiers and a cupola. Another angular structure, obviously brick, is marked '*prikazy*', and this time the design looks set to last. Meanwhile, there has been a significant change to the stone building, behind the Church of the Deposition of the Robe, that was last known as the metropolitan's residence. The international status of the Russian church must have improved, for this is now the palace of a patriarch.

The faithful map shows all of this, but despite all that it is misleading in a way that even Blaeu himself might not have grasped. The Dutchman's buildings cast compact, untroubled shadows, and yet the decades after Ivan the Terrible's death were among the most turbulent in the Kremlin's existence. *Kremlenagrad* is incomplete without that darkness, but to begin to look for it you need to know some history, and Blaeu was probably as hazy about Russia's as any other north-west European. As a map-maker, he would have been distracted, too, by all the new worlds of his day, for his was the golden age of European exploration. The coasts of continents as diverse as America and East Asia were gradually taking shape on paper with Dutch water-marks. These were fantastic places; exotic and terrifying. But the most eccentric sailors' tales of foreign lands could not have been more wildly wrong than the idea that the Kremlin of *Kremlenagrad* was orderly, immaculate, tranquil.

When Ivan the Terrible died, in March 1584, the boyars once again held Moscow's future in their hands. Even now, it is not easy to like the members of this jealous, arrogant elite. The French mercenary Jacques Margeret, who later headed the tsar's foreign troops, was never enthusiastic. The nobles he met were as soft as grubs. 'They go on horseback in the summer and in winter on sleighs,' he wrote, 'so that they get no exercise. This makes them stout and obese.'[4] A Dutch grain merchant, Isaac Massa, whose own well-fleshed features can still be studied in two portraits by Frans Hals, was no more flattering about them. 'The magnates', he decided in his memoir of Russia,

> lead a fairly unhappy life in this country. Obliged to be at court continually and remain standing for days on end before the emperor, they scarcely have one day of rest in three or four. The more they are raised in honour, the wearier they are out of anxiety and fear, and yet nevertheless they are constantly seeking to mount higher.[5]

In the boyars' defence, there was no obvious alternative. The Kremlin was not an arena that these families could simply leave at will. The ancient clans were bound to serve, and that meant they were trapped for life. Though ordinary people loathed them and believed they blocked free access to the tsar (who was essentially conceived as good), boyars (good and bad) had been governing beside the sovereign for ten generations. At the beginning of the seventeenth century, the question that had to be settled was whether one of them might finally ascend the throne in his own right.

The system was still based mainly on families, so it was notable that the man whose name featured so centrally on Joan Blaeu's map, Boris Godunov, came of a doubtful pedigree. Most other boyar families in the Kremlin had been there in some guise for centuries, and many were related or allied in complex ways. The Romanov clan, for instance, which traced its noble service back to the days of Ivan Kalita's eldest son, had junior branches whose members, by the 1580s, were almost equally eminent, including the Cherkasskys, the Sheremetevs and the Shestunovs. Towards the end of the sixteenth century, in the lifetime of boyar Nikita Romanovich Yurev-Zakharin, one of the Romanovs' most distinguished leaders, this clan did not disdain to build dynastic links with the Godunovs.[6] But other members of the old elite were more uneasy with the newcomers. The Godunovs appeared to be a vulgar brood. As the latest generation of them grew and flourished in the 1580s, the youngsters' talent and their quick success galled many who believed that every Kremlin prize was theirs by right of blood and history.

Boris himself grew up at the *oprichnina* court. It was not the most promising environment for a moral education, and to make matters worse, the wife that the young man's father chose for him seems to have been a latter-day Lady Macbeth. Mariya Godunova was the daughter of Ivan's most infamous enforcer, Malyuta Skuratov, and it was through that connection that young Boris and his sister, Irina, made much of their early progress in national politics.[7] They also made some powerful enemies, some of whom survived to shape the way their tale was told after their deaths. That is why, in subsequent accounts, there always seem to be at least two Boris Godunovs: a good one, enlightened and generous, and a murderer, the tragic anti-hero who later featured in Mussorgsky's opera.[8] What no-one ever questions, however, is that Boris was very rich. If anyone in the sixteenth-century Kremlin was the equivalent of a twenty-first-century oligarch, it was the clever, restless Godunov.

At thirty-three, Boris lacked natural grace. While some old clans could run to handsome, agile sons, the young boyar, at least according to Isaac Massa, 'was a man short in stature, fairly corpulent, with a somewhat round face'.[9] His wits were his fortune. He was the sort of man who quickly earns the loyalty of his officials: calculating, imaginative, and blessed with a memory for detail.[10] Few Russian rulers harboured larger plans for Moscow's spiritual primacy, and these, combined with his ambitions for the Godunov dynasty itself, gave young Boris a sense of mission.[11] Like several dictators of a much more recent age, he may also have reaped an unintended advantage from the disdain of blue-blooded rivals, although he shared their love of old-world style.[12]

The Godunovs' collective fortunes took a particularly promising turn in the last years of Ivan the Terrible's reign, when Irina Godunova married Fedor, the ageing tyrant's second son. The marriage, however, was far from conventional. Many accounts claim that Fedor was mentally handicapped, as simple and as helpless as a child. Whether this was true or not, the dying tsar thought it prudent to name a four-man regency council to protect the youth. Again, the Godunovs did well, for in addition to the princes Ivan Mstislavsky and Ivan Shuisky, its members were Nikita Romanovich Yurev-Zakharin and his ally, Boris Godunov.[13] The first test for these regents came while Ivan's body was still warm. One of the late tsar's former henchmen, Bogdan Belsky, took advantage of the general confusion to attempt a coup. The atmosphere was very tense – as it was bound to be while the succession was unclear – but then a rumour spread through Moscow that the *oprichnina* was coming back.[14] Even in a depressed and depopulated city, the prospect of more bloodshed and injustice was enough to provoke violence. Grasping for any weapon that came to hand – a pike, a club, perhaps a sword – the braver citizens made their way straight to the Kremlin to demand the truth, but as they mounted the bridge to cross the moat they found the huge gates barred. The regents' first full night of power ended in looting and at least twenty recorded deaths as the mob flowed back through the nearby rows of market stalls and past the arsenal.[15]

Behind those massive bolted gates, meanwhile, the council met continuously through the night. Belsky was sentenced to exile, but that still left the courtiers with the problem of a suspicious, volatile mob. Child-like or not, Crown Prince Fedor was now the key. As Ivan's heir (and people were already nostalgic for Ivan the Terrible, their late 'true tsar'), his presence offered an illusion of normality. The regents organized his coronation with an almost ugly haste. To an accompaniment of cheerful bells and showers of clinking silver coins, Fedor Ivanovich was proclaimed tsar on 31 May 1584. Significantly, Boris Godunov was the man who carried the new sovereign's sceptre, a service for which he was rewarded with the title of master of the royal horse, *konyushii*, the most prestigious of boyars.[16]

The last Daniilovich prince of Moscow, Tsar Fedor lived a pious, even contemplative life. He and Irina liked to pray, and no-one has ever managed to accuse them of any real malice. Secure in his own golden world, the tsar may not even have realized that his advisors were circling like vultures over an imminent kill. Outside his lavish fortress, however, the 1580s were proving to be unusually harsh and disturbing. Moscow itself was full of ghosts, its surviving population tormented by famine, fire and epidemic disease.[17] The 'little ice age' was just beginning, and crops were failing everywhere in Europe, but the hunger in the Russian lands followed years of terror and plague, and unrest made the climate problem infinitely worse. For one thing, thousands had left their homes during Ivan's reign, taking refuge in the borderlands to escape taxation or forced labour. Others, crushed by impossible debt, had sold themselves into slavery. Beyond the cities, peasants were still on the road, fleeing in their tens of thousands from the scourges of crop blight, debt and labour service. Most were making for the southern steppe and the Volga. According to one estimate, the acreage of land under cultivation in the north-eastern forest belt, including Vladimir, Suzdal and the Moscow region itself, dropped by 90 per cent in the decade after 1564.[18] Novgorod and its hinterland were virtually empty. The sun could have shone through the night for all the good it would have done to fields of weeds. However little there was left to steal, meanwhile, there were so many strangers everywhere that yet another bane of life was banditry.

Almost every class of citizen faced hardship. Ever since the days of Ivan III, the state of Moscow had expanded by conquering and suborning its neighbours, and the social costs of that approach were now becoming clear. Both local settlement and national defence, for instance, depended on the provincial gentry, the *pomeshchiki*, the men who had accepted smallish grants of land, often in the newly annexed territories and borderlands, in exchange for a continuing duty of military service. They were the sixteenth-century equivalent of patriotic settlers, but circumstances kept them from developing their farms.[19] The continuous wars of Ivan the Terrible's reign had demanded their participation almost without respite. In their absence, bonded labourers were supposed to cultivate the land and provide their masters with an income, but if the harvest failed the problems soon began to multiply. Estates turned into millstones as runaway peasants headed southwards to the rolling grasslands that most people now referred to as 'the Field'. Shouldering their former master's pike or axe, many of these fugitives joined the cossacks, the bands of outlaw horsemen who roamed the steppe like guerrilla gangs. But the state made no concession, in terms of service obligations, to the gentry militia-men, some of whom were now unable to cover the cost of their own food, let alone weapons or a horse. The peace-keepers were growing ever more demoralized, in other words, at just the time when outlaw bands were threatening security at home.

The militia was no more help when it came to facing foreign threats.

Indeed, their poverty was a guarantee that the Muscovite state would not keep pace with European military innovations. The corps of *streltsy*, the hereditary musketeers, were modern soldiers of a kind, but they formed only part of the army, and the firearms they used were still so unreliable, and at the same time so forbiddingly expensive, that the members of the gentry militia who fought beside them usually preferred to arm themselves with bows and arrows.[20] The foreign armies on Russia's frontiers were much better equipped, and most nursed more or less expansive plans. To the north, the Swedes harboured territorial ambitions in the Baltic, while Poland-Lithuania, to the west, eyed border towns across the rivers of Ukraine. The southern frontier was so exposed that even Moscow was not safe; in June 1591 a Tatar army led by Kazy-Girey reached the city's outskirts.[21] Other strategic centres, including Tula and Ryazan, were still more vulnerable, and slave-raids remained the curse of the Russian south for decades.

Whatever dangers the land seemed to face, however, the boyars never ceased to vie for power. While Fedor lived, the Godunovs and Romanovs behaved like life-long friends, but the princes Shuisky and Mstislavsky each believed the tsar's infirmity to be their cue to take control of Moscow's throne.[22] In 1585, it was Mstislavsky who made the first bid. When his plot failed, the Kremlin's governing council ordered the defeated boyar to become a monk, and ruled that his son, Fedor, could never marry.[23] This was a cruel punishment indeed; the idea was to make sure that the senior branch of the ancient Mstislavsky clan, whose royal service had begun in fourteenth-century Lithuania, would never produce another heir, let alone a new pretender.

Less than a year later, Prince Ivan Shuisky, a descendant of the sainted Alexander Nevsky, chose to prepare a coup of his own.[24] As usual, the plot began with malevolent rumours, and in the spring of 1586 there was a fresh panic in Russia's capital. Shuisky let the people think that Boris Godunov was preparing to usurp Tsar Fedor's crown. At this, the Kremlin tensed for civil war, and even the monks of the Chudov Monastery began to stock supplies of arms. Facing arrest and murder at Shuisky's hands, Godunov himself became so alarmed that he made secret approaches to England, which was already getting a reputation as the destination of choice for Russian potentates in crisis (the first would-be asylum-seeker in this line having been Ivan the Terrible). The boyar's escape-plan was not needed, but his rivals, aided by the metropolitan, Dionysii, certainly came within an ace of driving him from power.[25]

It may have been Tsar Fedor who ultimately saved him. On the pretext that Irina Godunova had not managed to produce an heir, the Shuiskys planned to engineer a royal divorce. Their anti-Godunov alliance grew stronger when they persuaded Fedor Mstislavsky that it could be his sister whom the tsar married next (a nice piece of poetic justice in view of the recent ban on his own right to a wife). The downfall of the Godunovs looked certain until the young tsar himself showed an unsuspected power of decision. To everyone's surprise, he refused to part with his wife, who was, in most respects, his best playmate as well as nurse. As the conspiracy collapsed, Boris and his Kremlin aide, the d'yak Andrei Shchelkalov, called in their debts, removing Dionysii from the metropolitan's seat, exiling several other leading priests, and starting an investigation at court. Six of the main conspirators were beheaded, and others, cast from the Kremlin and stripped of their estates, were exiled to the provinces.[26] The ailing Nikita Romanovich Yurev-Zakharin had died in April 1586. Of the four regents that Ivan the Terrible had originally appointed, only Godunov could now wield power.

Boris Godunov was not so foolish as to count himself secure. In a court riddled with intrigue, his regent's role was never guaranteed, while the country was beset with problems that resisted all reform. His government passed a series of measures to help the gentry by tying the peasants to their masters' land.[27] It also raised taxes and found labour for much-needed public works. Andrei Shchelkalov, described by Massa as 'a man of finesse, audacity and duplicity not to be credited', could squeeze money from anyone, even the Kremlin monks.[28] But no good works and no veiled threats could neutralize the opposition that his master faced. The church was full of discontent, for the priest that Boris had installed as metropolitan, his loyal henchman Yov, was widely viewed as an outsider, a man whose background had been tainted by a long association with the Godunovs. The boyar's next move, therefore, was a masterstroke.

In 1588, two years after the Shuisky crisis, the patriarch of Constantinople, Jeremiah, travelled to Moscow to petition for financial aid. Such missions had become a tedious necessity for Orthodox leaders from the Middle East, who were struggling to raise revenue under

Turkish rule. Jeremiah's first audience with Godunov and the *d'yak* Shchelkalov took place in July. Further conversations would be inescapable, but his plan was to return home before the first serious autumn rain. In the event, however, the patriarch and his suite were subjected to luxury house-arrest for nearly ten more months. Pretexts were found for each delay, and no-one mentioned *force majeure*, but as the weeks passed it became clear that Tsar Fedor's government (for which read Boris and Shchelkalov) would not release the visitors, still less afford their church financial aid, until certain conditions had been met. Months were wasted in the boredom of official politesse. Even if the foreigners managed to venture out, their path was always lined with Kremlin guards. If the Russians' purpose was to isolate their visitors from reality, the tactic worked. At one point, as if mesmerized by the Kremlin's splendour, Jeremiah started to play with the idea of moving his own patriarchal seat to Moscow in a bid to escape the Turkish yoke.

This was not Godunov's plan. The regent used a range of methods to make his points clear (Shchelkalov threatened to drown a member of the Greek delegation in the Moscow river[29]), and in time Jeremiah acceded to his wishes. In 1589, with the agreement of the ancient churches of the east, the leader of Russian Orthodoxy was formally elevated to the rank of Patriarch. Yov was enthroned in the Kremlin's Dormition Cathedral, and glory shone on smooth-faced Fedor for a second time. If Moscow had ever pretended to be a third Rome, the proof – and the responsibility – was evident now.[30] The creation of the patriarchate also added to the traffic in and out of Moscow's fortress; the Kremlin's opportunity to become a world-class centre of spirituality and culture had finally dawned.

The triumph did a lot to bolster Godunov's position, but the other testimony to his skills was more immediately visible. The regent was a large-scale commissioner of building-works. His main programme began in 1586. For nearly two decades to come, Godunov's architects employed a small army of builders, in the process providing work for thousands of hungry citizens at a time of economic stress. The projects sometimes took place far from Moscow, transforming landscapes in the provinces with brick and stone. But Godunov was also constantly aware of the Kremlin. Just before his death, indeed, his last construction scheme was meant to fix its place for ever as the capital of universal Orthodoxy.

The system for procuring builders was based in the Kremlin itself.

At the end of Ivan the Terrible's reign, with Moscow a semi-ruin, a Buildings Chancellery (the *prikaz kamennykh del*) had been added to the list of central government offices. Its main task was to manage the supply of skilled workmen. There was nothing particularly new about the idea that a craftsman might be liable to call-up on the crown's behalf, but the Buildings Chancellery made the system more official, and in Godunov's time it was tested to its limits. Under his regency, the Kremlin came to act as patron, master, and even the administrator of a sort of national apprentice-scheme. The labourers, whose trades were handed down in families, were drawn from more than twenty provinces. They included stone-masons, bricklayers and the men who worked the ovens and the quarries, and at times of need the *prikaz* could send its officials out to summon all of them to Moscow. From there, the men could be deployed to any site the tsar's officials had marked out for them, including cities in the provinces and new defensive forts. As a magnet for numerous grand projects, Moscow soon became accustomed to its builders' shanty-town, a makeshift settlement, well outside the Kremlin, that swelled each spring and shut down only when the frosts set hard.[31]

No labourer was likely to be rich, and members of the building trades were barely paid enough to feed and clothe themselves. But they had one unusual advantage, for they were exempt from tax. This privilege (which they shared with other specialists, including the *streltsy*[32]) was intended to recognize the fact that they were summer-migrants, and could not farm the land like ordinary peasants. What it also meant, however, was that they could make easy profits if they worked in their spare time. They cultivated kitchen-gardens round their settlements and sold the food. They also set up private markets, traditional Russian trading rows, and these could undercut tax-paying local businesses. In Tula the builders sold pots, in Vladimir footwear; in Suzdal they were noted for fur coats. Many were also willing to mend shoes and sheepskins, paint icons, fix tools or make furniture. When local people needed services like these, they knew exactly where to look, for the ground around the builders' settlements was always white with lime.[33] That dust must have got into everything in the summer of 1586: Boris Godunov had commissioned a new defensive wall for Moscow.

The massive enterprise involved enclosing 1,300 acres of the city in nearly six miles of fortified masonry. There were to be at least twenty-seven functional towers and ten sets of gates, beginning with an imposing entrance at the crown of the road to Tver. The architect was Fedor Kon, whose first clients (like those of many Russian masons) had been the monasteries.[34] But public works seem to have suited him. The peasants of the quarry-region, Myachkovo, were soon petitioning for help; the very bedrock of the meadows where their cattle grazed was disappearing on to builders' carts, and the fields for miles around were hard and sour with limestone dust.[35] When the new wall was finished, Moscow could boast three separate sets of fortifications – the Kremlin, Kitai-gorod, and Godunov's so-called White City – as well as a system of earthworks that stretched for miles beyond. But Kon was not allowed to stop until he had completed yet more walls, this time of wood, so that the entire city was enclosed.[36] The Kremlin's glamour was renewed, for the successive walls, like Chinese boxes, gave it the allure of a secret treasure.[37] In all, Moscow's fortification was an historic achievement, but it was not the epic project of the age. That prize went to the fortress at Smolensk, a strategic border city on the banks of the Dnieper, which in its time was the largest construction site in the world.

Moscow had ruled Smolensk since 1514. The city was wealthy and colourful, and its former suzerain, Poland-Lithuania, had not stopped coveting the place. Godunov's answer was to set about ringing it in four miles of sixteen-foot-thick walls, a scheme he again entrusted to Kon. At this point, Moscow's brick Kremlin was a century old, and siege-technology and guns had both evolved apace. The new design had to be more massive than Moscow's, less concerned with elegance, and sterner. The excavations for the fortification of Smolensk began in 1596, and from then until the project was completed in 1602, the Buildings Chancellery mobilized about ten thousand men. Between them, the labourers hefted at least a million loads of sand, while blacksmiths bashed out literally millions of nails. Like Fioravanti in Moscow, Kon built an on-site factory to make the bricks. His project called for 150 million of them, all of a regulation size; the ovens alone consumed such vast amounts of firewood that forests were cleared and the land left barren for miles around.[38] The awestruck locals, meanwhile, were forced to provide tools for an army of workers. For seven summers in a row, the deep ravine through which the Dnieper flowed rang to the sound of hammers and the slap and clatter of the trays of brick. Centuries later, Napoleon's Grande Armée and Hitler's Wehrmacht both spent harsh months in Smolensk, and neither treated the place with respect, but the remnants of Kon's walls endure, as obstinate as the sarsens of Stonehenge.

Whatever else he was doing, meanwhile, the regent Godunov always paid careful attention to the Kremlin. By the 1590s, his own palace there rivalled even Tsar Fedor's, and he staffed it with retainers whose titles mirrored those of the real court.[39] Across the square, he commissioned a team of the Kremlin's best artists to repaint the interior of the Faceted Palace, a task that called for more than fifty skilful icon-masters and quantities of expensive paint.[40] Years later, and before they were destroyed in a new round of improvements, the icon-painter Ushakov made careful drawings of these frescoes; he also added written notes. His records show that their artistic theme was the familiar genealogical fantasy: the Riurikids as heirs of Emperor Augustus. But one sequence was strikingly up to date. In it, Ushakov wrote, 'the Autocrat of All Russia [Fedor] sits on the throne, the crown on his head studded with precious stones and pearls ... On his right hand, next to his throne, stands the regent Boris Godunov.'[41] There were other boyars in the picture – the line stretched out to right and left – but Godunov had been made to look the tallest and by far the most magnificent.

It was a point that needed almost constant emphasis. The terror of the previous reign had steeped the Kremlin in malice. Aside from the unfortunate new tsar, the pawn in one of its most dangerous games was Ivan the Terrible's youngest son, Dmitry, the child of Mariya Nagaya, his last wife. In 1584, not long after the old tsar's death, the regents had exiled this infant, with his mother, to the city of Uglich, a move intended (at least ostensibly) to protect the fragile Tsar Fedor. Seven years later, when he was nine years old, Dmitry died in what was said to have been a freak accident. The enquiry that Godunov ordered into his death found no evidence of foul play, concluding instead that the child had cut his own throat while playing with a knife. Surprisingly, historians have tended to accept this tale, pointing out that Godunov had nothing to gain directly by killing Dmitry when Fedor was still alive and capable (perhaps with discreet help) of siring an heir.[42] But people at the time were far less gullible. Many believed an account spread by Dmitry's maternal relatives, the Nagois, who accused Godunov of attempting to poison the child before resorting to an assassin's knife. This was the story that Isaac Massa heard some years later, and the proof was said to lie in another terrible fire – the devil's work – that swept through Moscow two nights after the killing.[43]

In 1592, Irina bore Fedor a daughter, Feodosiya, but the infant's death, in 1594, again raised doubts about the future of the Godunovs. Fresh rumours of Irina's fall, and of her brother's imminent arrest, were whispered round the crowded trading rows.[44] In answer (or at least to reinforce a message that was being delivered on a more personal basis by the torturers that he had started to employ), Boris again began a round of building-work. The Kremlin was where power had to be defined, and so the site he chose was almost in the centre of it. The project was a new cathedral, and it was to be presented to the Ascension Convent as a pious gift in Godunov's name. The endowment of a religious building was not especially ambitious on its own (many boyars had built them before). What counted was that this one was the grave of Russia's grand princesses.

The scale of any major building was meant to advertise its patron's wealth, and there was nothing modest about Godunov's proposed cathedral. As its walls and cupolas rose within their cage of wood, however, the more specific implications of the regent's design-choice grew clear. His building paid an overt homage to the flamboyant Cathedral of the Archangel Michael, the tomb of Russia's male tsars, which had dominated the southern entrance to the Kremlin's Cathedral Square since 1508.[45] It is unlikely that Boris chose the blueprint by accident. Instead, his building, as a mausoleum for Russia's royal women and an assertion of the rights and status of the female line, deliberately echoed the striking appearance of the tsars' own burial place.[46] No woman had ever reigned alone in Muscovy (Elena Glinskaya had come close), but female sovereigns were not unknown in Europe, and Godunov had to believe that women mattered. After all, the one most closely linked to Russia's throne was his own sister.

Tsar Fedor died in January 1598. He and Irina never had a son, and so his death marked the end of Moscow's founding dynasty, the pure line of 'true tsars'. In the first hours, Boris is said to have tried to persuade his sister to accept the crown, but her answer, wisely, was to exchange her royal robes for a nun's habit and a life of prayer. Her brother followed her into the Novodevichy Convent, where he seemed determined to wait out the traditional forty days of deepest mourning. But ultimately the boyar's ambition prevailed. On 21 February, when a crowd of Muscovite petitioners and priests assembled at the convent doors, Boris Godunov finally agreed to end the dangerous uncertainty and take the throne. He even (literally) sat on it, but though he was now Russia's sovereign he made no swift move to be crowned. Instead, he forsook his beloved council chamber to nurture wider public acceptance and possibly to acquire a dash of military glamour. Boris spent part of the summer with his troops, ostensibly to stiffen their defence against Kazy-Girey.[47] It was only in September 1598 that he was crowned a tsar, in the Dormition Cathedral, by his political ally, the brand-new Patriarch Yov.

'The ceremony took place with a great show of splendour,' Isaac Massa related. The spectacle eclipsed even Metropolitan Makary's best efforts. The customary Russian symbols were, of course, evoked, but Moscow was now a patriarchate, and that meant that its tsar could claim the full imagined glory of Byzantium.[48] 'The crown', wrote Massa,

> was set upon [Boris'] head in the church of the Virgin by the Patriarch, surrounded by bishops and metropolitans, with all the prescribed ritual and a host of benedictions, together with the burning of incense. All along the road the tsar was to travel on the way from the churches to his palace at the crown of the fortress, they had spread out crimson cloth and covered it with gold; before the procession gold pieces were thrown down in handfuls, and the crowd fell upon them. . .

Money was not the only inducement on offer for this loyal mob during the eight-day celebration. 'At various places in the fortress,' Massa was told, 'they had placed great barrels filled with mead and beer from which all could drink ... The tsar ordered the distribution of triple wages to all those in the service of the state ... The whole country was glad and rejoiced, and everyone praised God for having granted the empire such a master.'[49]

The rejoicing was not entirely misplaced. Boris was one of the most gifted men who ever sat on Russia's throne. But he was also anxious to make certain of his right to rule. Some of his subjects could be bought with public works, others suborned with threats. Still, these were things a mere *d'yak* could have done. A tsar had to be seen in splendour, and that meant using the Kremlin. A crown was made, new jewels set, and Boris also accepted royal gifts, including regalia from Rudolf II's workshops in the Habsburg lands and a splendid throne from Isfahan.[50] But it was Ivan the Terrible's Golden Palace, with all the drama of the court, that made the deepest impression. When Boris received the Polish ambassador, Lew Sapieha, in 1600, Jacques Margeret observed each detail. The boyar tsar, he wrote, was

> seated on the imperial throne, the crown on his head, the sceptre in his hand, the golden orb before him. His son was seated next to him on his left. Seated on benches all around the chamber were the lords of the council and the *okol'nichie* [senior courtiers] wearing robes of very rich cloth of gold bordered with pearls, with tall hats of black fox on their heads. On each side of the emperor two young lords stood dressed in white velvet garments, bordered all around with ermine to the height of half a foot. Each wore a white tall hat on the head, with two long chains of enamelled gold criss-crossed around the neck [and over the chest]. Each of them held a costly battle-axe of Damascus steel on his shoulder, as if in readiness to let fly a blow, thus giving the impression of great majesty.[51]

The ritual and its setting were awe-inspiring, but Tsar Boris would have known of the constant plots and whispers out beyond the palace steps. Any boyar on the Russian throne was vulnerable, and a Godunov, still viewed by nobles with distaste, was at excessive risk. To protect himself, Boris created a network of informants and spies. His prisons filled, and several magnates felt the chill of imminent arrest. Servants were encouraged to inform on their masters, slaves on everyone in sight. The tsar himself grew increasingly reclusive, relying for information on the advice of his uncle, Semen Godunov, who ran the system of interrogations. Semen was no more than a torturer, and his cruelty further added to the number of the tsar's enemies.[52] For them, the Kremlin must have felt like a pit of snakes, but it was also the acknowledged centre of state and religious power. The opportunity to colonize it – to absorb two whole centuries of dynastic splendour into the Godunovs' pedigree – became the boyar tsar's obsession.

The drawing of *Kremlenagrad* dates from this time, and to be accurate it really should have featured carts and scaffolding and piles of bricks. As it is, the buildings that the map outlines include the tsar's most daring project in its final form. In 1600, Godunov ordered that two extra tiers should be added to the bell tower on the east side of Cathedral Square. The height was so vertiginous that even the scaffolding was a challenge, but soon the masons had begun their work, hauling bricks and lime to levels that no builder in the Russian lands had climbed before. The finished tower, an extension of Bon Fryazin's own so-called Ivan the Great, was nearly 270 feet high.[53] It was visible for thirty miles, and for centuries it was to be the tallest building in Moscow, surpassing Ivan the Terrible's Cathedral of the Intercession on the Moat (St Basil's) in height if not in bravado. Once he had made the famous tower his own, Boris ordered an inscription to be added. It was a proclamation to the world, and it is still there now, written on the uppermost tier in giant, gilded letters:

> By the will of the Holy Trinity, by the command of the Great Lord, Tsar, and Grand Prince Boris Fedorovich, Autocrat of All Russia, and of his son, the Orthodox Great Lord Fedor Borisovich, Tsarevich and Prince of All Russia, this church was completed and gilded in the second year of their reign.

'Boris hoped above all to appease the divine anger,' Isaac Massa concluded.[54] An observer from a different age might draw a parallel with twentieth-century cults of the leader's personality, but Boris did not have such far-reaching designs. The object was not to become a god, but just to occupy a higher plane of existence, a place where envy and conspiracy were impotent. And Boris would have used his eminence in creative new ways. The tsar's next projects included smart new buildings for the *prikazy* and playful battlements to top the walls that ran along the Kremlin's outer moat. Joan Blaeu's map shows both, but the most important structure of them all is missing, and was never built. It would have stood next to the enlarged Ivan the Great, which was intended to serve as its campanile. Its presence would have changed the Kremlin's geography for all time, focusing it on a new site. Where Ivan III had turned to Italy, Boris sent to James I of England in search of engineers with skills that his own subjects lacked (successfully: two of the country's most reputable builders arrived in Moscow in 1604).[55] The projected church was not to be like any other in the Kremlin. The tsar's intention was to build it large enough to hold thousands of souls, filling the citadel with ordinary Muscovites and inviting the entire Orthodox world to worship at the high altar of Russian faith.

What Boris had in mind was a cathedral for Moscow the Jerusalem, the holy city. His plan was to call it the Holy of Holies, and experts think it was designed in the image of the Church of the Holy Sepulchre. It would have been a place of pilgrimage, of majesty, and its completion would have set the seal on Godunov's dynastic rule. The shrines that the Daniilovich princes had built, including the Dormition Cathedral, would have been relegated to the second rank. By the time of Boris' death, in 1605, the new cathedral's general design had been approved, and a troupe of workmen at the site had assembled heaps of stone, lime and timber.[56] The tsar had also commissioned some opulent sculptures for the sanctuary. A reliquary was planned, a version of the Holy Sepulchre itself, and artists in the Kremlin workshops had created a pair of golden angels to stand guard at either end of it. The figures were life-sized, and one of them was said to have been placed in Godunov's own coffin when – as people later liked to say – his restless spirit rose to walk the earth after his death.[57]

This, then, was high tide for Kremlenagrad, a moment full of possibility. When that tide turned, the fortress closed its iron locks. The huge cathedral vanished without trace. The Kremlin is a place whose past is usually hallowed, but the Holy of Holies, that witness to the optimistic grandeur of the Godunovs, is all but absent from its chronicles. Even Andrei Batalov, who not only leads the Kremlin's architectural research effort but specializes in the age of Godunov, cannot be certain what it would have looked like if it had been built. *Kremlenagrad* appears in almost every guide to the Kremlin – the image is so well-known that readers tend to turn the page – but the real thing would have been terrifying at the best of times, and events were about to transform it, once again, into a theatre of the macabre.

According to Isaac Massa, Godunov's coronation oath had included a promise to shed no blood in Moscow for five years; an oath that he kept, the cynical Dutchman observed, by smothering and drowning his enemies or forcing them into monasteries.[58] His main rival, a close friend of the late Tsar Fedor, was the handsome Fedor Nikitich Romanov, the son of the old co-regent. The truce between the Godunovs and Romanovs had been abandoned when Tsar Fedor died. In 1600, Godunov's agents accused the older clan of using witchcraft, if not poison, in a plot against the ruling family. Boris ordered his men to burn the main Romanov residence in Moscow, purged the boyar council, and forced the forty-five-year-old Fedor Nikitich to take the vows of a monk (an irreversible transition to the church's world) under a new name: Filaret.[59] Whatever else the rival courtier might achieve, there was no further chance he could ascend the throne.

With that competitor removed, the skilful Godunov might yet have established a stable government, or at least cemented a more certain rule. But his hold on power was irreparably damaged by natural disaster. The summer of 1601 was cold and wet, reducing the yield of the toughest rye and wrecking some crops altogether. The winter that followed was colder and longer than the winters of the past, and then, in the summer of 1602, unseasonal frost and snow destroyed the harvest that a hungry people desperately needed.[60] The worst famine in memory took hold, and nothing Tsar Boris could do would make the fields green again. 'At about this time,' Massa explained,

> heaven afflicted the whole land of Muscovy with scarcity and famine such as history has never recorded ... There were even mothers who ate their children. The peasants and other inhabitants of the countryside, having consumed all their resources, cows, horses, sheep and fowls, without observing the prescribed fasts, began to look for vegetables such as mushrooms and other fungi in the forests. They ate them hungrily along with husks and the winnowings of wheat, cats, and dogs. Then their bellies swelled; they became distended like cows, and died swiftly in great agony. In winter, they were prey to a sort of fainting. They doubled up and fell on the ground. The roads were encumbered by bodies that were devoured by wolves, foxes, dogs, and all kinds of wild animals.[61]

As the countryside starved, Moscow's streets filled with beggars and fugitives. Massa was appalled. 'They had to organize teams of men who went every day with carts and sleds to gather bodies,' he wrote. They took this miserable cargo

> outside to large ditches in the open fields. There they were thrown in heaps, as is done with mud and refuse at home ... One day, I myself wanted very much to take some food to a young man seated in front of our lodgings, whom I had watched for four days as he fed himself on hay, dying of starvation. Yet I dared not do so for fear of being seen and attacked.[62]

The reproach implied by Massa's shocked and hostile tone should not detract from Godunov's record, for the tsar in fact made determined –

and expensive – efforts to avert calamity, at least in Moscow and the larger towns. At the start of the famine, in 1601, he passed laws to fix the price of bread. He also ordered his agents to hand out food and money to the starving, and in Moscow his men were soon feeding 70,000 people a day. Boris used his own funds, and his grain stores, to keep his people alive, and when they went on dying he paid for their shrouds. When the snow started falling in the summer of 1602, however, his soldiers were unable to stem the influx of refugees. Speculators converged on Moscow to claim the free food he intended for the city's poor. The tsar's own agents were the greediest of all. 'The poor, the lame, the blind, the deaf . . . fell dead like animals in the street,' Massa reported. 'With my own eyes I have seen very rich secretaries, dressed as beggars, slip among those receiving alms.' The people of Godunov's near-ungovernable capital must have wondered, at the height of the famine, if God were not punishing them for crowning a tsar who did not have genuine royal blood.

And then the portents started to appear. 'At about this time,' Massa relates, 'a series of terrible prodigies and apparitions occurred in Moscow, almost always at night and almost always in the vicinity of the tsar's palace.' The frightened guards maintained that 'they had seen a chariot in the sky drawn by six horses and driven by a Pole, who cracked his whip above the palace, crying out in such terrible fashion that several soldiers of the guard fled to their quarters in terror'. A scourge from Poland was indeed poised to destroy Boris and to unleash a war. The Dutchman (who had books to sell), described it as 'one of the strangest events to be recounted since the beginning of the world'.[63]

Tsar Boris had withdrawn from public life. The strain was telling on his health, but even in the deepest chambers of the Kremlin, his demons would give him no rest. The most persistent source of worry felt like vengeance from a ghost, for it concerned the shade of the dead boy, Prince Dmitry of Uglich. At first the tale was just a whisper, and Boris did no more than punish the gossips and spy on the crowds. But soon the facts were too disturbing to ignore. A man who claimed to be the last surviving son of Ivan the Terrible, the people's only living hope of a true prince, had entered Russia from Poland and was attracting followers in the south-west. Whatever his identity, the man himself was flesh and blood, and by 1604, when rumours that he had crossed Russia's borders reached Boris' ears, he had already raised an army with help from his sponsors in Poland-Lithuania. Boris attempted to dismiss the tale as a ruse by his enemies: the Poles would use a monkey to embarrass Russia if it suited them. Within a few months, however, the man who called himself Dmitry Ivanovich had established a court of his own on Russian soil. At the end of 1604, his army inflicted its first significant defeat on Boris' troops in a campaign to take Moscow and seize the crown.

No one can be sure who the self-proclaimed Dmitry really was. There is a general agreement that he was Russian, about the right age, and thoroughly familiar with the routines and hierarchies of Kremlin life. Some say he truly believed himself to be Prince Dmitry, and one historian, Chester Dunning, has recently broken with tradition by suggesting that he may indeed have been Ivan the Terrible's youngest son, smuggled from Uglich at the time of the supposed murder in 1591 and raised well out of Moscow's reach.[64] Godunov's agents spread a different tale, however, and it is still widely accepted. In this version, the so-called Dmitry is identified as a renegade monk, Grigory Otrepev, a scoundrel forced to take the cowl by his own father. The real Otrepev had lived in the Kremlin's Chudov Monastery until 1602, where he could well have learned the basic workings of the court.[65] But whoever he really was, Dmitry could be diplomatic, and he knew how to act like a tsar. He was also a fearless soldier, and his interest in military technology, combat and drill would later fascinate civilian Muscovites. These qualities, and the many discontents of Russia's people, helped to build support around him; his troops and executioners did the rest. He spent the winter of 1604 in the south, where opposition to Boris had long been strong. In 1605 his campaign for Moscow resumed in earnest.

Boris threatened death to any citizen who dared pronounce the false Dmitry's name. His agents organized an overblown victory parade (which fooled no-one) to force Moscow to celebrate the outcome of a minor skirmish in the south.[66] The tsar lost more support that day, and more again once the atrocities began. His henchmen maimed and butchered their first prisoners of war, and hostages were slowly burned alive or pushed under the river ice. The portents of doom persisted nonetheless. The coldest night of January 1605 brought a pack of wolves into Moscow, and a cemetery in the Kremlin itself was invaded by a band of foxes.[67] Meanwhile, more and more of Godunov's men defected, and the repeated questioning of rebel captives failed to expose Dmitry's real identity. Indeed, Ivan the Terrible's last widow (the real Dmitry's mother), now living as a nun called Marfa, was summoned to the Kremlin on a winter night (Boris' wife, Mariya, is said to have thrust a searing candle at her eyes), and even she refused to concede that the pretender was a fraud. In April 1605, and notwithstanding the attentions of two English doctors, Boris collapsed. The rumour that he had been poisoned was inevitable, but his death, almost certainly from a haemorrhage, may well have been caused by the anxiety that allowed him no rest.

Boris left a male heir, his son, Fedor Borisovich, and for a time the boyar elite in the Kremlin chose to honour this sixteen-year-old rather than face a vacant throne. But Fedor's claim had shallow roots, and there was little support for a second Godunov among courtiers who had suffered so deeply under the first one. Beyond the Kremlin, a hard-pressed population showed even less enthusiasm for the youth. At peasant hearths, and certainly round cossack fires out on the steppe, the talk was all of an imagined past, an ideal world whose details were so fuzzy that hope soon focused on the return of a leader that many chose to think of simply as the one True Tsar. This figure could have come straight from a fairy-tale (perhaps a dark one, since he was based on Ivan the Terrible), but the yearning for him was Dmitry's strongest card. Slowly, the military balance began to tilt in the pretender's favour. On 1 June 1605, Moscow reached a turning-point when a group of officials from Dmitry's camp gathered openly beneath the Kremlin walls to read a proclamation in their master's name. It urged every Muscovite to abandon the bloody struggle and swear allegiance to the real heir. 'God grant', ran the slogan, 'that the true sun will once again rise over Russia.'[68]

Moscow's population – encircled, hungry and sick of the fear and bloody spectacle of torture – needed no further encouragement. The Kremlin harboured their tormentors; this long day was their chance to act. A mob more than a thousand strong burst through the gates, and one of its first targets was Godunov's palace. The vanguard managed to arrest the dead tsar's widow, her son, and members of his inner circle, but others went on a looting spree, venting their wrath on anything Godunov might have touched. The discovery of alcohol brought chaos as the looters fought to get at the casks and barrels. In their excitement, some of the men took to drinking from their hats: at least fifty drank themselves to death in the Kremlin cellars.[69] At the same time, treasures and palace fittings, food and weapons were seized, disputed, and trampled or carried off; much of the gold was buried and lost in the months to come. It was the first day of Dmitry's rule – his succession was proclaimed from the Kremlin in the midst of the tumult – and it was the end of any Godunov Jerusalem.

Patriarch Yov was deposed and exiled. Tsar Fedor and his mother were strangled. The hated inquisitor, Semen Godunov, was captured, taunted and locked away to starve to death. Boris himself had been laid to rest in the Riurikid mausoleum in the Archangel Cathedral just over six weeks before. His coffin was removed (today, his remains lie outside the cathedral walls in the monastery complex at Sergiev-Posad). For a moment, it was possible to hope that the Kremlin had been purified, the royal line restored. The idea that Russia's murderous crisis might resolve if someone could create a rightful heir was appealing, but Russia would face years of civil war before it could agree about the candidate.

The newly proclaimed Dmitry's arrival in the Kremlin opened a fresh chapter in its international affairs. There had been talk of uniting the Muscovite and Polish crowns for generations. The argument for a Russo-Polish alliance, and even union, was clear. The two Slavic kingdoms shared a common history – the ancient Russian capital of Kiev lay in Poland-Lithuania – and the nobilities of the neighbouring courts were interrelated. But talks about union were often a cloak for larger diplomatic games (the agents of the Vatican were never far away). Both sides were also keen to chip away at their opponent's territory in the borderlands. As recently as 1586, Ivan the Terrible had proposed the candidacy of his son Fedor for the Polish-Lithuanian crown. That move had foundered with his own Livonian war. Now, under a new Polish-Lithuanian king, Sigismund III, the game unfolded with a revised set of aims.

Dmitry was a useful tool in the Polish schemers' hands. He owed his first success to Poles, the lords who had equipped him for his military campaigns. Some believe he acted on Poland's behalf throughout his life, and some allege he was a Catholic; he dressed like one, and shaved his beard, and did not hide his impatience whenever Moscow's priests intoned their lengthy prayers. He may even have convinced himself that a united Polish and Russian state could be a viable entity.[70] In Rome, the servants of the Catholic Inquisition kept an eye on his fortunes, prepared to overlook some wildness in exchange for the hope of allies near (or even on) the Russian throne.[71] What is certain is that there were numerous Polish agents at his court; they were housed inside the Kremlin from the start.

The foreignness of these advisors put the locals on their guard at once. No real Muscovite could think it seemly for a Catholic to tread the Kremlin's sacred soil, still less to trample on its customs, fasts and prayers. The same crowd that had swept Dmitry to the throne began to speculate about his morals once his retinue became ensconced. And the incomprehension was mutual. The gulf that separated Poles from Russians can be judged from the disgust with which the military officer Jacques Margeret (a Catholic) later dismissed the criticisms of Dmitry's conduct. 'As for the argument that [Dmitry] ridiculed the customs of the Russians and that he did not observe their religion except in form,' he wrote, 'it is not necessary to marvel at this – especially if one considers their customs and life-styles, for they are rude and gross, without any civility. And Russia is a nation of liars, without loyalty, without law, without conscience – sodomites, and corrupted by infinite other vices and brutalities.'[72]

Dmitry himself divides his chroniclers. Jacques Margeret loyally described him as 'wise, having enough understanding to serve as schoolteacher to his own council'.[73] But Margeret, who eventually became the head of Dmitry's palace garrison, was not objective; the story also persists that Dmitry was crude and licentious. It is said that the pretender debauched young women in his palace (and specifically its bath-house), including several Kremlin nuns and Boris Godunov's own orphaned daughter, Ksenia.[74] The space behind his lodging was turned into a bear-pit: on idle days, for his amusement, wild dogs were set on captive bears (and occasionally on humans).[75] According to another tale, the pretender's legs were so short that they waved in the air when he tried to sit on Ivan the Terrible's throne.[76] If that was so, it did not prevent him from issuing royal commands, and one of these involved a new palace. Conceived, they said, 'in the Polish style', it loomed above the Kremlin walls facing the Moscow river. Though it has since vanished from most records, its specifications sound lavish, for every nail and hinge was said to have been covered with thick gilt, and the stoves, in Massa's view, were works of art. The new tsar 'also caused magnificent baths and fine towers to be built', the Dutchman added. But clouds had gathered from the first. 'Although there were already vast stables in his palace compound,' wrote Massa, 'he had a special stable built close to his new dwelling. These new buildings had a number of hidden doors and secret passages, which proves that he was following the example of the tyrants, and that like them, he lived in perpetual fear.'[77]

The pretender's reign lasted for less than a year. His fatal mistake may well have been his choice of bride. When he accepted the help of the Polish noble Jerzy Mniszeck, in 1603, Dmitry had agreed to marry his sponsor's daughter, Marina, and in the spring of 1606 Mniszeck called in the debt. If Dmitry had chosen a Russian wife, and forged the right kind of dynastic link, the court might well have closed ranks round the self-proclaimed Riurikid, hoping to re-establish the familiar elite ballet.[78] Instead, in May 1606, Marina was summoned to Moscow with a spectacular retinue of Polish retainers and a horde of disorderly – and very foreign – wedding guests.

The bride's progress was sumptuous. The procession of gilded carriages, the liveried servants and the jewels alone cost several fortunes. Moscow was especially impressed by the horses, the coats of some of which had been transformed with red, orange and yellow dyes. The ten prize animals that pulled the royal carriage were 'spotted with black (like tigers or leopards), and matched so well that one could not distinguish one from another'.[79] Horses and all, the whole party, which was grander than the retinue of any bride since Sofiya Palaeologa married Ivan III, was accompanied by music, including flutes, trumpets and kettledrums, though this, the Russians thought, was a distraction from Orthodox prayer. The noise and swagger, however, were only the first of many insults. These Poles seemed to have come to stay. Even if they had enjoyed the pageant and the coloured horses, Moscow's people caught their breath when the baggage-train behind the guests began to disgorge household goods. The visitors were billeted on wealthy local families, and their hosts (who had not been given much choice) were shocked to glimpse bundles of weapons among the trunks and boxes that were being carried into their guest rooms.[80]

The next few days were even worse. It was not the fact of the Poles' persistent drunkenness (what Russian could speak out on that?), but its timing that caused such offence, the disregard for priests and icons, and the surprise (in a land of full-length robes) of strutting men in vulgar-looking breeches and high boots. On the day of the wedding, the crowds of common citizens, who had been shut out of the Kremlin for the ceremony itself, were horrified to learn that Catholics had taken the best places in the Dormition Cathedral. Isaac Massa reported once again that ominous clouds appeared in the sky, all seeming to come from the direction of Poland. A few nights later the moon turned the colour of blood.[81]

But murder, this time, was a Russian game. Since his arrival, Dmitry had failed to win the loyalty of the Shuisky clan, now headed by Prince Vasily Ivanovich Shuisky and three of his brothers.[82] Their long-time allies, the Golitsyns, had joined them recently in a series of assassination plots, none of which had come close to success. On the night of 15–16 May, six of their killers managed to break into the Kremlin, perhaps because Jacques Margeret had fallen ill (there was a suspicion of poisoning). But this attempt, like previous ones, was aborted. On 17 May the plotters struck again. Their group was led by prominent Shuiskys and Golitsyns in person, a clever ruse that encouraged the Kremlin guards to open the gates without question. Once inside, the attackers secured the citadel against potential rescuers and made their way towards the buildings where Dmitry usually slept. At the same time, at a prearranged signal, Moscow was wakened by the watchmen's bells, and warned that 'Poles' had invaded the Kremlin to kill the tsar. After weeks of tolerating their imperious guests, this was the only encouragement Muscovites needed. In the carnage that followed no fewer than five hundred foreigners (and not only Poles) were slaughtered.[83]

Behind the sealed Kremlin walls, meanwhile, the assassins closed in on their victim, who had sent his closest aide, Basmanov, to find out what was happening. The latter was killed as soon as he ran into the conspirators. Dmitry attempted to escape, as his door began to splinter under the intruders' blows, by jumping through an upper window. He must have hoped to disappear within the maze of buildings round the palace, but in his rush he slipped and broke his leg. Some of the *streltsy* tried to save him, but the invaders had the advantage, and though he pleaded for his life, the injured man was shot. At once the bodies of Dmitry and Basmanov were stripped naked, bound, and displayed with lurid mockery on a small table on the open space beyond the Kremlin moat. All Moscow had the chance now to inspect their so-called tsar. Isaac Massa examined the corpse 'with great interest', and reported:

I was able to convince myself that what I saw before me was the same tsar whom I had seen many times, the same who had reigned for a year . . . I counted his wounds. They were of the number of 21. His skull had been stove in from above, and his brain lay beside him.[84]

These details mattered because the body was to have an afterlife. Indeed, several corpses featured in the politics to come. First came a rumour that demonic flames had played around the gruesome figures on the Moscow square; then an unseasonal frost blasted the fields, as if in punishment for regicide. The boyar Vasily Shuisky, who now saw himself as tsar, blamed the misfortune on Dmitry's sorcery, and the pretender's body was thrown into a pauper's grave and, later, ceremonially burned. At the same time, a second corpse, this time that of a nine-year-old boy, was transported, with solemn reverence, from Uglich. The idea was to bring the true Dmitry home, to beg forgiveness for the sin of his murder, and to lay his bones to rest at last among his forefathers. The ceremony further damned the pretender who had stolen his name.

Shuisky had sent the Romanov Filaret to fetch the bones, a choice that kept the great priest out of Moscow and left the new tsar free to fill the vacant patriarchal office with a man of his own.[85] But whether he felt snubbed or not, Filaret performed his role with aplomb. He declared the body of the martyred 'Dmitry' (which may in fact have been that of a child Shuisky's men had murdered for the occasion) to be uncorrupted and sweet-smelling after fifteen years in the grave. Perfect childish hands still clasped a nut the young prince had been eating as he died. The carcass was now saint-material, and a procession accompanied the coffin on its progress to Moscow, arriving on schedule at the gates of the Kremlin. There, and all the way into the Archangel Cathedral, peacock ranks of bishops and court officials collected at the casket's side to marvel and to pray. Sick and injured pilgrims were beckoned into the coffin's presence and declared themselves healed; each new wonder was greeted by a loud peal of the Kremlin bells.

Jacques Margeret was among the unconvinced. The 'miracles', he wrote, were staged, and the corpse itself had soon decayed to such an extent that even 'massive quantities of incense' could not disguise the stench. This was no proof of holy grace but a 'vulgar show'. Stinking or not, however, Ivan the Terrible's last son was destined for the nation's pantheon. The child's body was buried in the catacomb of tsars, and no-one's doubts, then or later, prevented the newly created St Dmitry from acting as a standard-bearer for the Russian nation. His shrine still occupies a place of honour in the Archangel Cathedral.

The combatants in Russia's seventeenth-century civil war came from all classes and all regions of the Russian lands. It was not a simple class war – peasant against noble, city against countryside – but a conflict about legitimacy and justice that enlisted representatives of all classes on each of the many rapidly changing sides. Even within the Kremlin, there were nobles who supported the new tsar, Vasily Shuisky, and others who, at different times, pledged their allegiance to successive new pretenders or the Polish king. Some changed their minds several times. Filaret himself was captured by rebel troops and persuaded to serve a new pretender at a makeshift court, but the priest-politician eventually cast his lot with Sigismund III of Poland. Beyond the capital, the grievances of impoverished provincial gentry, peasants, cossacks and the landless poor alienated them all from Moscow's boyars, but that did not mean that they formed a single opposition force. In their struggle for a just order, for freedom and food, the common people and cossack armies ended up fighting on behalf of no fewer than eight self-appointed 'true tsars' between 1606 and 1612, and sometimes they fought for two at once.[86]

The first revolts began in the summer of 1606. City after city fell to rebel armies, mainly in the south, and all refused to swear allegiance to a vain and overfed boyar. Shuisky himself, in the unkind words of a modern historian, was 'short, stocky, balding and unattractive ... and looked vaguely ridiculous'.[87] Eschewing Dmitry's vacant palace, this unpromising tsar built himself new quarters in the Kremlin, but his tenure there, like his contested reign, was brief.[88] In July 1606, he had to barricade himself behind the Kremlin walls. For the first time, the cannon ranged around the royal fortress pointed downwards at the citizens below. At least two of the bridges that crossed the moat between the Kremlin and Moscow were also destroyed in preparation for a siege, and by autumn the capital was all but surrounded by insurgent troops. A serious food crisis loomed.[89] It was only by convincing Muscovites that the rebels were planning to slaughter all of them, women and children included, that Shuisky held the city at all that autumn. Meanwhile, the embattled tsar was forced to begin selling the contents of the Kremlin's fabled treasury. According to Isaac Massa, he raided the royal coffers for anything from gold to furs in his efforts to build support and pay his troops.[90] But he did not empty the strongrooms completely. That privilege was reserved for his successors.

The Moscow siege began in late October 1606, and its severity exposed Tsar Vasily to the capital's bitter criticism. Among his limited group of allies, the new patriarch, the ancient zealot Hermogen, became a most unlikely national hero. This seventy-six-year-old had joined the priesthood late in life, but he served it with a fanaticism that brooked no compromise with dissenters, appeasers, or foreigners of any kind. The insurgents, in his considered view, were Satan's creatures, a judgement that shored up the new tsar's rule for several months. Vasily, meanwhile, although no general himself, was wise enough to promote his talented nephew, Mikhail Skopin-Shuisky, to the most critical military command. By December 1606 the first insurgent army had been broken, its leaders divided, and Shuisky treated Moscow, yet again, to the spectacle of mass executions. Merchants and minor clerks alike grew tired of the sight of death as 15,000 cossacks were slaughtered. The ringleaders were publicly impaled.[91]

Tsar Vasily had few real friends. Some of the Kremlin's leading clans (especially the Golitsyns) saw their own members as alternative tsars, but most would have preferred a restoration of the former status quo, where they held power round the throne of someone they could all accept. There was frequent traffic between the Kremlin and the various pretenders' camps, but though a second 'False Dmitry' drew a hopeful suite to his court near Moscow, at Tushino, and though he was an Orthodox Russian (and thus a sort of patriot), he was unable to unite the many factions now competing for the capital. As the state of Muscovy continued to tear itself apart, Tsar Vasily approached the Swedes. In exchange for the Kremlin's 'eternal friendship' (and, by implication, eternal hostility to the Poles), Sweden pledged to help Shuisky to defeat the cossack insurgency and the hated pretenders. In 1609, a Swedish army duly marched south from the Baltic, its sights set on control of Novgorod.

But the Poles remained the real players in the battle for the Russian throne. No-one can be sure when the candidacy of Wladislaw, the son of Sigismund III, was first mooted, and in hindsight the choice appears almost defeatist. A deal with the Poles might well have brought peace to Muscovy, however, or at least supplied some decent troops to help shore up a restored throne. Wladislaw could also have founded a new dynasty, of impeccably royal blood, into which the boyar clans could marry once Vasily had been removed. In secret negotiations, the adherents of this option claimed to have extracted a promise from the fanatically Catholic King Sigismund that his son would convert to Orthodoxy before accepting Russia's crown. By the summer of 1609, however, Sigismund had taken the initiative himself. He already had spies in the Kremlin as well as troops in the service of the pretender at Tushino, but now he led an army of his own into Russia. His destination was Smolensk, which he intended to take quickly before continuing in triumph to Moscow. If Boris Godunov had not built that mighty fortress, the campaign might have ended differently, and certainly sooner. Instead, it took two years – and the loss of thousands of its citizens' lives – for Smolensk to fall to the Poles.[92] The Russians did not manage to recapture it for nearly fifty years.

The so-called Time of Troubles, which began with the doomed reign of Boris Godunov, was a saga of destruction, murder and betrayal, but its final chapter, in the Kremlin, was the darkest one of all. In July 1610, a group of boyars, with the support of church leaders and hand-picked citizens, drove Vasily to abdicate. They made sure of his permanent neutrality by forcing him to take the vows of a monk and all but locking him inside the Chudov Monastery. With the glum acquiescence of the city fathers, a seven-man council of boyars assumed interim power, ostensibly to prepare for the accession of Wladislaw.[93]

They may have been the wealthiest and most distinguished nobles in the land, but the boyars of this short-lived council were trapped within their Kremlin's own high walls, and trapped, too, by the mental habits that those walls had fostered over long decades. As detachments of cossacks, bandits and former slaves continued to ransack almost every suburb of Moscow, the seven council members could only cling to rule-books that they knew. Despite the fact that many Russians still seemed drawn to home-grown 'tsars' (Tushino had fallen, but 'Dmitry' remained at large until December 1610), the councillors could never contemplate a rough pretender on the throne. Nor could they imagine another form of power. Instead, they proposed, in the tradition of their ancestors, to dazzle the people with a new tsar, Wladislaw Sigismundovich, a royal heir, a fulcrum for the secretive, privileged and tightly regulated world they wished to recreate. Far from inviting Wladislaw to take the crown, therefore, they pleaded with him. Court officials were even tasked with listing the Kremlin's treasures (and the delights of its kitchens) as a form of enticement. Moscow's royal regalia – the sceptre and jewelled collar, the caps of Monomakh, of Kalita, of Godunov – were just the start; if the prince had acceded to the boyars' wishes, he could have wrapped himself in golden robes and fur-lined, pearl-trimmed, velvet cloaks. He also stood to inherit gold and silver plates and vessels, gemstones, sables and large quantities of cash.[94]

Instead of welcoming a prince, however, the Kremlin staff soon had to cope with a rabble of mercenary troops in need of winter billets. The boyar council turned out to be more afraid of its own people than of foreign soldiers. There were already some paid troops in the Kremlin, including Margeret's, but in the late summer of 1610 the council agreed to allow a Polish officer, the hetman (cossack chief) Stanislaw Zolkiewski, to move more troops into Moscow as a guarantee of public order. It was not a smooth operation, and at one point the city seemed about to rebel, but Zolkiewski eventually billeted parts of his army in the walled areas of Kitai-gorod and the White City and a final group, under his own leadership, inside the Kremlin itself.[95]

According to the hetman, the Poles behaved impeccably, but others reported arrogance, greed, and the burdensome demands that several thousand men were bound to make.[96] Patriarch Hermogen was prominent among those speaking out against the Popish horde, and as the long wait for Wladislaw stretched into months the old man started to attract a following beyond the Kremlin walls. His message, and the shame of citizens who feared their whole culture's collapse, stirred Orthodox resistance in the provinces. Then came the news that Sigismund had never planned to send his son, and meant instead to seize the crown himself. Hermogen leaked this from his throne in the Kremlin's Dormition Cathedral, thundering away about the dangers of Catholic rule. At the same time, the diplomatic Zolkiewski left the Kremlin. Control of its garrison was handed, at Sigismund's request, to a brutal officer called Alexander Gosiewski. His attitude to the job was typified by his (unsuccessful) attempt to cancel the Kremlin's annual Palm Sunday procession in the interests of public order.[97] Though he was also responsible for thousands of civilian deaths, few acts were better calculated to outrage Orthodox Russian souls.

Any pretence that Polish troops might act as saviours of Russia (an unlikely proposition at the best of times) was dissipated by events in the early spring of 1611. The foreign garrison in Moscow came to be regarded – by everyone except the handful of noble families whom they were protecting – as a hostile army of occupation. Beyond the Kremlin, and especially beyond Moscow itself, exhausted citizens in the provinces began to organize resistance movements whose aims were to expel the Catholics, defeat the scourge of banditry, and recapture their holy sites, including the Kremlin. The groups did not all work together, but for some insurgents, the liberation of the capital became a priority. In March 1611, soon after Easter, news reached the city of a breakthrough by Russian troops from Ryazan, and Muscovites responded with an attack that was intended to oust the Kremlin's Catholic garrison. Gosiewski's answer was merciless. The Kremlin turned on its own city with savage force. Jacques Margeret's memoir does not go into details, but another foreigner observed that when the French commander led his troops back into the fortress from one of its missions against the rebels, their clothes were drenched with so much blood that they looked like butchers.[98]

Gosiewski also ordered the destruction of any district where trouble-makers might have taken shelter. With the approval of the terrified boyars, parts of Moscow were set alight. 'Out of this,' wrote a German diplomat called Adam Olearius, who heard it all from witnesses two decades later, 'came such a colossal fire that the whole great city of Moscow, except for the Kremlin and the stone churches, was reduced to ashes in two days.'[99] Only the lines of ruined chimneys, like accusing fingers, suggested where rows of houses had stood before the massive fire took hold. For preaching his fierce anti-Polish views, Hermogen was imprisoned in the Chudov Monastery. What remained of Moscow was then looted over several days. When there was nothing left that looked worth stealing, the mercenaries dug in to wait for Sigismund behind the Kremlin's smoke-blackened walls. Sharing the fortress with them, the monks in the Chudov fasted and prayed, while just across the citadel's internal square, below Godunov's gleaming tower, the members of the boyar council, like the woebegone hosts of a squatters' commune, huddled with their skeleton clerical staff.

In 1611, the state of Muscovy ceased to exist. There was no legitimate government, no ruler, and the capital was occupied by foreign troops. Smolensk had fallen to the Poles, Novgorod was in Swedish hands, and much of the most productive countryside elsewhere had been abandoned or ruined by fighting. What saved the Russian lands from final dismemberment was not a tsar, nor the Kremlin's fabled charisma, but the people themselves. Hermogen, now starving to death in his cell, wrote letter after letter as he weakened, and his passionate calls to arms were smuggled out of the Chudov Monastery to monks and waiting citizens along the Volga and in the north-east. The Orthodoxy that he invoked meant a range of different things, but piety combined with guilt and shame, hatred of the devil and the foreigner, and love of homeland and the local saints made it a powerful mix. Among the thousands who heeded the call to liberate the Russian people was a trader in the Volga town of Nizhnyi-Novgorod called Kuzma Minin. By 1612, the army that he helped to found, led by the soldier-prince Dmitry Pozharsky, became the force the Poles feared most. Along with several other military bands, especially the one now under the command of the nationalist leader Prince Dmitry Trubetskoi, it might have established a separate state within the wider Russian land. Instead, the combined militia set its sights on the Kremlin. The truth was that no fortress in Russia could command a comparable measure of sacred power.

For another eighteen months, however, the Kremlin was still occupied by a dwindling band of foreign mercenaries. As ever, it was a little universe in its own right. Moscow had become a wasteland, food supplies were scarce, and no news of the future ever seemed to come, but like all armies the garrison complained the most when it was not paid. The boyar council had no cash to its own name, so it began to loot the Treasury. This was a quasi-government matter, so the first round involved melting the gold and silver plate down for coins. The money, struck in the tsars' mint in 1611, was stamped with the name of Tsar Wladislaw. But treasure has a magic of its own, and soon Gosiewski and members of the Russian elite were packing up sables (hundreds of them), removing gems, and helping themselves to bolts of velvet and fantastic golden robes.[100] Predictably, with such a glut, the price of gold and other treasure soon dropped heavily against more mundane goods, and gold chains scarcely bought a single cabbage, let alone a loaf of bread. If they could find a route out through the lines of walls, inventive troops now started to desert.

Even Gosiewski did not stay until the end. Before they quit the Kremlin in the spring of 1612, the hetman and his closest retinue removed the most valuable of the royal crowns, insignia and other precious items from the heyday of the Riurikids. The so-called Cap of Godunov, which blazed with two enormous Sri Lankan sapphires, was one of the occupiers' most valuable prizes, but the mercenaries also took a crown intended for the first Dmitry and a gold staff decorated with jewels.[101] The golden cap of Ivan Kalita vanished, too, and so did icons, crosses, gems and furs.[102] Some of this booty found its way across the border – two jewel-encrusted objects of devotion, an icon and a reliquary, landed in Munich in 1614, where they remain in the Schatzkammer of the Residenz[103] – but much was plundered by the cossack bands that preyed on any traveller who lingered on his journey west. And Russia was impoverished whoever took the gems. The looting of the Treasury was a primitive version of capital flight, and where the current generation has Swiss bank accounts, the thieves of 1612 buried any gold that they could not contrive to smuggle out. 'Unbelievable wealth, in the form of gold, silver, precious stones, and other valuable things, was seized and sent to Poland,' reported Olearius, and 'for amusement the soldiers loaded large single pearls in their firearms and shot them in the air.'

For several months after Gosiewski's departure, the remnants of the garrison clung on. By the summer of 1612, most of Moscow had been taken in the name of Russia's people, and only the Kremlin and Kitai-gorod remained in boyar and Polish control. Cut off from almost every regular supply, the Kremlin mutated from army slum to charnel-house. In September the first soldiers began to starve. A foreign merchant who visited the Cathedral of the Dormition discovered a sack full of human heads and legs in a shallow grave near the walls. Beyond the Kremlin, starving Muscovites stopped venturing out, for there were rumours that hungry Polish troops stalked the suburbs at night in search of succulent meat; the Kremlin itself became a symbol of dread. Behind its walls, the mercenaries fought over the bones of dead comrades, took shots at crows, and duelled for the corpses of the rats.[104] From 3,000, the garrison had shrunk to roughly 1,500 men. It took till October for the liberators to break through, and by that time the citadel was little better than a morgue.

No sacred site was undespoiled.[105] As they counted their dead, people were unlikely to mourn the precious manuscripts and books that had been burned, the history that they had lost for ever.[106] An outsider might even have thought that this was a good time for Russian patriots to start afresh. The people had rescued their country from destruction, the tsars were dead, and now a new sort of elite, perhaps some form of parliament, could plan a better, more enlightened future for everyone. But though the Russian people had indeed acquired a voice, the impulse of the time turned out to be conservative. The nation was still at war on many fronts (the Swedes and Poles each held substantial chunks of Russian territory), the Kremlin was a gaping ruin, and the old elite, the great boyars, had failed everyone. But for all that, the past – in foggy, tinted, and romantic form – seemed safer than divisive and untried alternatives. Of all the things that had been taken or destroyed in 1612, after all, it was not Godunov's sapphire crown, let alone the piles of plate, that people mourned. The loss that really rankled, as Russians prepared to build the Kremlin and their government anew, was Ivan the Terrible's cruel staff, the one that had been carved from the magical horn of a unicorn.[107]

5

Eternal Moscow

Four decades after the Troubles ended, a Syrian priest arrived in Moscow on the coat-tails of his father, the Orthodox patriarch of Antioch. He is known to Europeans as Paul of Aleppo, and his travels made a writer of him. Paul's charm was that he noticed things: the pearls and beading on a bishop's cope, the rancid smell of raw meat on a tribesman's breath. In our age of political correctness, you can read him for the grumpiness alone. As his visit to Russia dragged on, young Paul was nearly felled on several occasions by the strictness of his hosts' religious fasts. The stench of Russia's unwashed monks disgusted him. He found the interminable holy rituals exhausting too, and seldom seemed to end a day without complaining of his aching legs and back. And then there was the cruel, the intolerable cold; the poor Syrian's 'hands and feet and nose were nearly bitten off' by that on several occasions. The first of these, in early January 1655, was the result of an outdoor ceremony to mark the Feast of Epiphany. At the end of it, predictably, Paul and his father 'were so much affected by the cold, that we were unable to perform mass in the Cathedral'.

The ordeal took place around a platform on the Moscow river ice. From the first lines, the Syrian's description has an eerily familiar ring. Each January, he wrote,

> they construct a large inclosure of paling on this [Moscow] river, for it flows near the Imperial Palace; and the Patriarch goes forth with the Heads of Clergy and of the Convents, and the whole of the inferior clergy, in their robes, two and two, in grand procession to . . . the Water-gate. The Emperor follows them with his Great Officers of State, on foot, and wearing his crown; but at the moment they begin the Prayer, he uncovers

his head, and remains until the conclusion, thus exposed to the dreadful severity of the cold.

It happened that in January 1655 the tsar, Aleksei Mikhailovich Romanov (ruled 1645–76), was not in Moscow, but in any other year he would have waited for his icy dose of river water while the court stood by and watched. Thereafter, by custom, 'his majesty returns to his palace on his royal sledge, which is covered inside with red velvet, and is studded on the outside with gold and silver nails. The caparison of the horses is made of sable furs.'[1]

A century after the first Englishmen witnessed it, here was the Muscovite Epiphany ritual again. Here, too, were all the velvet and the gold, the courtiers, the splendid priests. The contrast with the Kremlin of just forty-three years previously could scarcely have been more extreme. In 1612, the idea of a royal sledge, and even of a royal backside to sit down in it, would have seemed almost ludicrous. There had been no tsar then, and it was far from certain that the Treasury still ran to a passable crown, let alone the gorgeous robes that courtiers had worn in other times. As the Syrians prepared to meet the sovereign in his Kremlin court in 1655, however, they laboured through the same long preparations as had Jenkinson and Chancellor a century before. They, too, were ushered into the Kremlin's awe-inspiring hall, where the tsar presided over a court of 'grandees . . . in dresses loaded with gold, pearls, and precious-stones'. Aleksei's crown, 'resembling a high calpack', was 'covered with large pearls and the most precious gems', and his yellow brocade cape was fringed with so much gold and lace and coloured stone 'as to dazzle the sight'.[2] A feast awaited in the Faceted Palace. 'The august Emperor was sitting in the centre,' his guest noted, 'at a large table entirely covered with silver.'[3]

For anyone who knew the recent history, this scene may well have appeared strange enough, but Moscow's air of timelessness was even more incongruous when set against the turmoil to the west. The English took things to extremes in their experiment with revolution, but by Paul of Aleppo's time the challenges to traditional authority were surfacing in almost every corner of Europe. Thanks to the likes of Galileo and Descartes, indeed, even the universe was threatening to break out of the frame that religion had made for it. The first half of the seventeenth century was a time of adventure. It was the era of the Pilgrim Fathers and

the *Mayflower*, of the Dutch in Connecticut and the first scholars at
Harvard. Explorers ventured north to Baffin Bay and south and eastwards to Tasmania; back home, in London and Paris, attempts were
made (with mixed success) to sell the public a new drink called coffee.
Most crucially of all, the science of war grew ever more sophisticated,
mainly because the European world was almost always under arms. The
guns that craftsmen made became more accurate, and battle-formations
grew ever more deadly. Soldiers were trained as professionals, drill and
discipline refined. The pace of change promised to make early modern
Europe richer and more powerful than any other region on the planet. In
this exhilarating context, the Russian court looked almost cataleptic.

The point, however, is that the illusion generated by the Kremlin was
a deliberate contrivance. Like the regalia and golden robes, the ceremonies that Paul described were replicas. The luxury of standing still
had not been open to Russia at the beginning of the seventeenth century
because it had no stable ground on which to stand. The old regime had
disappeared, the old landscape was wrecked. Perhaps in part because of
that, the ruling families longed for nothing more than the imagined ease
of their grandfathers' day. The civil war that had ended in 1612 had
never been a revolution, after all, and the new tsar's accession was not
a coup. As the smoke above the Kremlin cleared at the end of 1612,
there was no sense, at court or beyond it, that fresh ideas could possibly
be better than remembered pieties.[4] If anything, the trials of war had
reinforced the widespread yearning for a golden age, a time when the
True Tsar had sat in splendour on his throne.

The elite appeared to hold this line throughout the next half-century.
As Russia's government regrouped, the leading role was played, at first,
by the ancient ruling caste. A fragile order was restored, and the heirs of
the old nobility (and even some surviving members from the previous
age) clutched at the symbols, prayers and relics of the past in a bid to
shore up their pre-eminence. The tsar – once they had found their man –
was meant to guarantee stability; the church, which Hermogen had cast
in a heroic mould, would then oblige with all the settings and the bells.[5]
Throughout, another element of continuity was provided by officials
that the government employed. In 1613, more than half the staff of the
country's *prikazy*, far from all of whom were noble, had been working
in offices of some kind (not always in Moscow) since Godunov's time,
and clerical jobs themselves were more or less hereditary.[6] There were

no schools in the Muscovite state, let alone professional academies, so fathers trained their sons for the limited pool of posts. The country had been shattered and the Treasury was bare, yet here again was repetition, the memory of things as they were surely meant to be.

Once the new tsar had been named, setting a reactionary seal on the Russian nation's fate, the system in the Kremlin became rigid to the point of near-paralysis. Half-fearing that the people would denounce it if they glimpsed weakness or doubt, the court closed ranks. Priests returned to intone the ancient prayers at length, insisting on the perfection of Russia's faith. The practice of *mestnichestvo*, or rule by precedence, was reinstated in its full glory. But while the elite of both church and state hoped to hold on to their power and wealth by this rejection of unwelcome change, the world could not be kept at bay for ever. The success of Moscow's innovative neighbours was a constant reproach and also a threat. Inevitably, the Kremlin faced a distasteful, destabilizing choice. It could continue to cover itself in the moth-eaten glories of the past, thereby avoiding any return to the destructive uproar of the Time of Troubles, or it could engage with Europe, whatever the risks, and thus retain a place in it. The price of either course seemed far too high.

The occupants of the seventeenth-century Kremlin opted for a compromise. Instead of taking risks of any kind, they chose the cobweb mantle of nostalgia. Its dusty cloth was like a uniform for some, while for others it was fast becoming a sort of disguise, but either way, it was already very old. Each time a patch was added – a set of hastily drafted laws, a desperate attempt to bring the army up to date – the last authentic strands grew weaker still. The fabric could never have held indefinitely, and at the end of the seventeenth century it fell away completely to reveal a Kremlin primed to host its own version of absolutism, the innovative European form of monarchy embodied by the French Sun King, Louis XIV.[7] With new names in the royal chamber, a new army commanded by alien generals, and new cultural influences flowing in from its own fast-expanding territories, this incarnation of the Moscow fortress was a far cry indeed from the longed-for glory days of Ivan the Terrible and his fantastic golden court.

A nation's collective dreams are powerful, however, and if, one sleepless night, some *d'yak* had thought to check whether the illusion of eternal Muscovite dynastic splendour still looked convincing to the crowds beyond the Kremlin walls, he need have done no more than filch Paul of Aleppo's travel notes. It would have been no problem, back in 1655, to have found a civil servant who could translate from the Arabic. Page after page would have confirmed that the court's version of sacred continuity was still vivid enough to mesmerize the world. 'The origin of this Imperial Family of Muscovy is believed, by persons who examine the truth of history, to have been from Rome,' Paul of Aleppo had written. 'Observe how this august race, from that age until now, has been preserved in uninterrupted succession!'[8] However much the Kremlin changed, that chorus echoed underneath its walls for decades – centuries – to come.

In the winter of 1612–13, the mere thought of securing the succession might have chilled a Russian's bones. All the same, the country had to find a new sovereign, and the only hope of future unity was to consult a range of influential people, which meant convening an Assembly of the Land. It was called in November 1612 in the names of Russia's two main noble liberators, the princes Pozharsky and Dmitry Trubetskoi (the citizen Kuzma Minin, Pozharsky's ally and backer, carried no real official weight). Weeks after the scheduled opening date, in January 1613, hundreds of delegates converged upon the ruined Kremlin to deliberate. Along the way, their sledges had skimmed over forlorn graves, the snowy whiteness broken only by the wheeling parliaments of crows. The towns and villages the travellers passed were half-abandoned, and the households that remained all had bleak tales to tell. At the end of it all, Moscow could offer them little cheer. Burned, hungry and pitted with cannonballs, the city was desolate. As they assembled in the only space that could be patched up fast enough to hold them all – a chamber in the Kremlin's Riverside Palace – the delegates' mood was dour. These gentry, priests and loyal cossacks had paid a terrible price to secure Russia's future; now they picked their way through rubble. Even the quarters where they slept were semi-derelict. Since there was little shelter to be found outside the walls, many made do with unheated rooms in what was left of the Kremlin's old palaces and mansions.

The assembly's principal business was the election of a tsar. No-one considered parliamentary rule (the idea was shocking enough, thirty years later, in England), but Russian politics had shifted all the same.

The task of electing a sovereign was momentous in itself, but there was also a sense that Russia's people ought to shoulder some responsibility for making sure that any future government was just.[9] The front runner for the throne, at first, was Prince Pozharsky, whom many saw as the nation's ultimate saviour, but his humble blood ruled him out in the eyes of the old clans. Their choices included Wladislaw, Sigismund, and at least one member of the Habsburg dynasty, but speakers from less noble ranks declared all foreigners disqualified.[10] The patrician warrior Dmitry Trubetskoi looked better, but he turned out to have identified himself too closely with the tainted, pro-Polish boyars. Before long, the delegates started to look for the candidate who divided them the least, the most innocuous if not the most splendid. Their hopes eventually settled on a sixteen-year-old, the son of Filaret Romanov. His formidable father, who would have been a much more impressive contender, had been taken captive by the Poles in 1610 and had yet to return to Moscow. Without his protection, young Mikhail Romanov had the merit of appearing to be an entirely harmless (but blue-blooded) lamb.

Once the assembly had made its choice, a delegation went to Kostroma, the provincial city where Mikhail and his mother had lately taken refuge. They found a pale lad, indecisive and probably terrified. It was an inauspicious start, and Mikhail Romanov did not change much even after he was crowned. He ruled from 1613 until 1645, but there were always other voices in command. At first, these belonged to his maternal relatives, but then his father was released from Poland. In 1619, Filaret Romanov was installed as Patriarch, an office he had sought for years, and from that day until his death in 1633 the older man at last achieved his dream of Kremlin power.[11] Indeed, the title that Mikhail conferred on him, 'great sovereign', implying as it did a higher status than the tsar's, was a reflection of reality. Father and son were unequal in every possible respect. Where Filaret was strong and physically impressive, Mikhail was feeble, 'afflicted even when young with weak legs and a tic in the left eye', as Isaac Massa noted. 'He himself cannot write,' the Dutchman added, 'and I am not sure that he can read.'[12] The best that can be said was that he seemed to be gentle, at least from a distance. He was 'a lover of peace and amity with all Christian kings', his son's English doctor, Samuel Collins, later wrote, 'kind to strangers, and very religious'.[13]

The kindness, however, was conditional. Mikhail came to the throne of a country still at war with several foreign armies and also with itself. He owed his position – he owed his country – to groups of common citizens (such as the cossacks who had fought to oust the Poles), but his court had no intention of sharing power or dividing wealth. Few of the peasants who had helped to liberate Russia grew rich. Few even escaped the toils of serfdom. And in turn, because the country remained tense, the members of the court existed in a state of permanent suspicion. Trained in the schools of Godunov and Shuisky, their reflex was to repress all dissent. Most citizens accepted the idea of a new tsar, but any doubters were soon silenced, in the darkest prisons, by the percussive crack of their own bones. The new version of history was not imposed gently. Even the fact that young Mikhail had been elected was suppressed in favour of a trumped-up fable of divine grace.[14] It did not do to question this. Indeed, it would not do to question the Romanov tsars at any time to come. 'The Emperor has spies in every corner,' Dr Collins observed in the 1660s. 'Nothing is done or said at any feast, publick meeting, burial or wedding but he knows it.' And the Kremlin was jealous of its own secrets. ''Tis death,' the doctor continued, 'for anyone to reveal what is spoken in the Czar's pallace ... No-one dare speak a word what passes in their Court.'[15]

Romanov style was really novelty disguised as heritage. In 1613, the tsar-elect was fortunate that some of the royal regalia (including a couple of pieces that had started life as gifts to Boris Godunov) had escaped the looters, but as his coronation loomed, several other items had to be run up from scratch. There was a hitch when the craftsmen found that there was almost no gold left in the Treasury; they bought their metal from the local merchants in the nick of time.[16] But when Mikhail Romanov was finally crowned, the ritual emphasized continuity. After the ceremony in the Dormition Cathedral, for instance, the new tsar paid the customary respects beside the Riurikid tombs across the square in the Cathedral of the Archangel Michael; the Romanovs adopted all these bones (including that of the alleged Tsarevich Dmitry) as surrogate official ancestors.[17] Later, similar care was taken over Mikhail's wedding ceremonies, which took place in 1624 and again (following his first wife's death) in 1626. The senior official in charge of it all, Ivan Gramotin, scoured the palace records to find details of princes' weddings from the past, always careful to take note of the most effective gestures. He then inserted a series of calculated revisions, such as a larger ceremonial role for the Romanov family in the public scenes and an extra day of feasting for the city. The idea was to build support for the Romanov dynasty as a whole, and also to make it look every bit as royal, and as eternal, as its predecessor.[18]

Gold was not the only thing in short supply in 1613. So much wood had been looted and burned that the tsar had nowhere to sit, let alone to preside over his court.[19] Piles of rubble still littered the Kremlin's squares, the walls were stained with soot and ash, and several streets were physically blocked. The *prikazy* had been used as barracks, and when their liberators first returned they found the bodies of besieged defenders bundled at their feet.[20] The Kremlin was supposed to be a sacred place, but this fortress was gruesome and defiled. It was also very insecure. Gates were hanging loose, bricks missing, and some of the white foundation stones had become dislodged. The moat between the fortress and the public square was choked with rubble and carrion.[21] The prospect of rebuilding the symbol of Muscovite sovereignty would have challenged any government, let alone a stricken one.[22] In the first months of the new reign, taxes were raised seven times to help finance an urgent programme of repair.[23]

The work began at once, and the Faceted Palace was restored (or rather, patched) in time for Mikhail's coronation. But the task of rebuilding other quarters, to say nothing of giving the whole place a suitably royal air, was going to take much longer. In the past, of course, the Kremlin had burned down so regularly that rebuilding was almost routine. Muscovite craftsmen were used to working with the pre-cut logs from which even a large house could be built in hours. In 1613, however, there were almost no builders of any kind, and raw materials, including timber, had all but vanished from the land. Beams and doors were taken from the late Vasily Shuisky's palace to fix Mikhail's, and a set of lodgings for the tsar was ready in 1616, but recycled materials are seldom truly splendid. In any case, new fires gutted the palace buildings in 1619 and again (with even greater ferocity) in 1626.[24] The need for money and materials was insatiable. So was the hunger for skilled men. There was even a labour-crisis in the quarry-region of Myachkovo, which still produced the bulk of Moscow's building-stone.[25]

Mikhail Romanov's agents grasped at once that they would have to look abroad. A process started that would ultimately bring hundreds of foreign specialists to Russia, among them scores of talented artists and master-craftsmen. Many of these came for the money, for they were paid a reasonable rate and also given lodgings, food, and valuable bonuses such as fur and cloth. A man who made sure of a few trunk-loads of Moscow's fur for sale at home was bound to make a profit, and the trip was certainly an adventure.[26] For some, it was also a route out of trouble. Moscow provided a haven from Europe's Thirty Years War (1618–48). Instead of hiding from slaughter in Germany, a master-craftsman could join a lively and creative polyglot community in the tsar's employ that included the finest Russian artists and their colleagues from as far afield as Persia and the Caucasus. Other migrants came to flee the law, among them an Oxford jeweller whose father (as far as we know) had been arrested in 1608 for dealing in fake stones.[27] Though none lived in the Kremlin, the best craftsmen certainly worked there, as did many of the builders and the engineers (and foreign doctors, whose conditions were the best of all). Once more, and for the last time in its history, the citadel became a centre of artistic innovation on an international scale. In the process, it also opened Russia's gates to the new ideas and styles that foreigners were certain to import.

The most influential group of builders may well have come from England – or at least the British Isles. James I was keen to renew the trade relations that he had negotiated years before with Godunov. In token of his enduring goodwill, he sent experts to help with Mikhail's building-work as soon as the land routes were safe. The first, who probably took the merchants' road from Archangel, arrived in Moscow in 1615, and by the early 1620s, a number of 'English foreigners' were at work in the Kremlin. The best-known were one John Taler (or Taller) and a Scot, Christopher Galloway.[28] It is a pity that the records of their labours are so scant; it would be good to know how hard the court interpreters were made to work as anxious Russian *d'yaks* (and craftsmen) watched the Englishmen unpacking their set-squares and rules. Apart from a few account-books which say how much the top masters were paid, however, the only surviving witnesses are the buildings themselves.

The first new commission came from the tsar's father, Filaret. The patriarch wanted to create a landmark of his own, so he opted to extend the complex of buildings around the tower that his rival, Boris Godunov, had emblazoned in gold just two decades before. All gifts to churches were made as religious acts, and they were costly (in this case, roughly 3,000 rubles, which was an enormous sum), but Filaret's new bell tower was also a form of riposte. The building no longer stands, but records show that it too bore a portentous inscription. Where Tsar Boris' lettering had immortalized his own reign and the glory of his son, Filaret's triumphantly acclaimed Tsar Mikhail and his father. Eye-catching as that gesture was, however, the lost tower's architectural influence, at a time when there was so much other rebuilding to be done in Russia, turned out to be yet more immense. Partly because it had to house a single massive bell, its design (possibly by John Taler) was singular.[29] It rose into a spacious chamber and was finished with a decorative, tent-shaped roof. That silhouette, in new versions, was soon to pierce skylines in Moscow and for miles beyond.

It was as if the Romanovs, try as they might to cling to the past, were changing Russian culture and identity despite themselves. The royal family preferred to sleep in traditional wooden halls[30] but Mikhail's architects built him a new brick palace all the same, and its completion, in the late 1630s, marked a further development in Kremlin style. The royal chambers (*terema*; *terem* in the singular) were built on top of the ground floors and foundations of buildings that Ivan and Vasily III's Italians had erected in the late fifteenth and early sixteenth centuries, but though that gave them pedigree, the design paid little homage to the past. Constructed by a largely Russian team that included Bazhen Ogurtsov, Trefil Sharutin and Antip Konstantinov, as well as the mysterious John Taler, the so-called Terem Palace was a riot of intricate decoration, colourful and patterned like a westerner's fantasy of the Orient. The roof was gilded and the windows exquisitely glazed; each entrance and each architrave was sinuously carved, and most of the stone details were picked out in bright paints: blue, red, ochre, green and white.[31] The most luxurious interiors, which were completed in the reign of Mikhail's son, Aleksei Mikhailovich, were lined with German leather tooled with silver and gold leaf. By the 1660s, the doors, too, had been padded with gilded leather, and even the ceilings gleamed with silver.[32] The Russian builders incorporated half a dozen churches, whose cupolas topped off the structure in a rhythm of exotic forms. The most important chambers were restored in the last quarter of the twentieth century, and palace-visitors can find them now beyond the pair of massive lions at the turn of the stone stairs. The churches, on the other hand, are locked behind an ornate golden grille, albeit one of finest workmanship. The space is silent and the doors beyond are almost always sealed.

In Mikhail's time, however, the court was bustling, and it welcomed European craftsmen who could make machines. In 1633, the clock-maker and engineer Christopher Galloway installed a water-pumping system at the foot of the Sviblova Tower, which occupied a corner of the Kremlin wall above the Moscow river. Until that time, all water for the fortress had been lifted up by hand: henceforth the process would be mechanized. A few years later, Paul of Aleppo described the marvel. 'Having dug four or five large wells and built over them arches, hollow pillars, and canals,' he wrote, '[Galloway] set an iron wheel on the outside. Whenever they want water for any purpose, they turn this wheel with one hand, and the water flows out in great abundance.'[33] The new system made it possible to plant the palace terraces with hanging gardens, and later to add ponds to private courtyards on the upper floors. It was in one of these, allegedly, that the future emperor, Peter the Great, first tried his hand with a toy boat.

The most striking new building of all, completed in 1625, was the renovated and extended Saviour Tower. Its architects were forced to make it soar because the clock-mechanism that Galloway had started to design demanded a substantial inner room, while the large clock-face outside also needed some height.[34] Practical though it was meant to be, however, the structure could not have celebrated Moscow's overall rebirth with greater exuberance. Indeed, the celebration went a bit too far, for the tower's upper tiers were decorated with a set of naked human figures, *bolvany*, playful free-standing statues. Their nudity caused offence at once, and the figures were promptly dressed in cloth kaftans.[35] But this was a detail, and soon forgiven in the race to copy all those stylish curves and ogee lines. The first – and for some years the only – tall and pointed structure in the Kremlin walls, the tower's outline soon became the emblem of Moscow itself. Since Mikhail's time, it has featured in countless paintings and postcards, and it often represents the city for the television cameras of the world. In the 1950s, it inspired the 'Stalin gothic' style of Moscow's landmark skyscrapers.[36]

In part because of this iconic status, most textbooks attribute the Saviour Tower's design to a Russian, Bazhen Ogurtsov, occasionally giving some credit to the engineering Scot, Christopher Galloway. Recently, however, there has been a new interest in the building's forgotten western connections. One study, almost heretically, has compared it with possible ancestors in Tournai, Ghent and distant Aberdeen.[37] If anyone could ever find it again, an archival document, long since lost, might show that neither Ogurtsov nor Galloway designed the shape. Instead, that prize may well have to go to a man the Russian source named as Vilim Graf, another enigmatic member of the 'English-foreign' team that arrived in the wake of Mikhail's accession. The disappearance of the document that once named Graf has been convenient for extreme patriots, but it was probably lost in a genuine accident when the archives were moved in the early twentieth century.[38]

For his part, Galloway was fully occupied with clock-making. Mikhail Romanov had a passion for the things, and the Scottish master made several in Russia (including at least two for the Terem Palace). But Galloway excelled himself when he took on the commission for the most important one, which was to dominate the Kremlin's Saviour Gate. As he sketched out the first designs for this new clock, the existing model, which weighed almost a ton, was taken down and sold (for 48 rubles) to a monastery in Yaroslavl. Skilled bell-casters under the eye of master-campanologist Kirill Samoilov then dug the pits, created moulds, and poured thirteen new bells for its replacement.[39] In January 1626, the new clock was complete. The tsar and his father were so delighted that they rewarded their Scottish engineer with the pelts of sables and martens, a silver goblet, and yards of satin and damask cloth, a princely treasure that he was to receive a second time two years later when, after collapsing in yet another fire, the clock was restored, remounted and induced to chime again.

Unfortunately, even this second clock then suffered in a later fire, and in the end its famous face was lost. Reports from the 1650s, and a drawing in the memoirs of a traveller called Augustin Meyerberg (who visited Moscow in the 1680s), describe a generously proportioned circle finished in azure blue. Its whole surface was set with scattered silver stars, and at the top there blazed a golden sun and moon.[40] To any European who had seen the astronomical clocks of Prague or Venice, this artifice was not unknown, but even foreigners were fascinated by Galloway's mechanism. Instead of twelve divisions, his clock-face boasted seventeen, though in winter fewer than eight were actually used. The first hour (in Russian, one o'clock is still called 'the first hour') followed sunrise, the last finished at sunset. Moscow's latitude is 55 degrees north (the same as Edinburgh's and only 2 degrees south of Juneau in Alaska), so day-length (and the number of hours) varies considerably through the year. In the seventeenth century, a clock-keeper was paid to turn the dial on Galloway's clock twice a day so that the first and last hours would obey the sun.[41] Moreover, as Samuel Collins (himself from Braintree) observed a few years later, the dial itself, and not the (single) hand, revolved. 'In our clock-dials the finger moves to the figure,' he noted. 'In the Russian a contra, the figures move to the pointer. One Mr Holloway [sic], a very ingenious man, contrived the first dial of that fashion, saying, because they acted contrary to all men, 'twas fitting their work should be made suitable.'[42]

The metalwork for that great clock was almost certainly finished in the Kremlin itself. The reigns of the first few Romanovs were a golden age for the workshops that had flourished in the citadel (with interruptions) since the era of Ivan the Terrible. In the fifteenth century, these had started life as a royal armoury, but by the 1650s their ranks included gold- and silversmiths, jewellers, engravers, embroiderers, saddlers and tanners, as well as the full range of fine artists and experts in the creation and repair of weapons. The seventeenth century was not a time of boom – the army swallowed huge amounts of cash – but though the nation outside struggled with its taxes, the Kremlin workshops steadily grew in splendour.

Most of the raw metal was imported or recycled (silver-mining did not start in the tsars' lands till quite late in the seventeenth century), but the craftsmen worked hard once they got their hands on it. The Kremlin workshops produced everything from Russian royal crowns and diadems to robes embroidered with gold thread. Storage soon became a problem, but it was even more of a challenge to find enough space to carry out the work itself. The Armoury's main premises occupied a large three-storey building behind the Terem Palace (not far from the Trinity Gate), but smaller workshops were scattered round the palace precinct (the embroiderers worked near the royal women's quarters) and some of the heaviest metal-work, including the casting of cannon and bells, took place just beyond the Kremlin walls on the far bank of the Neglinnaya river.[43] Another little empire, this time dedicated to horses and carriages, nestled near the palace by the Borovitsky Gate. Its staff included goldsmiths and tailors as well as the masters who made saddles, stirrups, shoes and whips. By 1673, this Horse Chancellery, which eventually sported a gatehouse clock-tower in the finest European style, also employed eight veterinary specialists.[44]

The icon-painters occupied an entire floor of the main Armoury. It must have been a busy place, littered with the sea-shells that were used for mixing paint. The artists' duties included painting furniture and palace interiors and making architectural sketches. They also worked on military maps, so some were asked to travel with the tsar (it was in Polish-dominated Ukraine that Simon Ushakov, who headed the Armoury workshops between 1664 and 1686, came to see the art of the Catholic world at first hand[45]). Their main focus, however, was religious art, for which court masters could consult the thousands of icons that the tsars kept separately in the Chamber of Images (*obraznaya palata*). Some of these were very old, but the artists' exposure to masterpieces from the past did not make them mere copyists. Even at the beginning of the seventeenth century, distinctive colours and new forms had started to appear in Russian painting, and the innovative process never slowed. When the order came to renovate the frescoes in the Dormition and Archangel cathedrals, for instance, a team under the direction of Ivan Paisein produced a new interpretation of the damaged originals.[46] And because the Kremlin drew on talent from the entire realm, the freshly plastered walls became a sort of indoor master-class for a new generation of Russian painters.[47] By the 1640s, some of these had started to examine European masterworks (often thanks to engravings in the illustrated Bibles of Matthäus Merian and Johannes Piscator).[48] Slowly, the faces in the newest icons began to acquire contours, and impassivity gave way to a suggestion of emotion, even flesh. With a few distinguished exceptions, most of the icon-painters' patrons seem to have approved.[49]

The greatest changes of all, however, were prompted by the demands of Russia's expanding army. The Kremlin stores held glinting troves of armour: swords and daggers, axes, helmets, suits of mail, bows, arrows and guns in their thousands. Many were exquisite pieces designed for the tsar, though all were calculated to function in war. As late as the 1660s, swords and bow-and-arrow sets predominated in the collection, but most of these had started gathering dust. What counted now were muskets, carbines, pistols and artillery pieces. The tsars' workshops made hundreds of them.[50] It was one thing to manufacture a large stock of arms, however, and another altogether to put them to effective use on seventeenth-century battlefields. This was a lesson that the Russians had first learned during the Time of Troubles, when their country was invaded by the Swedes and Poles. As they faced professional troops from Europe for the first time, Russian *streltsy* and militia-men were appalled to find how ineffective their time-honoured methods of fighting had become. However much they might have disliked westerners, both Mikhail and then Aleksei Romanov were soon obliged to solicit their military advice.

The first group arrived in the 1630s. By then, officials from Moscow had scoured the Netherlands, England and the German lands in search of experts who might train and lead a Russian standing army. The days of traditional cavalry and *streltsy* units were drawing to a close; some of the latter ended up fulfilling their life-long service obligation to the tsar by working on his building-sites.[51] The foreigners set to their task at once, collecting over 60,000 men and stiffening their ranks with well-paid recruits from their own countries (Germans, mainly, but also numbers of Scots).[52] Most were equipped at the tsar's expense, and many of their weapons had been fashioned in his Kremlin Armoury.[53] By mid-century, Russia's army, according to one careful estimate, was regularly absorbing an eighth of the country's annual wealth.[54]

The reward came in 1654, nine years after Tsar Mikhail Romanov's death, when his son and successor, Aleksei Mikhailovich, recaptured Smolensk, the city that the Poles had occupied since 1610. The victory was a cue for the old world, the land of golden robes and gazing saints, to stage one of its final pageants. In years to come, it would be the sheer number of Aleksei's troops that outsiders admired.[55] But earthly things like manpower were not the point for onlookers that day. Aleksei's return was a festival of religious thanksgiving and dedication. Paul of Aleppo described the scene:

First came a banner accompanied by two drums beating, followed by the troops in three even ranks, in allusion to the name of the Trinity: if the banner was white, all the troops that followed it were dressed in white; if blue, those who followed it were dressed in blue; and so if it was red, or green, or pink, so as to include every possible colour. The order and arrangement appeared truly admirable, and they all moved forward, both infantry and cavalry, in the name of the Trinity. All the banners were new, having been recently made by the Emperor [i.e. the Kremlin workshops] before he set forth on his expedition. They were large, and much to be admired, astonishing the beholder with their beauty, the execution of the figures painted on them, and the richness of their gilding.[56]

The fall of Smolensk that was celebrated with those drums and banners paved the way for Moscow to negotiate for the control of Kiev (this was for a fixed term in the first instance) and also to extend into the territory of today's Ukraine and parts of White Russia (a region roughly corresponding to modern Belarus). Another Muscovite expedition had reached the shores of the Pacific in 1637, but victory in the west brought the vast continental power, which now ruled almost the entire Russian world, directly into Europe's orbit. It also brought Europe to the centre of the Kremlin court for good. Attracted by the prospects and the wealth, craftsmen and scholars from the ancient cities of Kiev and the old Rus south-west converged on Moscow in a renewed wave of intellectual and artistic migration. Unlike the specialists from England and the German lands, the new arrivals often came to stay, not least because they shared the Orthodox religion of their hosts. Their influence was unprecedented, for these people were insiders, not heretics. At the same time, however, their education and outlook were essentially European. No-one had guessed it, but the drum-beats of the holy court in 1655 would soon prove utterly inadequate to drown the clamour of relentless change.

For all the Kremlin's outward show of stability, the challenges were multiplying. Towards the end of Mikhail's reign, a Swedish diplomat even concluded that some form of uprising in Moscow was imminent.[57] Soon after, with a young Aleksei Mikhailovich on the throne, the prophecy was fulfilled. In 1648, the fortress was to witness violent revolt.

The Troubles had left the Russian people with a wariness of injustice and corruption round the throne. The death of the old sovereign brought these tensions to the surface. In the first years of Aleksei's reign, suspicion focused on a magnate called Boris Morozov. This man had been the prince's tutor, and he put that situation to good use. The late Tsar Mikhail's body was scarcely cold in 1645 when Morozov awarded himself the posts of Treasurer and head of several key chancelleries. His hold on Aleksei was further strengthened through their women: the two men married a pair of sisters, the daughters of a nobleman called Ilya Miloslavsky.[58] A delighted prince presented his tutor with a magnificent silver wedding carriage, covered inside and out with gold brocade and draped with costly sables. The upstart had soon built himself a palace in the Kremlin, installed his bride, and set about promoting his clients to influential positions at court. The most notorious of these were Levonty Pleshcheyev and Petr Trakhaniotov, another pair of brothers-in-law, and also Nazary Chistyi, a merchant who now doubled as a reforming bureaucrat. The conservative citizens of Moscow loathed the entire crew. Chistyi was closely associated with a hated new salt tax, but all four men were regarded as interlopers, cheats, and traitors to historic Russian ways.[59]

The sparks ignited on 1 June 1648. The tsar and his retinue had left the Kremlin on a pilgrimage, and as the royal group rode back an assembly of petitioners, greeting Aleksei with bread and salt, asked him to hear their grievances regarding 'the intolerable great taxes and contributions, whereby they were overburdened'. They also had a list of specific complaints about Pleshcheyev. Aleksei listened in surprise, promised to consider the petition, and rode on into the Kremlin, but as his horse trotted away from the crowd the boyars and the guards behind him turned on the protesters. The documents their leaders had prepared were destroyed on the spot, the petitioners who had come nearest to the royal party were beaten, and a number of the most vocal were arrested.

The next day, when Aleksei appeared on the steps of his Kremlin palace to attend a church service, he found a larger and more angry crowd in the square below. They wanted him to put Pleshcheyev, their current hate-figure, on trial. They wanted the tsar's views on their grievances, and they also wanted their arrested comrades to be freed. Aleksei withdrew into the palace, so it was Morozov's handling of this second incident that turned the public anger into violence. The shopkeepers, small tradesmen and artisans of Moscow pressed and jostled in the Kremlin square. Taking charge, Morozov ordered the *streltsy* to drive the malefactors out and lock the fortress gates, but the *streltsy*, whose hereditary status had been downgraded when the tsar's army was modernized, were no longer a reliable force. Instead of protecting the court, the elite guard turned on the man who had, as treasurer, reduced their wages. 'The musketeers refused the order from Morozov,' an anonymous Swedish writer recorded. 'Some of them went to His Tsarist Majesty and announced that they . . . would willingly . . . protect him, but that they had no wish to make an enemy of the crowd for the sake of the tyrant and traitor.'[60] More seriously still, the *streltsy* also told the crowd that they would take no steps to hold them back. 'The streltses,' runs another foreigner's account, 'whose pay being lessened and diminished, in so much, that they were not able to live by, took the Commons part.'[61]

The Kremlin now became a magnet for the protesters. The tsar appeared for a second time to remonstrate with the crowds, but his words had little effect. The mob stormed Morozov's palace. The treasure inside, seemingly massed at their expense, silver carriage and all, drove them to a frenzy, and

> all the stately and pretious things they found they hewed in pieces with shabolts and axes; the plate of gold and silver they did beate flat, the pretious pearles and other jewells they have bruised unto powder, they stampt and trampled them under feet, they flung them out of the windowes, and they suffered not the least thing to be carried away, crying alowd: To Naasi Kroof, that is to say, this is our blood.[62]

Real blood was also shed in quantities that day. Morozov managed to slip away, but one of his aides fell to his death as the boyar's Kremlin palace was looted. Nazary Chistyi, who had been in bed recovering from a riding injury, was tracked down to his hiding-place and beaten to death. The German diplomat and traveller Adam Olearius, from whom Chistyi had wrung a grievous bribe, described the scene with little sympathy. The victim's head, he gloated, 'was so battered that he could no longer be recognised. Then he was cast into a manure pit, and boxes and trunks were thrown on top of him.'[63] In desperation, the tsar agreed to surrender Pleshcheyev, and the wretched official was led out of the Kremlin through the Saviour Gate, accompanied by an executioner with an efficient-looking axe. Before the death sentence was even read, however, the mob had snatched the prisoner and clubbed him to death. 'His head was beaten to such a pulp that his brains splattered over his face,' Olearius recorded. 'His clothing was torn off and his naked body dragged through the dirt.'[64] The head itself was later hacked off by a monk, who muttered that the dead man had once had him cudgelled.

The Moscow crowd was focused, venting its rage on boyars, bureaucrats and a small group of the very wealthy. But someone was always bound to find supplies of drink. That afternoon, a posse of looters waded knee-deep in Morozov's wine, and some of these would later drown. Outside, the city was growing calmer, but the day's events held one last tragedy. By sunset fires had started in five separate places in Moscow. The blaze ripped through the sun-baked streets, killing hundreds, maybe thousands of citizens in its path. One writer estimates that up to 15,000 houses were destroyed; all agree that half the city burned.[65] Some people said that Morozov himself had set the fires to cover his escape, but others believed the blaze to have been a curse, insisting that deliverance depended on the burning of Pleshcheyev's bloody remains. The headless body was duly doused with vodka and dragged towards the embers. 'As soon as the body began to burn,' Olearius was assured, 'the flames began dying down before the eyes of the astounded spectators, and went out.'[66]

In the aftermath of the fire, Aleksei sent the patriarch, together with two popular boyars, to remonstrate with the protesters. Trakhaniotov, who had fled Moscow, was captured and brought back for execution, but Aleksei begged for Morozov's life in person, and as a compromise the treasurer was exiled to the Kirill-Beloozero Monastery 'in perpetuity'. In the short term, the protesters had won, a victory that paid off, literally, as cash was handed out and some taxes reduced. There was even an interlude during which more congenial leaders, including Nikita Romanov, the tsar's broad-minded uncle, replaced Morozov's men in the Kremlin. Foreign observers reported a widespread change of government personnel, but the reform was short-lived. By the end of October, Morozov had returned to Moscow, and soon after that he and his surviving associates were back in power.[67]

There were revolts in other towns, but the tsar himself still commanded a visceral loyalty almost everywhere. In 1649, a sober and determined Aleksei called another Assembly of the Land to codify the laws, establish social hierarchies, and draw some of the venom from the public mood. The crowd had called for justice and its tsar responded with a legal code. The document has become famous for the restrictions it placed upon the peasant serfs, whose very limited right to quit their landlords' farms was now removed entirely, permanently binding them to the land.[68] This was a gesture to the struggling provincial militia-men, and there were more, affirming a view of the social order that was meant to curtail further change. But the currents of unrest were not so readily stilled. The many pressures of this era – on *streltsy* burdened by unwanted innovation, on townsmen labouring to pay the ever-higher rates of tax, and always on the righteous Orthodox who faced injustice at the hands of evil favourites – threatened to erupt into violence at almost any time. For the rest of the century, the Moscow crowd remained a volatile and angry chorus underneath the Kremlin walls.

The most terrifying disaster was beyond human control, however. In 1654, Muscovy was struck by plague. Paul of Aleppo learned that nearly half a million had died, 'making the majority of streets empty of inhabitants'. Dogs and pigs were still devouring human corpses by the time of his visit, and the churches were 'destitute of clergy'. In Moscow itself, the city gates were 'silent for want of troops to guard them' and the streets 'frightfully desolate'.[69] The fear of infection was so great that the very doors and windows of Aleksei's palace had been bricked up to keep the miasmas outside. But locks across the Kremlin gates could not shut out this foe, and death rates among its monks and other residents ranged from 80 to 95 per cent.[70] The tsar, fortunately, was away from the city on campaign, and his family had escaped to safety, but by the time the plague had run its course, only fifteen servants remained in the palace. Aleksei's own deputy, Mikhail Pronsky, had died in September 1654, shortly after writing a horror-filled report to his tsar.[71]

The catastrophe prompted several more reforms. At a practical level, new regulations were introduced to stop further burials in selected Moscow churchyards, including almost all those in the Kremlin (though not the Archangel Cathedral). The ban remains in force: from 1655 the Kremlin virtually ceased to be a burial-site.[72] The tsar, meanwhile, indulged his hypochondria. Always entranced by herbs and alchemy of every kind, he sent his stewards to the borderlands to look for plague-remedies. In 1655, he approved a particularly extravagant order for three unicorn horns, two of the finest quality and one, for the women's quarters, of slightly lower grade. The price of the larger specimens alone was 5,000 rubles (compare that with the 3,000 rubles that it had cost to build Patriarch Filaret's lavish tower), but unicorn horn, as everyone knew, was a guaranteed remedy for plague. As the wild tribesmen of the south explained, you simply ground it into water several times a day.[73] Alternatively, there was always rhubarb wine. That, too, was a Muscovite speciality, and the tsar was jealous of the plants that grew beneath the Kremlin walls in his apothecary's garden.

*

The plague was thought by some to prefigure God's judgement on sinners; in this age of unrest, the fear of divine wrath was never far from people's minds. And the seventeenth century turned out to be a particularly testing time for the Russian church itself. A crisis in the 1650s shook the foundations of Orthodox, semi-theocratic Moscow, and it also cut quite literally through the centre of the Kremlin. The effects would prove irreversible, and so it was especially ironic that their basic cause was the church's obstinate refusal to countenance even the most benign of new ideas.

Since the time of its establishment in 1589, the Moscow Patriarchate had remained the only Orthodox seat of its kind outside Muslim control. Its leaders had been stubborn in their defence of the faith. With religious ferment spreading all across the Christian world, no border could stop all originality, but the Russian church put up a creditable fight. From Oxford and Bologna to Cracow, Europe's universities glittered with philosophers, but the Muscovites who marvelled over Galloway's clock and water-pumping system had no access to secular learning, and that was just the way the country's one true intellectual class, its priests and monks, still wanted it. Even their reckoning of time set them apart. They counted their years from the original creation of the world. Galloway might have left Scotland in 1620, but when he reached Moscow, like Alice falling down her rabbit-hole, he would have found himself in 7128. Russian theologians and popular mystics were fascinated by numbers – many were expert in the numerological aspects of the Book of Revelation – but Europe's rationalist mathematics seemed as threatening to them as black magic.

The effort to forestall polluting new ideas resulted in a chilly attitude to foreigners in the tsar's pay. Though Orthodox visitors were relatively innocuous, the church suspected other Europeans of heresy (Filaret had always reserved an especially potent venom for Lutherans) and they were known to drink for pleasure, smoke tobacco, and even to eat meat in Lent. Some employed Russian labourers and house-servants, placing the children of Orthodoxy in positions of subservience and exposing them to all manner of unspeakable contamination. Throughout Mikhail Romanov's reign, church leaders had condemned the easy contact between Russians and foreigners, but the profits involved (including those made by the tsar himself) were too attractive for legislators to resist. It was only in the wake of the 1648 uprising, when people started to question the foreign workers' tax exemptions, that real restrictions were at last discussed.[74] The church was quick to press its advantage. In 1652, the European residents of Moscow received an inconvenient new order. They were to quit their houses in the most expensive districts within four weeks, even if that meant selling them at knock-down prices. Henceforth, the government decreed, the 'Germans' were to live in a special new suburb beyond the Yauza river, a reservation where they could talk, smoke, shave, and even build their hateful churches without corrupting Russian souls.

The church's hostility to outsiders, however, was partly a reflection of deeper fears about the behaviour of its own people. No monastery wall seemed high enough to prevent Russian monks from catching sight of the lewd behaviour of Christmas crowds, and some had glimpsed overtly sexual games played in the winter gloom. 'Their dances', wrote Adam Olearius, 'include voluptuous movements of the body. They say that roving comedians bare their backsides, and I know not what else.' The Christmas carnival itself, a special season of misrule at which young men wore animal masks, suggested worse depravity: 'So given are they to the lusts of the flesh,' Olearius continued, 'that some are addicted to ... sodomy; and not only with boys but also with horses.'[75] Reformers were concerned as well as fascinated. In the early 1650s, they condemned almost everything from drunkenness to bagpipes, dancing, and the laxity of rural priests.[76] Despite the rules, the revels continued unabated.

When they were not denouncing folk religion, church leaders were tormented by a fear that they might inadvertently have strayed from the path of the true faith themselves. Their first contact with Orthodox clerics from Ukraine and White Russia gave Russia's bishops an unwelcome glimpse of the differences that had evolved between their own religious practices and everyone else's. Habits that had become traditional for Russians, including the way they crossed themselves, using two fingers rather than three, turned out to be corruptions of the true and apostolic 'Greek' religion. Mistakes had crept into their prized translations of the holy texts. Despite aspiring to the role of universal religious leader, Moscow discovered an embarrassing need for guidance (which explains what the patriarch of Antioch was doing in Moscow in 1655). When it joined the Muscovite state, the thriving city of Kiev added a new problem, because it boasted an impressive academy largely run by clerics. A province simply could not be allowed to rival Moscow in this way.

Among the priests who felt most keenly the desire to establish the pre-eminence and doctrinal perfection of Russia's church was Moscow's latest patriarch, Nikon. This man, perhaps the most ambitious ever to hold the office (although the competition could be close), was appointed in 1652. Well over six feet tall, he was as overbearing as he was intelligent. At first, Tsar Aleksei found welcome refuge in the man's decisiveness. Nikon was a scholar, too, and his library of books was rumoured to be the finest in Russia. But the new head of Russia's church also aspired to the authority enjoyed by an earlier priestly 'great sovereign': Filaret. At his enthronement, Nikon was said to have demanded that Tsar Aleksei 'obey him in spiritual affairs', which sounded almost like a bid for power. 'All this,' a foreign envoy noted eagerly, 'was promised.'[77]

The patriarch used showmanship to overawe. He employed the nimblest-fingered nuns to create his regalia. On Easter Sunday in 1655, he appeared in garments sewn with gold and precious stones worth a staggering 30,000 rubles; 'even Nikon finds some of his outfits too heavy', Paul of Aleppo wrote.[78] He also liked a good supporting cast, and often celebrated mass with seventy-five attendant priests. Like a pious tsar, and with similar funds, he founded a new monastery in the Valdai hills, near Novgorod, in 1653. Soon after, he commissioned a model of Jerusalem's Church of the Holy Sepulchre, and the copy was used in the design of his New Jerusalem Monastery, begun in 1656 on land belonging to the village of Voskresenskoe, forty miles west of Moscow on the Istra river. As Paul of Aleppo put it, having got the measure of his man, the patriarch was a 'great lover of buildings, monuments and collections'.[79]

But the Kremlin was the real base for Nikon's court. Although the site was getting crowded, Aleksei gave him some land, to the north of the Dormition Cathedral, so that he could realize his project for a holy capital, a world centre of Orthodoxy, within the fortress walls. The sovereign also lent him funds to build himself a palace complex, including several audience halls and new churches, the most famous of which was dedicated to the Twelve Apostles. More than a million new bricks were duly baked, German architects secured, and as the work progressed, Nikon was allowed to conscript some of the tsar's *streltsy* as labourers.[80] Paul of Aleppo visited the complex as it was being completed in 1655. 'It had seven halls,' he wrote, 'a bakehouse, and a large kitchen; so that the heat should ascend to the rooms above ... On the top of it he has raised a divan, looking over the country, and thence has made a passage leading to the Empress's palace, for the purposes of secret communication.' There were other halls, one of which was so extensive that its tiled floor was 'like a lake', and every room was decorated in the richest style. In a word, the Syrian concluded, 'these buildings are the object of wonder to everyone, for scarcely in the royal palaces is there anything to equal them.'[81]

When the din of the masons' hammers finally stilled, the patriarch moved in. A man whose out-of-town estates included about 35,000 serfs could pay for any luxury. Nikon's bakery supplied him with several varieties of bread and countless exquisite Russian pies, his brewery with kvass and beer. Meat was forbidden to any tonsured monk, but the patriarch's ponds and storerooms gleamed with fish, and his cooks prepared them in astounding ways, mincing the flesh and shaping it into the forms of lambs or geese, piling it into rare sea-shells, stuffing the smaller fish into the greater, and serving all on plates of silver and gold.[82] Fresh vegetables and fruit were grown on Nikon's farmland just beyond the city walls, but he reserved a special garden in his Kremlin grounds for choicer, usually imported, plants, spending a hefty portion of the church's funds on tulip bulbs.[83] At night, after his many prayers, the supreme leader of the Russian faith padded over the furs on his chamber floor to sleep between goose-feather quilts. There were rumours that he was not always alone. They said he entertained pretty young nuns.[84]

Whatever his own indulgences, however, Nikon demanded strict religious discipline from everyone else (he even scolded Patriarch Macarius of Antioch for taking off some of his heavy vestments in a private room). The penalties he favoured for the punishment of other people's moral lapses shocked his Syrian visitors. Almost every monastery they saw contained a prison, and these were full of monks who had been 'found in states of intoxication', many of whom were punished by being locked up and 'galled with heavy chains and with logs of wood on their necks and legs'. The head of the Trinity-St Sergius Monastery, possibly Russia's greatest, was sentenced to an exile grinding corn for the crime of taking bribes from the rich.[85] To maintain the new rules, the patriarch set guards at all the monasteries, and it was believed that these 'keep a strict watch by looking through the crevices of the doors; observing whether the inmates practise devotional humility, fasting, and prayer; or whether they get drunk and amuse themselves'. [86] At the thought of surveillance like that, the noblewomen in the Kremlin's more exclusive convent cells may well have paused between sips of their honeyed wine to suppress a shudder.

The next task was to sort out Russia's religious practice. To get that right, Nikon summoned experts from Ukraine, White Russia and the Orthodox patriarchates of the Ottoman world, all of whom passed intense weeks at his palace. Fresh reforms streamed almost daily from its audience hall. Priests were to adopt new vestments, including Greek-style cowls and skullcaps. There were to be new service-books, and scholars from Ukraine and White Russia were to work on new translations of the complete Bible. The sign of the cross was no longer to be made with two fingers but the corrected, 'Greek', three. In the field of architecture, Nikon called for an end to towered churches (these had been introduced in the reign of Vasily III, and the most prominent example was no less than the main tower of St Basil's). The patriarch's edict specified cupolas, and even decreed their number: one, three, or five. Changes like this (to say nothing of reformed service-books and vestments) overturned centuries-old Russian practices, many of which had been debated and approved in the days of the last True Tsar, Ivan the Terrible. The so-called Old Believers' subsequent attacks on the 'new' belief were based on that idea: only servants of the Antichrist, it was argued, would try to undermine historically sanctioned Russian liturgy and custom.[87]

Emotion, clearly, ran high in the world of faith. Nikon's dogmatism made him many enemies, most famously a senior priest called Avvakum, who referred to Russia's spiritual father as 'the Great Deceiver and son of a whore'.[88] The patriarch gave further offence by plundering several existing churches for the building-materials he needed for his projects at Valdai and Voskresenskoe. Personal issues – the jealousy of those he snubbed, the hatred provoked by his tyranny, resentment at the splendour of his earthly goods – deepened the rift within the church, beginning in the precincts of the Kremlin and spreading to the most remote provincial congregations. Once it had split, whatever the original reasons, the church could no longer sustain the fiction of its apostolic purity. And the dissident trend of Old Belief, which gathered pace in the 1660s, soon merged with a more general suspicion of government to feed a small but stubborn national counter-culture.[89]

Within the Kremlin, meanwhile, another duel, this time between the rival courts of Nikon and Tsar Aleksei, was now set to define the future boundaries of all spiritual power. The patriarch and Aleksei had once been friends. The two men dined together frequently, Nikon was like an uncle to the royal children, and the stone passageway between the two great palaces was warmed by many heavy-treading feet. Aleksei was so pious, too, that some privately dubbed him 'the young monk'. On each day during Lent, the greatest fast Russians observed, the tsar spent five or six hours in church and bent his body in prostration more than a thousand times.[90] Priest though he was himself, Paul of Aleppo was exhausted, but 'custom has made the [Russians] insensible of weariness. Our feeling was one of intense wonder and we never left the church but tottering on our legs after so much standing . . . We kept up appearances before them in spite of our inward rage and sufferings.'[91] 'Nightmarish religiosity' was the phrase that sprang to one historian's mind as he described Aleksei's court.[92]

Helped by the fact of Aleksei's own frequent absences at war, the relations between the two palaces remained cordial for several years. Inevitably, however, Nikon's dictatorial manner eventually paved the way for his political fall. His plan was almost certainly to turn the Kremlin into an eastern version of the Vatican, an international centre of religious faith where church, not state, made the main rules.[93] But Aleksei's position was too powerful, and the traditions of his court too well entrenched. Though no-one knows the exact cause of his rift with Nikon, the latter's refusal to appoint a bishop may have been involved. By 1658, the two men had stopped dining together. Aleksei also ordered that Nikon drop the title 'great sovereign'. In reply, the patriarch preached a sermon in the Dormition Cathedral in which he denounced the tsar for disloyalty, and a few weeks later, in the summer of 1658, he quit his palace and the capital. Ever the showman, however, he did not resign as patriarch. Indeed, basing himself at his New Jerusalem Monastery on the Istra, he continued to issue edicts as the leader of the Russian church.[94] He also allowed a corrosive rumour to circulate: it was said that he spent his days in heavy chains, punishing himself for abandoning his religious office because a feckless tsar refused to punish him in person.[95]

The battle of wills lasted for six more years. In the darkness before sunrise on 18 December 1664, however, a sledge from the countryside made its way towards the Kremlin bearing a heavily muffled passenger and a small group of attendants. Successive ranks of guards at the city's gates failed to recognize the grand old priest, who then took full advantage of the drama of surprise. Splendid in his pearl-encrusted pectoral cross and vestments, Nikon burst into the Dormition Cathedral and took over the service, dominating the vaulted space as if he had never left.[96] It was a challenge to both tsar and church, an assertion of the rebel's right to choose the terms on which he would perform his duties. Aleksei responded by summoning a court to rule on Nikon's future. The panel included boyars, members of the tsar's council, sixty-five senior churchmen, and the patriarchs of Alexandria and Antioch (Macarius and Paul made the journey to Moscow for a second time), and it met in December 1666, gathering in the palace banqueting hall. The outcome was never in doubt, especially as the foreign visitors, who needed Moscow's financial aid, would have known just what verdict they were meant to find. Nikon was declared guilty of leaving the Russian church 'a widow'. Before beginning his life-long exile, the big man was taken to a cell in the Chudov Monastery, and there his beard was cut off, his shimmering vestments stripped from his back, and his pectoral cross finally lifted from his neck.[97] His bid to turn his church into a kind of sovereign power had failed. The office of the patriarch itself would never quite recover from the blow, while the Kremlin – still a sacred site – passed decisively into the control of worldly masters.

The pace of further change was erratic, and the Kremlin continued to wear a mask of tradition, but by the 1660s the tsar's inner court was growing splendid on the wealth of its expanding continental empire. Aleksei's English physician, Samuel Collins, explained what he observed after his master's return from a campaign that had taken him to Vilno:

> Since his majesty has been in Poland, and seen the manner of the Princes houses there, and guessed the mode of their kings, his thoughts are advanced, and he begins to model his court and edifices more stately, to furnish his rooms with tapestry, and to contrive houses of pleasure abroad.[98]

Sure enough, in the late 1660s Aleksei ordered a major upgrade of the thirty-year-old Terem Palace, and especially of his own family's rooms. European trifles such as chairs, cupboards and even beds were not traditional in Russia.[99] Now everything was set to change. The private chambers were repainted, and where there had been flat religious scenes the walls now featured plants or planets in the sky. The current (short-lived) heir, also called Aleksei, was given an apartment decorated in imported blue and yellow silk and velvet. At the same time, tables and chairs, display cabinets and library shelves also entered royal inventories, though the tsar himself still slept 'in his shirt and drawers, under a rich sable coverlid, and one Sheet under him'.[100]

The purchase of those cabinets attests that Aleksei had become a collector, and like many other wealthy Europeans of the age, his tastes inclined to the exotic. Foreign agents were given the task of sourcing his treasures from lists that he dictated to his secretaries, and soon their efforts had produced a company of several dozen liveried human dwarves. The Kremlin's brand-new furniture was piled with tropical shells and fabulous tusks. The royal library began to feature a few books of European science, non-sacred volumes that stubborn followers of the Old Belief dismissed as 'excrement'.[101] Assisted by Samuel Collins, the tsar embarked on a series of scientific and alchemical experiments, to conduct which he imported a range of new devices – phials, metals, lenses and measuring instruments – from the German lands. These were exotica in their own right, and since they had no native Russian names, many were called by their original German ones, beginning a long tradition of importing German scientific terms into the Russian language.[102]

Collins was correct, however, to point out that Aleksei sought his real pleasures well beyond the stuffy confines of the Kremlin. Even after its refurbishment, the old fortress must have felt restrictive. In the 1660s, Aleksei abandoned plans to restore the interiors of several of its most important buildings, including the Faceted Palace, in favour of some projects of his own outside the walls.[103] He had always loved falconry, and his estate at Izmailovo, about five miles to the north-east of the Kremlin, was first developed for the sport. It expanded in the 1660s to include a palace and churches, a model farm, and even a small zoo, for which the tsar imported lions, tigers, polar bears and a pair of American porcupines.[104] The thick woods round another suburban palace, at nearby Preobrazhenskoe, also provided the tsar with sport and welcome fresh air. His most ambitious project, however, was a palace that he developed from yet another former hunting-lodge, at Kolomenskoe, to the south-west of the Kremlin on the Moscow river.

This new complex was conceived from the outset as a second, and more fashionable, royal court. The meadows by the river were a far cry from Versailles, whose transformation had begun in distant France, but the tsar's new palace incorporated every luxury his architects could think of. The main structure, which was completed in 1667, was entirely built of wood, and it featured elaborately gabled and shingled roofs, ornate carved windows and massive external stairs. The throne room was magnificent, and in emulation of ancient Byzantium, it boasted a pair of mechanical lions. Constructed out of copper and clothed in sheepskin, they stood on either side of Aleksei's royal seat, and at the touch of a hidden lever they rolled their eyes and roared, just as the original models had done.[105]

As the Kremlin's spell began to break, the tsar was not alone in aspiring to newly designed quarters. By the 1660s, government officials were also chafing in their antiquated rooms. Petitioners still brought their papers to the square beneath the bell tower of Ivan the Great. At times of crisis, the crowds still flocked towards the Kremlin palace steps. But the number of court chancelleries had grown at an astounding pace since Mikhail Romanov's accession, and his son had added more, many with ever-larger staffs.[106] The buildings where they worked had not been restored adequately since the Time of Troubles, and by 1670 some of the *prikazy* were in a dangerous condition. Accordingly, Aleksei's men laid plans to move both clerks and paperwork to more extensive sites in the White City and Kitai-gorod. The most ambitious of these relocations were delayed by cost, but moves on a smaller scale extended the visibility of government into the city.[107] At the same time, expansion also paved the way for the kinds of reform that only a large civil service can achieve.

The geography of power, and the symbolic resonance of the Kremlin, was changing for another group as well. The boyars who quit the fortress in the 1660s did so largely under pressure from the tsar. Though some substantial Kremlin mansions had been kept by members of the influential clans for centuries, Aleksei made a point of reclaiming any that fell vacant. His court was swelling round him, he was uninhibited about appointing new men to the highest ranks, and soon there were so many freshly created nobles that the old walls could no longer have contained them all.[108] The rest, now many scores of grand and titled men, colonized the streets of the White City, filling the district with mansions and palaces in the latest style and sweeping through it in a blaze of jewels to attend Kremlin events.

The display was no substitute for real power. The size of the court increased, but only a few truly counted in Aleksei's inner coterie, and feuds divided many of the rest.[109] While politics focused round the person of the tsar, however, wealth spread out across Moscow. The foreign quarter that had been set up in 1652, which now boasted several sumptuous mansions, became a patch of western Europe in the heart of an otherwise Orthodox realm. Far from isolating the infections of scientific thought and unclean diet, as conservatives in the church had originally hoped, it acted as a magnet for any wealthy Russian who dared to visit, the most famous of whom, from the 1680s, was the future Peter the Great. Behind their newly finished walls in the city centre, meanwhile, some of Aleksei's wealthiest nobles had taken to collecting, like their tsar, stuffing their luxurious rooms with globes and paintings, Baltic amber, European books and scientific instruments.[110]

A new passion for wealth and splendour, then, became detectable at court, adding a touch of worldliness to the pervasive Orthodox solemnity. In 1671, the atmosphere was lightened even further. Aleksei married for a second time, and his new wife, nineteen-year-old Natalia Naryshkina, introduced a bracing air of youth and optimism. It may have been her influence that inspired the tsar to experiment with Russia's first theatre. In 1672, he imported a troupe of German actors, providing them with a small stage in the palace at Preobrazhenskoe. The first show was forbiddingly austere – 'the tragi-comedy of Ahasuerus and Esther' – but the tsar was so transfixed that he sat and watched for ten whole hours.[111] The Miloslavsky mansion in the Kremlin, requisitioned by Aleksei in the 1670s (mainly to accommodate the huge number of adult women in the royal household), was adapted to incorporate a theatre a few years later, and given the delightful name of *Poteshnyi Dvorets*, the Palace of Amusements. (Much later, in the 1920s, this would be the building where the Stalins lived.)

The coming royal generation, too, showed promise and a potential for brilliance. Aleksei's brightest children were educated under the eye of Simeon Polotsky, a westernized cleric from White Russia, poet and graduate of the academy in Kiev (it was only in 1685 that Russia's own institution for higher education, the Slavic-Greek-Latin Academy, was founded in a monastery just outside the Kremlin walls). Though there is now some doubt about the story that this tutor taught his charges Latin, an innovation that would have given them access to the literatures of the Catholic world, their education did involve music and poetry as well as calligraphy and the mastery of religious texts.[112] After Aleksei's death, the reforms introduced by his heir, Fedor Alekseyevich (ruled 1676–82), reflected the progressive notions that he had imbibed. Fedor's advisors prompted him to abolish the use of torture in his prisons. They encouraged the wearing of shorter robes, a style that churchmen still considered lewd and scandalous. They also outlawed the stifling practice of *mestnichestvo*, the rank-bound system of appointments. One of this reign's most iconic acts, indeed, was the destruction of the Kremlin's precedence records. Promotion in the tsar's service, at court and in the army, was henceforth to depend mainly on merit as opposed to ritual status. The books themselves, those symbols of reactionary thought and practice, were burned.

'The seventeenth century,' a Russian historian observes, 'was an epoch marked by changes so radical that the very principles by which Russian culture defined itself were transformed.'[113] Moscow had witnessed all of this; its Kremlin nurtured much of the important change despite itself. But the old citadel continued to face both past and future simultaneously, as if its course were being set by a demented double-headed eagle. Most cultures evolve by increments, and the pace of change is often determined by the tastes of educated city-dwellers in organized professions or guilds. In Russia, there were no such groups, and the people's longing for stable and unchanging justice under God and tsar made innovations at the top seem positively dangerous. The tension could be so profound that some writers speak of a late-seventeenth-century cultural crisis.[114] Since they rejected every foreign innovation from tobacco to printed books, the Old Believers in particular were appalled by what they viewed as the apostasy, the decadence, of court life in this era. Their protest burned on for decades, but when it combined with more focused and material grievances the result was explosive. Old Believer influence was strong inside the hereditary corps of *streltsy*, and in 1682, the old world and the new collided in a bloody revolt.

The rising coincided with the death of Aleksei's successor, Tsar Fedor. The young man had been ailing for some time, but all the same there were rumours of poisoning. Worse, an elective assembly, convoked by the nobility and drawn from a narrow group within Moscow, broke the usual rules of succession when it announced an unexpected choice of tsar. After Fedor, the next in line was his brother, Ivan Alekseyevich (1666–96). This teenager was pious and dutiful, but he was also severely handicapped and physically weak. A son from Aleksei's second marriage, however, had impressed everyone who set eyes on him. In 1682, Peter Alekseyevich was just ten, but the assembly elected him unanimously.

It was a reasonable course, but some outsiders saw the substitution as a plot to unseat the true tsar, Ivan. Traditionalists also muttered that Peter's maternal relatives, the Naryshkins, were conspiring to take the throne. Disgruntled *streltsy* expected no less, and they seized the chance to scapegoat the unloved boyars for a range of other grievances that included the cruelty of their own officers, the 'Latin' innovations in the prayer book, the unhindered progress of the Antichrist and their own poor pay. Just weeks later, on 15 May, someone started a rumour that Tsarevich Ivan had been murdered by evildoers in the Kremlin. The date coincided with the anniversary of another alleged murder, the death of Prince Dmitry of Uglich, in 1591, and the obvious parallels were drawn. The *streltsy* overran the old fortress, first to discover the truth (they were allowed to see the live Ivan) and then to vent some pent-up rage. Their victims included the unpopular head of the *streletskii prikaz*, Yu. A. Dolgoruky, against whom they had genuine grievance. But the musketeers also turned on the relatives and supporters of the supposed 'usurper', Peter, including his uncle, Ivan Naryshkin, who was believed to have tried on the crown and now died on the pikes for it. A number of other unfortunates, including several foreign physicians, were hounded to their deaths for sorcery and poisoning. Traditionalists to the last, the *streltsy* hacked most of their victims to pieces by hand.[115]

The tsar-elect, Peter Alekseyevich, was also brought before the terrifying crowd. At one point, the ten-year-old was standing next to his mother and a powerful kinsman, Artamon Matveyev, when rough hands seized the latter and threw him to his death among the knife-sharp blades in the palace square. Some think this early horror followed Peter through his life; his manic stare and twitching muscles later alarmed the foreign visitors who noticed them.[116] But at least he lived, and he was even permitted to take his crown. After frantic negotiations, the court agreed to anoint both boys at once (a double throne was made for them in the Kremlin workshops). Since one was a simpleton and the other a child, Aleksei Mikhailovich's formidable daughter Sofiya, Peter's half-sister, promptly assumed the powers of regent. In fact, this was the solution for which the ambitious and educated princess had been scheming all along.

Throughout Sofiya's regency, the Kremlin stood for Muscovite tradition in a city whose court continued to be torn between the old world and the new. Thick-set and bearded men, their long robes glittering with pearls, could be observed through steamy windows in the palace, but the forward-looking were now learning German in the foreign quarter's smokiest taverns. Dressed like an empress, Sofiya ran a dazzling government with the aid of her advisor, Vasily Golitsyn. Its high point, in 1686, was a Treaty of Eternal Peace with Poland. The terms, which were generous to Russia, included the transfer of Kiev to the Muscovites in perpetuity.[117] Closer to home, and following a major fire in 1682, Golitsyn (whose own mansion was as sumptuous as any royal house) supervised much-needed renovations in the Kremlin, including repairs to the Faceted Palace. The work added complex new detail to a building from the age of Ivan III.[118]

But the Indian summer of Muscovite Russia was destined to be brief. Peter's star was rising. The young man spent his teens in the suburban residence at Preobrazhenskoe, the name of which, appropriately, derives from the Russian for 'transfiguration'. The pious streltsy, with their fixation on words and symbols, would have been well advised to notice that. As tsar, Peter would overturn their traditions and then destroy their entire world. One of his earliest acts was an assault on the notion of time itself. He soon despatched the church's calendar, bringing Russia more closely into line with Latin Europe and the anno domini. He also got rid of the azure clock over the famous Saviour Gate. When it came to machines of any kind, this emperor had northern European tastes. In the next century, the Kremlin clock that he commissioned in Amsterdam would cut each Russian day and night, with military precision, into twelve exactly equal hours.

6

Classical Orders

On 6 January 1696, the twenty-nine-year-old co-tsar Ivan Alekseyevich attended the annual Epiphany service on the Moscow river. The tsar himself wore gold, the court their splendid damasks and their furs. There were glinting lines of *streltsy*, cantors, icons, priests in pearl-encrusted robes. It was a classic celebration of the feast day, and it was also one of the last.[1] Just over three weeks later, on 29 January, Tsar Ivan died. By custom, the funeral had to be held within twenty-four hours; Ivan's took place the following afternoon. The corpse was washed and wrapped in golden cloth. It made its final journey on the royal funeral sledge, a mere few dozen yards across the square, to the sixteenth-century Cathedral of the Archangel Michael. The patriarch presided, and the coffin was accompanied by a procession of icon-bearing priests. Their every step towards the tomb seemed to be answered by the rhythmic tolling of a bell. Behind the sledge came the lay mourners, all in black, chief among whom was the dead man's half-brother and co-tsar, Peter, and also (well behind the men), his widow, the doughty Praskovya Saltykova.[2] The Kremlin nuns sang burial hymns (they later presented an itemized fee). There were candles, icons, incense, prayers. There was also, probably, a spike in crime. Solemn royal events like these were almost always a bonanza for the city's murderers and thieves.[3]

Twenty-nine years later, in the chill of another northern January, the funeral candles were lit again. In the brand-new city of St Petersburg, four hundred miles north-west of Moscow, the late Ivan's erstwhile co-tsar was dead. This time, there would be no procession and no burial in the Kremlin. Indeed, the funeral did not happen at all for several weeks. In a complete break with the tradition of centuries, Peter's corpse was put on display in a special hall in St Petersburg's new Winter Palace.

There were icons and prayers, but the open casket also lay among a fine collection of military honours, and the backdrop included classical columns and a set of four white pyramids.

There was no precedent for this strange scene. The late emperor's advisors had to invent the pageantry themselves. Having agreed that Peter's body should be interred in the new Peter-Paul Cathedral, their problem was to arrange a procession from the hall where he lay in state to the mausoleum on the other side of the frozen River Neva. On the day of the funeral, 10 March 1725, there were drummers and even trumpeters at the head of this cortège. The *streltsy* had been abolished years before, so the route was lined with 10,638 uniformed troops in the new style. A counterpoint to the inevitable tolling bells came from the deeper bass of cannon on the nearby fortress walls; these fired at one-minute intervals for what seemed like hours as the line of courtiers, priests, military officers and foreign guests made their way over nearly half a mile of ice.[4] There was no patriarch, there were no nuns. The sight would have been unimaginable thirty years before.

The eighteenth century was the Kremlin's classical interlude. For five hundred years, the citadel had carried Moscow's royal culture like an ark, preserving the illusion of genetic continuity throughout a grand succession of catastrophes. During Peter's reign, many of the fragile trophies of that past were washed away as a reforming tide engulfed court politics and high culture. First came the liquidation of the *streltsy* and the complete shake-up of the court. Then the office of patriarch was abolished, while further moves reduced the church's power and wealth. But the most far-reaching of Peter's reforms was the decision to shift his court to St Petersburg, leaving the Kremlin orphaned and marooned. By the time his grandson's wife, the German-born Empress Catherine the Great, assumed the throne in 1762 the citadel was no longer the religious and administrative heart of a backward-looking government. Instead, it had become another site for the display and exercise of power, essential for some ceremonial purposes, expensive and magnificent enough, but not the sort of thing a Royal Person wanted every day. It had its uses, it was full of historical curiosities, and the troublesome Muscovites remained attached to it, but try as One might (and One certainly did) it was an impossible place in which to conduct any kind of civilized life.

*

It is always hard to picture the historical Kremlin, not least because the current incarnation is so memorable. The fact that there were so few drawings, and certainly none that used the European techniques of perspective, makes the task harder still. But at the start of Peter's reign, in the final years of the seventeenth century, the images began to change.[5] Peter was the first Russian ruler to encourage the arts of printing and engraving on a serious scale, and certainly the first to put them to secular use. It was a Dutchman, Adriaan Schoenebeck, who taught him what a good engraver could achieve.[6] Schoenebeck's stepson, Pieter Picart (1668–1737), and Russian colleagues such as Ivan and Aleksei Zubov, went on to record all of the most important landscapes of Peter's reign, including (in 1707–8) a famous *View of Moscow from the Stone Bridge*.[7] Thanks to perspective, and thanks also to the rigour of the artists' training, the Kremlin was captured in three dimensions at last, and in years to come the size and quality of paper available to the country's elite printers began to permit a broad, even a comprehensive, view.

When I try to grasp what it was like to live inside the Kremlin during Peter's reign, however, I still find monochrome engravings strangely dumb. They are beautiful, of course, but part of their beauty is their very poise. Classical landscape-artists were not really trained in the chaos of cultural meltdown. For that, I think, we need to imagine sound. Peter loved noise. Indeed, he made so much of it that Kremlin residents may well have waved him off in dazed relief each time he saddled up for the two-hour ride to the royal hunting estate of Preobrazhenskoe. It was there that he preferred to spend his leisure time, especially until the later 1690s. Once he was gone, the Kremlin saints could sleep safe in their silver crypts, while priests and monks filled the surrounding air with unaccompanied, mesmeric, chant.[8] Across the square and up canopied steps, meanwhile, the royal women were disturbed by nothing more strident than the protests of their captive parrots. There were church bells, of course, and the chiming of Galloway's clock, but these were noises that the Kremlin staff controlled. The fortress was accustomed to being the master of its own soundscape.

The first intrusion may have been the banging of a child's drum. Even as a boy, Peter played soldiers with the palace dwarfs, but as he grew the make-believe became more serious. This tsar was always drawn to guns and ropes and bags of tools. By his early teens he had created two regiments at Preobrazhenskoe. Although they were dismissed as play-soldiers at first, the Semenovskys and the Preobrazhenskys were the forerunners of his future elite Guards. Their ranks included a group of his own friends, some idle members of the palace staff, and a sprinkling of regular soldiers and foreign officers, but their exercises quickly ceased to be mere games. The cannonballs that Peter's soldiers fired were real; his bullets sometimes left men bleeding in the grass. Peter himself often played the role of bombardier, a rank and filer who took orders from above, but no-one ever doubted whose authority could kill.

Despite his preference for Preobrazhenskoe, the co-tsar did not shirk his duty to the throne room.[9] He made the short ride to the Kremlin regularly, and by the end of the 1680s his lanky, awkward presence had come to dominate the royal council there. His marriage, in 1689, followed Kremlin protocol. But no concession to tradition could forestall the plots against him by his sister, the regent Sofiya, and her close friend, Golitsyn. An August night in 1689 was interrupted by desperate hoof beats as Peter fled Preobrazhenskoe (allegedly in his nightshirt) after hearing that *streltsy* had been sent to kill him. He did not stop until he reached the Trinity-St Sergius Monastery, forty miles outside the capital. From there, he summoned the entire court, much as Ivan the Terrible had done when he forced the boyars to take the same north-eastern road in 1564. By 9 September, Peter had effectively seized power from beyond the Kremlin walls, dispelling any possibility that his sister might convert her regency into a life-long reign. Golitsyn was arrested and exiled, Sofiya faced genteel disgrace.[10] For a time, co-tsar Ivan excepted, the royal palace was a shell, a cage for royal women and exotic birds.

The silence was not fated to last. In 1690, Peter's first child, a son called Aleksei, was born. As if to drown the freshly swaddled infant's cries, the Kremlin bells began to ring, and priests in white and gold intoned the customary prayers. But Peter's tastes ran to explosive kinds of noise. As one observer reported: 'Foreign-led infantry regiments were drawn up in the Kremlin, presented with gifts and vodka ... and ordered to fire off rounds of shot, disturbing the peace of the saints and ancient Tsars of Moscow.'[11] It was a foretaste of the great cacophony to come. The most annoying rattle at the fortress windows in the summer of 1696 was caused by heavy builders' carts, using its precincts as a shortcut, especially when the tsar was not at home.[12] But then, in January 1697, Peter staged a spectacle to celebrate his recent capture of the Black Sea port of Azov from the Turks. His father, Aleksei Mikhailovich, had chosen to lead his troops in the old way, a re-enactment of scenes from Jerusalem, when he returned in glory from Smolensk in 1655. Peter shared his father's faith (he never wavered in his Orthodox religious practice), but the metaphors he favoured where the army was concerned were those of imperial Rome. The Saviour Gate, so central to court rituals in other times, was not included in his ceremony, and his parade did not restrict itself to the hallowed precinct, between the Saviour Gate and St Basil's Cathedral, that was now starting to be called Red Square. Instead, Peter's event-master chose a piece of open ground and commissioned the Kremlin artists to build a classical triumphal arch (they had to work from drawings, for it was a new idea), complete with images of Mars and Hercules and most un-Russian laurel-swags.[13]

The arch itself praised earthly power. It also liberated the victorious tsar from Kremlin geography, Jerusalem and all, for now he could stage his triumphal celebrations anywhere – he just needed a decent space – and he could fill the whole city with noise. By day, there were drums, cannon and trumpets as the festivities continued on his chosen site. By night, Muscovites heard the crack of fireworks. 'If you would please a Russian with music,' Dr Collins had written years before, in Peter's father's reign,

> get a consort of Billingsgate nightingales, which joined with a flight of screech owls, a nest of jackdaws, a pack of hungry wolves, seven hogs on a windy day, and as many cats with their co-rivals, and let them sing lachrymae, and that will ravish a pair of Russian luggs, better than all the music in Italy.[14]

The secretary of the Habsburg mission in Muscovy in the 1690s, Johann Korb, was hardly kinder. 'The sound of Russian music in general is so displeasing to the ear that it is . . . calculated to sadden than to rouse to martial daring,' he wrote. But Russians knew how to be loud: 'Their chief instruments are fifes and kettle drums.'[15] The Azov celebration added day-long peals of the Kremlin bells, the stamp and flare of horses on parade, barking dogs, and endless ranks of marching boots. Aside from the destructive roar of flames, it must have been the brashest sound Moscow had heard for decades.

When the last firework had shrunk to ash, the noise subsided round the Kremlin for a time. But life was different out at Preobrazhenskoe, and certainly in the fabulous mansions of the nearby German quarter.

It was there, and mainly in the palace of the Swiss-born soldier Franz Lefort, that Peter first heard European music, the strings and woodwind from another world. Even the loudest instruments were drowned, however, by the irregular explosions of ear-splitting masculine laughter that always seemed to accompany them. Peter established a parodic court, the 'All-Jesting and Most Drunken Assembly', and its amusements were scandalous. In 1699, Korb reported a party in Lefort's mansion that included 'a sham Patriarch and a complete set of scenic clergy dedicated to Bacchus'. Peter's former tutor, Nikita Zotov, was

> decked with a mitre, and went stark naked, to betoken lasciviousness to the lookers-on. Cupid and Venus were the insignia on his crozier, lest there should be any mistake about what flock he was the pastor of. The remaining rout of Bacchanalians came after him, some carrying great bowls full of wine, others mead, others again beer and brandy.

The church had called tobacco 'Devil's incense', but Peter loved the stuff. Korb noted that his revellers were provided with 'great dishes of dried tobacco leaves, with which, when ignited, they went to the remotest corners of the palace, exhaling those most delectable odours and most pleasant incense to Bacchus from their smutty jaws'.[16]

Traditionalists, of course, were horrified. It was not change itself (which even the blessed Tsar Aleksei had embraced in his later years), but Peter's pandemonium that shook the walls. In the rich candle-light inside the Kremlin, bearded shadows bent and merged, their whispers lost in the deep velvet and the swelling prayers. This was Russia, after all, and people had been flogged for lesser outrages than Peter's. But that was just the point. Peter's court broke the old rules on purpose. Each member of it, whether he had been born a prince or the son of a baker, was there by Peter's grace and favour. Where formerly the tsar's elite had been called to attend ceremonies in the cathedrals and palace halls, this one required its members to join in drunken games. There was no other way to stay close to the sovereign. And Peter could dictate and change the terms at will; his followers walked a fine line between devotion and blind terror almost every time he raised a cup.[17] No-one could ever feel completely safe. Nikita Zotov, the naked 'Prince-Pope' in Korb's shocked memoir, was later forced, as an old man, to undertake a humiliating mock-wedding for an audience of guests wearing grotesque masks and accompanied by groups of performing bears. There was even a joke orchestra, whose members blew on pipes and hooters and banged the palace plates.[18]

The opposition, drawn from conservatives, disgruntled *streltsy* and die-hard supporters of Sofiya, grew and began to develop plans. But first came a surprising interlude. In March 1697, Peter left Russia altogether. No tsar had travelled abroad since the era of the Golden Horde, but this one was not bound by precedents like that. He gathered a collection of about two hundred young nobles, put Franz Lefort and two of Moscow's own best diplomats in overall charge, and set off for Europe under the assumed name of Peter Mikhailov (which fooled no-one). In part, the Grand Embassy was a fact-finding tour, a chance to learn at first hand about ships, science and European manners. For Peter Mikhailov, it was also another so-called game, and he spent weeks in Dutch and English shipyards, often living as a common seaman. But Russia's unconventional sovereign was also careful to pay his diplomatic dues, and his delegation spent time at William III's Kensington Palace (the tsar actually lived in Deptford), and also in Habsburg Vienna. Peter was still at the Austrian court when he learned that Moscow's German quarter and his throne had been the targets of a *streltsy* putsch. By the time the news reached him in the summer of 1698, the worst was over. His loyal generals, including Aleksei Semenovich Shein, the hero of Azov, had taken charge of the military situation at once. The bacchanalian 'Prince-Caesar', Fedor Romodanovsky, in his capacity as Peter's deputy and secret-police chief, had already begun the hunt for conspirators. Still, it was time to return home.

The tsar abandoned his foreign adventure at once. He rode directly to Moscow, completing the journey in four weeks, and reached the Kremlin at night. According to Korb, Peter slipped into the fortress unannounced, 'taking advantage of the shades of night', to see his 'darling little son, kissed him thrice, and leaving many other pledges of endearment, returned to his wooden dwelling [Preobrazhenskoe], flying the sight of his wife, whom he dislikes with a loathing of old date'.[19] Evdokiya Lopukhina, the wife in question, was innocent of any conspiracy, but her conservative manner and uncongenial extended family left Peter cold. By now, too, the tsar was deeply involved with his German mistress, Anna Mons, a resident of his beloved foreign suburb. Until the following spring, when Peter forced Evdokiya to take the veil, the Kremlin, with its stifling *terema*, was the best place in which to abandon her.

1. Simon Ushakov (1626–1686), *The Tree of the State of Muscovy*, 1668.

2. Kremlin Cathedral of the Dormition.

3. Sixteenth-century Moscow School: *The Entry into Jerusalem (Palm Sunday)*.

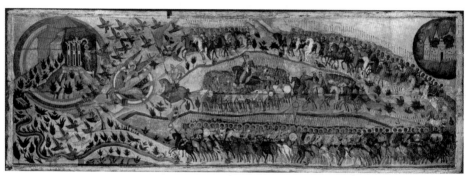

4. *Blessed Be the Hosts of the Heavenly Tsar* (mid-sixteenth century).

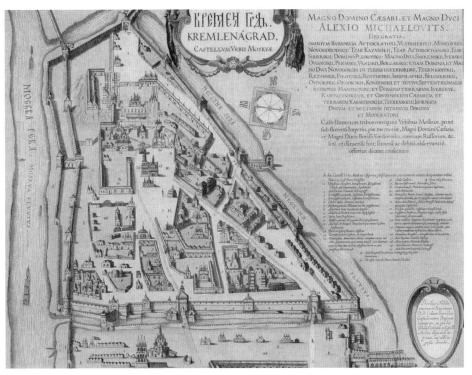

5. Joan Blaue's *Kremlenagrad* (1662).

6. Bell tower of Ivan the Great.

7. Celebrations in the Faceted Palace for the coronation of Tsar Mikhail Fedorovich Romanov, July 1613.

8. *A Palm Sunday Procession before the Kremlin*, drawing based on sketches by the German diplomat Adam Olearius (d. 1671).

9. Pieter Picart (1638–1737) and students, *Panorama of Moscow in 1707* (detail).

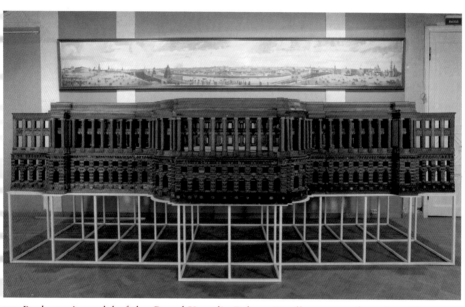

10. Bazhenov's model of the Grand Kremlin Palace. Finally approved version: The central part of the façade from the Moscow river, 1772–3. Scale 1:48.

11. Bazhenov's model of the Grand Kremlin Palace. First version: View of a fragment of the central part from inside, 1769–73. Scale 1:48.

12. Johann Christian Oldendorp, *The Fire of Moscow in September 1812*.

13. Fedor Yakovlevich Alekseev, *Cathedral Square in the Moscow Kremlin* (early nineteenth century).

14. Jean-Baptiste Arnout's view of the Kremlin and the Saviour Tower.

15. A view of the Patriarch's Court, F. Dreher after F. G. Solntsev (1801–92).

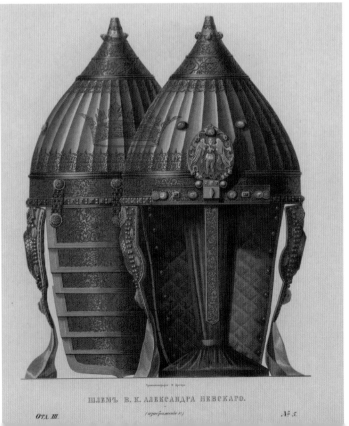

16. The helmet of Prince Alexander Nevsky, F. Dreher after F. G. Solntsev (1801–92).

ШЛЕМЪ В. К. АЛЕКСАНДРА НЕВСКАГО.

September was the start of old Russia's New Year and Peter planned to make it unforgettable. He had scarcely dismounted in the yard of his suburban palace when he called for barbers. Archaic Russia had stood up to the new reign for the last time. On 26 August 1698, when Moscow's elite flocked to make its ritual prostrations to the tsar at Preobrazhenskoe, Peter's strange campaign began. He wanted his subjects to look – and think – more like the Europeans he had just been visiting. The first beards to come off were those of Romodanovsky and Shein, but Peter's gaze lingered for longer on the doubters and opponents in the throng. As the new year dawned, a pale-chinned Shein put on a massive feast. 'A crowd of Boyars, scribes, and military officers, almost incredible, were assembled there,' Korb recorded. 'And among them were several common sailors, with whom the Czar repeatedly mixed, divided apples, and even honoured one of them by calling him brother. A salvo of twenty-five guns marked each toast.'[20] Forced laughter also echoed round the hall. By dawn, hundreds of faces had been exposed by the barber's blade.

The *streltsy* were next on Peter's list. The announcement was made at Preobrazhenskoe, but its reverberations echoed everywhere. 'Around my royal city,' Peter wrote, 'I will have gibbets and gallows set upon the walls and ramparts, and each and every one of the [rebels] I will put to a direful death.'[21] In fact, the inquisitors had already begun their work, torturing the *streltsy* in batches of thirty. The object was to find out who had put the soldiers up to their revolt, but torture also showed the world who was the boss. 'Scourged most savagely with the cat,' Korb reported, 'if that had not the effect of breaking their stubborn silence, fire was applied to their backs, all gory and streaming, in order that, by slowly roasting the skin and tender flesh, the sharp pangs might penetrate through the very marrow of their bones.'[22]

The ultimate quarry was none other than Sofiya. Peter had assumed her guilt from the outset, imagining her to have been the instigator of the plot to remove him, and much of the torture was aimed at nailing the case against her. Predictably, the inquisitors achieved their goal, and the former regent was sentenced to spend the rest of her life as a nun in the New Convent of the Virgin. This compound, like the Kremlin, was a quiet and exclusive place in normal times, but no walls could keep out the bitter sounds of Peter's vengeance from the streets beyond. Once he had finished his enquiries, the tsar ordered the *streltsy* settlement, on the south bank of the Moscow river, to be razed and burned. At the same time, his hatchet-men began their work. Many *streltsy* were hanged, some broken on the wheel, and a number beheaded. Peter himself played executioner at times, for he delighted in the thud and splatter of an axe. Romodanovsky, Lefort and several other noblemen joined him, for the torture and the killing, like barbering and drunken feasts, were treated as another test of loyalty.

The scenes of butchery were enacted every day, including Sundays. In all, 1,182 *streltsy* were executed, some at Preobrazhenskoe and some beneath the Kremlin walls. As Peter had ordained, the broken bodies were displayed on gibbets and the severed heads were speared on pikes. Some were strung up for Sofiya to contemplate through the small windows of her convent cell. But many were skewered on iron hooks along the Kremlin walls. At dawn, the air vibrated with the wing-beats and the squabbles of the feasting crows. There was a saying in Moscow for many years to come: 'Wherever there's a battlement, there's [the head of] a *strelets*.'[23]

On 19 December 1699, the people of Russia received an order to celebrate the next New Year on the unaccustomed date of 1 January. There were to be fireworks and festivities and the artillery were to blast away on Red Square for an entire week. 'As a gesture of merriment', the tsar instructed, citizens were to wish each other a happy new year whether they liked it or not, and everyone was urged to decorate their homes with festive trees like pine or spruce. The wealthiest were ordered to open their houses and offer hospitality to all.[24] The great reformer had embarked on a headlong race to learn from Europe. Four days later came an order telling nobles how to dress, insisting on short (scandalous) 'Hungarian' coats, with tailors' dummies placed on display so that his subjects could see exactly what their tsar required.[25] Although the Kremlin remained a segregated and conservative environment, the pampered and secluded women of the old elite would soon be bullied into giving up their veils. The bitterest opposition came from those who adhered to the Old Belief. In their eyes, Peter was at best a changeling (a 'German') and at worst the creature of the Antichrist.[26] The heavy clomping of his foreign boots, the pious murmured knowingly, was nothing other than the devil's own hoof-beat.[27]

Not all Peter's reforms hit Russia out of the blue. The church had been in turmoil since the days of Filaret. The tsar's impatience with clerical meddling (he had dismissed the patriarch's attempt to save the *streltsy* in 1698[28]) reflected a broader eighteenth-century consensus that religion should be confined to its own, rapidly shrinking, spiritual sphere.[29] And the point of many other changes was the need for military reform. Ivan the Terrible's reign, and the succeeding century of trouble and revolt, had stalled all possibility that Russia might become a modern European state. Thereafter, reformers had been thwarted by their colleagues' fear, and often also by a lack of money. But Russia could not stand up to the Europeans if it did not regroup and rearm. Merely to hold on to Ukraine (and Peter always wanted more), the tsar needed to bring his armies, and the fiscal arrangements that supported them, into line with those of powers that confronted Russia across the Dnieper and the Don. Peter's radicalism certainly offended and shocked some of the Muscovite elite, but their own collective sense of purpose had become so weak that they could not agree to resist him.

The style and scale of change effectively amounted to a revolution. Classical references – to Bacchus, to Victory, to Jupiter – are so familiar that it is hard to imagine the shock of their appearance in late-seventeenth-century Russia. Up to that point, few Russian nobles had set foot abroad, and almost none had the least idea about classical art or poetry. Those who listened to their priests would have considered statues (whether clothed or not) to be idolatrous. As for the mass of Russia's people, the citizens who bowed and crossed themselves whenever they walked past a church, Rome and all its heresies were abhorrent. But in the early eighteenth century, an entire pantheon of antique deities, centuries of classical art, and bewildering multitudes of figurative statuary, much of it in celebration of the female nude, burst into Orthodox Russia with the suddenness of an invading horde. As Lindsey Hughes, Peter's British biographer, perceptively observed, no-one outside the court elite could even understand the references. When a clerk was cataloguing recent acquisitions to Peter's Armoury collection in 1701, he listed a silver globe, on top of which were seated 'two men: one large one in a hat, with wings on his hat and his feet'.[30] He clearly had no idea that the figure in question was Mercury.

New buildings changed the feel of Moscow on an even grander scale. First came the Sukharev Tower, which Peter commissioned in the 1690s. Originally a gatehouse on the road that he had ridden to the Trinity-St Sergius Monastery, this became a landmark as imposing as the Kremlin's Saviour Tower. From 1701, its third floor housed Peter's new School of Mathematics and Navigation, while its upper chambers were used as an astronomical observatory.[31] Another tower (at just under 266 feet, briefly one of Moscow's tallest) belonged to a church on the city estate of Peter's favourite, a courtier of humble origins called Alexander Menshikov. Until it was reshaped by lightning, its narrow spire prefigured those of the future St Petersburg. Peter himself ordered transformations on the margins of Red Square, first by removing (yet again) the hazardous impromptu market that spilled into it and then, in 1699, by constructing an imposing three-storey pharmacy, part of a wider campaign against folk remedies and general peasant ignorance.[32] As the ever-caustic Korb observed, not all were pleased. 'Formerly the people used to live to a great and reverend age, using nothing except simples,' the Habsburg diplomat recalled. 'Now they die in a more costly fashion, and, as some complain, much earlier.'[33]

In the midst of all this rebuilding, in June 1701, the Kremlin was all but consumed by a particularly devastating fire. The flames swept through the whole fortress, destroying every wooden mansion and gutting even the stone ones. For years to come, some palace buildings were left without roofs, doors or windows. Many offices of the *prikazy*, including the prestigious Foreign Affairs Chancellery, were burned to the ground, and though rebuilding began in 1703, not all were restored. Large numbers of officials were left to improvise accommodation or to move out in search of better premises in Kitai-gorod and the White City.[34]

But Peter viewed the devastation as an opportunity. Almost at once, he ordered the most severely affected site, a large triangle near the Nikolsky gates, to be cleared, and in January 1702, Kremlin staff began to record the arrival of 'all manner of supplies' for an enormous new building.[35] The proposed arsenal was to be Peter's landmark in the Kremlin. An engraving by Adriaan Schoenebeck shows an entrance flanked by classical columns and pediments, Roman gods, and a fearsome double-headed Russian eagle. Beneath the eagle, twenty-six crests, representing Russia's expanding list of provinces, were added after consultation with the Foreign Affairs *prikaz*.[36] The local masons protested when a Saxon, Christopher Conrad, was hired to oversee the work, and more recriminations followed in the winter of 1713, when the half-completed roof caved in.[37] It was another ten years before the scaffolding came down, but by that time there was no resisting the imported European style.

The new brand of classicism was an awkward fit inside the Kremlin, and the truth was that a tsar who wanted wide streets and straight building-lines could never have lived in comfort in the venerable fort. Peter yearned to find a place for his own version of Moscow's German quarter, a suburb so neat that an Italian visitor thought the houses 'looked like caskets'.[38] The tsar imagined nights spent in the mixed (and raucous) company he had kept with Franz Lefort, days passed in the style of the court he had seen in Habsburg Vienna. From that perspective, the Kremlin was no better than a nagging maiden aunt who stubbornly refused to die (but whose riches were too precious to renounce entirely). When he rejected the constraints of the old place, Peter broke the mould of Muscovite politics. Soon, he would start presenting himself as Peter I, dropping the formal patronymic favoured by his predecessors. No longer tied to genealogy, no longer servant to the ancient sites and sacred rituals, he could determine for himself where power was to be exercised, what symbols it would develop, and also how to use the Kremlin spaces whose disposition had prescribed, for centuries, the rituals of his forefathers.[39]

He would, of course, build a new capital as well. The most protracted military campaign of Peter's life opened with an alliance against Sweden in 1700. The tsar's Grand Embassy had visited Riga on its European tour, and Peter now claimed that the Swedes had slighted him. There were also rumours, probably fabricated, that the Swedes themselves were preparing to attack Russia's northern trading cities, including Novgorod, Pskov and Archangel.[40] In reality, Peter and his allies, Christian V of Denmark and Augustus II of Poland and Saxony, may well have decided to take advantage of the inexperience of Sweden's new ruler, the eighteen-year-old Charles XII. But the calculation backfired. The austere Swede proved an even more determined warrior than Peter, and in November 1700 the Russians, who had fielded four times as many troops as Charles, sustained a punishing defeat at Narva on the Baltic coast. More than 10,000 Russian lives were lost, 150 Russian cannon captured, and Peter (shamefully) was forced to flee.[41] Russia's military iron age began with a catastrophe.

The victories that followed probably owed more to Charles' low opinion of Peter than to any Russian prowess in the field. From 1701, the main part of the Swedish army was occupied in wars with Poland and Saxony. Confronted with a smaller force, the Russians won a series of battles, capturing the fortress of Nöteborg on Lake Ladoga in October 1702. The following spring, Russian troops took a Swedish settlement called Nyenkans further down the River Neva. After a boat-trip to assess the strategic possibilities of the low-lying delta, Peter chose an island downstream, which the Finns called Yannisaari, for his own defensive military fort. The site was dedicated by Russian priests on Peter's name day in the summer of 1703. Poor as it seemed, remote and bleak, this was the future kernel of St Petersburg.[42]

Moscow paid an ugly price for these adventures. For years, there was a real danger that the Swedes might strike directly at the Russian capital. The renaissance Kremlin would have been an easy target for their European guns, so Peter ordered that the citadel should be refortified. In 1707, he brought his best siege-engineers to excavate and build eighteen massive bastions to Dutch designs.[43] The work meant shifting mountains of soil and timber in the centre of Russia's busiest city, displacing street vendors and merchants' halls, and even ploughing up Aleksei Mikhailovich's beloved apothecary garden. At first, the builders dragged their feet, constrained by lack of money, but in October 1707 Peter's son, Aleksei Petrovich, suggested that each bastion be assigned to a specific boyar. The list that was eventually approved reads like a last roll call of historic Muscovy – the first two bastions were assigned to Peter and his son, but then came Golitsyn, Dolgoruky, Saltykov, Prozorovsky and all the great dynastic names.[44] It was the most ambitious addition to the Kremlin's fortifications since the time of Ivan III. Thirty thousand labourers were involved in the project, which was the largest of its time in Russia. When it was finished, a jumble of civil buildings and market stalls had been swept aside, and the Kremlin was trapped behind a double row of freshly turned ramparts.[45] The change reflected recent European military science, but it cut through the medieval city-centre like a scar.

Peter's armies ultimately won. In June 1709, a Swedish force under Charles XII's leadership was defeated at Poltava in central Ukraine. The celebrations were compulsory, lavish, and loud. There were fireworks and cannon-rounds, fanfares, drummers and Russian pipes. The centrepiece, in January 1710, was a triumphal procession through Moscow. Peter entered his capital on horseback behind the Preobrazhensky regiment, his route adorned by seven wooden arches in the classical style with inscriptions praising Russia's 'Mars', its 'Hercules', the emperor who conquered like a Roman god. The temporary structures cost small fortunes to design and build, but Russian nobles now vied jealously to pay for them. Aleksei Zubov produced the usual commemorative engravings – orderly, narrative, classical in design – and they show processions in the European style, devoid of long robes, fur hats, or hirsute boyars.[46] Every detail was carefully recorded, from the sword in the hand of a carved gladiator on an arch to the tricorne hats that the real soldiers wore, but the Kremlin, landlocked relic of a different age, barely figured anywhere at all. Peter used the fortress merely as an extra prop. Its towers made a good support for garlands, and its gates looked grand when they were lit with thousands of his multi-coloured lamps.[47]

Peter's foreign policy ensured Russia's place at the European table. Muscovy was all but forgotten as a new imperial Russia took the stage. From 1721, when Peter signed the Peace of Nystad with Sweden, the Russian empire, which already stretched from the Pacific to the Dnieper, came to embrace the Baltic coast from Vyborg to Riga, parts of Karelia, and islands in the Baltic Sea. At the heart of it all, however, the Kremlin entered an age of eclipse. The turning point was probably 1711, when the bulk of government business shifted to St Petersburg. As Peter departed from Moscow, so did his wife, his family, and the usual troupe of guardsmen, flunkeys and informers. The citadel of the old state must have felt strangely empty.

The noblemen themselves were torn between the comforts and familiarity of Moscow and the chance of promotion at Peter's Baltic court. In 1714, Peter resolved the matter for at least a thousand of them when he issued an order that forced them to relocate, with their households, to his new city on the Neva. According to a survey of 1701, there were forty-three significant households (*dvory*) inside the Kremlin walls at the start of Peter's reign, five of which were headed by courtiers and the other thirty-eight by elite priests.[48] Thirty years later, however, even that small total had been cut to ten. There had also been a reduction in the number of wealthy courtiers living at expensive addresses nearby.[49] Everyone complained about the thieves and ruffians who seemed to have replaced them on Moscow's exclusive and once-fashionable streets.[50]

Moscow remained the 'first' capital, but over time less and less of the sovereign's business took place in the Kremlin itself. For years, Peter had held his meetings at Preobrazhenskoe; he issued numerous decrees from there. Only the great files of paper stayed in the Kremlin, stacking up in requisitioned rooms, many of which had never been designed as offices. To add to the problems of co-ordination, especially in war-time, Peter was constantly on the move. In 1711, in the interests of efficiency, the tsar created an entirely new body, the ten-man Senate, whose task it was to run the country on a daily basis whenever he was on campaign. For two years, this met in a building behind the Kremlin's Annunciation Cathedral, but when the Senate moved north, all that was left (apart from a new, less glamorous, government for Moscow) was the paper. In years to come, reports would start alluding to activities by mice.[51]

As part of the same reform, the *prikazy* were replaced by 'colleges'. Far from making government simpler, this second move led to a multiplication of offices, many of which remained in Moscow or retained an extensive set of sub-departments there. The noble politicians might have left, in other words, but those of lesser rank now moved into the fortress, installing servants, horses and wives. A number of palace buildings – notably those that had once served as bakeries and stores – were transformed into office-blocks and even unofficial tenements.[52] With the administrators came the need for facilities, including a prison for offenders awaiting sentence and several sets of public stocks. A tavern sprouted up as well.[53] The royal apartments themselves were untouched, but even that, in a city of cold and damp, amounted to a death sentence. By the end of Peter's reign, large parts of the old Kremlin palace were uninhabitable.

Meanwhile, to pay for Peter's war, a team of bureaucrats was charged with squeezing money from the two great Kremlin monasteries. In requisitioning a portion of monastic wealth, the emperor was only continuing policies his father and others had begun, but his style was unapologetic. In 1699, for instance, as part of a wider review, the Kremlin cathedrals and monasteries alike found their spending and tax privileges under scrutiny. Among the claims that were dismissed was one from the Annunciation Cathedral. It turned out that its staff had been submitting an inflated candle order for years, supposedly to provide spares in case the usual ones miraculously self-ignited.[54] Two years later, when the Patriarchal court was abolished in favour of a Monastery Chancellery, church income began to be collected centrally, and in 1706 the Kremlin's religious foundations, like all others, lost the tax exemption that had allowed them independent control of land and serfs.[55] In 1721, Peter finally abolished the patriarchate altogether, and the grand buildings that Nikon had built in the 1650s were reassigned. Church leaders now met as a committee, the Holy Synod. The atmosphere was muted, even drab, for bureaucrats will always lack the charisma of wonder-working saints. And Peter changed the rules for verifying miracles, which meant that almost nothing qualified for years.[56] Moscow still had its metropolitan, a man to lead cathedral prayers and the processions at great feasts, but the patriarch's seat in the Dormition Cathedral remained empty.[57]

With that, the meaning of the citadel itself began to change. To some, it was a landmark and a talisman, a jewel; but by the early eighteenth century it was also possible to view it in a very different light. Eternal Moscow was a myth; Peter's reforms had proved that people could be forced to live in rapidly moving secular time. The past, meanwhile, had finally turned into history. It was a new diversion for the emperor and his close friends. Peter initiated a series of measures to catalogue, preserve and explore what he referred to as 'curiosities'.[58] He began, in 1701, by ordering his palace workshop staff to create an inventory of the Kremlin's treasures, possibly with a view to raising cash. At a time when the wealthiest man in Russia, Sofiya's co-plotter Vasily Golitsyn, had just forfeited estates worth 71,000 rubles, the value of Peter's treasury was estimated at approximately 250,000 rubles.[59] A century after the Time of Troubles, when so much had been lost or looted, this was a satisfying tally. And the list itself may well have piqued the emperor's interest. In Europe, he had visited palaces where treasures were prized, and not as holy objects, nor as cash deposits in the safe, but as pieces of art. In 1718, Peter had parts of the Kremlin treasury displayed, commissioning glass cases for the choicest items.[60] Gold cups, pearl robes and jewelled swords, recently part of ceremonial life, were now available for his guests to admire like the relics of a vanished civilization.

Peter also ordered his empire's churches, cathedrals and monasteries to submit their most interesting parchments and papers to the Senate for scrutiny and possible copying.[61] Historically, it had been the Russian church that kept the records of the past. The Holy Synod still resisted the idea that anyone might be allowed to work through the material and write a book (its condemnation used words such as 'pointless' and 'deceitful'), but Peter's new collection formed the basis of a valuable archive for the historians of later times. A reform of the alphabet in 1708, aimed at creating a rational script for government, made many older documents seem more exotic still. And then there was a treasure-hunt, also inspired by the idea of half-forgotten manuscripts. For years, there had been rumours of valuables and a priceless library, a collection saved from lost Byzantium and brought to Moscow by Ivan the Terrible's grandmother, Sofiya Palaeologa. Long buried somewhere under the Kremlin, its fabled riches now began to beckon the impious Kremlin residents of this very different age. The first search was initiated by Fedor Romodanovsky, who used the excavations for Peter's arsenal as an opportunity to hunt for hidden vaults (he later claimed to have discovered two complete underground palaces, but the story has never been corroborated). In 1724, a *d'yak* called Osipov began a second dig around the Tainitsky gates, which was continued, with the blessing of the Senate, a decade later. A lot of tired servants moved a lot of soil, but nothing was found.[62] The rumours and the dream, however, would prove more durable, over the centuries, than any cache of old vellum.

The Kremlin was becoming a visitor attraction. Peter even introduced an entrance charge. Worldly though he was, the Habsburg envoy Johann Korb was impressed after his tour of the relics and icons.[63] But signs of neglect were everywhere, from gardens 'going to ruin on account of human sloth', as he observed, to royal apartments falling victim to burst guttering and moss.[64] By mid-century, the Kremlin was decaying into Russia's Fontainebleau, the poor relation to St Petersburg's Versailles. Indeed, a Russian nobleman who visited the old French palaces at Fontainebleau in 1756 (travel abroad was almost commonplace by then), wrote that he felt 'as if I were in Moscow in the Kremlin palace. There is no symmetry of any kind; it's mostly chambers and entrance-ways. In a word, every single prince seems to have built something somewhere by whatever architectural rules happened to prevail.'[65]

Inconvenient though it was, the Kremlin was never totally abandoned. The citadel had two main symbolic uses in the new imperial Russia. In the first place, it was still a valued symbol of apparent continuity. In the decades to come, there was no better place to crown a tsar, especially when the candidate was mad, female, illegitimate, or a suspected regicide. And the Kremlin also mattered because it was the heart of Moscow;

no-one ever held Russia without that capital's support. In 1718, when Peter disinherited his eldest son, Aleksei, he chose to hold a trumped-up treason hearing in the Kremlin's banqueting hall; it was a way of facing down the simmering opposition of a city that had not grown used to bowing to St Petersburg (and still, perhaps, believed in royal primogeniture). On 3 February 1718, the court listened in silence as a tearful Aleksei renounced his claim to the throne. The new heir, Peter's infant son Peter Petrovich, was proclaimed in the Dormition Cathedral immediately afterwards. Beneath the Kremlin walls, meanwhile, the fact of Peter's absolute personal rule was emphasized to every Muscovite bystander by the elite guards who patrolled day and night in groups of five or ten.[66]

The choice of Moscow for the first of the new era's coronations was also politically inspired. Aleksei died in St Petersburg in June 1718, quite possibly at his own father's hands and certainly after weeks of the torture that his father had supervised. But the tsar-elect, Peter's adored Peter Petrovich, did not survive beyond his infancy. In his last years, Peter the Great was left without an obvious heir. Whatever happened, he would have to make a choice, and his people would have somehow to be induced (even after his death) to accept it. The court ideologue of the time, Feofan Prokopovich, produced the necessary legal reform (it stated that each tsar henceforth should have the right to name his own successor), but legitimacy needed more than the mere letter of the law. By 1722, Peter had decided to trust his empire to his second wife, Catherine. This woman, born Marta Skavronska, came from provincial Lithuania and had started life as a laundress. Her origins, however, were only one of many possible objections to the idea that she might reign as Russia's empress. No woman (with dubious exceptions such as Elena Glinskaya and Peter's half-sister Sofiya) had ever ruled the Russian lands. And Peter wanted to crown her himself. There was no patriarch to preside, no dead tsar to replace, and no cluster of golden-robed boyars to kiss the cross. Legitimacy was the central problem, so Peter wisely gravitated to the Kremlin's Dormition Cathedral for the ceremony. Every new sovereign after him would do the same.

The script, the symbols and the velvet uniforms were all Petrine creations. The preparations for Catherine's great day were as thorough as Makary's plans for Ivan the Terrible, and the atmosphere was probably as tense. The ceremony was planned as a 'coronation' (*koronatsiia*), a European term that Peter chose in favour of the traditional Russian *venchanie*. Having set their faces against one tradition, however, the members of the coronation commission were careful to combine the most impressive European borrowings with concessions to Russian taste. While reading all they could about the customs of ancient Rome and the Holy Roman Empire, Peter's advisors also studied old Byzantium, for this at least was one place where women had ruled as empresses.[67] They observed that regalia were central, and while they could make use of an existing sceptre and orb, they decided to commission a new crown, since the traditional Russian jewelled cap lacked the desired elegance. A jeweller called Samson Larionov, whose trade was 'to make things with diamonds for her imperial highness', was approached in deepest secrecy. His commission was to produce a crown that would appear, when finished, 'as if old, and not newly-made'.[68]

The Kremlin buildings also needed work, and the preparations began in 1722. Staff were drafted to the Kremlin workshops, which had seen little business for a decade. They began with the refurbishment of the Faceted Palace. In the years between his accession and departure for St Petersburg, Peter had allowed this space to be used for theatrical performances. As a result, the remnants of the old frescoes had suffered irreparable damage, and now there was neither the time nor means to restore them. Instead, as court engravings show, the venerable walls were covered with cloth and the carved detailing given an entirely new look with red and gold paint.[69] The banqueting hall received the same kind of well-meant attention. As the painters whitewashed and made good, other craftsmen worked to build the thrones, walkways and galleries that would be needed for the sovereigns and their guests. The schedule was tight, and no allowance was made for refurbishing the Terem Palace, which gaped on to Cathedral Square like a sightless guest. Someone estimated that it would cost 50,000 rubles merely to repair its window-frames.[70]

On 5 May 1724, Moscow was woken by the sound of trumpets. For forty-eight hours, the heralds announced the coronation to a city and its numerous expensive visitors. The Kremlin bells might ring as they had always done, but this was a new kind of pageant, and Peter intended to shake the old stones to the ground. On 7 May, Peter and Catherine entered the cathedral in a spirit very different from that of Peter's own coronation three decades before. Instead of *streltsy*, there were members of the newly formed Guards regiments; instead of robed boyars, a line of courtiers in European dress. The crowd, indeed, included many foreigners, not least the families of Peter's married daughters. As to the principals, Catherine herself wore an embroidered purple robe with gold trim, imported from Paris, and Peter a kaftan and breeches in sky-blue silk, embroidered in silver, topped off with a matching hat with a magnificent white feather. Led as it was by uniformed marshals and Peter's closest aides, the procession gleamed in rainbow hues, a far cry from the golden monochrome of Peter's youth.

The assembly was also a more diverse social mix than Moscow's cathedrals had seen on previous occasions. The courtiers included many who had never waited for promotion through the ranks of the old clans. There were new names, new manners and a new swagger. Even more significantly, it was Peter, not the church leaders, who took the central role. The archbishops said their prayers, but it was he who created the new empress as she knelt at his feet to receive the imperial crown, that old-new masterpiece 'adorned with pearls, diamonds, and a huge ruby of marvellous beauty larger than a dove's egg'.[71] The cathedral was silent as Peter stooped to place the diadem on his wife's head, but signallers outside were waiting to order the first cannon-blasts at once.[72]

The emperor had been unwell for months, and the proceedings in the Dormition Cathedral marked the end of his public involvement that day. But Catherine still had some important appointments to keep. Like every tsar of ancient Muscovy, the former laundress planned to visit the tombs of her adoptive predecessors. Walking under a golden canopy supported at each corner by hand-picked stewards, she led her retinue across the square towards the Archangel Cathedral. Inside, she communed with the spirits of Ivan Kalita, Dmitry Donskoi and Ivan the Great. She even offered prayers to Ivan Alekseyevich, the half-brother who had once ruled at Peter's side. It was a theatrical tour de force, a grafting on to Moscow's past; in the trance-like atmosphere of sacrament, the new empress may even have been partially sincere about her place in this bizarre succession. The irony was compounded by Catherine's special reverence for the boy-prince Dmitry of Uglich, whose supposed corpse had played such a peculiar role in the legitimacy struggles of the 1600s.[73]

The day ended with feasting and more fireworks, but Moscow itself was the backdrop, rather than a participant, throughout. Where previous coronations had been accompanied by gifts of food and drink for its citizens, this one was a party for Peter's elite. For those who had been living in the Kremlin, and for those who worked or prayed in it, the quick and superficial renovation of selected buildings had been strange, but the sudden arrival of a colourful, strutting court was more like an invasion. The newly widened, newly tidied central streets were flooded with alien silks and liveries. Broad-shouldered guards in uniform held ordinary citizens at bay. And when the court had left, grumbling about the damp and the inconvenient rooms, the Kremlin slipped back into ineluctable decay.

The tone was set for the imperial era. From the early eighteenth century until the end of the nineteenth, a succession of autocrats – male and female, rapacious, crazy, foreign and sometimes even competent – chose to hold their coronations in the Kremlin. With very few exceptions, they opted for smarter accommodation (and more congenial company) when the time came to select their final resting-places, and almost all were interred in St Petersburg. But at the start of every reign, and often as the Guards had barely sheathed the weapons that had brought the winning candidate to power, the court splashed out on new costumes and made its way to Moscow for a round of coronation balls. In the Kremlin, the cathedrals were repaired and swept, damp patches screened, and kitchens stocked for epic catering campaigns. Across the old White City and Kitai-gorod, a swarm of squatters (some quite affluent) were bundled off to the country, and rooms prepared for fancier, and more exigent, inhabitants. Almost every court grandee had lodgings in Moscow – many retained mansions in the ancient capital – but to read their complaints and gossip is to sense a collective intake of breath as each prepared to suffer the expected chills and grime, the inconvenience, and the inevitable smell of shit.[74]

The compensation, between the formalities and balls, was that many could relax. Russia's first capital had managed to retain a comfortable air of shabbiness, of village anarchy, that greeted starch-faced courtiers with the warmth of an apple-cheeked old nanny. In 1762, when the obligation to serve the tsar at court was finally commuted, and noblemen could choose to live exactly where they wished, many left St Petersburg for the old capital at once.[75] 'They here support a large number of retainers,' an English traveller remarked, 'gratify their taste for a ruder and more expensive magnificence in the antient style of feudal grandeur, and are not, as at Petersburg, eclipsed by the ... imperial establishment.'[76] The empress Catherine the Great (ruled 1762–96) agreed, noting in her own memoir that Moscow's nobility 'would happily spend their entire lives being taken about all day in a coach and six ... which hides from vulgar eyes the master's own dirt and the disorder of his household in all matters and especially its economy'. Even Moscow's noblewomen seemed to disgust her, for their heavy jewels and sumptuous clothes ('superb', the sharp-eyed Catherine observed) looked vulgar and incongruous when their servants were so ill turned-out, and even barely clean. 'You would hardly dare to say,' the empress concluded, 'that they were people like us.'[77]

But the first capital was not a backwater. Indeed, the eighteenth century saw its nobility at its most brilliant, as if the old elite had needed nothing more than Peter's death to start adopting voluntarily the lessons he had sought to force on it. A lively mood pervaded Moscow's salons (themselves unthinkable as a concept just a few years before); people read and argued, flirted, and sent smart sons off to do the European tour. An architectural school, headed by the influential Dmitry Ukhtomsky (1719–74), was opened near the Kremlin in 1749, and in 1755 Moscow also became the site of Russia's first university.

One topic for the soirées was the rediscovery of ancient worlds. In 1738, the whole of Europe (in which Moscow now counted itself) had watched enthralled as workmen digging near Naples began to exhume the city of Herculaneum, buried under volcanic ash since the eruption of Vesuvius in the first century. When a Spanish expedition unearthed Pompeii a decade later, Russian nobles were among the first to sketch and document the site. This could have been the start of similar excitement over Russia's past, and a series of geographical expeditions led by Vladimir Tatishchev indeed explored some Russian sites, including medieval Vladimir. But what these pioneers would find was hardly as satisfying. Not only was the style perplexing (there was no order, there was no geometry, no balance), but what remained was disappointing, largely built of perishable wood.[78] By common consent, classical Italy was not only better preserved but also far more picturesque.[79]

Cities and their buildings were on everybody's minds. St Petersburg had been a splendid project (or so it seemed in retrospect), and other centres now aspired to the same style. At this point it was natural for Russian planners to look to Europe for their inspiration. The fashion had been set by Peter the Great, who personally supervised the first Russian edition of Giacomo Barozzi da Vignola's famous treatise, *Canon of the Five Orders of Architecture*, in 1709. The work explained the rules of symmetry and proportion, it insisted upon measurement (rather than the usual guesswork and improvisation), and with its prescriptions for style it became the eighteenth-century Russian architects' bible.[80] By mid-century, it was also part of any sophisticated education to have read the works of Vitruvius and Palladio. As for the improvement of existing sites, many Russian travellers to Rome were particularly struck by Michelangelo's restoration of the Capitoline Hill. In 1763, the medieval city of Tver burned to the ground. The project to rebuild it was an opportunity to test the lessons that had just been learned. When the new centre rose on faultlessly neo-classical lines, with wide streets and a spacious elegance, it was acclaimed a triumph. Tver's airiness exposed the rambling, muddy chaos of its sister towns. The race was on to turn all Russian cities into paragons of European order.[81]

But that still left the problem of the old Kremlin. While Moscow's educated class debated plans to make their city rational, the simple people (who outnumbered them) clung to their beloved religious sites.[82] Successive rulers improvised. At the end of the 1740s, for instance, the empress Elizabeth (ruled 1741–61) instructed her favourite architect, Francesco Bartolomeo Rastrelli (1700–71), to build her a new Winter Palace in the Kremlin. Completed in 1749 (and rather more modest than its St Petersburg namesake, also built for Elizabeth by Rastrelli), this largely wooden building, which rambled over several wings and seemed to flummox visitors, survived till 1838. In 1812, it was here that Napoleon would spend several awkward weeks waiting in vain for Russia's surrender to the Grande Armée.[83]

The Winter Palace did not make the Kremlin a convenient place, and it fell to Elizabeth's successor, Catherine the Great, to grasp the nettle of improvement on an epic scale. There is some irony in this, since the German-born empress was so decided in her aversion to Moscow. Her impressions of the Kremlin had not been improved by visits during Elizabeth's reign, nor by the illness that she suffered there as a young bride (as a result of which her head had been completely shaved). The ever-industrious Catherine considered Moscow to be a 'seat of idleness', and even its precious history seemed to hold little charm. 'Never can a people have been confronted by more objects of fanaticism,' she fulminated, 'more miraculous images at every step, more churches, more men of the cloth, more convents, more of the faithful, more beggars, more thieves, more useless servants in the houses – and what houses, what dirt . . .'[84] For all that, Catherine understood that Moscow's iconic fortress occupied a special place in Russian hearts. She chose the city for her coronation, she remained in the capital for months thereafter, and she returned several times for state affairs over the course of her reign. When it came to parks and landscape and exotic halls, no European ruler of the time was more ambitious.[85] Her principal efforts focused on St Petersburg and the suburban palaces with which she planned to surround it, but she could not leave Moscow alone.

Catherine had originally come to Russia (at the age of fourteen) as Princess Sophie Fredericke Auguste of Anhalt-Zerbst. It was her destiny to be a royal bride, the consort of Peter the Great's unattractive grandson, the future Peter III.[86] She was already estranged from him in 1761, when a committee of architects was appointed to advise the Moscow Senate on the condition of the Kremlin in readiness for the young tsar's coronation. It was a troubling subject, for the citadel had suffered yet another devastating fire in 1737. As a result, the frescoes in the main cathedrals needed urgent renovation, not least because the fire-damaged ceilings often let the rain and snow-melt pour right through, to the point of disrupting services inside.[87] The ancient Cathedral of the Saviour in the Forest had full-grown trees emerging through its roof.[88] Elsewhere, the damage was so ugly that it had become customary, on state occasions, to erect temporary hoardings to conceal the worst-affected buildings, which included Peter the Great's Arsenal.[89] Russian craftsmen were adept at hiding rubble and fire-blackened stones behind enormous gold-trimmed banners, but it was clear that money needed to be spent quite soon.

In the event, it was not Peter III (who was murdered), but Catherine herself who swept up to the Kremlin gates to star in a protracted round of coronation celebrations in September 1762. The ceremony was lavish by any standards, even Russian ones.[90] Catherine's imperial crown, completed specially for the occasion, included nearly 5,000 diamonds; the rest of her outfit (the dress was a spectacular confection in silver brocade with an ermine trim) cost at least 20,000 rubles. These sums could have paid for a lot of guttering and paint. But though the pageantry was breathtaking, the slow decay behind the scenes continued for some time to come. It was not until eight years later, in 1770, that Catherine finally approved a schedule for the renovation of the main cathedrals. Only sober and pious artists, she wrote, were to work on them: 'the type of people that you find in monasteries'. These persons were to understand that the renovations should be completed 'without revision and where there is gold it must be replaced and not with yellow paint'. But Catherine also approved the use of modern oil-based pigments (they lasted better, after all). She could not have known, but these were guaranteed to wreck the ancient plasterwork. Her intervention also set a precedent. The frescoes were retouched and cleaned for almost every coronation to come, with the result, by the early twentieth century, that it was a struggle to imagine the originals behind the garish oils.[91]

And there was still a lack of space – of really imposing space – for state events. Elizabeth's palace was small (by imperial standards, that is), the old *terema* were uninhabitable, and the Faceted Palace was cramped and antiquated. Aleksei Mikhailovich's wooden palace at Kolomenskoe, meanwhile, which Catherine had hoped to use, was in such a dangerous condition that the empress ordered its demolition.[92] In 1767, when Catherine, influenced by the teachings of her friends the Paris *philosophes*, convened a Legislative Commission to deliberate on Russian government, the Kremlin could offer only the most basic facilities. Indeed, the 460 delegates had no option, at first, but to gather in the Chudov Monastery, and their first meeting with Catherine, 'the new Justinian', held in a seventeenth-century audience-hall, lacked the required elegance. The whole assembly, complete with a small army of staff, eventually decamped to St Petersburg.[93]

In Catherine's splendid new age, the Kremlin's dilapidation amounted to a national disgrace. What the empress required, what Moscow needed, was a setting for truly royal gatherings: a palace and parade-grounds, squares, and at the very least a decent meeting-hall (provisionally described as 'the attendance place'). The question of the architect was next, for this was a project of imperial proportions. The right man for the task was Vasily Bazhenov (1737–99). Widely tipped as Russia's creative star, he had won a prize scholarship to Europe as a youth, garnering acclaim (and a medal) in Paris. In Italy, he had been voted into both the Bolognese and Florentine academies. He was fascinated by St Peter's basilica in Rome, and inspired by architecture's potential for emphasizing empire and enlightened power. A Muscovite to the core, however, Bazhenov had grown up in and around the Kremlin. No commission was more appealing than the chance to transform its iconic site, perhaps even to become Moscow's Michelangelo. In place of Ivan III's Third Rome, Bazhenov imagined a successor to the first, the imperial, original. The secular empire of reason, not inward-looking theocracy, was his ideal. Tellingly, he considered Peter's classically inspired arsenal to be the finest building on the Kremlin hill.[94]

In 1768, Bazhenov accepted a commission from the government's 'Kremlin expedition'.[95] Inspired by the success of Tver, a small group under Catherine's eye asked him to prepare a report, to schedule essential renovations, and to make a plan for new accommodations. But Bazhenov was not to be contented with a few repairs and a new audience hall. His critics in St Petersburg, including the poet Gavrila Derzhavin, scented disaster. From what they heard, the plans were so ambitious that they seemed to challenge nature itself.[96] This was no more than Europeans from Christopher Wren to 'Capability' Brown had been doing for decades, and it was exactly the trick that Rastrelli had performed in the Baltic marshes of St Petersburg. But this was Moscow, and from the outset Bazhenov's project was a controversial one.

He started with a site survey. Since Peter's time, Bazhenov knew, there had been plans to change the Kremlin's axis, to make a new grand entrance near the arsenal, so that the fortress, once built to protect Moscow from armies that came from the south, would turn north-westwards towards St Petersburg.[97] Bazhenov toyed with this idea, but soon rejected it in favour of a grand façade along the Moscow riverbank on the side that looked out over the district of Zamoskvorech'e. This orientation, facing south, would afford the new palace a splendid entrance by the water. Inside, meanwhile, there would be room for several impressive squares (or rather, an oval, a circle and a diamond-shaped parade-ground). The cursed mud would disappear for ever under geometric marble slabs. The proposed palace – a huge building – might rise upon a spectacular ground-floor colonnade that could run for half a mile. Although a massive structure, it would then appear to float, so light would its proportions be; it could have wings and cupolas, it could outshine St Peter's basilica in Rome. As Bazhenov's pencil flashed across each page, the plan emerged for Europe's largest palace-complex, a second Capitoline Hill. It was, of course, unfortunate that there was an ancient fortress wall and towers in the way. But the same problems must once have faced the improvers in Rome.

The *prikazy*, long ruined, were the first to go. More contentious was the removal of a cathedral dedicated to the Chernigov martyrs, but the sixteenth-century edifice had suffered from decades of neglect and its structure was becoming hazardous. That gone, the wreckers started on a stretch of wall and three of the towers on the Moscow riverbank. As far as Bazhenov could tell, Catherine was enthusiastic. She even intervened to make sure that the kitchens would be handy for the proposed banqueting-hall, and at first she studied every detail of the excavation plans. It looked as if the whole of central Moscow would be realigned, as if Tver's lessons had at last been learned.

Bazhenov was a man possessed. Now that he had an overall vision in his mind, he threw himself into making a detailed model of the new complex. Indeed, he made two models, for the first was rejected by his patron, the empress, after which he patiently began again. For years, he was preoccupied with shapes, installing his design team in a specially constructed model-house (between the arsenal and the Chudov Monastery), which itself had fifty-three windows and took a whole year to build. The Lilliputian palaces that rose inside were masterpieces. The modellers needed well-seasoned wood, so Bazhenov requisitioned timber from demolished Kolomenskoe. When each shell was complete, his team mixed plaster for the tiny mouldings, and real marble was added in some places to test its finish and hue.

The architect needed to be certain of the play of light and colour everywhere, so artists worked beside his draughtsmen from the first. Their task was to create a set of elfin versions of the future wall and ceiling panels for the interiors, perfect in every detail. Catherine put her foot down when she heard that 'finished paintings' were being created, at her expense, for a mere maquette, but by this time the sum of 60,000 rubles had already been poured into Bazhenov's miniatures.[98] The models were so lifelike that they became tourist attractions in their own right. They also constituted a kind of advanced architecture school: the brilliant Matvei Kazakov, Bazhenov's deputy, used them to train young draughtsmen as they worked on them. The plans provided a beautiful focus for reformers' dreams. Catherine herself decreed that Bazhenov's model-house should be open for viewing by the public, 'except for the baser sort'.[99]

The plague that hit Moscow in 1771, however, respected neither class nor education. It was deadly even by eighteenth-century standards, and by the time it had run its course, about a quarter of Moscow's population (or just under 57,000 people) had perished.[100] At the height of the infection, in August–September 1771, as many as nine hundred people were dying in the city every day, and the survivors trembled in panic. A riot broke out when a rumour started that plague spots had appeared on the icon of the Virgin that was kept in a public chapel not far from the Kremlin. Crowds began to gather – and to spread the plague – beside one of the city's principal gates. Moscow's archbishop, Amvrosii, ordered the contentious icon to be secured inside the Chudov Monastery till the epidemic was over, but this act, a violation of the people's right to see, worship, and even touch their Virgin's painted face, provoked a fatal uprising. 'Moscow is a crowd,' wrote Catherine to Voltaire, 'and not a city.'[101] A mob stormed the Kremlin and broke into the monastery, later hunting down and murdering Amvrosii himself.[102] Through it all, Bazhenov stood guard in the model-house, keeping watch over his latest prototype as the rioters surged by outside. His pupils whispered that he was ready to defend it unto death.[103]

His work on the project did not resume until the start of 1772. In sombre but determined mood, Bazhenov tested samples of the pale Myachkovo stone, he built a brickworks, and his men made progress in shoring up the historic buildings (notably the three great cathedrals and the bell tower of Ivan the Great) that every Russian always wished to save. He must have paused and worried when he learned that the first cracks had appeared in the Archangel Cathedral walls. It was at this point that the bulk of the demolition-work along the riverbank was carried out, giving a fine view of the old building, but disturbing the groundwater and the underlying rock. Despite all that, on 9 August 1772, the first foundation stone was laid. A giant square was cleared for the ceremony, in each corner of which stood Doric columns respectively dedicated to Europe, Asia, Africa and America. One of these bore an inscription in alexandrines comparing the Kremlin with the finest buildings of classical Greece and Rome. As the first trench was dug (appropriately nearest to 'Europe'), a participant recorded that 'joy was written on every face, combined with the wish to see the happy completion of the building'.[104]

But Catherine was losing heart. The empress was absent from both Bazhenov's dedication-galas, and notably from the one in June 1773 when the architect himself laid the ceremonial bricks, with their emblems of Catherine and her son, Paul, that were to form the basis of the palace's principal wings. The grandeur of this occasion already belied a troubling lack of funds. Bazhenov's critics were also beginning to draw their sovereign's attention to the likelihood of further damage to the Archangel Cathedral. The architect travelled to St Petersburg, perhaps to plead for cash, but the strain proved overwhelming and he became so ill that work was halted for several months. Nature, as the sceptics had predicted, was proving stronger than the human will. A change in fashion also doomed the great palace. As Europe's fascination with the ruined and the exotic grew stronger, Catherine's tastes were changing. She liked a bit of gothic now, she wanted to explore chinoiserie.

Bazhenov never built his palace. His principal legacy in central Moscow is a stunning private residence, the Pashkov House, which stands on a hill opposite the Kremlin (and is now part of the Lenin Library). Instead of transforming the Kremlin, the Muscovite genius was assigned to projects at Tsaritsyno, a site outside the city that Catherine imagined as a sort of grand country retreat. He planned a range of gothic park-buildings for that, but they were never completed. As for the Kremlin, Bazhenov's most enduring contribution was his fantastically detailed model. In a later age, this was displayed in the Kremlin museums, but it was an inconvenient object to exhibit, needing an entire hall to itself. In the Soviet era, it turned up in the Don Monastery, a nationalized space which at least had a large enough room (the former cathedral) in which to display it. But when the monks returned in 1991, the model disappeared again for twenty years. It was only in the summer of 2012 that parts of it finally emerged into the daylight of Moscow's Shchusev Museum of Architecture. The museum has no single gallery with the space to display it all, but something of its severe glory can at last be glimpsed, albeit as a series of broken sections in two separate rooms.

It was not Bazhenov who ultimately solved the problem of the Kremlin's new 'attendance space' but his pupil and colleague, Matvei Kazakov. The son of a sailor, this man – who had never travelled beyond Russia (and had not even seen St Petersburg) – originally trained in the Ukhtomsky architecture school. His early work included some buildings in Tver and also conservation in the Kremlin itself. More recently, he had worked with Bazhenov on the unbuilt palace, and it was often he who supervised the real work, from stone-cutting to the preparation of foundations. A draughtsman of unusual talent, Kazakov also drew numerous Kremlin scenes, including the restoration of the Cathedral of the Saviour in the Forest, which he directed, and also every stage in the unfolding saga of Bazhenov's plan.[105] When Moscow's new archbishop, Platon, was looking for an architect for his official residence, the site for which, next to the Chudov Monastery, had been approved by Catherine herself, Kazakov was an obvious choice. This so-called 'Chudov Palace' was completed in 1776, and though its occupants complained about the noise that nearby cannon made on public holidays, it soon became the most comfortable address in the entire fortress.[106]

In 1776, Kazakov won an even more glittering prize: the commission (which Bazhenov had not managed to fulfil) for the new attendance-place. The building is still among the most beautiful on the Kremlin hill. Now known as the Senate, it is a triangular structure of neo-classical design, topped with an elegant dome that is just visible above Red Square. When it was opened, its magnificent audience-hall, eighty-nine feet high and eighty-one feet wide, won universal praise, as did the gracious scale of its internal courts and handsome upper rooms. Kazakov's Senate was to be a model for neo-classical buildings across the Russian empire, and the architect went on to beautify his native Moscow with a new home for the university (1782–93), a grand building for assemblies of nobility (1793–1801), and numerous private houses of palatial proportions.[107]

There was some question, nonetheless, about the Russianness of the new style. The eighteenth century in Russia has been described as an era of 'imitation and apprenticeship'.[108] If the state of Muscovy was like a tree, then Peter's goal was to create a brand new graft, keeping the virile rootstock but exchanging the visible top-growth for something more productive and possibly more appealing. The new plant blossomed under Catherine, but it was still an experimental hybrid. The question of Russian identity was complicated, and in the coming age of the nation-state, the autocracy's very success, and its imperial expansion in particular, made the issue still more complex. By the time of Catherine's death in 1796, her court conversed and wrote in French. The empire that she governed from St Petersburg was no longer wholly Russian, either, and included large parts of Poland, the former khanate of the Crimea and parts of the Caucasus, as well as territories in Siberia that stretched as far as the Pacific coast. Only the state itself united these; there was no single culture for the entire space. Russia faced a dilemma. No longer content to be an apprentice to Europe (especially as France dissolved into revolution after 1789), it would attempt to revert to its roots, reviving a half-forgotten language and an eclectic range of visual styles in pursuit of prized uniqueness. But Peter's hybrid had evolved too far. Whatever traditions might still persist among the peasants closest to the soil, the scions of Russia's cosmopolitan elite, the courtiers and guardians of the Kremlin, could not abandon all the new things they had learned. The only route back to old Muscovy was in romantic dreams.

7
Firebird

A courtier whose business took him to Moscow at the beginning of the nineteenth century would probably have welcomed the journey. For one thing, it meant escaping from St Petersburg, where everything cost twice or three times the accustomed price and life revolved around display. And then there was the visceral, the almost atavistic draw of the older city. As the English engineer John Perry observed, 'Mosco is the native place which the Russes are fond of ... they have here all their comforts.'[1] The time-worn capital was Russian to the core. Despite a string of energetic schemes in Catherine's time, no planner had managed to tame it. Its courtyards were a jumble of the rustic and the new, there was a reassuring barnyard smell, and even major thoroughfares were blocked at frequent points by relics of defensive wall and the polluted coils of rivers.[2]

For all its brand-new mansions with their colonnades, the place continued to strike visitors as medieval. After a century of legislation calling for stone and brick, three-quarters of its buildings were still built of wood, including the new theatre.[3] A recent run of pipes now brought fresh water from a village twenty miles away, but at sunset, and even close beside the Kremlin, there were always women with baskets of laundry and carters with their thirsty horses crowding on the sloping riverbanks. In the ramshackle trading rows, pie-sellers jostled between stalls laden with everything from cloth and paper to knives and sweet long yellow melons. It was a place where a man could wear his second-best boots, the comfortable ones, and where he could afford to waste an hour in the bookshops on Nikolskaya street or reading the newspaper, *Vedomosti*.[4]

In 1810 Moscow was the largest and probably also the wealthiest city in the Russian empire. Its population, calculated in 1811, was just over 270,000, but the numbers fluctuated sharply by season. Although it was the second capital, it was mainly a winter city, a place where provincial nobles spent the colder months, complete with their retinues of servants and the tradespeople who surfaced in their wake. And it was also an increasingly cultured place, boasting Russia's first university and three academies, that wooden theatre, fourteen printing presses, and, for the nobility and wealthy merchants, separate and exclusive clubs.[5] The rich might be wealthier than ever, but they no longer enjoyed their old monopoly on civilized discourse. An entirely new class, the intelligentsia, had made its entrance in recent decades, and though their influence remained quite small, the pallid, intense, ink-bespattered types now made up almost 4 per cent of the city's population.[6] The largest social group, meanwhile, included servants, traders and petty craftspeople, all of them serfs whose obligations included annual payments or indentured labour in their lord's service. A single nobleman might run his Moscow household with several hundred staff of this kind, ranging from cooks and nursemaids and the lad who swept the carriage yard to the members of his serf-choir and even his serf-artist. None of these people was free to leave, or even, in most cases, to marry without permission. Their slavery was something that a few of the more thoughtful of their masters were beginning to find uncomfortable.[7]

In all seasons, males outnumbered women in Moscow, sometimes by more than two to one. The reason for that was the growing practice, among serfs, of earning the cash to pay their obligations by leaving their villages to seek work elsewhere, usually in the quietest months of the agricultural year. At the turn of every season, there were thousands on the roads, walking between Moscow and the provinces, their efforts justified by the small sums they earned by selling shoes or mending roofs or even seeking work in factories. As well as hosting trade on a grand scale, Moscow was becoming a centre of paper-milling and textile production. By 1812, there were more than four hundred factories in the old capital, and to Catherine the Great's disgust, some had been established in the city's ancient centre.[8] There were also military barracks, parade-grounds, and, to cater for the famous Russian soul, innumerable monasteries.

At the top of this uneven social pile, the world seemed to belong to Moscow's tiny elite of noblemen.[9] More at ease than in the past, free to enjoy the best that Europe could offer of art, of fashion and of luxury, the members of this gilded class devoted much of their lives to elegance. They gambled and they drank champagne, but the Europe that they knew so well had also taught them to converse for fun. As they gathered in the fashionable new salons, their talk was of culture, language, Russia's future, and, increasingly, its past. If they ventured into prose, a longing for history (and, in some cases, an obsession with death) imbued the writing with a Romantic quality that recalled the great Germans – Schiller, Herder, Goethe – that so many had begun to read.[10] But even if they wrote in Russian, as opposed to the politer French, most were looking for echoes of Italy, or for a gothic shiver of delight, when they began to praise landscape. Poetic writings by the likes of Gavrila Derzhavin (1743–1816) and Konstantin Batiushkov (1787–1855) were among the finest, but all the same they tended to evoke a predictable range of European, as opposed to Russian, scenery, and they did it using Greek and Latin verse-forms.[11]

The sentiments these poets were supposed to feel on viewing Moscow would also have been standard fare for other Europeans of the time. Lyrical odes came easily to the era's sensitive travellers, and most shared an enthusiasm for mournful groves, shepherdesses and the ruins around Athens, Rome and the Bay of Naples.[12] Indeed, it was precisely to find an echo of those antique sites that Russian visitors wandered the Kremlin in the last years of the eighteenth century.[13] True, there was always bustle somewhere on this particular hill. The Kremlin's monasteries hummed with holy business, the cathedrals could draw massive crowds, and the more sinister corners harboured vagabonds and cut-purses. 'The worst den of thieves in Moscow' was one contemporary's view of the old place.[14] But a literary soul could always find a quiet space, and if he liked the feel of ruins he might step into a palace yard. The pressures of the city really could give way to silence there. The *terema* were almost derelict; of the older buildings, the Faceted Palace alone continued to play host to court events. Aleksei Mikhailovich's Poteshnyi Palace, also in very poor repair, was patched up for the newly created Kremlin commandant in 1806, but though it accommodated several noble families from time to time, it was never exactly teeming.[15] The eye could rest contentedly on the building that Rastrelli had designed for Elizabeth in the 1740s (though it was now considered cramped), while the service quarters behind it, which housed army officers and senior Kremlin staff, could easily be ignored (as could the heaps of rubble in the grounds nearby[16]). In all, the place was definitely romantic, if not quite up to Italian standards, and its ruins held a touch of pathos and more than a pinch of oriental spice.

In the middle of the eighteenth century, as a young bride, Catherine the Great had lamented the Kremlin's various discomforts in her letters. When her son, the emperor Paul, was crowned in 1797, large numbers of the royal party preferred to reside outside the citadel for the same reasons.[17] But romance, the lure of gothic sensation, was already drawing others to the ancient site. When she arrived in Moscow for the new tsar's coronation, Princess Golovina complained, as most did, about the lack of dressing-rooms and boudoir-space, but she allowed herself to be enchanted by the overall impression of the citadel. 'You would have to have the talents of an historian to describe in mere words all the awe that the Kremlin instils,' she wrote in her diary that spring.

> You would need the pen of a poet to extol the impressions that this ancient and wonderful place plunges you into, this cathedral, this palace, the gothic style of which with its terraces, railings and vaults gives it an air of fantasy and which in its height stands lord above the whole of Moscow.[18]

The princess had no real desire – and no obvious means – of exploring the Kremlin's past with any precision. Her response was based on a fantasy, and it combined a well-bred classical sensibility with an inchoate (but conservative) nationalism and a good (safe) helping of the macabre. For her, as for so many others at the court, the Kremlin had become a prop for a new brand of theatre. In the wake of the French Revolution, Catherine's heir rejected anything that smacked of liberal cosmopolitanism. Instead, Emperor Paul made a point, on his accession, of reaffirming his connection to the spirit of old Muscovy. When the time came for his coronation, he chose to enter the ancient Russian capital on Palm Sunday, creating echoes of festivities from centuries before. 'The procession', Golovina wrote, 'was colossal.'[19] The ceremony itself, with its overtones of rebirth and divine nomination, took place on Easter Day.[20]

As a literal re-enactment of the past, however, the pageantry was inconsistent. Paul rode into the Kremlin to be crowned (whereas tsars of old had walked); he lined the squares with modern guns; and soon he was exploring plans to rebuild the entire site. The architect he chose was Kazakov, and the brief included a new palace, a riding school and hanging gardens.[21] If this tsar had lived, a round of demolitions would almost certainly have followed, and some of the cleared space would have been used as a parade-ground for his beloved Prussian-style troops. As it was, however, even his plan to remove Peter the Great's now derelict earth bastions, approved in 1799, was postponed and then forgotten.[22]

Paul was never a popular ruler. Personally, he seemed to combine the worst qualities of a spiritual mystic with the sadism of a sergeant-major, while his Francophobia (which was at least as much about his mother as about Robespierre) was jarring to a court raised on the *philosophes*. Catherine had encouraged the fashions and tastes of Paris, recoiling only at the prospect of an uncouth mob; Paul, however, was part of a reactionary group that rejected the entire culture of the regicide French.[23] His subjects were forbidden to use any word – such as 'fatherland', 'citizen' or 'club' – that he suspected of revolutionary overtones. Under his increasingly repressive regime, guest lists for balls and soirées required prior approval, and even music was subject to censorship. A great lover of uniforms and boots, Paul also imposed his own views on the nation's clothes. Round (as opposed to three-cornered) hats were banned on political grounds, and fashionable tail-coats were magnets for his gendarmes, many of whom carried shears so that they could chop off the dandyish flaps of cloth on the spot.[24]

There was an obvious precedent here – Paul was a great admirer of Peter the Great – but where Peter's reforms had transformed an empire, Tsar Paul's merely looked spiteful. His enemies gained confidence each time he made them watch him strutting with the troops. If the conspirators delayed, it was only because they could not act without the consent of the presumptive heir, Alexander Pavlovich, the tyrant's eldest son; but by March 1801 even that young man had stopped objecting to the idea of a merciful arrest. The final act, however, was neither humane nor particularly just. The textbooks usually describe it as a 'scuffle', thereby evading reference to bloodshed, let alone premeditation. In reality, a group of courtiers burst into the emperor's bedchamber at night on the pretext of arresting him. When Paul tried to hide behind a curtain, one of them grabbed a heavy snuffbox and aimed it at his head. The rest then fell upon the injured man and beat him to death, though none would ever admit to having struck the fatal blow.[25] The murder was never investigated. It ought to have ranked among the most popular crimes in Russian history (an interesting shortlist to compile), but instead it became another cursed regicide, and for decades to come the site of the killing, in St Petersburg, was shunned by princes and passers-by alike.[26]

The new emperor, Alexander I (ruled 1801–25), had been Catherine's favourite grandson. Sensitive, intelligent, but famously weak-willed, the twenty-five-year-old may well have regretted his own, albeit passive, part in his father's murder. At best, it was an inauspicious start to the new reign, but contemporaries chose to overlook the tragic portents as they prepared to welcome their new ruler. 'You shine like a divine angel / With goodness and beauty', the historian Nikolai Karamzin wrote in an ode on Alexander's accession to the throne.[27] 'What a beauty, and in addition what a soul!' declared another noble fan; another likened him to Apollo.[28] Though Alexander himself insisted that his coronation should be a modest and businesslike affair, so many flocked to Moscow for the occasion that the city's population temporarily doubled.[29] In the imaginations of his people, if not in practice, the new emperor promised a fulfilment of the hopes raised by Catherine the Great, a golden age of reason and justice. There was talk of the emancipation of the serfs, of law-codes and prosperity. For months, enormous crowds would gather just to see the young man's face.

The cloud on the horizon was a European of humbler birth: the upstart Corsican, Napoleon. This brilliant strategist had made himself master of most of western Europe. He had overturned the last revolutionary regime in France, crowned himself emperor, and now behaved as if he were the equal (or superior) of any autocrat in the known world. His success, and the relatively enlightened use that he was deemed to be making of it, had earned him respect, and in some quarters adulation. He seemed to be a hero for the time, a man who could talk to a foot soldier as easily as he could snub a prince of royal blood. By 1806 he had defeated almost every army in Europe (including Russia's), dictated a new continental order, and presided over the dissolution of the thousand-year-old Holy Roman Empire. The Francophiles within the Russian liberal elite were mesmerized, though they could not always approve. In Moscow, however, which had always preferred the cultures of Germany and even England to the Gallomania of St Petersburg, the French advance seemed like a call to patriotic arms.[30]

A new topic began to circulate at the Thursday soirées in Moscow's salons. The talk was now of nationhood. American independence had opened a debate about citizens and their right to rule, while the French Revolution and the new French emperor had brought the same issues to the heart of Europe. As the world blazed, Russian patriots divided. Some were inspired by the Napoleonic vision of orderly new governance, but many counterposed the vigour of the Russian state to the decadence that had doomed so much of Europe to the Corsican's control.[31] It was admittedly a problem that Russia's courtiers still corresponded, flirted and worried in French; there was no real Russian literature, no native high culture. But Russia was a mighty state, and patriots began to extol its specific virtues. They decided that autocracy itself was the measure of their land's historic greatness. The strong state, Russian-style, might even turn out to represent Russian culture's highest achievement, though the nation's Orthodox faith ran it a close second. Sergei Glinka, elder brother of the composer, was one of the earliest advocates of this sort of line in Moscow, but its most famous exponent, and certainly the most prolific, was the historian Nikolai Karamzin (1766–1826). His *Notes on Ancient and Modern Russia* appeared in 1811, taking an anti-European line and praising the Romanov dynasty even before Napoleon had crossed into Russia.[32]

The state that Karamzin envisioned was firmly rooted in the past, and history became a tool for exploring its virtues. The historian's greatest work, his multi-volume *History of the Russian State*, took decades to complete, but beyond the walls of his study, interest in the Russian past, almost always from a nationalist point of view, was gaining a wide popularity by 1812. An elite that had forgotten how to read pre-Petrine script began the painful task of understanding it. A century after Peter the Great's alphabet reform, the documents he might have read with ease perplexed his successors and then fascinated them. Old papers were collected, stacked in wooden cupboards, pored over. The Society for the Study of Russian History and Antiquities was founded at Moscow University in 1804, and noble amateurs began to edit and publish medieval chronicles at the same time.[33] Before the people's very eyes, a history that had been lost – its records burned, buried, or rendered indecipherable – was gradually, and thrillingly, rediscovered. It would be years before the bones of Russia's real past were finally unearthed, but research had certainly become respectable.

Old buildings, too, began to draw the antiquarians in their pince-nez: Russia's architectural heritage was better studied in the first decades of

Alexander's reign than it had ever been. But ruins were not always destined for faithful preservation. The Romantic approach was not about
conserving history but rather about feeling it. This was a generation
that clung to its best-loved symbols and landmarks, wrote odes to
ivy-covered stones, and discarded the inconvenient, the unsightly and
the frankly hazardous. If real things were not sensational enough, the
romantics were also prepared to alter them. It was at this time, the
beginning of the nineteenth century, that the gaudy exterior of St Basil's
Cathedral on Red Square was briefly painted white 'for authenticity'.[34]
The idea of a public record, greater than each private person's interest
or taste, had yet to grip Muscovite minds. In 1806, when many of the
Kremlin's medieval treasures were moved to new quarters, its commandant felt obliged to issue a specific order forbidding his staff from
selling off the small (and thus conveniently portable) items of the
hoard.[35]

In the midst of all this, Alexander's coronation provoked the usual
rash of anxieties about the dilapidated state of the Kremlin, and the first
decade of the new reign saw demolition in the fortress on an ambitious,
even reckless, scale. In charge was Petr Stepanovich Valuev (1743–
1814), a former protégé of Tsar Paul's whose priorities may be guessed
from his choice of adjectives to describe the structures within the royal
compound: 'ruined', 'dangerous', 'dirty' and 'disorderly'.[36] The Kremlin
walls themselves, of course, were now such powerful symbols of Russia's antiquity that they were repaired, stabilized and cleaned in readiness
for the coronation, but other buildings, including the Sretensky Cathedral (built by Ivan the Terrible) and a crumbling tower above the
entrance to the *terema*, were demolished without scruple (the fabric of
the tower, along with that of Boris Godunov's Kremlin palace, was later
sold). Beyond them, just below the Kremlin walls, two of the oldest palace smithies were knocked down as an eyesore.[37] The Vodovzvodnaya
Tower, on a corner near the riverbank, was demolished and rebuilt in
1806, while Empress Elizabeth's palace was extended with an upper
storey and a colonnade. The total cost of repair work within the citadel
amounted to 110,000 rubles between 1801 and 1809.[38]

Improvements in the spirit of order and harmony were generally welcomed by the better sort. Whenever a ruin was lost, new public spaces
could appear, and sometimes these were popular. In 1808, Valuev's men
demolished a stretch of seventeenth-century city wall, long crumbling

and for years a refuge for criminals and fly-by-nights. Though any change drew anxious gasps, the public was won over to the loss of this landmark when the plans for Moscow's first ever pleasure-ground were unveiled in its place. The park, complete with fountains, was a space where Muscovites could take the evening air, no doubt flaunting the new outfits that they had imported from France. 'Few people were worried about what was happening in Europe,' wrote a contemporary. 'Everyone was busy with the great event of the day – the opening of the new Presnya ponds pleasure-ground.'[39] The first of Moscow's tree-lined boulevards, Tverskoi, was also completed at this time, making the city-centre even more inviting on a summer's night. By 1811, on the eve of Russia's patriotic war, the leisured class of Moscow must have felt uniquely privileged. One thing the planners had forgotten, oddly, was to institute a system of fire insurance.

What put an end to this dreamlike interlude was a visit by the tsar himself in July 1812. The military situation had worsened dramatically. Relations between Alexander I and Napoleon had grown tenser and then snapped between 1809 and the summer of 1812. No-one could really have said what the French emperor hoped to gain by invading Russia, and it would have been as difficult to state exactly what was in the Russians' minds as they failed to make peace with him, but a series of alleged insults, inflated slights, economic strains and territorial anxieties gradually led the two courts to the brink of confrontation. In view of the slaughter to come, the diplomatic failure was not so much a sleepwalk as a *danse macabre*. In the winter of 1811–12, the French began to assemble the largest army that the world had ever seen, a multi-national force drawn from the whole breadth of Napoleonic Europe and for ever famous as the Grande Armée.[40] The host crossed on to Russian soil on 24 June 1812: Midsummer's Day, a fine season for Russia's wars. Four days later, Napoleon himself rode into Vilna.

The invasion came as a shock to Alexander, and for some days it was feared that he might try to lead the military response. Happily, he was persuaded instead to focus on mobilizing the nation's spirit. His visit to Moscow in July was calculated to shake the city from its torpor and also, in view of the French emperor's talent for rousing common people to revolt, to quell emergent pro-Napoleonic sympathies. In both respects, it was a success. Huge crowds pressed round the handsome sovereign wherever he went; the Kremlin itself was packed to the limits. In ballrooms and along the tree-lined boulevards, the pursuit of elegance gave way to a new fashion: patriotism. 'The dandies stopped showing off,' a satirically minded Alexander Pushkin later wrote. 'Mr so-and-so emptied his snuffbox of French snuff; another burnt a dozen French booklets; yet another gave up Chateau Lafitte and took to eating cabbage soup. They all vowed never to speak French again.'[41] Many offered funds, serf-soldiers, and even their own services to the national cause. Purple silk tents were erected in the city's squares, and young men queued in jaunty lines to sign up for the tsar's army. At the same time, however, and despite the talk of Moscow's glory, others were making their plans to flee. It looked as if Napoleon might head their way instead of to St Petersburg.

The news would soon confirm that fear. The Grande Armée seemed to advance unchecked, and soon it had reached the walls of Smolensk. The French were determined to take the fortress city as they headed east; it was to be a forward base, a centre for supplies. In August 1812, Napoleon expected the old place to fall at once, perhaps even to welcome an army that promised brotherhood and liberty to enslaved people everywhere. What followed, however, was worse than simple resistance. The massive walls above the Dnieper repelled the initial light attack. Then, perhaps because of random sparks (or possibly, unthinkably, through arson) a fire broke out which, as one witness later wrote, 'rose in whirling and destructive grandeur ... and consumed Smolensk amidst ominous and awful crashes'.[42] Napoleon was gratified, comparing the sight of the burning city to 'the eruption of Vesuvius'.[43] But his aides saw their future supply base going up in flames, and with it the best hope that Russia's people might have welcomed Napoleon's version of liberty.

As the fires cooled, the French officers made a brief tour. Many of Smolensk's prosperous residents had fled before the enemy arrived, but hundreds had been trapped inside Boris Godunov's Russian bricks. The sights were sickening even to the most war-hardened of veterans. 'Like thousands of others,' a German soldier in the French army recalled, 'I was marching along when, between two burned-out houses, I saw a small orchard whose fruit had been carbonised, underneath the trees of which were five or six men who had been literally grilled.'[44] In Moscow, news of the fire spread like a plague. Accounts of pitiless flames and searing heat needed no elaboration in a city with Moscow's history. That very day, the price of hiring a horse in the old capital increased four-fold, and by nightfall the roads leading out of it were choked with carriages and carts.[45] Most people headed south and east, towards Rostov, even Kazan. In the Volga town of Nizhnyi-Novgorod, the rents on summer homes tripled overnight.[46]

Moscow's defence depended on two men. Military operations were entrusted to Prince Mikhail Kutuzov, a veteran of Russia's Turkish wars and more recently of a failed campaign against Napoleon in Austria. A former governor of St Petersburg and Kiev, Kutuzov understood the strategic and psychological importance of Moscow, but his priority was the survival and ultimate victory of Russia as a whole. Meanwhile, the civil government of Moscow depended on the wealthy and conservative Count Fedor Rostopchin. Complacent in the early months of 1812, this man now dedicated himself to the patriotic cause, insisting even after the disaster at Smolensk that he would never hand the keys of Moscow to the French. That promise was eventually honoured, though few at this point could have imagined how exactly the count meant to fulfil it. For the present, he continued to prepare for Moscow's defence. Though almost everyone with the means to do so was making plans to flee, the remaining inhabitants, described as the poor or 'dark people', were issued with arms. The Kremlin cannon, once again, were cleaned and trained towards the streets.[47] The governor's patriotic stand earned him a hand-written letter of thanks from his emperor on 6 September. Like so much else in Russia at the time, it was written in immaculate French.[48]

The harvest season of 1812 was glorious; the fruit – apples and plums – conspicuously good.[49] Away from the fighting, it was easy to ignore the danger that now threatened tens of thousands of young soldiers' lives. In Moscow, rumours of all kinds were circulating; the temptation to hope, to cling on till the last, kept a few stalwarts in the city even now. Kutuzov himself was sanguine, repeatedly promising to hold the capital at any cost. On 7 September 1812 he took his troops into the bloodiest one-day battle that Europe had ever seen. The duel for Moscow, at Borodino, near Mozhaisk, was sheer butchery. The fighting was vicious, with near-continuous artillery fire, in a restricted space, from dawn to dark. The total Russian losses have been estimated at 45,000, French at 28,000, but the figures give no sense of the carnage or the waste.

Napoleon inspected the field, as was his habit, after the guns had stilled. 'Every thing concurred to increase the horrors of it,' one of his aides, Comte Philippe-Paul de Ségur, was later to recall. 'A lowering sky, a cold rain, a violent wind, habitations in ashes, a plain absolutely torn up and covered with fragments and ruins ... soldiers roaming every part among the bodies of the slain and emptying the knapsacks of their dead comrades to procure sustenance for themselves.' Many took shelter under heaps of dead, and one Russian was said to have survived for several days inside the ravaged carcass of a horse, gnawing on the exposed flesh. The following spring, when the Russians finally cleared the field, they would bury a total of 35,478 horses, but there were even more human corpses.[50] In late October 1812, when the French army was retreating, the troops would start suspecting they had stumbled on the former battlefield when they noticed dark flocks of wheeling crows against the white background of snow. In the path of the soldiers' weary steps, the smooth landscape soon started blistering with numberless half-buried grisly shapes.[51]

On the night of the battle, Moscow kept vigil by holding a religious procession in the Kremlin and around Red Square. The faithful crowded into the Dormition Cathedral for prayers; others volunteered to tend the 22,000 wounded – the shells and massive bullets left appalling injuries – who had already arrived in the city's hospitals and temporary wards.[52] In truth, however, Moscow was now almost defenceless. Rostopchin still averred that it would stand, but even as he spoke, the order had been given to pack and evacuate the city's historic treasures. Jewels, icons and gold from the Kremlin were carted south and east to the Volga and Vladimir; other items, including parts of the Chudov Monastery archive, were interred underneath the Kremlin walls.[53] But there was very little time. On 13 September, as some of his aides were preparing to engage with the French again, Kutuzov announced his decision to abandon the old capital. 'Moscow is not the whole of Russia,' he explained. 'To save Russia we need an army; to save the army we must give up the idea of defending Moscow.' That evening, Rostopchin, spluttering with rage, was obliged to order a more general retreat, including that of the Kremlin garrison. They marched out to the strains of a military band, reportedly because 'according to the code of Peter the Great, a garrison abandons a fortress to the sound of music'.[54] All too soon, however, the drumming and the marching boots gave way to silence.

As the last soldiers strode away, it was Rostopchin's turn to quit Moscow. Among his final acts was an order to withdraw the fire-brigade and sink the city's fleet of fire-boats. He also had the prison-gates unlocked, and the upshot was a night of looting, the scale of which remains unknowable. The liberation of what witnesses described as Moscow's 'dirty, disgusting mob', however, and the arrival of additional opportunist looters from the surrounding countryside, would help Rostopchin's planned reception for the French. He left a notice hinting about what he had in mind, addressed to the invaders, on the gate of his own estate at Voronovo, to the south-west of Moscow:

> For eight years I have improved this land, and I have lived happily here in the bosom of my family. To the number of one thousand seven hundred and twenty the dwellers on my estate are leaving it at your approach, while, for my part, I am setting fire to my mansion rather than let it be sullied by your presence. Frenchmen! In Moscow I have abandoned to you my two residences, with furniture worth half a million rubles. Here you will find only ashes.[55]

For the soldiers in the Grande Armée, however, those residences still seemed good enough. Many officers were so confident about the pleasures ahead that they had packed their bags with evening dress.[56] Their first sight of the Russian capital promised not to disappoint. The comte de Ségur remembered the scene until he died. Before us, he wrote,

> was an immense and singular assemblage of some two hundred and ninety-five churches and fifteen hundred splendid habitations ... They were grouped around a lofty, triangular palace ... and a vast bazaar, a city of merchants, exhibiting the opulence of the four quarters of the world. These buildings, shops as well as palaces, were all covered with polished and coloured plates of iron ... A single sunbeam made this superb city glitter with a thousand varied colours; and the enchanted traveller halted in ecstasy at the sight ... Over this immense and imposing theatre we conceived ourselves moving in splendid procession amidst the acclamations of surrounding nations.[57]

Here at last was a cause in which exhausted soldiers could believe, a reward equal to the price in blood and effort and months on the road. Napoleon, no stranger to the capture of great cities, paused to await the usual delegation. It was only after a long interval, when no-one turned up with the city's keys, with bread and salt, that the depth of Moscow's silence started to impinge. The stillness held, uncannily quiet, and not until the French approached the Kremlin itself, the gates of which were bolted, was it broken by 'the most savage yells' from within. The fortress had not quite been abandoned – five hundred or so soldiers had stayed inside when the main convoy left – and these had been joined by a crowd of disorderly civilians, men and women, all of them in 'a state of beastly intoxication'. Their curses ('horrid imprecations') now rained down upon the French. Moscow had fallen without a shot, but it took cannon-fire to open the Kremlin gates, and even then one of the defenders flew at a member of Napoleon's advance guard, fighting even with his teeth as Frenchmen piled in to disarm him.[58] The conqueror's grand entrance, through the Borovitsky gates, was thus delayed, but his satisfaction at taking the Russian citadel remained undimmed. 'Napoleon's earlier hopes,' Ségur observed, 'revived at the sight of the palace, at once of Gothic and of modern architecture, of the Romanovs and the Rurics.' The throne was still in place, he found, and even the Kremlin's innumerable clocks were ticking.[59] 'The city is as big as Paris,' the emperor wrote to his wife. It seemed 'provided with everything'.[60]

That very night, however, the picture changed. While Napoleon rested in the Kremlin, surrounded by the flower of his army, his sentries on the high brick walls noticed a new glow in the Moscow dark. There had been several small fires since the French arrived, and each had been blamed on the carelessness of troops. This time, by almost all accounts, the blaze was being set deliberately, a co-ordinated campaign of arson that made the best use of an equinoctial wind. 'All the narrators had remarked men of atrocious look and tattered garments,' Ségur later wrote, 'roaming around amid the flames, and thus completing a horrid image of the infernal world.' A fiery ball settled on the palace of Prince Trubetskoi, burning it down. At this signal, the Bourse was torched; witnesses reported seeing Russians dressed as policemen stirring the flames with tarred lances. The French hacked at the most obstinate of these arsonists with sabres, but gruesome chopping could not cut the torch from every fist.[61] In the space of an hour or less, the blaze turned to a steady roar, punctuated by explosions and the clatter of collapsing masonry and metal roofs. The French emperor and his aides were in acutest peril, for there were still explosives in the Kremlin arsenal, and they themselves had recently brought a battery of artillery into the fortress, stationing it, for safety, under the palace windows. For a whole night and through the next morning, the future of Napoleon's campaign, and his very life, depended on the vagaries of airborne sparks.[62]

For some hours, the emperor stayed in his palace suite, pacing the wooden floors and watching through each window as he passed. The longed-for treasure shrivelled up before his eyes; he cursed the Russians for their barbarism. Despite entreaties from his aides, however, he refused to make an early move. By the night of 15 September, as one of his officers recalled, the firestorm was so bright outside that it was possible to read by its light without the need for oil lamps. But the next day was the worst of all. Even Napoleon could not hold out when the Kremlin arsenal finally caught fire. A decision was taken to withdraw, to make for the Petrovsky Palace on the Petersburg road. By this time, however, the citadel, as Ségur wrote, was 'besieged by an ocean of fire'.

None of the Kremlin's principal gates was usable, but the occupying troops eventually came upon a postern gate in the rocks on the side above the river. It was one of the Kremlin's secret routes, a legacy of centuries of improvised repair and alteration, but as they closed it behind them, the imperial party discovered that they were scarcely any better off. The city they had gained was a burning wasteland; featureless. 'A single narrow street, crooked, in every part on fire, presented itself to our notice,' Ségur continued,

> but it seemed rather an avenue to hell before us than a way to escape from it. We were walking on a soil of fire, under a sky of fire, and between walls of fire. A penetrating heat was ... almost destroying our eyes, which yet it was necessary to keep open ... A devouring air, sparkling ashes, detached flakes, made our respiration short, dry and gasping, and already suffocated with smoke.[63]

The French elite escaped that day, helped by a local man who knew the routes, but thousands of others remained trapped, condemned to the most cruel death. Ségur's account must be balanced with those of Russian witnesses, which tell of French troops running riot: looting, brutalizing, taking their revenge. They treated every Russian as a suspected arsonist. Some were held as prisoners of war; others were cut down on the spot.[64] For the survivors, huddling in the reddish dark, the only refuge from the heat and falling debris proved to be the cemeteries. After six days of fire, the worst Moscow had ever seen, strings of pitiful figures, as insubstantial as ghosts, emerged into the wreckage of their city. Even when the smoke had cleared, the ruins stank of rot and soot and death; the stench was nauseating several miles away.[65] There was scarcely a green leaf anywhere, hardly a tree to punctuate the horizon. A bitter economics ruled. Anyone could snatch a fine snuffbox or set of silver spoons, but food of any kind was almost unobtainable. In the fields beyond Moscow, groups of French troops built their campfires out of mahogany furniture and gilded window-frames. When it was time to eat, however, their only hope was rotten horseflesh.[66]

In the midst of desolation, the Kremlin still stood more or less intact, a symbol to Russians, a landmark for the homeless, and a magnet, more immediately, for the returning French. Napoleon moved back to the citadel on 18 September. His mood had soured, and two days later, his bulletin announced that 'Moscow, one of the most beautiful and wealthy cities of the world, exists no more.'[67] Despite that loss, however, the Corsican persisted with a doomed attempt to build some kind of life among the ruins. Though almost none of the local population supported it, a Moscow government was decreed, with orders to collect the corpses and maintain the peace. Theatrical performances were commissioned, and concerts, featuring an Italian soloist with piano accompaniment, were held in the Kremlin palace to help pass the nights.[68] The decision to indulge in makeshift luxury, bizarre enough at any time, turned out to be one of the most disastrous of Napoleon's entire career. As the milder days of autumn faded, so did the last options for the French. Napoleon could surely not have hoped to feed and lodge his army in this city through the winter. There was almost no fodder for the vast stable of horses, either. A retreat was inevitable, and the sooner it began, as Napoleon himself later conceded, the better his army's chances would have been. For now, however, the general sulked, spending long hours over his food and settling his stout frame along a damask-covered chaise, novel in hand, throughout the heavy interval of afternoon.[69]

Back in what was left of the real Moscow, the French had started to exact their price. In addition to the furs and trinkets and the cashmere shawls that they had looted, Napoleon's men were encouraged to pack up or desecrate anything that might seem precious to the hateful Russians. The systematic desecration of the Kremlin followed. Stories abound of horses stabled in its churches, of gold and silver melted down (an on-site forge was constructed for the purpose), and of violating fingers probing the coffins of the ancient saints. The 'beasts' were even said to have cut the head off the revered corpse of Tsarevich Dmitry.[70] Napoleon set his heart on the gold cross that glinted on the top of the Ivan bell tower, and he ordered it to be brought down, packaged up, and carted off to decorate the Paris Invalides. When it reached the ground (in several pieces), this particular treasure turned out to be no more than gilded wood. Still, by ripping out assorted icon-mounts, lamps and palace fittings, the French managed to melt down a total of 325 poods (11,700 lbs) of silver and 18 poods (648 lbs) of gold. These figures, which are cited in every Russian source, were established with the help of a set of scales that the French set up in the Dormition Cathedral. One of the columns was said to have carried a scribbled record of the tally for decades afterwards.[71]

As the occupation dragged on, even Napoleon grew impatient, drilling and inspecting his troops more frequently by the day. Kutuzov's Russians, too, had regrouped; in the second week of October, an advance-guard of French soldiers heading west was trapped and slaughtered. When the first snow fell on 13 October, Napoleon finally gave the order to prepare for retreat. Encumbered by lines of laden carts and sagging bags of treasure, the Grande Armée was ready to go home. But the French emperor had yet to satisfy his hunger for revenge. As his retinue filed out of the gates on 19 October, he left instructions that the Kremlin should be mined. Obediently, his sappers, led by Marshal Mortier, laid barrels of explosive under the Faceted Palace, the arsenal, the larger defensive towers and the bell tower of Ivan the Great. According to Ségur, at least 183,000 kilos of explosive were stacked up in the subterranean palace vaults.[72] Two days later, at 1.30 in the morning, a mighty explosion shook the earth; windows shattered for miles around, and several onlookers, hurrying to the scene, were injured by the flying glass and rubble from successive blasts. A party of looters who had entered the Kremlin as the last French left were hurled into the air; as Ségur has it, 'mutilated limbs, mixed with the fragments of the building, and with broken [weapons], fell far and wide in a frightful shower'.[73]

Napoleon heard the explosions from a bivouac twenty-five miles away. He issued a proclamation at once, echoing the language he had used after the Moscow fire. 'The Kremlin, ancient citadel, coeval with the rise of the [Russian] monarchy, this palace of the Czars, has ceased to exist.'[74] It was a bold and angry statement, but it was not true. The arsenal was indeed a ruin; the Faceted Palace had burned. One of the outer towers had collapsed to its foundations, the Nikolsky gates and several other towers had been wrecked, and the iconic bell tower of Ivan the Great had suffered extensive damage, including the loss of the adjoining Filaret Tower. But the mines had only wounded, not destroyed the fort.

The damage to Moscow as a whole was far greater. In the weeks after the French retreat, Muscovites cleared 11,959 human corpses and the bodies of 12,576 horses. Here and there, sinister piles of blackened flesh had blocked entire streets.[75] Though parts of the city had escaped the fire with little damage, most of the central districts had been razed. On Tverskaya street, only twelve houses had survived, and only two still stood above the ruins of Kitai-gorod.[76] 'The whole of the left bank of the city was exactly like a big black field,' a witness later wrote. 'Many churches were standing, but round them lay the burned-out wrecks of houses: here and there a stove might stand, here a sheet of metal roofing; sometimes the house had survived and the outbuildings were gone, elsewhere only an outbuilding survived.'[77] In all, roughly 6,500 of the 9,000 major buildings in the city had been ruined.

Returning refugees, the *beau monde* of the old Moscow, were often the most bitter when the truth struck home. As an uncle of the writer Ivan Turgenev put it: 'The thirst for revenge is a source of glory and the future guarantor of our greatness. No-one wants peace.'[78] Moscow's fiery crucible certainly burnished the rhetoric of nationalism, but as ever the longer-term material effect depended on a person's status. The price that ordinary Muscovites had paid – the poor who lacked the means to regroup and rebuild – was incalculable. Large numbers – ten thousand or more – of Moscow's wealthy merchants also faced ruin; their stocks as well as their grand homes were lost, and many eked out livings in the common trading-stalls for the rest of their days.[79] But the real elite, the Stroganovs and Trubetskois, the top tier of the court, absorbed its losses from the safety of alternative estates. Though they attended the sumptuous commemorative ceremonies in the Dormition Cathedral in decades to come, and though they flocked to admire any newly painted portrait of the war heroes, the great magnates escaped with little lasting damage to their livelihoods, and in time many built new mansions even grander than the ones they had lost. The rift with the French would soon close. Contention still lingers about the causes of the Moscow fire, but Ségur could claim to have his version from the horse's mouth. Rostopchin moved to France in 1815 and he met and talked to Ségur there. In time, they even became kin, for Rostopchin's daughter married Ségur's nephew.[80]

The process of rebuilding Moscow began in an atmosphere of shock. With Russian troops still in the field (and Frenchmen still on Russian soil), there were no easy triumphs for the citizens at first. The Kremlin was hastily locked; that winter it would serve, among other things, as a depot for any valuables that honest people found and handed in.[81] But it was also a semi-wreck, and far from totally secure. The patriotic heroism that was supposed to have been kindled by Moscow's flames was not universally shared. Even the police resorted to looting. Mere survival came first for almost everyone. As peasants from surrounding regions converged on the city to pick the ruins clean, there was also a good deal of cynicism and simple greed.

But their suffering had strengthened many people's Christian beliefs. There was a sense, expressed by Sergei Glinka among others, that Russia, in its Christ-like guise, had sacrificed itself (and certainly Moscow) to save a sinful Europe from destruction.[82] For many, too, the saints were still performing miracles on Moscow's soil. 'And the thing that I would not believe if I had not seen it with my own eyes,' a Russian investigator wrote to Rostopchin after the French sappers' parting explosion,

> was that despite the terrifying quake, which broke the windows in almost all the houses in Moscow and could be heard 40 *versts* [26 miles] away, the miracle-working images of the Saviour at the Saviour Gates and of Nicholas the Wonder-Worker on the Nikolsky gates not only escaped any damage, but the lamps that hung in front of them and still do hang, and even the glass that covers the images themselves, did not get broken.[83]

By a further miracle, the bodies of the saints themselves had also more or less escaped unscathed. Moscow's metropolitan assured his flock (revealing a bizarre sense of priorities on someone's part) that the mortal remains of Tsarevich Dmitry had been carted out of the Kremlin before the enemy forces arrived (this honour he would later share, in different times, with Lenin). Whichever corpse's head the French troops had cut off, it was not the one that Russians ascribed to their dynastic saint.[84]

The sacred mysteries at the heart of Moscow's fortress, at least, had survived. Exactly what role they played in the lives of starving, frightened survivors during that homeless winter is unclear. The ragged did not leave memoirs. But when Russians of a different class began to tell the story of the fire, the key to Moscow's resurrection seemed to be the city's soul. 'In the month of October,' Tolstoy would write forty years later, 'without a government, without church services or sacred icons, without its wealth and its houses, Moscow was still the Moscow it had been in August. Everything was shattered except something intangible yet mighty and indestructible.'[85] That 'mighty' thing, perhaps, was the very folk-belief, the visceral affection for familiar saints and local shrines, that planners and enlightened courtiers had been dismissing for so long. A few years later, in the middle of the nineteenth century, Tolstoy's would be the generation that rediscovered it.

In the first months after the fire, however, the main priority was rebuilding. In May 1813, Alexander I convened a special commission to begin work on the city's reconstruction. The first plans were ready that autumn. Large-scale work started in 1814, but it would be some time yet before the main squares and boulevards stopped looking like a giant building-site, and longer still before the city's population had recovered to its pre-war high.[86] The tsar himself did not visit for three more years. By that time, though there were construction projects everywhere, the immediate evidence of death and looting had been swept away.[87]

Moscow must have felt unusually spacious for a while. Clutter and rubble gave way at last to new, elegant squares. Three generations of architects were finally vindicated as Red Square acquired its current shape and the Kremlin ceased to be an island surrounded by moats. Peter's earth bastions were demolished, and the Neglinnaya river was piped underground to make way for twenty-two acres of new gardens, the Alexander Gardens, at the foot of the Kremlin walls.[88] These were designed with overtones of Italy, complete with landscaping, fountains and grottoes. 'Moscow is becoming beautiful,' the city's postmaster wrote to his brother in 1820. 'They are making a park round the Kremlin walls that will be no worse than the Presnya ponds.'[89] The improvements were so radical that some outsiders found them disconcerting. In 1839, a Frenchman, the marquis de Custine, on a visit from Paris, could scarcely hide his amazement. 'What would Ivan III have thought,' he asked, 'could he have beheld at the foot of the sacred fortress, his old Muscovites, shaved, curled, in frock coats, white pantaloons, and yellow gloves, eating ices . . . ?'[90]

The commission for Moscow's reconstruction functioned until 1842. As it closed its books for the last time, its members could congratulate themselves. The fire had proved to be an opportunity. The planners had swept away much of the city's medieval jumble, at least in the centre. The village feel had been replaced, the dream of neo-classical order realized. Strict regulation made sure that most new building followed a prescribed pattern, giving the city an unaccustomed harmony, while the sprawl was tamed by grouping houses on to smaller, more regular plots. The city's isolation from St Petersburg had also been reduced, for the capitals were now linked by a public stage-coach service, the horse-drawn diligence, meaning that anyone could make the journey in two or three days. It would not be long before that time was reduced even further: in 1851, a new railway line, one of Russia's first, was opened between the cities, again promoting commerce and sparking a local building-boom.[91] Among Moscow's other new amenities were extra street lights (fuelled by oil), better drains, new fountains, and a fire service staffed by more than 1,500 men and 450 horses.[92]

The Kremlin itself was reserved for the attention of a special commission whose brief was not rationalization but authentic reconstruction. The point was to preserve and cherish the monument that had come, as no other, to define Moscow and even Russia. While the city round it modernized along the now-familiar neo-classical lines, in other words, the Kremlin's meaning shifted subtly; as a national emblem it had to reinvent itself in national guise. Its morale-boosting value was so widely recognized that a lavish budget for restoration was approved despite the other claims on imperial funds. By the end of 1813 the architects had spent 294,500 rubles (a prince's fortune) on the restoration of the cathedrals alone.[93] In their search for authenticity, some experts, including the Italian-born Dementy Zhilardi, consulted the drawings and ground plans that the pioneering architect Ukhtomsky had created half a century before. Even where there had been extensive damage, builders were encouraged to preserve foundations and original courses of stone, and where new building was inescapable, as was the case with several of the fortress towers, they were supposed to copy anything that had survived. The silhouettes, as they rose against the bare skyline, meant more than they had ever done to local people on the streets below.

But the more observant might have noticed something odd about the shapes of the new spires. The architects of post-war Moscow, like Russian intellectuals more generally, were eager to repair the nation's most historic monument in an appropriately Russian manner. What that meant in practice, to a generation that considered it a compliment to improve on legacies from the past, was that the builders who restored the Kremlin adopted a Romantic, even gothic, style. Osip Bove, a student of Kazakov, gave the Nikolskaya Tower a new (and unprecedented) decorative spire; St Petersburg's Karl Rossi designed a confection in stucco, domes and yet more pseudo-gothic detail for the Ascension Convent. The finished church, dedicated to St Catherine, was so ornate (and so prominent, lining the main route into the Kremlin from Red Square) that even at the time it was considered incongruous. The same criticism was levelled at some of the proposed replacements for Filaret's ruined building, adjoining Ivan the Great, but the most extravagant plans here, complete with gothic towers and classical friezes, were rejected in favour of a simpler and more sober building by Zhilardi based on drawings from the 1750s.[94]

Among the most controversial ruins was the Cathedral of Nikola Gostunsky, which dated from 1506 and housed an icon of Nikola, the people's best-loved saint. This building stood on open ground beyond the Ivan bell tower. Prominent and fragile, it had suffered badly during the French occupation, and in 1816, on the eve of Alexander I's long-awaited visit, the planners viewed it as an eyesore rather than as a national treasure. Some members of the Kremlin commission advocated reconstructing it, perhaps as yet another exercise in the pseudo-gothic style, but others saw the site's potential for large military parades, and it was this group that eventually prevailed. The old cathedral was demolished by a group of soldiers under orders from the city architects in August 1817.

But knocking down a church of such great age, a symbol of the very spirit Muscovites had suffered to protect, was not straightforward. As Valuev had discovered ten years before, the Kremlin's buildings had become everyone's business, and after 1812 there was a sense that Moscow's surviving monuments might belong, in part, to its people. The metropolitan, Avgustin, had the solution. A century later, it was to become the tactic of choice when Stalin's young communists had a church to destroy. 'I agree [to the demolition],' the metropolitan wrote, but only on condition that you undertake the work at night and that by morning they have not just demolished it but the site is completely cleared and everything removed so that there should be no indication left that a cathedral was ever there. I know Moscow: if you start knocking something down in the usual way you will not be able to stifle the rumours. You have to take them by surprise and then they all keep quiet.[95]

It was a shrewd, if not exactly democratic, view. Avgustin found, just as the Bolsheviks later would, that a building really could disappear from memory.

The Kremlin as a whole seemed quite complete without the old landmark. To judge by the surviving paintings, the citadel emerged from the age of repair with real elegance, though artists tended to paint out the rubbish-heaps and scaffolding. Most images from this era show the fortress rising white and gold above the city, although at one point the brickwork was actually painted a shocking blood-red.[96] This was definitely a landscape that belonged to the rich and educated, to noblemen and ladies of the better sort. It is through the artists' eyes that we glimpse the well-dressed crowds: the gentlemen with their top hats and shiny canes, the ladies in their bonnets, gloves and crinolines. They could be leading citizens of any European state, and there is little sense of Russia (let alone romantic Muscovy) about their world. What sets them apart is not their nation's history but their present-day wealth. Horse-drawn carriages race past the convent gates while uniformed Kremlin guardsmen stand to attention, swords at their sides. The sense of exclusivity is emphasized by the long stretches of iron railing and the sentry-boxes with their bright diagonal stripes. A watercolour from the 1820s by Osip Bove shows the restored expanse of wall along Red Square, and also (a personal triumph, for he had fought to introduce them) the freshly planted lime-trees round the old ramparts.[97] The fortress had become a place where the elite could promenade. They soon flocked there, sporting their lapdogs and their parasols.

The Russian nation clearly needed something else, not just this theme-park for the leisured rich. The memories of 1812 were everyone's. By all accounts, Alexander himself disliked the story of Moscow's great crisis, preferring to think about his more victorious moments (and especially his entry into Paris, at the head of his troops, in 1814).[98] But tens of thousands of victims, and Moscow's own ashes, were not easily forgotten. In a brief interlude of messianic passion, the emperor allowed himself to be inspired by visions of the Russian people and its mystic sacrifice.[99] In 1813, his court announced a competition for a permanent memorial to the epic of 1812. Significantly, there was no plan to build it in the Kremlin itself; Alexander refused to contemplate such an upheaval. Instead, a site – and an idea – had to be found in Moscow, and to Moscow it would then belong.

Buildings, portrait galleries, fountains, statues and parks were all sketched and discussed, but eventually it was agreed that the central landmark should be a cathedral, a holy building dedicated to Christ the Saviour. The first round of the competition came and went. Preliminary drawings, which ranged from a version of St Peter's basilica to Giacomo Quarenghi's take on the Pantheon in Rome, were soon dismissed.[100] As universalist ideas like these were aired in St Petersburg, however, Moscow's thinking took a nationalist turn. In 1818, a statue to the victors of 1612, Minin and Pozharsky, was installed on Red Square. It had been designed for Kuzma Minin's city, Nizhnyi-Novgorod, but in Moscow it came to stand for a nation that was Orthodox, conservative, and proud.[101] Tellingly, the helmet that the bronze Pozharsky cradled in the crook of his left arm was deliberately based on an original (mistakenly) thought to have belonged to Alexander Nevsky.[102]

In the next few years, the victory over Napoleon would inspire numerous buildings across Russia, including St Petersburg's Kazan Cathedral (which housed the banners captured from French troops and also the keys to many of the cities that the invaders had occupied). But the scheme for Moscow's own shrine continued to stall. The architects, it seemed, were torn between the old 'classical' world and Moscow's new, ultra-Russian, nationalism. In 1817, however, Alexander finally approved a plan to build the cathedral in the universal European (as opposed to an identifiably Russian) manner. The winning entry, by the architect Alexander Vitberg, was scheduled to tower above Moscow from a site on the Sparrow Hills. Vitberg himself described its style as 'Egyptian-Byzantine-Gothic', and though the idea is hard to visualize, his sketchbooks show just what he meant.[103] The building – which would have been vast – included obelisks and columns and a huge Byzantine dome. Its spirit was international, and it was meant to be inclusive rather than purely Slavonic. But tensions built around the project from the first. Though cash was found, and 11,275 unfortunate serf-labourers were assembled for the long task of constructing it, Vitberg's vision was never realized. Alexander I died in 1825. His heir and brother, Nicholas, was never one for universal brotherhood.

The marquis de Custine visited Russia in 1839. Something of a social outcast in France, where his homosexuality had brought censure and considerable personal pain, he was looking for a subject for his real passion: writing. The empire in the east was no longer a provincial outpost; in the aftermath of Napoleon's defeat, most people knew it as an arbiter of European politics. At the same time, its huge size and its untapped power were fascinating. As Ottoman Turkey continued to decline, Russia looked set to take its place, straddling the frontier between Europe and Asia, holding the line between the world of modern comforts and the seething, tempting, maelstrom of the Orient beyond. Like many Europeans of his time, and certainly the French, Custine was hoping to find some first-hand oriental barbarism for his book, and like many other visitors to Russia with that mission, he ended up perplexed.

There were the usual inconveniences. Every traveller to Russia seems fated to describe vast spaces, an extreme climate, and the extraordinary drinking-capacities of the Russian male. In some ways, these, and even the attentions of an ever-watchful state police, were just the things Custine was looking for. He also found much to admire in the new emperor, Nicholas I. This tsar was handsome, if severe; he bore himself as a true despot should, frowning from the strain of responsibility; and though he wore a corset, which Custine deplored, from the neck up he looked noble and even 'rather German than Slavonic'.[104] The singularity of the emperor's power, his absolute but lonely eminence, was mesmerizing. 'If I lived in Petersburg,' Custine remarked, 'I should become a courtier, not from any love of place or power, nor from any puerile vanity, but from the desire of discovering some road that might reach the heart of a man who differs from all others.'[105]

When it came to authentic local colour, however, the foreigner found the court in St Petersburg to be Janus-faced. It had taken a real effort on the part of Peter the Great, of the reformers in the age of Elizabeth and Catherine, but by 1839, when Custine visited the country, Russia was almost as European as it is today. Its businessmen made money out of European trade, its libraries were stocked with European books, and its young nobles travelled just as any other wealthy Europeans might. Even those who stayed at home continued to take whatever they saw fit from Europe, from fashion to technology and even (with explosive results) political ideas. Against this background, Nicholas encouraged Russian nationalism, but his variant on the theme was specific. In 1833, his conservative advisor, Sergei Uvarov, defined Russian nationhood in terms of 'Orthodoxy, Autocracy, Nationality'. 'The trick,' as the musicologist Richard Taruskin has commented, 'was to associate love of country not with love of its inhabitants but with love of the dynastic state.'[106]

Custine accepted the autocratic politics as part of his tourist package (it is a deal that foreign visitors have gone on striking ever since), but what he really revelled in was the official promotion of Russianness. Though it was never more than costly palace make-believe, court life had certainly acquired a nationalist veneer. Flying in the face of decades of sophistication, Nicholas introduced a 'national' dress-code for certain court functions. Mistaking this innovation for something timeless, Custine described the elaborate head-dress that elite women had lately been obliged to wear: 'it is very ancient,' he wrote, 'and gives an air of nobleness and originality to handsome persons'. At the wedding of a royal princess, he was also delighted to observe 'the Russian, that is to say, the Persian, costume of the men'. These people, 'in their long robes and brightly-coloured girdles ... created the illusion of an immense Turkey carpet'.[107] What troubled the visiting Frenchman was not the exotic and alien, but rather the Europeanness of the court: the extent to which, in Catherine the Great's shadow, the 'enrolled and drilled Tatars' aspired to a civilized life. 'I do not reproach the Russians for being what they are,' he explained, 'what I blame in them is, their pretending to be what we are.'

It was a sentiment that some of Russia's own elite were coming to endorse. In an age when every educated citizen was discussing the country's future, a range of thinkers saw salvation in the traditional, the Slavonic, and the Orthodox. Moscow was such people's true spiritual home, and by Custine's time, the city had become a Mecca for conservative historians and philosophers. Among these were the antiquarian Ivan Snegirev, who also worked as a literary censor (one of his projects was to check the Bible for sedition), the artists and restorers Fedor Solntsev and Alexander Veltman, and patrons of theirs from the Golitsyn and Stroganov clans.[108] These people's lives revolved around historical research, religious ritual, and loyal service to their emperor. It was to find their kind of Russia that Custine set off for Moscow.

He was not disappointed on his arrival in the old city. 'The first view of the capital of the Slavonians,' he wrote,

> rising brightly in the cold solitudes of the Christian East, produces an impression that cannot easily be forgotten ... The whole plain is covered with a silver guize. Three or four hundred churches ... present to the eye an immense semi-circle, so that when approaching the city, towards sun-set on a stormy evening, it would be easy to imagine you saw a rainbow of fire.

Even greater thrills awaited in the city's heart:

> The citadel of Moscow is not merely a palace. It is the bulwark of Russia, the revered asylum in which sleep the tutelary saints of the country, it is also the prison of spectres ... In this prodigious creation strength takes the place of beauty, caprice of elegance: it is like the dream of a tyrant, fearful but full of power; it has something about it that disowns the age ... an architecture that has no connection with the wants of modern civilisation: a heritage of the fabulous ages, a gaol, a palace, a sanctuary, a bulwark against the nation's foes, a bastille against the nation, a prop of tyrants, a prison of peoples.[109]

The problem, at least from the romantic point of view, was that Nicholas had plans to bring things up to date. The autocrat had always felt at ease in Moscow. In 1818, while Alexander was still emperor, he had taken over the old Chudov Palace, the building that Kazakov had created for Archbishop Platon in 1776, and rather than moving out of it on his accession, he had extended and adapted it several times. For all his efforts, however, the building, which was now known as the 'Nicholas Palace', was feeling, as he put it, 'inconveniently small'. A new residence was required, especially since he planned to spend more time in the historic city. 'We will show you the new works that we are making in the Kremlin,' Nicholas promised Custine. 'My object is to render the architecture of these old edifices better-adapted to the uses now made of them.'[110] The Frenchman was horrified. 'This is a profanation,' he wrote. 'Were I the Emperor, I would rather raise my palace in the air, than dis-turb one stone of the old ramparts of the Kremlin.'[111]

It was a classic foreigner's misapprehension. Where Custine saw a site as fabulous as old Peking, a treasure-house if not exactly a theme park, Nicholas saw his patrimony, and he also saw a catalogue of disrepair. Since he entirely shared the conservatives' reverence for Muscovy, he did not plan to rebuild in a European style. Russia's ancient architecture, as every Slavophile agreed, embodied the essence of its spirit for the modern age. And that same spirit could be used to build anew, or, as one conservative put it, 'to teach the newest generations about the solidity and moral strength of Russia'.[112] Along with Muscovy, the other model for the builders was Byzantium, for there, surely, lay the ideal image of a strong, Orthodox state, a spiritual empire, the prototype for everything that Russia's governors now wished to counterpose (again) to Popish and Protestant Europe. There was not much of old Byzantium left to copy by the 1830s, but the idea was everything.

The pastiche Russian style that Nicholas admired evoked its adoptive antecedents with a blatant disregard for history or taste. The strident, even xenophobic Russian chauvinism, the Slavophilism, of Nicholas' time was deliberate and selective. It was also an elite pose, the cost of which, in terms of stalled reform, was largely borne by the poor. That pose, however, soon became a habit. The Grand Kremlin Palace was to be one of its most conspicuous monuments, the architectural equivalent of dressing sophisticated (and French-speaking) courtiers in 'national' costumes.

The supervisor of Kremlin buildings, Baron Bode, watched Nicholas take his decision. 'In the autumn of 1837,' he wrote,

> the Emperor came to Moscow. His Majesty having found the ancient palace too ugly and small, walked round it, beginning with the boyars' terrace, where there were plans to build a new great hall. Seeing all the inconveniences of this project, and those of making the throne room larger, the Emperor, coming to the end of the reception rooms, that is to say to the study of the late Empress Mariya Fedorovna, stopped, examined the plans, and gave an order to add to the palace a new great hall [currently the Throne Room or St Andrew's Hall] . . . Meanwhile, it was pointed out to the Emperor that the old [Elizabeth] palace was falling into ruin. This palace had been rebuilt in great haste after the 1812 fire, in 1817, for the arrival of the late Emperor Alexander I . . . After a detailed examination of the ceilings and roofs, the [engineers] were persuaded of the impossibility of guaranteeing the security of the palace in regard to

future fires. It was probably this last that decided the Emperor to have a new palace built, more solid and in greater conformity with the grandeur of the first capital.[113]

The next stage was to find an architect, and though several worked on the palace in the next decade, none would bear a greater responsibility than Konstantin Ton (1794–1881). His name would become synonymous with the pseudo-Byzantine architectural style that epitomized Nicholas I's official nationalism in the middle of the nineteenth century, but Ton was no vulgar Slavophile. He trained in St Petersburg and spent his formative years, in professional terms, working in Europe. By the time he came to Nicholas' attention, he had worked in Paris and also in Rome, where he had helped restore an ancient palace on the Palatine Hill.[114] But Ton knew how to meet the needs of Russia's autocrat. His work in Moscow, which included the majestic railway terminus (1844–51), combined a homage to imagined pasts with all the comforts of modernity. Riurikid Muscovy was a direct inspiration (Ton made a study of its old churches), and more distant antiquity – in its autocratic, Orthodox variant – was conjured by Byzantine domes, an exercise that always called for quantities of gold. Most critics comment that the results lacked the elegance of Moscow's real medieval buildings. One specialist refers to Ton's work as 'a horizontal, earthbound mass', another writes of 'arid grandeur'.[115] But Ton's two greatest buildings were designed to satisfy the tsar's demand for space – and for magnificence – while also celebrating the very past that their construction swept away.

The Grand Palace was not the architect's first Moscow commission, and nor was it the most famous. In 1831, Ton had started work on an alternative Cathedral of Christ the Saviour to commemorate Moscow's 1812. This time, the current emperor approved, and the site, not far along the Moscow river from the Kremlin, was easier to develop than Vitberg's abandoned terrace on the Sparrow Hills. The new building was to be a vast Byzantine-style basilica (some antiquarians preferred to call it 'old Russian'), a monument to the Russian state rather than to Russia's people.[116] Technologies that Ton would hone on Moscow's railway terminus came in particularly handy when the time came to secure the dome. But even this ambitious architect could not devote himself to two monsters at once. For much of the 1840s, his focus shifted from the new cathedral to his palace on the Kremlin hill.

The work was taxing, costly, and boundlessly frustrating. Every contractor wanted to choose his own workmen (Ton himself liked railway engineers), co-ordination was a nightmare, and the costs spiralled from month to month.[117] Nicholas was a problem, too, for he took a maddening interest, demanding frequent reports and giving endless pettifogging orders. Each time poor Ton, who was exposed to every Russian winter chill, missed a few days at work, he felt bound to apologize like a schoolboy.[118] From his base in St Petersburg, Nicholas tried to specify the flooring and the tiles, asked endless technical questions about the heating, and checked the progress of the kitchens and the chimneys and the drains. He was also very keen to track the mounting cost. As Bode carefully explained: 'His Imperial Majesty took a personal involvement in practically every detail, and from the beginning to the end of the works everything was done according to His Imperial Majesty's instructions.'[119]

The central problem was the site itself. Nicholas wanted his palace to stand on the south-west corner of the Kremlin hill, but any building there was always going to impinge on older palace buildings and the churches that formed part of them. A giant office tower in the middle of the Vatican could not have made a bigger splash. Ton's solution was ingenious. He would incorporate selected key structures in his design. Like fragile creatures fossilized in rock, the Faceted Palace, parts of the Terem Palace, and numerous churches – including several of the Kremlin's oldest – were engulfed within the new structure, more or less becoming part of it. The new sections of the palace connected to the old by means of a ceremonial staircase and a domed reception hall. The Saviour in the Forest, the oldest church on Kremlin soil, ended up in a courtyard, with Ton's walls looming over it on three sides. The golden palace of the Moscow tsars was buried underneath St George's Hall, the reserve palace below Ton's new St Andrew's Hall, and the historic boyars' court beneath a hall named for the Order of St Vladimir. An illusion of continuity prevailed. Even the old hanging gardens were remembered by a steamy glasshouse filled with palms. It was a clever approach, but not all visitors were pleased. 'How the Russian committee of taste could have induced themselves to set up an eyesore of such gigantic proportions on so holy a spot,' the earl of Mayo wrote after a visit that took place while the work was still in progress in 1845, 'can only be conceived by those who have mused upon the edifices of Trafalgar Square.'

When it was opened, in 1849, the Grand Kremlin Palace was the largest building on the Kremlin hill, and it remains the most imposing. In that respect, it perfectly embodied the values of its imperial patron, though the aforementioned earl of Mayo cannot have been the only person to think that it looked 'more like a Manchester cotton-factory than the Imperial residence of the sacred Kremlin'.[120] The finished colossus, which cost about twelve million rubles, boasted the largest audience hall that Russia had ever seen, a massive space that was nearly two hundred feet long and three times the size of the Faceted Palace. And this was only one of five such spaces; the place could swallow several separate crowds at once. In addition to these public rooms, the building also included seven hundred private apartments.[121] The most elegant of these, separate from the main residential wing, were reserved for the imperial family itself. The tsar was a great champion of married bliss.

By all accounts, Nicholas was delighted. On the occasion of its formal opening, he described his Kremlin palace as

> a beautiful architectural work, which will be a new ornament for my beloved ancient capital, the more so because it harmonises entirely with the buildings that surround it, and which are sacred to us, as much for the secular memories that are attached to them as for the great events of our national history.[122]

He timed its opening to emphasize that sacredness. The Grand Kremlin Palace was inaugurated in 1849, at Easter, and the emperor and his family made their Easter devotions in the restored Church of the Saviour Behind the Golden Grille, Tsar Aleksei Mikhailovich's favourite place of worship and now physically part of the new building. It was the first time a Russian ruler had spent Easter in Moscow since Paul's coronation in 1797, and the first time that the Saviour Church had been fit to receive such a distinguished party in decades. The new metropolitan was effusive. His sermon explained that,

> Sovereigns, like private individuals, build their houses to have a home that is peaceful, pleasant, suitable for their rank and in conformity with the needs of their social engagements. But these things were not enough for our Tsar, who does not wish to live a life apart, but wishes to live in

complete unity with his people and his empire. He consented to wish that his dwelling should symbolise the Tsar and the Empire and made a Tablet of Commandment or a Book in Stone, where can be read our present grandeur, the venerated memory of the past and an example for the future.[123]

This 'venerated memory', however, turned out to be selective. What Ton's great palace really did was to create a new Kremlin, renovating and giving precedence to sites that were considered important and singularly disrespecting others. Aleksei Mikhailovich's Saviour Church, like several others in the palace, was given a new prominence as well as a more elegant general environment. New roofing was also designed to resist the vexatious leaks. But one of the oldest churches on the Kremlin site, an ancient foundation dedicated to St John the Forerunner, was demolished. With it went a whole chapter of Moscow's pre-Mongol history, as well as many memories of later palace life.

The Church of St John was a fifteenth-century masonry building near the Borovitsky gates. It was not striking in itself, but it may have marked the first religious site on the entire hill. The usual history of fire and redevelopment had altered its original appearance, and even antiquarians were only lukewarm in their praise, but the site, all Muscovites agreed, was sacred. In 1814, during renovations, wooden posts found near the building led to speculation that this had been the site of Peter the Wonder-Worker's Kremlin residence.[124] Ivan Snegirev described it as 'the oldest of churches', and others noted that its festival, St John's Day, coincided with the midsummer feast of Ivan Kupalo, a pagan holy day that Russian folklorists had just begun to rediscover. Everyone's excitement increased after the church's eventual demolition, when bones, including a horse's skull, were found in the deepest layers of earth beneath, suggesting – so the experts hoped – that the place had once seen animal sacrifice.[125]

A young employee in the Kremlin's armoury museum called Ivan Zabelin later recounted what happened. In 1846, Nicholas I, on a visit to inspect the progress of his building work, observed that the old church obscured a particularly lovely view of his new palace from Moscow's Stone Bridge. The bridge was a fixture and the palace his pride, so the church would have to be moved; he left the details to the architects. Only the fear of popular outcry – that lesson from Valuev's day – delayed immediate destruction. But even Baron Bode agreed that the church was too fragile to move intact. Its demolition was approved instead, with plans to transfer the church's sacred objects to a room above the Borovitsky gates. The only other concession offered was that a plaque might one day mark the site where, so the experts all supposed, Muscovites had prayed since their original conversion to the Christian faith.[126]

'When they demolished the church,' Zabelin wrote, 'the view from the other side of the river was even more unsightly. A curved space, wide and empty, opened up on Moscow's most ancient site, between buildings, which, running as they also did along a curve, lacked any kind of regular facade.'[127] Custine was equally dismissive of the grand new style. Although he lacked Zabelin's sense of history, he had the same distaste for new white slabs. He studied the flat surfaces and solid lines on the plans of Ton's palace and concluded, disgustedly, that 'all who preserve any sentiment of the beautiful ought to throw themselves at the feet of the emperor and implore him to spare his Kremlin ... He is destroying the holy ramparts of which the miners of Buonaparte could scarcely disturb a stone.'[128]

8

Nostalgia

The search for an authentic Russia released a new kind of energy. Imported ideas engaged and collided with recovered Russian ones to create the conditions for a cultural golden age. From Alexander Pushkin to Lev Tolstoy, from Glinka to Tchaikovsky, the arts attained an excellence that few in Europe at the time could rival. Whatever Custine might have wanted, too, the creativity was not confined to obviously 'national' themes, and much of it transcended politics and even questions of identity.[1] One branch of late imperial Russian cultural life, however, at least as it developed in Moscow, concerned itself with little else. The nineteenth century was the golden age of Russian history, an age that began with Nikolai Karamzin and ended with the readable, wide-ranging work of Vasily Kliuchevsky (1841–1911). Between the two stood another giant, Sergei Soloviev (1820–79), the author of an encyclopaedic narrative history of Russia in twenty-nine volumes. He had material to write much more, but he died, in mid-sentence, at the age of fifty-nine.[2]

Today, much of this writing has a dated, rather heavy feel. Like Karamzin, Soloviev was the sort of person Josef Stalin later called an archive rat. His output, rapidly produced, makes little enough concession to the reader, while that of his less-talented contemporaries, though full of information, is often genuinely turgid. For years now, hardened Moscow library staff have been shrugging in sympathy as they hand me volumes that have not been ordered, and certainly not read, since well before we were all born. In the second half of the nineteenth century, however, there was something really thrilling in the process of discovery. It was not just that the stories themselves were dramatic (although that certainly helped). The point was that history really mattered. The past, the Russian past, was now the raw material for nationhood, and while a writer of Fedor Dostoevsky's calibre might think of everything in terms of spiritual philosophy, those of a more prosaic stamp needed their facts. In nineteenth-century Moscow, historians were there to help, inspiring readers with the evidence that Russia's entire course on earth – as witness the pre-Petrine past – was sacred, precious and unique.[3]

By definition, systems of dynastic rule must always emphasize their continuity. The Kremlin had been an important witness to that tale – and also a main theatre for state display – for centuries. Even in the heyday of St Petersburg, despite the renunciation of Moscow's customs, dress and calendar, the ancient capital as a whole had played an important role in the idea of Russian nationhood. But as St Petersburg began to breathe the aniline air of Europe's industrial revolution, Moscow came to represent the place where Russia might still be most real.[4] Peter the Great's reforms were not exactly regretted, but nostalgia grew for a Slavic authenticity that many believed to have been lost. In Moscow's salons and, increasingly, in libraries, conservatives reconstructed their collective past as a tale of new Byzantium, Third Rome and holy empire all in one. In the Kremlin, which was one of the movement's most important sites, historians and artists worked together to restore old buildings, establish museums, and get to grips with the archives.

By the second half of the nineteenth century, Moscow had become an epicentre of activities that spanned the disciplines of history, archaeology, architectural preservation and even folklore.[5] Its university hosted the gatherings where papers were read (and provided both Kliuchevsky and Soloviev with their prestigious chairs); its wealthy nobles bought and preserved whole archives, encouraged scholars, and collected art. In 1861, the city took delivery of a treasure-house of books and objects from the deceased Petersburg antiquary Count Nikolai Rumyantsev, and other noble patrons purchased manuscripts that might otherwise have disappeared. Most, in the tradition of aristocrats at any time, were willing to open their collections for (some people's) scholarly research.[6] For artists needing more material support, Moscow was now also home to patrons of a modern kind, the empire's richest and most ruthless merchants and industrial entrepreneurs. The best known was probably the merchant-magnate Pavel Tretyakov, who laid the basis for the city's pre-eminent gallery of native art when he presented Moscow with his collection (and a building in which it could be housed) in 1892.[7]

The extent of cultural change was increasingly reflected in the atmosphere at court. There was a yearning for the purity of former times, which were imagined as an age of pious riches. By the end of the century, God's last anointed tsar, Nicholas II (ruled 1894–1917), had even managed to convince himself that simple people could adore him with a simple love.[8] Nostalgia (the original meaning of the word links it with homesickness) was almost the sum of his politics. In April 1900, Nicholas celebrated Easter in Moscow. He was the first tsar to do so since Nicholas I had opened the Grand Kremlin Palace in 1849, and the occasion was a landmark in his private spiritual life. As he wrote to his mother, he and his consort, Alexandra, 'spent the best part of a day' visiting the Kremlin's holy places and 'deciding which church we shall attend for Morning Service or Mass or Evensong ... We also read a good deal of history about the "Times of Moscow" [i.e. Time of Troubles].' As he added, 'I never knew I was able to reach such heights of religious ecstasy ... I am so calm and happy now.'[9]

The new tsar's Muscovite romance continued. In 1906, the tenth anniversary of his coronation, Nicholas' famous jeweller, Carl Fabergé, created one of the most celebrated of his renowned Easter eggs, based on the Kremlin and its Dormition Cathedral.[10] The charming trinket was the tsar's gift to his consort that year, but it was far from the sum of their nostalgic pleasures. In February 1903, for instance, the couple had presided over an unforgettable Muscovite costume ball at which the guests had all appeared in authentic-looking seventeenth-century robes. As Nicholas noted in his diary, 'the hall looked very pretty filled with ancient Russian people', while one witness described the scene as 'a living dream'.[11] Though Russia teetered on the brink of civil unrest, a series of historic gala jubilees followed throughout the reign, the most spectacular of which was the tercentenary of the Romanov accession in 1913.[12] After a royal progress through the land, this culminated in extended celebrations in the Kremlin.[13] Moscow's loyal historians were ready with a special exhibition to accompany the banquets and the balls, a full-scale celebration of Muscovy that featured 147 rare pre-Petrine icons as well as fabrics, silver and a display of original documents. Many of the items had been loaned from private collections in the city. For the elite, even the bourgeoisie, the celebration of the golden past had turned into a patriotic act.[14]

In general, the past seemed to appeal the most to those who feared prospective change. The nineteenth century is often associated with the stress and transition that produced such radicals as Alexander Herzen (1812–70), Mikhail Bakunin (1814–76), and Georgy Plekhanov (1856–1918), respectively the founders of Russian socialism, anarchism and the Russian Marxist movement. By the 1900s, Russia could boast several different brands of revolutionary party, numerous would-be political assassins, and a fledgling trade-union movement. At the time, few of Moscow's more prosperous types – its notaries and professors, its businessmen with their new money and hand-rolled cigars – spared much thought for the greasy youths and home-made bombs. Almost none had heard of communism, and most thought of revolution as a horror once inflicted on the French. There were many – including several historians – who regarded the impulse to commit acts of terror as a kind of psychological illness.[15] But the injustice and inflexibility of tsarist rule unquestionably drove enlightened Russian citizens to near-despair, and hardship was a real spur to clandestine, illegal, labour organization.

On Moscow's streets, however, and in the basement rooms where people lived without cigars, the talk was seldom about revolution, let alone Karl Marx. The city's population boomed, increasing by 65 per cent in the decade after 1861 and comfortably exceeding a million by 1902.[16] The newcomers who hung around the taverns, markets and pavement stalls might have been poor, but most could still afford cheap souvenirs.[17] Old photographs – the Russians loved them – show turn-of-the-century crowds against a city lined with shops and signage, and folklore and history are suddenly everywhere. Some of the posters and advertisements bore images derived from fairy-tales (the water-spirit, *rusalka*, was popular), and some showed landmarks like St Basil's and the Sukharevka Tower, but the Kremlin was a recurrent, an inescapable, motif. It featured in picture-postcards, magazine-covers, and on the lids of decorative chocolate-boxes. It also turned up on thousands – millions – of icons. By the 1890s, the workshops in Palekh and Mstiora were turning these out like bars of soap; the craftsmen in a single village (Kholmy) could produce as many as two million in a year, and they soon began using the Kremlin's image as a shorthand for holy Russia.[18] As time went on, the fortress also started to feature on mass-produced scarves and postage stamps, on printed calendars and the covers of souvenir theatre programmes.[19] Russian style had, in effect, become a brand, and the Kremlin was its instantly recognizable trademark.

*

That style, however, was a nineteenth-century invention. It drew on early works of art, the products of an age as yet unsullied by the neo-classical revolution, it drew on Russia's scattered churches, peasant costumes, and icons from a range of different schools, but the nineteenth century's achievement was to interpret and synthesize these diverse, eclectic, and not always truly Russian objects into an entirely novel artistic idiom. Distinguished by a weakness for the onion dome and *kokoshnik* (the decorative Russian corbel arch), the fashion was far from austere. Magpie-like, its exponents collected everything from peasant woodcarvings to drinking-cups, and that was where the treasures of the Kremlin played their role. Largely untouched, and often prey to mice and rot, the relics of pre-Petrine Muscovy that the fortress contained had been little more than lumber for a century; at best they made a collection of random curiosities. The process of their rediscovery took decades. But in the end, a neglected assortment of icons and decorative weaponry, a trove of awkward, heavy ceremonial regalia, and the motifs in a set of semi-ruined buildings emerged as the inspiration for a nation's cultural revival. Elaborate and faintly exotic, its colours, shapes and lettering have gone on symbolizing Russia, to itself and others, ever since.

The objects in the Armoury Chamber had swum into official view on several occasions since the days of Peter the Great. As early as 1755, a palace official called Argamakov had argued for the creation of a permanent exhibition space. But it was only in 1801, when Alexander I, on the eve of his coronation, began to take an interest that the condition of the Kremlin collection attracted any serious concern.[20] It turned out that there were thousands of objects, almost jumble, in the Kremlin's various strongrooms. Icons were more or less familiar, but the original purpose of some of the rest remained a puzzle. An eye-catching golden ewer, the metal twining round a large exotic shell, was one such mystery, but even the more familiar objects could be difficult to identify precisely.[21] The collection included elaborate religious vestments, not least some pearl-encrusted mitres from the seventeenth century, but then there were the jewelled tankards and court plate, drinking-vessels adorned with niello work, quantities of swords and bows, saddles, harness and decorated horse-armour. None of this had been examined for decades. Some things were literally falling to pieces.

As soon as the collection had been noticed by St Petersburg, questions started to be raised. One thorny issue was the cost of curatorial staff. Their numbers, the accountants saw, seemed to have mushroomed even as the collection continued to decay. The supervisor of all Kremlin works, tidy-minded Petr Valuev, promptly reorganized both staff and treasure, though he thought that all 'useless' objects should be sold.[22] It fell to others to see the real value in the old robes and the tarnished swords. One hopeful theory, proposed by no less a person than the president of St Petersburg's Academy of Arts, Aleksei Olenin (1763–1843), was that a true study of such objects would reveal the classical (i.e. European) origins of medieval Russian culture, establishing a long-lost link to Europe's common ancestors in Greece and Rome.[23] It was a tempting idea at the time, and in 1806 the tsar commanded that the remaining objects in the Armoury and associated workshops should be put in order pending more investigation.[24]

Olenin worked in the collection from 1807, joining a small group of other experts and enthusiasts, and the first catalogue, prepared by A. F. Malinovsky, was published that same year. The task of establishing the authenticity of anything was complicated by the eagerness of wealthy patriots who proffered items from their own strongrooms, and even by a few donations from public-spirited peasants, who came to Moscow bringing objects they had turned up in their masters' fields.[25] In 1810 the architect I. V. Egotov completed a special building, in the finest neo-classical style, to house it all. Valuev assumed the role of curator, a task he fulfilled with his usual energy.[26] But the collection's troubles continued. First came the panic and last-minute packing as Napoleon advanced; the treasures that came back from Nizhnyi-Novgorod in 1814 had been so roughly handled that some of the most delicate items, including fabrics and porcelain, had been damaged beyond repair.[27] To compound the losses, a good number of smaller items, including collections of rare manuscripts (and also including Karamzin's own archive), had disappeared when Moscow burned.

The destruction was catastrophic – by 1814 the palace collection must have felt like the salvage from some great shipwreck – but Napoleon's invasion of the homeland inspired a new respect for the legacy of old Russia. People might not know quite what an object was, let alone how best to place it in context, but a new sense that Russia had its own art, in style and spirit different from that of Europe, was detectable at court and among some intellectuals. The accession of Nicholas I in 1825 was not untroubled, sparking a failed revolt by disaffected members of the Russian intelligentsia, but that, too, gave an impetus to patriots. The emperor harnessed their enthusiasm in his political programme, encouraging Russian-centred art and style at court as eagerly as he bore down upon dissent. The precise story of this Russianness, however, was a problem that forced Nicholas to take advice, especially from his court antiquarians. It was confusing enough to have to deal with unintelligible script, for Old Russian was almost Greek to Nicholas' generation. But there were also tough questions to be answered about provenance; unless there was crystal-clear documentation, it was almost impossible to determine the date of anything.

Nicholas was not a scholar, and his interest was always pragmatic. Faced with this collection of treasures, whose use and origin were often unknown, his priority remained the promotion of official nationality, and to that end he needed someone who could interpret the past. Olenin knew exactly whom to recommend. In the 1830s, he encouraged his emperor to hire the award-winning artist Fedor Solntsev (1801–92) to explore and record the Kremlin collection.[28] In later life, Solntsev would recollect that his commission had been to document Russia's 'ancient customs, dress, weaponry, church and imperial accoutrements, everyday objects, and archaeological and ethnographic information' from the sixth to the eighteenth centuries.[29] His execution of that mammoth project (if not his actual name) would soon be famous, and it still shapes most people's idea of 'real' Russian style.

Solntsev's work was not confined to copying; the tsar additionally commissioned him to create a series of Russian motifs to decorate a new 'Kremlin' porcelain dinner service comprising five hundred settings. The work took sixteen years to complete (the final pieces were fired in 1847), but the service was spectacular, and would be used whenever the court wanted a Russian nationalist theme, most notably at the Romanov tercentenary in 1913.[30] A second service, this time for Nicholas' son, Grand Duke Konstantin Nikolaevich, was fired later in the 1840s. For both commissions Solntsev drew on his explorations in the Kremlin, and though some of the objects that he copied had been made by foreign masters in the tsar's employ (or, at least, by Russians working under instruction from Germans, Scots and Persians), the porcelain became a landmark of national art. A whole series of Kremlin plates, for instance, followed seventeenth-century designs, while the distinctive shape of the so-called 'Alexander Nevsky' helmet (which had, ironically enough, been made at a nostalgic moment in the reign of the first Romanov tsar) was recycled to inspire the lid of Grand Duke Konstantin's new coffee-pot.[31]

In 1834, a very busy Solntsev was also charged with the renovation of a suite of rooms associated with Mikhail Romanov in the old part of the Kremlin palace.[32] The *terema* became – and still remain – a showcase for his new, imagined, version of the past. The colours on the walls and tiles were deep and rich, the patterns intricate, organic, as if inspired by the meadow-flowers in a Russian fairy-tale. Some of the design was authentic (Solntsev retrieved and copied anything that had survived), but much was improvised, and some relied on flights of creative imagination. The furniture, for instance, included Solntsev's copies of pieces rescued from Kolomenskoe, but the heavily draped beds – never a feature of the real *terema* – had no historical connection to the chambers where they were to stand. The colour-scheme, favouring deep red and green, was also chosen to evoke the romantic feel that Solntsev wanted.[33]

In all, the restoration, which also involved architects like Ton and F. F. Rikhter, was almost as creative as a brand-new design. By indulging a fantasy, the artist and his allies were making a sort of fake (in this regard, Solntsev has been likened to Britain's Augustus Pugin and France's Eugène Viollet-le-Duc).[34] But that fake was immensely influential, and it remains, for most, the closest they will ever get to a sense of the Muscovite past. Another outcome was the rediscovery – in many ways, the reinvention – of the Kremlin as a work of art. This coincided with a wider acceptance of native landscape, for by the 1850s even Russia's aristocracy had begun to accept that the silver birches that grew everywhere on their estates could be as scenic as any cypress-grove in Italy.[35]

The Kremlin became a treasure-house for the resurgent culture. Russians were used to looking at classical and fine European art, but now they could take pride in every home-grown masterpiece. When the final book in Solntsev's most extensive collection of watercolours, the six-volume *Antiquities of the Russian State*, appeared in 1853, it marked a watershed in art appreciation and in taste, and most of the objects it showed were treasures from the Kremlin Armoury. Here was the famous fur-trimmed Cap of Monomakh, but here, too, were the details of embroidered fabrics, the handles of swords, lamp-holders, coach-work, decorative saddlery. The colours were brilliant and clear, featuring red, gold, emerald and ultramarine. In Solntsev's hands, each venerable piece had acquired a perfection so dazzling that it banished any lingering thought of cultural inferiority, let alone mildew.[36]

In reality, however, moth and fungus were making fresh inroads into the collection even as Solntsev worked. The culprit was the 1810 museum building itself. Egotov, fearing fires, had deliberately built it without stoves, and by the 1830s the pervasive damp looked set to destroy whatever the mice and Napoleon had overlooked. Such ravages were intolerable in the age of Russian nationalism, so Nicholas I approved a project for an entirely new museum. The site that was identified, beside the Borovitsky gates, allowed Konstantin Ton to build it as an annex to the Grand Palace.[37] The new building shared the same style, the same solidity, and (like the palace) it occupied a site of unique archaeological significance. That site, sadly, was surveyed and excavated in haste, and if there had once been an ancient road or hermit's cave underneath it, Moscow was never to find out. Nor would local antiquarians get the chance to explore the ruins of Godunov's palace, the last major building to have stood there.[38] Another disappointment came in 1851, when the staff in Ton's new Armoury Chamber museum discovered that no provision had been made in it for conservation work. They were already feeling underpaid, but now the only space where they could clean, repair or study their objects was in a basement of the adjoining Grand Palace.[39]

If anything, when the museum was finished, the Kremlin felt more like the exclusive property of the Russian tsars than it had ever done. Experts who worked there often arrived to find the building locked without notice.[40] As for the public, entrance was limited, mainly, to Muscovites and special, pre-vetted, guests. A fairly liberal system was introduced under Nicholas I's successor, Alexander II (ruled 1855–81), but from the 1880s the palace imposed firmer controls. Entry-tickets could be obtained only from the police administration, and the procedure would have made today's restrictions appear light. In 1914, potential visitors had either to provide proof that they lived in Moscow or, if they were not locals, to apply in writing (to a separate office in a different building) two weeks in advance of any planned visit.[41] The museum's opening hours – 10 a.m. till 2 p.m. three days a week between September and May – limited visits even more. Despite all this, the Palace and Armoury together received an annual average of about a quarter of a million visitors in the last years of tsarism.[42]

For foreigners, the rules were different, and showed how closely Russia's newly created nationalism was connected to the official Orthodox Church. When a selection of the Armoury's treasures was earmarked for display at the Paris Exposition of 1867, the Russian authorities refused to allow the items to travel, pleading that sacred objects should not be treated as exhibits for the vulgar gaze.[43] The Paris public had to be content with a set of drawings. It had been fine to sell some pieces of the same trove sixty years before, and it was not unusual to find an item mouldering in basement rooms, but foreigners, even curators and specialists, could not examine anything unless they made the effort to present themselves to the Moscow police.

For those who managed to procure their ticket, however, the Armoury offered glimpses of another world. It was a Romanov family collection, the private property of a royal dynasty, and that lent it an eclectic and unbalanced air. Indeed, it was not even quite complete, for in 1858 Alexander II ordered that some of the objects, selected silver plate and furniture, should be removed to furnish a museum-project of his own, the restored house of the Romanov boyars on nearby Varvarka street.[44] Some other gaps were suspiciously like unsolved crimes: small gems, pocket-sized ones, were rarer than the massive, famous jewels that could never have been sold. Weapons and transport featured prominently (a whole room was devoted to ceremonial coaches), but there was little trace of any routine palace life, especially that of royal women. A room was set aside for Bazhenov's extravagant model Kremlin, an object that was fast becoming the white elephant that it still remains, and beside it stood the older model of the palace at Kolomenskoe, a relic of Muscovy that now seemed closer to the nation's heart. The most glamorous attractions were the celebrated gems, including the royal regalia. Two rooms held these – there was a special case just for the Cap of Monomakh – and visitors could also view the coronation robes. To these were added diplomatic gifts, including unique inlaid thrones from Isfahan, one made for Boris Godunov, the other for Alexei Mikhailovich, a carriage given by England's King James I, and the finest collection of Tudor English silver in the world.[45]

Despite the new level of interest, the Kremlin was hardly a public institution and certainly not a museum. Its fate depended on decisions made at court, in St Petersburg, and on whatever budget the administration there could spare.[46] Fortunately, three out of Russia's five nineteenth-century emperors harboured a real fondness for Moscow, and even the reforming Alexander II, who was born in the Kremlin's Nicholas Palace in 1818, referred to the city (which he did not like) as 'my native land'.[47] The years of ivy-covered neglect were coming to an end. 'As Moscow is the heart of Russia,' a guidebook of 1856 solemnly explained, 'so the Kremlin is not only the heart and soul of our white-stone Moscow, but also the seed from which our Russian Tsarism has grown.'[48] The piety was genuine, but it was fast becoming an anachronism. Europe was changing, and even white-stone Moscow would not stand aloof. Eighteen fifty-six was the year when Henry Bessemer's new steel process promised to revolutionize manufacturing across the world. The tale of humanity itself was being rewritten. Just outside Düsseldorf, near Erkrath, some workers had just found parts of a skull that later formed the standard for Neanderthals. Three years later, in 1859, Charles Darwin was to publish his shattering book, *On the Origin of Species by Means of Natural Selection.*

However hard conservatives might try, there was no way to hold back an advance of progress on this scale. In the age of steam, a political system that was based on coercion and political repression, even one that was oiled by regular doses of Holy Russian sentiment, could only overheat and stall. The more thoughtful members of Russia's political class had grasped this by the reign of Alexander I, and in 1855 the death of his obstructive successor, Nicholas I, opened the way to limited change. The greatest single measure of reform (whose fiftieth anniversary, in 1911, was one jubilee that the Romanovs chose to ignore) came six years later, in 1861. When he succeeded his father, Alexander II had made it clear that he intended to abolish the institution of serfdom. It was a reasonable, almost irresistible, decision, long-discussed. It was taken at a time when slavery was being challenged across the civilized world. Predictably, too, conservatives were appalled. In Russia's case it looked as if their cause had been betrayed by the sovereign himself. 'Woe to Russia,' wrote one Moscow-based historian, 'if it knocks this pillar away of its own accord and breaks the centuries-old bonds of reciprocal benefit.'[49] If Karamzin had lived, he would have written much the same. 'Serfs can be liberated,' he had once quipped, 'as soon as it is possible for wolves to be fully fed while sheep remain uninjured.'[50]

In fact, the emancipation manifesto was limited, complex and cautious, a far cry from the principled stand of anti-slavery campaigners in the English-speaking world. But the end of serfdom constituted an epic break with the past, and it was followed by a programme of important further change. In the next few years, Alexander II signed laws providing for limited local government, extended education provision and far-reaching legal reform, including jury trials. He might have gone yet further if the political mood had not been soured (to put it mildly) by an attempt on his life in the spring of 1866. Already depressed by the death of his eldest son, the heir-apparent Nikolai Aleksandrovich, the previous year, a shocked Alexander II now began to rely almost exclusively on a conservative clique of advisors.[51] The next fifteen years were punctuated by explosions, shots and the ring of hammers on hangmen's scaffolds. But this repressive war on terror proved futile, and in March 1881, despite the efforts of his spies, the emperor, now in his early sixties, was blown to pieces by a bomb laid for his carriage as it travelled through St Petersburg. It took him several hours to die, and the scene (especially the blood) haunted the shocked imaginations of his loyal subjects everywhere. The royal family itself could scarcely bear to speak of it.

Alexander II's heir, Alexander III, never forgot that he owed his throne to his father's agony. He was an uncompromising reactionary, and his reign was to be one long tale of arrests, forced emigration and penal exile, censorship, hypocrisy, and the pervasive use of informers. But it began with a coronation. The event was delayed until the spring of 1883, and the interval allowed the palace craftsmen to adapt the setting to new tastes. Since Peter the Great's reign, the Faceted Palace (which had at times done service as a theatre) had been whitewashed inside, lined with fabric and hung with classical medallions.[52] In preparation for his coronation feast, Alexander commissioned a group of icon-masters from Palekh to restore the interiors 'to the old appearance that they had in ancient times'. The team, led by the Belousov brothers, toiled for months, working largely from Ushakov's seventeenth-century drawings, and though the results lacked subtlety (they remind me of the pre-Raphaelite Brotherhood's pastiche medievalism), the lines of old-time princes and boyars certainly evoked the saintly era of dynastic rule.[53] The diners who gathered inside on the coronation afternoon sat among richly painted walls. In the centre of the room, they could admire the tiers of shelves that groaned, as in the distant past, with antique gold and silver from the Kremlin hoard. Outside, there were no Latinate triumphal gates, and even the lavish commemorative album from the occasion had an elaborately Russian, not classical, graphic design.[54]

The timing of the coronation coincided with the opening (at last) of the Cathedral of Christ the Saviour. As a monument to the redemptive power of the people's sacrifice in 1812, Ton's vast shrine might, in other circumstances, have seemed to challenge the Kremlin's dominance of Moscow's sky. It housed important relics from the war, and its walls bore a carved list of the names of the fallen. The building could accommodate 10,000 people, and its cupola, an unsung miracle of nineteenth-century engineering, was higher even than the landmark bell tower of Ivan the Great. The original plan for the cathedral's gala opening was to have involved cannon, trumpets, and the premiere of Tchaikovsky's 1812 overture. But Alexander II's assassination forced a delay, and even a rethinking of the symbolism. On 30 May 1883, as the new imperial family and the lines of ministers and priests processed from the Dormition Cathedral to Ton's building and back, it was clear that, in this new age of reaction, the cathedral's role would be to extend the dynasty's imperious reach along the river, consuming Moscow's public space in the service of autocracy.[55] Years after his death, on 30 May 1912, a colossal statue of Alexander III was unveiled at the top of the cathedral steps. Nicholas II and his wife (in a delightful white toilette, complete with parasol) were there to watch, and so were all the priests and advisors, but as the monster loomed above the crowds, glaring at Moscow and the Kremlin from its massive throne, it looked as if the city had been conquered by a giant.[56]

By then, however, the Kremlin had acquired a giant of its own to even out the competition. Today, the most famous monument to the assassination of Alexander II is in St Petersburg. Alexander III commissioned the shrine, now known as the Church of the Saviour of Spilled Blood, in 1883, and it was built in an uncompromisingly nostalgic (for which read pastiche) neo-Russian style, complete with colourful mosaic panels and the standard-issue onion domes. But while St Petersburg endured years of disruption during the construction of that (and still endures the finished building), Moscow's elite found its own way of commemorating the murdered tsar. S. N. Tretyakov, the brother of the art-collector, took the initial lead, and it was his idea that any monument should stand near the Kremlin palace where Alexander II had been born. The site of the old *prikazy* looked just right, and then a ground survey added an appropriate *frisson* by turning up hundreds of skeletons, suggesting hurried burial, perhaps during a Mongol raid.[57] This bloody precedent was a good start, but though it sanctified the site it did not help much with the future monument's design. Statues were not in keeping with the old Kremlin, and Alexander had never been a robes and candles man. In the end, it took three competitions and a lot of argument to settle on a winner, by which time the project – which those involved seemed to treat as a spiritual test – had taken on grotesque dimensions.[58] It had also acquired a royal patron in the shape of Alexander III's own brother, the pious, prim and reactionary Grand Duke Sergei Aleksandrovich, who became governor-general of Moscow in the spring of 1891.

The first stone for the Kremlin monument to Alexander II was laid, to the sound of bells and a full 133-gun salute, on 14 May 1893 (the buried skulls, meanwhile, were borne off quietly to Moscow University). Five and a half years and just under two million rubles later, in August 1898, the finished structure was opened by the new tsar, Nicholas II. Towering above the Moscow river, especially when illuminated at night, its centrepiece was a bronze statue of the murdered emperor roughly four times natural size. Leading up to that was an open-air gallery lined with 152 columns, a pointless space that Muscovites were quick to dub 'the bowling-alley'. Pink granite from Finland completed the ensemble, which even the most sheepish members of Moscow's intelligentsia were known to hate. Inside, meanwhile, the theme was romantically historical. A team of artists had created a mosaic cycle within the colonnade to lead visitors through nine hundred years of supposedly continuous Russian history. The starring roles were played by thirty-three officially approved rulers from Vladimir to Nicholas I and finally – glancing outside – by Alexander II himself.[59] The main inscription on the façade ran: 'To Alexander II with the love of the people.'[60]

Strangely, once they had lived with it for a few months, large numbers of ordinary Muscovites seem genuinely to have made the Alexander monument part of their lives. It was secular and accessible, and the view from the top was great. The paved space underneath the colonnades became a favourite for ladies seeking to enjoy the sights and also for the gentlemen who idled round to wait for them. Thousands of humbler mortals treated the mosaics as a useful introduction to their nation's history, or at least as a place to take their visitors when the weather was wet. One of Moscow's nimbler textile factories cashed in, and began marketing a woven headscarf that featured the monument (in red, on a cream ground) surrounded by a tasteful greenish border composed of the royal portraits rendered as a series of medallions.[61]

This comfortable version of the past grew ever more alluring as the pace of economic change increased. As Moscow's population boomed, and new smokestacks and loud machines intruded on its calm, the attractions of nostalgia grew ever more powerful. So did the threat to the people's sense of Russianness from endless tempting foreign goods and brash ideas. The Kremlin itself was not safe. In 1893, a citizen called Kozhevnikov drew attention to the citadel's poor state compared with the Upper Trading Rows (now known commonly as GUM), the glass and iron palace that now challenged it across Red Square. With so much building going on, so much regeneration, the Kremlin urgently cried out for help; its renovation, Kozhevnikov wrote in an essay published in the journal *Russian Archive*, amounted to 'the sacred duty of sons before their fathers'. 'To become what they should be,' he continued, 'the Kremlin walls should not be whitewashed, nor painted, but they should be artistically decorated with hand-painted illustrations ... all around and from top to bottom ... showing scenes from the drama of Russia's history.' The themes proposed were patriotic: Russia's heroic stand at the crossroads of the continents, its history of holy struggle and its war against infidels, Asians, and (wrote Kozhevnikov) the 'armies of fanatical Islam'.[62] The idea seems outlandish now, but at the time there would have been a stampede if an artist had been called upon to do the job. The pack might well have been led by two brothers, Victor and Apollinary Vasnetsov (1848–1926 and 1856–1933 respectively), whose work in these years included paintings, ceramics, carved wood and even architectural designs that gave the nation just the Muscovy it seemed to want.[63]

Real Kremlin life was no romance, but nor was it in keeping with the new commercial frenzy out on Moscow's streets. The pace of life had slowed in the fortress since the building of St Petersburg. By 1909, the Chudov Monastery, which at its height had been home to three hundred monks and their servants, housed only seventy-two men, of whom twenty-three were non-religious palace staff.[64] The Ascension women's monastery had declined in the same way; by 1917 its complement had dwindled to just fifty-one.[65] Both institutions had been forced to find new ways of generating revenue since their heydays, the men by selling candles, holy books and consecrated bread, the women by weaving palm crosses and making artificial flowers for sale.[66] Meanwhile, though ceremonies for the tsars were still magnificent (and the Synod choir, which sang in the Dormition Cathedral, remained a wonder of Moscow's cultural life), the daily services in many Kremlin churches were perfunctory. 'The service was crude,' one visitor recalled after attending vespers in 1911, 'the deacons and the singers had the most disagreeable bass voices, the church was empty and dark, and the whole thing had a most disagreeable effect on me.'[67]

Outside the confines of the church, on land where weeds and even full-sized trees had lately grown, a dull parade-ground order now ruled almost everywhere. Though visitors, if decently attired, were permitted to stroll about the hill by day, Cathedral Square itself was enclosed by railings and guarded by a row of sentry-boxes. All gateways and main thoroughfares were locked at night. The guards belonged to the permanent palace staff, all of whom were carefully screened for deviant political views. The other residents included policemen and grenadiers, but the Kremlin's full-time population also numbered several doctors and architects, a midwife, and at least seven accountants. An army of servants (known, to their own well-documented discomfort, as 'lackeys'[68]) completed the population. Many lived on the site itself – there were about two hundred such official residents in 1905 – but conditions were modest (few occupied more than one small room) and the atmosphere could be more or less subtly oppressive. Even occasional overnight visitors were watched and sometimes subject to arrest.[69]

The staff themselves led languid, even boring, working lives. In 1862, Sofiya Behrs, the daughter of a resident palace doctor, held her wedding in a Kremlin church. The groom was Lev Tolstoy, who later used the scene (complete with his embarrassing last-minute search for a clean shirt) when he described Kitty and Levin's marriage ceremony in his novel *Anna Karenina*. Like the fictional Kitty, the real Sofiya had spent the entire day in tears, but she managed to control herself in the presence of 'a great many strangers, palace employees mostly' who gathered round to watch. As Tolstoy put it, 'Those who had arrived too late to get into the middle of the throng pressed round the windows, pushing and disputing and trying to peer in between the bars.'[70] There was normally so little for such people to do that when the imperial family needed to accommodate large numbers of important guests (as they might on almost any state occasion), the Kremlin's less important residents – whole families – were obliged to vacate their rooms, sometimes for months at a time.[71] 'Kremlin life is oppressive,' Tolstoy's new wife reflected on a return visit to her parents' apartment. 'It evokes the oppressive, lazy, aimless life I led here as a girl.'[72]

The circumstances were not conducive to determined effort. It must have felt quite strange to quit the city for the Kremlin's tranquil squares, nod at the sentry, and to step inside the Armoury archive. The building was magnificent, a blaze of gold; the ill-lit desks, by contrast, narrow, cluttered and austerely functional. And yet the nineteenth century's nationalist historians could not keep away from the fortress, for besides its gems and lavish gold, the Armoury's other major treasure was its store of documents. The majority of these papers had started life in Muscovite *prikazy*, and had been shifted, like unwanted baggage, from shelf to store to strongroom as the Kremlin landscape changed. The collections included account-books and treaties, details of fire legislation, and the names of every foreign worker in the Kremlin's hire. The paperwork was incomplete – parts of the archive had burned and other documents had disappeared in the many government reorganizations of Romanov times – but this was raw material for real professional research. While lackeys next door in the palace rubbed a languid thumb across the silver spoons, a new team of historians began to write.

They did not get to work in special light or pull on clean white gloves. They were not like the specialists who use archives today, and they tended to share a particular outlook and cast of mind. The older generation was represented by Ivan Snegirev (1792–1868), historian, ethnographer, official censor and arch-conservative. A professor in Moscow by the 1830s, his output included historical accounts of famous monuments, among them several of the Kremlin churches, and news of his efforts soon reached as far as London's British Museum. Snegirev took great delight in decoding the documents that wealthy patrons could not read ('they say the writing of the seventeenth century looks like shorthand,' he wrote in 1841[73]), and used that skill to open doors into the lost world of pre-Petrine tsars.

As his diaries show, however, Snegirev's was a spiritual, not merely scientific quest. He was a regular attender at both the Chudov Monastery and the Dormition Cathedral, and his love of dusty papers was part of his deep religious faith. He read and wrote, in other words, in search of the imagined city, saint-filled and still untouched by Europe, that had produced the art and religion he loved. Beyond the church, his circle included many of Russia's conservative patriots as well as the cream of artistic Moscow. He spent evenings in the company of the writers Sergei Glinka and Ivan Turgenev, he dogged Fedor Solntsev round the Kremlin, and he lectured Konstantin Ton about the building he was planning to erect. The writer Alexander Veltman (1800–70), later curator of the Armoury Museum, became a friend, as did the noblemen – mainly Golitsyns – who sponsored Snegirev by buying ancient manuscripts for him to decipher. His wife, however, was no admirer of his monkish tastes, and in return he found her wild and vulgar, even slightly mad. On a day-to-day basis, he took refuge in libraries. 'I got on with my own affairs,' the historian wrote in January 1843, 'which my wife greatly obstructed.'[74]

As well as cultivating the elite, Snegirev used his influence to encourage talent and attract new minds to his projects. Among his protégés was a penniless young man from Tver called Ivan Zabelin (1820–1908). In 1837, when the latter was forced to abandon his studies for lack of funds, Snegirev took him on to work with documents in the newly accessible Kremlin archives. In compensation for his meagre pay, the youth was given rooms in the Cavalry Building behind the Kremlin palace, and he took the opportunity to immerse himself in the lives of dead Muscovite tsars. He would give his best years to that subject, though he also led successful archaeological expeditions to the Crimean steppe.[75] Snegirev approved Zabelin's first publication, an article based on Kremlin papers, in 1842. Exactly twenty years later the younger man completed his first masterpiece, a study of the seventeenth-century Kremlin called *The Home Life of the Muscovite Tsars*.

Snegirev and his protégé lived in a world apart from liberal reforms and revolutionary politics. For Snegirev, patriotism was a holy duty almost indistinguishable from religious service. In 1855, for instance, on the day after the death of Nicholas I, while the bells rang and the cannon boomed above the shocked, clamouring crowd, Snegirev joined a select group of Moscow's elite in the Kremlin's Chudov Monastery to hear the imperial succession manifesto. The sombre mood there was far more to his taste than a noisy crush among the mob. 'It is remarkable,' he noted, 'that Nicholas I died on the very same day and hour (Friday at noon) that Christ suffered for us when He was on the cross.'[76] It did not matter that the late tsar was a prig, nor that he had demolished large parts of a building Snegirev revered. A loyal subject was supposed to view the dead ruler with religious awe.

Zabelin's patriotism was much less spiritual in tone. He was no lover of Nicholas I, and wrote accusingly about the damage that the emperor had caused with his ugly Kremlin palace and the botched repairs. As the son of poor parents, he greeted the emancipation of the serfs in 1861 with tears of joy, although he then stopped short of any further liberal demands.[77] Like Snegirev, however, he certainly believed that Russia was a nation with a destiny. His pet hates were the student radicals, the future gravediggers of tsarism. He also condemned the substantial band of émigrés who wrote critically about Russia from the comfort of western European cities. Citing a Russian proverb, he observed that 'you must not carry arguments out of the hut'. But the concepts that had done the most to pollute national life, in his view, had originated among the tsar's Polish Catholic subjects, a large minority in the empire with strong connections to Europe. 'Freedom, independence, self-reliance, self-government,' he wrote disparagingly in 1861, 'this is the miasma of our ideas at the moment, like an epidemic.'[78]

Chauvinism like this was the hidden poison in neo-Russian thought. A search for cultural purity could easily go wrong, a love for all things Russian degrade into resentment of the foreign and the unfamiliar. The canker of anti-Semitism had established itself all over nineteenth-century Europe, but in Russia the wildest spores were deliberately cultivated. Indeed, the Russian version was so unapologetic that in 1891 Alexander III's brother, Grand Duke Sergei Aleksandrovich, felt able to demand that Moscow should be cleared of Jews as a precondition for his acceptance of the post of governor-general in the city. Even more surprisingly, perhaps, the city authorities were willing to comply, and in 1891–2 two-thirds of Moscow's Jewish population were driven from their homes by local police. More than 15,000 people were forced to survive on the roads, dependent on the fragile mercy of provincial life.[79] It was a strange way to attempt to win the people's loyalty and love, but a caste of Muscovite chauvinists approved. Zabelin was more imaginative (compared with the grand duke this was not saying much), but in

1905, when his beloved Moscow dissolved into violent revolution, the old man blamed the 'eternal Jew [*vechnyi zhid*] with his intrigues', and notably 'the Jewish [*zhidovskie*] newspapers'. In private, Nicholas II had decided that 'nine-tenths of the trouble-makers are Jews',[80] and Zabelin (independently) agreed. 'We have had the Pechenegs,' he noted in his diary, 'the Polovtsians, the Tatars, the Poles, a score of different Europeans under the leadership of the enlightenment French. Now we have the revolutionary invasion of the Jews . . . presenting the Russian people as the most worthless of the worthless.'[81]

This was taking nostalgia into the realms of deep despair: fomenting hatreds, abusing history and building false, murderous, pride. But at this time its very intolerance actually added to the appeal of Russian style, at least in conservative circles. The nationalist movement is difficult to like, but in the nineteenth century's final decades it seemed no more abhorrent, to most people, than Russia's own version of England's Arts and Crafts movement. By 1900, the taste for so-called 'Russian revival', for the shapes and forms of Muscovite high art and recovered folklore, was influencing everything from painting and architecture to journalism, literature and textile-design. As the chairman of the Moscow Society of Architects complained in 1910, 'material from the past' exerted such a hold on the national imagination that it was all but impossible to say 'a new original word'.[82]

The first Imperial Russian Archaeological Society was founded in 1846, by the grace of the emperor, Nicholas I, in St Petersburg. Moscow followed suit in 1864, but the interests of the Imperial Moscow Archaeological Society would turn out to be distinctive.[83] A well-earned reputation for documentary research turned the society into one of the most influential voices for architectural conservation in the empire, though its ultimate campaign, a project to repair the Kremlin's Dormition Cathedral, remained at best controversial and at worst destructive.[84] In 1918, under a different regime, the members of Moscow's post-revolutionary artistic elite condemned its treatment of the frescoes as vandalism – the restorers should have done no more than scrape back later paint to uncover the earliest layers – but the damage might have been much worse. Church leaders had wanted to redecorate the Kremlin's most famous interior with Byzantine mosaics: repainted frescoes were far less incongruous. Members of the society also won an argument about the socle, the base on which Fioravanti had designed the building in the fifteenth century, and by the outbreak of the First World War, a team of engineers had managed to lower the whole of Cathedral Square, returning the landmark to its original proportions.[85]

The path that led the society to such achievements was far from smooth, however. Zabelin, a noted archaeologist in his own right, attended the Archaeological Society's first major congress in 1869, surely a key moment in the city's relationship with its own past. It was, for him, a cruel disappointment. Like many such meetings before and since, this one felt – as he put it – like some kind of livestock exhibition, a tedious parade of narrow, self-regarding personal displays. 'It is boring even to record it,' he wrote in his diary. 'No-one has a clue about the discipline.' With pardonable rancour, too, he noted that the great historian Mikhail Pogodin (1800–75) had not mentioned his own *Home Life of the Muscovite Tsars*.[86] But pompous men with gold watch-chains (Solntsev was there) were not the sum of the society's problems. From sentimental archaizing to the caprice of the tsar, its projects always had to overcome the most frustrating obstacles, and none faced more of these than its first and greatest scheme of all: the construction of a public museum beside the Kremlin.

When Alexander II let it be known that he wished to found such a museum, what he imagined was a series of displays that would tell Russia's history through the lens of war. The Archaeological Society convened a committee under the chairmanship of Prince Aleksei Uvarov in 1869, and soon its members were thinking hard about objects and their value to a fact-hungry public. The narrative of progress, romance, and Russian uniqueness was never questioned, but the museum soon moved away from Alexander's puerile focus on the military. The committee preferred to widen its remit to include the whole of Russian history, and Moscow's story above all. The proposed building, which was to be opened in honour of Tsarevich Alexander Aleksandrovich (the future Alexander III), soon became known simply as the Moscow Historical Museum.[87]

The society's progress was painfully slow. One source of delay was the Polytechnical Exhibition of 1872, a brilliantly successful event held in the public spaces round the Kremlin to mark the bicentenary of Peter the Great. Attractive stands in lavish temporary pavilions invited Muscovites to explore the finest achievements of science (including history), and the exhibits, which included recently discovered documents and ancient seals from inside the fortress, were the talk of the city.[88] The public appetite had certainly been whetted, and the historians were eager to seize the initiative. As the marquees and the coloured lamps came down, members of the Archaeological Society were pleased to learn that some of the most interesting items from the exhibition had been earmarked for permanent display in their museum, and also that their new building had been assigned a whole block at the north end of Red Square. This was a stone's throw from the Kremlin, which gave the advocates of fashionable Russian style an extra reason to base the museum's design on it. Conveniently forgotten was the fact that many of the most iconic features of that fortress had been shaped by the ideas of foreigners.

The competition among architects was fierce. Among those who submitted designs were Fedor Shekhtel (later famous for his interpretations of Russian *moderne*, a kind of Art Nouveau) and Nikolai Shokhin, one of the architects of the eye-catching new Polytechnical Museum. The winner, however, with a design called 'Fatherland', was Vladimir Shervud (Sherwood), a Russian of British descent. His eclectic plan was purely and quintessentially Russian, at least as people of the time chose to interpret that, and the Kremlin clearly served as inspiration. Arched windows and a tented roof, elaborate gables, twining curves and gothic porches: Shervud's design had everything except coherence. Zabelin (to his credit) remained unconvinced. At an early meeting of the management group, he noted that the style amounted to an assemblage of disparate and mismatched parts, observing mischievously that the facet-detail of some of the stonework was based on old Italian designs. 'They don't exist in Italy,' a bigot from the nationalist camp snapped back, 'and since Aristotele [Fioravanti] built in the Russian style, the [facets] must be Russian.'[89]

More arguments awaited when it came to fitting out the exhibition halls: this, after all, was a rare chance to make a definitive intellectual statement at public expense. Experts of widely differing views threw tantrums over questions like the place of Europe, the relevance of common people, the place to be accorded to military affairs, and (of course) the rules for admission. But in the end, the museum was largely shaped by Zabelin's sensibility, especially after he became its executive director on Uvarov's death in 1884.[90] The rooms were beautiful, painted in bright colours, an inviting place for a stroll whatever you wanted to see. Muscovites flocked to the galleries in droves, and as they toured the spacious halls they were introduced to a thrilling, and an unsuspected, world. Dinosaur bones, they learned, had been found in their own forests. Urn burials had taken place in lost kurgans not far from the Tver road. Traces of pagan sacrifice, meanwhile (and, more prosaically, old coins), had been extracted from under their very streets.[91]

This sort of thing was much more fun than any list of stuffy tsars. Although the Archaeological Society spent relatively little of its effort on fieldwork, Zabelin had always insisted that archaeology and history were 'the right and left hands of the same scientific organism'.[92] The notion gave the Kremlin a peculiar allure. In normal times, the palace administration did not permit excavation of any kind on the hallowed hill. For the most part, digs could only accompany scheduled building-work, which limited the scientific possibilities.[93] But no-one could deny that there were treasures to find. In the 1830s, when Ton had begun to prepare the site of the old palace buildings for his great monolith, the experts had gathered like so many crows. Among their first discoveries, in 1837, was a complete and intact vanished church. In the fourteenth century, Dmitry Donskoi's pious wife, Evdokiya, had built it in the name of the Raising of Lazarus, a name that imbued its rediscovery with a certain pathos. When the forgotten building was unearthed among the palace foundations, Muscovites began to ask what else might have gone missing there.[94]

The answer was that there were relics from pre-Mongol times, to say nothing of later items of enormous importance. Among the most impressive of these, also turned up by Ton's palace building-works, were a series of horizontally laid oak beams of massive size. According to Zabelin, these must have dated from Ivan Kalita's reign, and were the remains of the oak wall he had built around the stronghold in the winter of 1339.[95] Their placement, and the evidence of deep earth-workings along a line from the Borovitsky to the Saviour gates, allowed historians to picture the size and shape of the original fortress, which turned out to have been more modest than they had assumed. Smaller objects offered clues to the lives of the citadel's first occupants. There was silver jewellery from pre-Mongol Rus, a selection of coins, and even an empty vault, the purpose of which, since its contents had long since decomposed, must once have been to store grain for an early population of settlers.[96] In 1847, the demolition of the Church of St John the Forerunner, by the Borovitsky gates, yielded yet more silver coins and a pair of earrings. When the newly founded Archaeological Society turned its attention to those, excited specialists began to claim that the Kremlin must have been occupied in the ninth century, and even that it may have been the site of pagan rituals.[97]

By far the most dramatic episode, however, began in 1891, when a professor from Strasbourg named Eduard Tremer turned up in Moscow, ostensibly on the trail of a rare book. His tale gripped the city, for Tremer claimed that he was looking for a volume that had entered Russia in 1479, in the train of Sofiya Palaeologa.[98] As the heir of Byzantium, he explained, she had brought with her a collection that included books in Greek, Latin, Hebrew and Aramaic, codexes, rare manuscripts and classics long-since lost. There were alleged to be at least eight hundred items, a figure that had been corroborated in the sixteenth century by courtiers like Andrei Kurbsky and Maxim Grek. Sofiya's unlettered husband, Ivan III, had found no use for the books, and his son, Vasily, had been too busy hunting to sit down and read. Ivan the Terrible, however, was said to have admired them for their beauty and, potentially, as texts. The collection formed the core of his fabled library, an inheritance so valuable that he refused to part with it. In the 1550s, he invited a German called Vetterman to translate the antique scripts into Russian. The sage duly appeared in Moscow and was introduced to the great collection, but he proved unwilling to submit to Ivan's rules. Refusing to work in the secret darkness of a vault, he offered instead to purchase the hoard. Ivan fell into one of his rages, dismissed him (a light punishment for the time), and had the entire library, which was stored in two massive stone chests, consigned to a chamber under his fortress and locked behind a set of iron doors.[99]

Tremer directed his audience to an article in the pages of an obscure journal that had been published in 1834. Its author, one von Dabelov, was a professor from the Baltic city of Dorpat. In the course of his research in Riga, Narva and Reval, Dabelov wrote, he had found several old notebooks, some parts of which bore writing that looked like Ivan the Terrible's. Deciphering the rest, he concluded that the notes were fragments of a lost list that Vetterman had prepared during his brief stay in the Kremlin in the 1550s. The catalogue included at least eight volumes of classic history, including one of Cicero's; there were also autograph manuscripts by Tacitus, Sallust and Livy, a copy of Justinian's *Codex*, and parts of Virgil's *Aeneid*. The Greek texts supposedly included lost works by Aristophanes and Polybius, and there were many other items from the court library of Constantinople.[100]

Von Dabelov had vanished into Dorpat's mist, but Tremer, turning up when Moscow's ear was tuned to history, became a celebrity. He told the public that he had found documents in Leiden that looked like parts of a fourteenth-century copy of an older manuscript. He had come to Moscow in search of the rest, for he believed that the larger part of it was probably in Moscow and must have arrived with Sofiya. The text he was after was a lost section of the *Iliad*, rumours about which, as he understood, persisted among archivists in the Kremlin.[101]

The idea of a library of priceless works caused a sensation. Emotive pieces appeared in the Moscow press, and disputes of a more pedantic kind were to fill the learned journals for years to come.[102] Sergei Aleksandrovich, the reactionary governor-general of Moscow (and by now Zabelin's boss as Director of the Historical Museum), at once formed a commission to explore the evidence and advise on the necessary excavations. This was chaired by Prince Shcherbatov and included a sceptical Zabelin, both also representing the Historical Museum. Under its supervision, workers dug under the Kremlin's most historic towers, exposing subterranean defensive works but finding no trace of the sealed doors. They made a new effort to uncover the passageways that might once, in medieval times, have linked strategic palace buildings, paying special attention to the Archangel Cathedral, since some assumed the books to have been buried close to Ivan's grave. The work was not entirely fruitless: it uncovered several lost buildings, including the foundations of the fifteenth-century Treasury.[103] What the explorers never found, of course, was Ivan's library.

The establishment of the Historical Museum was an epic labour in itself, but the industrious Zabelin also continued to publish. His last major work, *The History of the City of Moscow*, appeared in instalments between 1902 and 1905. The book was written under the supervision of the Moscow City government, the wealthy and august Duma, and its purpose was to foster civic pride.[104] But though the city was officially his theme, Zabelin chose instead to write a history of the Kremlin in the guise of a walking tour. The citadel had been his first love, and now he brought together a lifetime of anecdotes, the fruit of decades of original research. His book contains accounts of court life, government, and even prisons. It combines a knowledge of architecture with a sense of drama and spiritual destiny. Detailed and scholarly, it is also a hymn to the Kremlin of martyrs and Russian heroes, and that explains why, in the early twenty-first century, the new age of historical chauvinism, the book has been reprinted several times.[105] But Zabelin's was not the ultimate account of the tsarist Kremlin. That laurel belongs to the work (now also reissued) of Sergei Bartenev (1863–1930).

Bartenev was the son of a prominent Moscow historian, Petr Bartenev, the founding editor of the journal *Russian Archive*. From such beginnings, naturally, the younger man rejected history in favour of music and composition. But the Kremlin exerted a special pull on him, and eventually he joined its staff as a curator. In 1912, he published his best-known book, an elegant history of the Grand Kremlin Palace, printed in both Russian and (for twice the price) French. The volume covered the history of the site, including a survey of the original stone palace of Ivan III, before taking its readers on a stunning tour of the current palace, its churches and its ceremonial halls. There were numerous black-and-white photographs, some of which now constitute the last pre-revolutionary record of buildings, such as the Saviour in the Forest, that were later destined for extinction. The book did not discuss the recent restoration-work (interiors were shown as if they were perfectly preserved versions of their original selves), but it certainly encouraged Russian hearts to swell.

Bartenev's most ambitious scheme, however, was a projected three-volume history of the entire Kremlin: *The Moscow Kremlin in Old Times and Now*.[106] Though only the first two volumes ever appeared, this work was as compendious as any encyclopaedia. Its readers, if they had a desk of sufficient size, could find in it the exact dimensions of every battlement and tower. They could discover how the walls were built and roofed, what kinds of foundation were dug, and often who exactly paid for what. If they preferred to read chronologically, they could follow the stories of the Moscow tsars, and they could picture all of this with the help of five hundred years of maps and drawings, Russian and foreign. Bartenev cited experts like Karamzin and Kliuchevsky, but he also incorporated lengthy excerpts from original documents. The book was almost unreadable, and it could only have been written by someone who lived in the Kremlin and had been more or less seduced by it. In fact, Bartenev worked with the official blessing of the Kremlin's chief administrator, Prince Odoevsky-Maslov, and the two were neighbours in the Kremlin's Cavalry Building.[107] *The Moscow Kremlin* reflected the academic spirit of its time but also the nineteenth-century's main fantasies about the Kremlin as a place, including a meticulous, almost religious, deference.

Bartenev's *Moscow Kremlin* was written in the florid language of Russia's nineteenth-century court, but anyone can still enjoy his most original idea. It is a map, a plan of the Kremlin on which are superimposed the outlines of every known structure, whether lost or extant. Four colours – red, yellow, blue and green – provide a chronological guide, existing buildings featuring in red and vanished medieval buildings (the oldest) in green. The map is very large, over three feet square, but the detail is so fine that it takes a magnifying glass and patience to discern the names and dates of individual monuments. With these, you can make out the courts of fifteenth-century boyars, the ghosts of churches, the rectangular outlines of the old *prikazy* and the folds of Peter the Great's bastions (the latter yellow, since they dated from the neo-classical age). The complex shapes of long-demolished palace buildings also feature, coloured blue, beneath the red lines of Ton's much more recent structure. It is a fascinating, utterly absorbing document, and it is still in use. On my first day as a researcher in the Kremlin library, the staff brought me a mounted copy, larger than a table-top, and left it by my desk for reference.

Like most historical sources, however, this beautiful object has to be read critically. Bartenev's map does not show the Kremlin as he knew it, or even as it grew and altered through history, but as he wanted to imagine it. The historical developments, even the loss of churches or the disruption caused by Peter the Great's earthworks, all point to a noble outcome, a beautiful present. In reality, there would have been uncertainties, not tidy lines, at almost every point. More seriously, the map offers no trace of the pervasive clutter of encroaching modern life. One thing that it carefully overlooks, for instance, is the coal-burning electricity generating station that had recently been completed in the Kremlin grounds. Built to power the illuminations at the coronation of Tsar Nicholas II in 1896, it remained a semi-secret, almost shameful, addition to the palace complex, not least because the city as a whole had four more years to wait for its first power-station.[108] Indeed, most streets remained in the gas age (or that of candles and oil) until the 1920s. The Kremlin's new facility caused so much confusion that it took years for palace officials to decide upon the uniforms that its technical staff were to wear. It was a question they were still discussing when the monarchy collapsed in February 1917.[109]

Another subject that Bartenev's map does not discuss is architectural style (as an existing building, Ton's new palace is shown in the same triumphant red as the ancient Dormition Cathedral), and it passes no political comment. So it takes a reader with some knowledge of the space to understand the meaning of a small red outline, marked with the symbol that the author used to indicate a consecrated site, in the middle of Senate Square. It was, in fact, another monument, a substantial metal cross in the Russian revival style, designed by Victor Vasnetsov to mark the site of a murder that had horrified conservatives and loyal Russian patriots. In 1910, the date of Bartenev's map, the monument was only two years old, and its story would have been fresh in the minds of every Kremlin resident.

The drama began in January 1905, when Grand Duke Sergei Aleksandrovich, whose reactionary views had made him a prime target for terrorists, had moved into the Kremlin's Small Nicholas Palace (so-called to distinguish it from the Grand Palace that Nicholas I had later built) for his own protection and that of his family and staff. The grand duke's fortunes had taken a dive since the accession of his nephew, Nicholas II. Devoted husband though he was, and thoughtful master to his own immediate retainers, his inflexibility as an administrator was rapidly becoming an embarrassment at court. On 1 January 1905 he resigned as governor-general of Moscow, but the threats to his life continued.

Grand Duke Sergei was about to become the first royal victim of the coming revolutionary storm. The Russian nationalist project had not succeeded in including everyone. The mass of Russia's poor was not convinced; historic art did nothing for the workers in their airless dark or peasants struggling with debt. Such people might enjoy a festival, they might turn out to cheer their tsar, but the grinding hardship of their lives attracted them to any revolutionary spark. Among the most alienated were the students, disgusted by the empire's repressiveness, its chauvinism, and its complacent assumption that the poor deserved – even enjoyed – their fate. In 1904, a war with Japan revealed the full extent of Russia's weakness. Again, it was the poor who bore the brunt, enduring food shortages and extended working hours as well as providing the bulk of the foot soldiers who would have to die. The imperial elite consistently underestimated the public mood, ascribing any protest to the work of isolated malcontents. In January 1905, a peaceful crowd of protesters in St Petersburg was hacked to pieces by the tsar's cossacks. This atrocity, universally known as Bloody Sunday, became the rallying cry for a nationwide revolt. The pressure of the public's rage was one of the reasons why, back in Moscow, Sergei Aleksandrovich, daily expecting an attack, had started to forbid his adjutants to share his carriage, fearing for their lives.

The assassin, Ivan Kalyaev, was a member of the Socialist Revolutionary Party, a group whose aim was to destroy the current system in the name of the peasants. He had made several visits to the Kremlin – his face was a familiar one – but when he walked through the gates on 17 February 1905 the newspapers that he habitually carried concealed a bomb. No-one looked too closely that cold afternoon. The grand duke's carriage-wheels crunched over snow, his coachman whipping the horses towards the Nikolsky gates. As the carriage rounded the Senate building, Kalyaev threw his bomb, killing the victim instantly by blasting him to bits. The grand duke's widow, Elizaveta Fedorovna, who had heard the explosion, rushed out of the palace where the pair had been eating lunch a short time before and threw herself into the bloodstained snow, gathering up the pieces of her husband's corpse. A schoolboy later remembered how he and his friends found more scraps of flesh during a sledging expedition the next day. Some of the grand duke's fingers, still wearing their heavy rings, were blown on to the Senate roof.[110] It is the sort of detail that could never feature on Bartenev's map.

The revolution of 1905 hit Moscow with punitive force. Neither the imperial authorities nor the Duma was prepared for the strength of public outrage. The bourgeoisie itself was divided, some joining the calls for reform while others condemned any proletarian demand as insurrection. Zabelin, by now an old man, wrote a dismal list of words in his diary, the lexicon of a changing world. 'Revolution,' he began. 'Bureau – resolutions – petitions – delegates – cadres. Qualifications. Functions. To function. To get qualified. Provocateur.' Later that season he thought that everyone has stopped asking; instead they importunately DEMAND that their lives must improve, that the working day should be reduced and wages raised, and they demand this AT ONCE. They also demand the introduction of a democratic republic AT ONCE. Russia [*Rus'*] has become a madhouse . . . it's like an epidemic of plague or cholera.[111]

But this, of course, was no passing affliction. In January 1905, a third of Moscow's workforce went on strike in protest at the Bloody Sunday massacre in St Petersburg. By spring, the public mood had hardened even further, and political parties on the left, including democrats and socialists, had gained considerable ground. The most extreme conservatives responded by arming themselves, and Russia saw a series of clashes between the protesters and vigilante groups such as the Black Hundreds, a nationalist and anti-Semitic band of thugs. In Moscow, these were rallied by *Moskovskie vedomosti*, the newspaper of choice for people like Zabelin. The pogroms that disfigured other Russian towns were only averted in Moscow because it had already lost most of its Jews. In vain did the prime minister, Count Witte, warn the tsar against 'finding an energetic soldier to crush the rebellion by sheer force'.[112] All Nicholas could think of was repression; the coming months destroyed his dream of a mystical union with the people. In the face of blatant state brutality, the workers, and even Duma members, responded with further strikes, and by October the entire city was at a standstill. Only the army and police seemed to share the emperor's view that the best answer was to use the troops. Nicholas II confessed as much in a letter to his mother, whining that 'I had nobody to rely on except honest [police chief] Trepov'.

Witte did at least persuade the tsar to grant a constitution, and the declaration, in October 1905, brought the crowds out yet again, this time in celebration. But the 'abscess', in Nicholas' phrase, had not been 'lanced'.[113] Extreme-right brutishness provoked the next outburst. On 18 October, the day after the reading of the constitution manifesto, right-wing vigilantes killed a leading Moscow socialist, Nikolai Bauman, sparking renewed conflict. That winter, as the city teetered on the brink of anarchy, there were yet more mass strikes, and barricades went up in the workers' districts.[114] The year ended with pitched battles on Moscow's streets. Trepov and the cossacks had imposed order by late December, but the regime had lost moral authority. In the years to come, protest was silenced by arrest and the enthusiastic use of hanging, but in the workers' districts there would be no toasts to the Kremlin.

From this point, it would be easy to look ahead for signs of the catastrophe to come. The revolutionary leader Leon Trotsky later called 1905 a 'dress rehearsal', but the streets of workers' red flags that autumn did not lead in a straight line to Bolshevism's own Jerusalem. Even in the nine years that were left before the First World War, there was time and space for the likes of Bartenev to make their maps, nostalgic and romantic, and for publishers to print (and sell) Vasnetsov's paintings of the medieval Russian world.[115]

But the hour has come to take leave of nostalgic dreams. As the curtain begins to fall for ever on the tsars' Kremlin, there is barely time to linger on the last ever coronation, which took place in 1896. The crowning of Nicholas II was an event that focused on the mystery of sovereignty, the sacred bond that joined the tsar and people.[116] Its precedents reached back to a fantasy of Byzantium, 'the ideal Christian state', and through that to a world that shone with a much brighter light than humdrum Europe and its tedious middle class.[117] The lucky guests who received the coronation albums where these sentiments appeared could remind themselves in advance about the continuities with coronations of the past. The books, in finest reinvented Russian style, were full of splendid pictures, including several of the previous two coronations, and the text included a vivid thousand-year history of the ceremony (not entirely inaccurate) to instil the required sense of awe. Each item of regalia was carefully described, each gesture analysed. The very weight of the volumes, and the luxurious paper inside, might well have been enough to make recipients catch their breath.

The press – the world's press – joined the commentary, listing past tsars and noting the precedents for every detail of the pageantry to come. In Russia, a number of cheap histories were also printed to satisfy public demand. One such, Tokmakov's *Historical Description of Every Coronation of the Russian Tsars, Emperors and Empresses*, reads like a literal record, despite the fact that almost every detail from before Peter the Great was still conjectural. There was even a portrait of Riurik, with dates, though no-one could be sure he had existed, let alone what he looked like (uncontroversially enough, the artist showed him dark-eyed, with moustache and beard).[118] The other fixation was with continuity, lingering on the stories of dynastic tombs and the thrones of the

Romanovs. As for the Dormition Cathedral, whose domes still leaked pending the Archaeological Society's great repair, the coronation album described it as 'modest in size but great in its historical significance and in its ordinances, the most precious heart of Russia, and of its first capital, Moscow'.[119]

Public excitement gathered pace, but Nicholas himself had little appetite for the coming display. As he wrote to his mother in the spring of 1896, the preparations were full of reminders of his father's coronation and, thus, inevitably, of his recent illness and death. 'Darling Mama,' he confided on 27 April,

> I believe we should regard all these difficult ceremonies in Moscow as a great ordeal sent by God, for at every step we shall have to repeat all we went through in the happy days thirteen years ago! One thought alone consoles me: that in the course of life we shall not have to go through the rite again.[120]

It was one of his few prescient comments, but it did not help much when the day arrived. The new emperor found the lengthy ceremonies tiring. The robes that had been sewn by armies of industrious nuns were heavy, and he worried, too, about his proud wife in her cumbrous gown. His compensation, as always, was the 'sea of heads', his people massed to show their love for him. Thousands crushed into the restricted precincts of Cathedral Square: invited dignitaries, uniformed guards, and representatives from every corner of the empire. As the Kremlin's famous bells rang out, Nicholas could have imagined himself at the centre of a timeless pageant, holy and suffused with light, as if a medieval painting – though not the kind with bloodstained swords and torture-scenes – had sprung miraculously to life.

But the bright tableau was soon marred by the news of mass deaths at the people's coronation party on Khodynka field. The day had not been meant to go this way. The idea had been to put on a traditional coronation feast, the ritual gift Muscovite tsars had always offered to their subjects. As London's *Times* had noted (in its smuggest tone): 'No less than five thousand poor people will be housed and fed during the stay of the Czar and the Czarina in Moscow, and on the day of the coronation there will be a grand dinner given, at which ten thousand poor people will be present.'[121] But the feast laid on for Muscovites, the open-air coronation feast, had gone very wrong. At dawn, stampedes of revellers had surged towards the booths where food and coronation mementoes had been set out, and before the appalled gaze of the world's journalists, the crowd had become a mass of bodies; wounded, trampled and dying. Some later blamed the panic on a rumour that there would not be enough food, and many later drew attention to the treacherous, uneven ground. As people fell, there was no hope of saving them. 'Probably some 2,000 persons perished on the spot,' wrote the London-based *Graphic*, 'while many of the 1,200 in hospital are not expected to survive.' Many of the corpses were 'so disfigured and stripped of clothing that identification was almost impossible'.[122]

While Moscow's cemeteries filled with dead, however, the Kremlin glittered like a Christmas tree. It was traditional for lamps to burn at coronations (the illuminations were one thing that even Alexander III had not skimped on), but these dazzled the crowds, bathing the halls in artificial light for the benefit of invited guests and conscripting even passers-by to the festivity. The empress Alexandra had thrown the first switch, lighting the bell tower of Ivan the Great and then the Kremlin's other main historic sites. 'Like diamonds, rubies and emeralds among a mass of other precious stones,' wrote one admiring chronicler, 'Ivan the Great and the Kremlin towers stood out above the illuminated capital and its sea of lights.'[123] The Russian national colours – red, blue and white – picked up the fabulous outlines against a background of low springtime clouds. The evenings that May were damp, the public mood sombre and pained, but through it all the fortress blazed above the huddled roofs like a child's fantasy castle, a dream home for the prince and princess in a fairy-tale.

9

Acropolis

Conservatism was not the only cultural news in Nicholas II's Russia. An urgent, vigorous demand for change had also found its voice during the nineteenth century. The outside world woke to the signals of this rather late. It even took its time to notice how creative the effects of restless energy could be. In May 1913, as every textbook lovingly records, Igor Stravinsky's ballet *The Rite of Spring* opened in Paris, designed and performed by Sergei Diaghilev's brilliant Ballets Russes. As sinuous woodwind solos drew them into a scene of abduction and sacrifice, an audience that included Maurice Ravel and Gertrude Stein, to say nothing of the dance critics of every newspaper from the *New York Times* to *Le Figaro*, recoiled in shock. Some later praised the pagan wildness on the stage, but many chose to be affronted by a spectacle of barbarism.[1] If they had known their Vasnetsov, or studied recent Russian art, the critics might have been a little less surprised. Today, the production, though innovative as ballet, resembles nothing quite so much as a late-nineteenth-century essay in folklore and archaism.[2] The menace it implied, moreover, was symptomatic of many other public debates in Russia, where conflicts were developing that would last far longer than the dance-writers' outburst in the cultural press. In politics as in the arts, the empire had reached breaking-point.

An exhibition that opened in February 1914 brought some of the tensions to the surface, at least as far as painting was concerned. The Society of Lovers of the Arts on Bolshaya Dmitrovka had been decked out with jaunty yellow flags for the occasion, and although visitors were sparse, the artists themselves were enthusiastic. Several members of the group involved, which called itself the Knave of Diamonds, had worked in France, and one of them had persuaded Picasso to send a canvas to the show. There were also contributions by Georges Braque and Henri Le Fauconnier, but the bulk of the display was local work. Bright colours filled the air like unexpected music; Aristarkh Lentulov's canvas of St Basil's Cathedral, for instance, managed to be even more effervescent than the building itself, and his cubist Moscow positively blazed. Still, many critics failed to pick up on the vigour of it all. They noted that the group had a strong taste for *nature morte* ('there are a lot of apples'), but complained that its more ambitious paintings failed the naturalism test. Some works really did defy all reason. One canvas, for instance, was covered with some greenish geometric shapes, in the centre of which the artist had added a lifelike lotto ticket. On checking the catalogue, it turned out that the subject was meant to be *A Lady in a Tram*.[3] Its artist, Kasimir Malevich, was a man who upset fellow-painters, let alone critics. 'Creation,' he was soon to write, 'is present in pictures only where there is form which borrows nothing already created in nature.'[4]

Moscow rediscovered its vigorous imagination in the age of the avant-garde. The city hosted innovators of all kinds, from the composer Alexander Scriabin to the theatrical director Konstantin Stanislavsky. The architectural legacy of the time, preserved in the brick and curved wrought iron of Fedor Shekhtel's mansions in the *style moderne*, still brings most visitors to a full stop, amazed to find pink walls and painted flowers in the streets near Patriarch's Ponds. Discredited though they appear today, the political and social hopes of these decades were just as thrilling. Science, art and social fantasies combined: optimists dreamed of universal happiness, abundance, immortality. The same philosopher could write of folk crafts and space-travel to Mars, the same artist consider colour's psychic resonances and a plan for self-propelled air flight. Even the Kremlin played a part, for one visionary, inspired by Russia's spiritual path, proposed its domes and towers as the architectural prototype for a string of utopian communes.[5] For him (and for countless others), the citadel's iconic silhouette was not so much an heirloom as the pointer to a future in which Russia's unique spirit could redeem the world. Almost anything seemed possible, and hope, unrealized and unexamined, seemed to unite the fantasists in common cause. Beneath the high, forbidding, very un-utopian walls of the real Kremlin, the energy of Russia's silver age rolled out in rainbow colours as much as those percussive, shamanistic chords.

It helped that these were also times of economic boom. By the beginning of the twentieth century, the Muscovite elite was almost entirely made up of families whose wealth derived from trade, industry and investment. The millionaire Tretyakovs and Ryabushinskys, the Morozovs and the Botkins had real political clout, and their people dominated the city's governing chamber, the Duma.[6] Many were imaginative public givers, and it was they who paid for the new concert-halls and art galleries and the experimental theatre where plays like Anton Chekhov's *Cherry Orchard* were premiered. Among their other plans was a scheme for an underground transport system, the metro, which engineers hoped to open in 1920.[7] Technology like this allowed the city to expand in every plane. In 1916 alone, the tram network accounted for 405 million journeys, more than 300 for each citizen.[8] Another new technology, the elevator, inspired a revolt against the constrictions of the ubiquitous faux-Byzantine building style. 'With the beginning of the new century,' wrote Boris Pasternak,

> everything changed as if by magic. Moscow was suddenly gripped by the spirit of trade and commerce of the great capital cities ... Before you knew it, there were gigantic brick buildings soaring skywards on every street. At that moment Moscow – and not, as hitherto, St Petersburg – gave birth to a new Russian architecture, that of a young, modern, vigorous metropolis.[9]

The fruits of the city's rapidly expanding growth were not equally shared. The hatreds of 1905, repressed and silenced by police, smouldered like embers waiting for a draught. In places they were kept alive by groups of revolutionaries, and notably by Marxist activists of various types, some of them aligned with larger, illegal, parties. Injustice helped write their agenda, and it gave them a potential constituency of millions. The poor, of course, had little power themselves, a fact that also helped explain the neglect and degradation of the districts where they were condemned to live. In Moscow alone, a chronic shortage of housing obliged them to pack into basements and barracks, renting beds for periods of hours and sharing bugs along with their political ideas. Not surprisingly, the city had one of the highest death-rates in Europe.[10] The prime causes were soaring levels of infant mortality and a general lack of clean water and sewers, but it also mattered that labour legislation was almost unknown, industrial accidents routine, and that the city suffered from a perpetual lack of hospital beds.[11] The gap between rich and poor was flagrant, provocative and growing.

And then, without a thought for art or bread, Russia entered Europe's war. 'Let the unity of the Tsar and His people become yet stronger,' Nicholas II declared in his manifesto. 'Let Russia rise as one person.'[12] Like those of every other European nation, his subjects drank deep on such rhetoric, forgetting other troubles for one final, fervent season. Austria's Archduke Franz Ferdinand was shot on 28 June 1914. On 23 July, Serbia received an Austrian ultimatum threatening punitive war. The Serbs appealed for Russian help, and St Petersburg, dreaming of Slavic brotherhood and Balkan influence, responded. Russia's general mobilization began on 30 July. In August, Moscow put out its national flags, began collections for the war effort, and cheered each new batch of recruits as they marched past the Kremlin walls.

The citadel had lately seemed irrelevant to Moscow's modern businessmen. Real life had focused on the banks, the trading rows, the restaurants and theatre stalls. But the war gave the Kremlin a renewed importance; a practical role to equal its ceremonial one. Safe from enemy machine-guns, it found its place as the repository of Russia's crown jewels and the bulk of the nation's gold bullion. A special strongroom was prepared to house the treasures of imperial St Petersburg and also the state gold-reserves of vulnerable allies like Romania.[13] Meanwhile, the Kremlin's status as an imperial palace, the property of the tsars, allowed the Romanovs to put it to a novel use. In 1914, the empress Alexandra ordered that a hospital for officers should be created somewhere on the Kremlin hill. The concession to mere citizens was a serious one, implying profanation of the consecrated ground, but the idea was to emphasize the sacred nature of this war. There was also something intimate, a direct personal link, in a hospital that bore the empress's name. Fifty beds were envisaged, though a contingency was proposed 'should all of these be occupied'.[14] As the first casualties arrived, the empress requested that she be informed of each officer's name and the details of his wounds. The impression that these men were almost family could only have been reinforced at Easter 1915 (and again in 1916) when each of the patients in the Empress Alexandra Fedorovna hospital received a personal gift, a small china egg, hand-decorated with the imperial coat of arms.[15]

What started as a noble act, however, soon became absurd. Russia's war was a disaster. The troops were brave – their courage in the face of death was legendary – but they were not prepared to fight this bitter war. In the first year alone, their losses were about four million men.[16] The soldiers fell to better-equipped and better-led opponents, to poor transport networks on their own side, and to the ebbing of morale. If the empress had taken the time to read the reports on 'her' officers, she would have been alarmed at the details of shell-wounds, head injuries and amputations. The Kremlin hospital began its life in the spirit of Marie Antoinette's toy farm in eighteenth-century Versailles, complete with snowy palace linen on the beds, but it ended in chaos and squalor. The plight of the casualties was desperate, their numbers overwhelming. Distracted by problems at court, the empress lost interest, leaving the enterprise to Moscow's city government.[17] Poignantly, the establishment of Alexandra's Kremlin hospital had displaced a little-visited and rather drab museum, a collection dedicated to Moscow's war of 1812.

The Russian revolution of 1917 changed the Kremlin's reputation fundamentally, for ever linking it with the red flag. The opening events in that drama, however, took place in St Petersburg, whose German-sounding name had been changed, on the outbreak of war, to the more Slavonic Petrograd. That bracing rebaptism aside, the city's patriotic enthusiasm had evaporated as rapidly as Moscow's after 1914. From national politicians in the Imperial Duma to the factory workers who supplied the troops, the ranks of those who had lost faith in Nicholas II seemed to swell by the day. The tsar had taken personal command of the armed forces in September 1915, a move that doomed the war effort and then the monarchy itself. Once he was giving orders at the front, every new defeat appeared to be his fault, while back at home his government lurched from crisis to crisis under the doubtful leadership of a succession of unpopular ministers and his foreign-born consort, 'the German woman', Empress Alexandra.

The centuries-old institution of tsarism was not broken in battle, however, but by a poor supply of bread. There had been hunger in the capital for months, largely because of failures in the transport system. But the catalyst was an unexpected change. On International Women's Day, 23 February 1917, the crowds were ready to forget their troubles for a moment and join peaceful marches in the name of equal rights. The demonstrators were surprised to meet no credible resistance from the tsar's cossacks. That absence of repression, combined with real grievances about their food and freedom, encouraged larger crowds to turn out in the next two days, and soon the city-centre streets were more or less in the protesters' hands. On 25 February, a fatal intervention by Nicholas II turned this turbulence into a revolution. From his headquarters at the front, the tsar unwisely ordered the chief of the Petrograd Military District to 'put down the disorders by tomorrow'. Bloodshed ensued, exactly as in 1905, but this time many garrison troops, including large numbers of teenage conscripts, were starting to become as disaffected as the crowds.[18] Almost overnight, thousands joined Petrograd's workers in denouncing the tsar's brutality and manifest injustice. As the instruments of state control dissolved under the people's very eyes, old fears and prohibitions seemed to melt. In early March 1917, Nicholas II, the last Romanov tsar, was forced to abdicate.[19]

Rapid negotiations followed, as a result of which the Imperial Duma stepped aside to make way for a new Provisional Government. Besuited politicians, already yesterday's men, chiselled away at its legal details while the people who had forced the pace – the lanky boys and tired women, the soldiers and the dissident police – gathered for stormy, jubilant meetings, passing ambitious resolutions about everyone's freedom and rights. Many formed self-governing councils, or soviets, at their places of work. These also spent their days and nights in ardent, impromptu debate. However hungry everyone remained, the mood in the city was optimistic, even celebratory. No-one imagined how hard the road ahead was likely to be. Even the war seemed winnable. Russia had become a republic.

Moscow followed the imperial capital's lead with little protest. At one point, its police had been preparing to resist all change, but when the news of Nicholas' abdication reached the city, the old order fell apart like a moth-eaten curtain. A British businessman, Allan Monkhouse, turned up at the factory that he managed to find the engines strangely silent. When he asked a group of workers what had happened, they replied 'in chorus, and in one word, "Freedom."'[20] The squares outside were already filling. 'The majority of the crowd consisted of people who that morning had been praying for the good health of the imperial family,' a Moscow worker, Eduard Dune, would later write. 'But today there was a festival on the streets ... I scented that atmosphere of joy, when everyone you meet seems close to you, your flesh and blood, when people look at one another with eyes full of love.'[21] By afternoon, the prisons had been opened and the victims of tsarist repression were free. Quick-witted entrepreneurs piled their stalls with lengths of red calico ribbon; the stock was cleared in minutes, and eager revellers started tearing the strips into smaller shreds so that all could wear the revolution's badge.[22] Even the crack troops who had been sent to quell the carnival ended up marching into town with red scraps tied to their bayonets, cheerfully singing the 'Marseillaise'.

The liberation of Moscow did not involve the royal family, most of whom were still in Petrograd, but the Romanovs' citadel and residence could not remain untouched for long. Less than four days after the tsar had gone, Moscow had a new city government, complete with brand new rubber stamps and an impressive supply of headed paper. The decrees rolled out like ticker-tape, establishing committees, approving freedoms, and outlining new rights. It did not take long for the Kremlin to appear on an agenda. As a former royal property, it was no longer owned by any dynasty or clique. Instead, the new administration annexed it in the name of democratic Moscow, dismissing the palace employees, as stooges of the fallen tsar, in the same breath.[23] As far as the revolutionaries were concerned, that was the job done for the coming months.

The decree that claimed the Kremlin on behalf of Moscow was meant to be another blow for freedom, but like so much in these dramatic weeks it was ill-conceived. The great walled complex was not so easy to reform. For one thing, there was all that treasure, huge repositories of gold. The streets outside the citadel were thronged with people, there were firearms and former prisoners about, and the maligned palace staff were quick to point out that no-one was as qualified as they to take care of the fortress and the valuables inside. The new administration drew back, and soon Prince Odoevsky-Maslov, who had managed to keep his post of Kremlin superintendent (and his Kremlin residence), was giving orders of his own. Whatever Moscow's government might think, the prince made clear that no item of palace property was to be handed out, even to the city's military officials, without his written approval. He also stipulated, with icy confidence, that any object that had disappeared in the first hours of revolution (the list included many of the palace horses) should be returned at once.[24]

The Kremlin's humbler staff were also making plans. In April 1917, they formed a union. Its demands included fair pay, job security and, movingly, the right that palace servants should not be known as lackeys.

Their salaries had not been raised since 1902, retainers wrote, and were also much lower than those of their counterparts in Petrograd. It would be good to put that injustice to rights, but in the short term most were keenest to protect their pensions and to hold on to their rooms. At a time of rent-inflation and social uncertainty, even a basement in an old building was an asset.[25] Odoevsky-Maslov tried to find the instigators of the new union, but there is no record of disciplinary action.[26] That spring, after all, he needed every available pair of hands to defend the old place, a purpose that was also best served if its routines stayed intact. The calls for higher pay and guaranteed retirement echoed into empty air, but the staff dug into their small flats, found floor space for their homeless friends and relatives, and waited to see what would happen next.

For Moscow's artists, however, these were forward-thinking times. In April, a meeting to discuss their role in the new state was so over-subscribed that it had to be held in a building usually reserved for the popular Solomon's Circus.[27] Three thousand people came to share their views about democracy and art, discussing everything from theatre and music to the future of books. Malevich and his visionary rival, Vladimir Tatlin, were both present, as were some members of the Knave of Diamonds group (notably Petr Konchalovsky), but so – in rather different clothes – were figures like the millionaire collector Sergei Shchukin (for whom Matisse had just painted a version of *La Danse*) and the curator of the Tretyakov Gallery, Igor Grabar, celebrated author of a recently published history of Russian art.

Apart from the excitement of the hour, what brought these very different characters together was the opportunity to remake Russia's cultural life. The idealists among them talked about the creativity in every soul, and there were many fervent promises of clubs and education for the masses. That still left the orphaned Kremlin looming like a beached hulk on a fairground site, but happily the avant-garde had long nurtured a plan for it. The idea was to transform it into the heart of a vast super-museum, a space that would incorporate the existing Historical Museum and several city-centre mansions (including, later, Shchukin's own) as one enormous and inspiring complex. In his more expansive moments, even stuffy Grabar called the Kremlin 'Russia's acropolis', and the term caught on. The citadel, freely open, could show the best of everything (Grabar already had a selection in mind); the huge exhibit would take its visitors on a journey towards the future of the world. A letter Grabar wrote that June to Alexander Benois, who had been put in charge of Petrograd's Hermitage, radiated creative optimism.[28] Benois could have assured him of similar moves in the other capital by a group around Maxim Gorky, including figures such as Ivan Bilibin, Fedor Shalyapin and Vladimir Mayakovsky.[29]

For Grabar as for Benois and his friends, however, the priority was to preserve the treasures of the past. Other artists might have dreamed of shattering history altogether, transforming everything from poster-art to living-space, but Grabar was more interested in protecting the Kremlin and its contents.[30] In this devoted enterprise, he was assisted by the numismatist V. K. Trutovsky, a leading light of the Moscow Archaeological Society, who went on to become the Armoury's first curator in the new era.[31] The Moscow authorities were intrigued by Grabar's planned acropolis as well, but there was never any time or cash to sort things out. Like Petrograd, Moscow awaited the convocation of an elected Constituent Assembly, whose role would be to create a legal basis for the infant state, and meanwhile Russia as a whole was still at war. The hard-pressed city government, with few rubles to spare for building-maintenance (and none for more utopian schemes), devoted part of the summer of 1917 to selling off exotic plants from the palace hot-houses.[32]

By autumn, then, much had been said but nothing really decided, in which respect the Kremlin was no different from almost every other institution in the land. With hindsight, it is clear why Russia's democratic revolution failed. Euphoria was wonderful, but it could not cover up the nation's differences for long. The Provisional Government, unable to guide the country out of war and desperate for guns and bread, lurched back towards repression, increasing working hours, punishing strikers, and threatening the revolutionary left. Its commitment to property and to the bourgeoisie deprived it of the chance to begin land reform in the countryside (a major omission in an empire of peasants) and left it without appetite for a rebalancing of labour rights. By September, even the eight-hour day appeared too radical for this well-meaning but frail administration. Its conservatism could only help the parties of the left, including well-organized groups of Bolsheviks operating in the major cities and among conscripts in the army and fleet. More generally, the soviets, the councils that the people had elected for themselves, grew ever more confident, and, in political terms, more effective. They, and not the Provisional Government, spoke with democracy's legitimate voice. The news from the front line grew blacker by the week. The people's army had started to desert. In October 1917, as political leaders in the soviets prepared to meet for their Second Congress, an event quite independent of the tired Provisional Government, nothing but official purple ink could block their route to power.

The soviets had elected an assortment of delegates to their national meeting, and the Congress, itself a cubist patchwork of political parties, looked set to debate a full spectrum of hopes. The left predominated, but its parties did not speak with a single voice on anything from property rights to Russia's obligation to go on fighting the war. To forestall what he considered to be time-wasting debate, the Bolshevik leader, Vladimir Lenin, pre-empted the Congress (and usurped the people's democratic rights) by seizing power on the eve of its official convocation, storming the Winter Palace in the name of the workers, soldiers and sailors while in fact staging a single-party coup. On 25 October 1917 old style – 7 November by the calendar his government later introduced – Lenin issued a manifesto that declared Russia to have passed into the people's hands. His slogan, 'All power to the soviets', implied a broad-based workers' administration. In fact, what was intended was a Bolshevik directorate, a dictatorship of the proletariat, with fuller details to be decided at some time in the future. As one of the participants conceded in old age, the Bolshevik elite, determined though it was to obtain power, 'had only the vaguest notion' about what to do with it afterwards.[33] In the earliest days, Lenin's party could scarcely even claim complete control of Petrograd. Before they could make any progress, Bolshevik supporters, organized (and almost always armed) into units called Military-Revolutionary Committees, faced the challenge of consolidating their rule. No city that they had to take was more important than Moscow.

The counter-revolution that awaited them in the old capital was led by the city government itself, and it recruited scores of volunteers – mainly military cadets – as soon as the news from Petrograd arrived. On the Bolshevik side were professional revolutionaries, workers (the so-called Red guards) and also a number of soldiers opposed to any continuation of the war. All were supplied with lethal quantities of arms; grenades and bullets had been disappearing from the factories since spring. The fighting was in earnest.[34] As Russians shot at Russians, however, the city itself continued to operate. On one of the darkest days, Allan Monkhouse saw a performance of *The Cherry Orchard* at the Moscow Arts Theatre, though his journey home was interrupted by a sharp burst of machine-gun fire.[35] Street urchins dared each other to dash past the bullets on the corner of Nikitskaya street; the careless risked a pointless death.[36] Fierce battles were fought round the city Duma and the telegraph office, but the epicentre of the struggle was the Kremlin.

The Reds had occupied the citadel as soon as Lenin's signal had reached them from Petrograd. The problems started when they could not hold it. A detachment of military cadets and anti-Bolshevik troops (often called 'Junkers' in later Soviet accounts) resorted to a simple ruse: their leader, Ryabtsev, marched up to the gates and told the occupying forces that their coup in Moscow had failed. The Bolshevik regiment in the Kremlin, like so many gullible defenders of the past, opened the Trinity gates, and Ryabtsev promptly stormed the citadel and threatened those inside with lynching. His men dug into the Small Nicholas Palace, took the remaining Reds hostage, and placed sentries at every gate. The gold reserve, according to some witnesses, remained untouched, but any weapons in the arsenal were quickly commandeered.[37]

It was obvious that the Bolshevik hold on Moscow would not be secure until the Kremlin was recaptured, but the methods that the Reds now used appalled almost everyone. Soon after Ryabtsev's triumph, artillery based on the Sparrow Hills began to shell the venerable walls. It was as if the holiest site in the land were being desecrated; there were even rumours (incorrect) that St Basil's lay in ruins. Russia had not managed to find the ammunition to win the European war, remarked a Kremlin priest, but the people did not seem to lack the means to shoot at one another.[38] For a few hours the Bolsheviks ceased fire, horrified at the damage they might be causing, but the artillery commander, a Bolshevik professor of astronomy called Shternberg, eventually overruled his comrades' protests and trained his guns at the fortress for a second time.[39] When news of the shelling reached Petrograd, the new education commissar, Anatoly Lunacharsky, tendered his resignation in disgust. 'My cup is full,' he wrote. 'The Kremlin, where are gathered the most important art treasures of Petrograd and of Moscow, is under artillery fire ... I can bear no more.'[40]

In fact, the Junkers had surrendered that same day (and Lunacharsky promptly snatched his job back). The fighting had lasted almost a week, however, and hundreds of Muscovites had perished. In the palace yards behind the Kremlin walls, corpses now lay stiff in pools of blood. Moscow's proletariat mourned the victims of counter-revolution; the bourgeoisie its fallen students and its vanished hopes. The dead cadets, who gave their lives, as one of the city's conservative history professors lamented, 'for god knows what', were buried on 13 November (old style). There was a long funeral service in the city-centre Church of the Great Ascension, but afterwards it was difficult to find a graveyard whose owners were willing to accept the coffins, for the counter-revolution had become divided and afraid.[41] The workers, however, were buried in some of Russia's holiest soil, for their graves were dug at the base of the Kremlin walls. It was a site that only recently had seen a royal dais for the lines of soldiers going off to fight.[42] This time, a stalwart of the revolution's corps of artists, architect Pavel Malinovsky, was recruited to design the props and the memorial parade.[43]

The American journalist John Reed travelled to Moscow from his base in Petrograd to watch this funeral. On 10 November, he witnessed 'a river of red banners' as the city's grieving people, choreographed by Malinovsky, streamed through Red Square in their thousands. The night before, Reed had picked his way along the darkened walls with a student guide, carefully following the sound of shovels to reach the site of the common graves. 'We looked down', he wrote, 'into two massive pits, ten or fifteen feet deep and fifty yards long, where hundreds of soldiers and workers were digging in the light of huge fires.' One shift was not enough to finish a job on this scale, and as the journalist turned to leave, he saw a new group arrive, pick up the tools, and begin 'digging, digging without a word'. That way, despite the snow and darkness, the pits would be finished by dawn, ready for the weeping lines of mourners and the red-draped coffins, the 'wreaths of hideous artificial flowers' and the sea of improvised red flags. The location alone confirmed the scale of change in everybody's lives. As the student had explained to Reed, gesturing towards the piles of earth, 'Here in this holy place, holiest of all Russia, we shall bury our most holy. Here where are the tombs of the Tsars, our Tsar – the People – shall sleep.'[44]

There were no priests beside this grave. At a specially convened meeting on 9 November, the church had condemned the interment of humble folk in sacred soil, though it offered to neutralize that blasphemy against the tsars and saints by organizing prayers and a procession. Its blessing was forbidden by Moscow's revolutionary government. On 21 November, when church leaders nevertheless attempted to process to the grave and sprinkle holy water, they were met by Soviet bayonets.[45] In years to come, however, the site became a new kind of religious symbol, a relic for the communists to tend. Its martyrs lent solemnity to all Red Square parades, their sacrifice transformed, like Christ's, into a holy act. The new regime was laying claim to history, as keen to sink its hungry roots into the holy earth as any tsar. But though the site was historic enough, and hallowed over centuries by rituals like the Palm Sunday procession, Moscow's workers might have noticed that the graves themselves were outside, not within, the Kremlin walls.[46]

As they attempted to consolidate national power, the Bolsheviks played down the destructive effects of their artillery. The Kremlin, they insisted, had not suffered very much in the battle for Moscow. Grabar, now working for the new regime, insisted that the damage was less regrettable than the previous decade's heavy-handed restoration-work.[47] The truth, however, was far less benign. Even the most starry-eyed of the new regime's admirers had to admit, albeit privately, that the condition of the Kremlin was a national disgrace. Bolshevik artillery had shot out the main cupolas of the Dormition Cathedral and the walls of the Twelve Apostles Church. The two other historic cathedrals, the Annunciation and the Archangel Michael, were pock-marked, and there were bullet-holes and shell-damage in the walls of both monasteries and on the iconic bell tower of Ivan the Great. The Kremlin walls had been breached in several places, and several towers had almost collapsed. By a miracle (or so most people thought) the icon of St Nikola that hung above the Nikolsky gates had escaped, as it did in 1812, but the wall behind was cracked and charred. Inside the buildings, icons and books lay under piles of rubble. The arsenal had been plundered, as had the patriarch's sacristy with its pearls and gold. Elsewhere, shards of glass, wood-splinters and gaudy fragments were all that remained of palace treasures and church furnishings.[48]

Despite a dizzying legislative schedule (and with no budget), Moscow's newly empowered Bolsheviks enlisted protection for the wounded buildings and the treasure that they stored.[49] For a few exciting days, Kasimir Malevich was given control of the art, but that was never going to work. The man who later called on the hungry to 'burn Raphael in the name of the future' was soon steered towards more suitable tasks. Grabar, assisted by a group of artists that included the cubist Knave Lentulov, was summoned to help, but progress really called for central government support.[50] Eventually, a caretaker administration moved into the Cavalry Building, sailors and riflemen with good revolutionary credentials but no sensitivity when it came to antiques. Fortunately, most of the ordinary palace staff were still in post, guarding what was left of the imperial heritage, but it was unclear how and when they would be paid. Perhaps to compensate for that, some colluded in rackets, pilfering any portable objects and smuggling the remaining guns out of the arsenal.[51] They soon taught their friends how to find the hidden passageway that had been built to service the coal-fired power-station near the Trinity gates.[52]

Barter and crime were emblematic of the times. As Russia's formal economy ground to a halt, its banking and production paralysed, an unofficial market sprang up, exchanging rings and watches for food, weapons for train tickets, fur coats for lumps of coal. Though diamonds could be bought on the meanest street, bread became almost unattainably expensive. Even a worthy like Grabar might have been tempted into some sort of illicit trade, for by the spring of 1918 the price of a loaf was soaring well above his daily pay.[53] Later, the new government issued orders to nationalize the mansions of the wealthy, together with their contents, and that added a fresh tide of luxury goods, this time looted by semi-official mobs. In this bizarre economy, a brooch or necklace, once a treasure, might be sold for scraps of food, enough to sustain a body for a few hours. And in the short term, many gangs were interested more in vengeance than profit; no-one knows how much the angry mobs destroyed in the winter of 1917–18. The danger was that items of real artistic or historical significance to the nation might vanish altogether. Many did: a typical loss, stolen from the Kremlin itself, was a gold reliquary, or zion, dating from 1486, a rare example of medieval gold-work by Russia's own master-craftsmen.[54]

The answer was to put an irreproachable Bolshevik in charge, but Lenin's team in Petrograd took several months to organize itself. In that time, there was hardly a museum in the land whose staff could be absolved entirely of pilfering. But as Russia's Orthodox prepared to celebrate their Christmas, the resolutions finally began to flow, and on

5 January 1918, Lunacharsky turned to the Kremlin itself. His decree stated that 'All structures within the territory of the Kremlin, artistic and historic monuments, regardless of their original ownership or the fact that they are used by specific departments or institutions, not excluding the churches, cathedrals and monasteries, constitute the property of the Republic.'[55] The priority now was to save the People's artistic heritage from the people themselves.

It was a classic test of new state power, and the Bolsheviks barely passed it. A new body, the People's Commissariat for the Preservation of Historic and Artistic Monuments, was formed to prevent the activities that were threatening to destroy the nation's inheritance, chief among which was simple vandalism. 'The hatred that the Russian people feel towards the previous owners ... should not be directed towards innocent objects,' Lunacharsky ordered.[56] The country mansions went on burning nonetheless, and looters gathered at the gates of the great palaces in town. The cherished plan to turn the Kremlin into a museum was going to have to wait. For now it had to re-enact its less glamorous role as a giant safe for Moscow's valuables. Indeed, the Moscow branch of the new Monuments Commissariat was already known simply as the Kremlin Commission because so many crates of recovered loot were being stored inside the fortress. Its head, the man in charge of Moscow's entire heritage, was Pavel Malinovsky.

For the forty-nine-year-old architect, the high point of whose work to date had been a summer mansion for a provincial flour-merchant by the name of Nikolai Bugrov, the new responsibilities were heady. For just under two years (until someone better-connected grabbed the job), Malinovsky was responsible for the contents of all Moscow's museums and libraries, galleries, mansions, and the whole of the Kremlin. As everyone anticipated, he based himself in the citadel, though his presence there was not universally welcomed. A member of his team arrived for her first day at work to find the whole place deserted. Knock as she might at several doors, no-one would direct her to Malinovsky's office ('sabotage', the commissar confided when they finally sat down).[57] Although he was their only hope, Moscow's conservative establishment, the art-experts and academics whom he had upstaged, regarded their new comrade as an interloper and busybody: 'a repulsive, ugly little man who does not inspire trust'.[58]

Even more annoying, at least to any other self-appointed guardian of

Russian culture, was the next addition to the staff in the Kremlin's Cavalry Building. Malinovsky's deputy was to be a second-rate artist called Evgeny Oranovsky ('a complete fool, and probably malicious as well'[59]), and his task was to log and conserve Moscow's treasures, including everything that Red guards brought to him.[60] The point was to prevent destruction, export and black-market trade, and to that end no painting and no trinket was supposed to evade him. If citizens wished to keep objects of historic or artistic value in their homes, and even if the curators of established museums wished to retain their collections, they were now meant to apply for documents from Oranovsky's hand. Unregistered valuables would all be liable to confiscation. Registration was invited at the Kremlin itself, Tuesdays, Thursdays and Saturdays only, 12.30 to 2 p.m.[61]

'Every day a new decree,' a Muscovite scrawled on one of the city's houses, 'but still there is no bread.' The decrees certainly abounded. At the same time, however, even officials seemed confused about the status of nationalized property, including anything that Moscow's richest citizens might have left behind when they prepared to flee the country. In the confusion, mountains of jumbled objects cluttered Oranovsky's little office every morning.[62] Among the looted ('conserved') items on his list by early January 1918, many of them stacked in crates in the Kremlin's Armoury Chamber, were European paintings, antiquities, and 30,000 books from the library of Aleksei Uvarov, the late founder of the Moscow Archaeological Society.[63] In March the officer in charge of the Kremlin arsenal wrote to complain that so many things – including instruments from a local church orchestra and a batch of radio-telegraph equipment – had been brought there in error that there was no space left for his men to work.[64]

Oranovsky's style of operating can be judged from his memoir. Searching the Grand Kremlin Palace in his first weeks, he and his men discovered a cache of valuables that the Provisional Government had moved to Moscow for safekeeping earlier in 1917. There was porcelain and there was gold, but there were also cases of fine wine, which, being Bolsheviks of the hard school, the men regarded as a form of temptation rather than treasure (or art) in liquid form. Oranovsky ordered the entire supply to be poured into the palace drains. As he wrote, not without pride, 'The drunken aroma of those wines infused the palace for many a month.'[65]

And there were further bright spots in the dutiful hack artist's life. The Armoury Museum's curator, Trutovsky, was a consistent ally, and a Kremlin priest, Archimandrite Arsenii, facilitated some co-operation by the church. In February 1918, the aristocratic owner of the Kuskovo estate, a palace in stunningly landscaped grounds on the edge of Moscow, applied in person for his help in saving a collection of rare porcelain.[66] More frequently, however, Oranovsky worked in an atmosphere of suppressed rage. Beyond the Kremlin, wealthy people knew him as the man who checked the contents of their private safes, helping himself (or the new state) to anything that could be classed as art before Lenin's secret police seized the rest. Moscow's remaining artistic elite – still reckoning itself to be the only possible custodians of art and books – detested him, and poked fun at his boorish manners and his fondness for dining off the palace china.[67] No-one really wanted him to take their things. In the circumstances, there was something heroic in his zeal throughout that hungry winter, the long hours that he worked in those unheated rooms, his passion for 'conserving' treasures that the Bolsheviks might otherwise have sold for cash. He fought against the dealers and insulting crowds and even the police. Among the pieces that his men snatched from the latter in 1918 were two handguns set with diamonds, the property of the celebrated army commander General Brusilov.[68]

No-one felt like a hero on the bleaker days of that first winter, however. The monks and nuns, the archivists, the painters and the palace staff made tea, lit tiny stoves, and shivered in the undiscriminating cold. Though Moscow's artists were still dreaming of their avant-garde acropolis, it took a strong faith, whether religious or political, to believe in a bright future for the Kremlin in the early months of 1918. The interiors were dim, even menacing, though loyal servants of the old regime attempted to protect the sacred rooms with locks. Churchmen made plans to bury their treasures, and rumours that they had already started taking some along a secret tunnel underneath the walls abounded. But it was the disorder that was most apparent. There were no corpses outside the palace windows now, but the rubble had not been cleared, and nor had the refuse that was piling up in the snow, attracting hooded crows and rats. Whenever there was a slight thaw, the gateways slithered into mud, and a lake collected in the square, reflecting the bell tower of Ivan the Great in frothing sludge. As one of Lenin's aides later remarked, shamelessly shifting the blame, 'Napoleon left the Kremlin in 1812 in no more littered, ruined and dirty a state than the gentlemen Junkers did [in 1917].'[69]

It was a winter when the Kremlin's future could have taken many turns. There was still a lingering chance that it might have become a museum-park; it was fast turning into a fortified bank for the nation's valuables in any case. But though its masters talked about repair, little was done, and the Kremlin could just as well have succumbed to another fire or crumbled into semi-ruin.[70] It was not until four months after Lenin's coup that its fate was settled. By then, a civil war was pressing on the Bolshevik elite. They needed a secure stronghold, and they also needed a more centrally located capital city from which to extend their territorial control. Moscow offered both, and it also had something more, for the place was lively with historic resonance, an asset that had rescued several fragile regimes of the past. Petrograd had served its turn as the cradle of proletarian revolution; Moscow was the mother of the Russian people's lands.[71] Privately, Lenin disliked the place, but there was little real choice.[72] In February 1918, the Bolshevik government secretly agreed to move its capital back there.[73]

The relocation involved several hundred souls, including the entire membership of newly formed organs of government like the Central Executive Committee and the Council of People's Commissars, together with the most essential of the many staff who worked with them. At the centre of it all was Lenin himself, a figure now so precious that he was protected like the queen bee in a hive. The logistical anguish of moving an entire war-time government was as nothing compared with the anxiety for Lenin's life. In the end, the relocation plan was kept secret, disinformation (including a denial that the government would ever move) was dropped into any listening ear, and even government personnel (including Lenin) were not told in advance exactly how and when they were to travel.[74] To further distract would-be assassins, Lenin's colleague, Vladimir Bonch-Bruevich, arranged for the members of the Central Executive Committee – politicians, soldiers and sailors – to make a decoy journey in railway-carriages requisitioned from the tsar's own stock.[75] The epic move, involving two entire trains, took place on a Sunday, 10 March, with much official bustling and cross-checking before the passengers could settle into the deep leather and the monogrammed moquette.

Travelling with his wife and sister in a less conspicuous train behind the other two, Lenin arrived in Moscow the following night. It is likely that he had always hoped to make the Kremlin his base in the city, and the Cheka, the agents of security and (later) terror, had duly placed it in a state of siege.[76] From March 1918, access to the fortress was restricted to persons in possession of a pass, the coveted *propusk*, and these were issued only by the Kremlin commandant.[77] A former sailor, Pavel Malkov, was given this job, working closely with the secret police in a role whose powers paralleled (and soon exceeded) those of Malinovsky in his art empire. Living conditions in the Kremlin remained squalid, however, and Lenin and his entourage arrived before the telephones and new guard-posts had been set up. Like many other top officials, the leader of the first proletarian revolution in the world spent a first night at the five-star National Hotel. His neighbours included other Bolshevik luminaries, and more had been accommodated in the nearby Hotel Metropole (splendid but shell-damaged) and in the rather less grand Hotel Lyuks.[78]

In the years to come, as government swelled and more and more officials, time-pressed and self-important, moved to the Bolshevik capital, former hotels and even former mansions would be used as top-grade government billets. Their china and linen, marked and crested, were distributed to ambitious provincials, many of whom had arrived in the capital with little more than a change of clothes.[79] Accommodation soon became so scarce that people were grateful for a shared room, while an apartment was a real luxury. But every politician, however comfortable they found the erstwhile quarters of the bourgeoisie, eventually aspired to live inside the Kremlin. It towered over everything. When the great gates shut, as they were soon to do on all but those entrusted with the new elite's official pass, the city almost disappeared from view; the Kremlin's elevation minimized its ant-like striving and its small despairs. You were either in or you were definitely out.

Lenin asked to move in after just one night. His aides had planned to give him an apartment and offices in the Senate, but the suite would still take some weeks to prepare, and he was so impatient that a temporary set of two rooms had to be cleared in the Cavalry Building.[80] This was a bad omen for Oranovsky and his staff. Their work (which also brought them into conflict with the well-connected art dealers who were raising cash for Lenin's cause) was already under scrutiny, and now their space seemed set to disappear. But Lenin did not remain in his two cramped rooms for long. Later that year, as planned, the leader moved into more generous and permanent lodgings on the third floor of the Senate, a suite where he could have a library and where he and his wife, Nadezhda, kept a much-loved cat.[81] Among the modern touches were an Erickson lift and an indoor toilet (Ideal Standard) in a heated room.[82] But Lenin also craved the fresh night air, and in 1920 his Kremlin apartment was extended with the addition of a makeshift study on the roof, concealed within the folds of the great building. Here he liked to rest each evening, lulled by the stillness of a city paralysed by civil war. Eighty years later, the curator of Lenin's Kremlin apartment museum was nostalgic for that rooftop space. It was a relic of the first heroic days, before a time came when the leaders could build anything they chose.[83]

Government, of course, was the priority, and that meant meeting-rooms and offices. The Senate had always housed assemblies – that was its purpose – so it was a natural location for the new revolutionary cabinet. The Council of People's Commissars met in a long room, its members choosing leather chairs around a baize-covered table. At one end was an old-fashioned Russian stove, and it was here that the smokers had to sit so that their habit did not trouble the famously clean-living Bolshevik leader.[84] Larger assemblies, the Congresses and Conferences of the Bolshevik Party that were held in more or less alternate years, were sometimes fitted into the Grand Kremlin Palace. Since these could last for several days, a canteen had to be provided, and someone chose to use the fifteenth-century Faceted Palace for that. Soldiers in their grubby jackets jostled party officials, always talking and always in a hurry. By 1922, despite the discreet efforts of the palace staff, there was soot on the historic walls and spots of grease on the carpets and parquet. Steam had lifted antique plaster from the walls and cigarette-smoke had thickened the air. Nearby, a group of several palace rooms, including a church, was being used to dry residents' laundry. The windows were left open summer and winter, and, as an inspector later wrote, the snow and wind were making sure to finish any damage that had not already been accomplished by the occupants.[85]

The frantic pressure on Kremlin space left little time for sentiment. Government workers needed lavatories and typing pools, secret police needed cellars, everyone needed cleaners and maintenance-staff, and then there were the soldiers, the garrison, together with their bulky and explosive weapon-stores. The land outside was wracked by poverty and civil war, but members of the new elite employed maids, some added cooks, and Lenin himself had a loyal chauffeur, Stefan Gil. The old palace staff, meanwhile, had also managed to cling on, and some were even starting to teach their new masters how to use the china and the knives and forks.[86] By the middle of 1918, the Kremlin teemed with housekeepers and drivers, resident bodyguards, and nannies for the children of not one, but many new-style ruling families. That summer, there were 1,100 people living in the Kremlin, 450 of whom had moved in since the revolution.[87] Additional personnel and servants increased these numbers to 2,100 by the end of 1920. The old Kremlin, with its official complement of just two hundred staff, had never witnessed such an influx. The assorted inhabitants were crammed into 325 apartments, not all of which were really fit to live in.[88]

Leon Trotsky, whose role in these early months was almost as important as Lenin's, took to the new environment with ease:

> With its medieval walls and its countless gilded cupolas, the Kremlin seemed an utter paradox as the fortress for the revolutionary dictatorship ... Until March 1918 I had never been inside [it], nor did I know Moscow in general, with the exception of one solitary building, the Butyrsky transfer-prison, in the tower of which I had spent six months during the cold winter of 1898 to 1899.[89]

Now he was living in a world of gilded mirrors and Karelian birch: 'The aroma of the idle life of the master class emanated from every chair.' An ornamental clock, decorated with the figures of Cupid and Psyche, stuck in his memory. Soon after he moved in, its chimes had broken into one of his snatched business conversations with Lenin. 'We looked at each other', Trotsky wrote, 'as if we had both caught ourselves thinking the same thing; we were being overheard by the past, lurking over there in the corner. Surrounded by it on all sides as we were, we treated it without respect, but without hostility either, rather with a touch of irony.'[90]

A different mood afflicted those who had to fight to win a room. From the accommodation point of view, there were only three viable buildings: the Senate, the Cavalry Building, and part of the Grand Palace. Many of the rest, including the Small Nicholas Palace, were too badly damaged for any use (though Lenin tried to overrule the experts several times[91]), while detachments of Latvian guards now occupied the barracks. Trotsky's sister Olga and her husband, Lev Kamenev, moved into the Cavalry Building (they were so grand that they disdained to pay their rent), and so, for a while, did Stalin, who briefly shared a lodging with his future henchman Vyacheslav Molotov. Others, including the proletarian poet Demyan Bedny, were given rooms on the 'Frauleins' corridor' of the Grand Palace. It was an extension that lacked proper sanitation and seemed to be permanently cold.[92]

Both Malkov and his comrade Malinovsky joined the hunt for space.[93] While the architect explored the palaces, Malkov's attention was directed at the church. As he recalled, the Kremlin's religious residents, 'all flapping in their black ... lived by their own rules and took no notice of ours'. Worse, 'I had to provide these people, most of them enemy brothers, with permanent and single passes to the Kremlin: how do you protect the Kremlin from hostile elements that way!'[94] It was common knowledge that valuables were disappearing under the priests' flapping cloth. On one occasion, Malkov claimed to have exposed the church's 'fortress' in the city, stuffed with smuggled treasure from the Kremlin. Partisan though he was, the tale was true. An archive document from April 1918 confirms that Malkov's police indeed 'repossessed' a cache of items from the Chudov's inventory, among which were thirteen crosses, four golden icons, seven diamond-encrusted mitres, a gold star, and a golden box containing holy relics. Believers had also removed five chalices, two gospels, lamps, mitres and other valuables from the Ascension Convent.[95]

The Bolsheviks condemned the whole tribe of churchmen as spies. In July 1918, Malkov was mandated to expel most of the Chudov's monks, though a separate enquiry continued in the women's case.[96] By late July, about a third of the Kremlin's monastic residents had gone, but the core of men and women that remained included the most stubbornly pious of all.[97] These people argued – and truly believed – that their duty was to pray beside the ancient shrines. They also promised that they worked in other ways, physical ones, baking communion bread and scrubbing their cells. The nuns' days were numbered, however, when an official called Kuznetsov reported to his masters in the late summer. Only thirty-six women were left in the Kremlin convent, he noted, and most of those were old, too decrepit to carry out the advertised monastic chores. At least nineteen of them were over fifty, an age at which, as he put it, 'a woman is considered unfit for work'.[98] On that undignified note, a religious tradition that had flourished on the Kremlin hill for six hundred years was brought to an end.

Malkov could now use some parts of the old convent as rooms. But the pressure on space continued to increase remorselessly, and the cramped conditions left the Kremlin seething with rivalry. The situation came to a head when Trotsky's wife, Natalya Ivanovna, took over the plum job that Malinovsky had been doing running Moscow's art. The new governing lady was taken with the idea that the palace could be turned into a museum. In 1920, that belief led to a bitter argument with Stalin. At issue were rooms in the wing that led from the Grand Kremlin Palace to the Armoury Chamber. The rooms themselves were covetable: elegantly furnished and flooded with light. Lunacharsky was already in residence, and one or two nearby suites had been occupied by other fortunate comrades, but Natalya Ivanovna was not pleased to learn that the boorish Georgian commissar wanted to join them. As she explained in her letters to Lenin, the annex opened straight into the treasure-house of the Armoury Chamber. It ought to be part of a great museum, it should be sealed off, and anyway it was inconvenient and 'hellishly cold', for there was neither heating nor modern plumbing.

The argument involved such major players that Lenin was forced to adjudicate personally. He made a few enquiries and discovered to his horror that the use of the royal apartments as emergency residences had resulted in 'samovars being placed under eighteenth-century Gobelins [tapestries] and baby-clothes being dried over Augsburg tables'.[99] It was a fire-hazard at the very least. Stalin was not permitted to annex the gracious rooms, and other colonists were soon moved out. From Stalin's point of view, however, the story did not end in defeat. In 1921, when he returned from the civil war's southern front, the leader rewarded him with apartment No. 1 in the so-called Poteshnyi Corpus, part of Aleksei Mikhailovich's crumbling Poteshnyi Palace. It was a large flat, grand enough for the servants and children to have their own rooms, but its place in Lenin's affections, its status as he signed it off to Stalin, can be judged from the fact that the previous occupant had been a woman very close to Lenin's heart: his alleged mistress, the beautiful Inessa Armand.[100]

'Around the city, many talked of orgies in the Kremlin,' a Red guard wrote in his memoir of these years. He was not talking about sex (that would come later), but about the greatest issue in most people's lives at the time: food. 'The Russian intelligentsia,' he went on, 'knowing that the treasures of generations of Russian tsars were preserved [in the Kremlin], assumed the Bolsheviks must be stuffing their faces.'[101] At a time when the whole country was starving, such rumours were not only natural but damaging. Beyond the Kremlin walls, in a land of failed harvests and abandoned farms, the average Muscovite was eating a mere 1,700 calories a day by 1918, close to starvation rations.[102] Any guaranteed supply, however simple, was a luxury. Hot meals were one of the perks of Kremlin life. But it was a far cry from the bacchanalia of later Soviet times. Junior Kremlin staff had only the most basic food, and even the elite ate modestly at first. 'Instead of fresh meat,' Trotsky wrote, 'they served corned beef. The flour and the barley had sand in them. Only the red Ket caviare was plentiful, because its export had ceased.'[103]

Austerity, however, did not last for long. It took just months for a hierarchy to form behind the Kremlin walls, for 'higher' staff to lord it over 'lower' ones and for almost everyone to start living better than the lesser mortals in the world outside. The excuse was that busy public servants should not waste their time on practicalities, but the effect was an inflation of luxury. Under the soviets, the people themselves were supposed to be the new tsar, but in this respect at least their leaders were content to act on their behalf. The rumours of privilege that were circulating in Moscow by 1920 had become so poisonous that Lenin created a special commission to investigate and report.

Its findings painted a picture of self-righteous and growing excess. The bulk of Kremlin staff ate in the Central Executive Committee canteen, where each person was allowed just over 100 grams (roughly 4 ounces) of meat or fish at a sitting. There were also rations for bread, vegetables, rice, butter and sugar, none of which was orgiastic by any measure. What really might have sparked a riot was the list of items set aside for the elite. Ministers in the Council of People's Commissars were thought to need 300 grams (12 ounces) of meat or fish at every meal, twice the other staff's generous ration of rice or macaroni, and four times the regular amount of bread.[104] No later document would ever show that these amounts had been officially reduced.[105] Instead, the privileges multiplied. Elite families who found life in the Kremlin inconvenient, for instance, could soon take a generous hamper (and servants) to their country homes. By the early 1920s, the out-of-town mansions of former millionaires, most famously that of an oil magnate called Zubalov, had been assigned to Russia's Stalins and Dzerzhinskys. From 1918, when he went there to recuperate from bullet-wounds, Lenin himself spent increasing amounts of time at Gorky, taking the air in a mansion that had lately belonged to a General and Mrs Reinbot.[106]

The country houses on the estate at Zubalovo provided the setting for many of the parties and the fragrant summer days that Kremlin children of the 1930s later recalled in their memoirs. Even in Lenin's time, the provision for what were euphemistically known as state rest-homes was generous. 'We'll spend gold on this,' Lenin had promised in May 1918, 'but the rest-homes will only be model ones if we can show that they have the best doctors and administrators, and not the usual Soviet bunglers and oafs.'[107] The leader also wanted a secret transport connection between any retreat-complex and the Kremlin, but for the present his charmed elite made do with a small fleet of cars. You might have found them if you had walked past the Cavalry Building, behind the so-called 'children's wing' of the palace, and through a stuccoed arch. The garages were ramshackle buildings, reeking of petrol-soaked rags, and they included a yard for lorries, armoured cars and other big mechanical beasts. A neglected corner behind them provided Malkov with the quiet spot he needed in 1918 when he received the order to shoot Lenin's would-be assassin, Fanya Kaplan, an execution that he tried to disguise by running the engines of several lorries before he opened fire. It was also somewhere around here that he poured petrol over her remains and burned them.[108] Nearby, meanwhile, in readiness for the Kremlin's new masters, there gleamed a row of Packards, a Rolls-Royce, and, until it was taken from Lenin's chauffeur at gunpoint in March 1918, at least one of the tsar's own favourite Delaunay-Belleville limousines.[109]

The cars were kept inside the walls because the Kremlin's latest tenants were afraid of everything from theft to kidnap and assassination. These fears were fully justified. When the government moved in in March 1918, the worst period of the civil war had barely started; in the months to come there would be fighting on the Don, in the Urals, Siberia, Ukraine, and even close to Moscow. Trotsky helped to take the Soviet people out of Europe's war, but that decision, too, proved controversial. The treaty with Germany, signed at Brest-Litovsk in March 1918, provided for the surrender of some of the Russian empire's richest land (in Poland, the Baltic and Ukraine), and it was also a betrayal of existing alliances. At the same time, the new regime's social programme was earning it enemies in every wealthy street closer to home. The hapless population, caught in the middle once again, fought sometimes for its land or kin, sometimes for Lenin's promises, and probably most of all for sheer survival. Supported, on and off, by the British, the Americans, and even the French, an ill-assorted collection of monarchists, nationalists, local patriots and anarchists aligned themselves against the Reds. At one dark moment, in the early summer of 1918, the crisis grew so threatening that Lenin ordered the pre-emptive murder of the entire royal family, who had been imprisoned in a mansion in the Ural town of Ekaterinburg. His officers promptly complied. Moscow's own emergency came in 1919, when the White general, Anton Denikin, closed in from Tula and Orel, forcing the new capital to prepare for a siege.[110] Hostilities continued into 1921, wrecking a land and a generation already harrowed by world war.

The struggle for Russia's future saw the burning of whole villages, the massacre of children; it witnessed every imaginable cruelty from mutilation to cannibalism. The conflict took the art of murder to extremes, impressive even to a people reared on tales of medieval saints. But violence was not the only tribulation that the citizens of the new Soviet state were now about to face. The First World War bequeathed an influenza epidemic, and Russians, like everyone else, died in their tens of thousands. Meanwhile, the mass movement of refugees provided easy routes for the spread of other scourges, including dysentery, typhus and cholera (two disinfection chambers were introduced to decontaminate visitors to the Kremlin[111]). No-one can be sure how many citizens of Lenin's new republic died, for records were impossible to keep, but it is thought that between nine and fourteen million perished in the years 1917–21.[112] A further two or three million fled, some to Europe, others to China. For those who remained, the future looked bleak. Moscow itself had emptied, its population falling by about 50 per cent. The survivors were thin and hollow-eyed, watching events with caution, confused and afraid.

The new regime could not survive without these people's physical support, their labour and their combat skills. But it also needed something that was even more unlikely in the circumstances: revolutionary true belief. Lenin's ambition, after all, was nothing less than the remaking of the world. Military victory was crucial to his cause, and the Red Army, masterminded by Trotsky, fought an effective if at times desperate campaign to defeat all forms of organized counter-revolution in the field. Behind the lines, however, and certainly in Moscow, it was the Cheka, Felix Dzerzhinsky's so-called Extraordinary Commission, that was the more conspicuous instrument of the new age. More war-like than secret police, more ruthless than most armies, its tools included terror, intimidation and butchery on a gruesome scale. In August 1918, prompted by the successful assassination of a leading Petrograd Bolshevik and the attempt on Lenin's life in Moscow, it unleashed a programme of wholesale execution. The bodies, thousands of them, were often left exactly where they fell. The idea was to teach survivors how to think, and as cultural revolutions go, it was a textbook case. The victims included entrepreneurs and priests, White-guardists, even shopkeepers. In the late summer of 1918, the sunlight glittered every morning over teeming clouds of blowflies.

Whatever else bullets could do, however, they were not enough to win most people's hearts. And this was a problem, for the Bolsheviks were not mere thugs. On paper – and in some places in fact – they were a government of visionaries, and this was where Russia's creative artists were supposed to help. The optimists in the art world had been jubilant in 1917, seeing the revolution as their chance to follow long-held fantasies and remake human life. It took them some years to realize that their new patron was a traditionalist at heart, that Lenin's dreams were rusty things, not headed for the stars. Space-ships and cubist paintings were beside the point. As everyone discovered in the end, Marxism saw progress as a single one-way track, along which the world's people juddered forwards, stage by stage, like the travellers in an old bus with stubborn gears. The artists' only real job was to get the grumbling passengers to stick to the right route. To that end, their first task was to create a new canon of saints and fallen heroes, communist-style, for this was thought to be the best way to inspire a superstitious, doubting populace. Like the courtiers of almost every old-time tsar, in other words, the servants of this revolutionary government were asked to find a way of turning Russian history to practical use.

The 'feudal' Kremlin, bastion and symbol of the former age, was obviously a good place to start, as was Red Square as well as almost all central Moscow. These sites were ones where history could be reinterpreted on a serious scale. The work began in November 1917 with the martyrs' requiem around the Kremlin graves, and it continued when the first red flag was hoisted on the Senate roof. Covetous eyes were no doubt squinting up at the tsars' double-headed eagles even then, for they presided all too visibly above the proletarian citadel, but first there were more obvious targets to consider. In April 1918, a decree from the Central Executive Committee, approved by Lunacharsky, ordered that monuments thought lacking in artistic merit – equestrian statues of recent tsars being a case in point – should be removed without delay. In their place, new works, designed to glorify the values and heroes of the revolution, were to be planned and erected with all possible speed. The commissars announced a series of artistic competitions, which, it was hoped, would attract a new kind of entrant, not the usual self-perpetuating circle of bourgeois aesthetes. It was also hoped (indeed it was decreed) that the contestants would restrict themselves to cheap materials. The winning designers, whatever their background (and with luck it would be proletarian), would receive the funding to create the first iconic symbols of the new, popular, past.[113]

Predictably, demolition was by far the simplest part of the enterprise. At the end of April 1918, Lenin came upon a group of lads from the Kremlin garrison labouring over something heavy. The story goes that they had taken the initiative to remove the cross from Vasnetsov's neo-Russian monument to the murdered Grand Duke Sergei Aleksandrovich. The entire structure was soon gone, and Lenin talked of replacing it with a memorial to the grand duke's assassin, Kalyaev.[114] Other tsarist carbuncles, including the statues of Alexander III (beside the Cathedral of Christ the Saviour) and Alexander II (in the Kremlin), followed the duke's cross into a cart, though someone managed to make off with all the metal from the latter, probably with help from members of the Kremlin guard.[115] But the task of making new things was perplexing. Revolutionary art was meant to be iconoclastic, and in the spirit of the times the people themselves were given the task of selecting the winning entries in the competition for new monuments. But the artistic instincts of some workers and most peasants were conservative. The road that led to all those dreary busts of men with beards – Marx, Lenin, even Spartacus and Tchaikovsky – began with that contradiction.

Lenin's own tastes, in sculpture as in so much else, were those of a provincial schoolmaster. In consultation with a young architect, N. D. Vinogradov, he compiled a list of the historical figures whose busts he wished to see on Russia's plinths, and he also demanded that instructive inscriptions and bas-reliefs should be fitted to prominent buildings, starting with the Kremlin. It was Lenin, too, who requested that a large statue of Tolstoy be erected opposite the main doors of the Kremlin's Dormition Cathedral.[116] Today, such monuments – and, of course, similar statues of Lenin himself – are the very stereotype of Soviet art, but the early 1920s in fact brimmed with far more exciting, even shocking, schemes. From Lentulov and Malevich to Vladimir Tatlin, the innovators longed to do their work. The proletarian poet Mikhail Gerasimov tried at one point to represent the Kremlin as a giant dynamo, electrifying the nation's soul with a new kind of magnetic energy.[117] Lenin was left fuming in his room. No-one seemed able to produce a bust of Karl Marx when he wanted one.[118]

The most immediate pressure in 1918 came from the revolutionary calendar, for the workers' carnival, the first great festival of the world's first ever proletarian revolution, was due to be observed on 1 May. Moscow had been the capital for just three months, but Lenin was always sensitive to crowd propaganda, and that meant a Red Square parade. The Kremlin had to show a revolutionary face. To design the pageant, the Bolsheviks hired two famous brothers, the artists Leonid and Victor Vesnin. Money was promised, leave secured, and Pavel Malkov scoured the city for strings of bunting. By late April, the carpenters were putting up the scaffolding and building a stage. There were boxes of flags and yards of rope everywhere. The basement workshops near the Kremlin walls were cleaned, and groups of women turned up every day, their faces set on business.

The women's job was to sew together enormous sheets of red fabric, the aim of which became clear when the sun rose on the festival morning. Remarkably, the Kremlin's round Kutafia Tower had been entirely wrapped in the red cloth. A double row of red flags led from it to the Trinity Tower behind, creating a scarlet corridor into the Kremlin itself. Evergreen garlands promised spring and natural abundance, while fiery banners proclaimed the freedom of labour and the victory of the Soviet republic. But the mournful theme of sacrifice was kept in mind. The martyrs' graves beside the Kremlin wall were turfed for the occasion and heaped with fresh flowers. Every group, as it marched past, lowered its flag or banner in respect, and black flags lined the Kremlin walls behind the mounds of earth. In August, when the Kremlin's Saviour Tower and clock were being repaired, a mechanic reset the famous bells. For years to come, they played a brisk, loud rendering of the 'Internationale' at 6 a.m., but at 9 a.m. and again at 3 p.m., whenever the new government required, they also played a funeral march.[119]

Just days after that May parade, a memorable religious service took place in the Kremlin. For centuries, Muscovites of a certain class had converged on the Dormition Cathedral for the greatest festival in Orthodox religion, the Christian celebration of eternal life. For centuries, too, a procession of the cross, joined by hundreds of the faithful, had brought the Easter message to the streets with icons, chanted prayers and lines of priests. It was a feast more sacred and probably even better loved than western Europe's Christmas, and in 1918 it fell just after the Bolshevik May Day. That coincidence may have helped persuade Lenin to issue a special permit for the Dormition Cathedral to be opened for the usual service and procession.[120] Oranovsky, with his responsibility for Kremlin treasures of all kinds, remembered the episode as the most stressful of his life, the Latvian riflemen standing a tense guard as the great bells rang and the crowds filed in. The Kremlin would not see another Easter like it for seven decades.[121] There would be no repeating all that bustle, not with the leaders' lives at stake, to say nothing of the gold and sacred art. A request to hold a smaller procession in November 1918 was refused, by Malkov, on the pretext that the church's erstwhile property in the Kremlin was being catalogued.[122]

Outside the Kremlin, meanwhile, the contest for Russia itself grew ever more bitter. The church was fast becoming the Bolsheviks' only major rival for the nation's soul. In 1917, before the Bolshevik coup, it had been possible for lay people to hold utopian and Orthodox ideas simultaneously, to celebrate May Day and Easter in the same spirit of hope. Even pioneers like Tatlin had Orthodox roots, and many of the avant-garde had found their greatest inspiration in old icons. Lenin's party refused these divided loyalties. It is likely that it killed at least 9,000 priests, mainly in 1918; as Lenin remarked, 'the more representatives of the reactionary . . . priesthood that we can shoot . . . the better'.[123] And saints themselves were seldom better off. In the spring of 1918, a group of devotees, alarmed by the Kremlin's closure, asked to take charge of the remains of Metropolitan Aleksii, the founder of the Chudov Monastery, and to remove the coffin for safer keeping elsewhere.[124] It was a modestly worded request, framed to spare the leader any inconvenience. The believers' point was that Aleksii's body, like those of other Kremlin saints, had to be tended, for the holy man was truly present, uncorrupted even by the scourge of death. A note in Lenin's hand instructed his aide to reject the request. Instead, the coffin was to be opened at once and the contents examined in the presence of witnesses.[125] The arrangements took a little while, but in 1919 a group of 'scientific' Bolsheviks unwrapped and exposed Aleksii's remains as part of a nationwide campaign against the cult of the pre-revolutionary saints.[126]

These cruel gestures helped to crush the practice of one kind of faith, but Lenin's party had yet to establish anything substantial to put in its place. That priority largely explains Lenin's impatience about monuments. Although his campaign for 'monumental propaganda' had been launched in April 1918, by late May there were still no Marxes on the plinths round Moscow. Lunacharsky and Malinovsky both faced his 'surprise and indignation' at that point, and soon the leader was demanding that the slackers should be named and imprisoned. By mid-July, every sculptor of any note was busy carving his designated personage. Marx, Engels and Auguste Blanqui were at the top of the list, but Brutus and Robespierre, as well as Chopin, Voltaire, Beethoven and Lord Byron were also represented. As ever, finding female subjects to balance the inevitable regiments of men was tricky for the committee in charge. On a list that ran to sixty-two names, only one (the revolutionary populist Sofiya Perovskaya) was a woman. That may be why the ever-helpful Oranovsky got the job of sculpting the late actress Vera Komissarzhevskaya, who had played the role of Nina in the first run of Chekhov's *Seagull*.[127] With her nomination, the female contingent was doubled, but everything from lack of paint to sheer incompetence still threatened the scheme. In September 1918, a bust of the eighteenth-century social critic Alexander Radishchev (sculpted by Leonid Shervud, the son of the Muscovite architect) simply disappeared before it could be unveiled. Lenin heard the report on that with 'deep revulsion of spirit'.[128]

To be sure, there were some triumphs to record. In the spring of 1918, the sculptor S. T. Konenkov ('Russia's Rodin') had accepted the task of designing the Kremlin bas-relief Lenin so craved. Ostensibly, its purpose was to honour 1917's fallen, but the more profound objective was to upstage the Christian icons before which the faithful (and even the not so faithful) still paused and bowed and silently crossed themselves. In November 1918, Konenkov's answer, an angel named 'Genius', was unveiled. The work was made of forty-nine separate brightly glazed pieces, but its style owed more to folklore than to cubism. The background was a rising sun, and the figure held a red flag in one of its giant hands and green palm fronds in the other.[129] The architects and sculptors of the avant-garde were on notice; their task was not to express spiritual truths or individual creativity but to educate the Russian masses. The avant-garde magazine *Lef* might proclaim that the time had come to move beyond the conservative art that had always 'required' a 'passive mentality, soft as wax'.[130] But Lenin's motives were less pure, and the ultimate results were not utopian.

The final skirmish in this battle for the nation's soul was the darkest of all. As the fighting in the civil war subsided, a famine as merciless as any Old Testament plague swept over Russia. The suffering was at least as great as any witnessed in the recent war, moving donors as diverse as the United States government and the pope to extend generous material aid.[131] In Russia, the Orthodox Church, though stricken itself, offered to raise money and to help distribute food. Its leader, Patriarch Tikhon, went as far as to make a list of valuables that parish churches might offer to sell as part of the appeal for funds.[132] Ignoring this, Lenin demanded that all church assets be seized. Their cash value was scarcely the point. 'It is now and only now,' he explained in a secret directive, 'when there is cannibalism in the famine regions and the roads are littered with hundreds if not thousands of corpses, that we can (and therefore must) carry through the confiscation of church valuables with the most rabid and merciless energy.'[133] The civil war was almost won, and this last effort, from Lenin's point of view, would guarantee a victory.

The decision to liquidate church assets was taken in the Kremlin at the end of December 1921. Directed by an impatient Trotsky, the Central Executive Committee laid careful plans to avoid resistance, to the point of stipulating that the requisitioned treasures should be moved about on passenger trains, not goods wagons. The public response fully justified such precautions. Even in Moscow, where the preparatory agitation and propaganda had been thorough to the point of saturation, the requisitions sparked heart-rending protests. It was not clear to anyone why treasured objects should be snatched away, especially as there was still no bread. 'The starving need food, not gold,' the workers in one factory resolved, and some dared to suggest that the famine was the fault of the 'bourgeois' in the Kremlin. If Lenin and his crew resigned, they whispered, we might get a government that could feed us all.[134] This kind of talk put Bolshevik nerves on edge: it was the breath of civil war, the poison of White guards and priests. *Izvestiya* urged workers and peasants to 'burn out' the priestly counter-revolution 'with a hot iron'.[135]

In the late spring of 1922, Moscow let its gunmen loose. Armed gangs arrived to seize and package gospels, icon-mounts and chalices; churches were searched, opened coffins left gaping. Believers wept as lead and silver coffin-lids were carried off, sometimes from local churches and sometimes from the great cathedrals of Russia's walled cities. In Petrograd, a particularly eager team prised open coffins in the Peter-Paul Cathedral. They ripped a string of pearls from the long-dead neck of Catherine the Great, but when they opened Peter's coffin and were confronted by the formidable and surprisingly lifelike body inside they stepped back, abandoning the mission in terror.[136] It was a rare victory for the old regime. Elsewhere, the Reds were ready with machine-gun fire. Busy though he should have been, Lenin demanded to be informed 'on a daily basis' about the number of priests who had been shot.[137]

The Kremlin churches were not exempt from general attack. Indeed, the accusation that the 'high-ups' were living like tsars helped seal their fate. The Moscow public watched as icon-lamps and canopies were torn from the Kremlin walls. Grabar's written complaint about the consequent exposure of late-fifteenth-century paintings, so fragile that they could not be expected to survive in the open air, never received an answer.[138] In Aleksei Mikhailovich's favourite palace church, the Saviour behind the Golden Grille, a silver iconostasis that held works by Ushakov and his contemporaries was dismantled for melting down. Silver doors and decorated reliquaries in the Chudov Monastery were also forfeit. But despite all the destruction, the total haul from the Kremlin, in bullion, was less than had been taken by Napoleon.[139] And at a time when the depressed world market was already flooded by Russian loot of every kind, half a ton of gold was never likely to secure the revolution anyway.

The whole campaign against religious art ran counter to the Soviets' economic interests. A better-informed government might have taken the time to assess the value of artistic treasures, of relics, unique icons and even minor works of sacred art. Attempts to do this often foundered on the zeal of local requisition teams, who just grabbed everything, regardless of instructions about fine objects, waving the loaded crates off to the foundries without a second look.[140] Among the few officials who could influence the process, a weary but tight-lipped Grabar attempted to step in and save some of his nation's precious heritage. He even pleaded with the state's broker to pause for a while, to wait while he and his colleagues taught Europe how to understand (and pay for) Russia's great religious art.[141] But Bolshevik bull-headedness prevailed; this was the liquidation of the church, the death of God, not just an exercise in fund-raising. The great icon collections of the world – including those in Sweden and the United States – date from this season of fire-sales. Some treasures, including many of the embroidered vestments in Washington's Hillwood Collection, were bought in the Moscow equivalent of charity shops.

The experts could insist only that the very finest and most famous objects be assessed in the Armoury Chamber. In all, over 10,000 individual pieces of church art were unpacked in the museum in the nine months of the campaign. But it was impossible to track and save it all. Grabar spent sleepless nights defending items that might otherwise have disappeared, chasing each new consignment and almost physically snatching some things from the smelting flames.[142] It was exhausting and depressing work, but like everyone else in the artistic community, he was trapped, for the Bolsheviks were the only patron left in town. Conservators could either work with them or they could take a bullet with the priests.

While one religion suffered these repeated blows, another – or at least a system of belief – enjoyed the most overt state patronage. Bolshevism was neither unworldly nor ethereal, however, and its holiest symbol, after 1924, was Lenin's tomb. 'One day,' Lenin's comrade Leonid Krasin declared, 'this spot will hold a greater significance for mankind than Mecca or Jerusalem.'[143] On Lenin's death, his grieving colleagues chose a burial-site for him beside the people's graves of 1917, and to mark it, the committee hired Aleksei Shchusev, an architect whose inspirations (like Vitberg's back in 1813) included the Egyptian pyramids.[144] Shchusev's designs (several mausoleums were built, first in wood and then in marble) proved dignified, if stark, and the tomb itself was so sacred that it entirely upstaged the existing martyrs' graves, which were transformed into a row of faceless geometric blocks. It also superseded Konenkov's multi-coloured bas-relief, which now looked positively light-minded by contrast with the shrine.

From this time on, the Kremlin would again belong exclusively to the elite. There was no further spontaneity around its walls. The revolution had been fought for many things, but in the end the victory went to a rag-tag group of fixers, thugs and managers. In the ruthless and utilitarian atmosphere of the coming age, the avant-garde did not appeal, and its plans for the Kremlin were shelved along with many of its other more utopian hopes. The process took a few more years, for dreams die more slowly than human beings, but by the end of Soviet Russia's first decade, the short, hot Indian summer of the acropolis Kremlin had finally drawn to a close.

10

Red Fortress

Guarded and sealed, the Kremlin of the 1920s must have seemed like a remote and anti-human place. Beneath those formidable walls, however, Moscow was still lively with the revolution's energy and hope. The early 1920s were a heyday for utopians, and the times were also reasonably kind, for a while, to the thousands of Muscovites who engaged in small-scale trade. While the artists and dreamers sketched their plans for futuristic, high-rise lives, the tradesmen (who were far more numerous) got on with buying, selling, and scraping a living from stalls and pavements in the real world. Alongside both, a tight-lipped piety could still be found behind church doors, and any walk in the city, however short, involved at least one encounter with Orthodox religious faith. The German socialist Walter Benjamin was swept up and delighted by the chaos of it all. The Moscow of 1927, he wrote, was a place where life went on 'as if it were not twenty-five degrees below zero but high Neapolitan summer'. The only things that made him nervous were the countless shrines. Moscow's cupolas and golden domes reminded Benjamin of an 'an architectural secret police'. The inner rooms below, he feared, were probably 'fit to plan a pogrom in'.[1]

Moscow remained a composite of old and new, but for a time the frankly makeshift seemed to have the upper hand. It was one of the many problems that frustrated the revolution's more enthusiastic supporters as they began to craft the world's first ever workers' state. Far from enjoying leisure, health and universal brotherhood, the Soviet paradise seemed constantly beset by demons. In Moscow, the most troubling of these were housing, health and jobs. The mass exodus of the civil war years was soon forgotten as the city's population began to spiral upwards. In addition to the bureaucrats, secret police and Party men, tens of thousands of migrants arrived in the capital each summer, all hoping for seasonal work and all needing a bed. Unemployment rose four-fold between 1921 and 1927; in early 1929, it peaked at nearly one in three. Working or not, everyone needed transport, doctors and food, and urban services were soon under critical strain. 'What kind of socialism is it,' a speaker asked at a meeting for factory workers in the spring of 1926, 'when the workers get forty rubles for their physical efforts and the people in power get three hundred rubles for showing us the path to socialism? It's turned out to be just like the past, when priests showed everyone the way to heaven.'[2]

The project to transform Moscow was clearly urgent. The challenge was also a stimulating one, however, and it attracted some of Europe's most ambitious men. In the 1920s and 1930s, a list of stars including Erich Mendelsohn, Walter Gropius and Le Corbusier proposed new buildings for the socialist capital and also large design concepts of a more general kind. The local Soviet architects were also buzzing with ideas. Freed from the old constraints and tastes, innovators like El Lissitsky and Konstantin Melnikov began to plan glass skyscrapers and whole suburbs on stilts. There was even a 1920s version of the garden city, zoned to provide space for industry and workers' homes.[3] Money was tight, and only a fraction of these schemes was ever completed, but the inter-war decades of the twentieth century were probably the only time in the history of Russia when its architects managed to lead the world rather than running after it.[4]

At first, too, the revolution brought some pickings for the conservationists. As Igor Grabar had perceived, the state's determined seizure of the assets of the very rich was like an open invitation to explore their properties. Even the church could not exclude the expert teams. The only real requirement was a permit on the necessary form. Since he could almost print these for himself, Grabar found time in a packed official schedule to supervise the wholesale stripping of old plaster. What he was looking for was genuine Russian art, by which he meant the medieval stuff, and to find it he was ready to destroy almost anything that was not at least a hundred and fifty years old. Others also grasped this rare chance to explore. From 1923 to 1928, for instance, a team led by the architect Petr Baranovsky worked to unveil the long-lost mansion of the seventeenth-century magnate Vasily Golitsyn.[5] They found it by chipping stucco from a squarish city-centre block, uncovering the old windows, and knocking down an ugly service extension. Apart from its obvious historical importance, the resulting structure was a rarity in a city that had lost so much of its heritage, and almost everyone was delighted.[6] Even the secret police joined in, although for them the most important thing was to make sure that they had complete control of any secret passage that Golitsyn and Grand Duchess Sofiya might have built between the mansion's cellars and the Kremlin.[7]

The transformation of the city, then, was not steered by some sinister cabal. At first, the whole thing even lacked a rational design. As some old structures were being resurrected, others were about to be torn down. The demolition started in 1922 with a nineteenth-century chapel dedicated to Alexander Nevsky, which someone in the futurist camp complained was blocking traffic in a city-centre street. The church was powerless to answer back, and Grabar, in his role as the city's artistic consultant, did not protest, because the building was an ugly one. The chapel was quickly razed, a decision that opened the gates to a flood of similar plans.[8] Grabar soon seemed almost elated. It was not just that he disliked virtually everything that had been constructed since the days of Konstantin Ton. He was also happy to approve the demolition of a treasured older building if he could salvage the materials for a more attractive or high-profile scheme.[9] The iconoclasm of the 1920s was, for him, a straight case of win-win: a conciliatory attitude to the new regime helped keep him in his enviable job, while he could look forward to frequent bonuses in the form of recycled bricks for renovation projects of his own.[10]

By 1927, however, the pressure to accept whatever change the new regime required had started to make some other people in the conservation camp highly uncomfortable. That year, they attempted, unsuccessfully, to prevent the demolition of the last of Moscow's grand baroque triumphal arches, the so-called Red Gates. Some then joined a collective body, *Staraya Moskva* (Old Moscow), to protect the best-loved landmarks that remained. Petr Sytin, the author of several important histories of Moscow, was particularly fond of Peter the Great's Sukharevka Tower, which he imagined as the focus of yet another new museum. Petr Baranovsky, who had led the work on Golitsyn's mansion, devoted a good deal of precious time to the Kazan Cathedral, a much-altered seventeenth-century building on Red Square, restoring it with every care for the original design. Other architects worked just as scrupulously on the Kremlin's Chudov Monastery, whose main churches (now free of monks) were landmarks of Old Russian style. Like St Basil's Cathedral and the Kremlin walls themselves, these were the people's basic heritage, and Moscow seemed impossible without them. But a turning-point was looming, and the catalyst was probably the tenth anniversary of the Bolshevik revolution in November 1927. Soon after that, the restoration workshops in Leningrad (the erstwhile Petrograd) were closed, leaving the old imperial capital to rot. Elsewhere, and even in Moscow, the pressure to 'cleanse' (that is, remove) religious buildings and imperial sites increased. And a worrying rumour had begun to spread to the effect that Lunacharsky, the conservation-minded Education Commissar, was about to fall.[11]

When Stalin announced his plans for drastic economic change, the advocates of cultural warfare were enthralled. The blueprint for the country's transformation was a Five-Year Plan for industry and agriculture, launched in 1928. This envisaged an entirely new Soviet economy, a dream (or nightmare) of huge factories and power-plant, of tractors moving in formation over golden miles of wheat. Stalin ordered the forced collectivization of millions of private farms, followed by the state-led requisitioning of grain. The implications for anything old or faltering were obvious. An ideology that could justify the deaths of millions of peasants in the name of the future could hardly let its progress founder at the sight of ancient walls. The sound of dynamite reverberated through Moscow. It was a second revolution, the so-called 'great break' with the past, and five years later, victory was declared. The final plan for Moscow's reconstruction ('an attack upon the old') was not approved until 1935, but by then the landscape had completely changed. 'Old, feudal, noble, merchant and bourgeois Moscow grew and developed slowly,' announced the journal *Class Struggle* in 1934. 'But the victory of the proletariat has opened new pages of world-historical importance here . . . in the name of Stalin a new stage in the construction of the socialist capital has begun.'[12]

Among the losses was the Sukharevka Tower, which was demolished on the now-familiar pretext of improving traffic flows. In 1934, Baranovsky's lovingly restored Kazan Cathedral was commandeered as a canteen for the men who were digging metro tunnels, and two years later it was destroyed completely, ostensibly to ease the path of vast Red Square parades.[13] Even Golitsyn's rediscovered palace was blown up, this time to make space for a monumental bank. At one point, at a planning meeting where models of city-centre buildings were being placed on a paper map, Stalin lifted the miniature St Basil's from Red Square, briefly considering how things would look if it were gone.[14] The church was spared, but Moscow lost hundreds of other historic buildings, as well as many of the winding central streets and leafy courtyards that had fed its village soul. At best, some civic monuments were mounted on rollers and relocated when the time came to widen a boulevard; the governor-general's house on Tverskaya, originally built by Kazakov, was moved this way in 1937, as was the former English Club.[15] But the result was an intimidating emptiness, as devoid of comfort and character as it was of shady trees. Stalin wanted space for all the tanks and marching troops; his heirs still live with the windswept results.

With or without the tanks, however, most religious monuments were doomed. In the outright war that economic transformation required from 1929, loyal citizens had to prove themselves actively anti-religious. 'Dynamite', one such class warrior announced, 'has become a real ally in our uncompromising battle against Orthodoxy.'[16] In six months during 1929 alone, four hundred religious buildings in Moscow were closed, including the last working church in the Novodevichy Monastery.[17] In July 1929, one of Moscow's most revered shrines, the Chapel of the Iberian Virgin, was demolished to ease large-scale access to Red Square. It was high time, the planners must have argued. This chapel blocked the free passage of crowds. But in secret, Moscow's new rulers were also worried by its spell, which was so strong, even this late in the new age, that marching communists, red flags and all, were sometimes seen to cross themselves as they passed by.

Strong passions could be harnessed on all sides. Christians felt besieged and trampled, but the Bolshevik elite, taking decisions for their own half-secret purposes, tapped into a movement that was as genuine and deeply felt, in the cities at least, as that of the Orthodox believers in the other camp. In 1929, an 'anti-Christmas' demonstration in Moscow's principal city-centre park attracted 100,000 participants. 'Anti-Christmas' and 'anti-Easter' marches in the next two years were similarly popular.[18] Having endured decades of repression and even violence at the hands of the inquisitors of the old regime, the anti-clerical working class was euphoric. The atheists in its ranks might have been confused about some issues – they never quite got used to the finality of godless death – but they knew that they had finished with the priests and rote-learned prayers. Their cycling festivals, open-air picnics and banner-waving parades were certainly sponsored by the government, but the force of this revolution came from real Russian souls.[19]

It was not long before attention turned to the most grandiloquent religious building in Moscow, Konstantin Ton's Cathedral of Christ the Saviour. Even after 1917, the building was a focus for the fragmentary religious life that still endured. The famous choirs still sang there when they could, and until 1929 the faithful continued to queue at its great doors for evergreen branches and Christmas blessings. Unlike the Kremlin that it faced, however, this building was not really capable of reinvention, for no-one could believe for long that the cavernous interior, marble and all, would make a splendid workers' club. In 1931, when the planners were looking for a site for their showpiece Palace of Soviets, the decision was taken to have it demolished. By this stage, the city's countless Orthodox believers had learned to be cautious. Very few dared to protest. The ageing artist Apollinary Vasnetsov tried to defend Ton's domineering structure (and the art inside), but his argument was based on heritage, not faith. 'It is easy', he wrote, 'to demolish, but when a cultural and artistic monument has been destroyed without trace it will be too late to be sorry.'[20]

The Party newspaper, *Izvestiya*, refused to print Vasnetsov's letter. This was the clearest signal that the demolition had been approved (if not instigated) at the highest level. The massive structure, seven decades in the planning, was gone within the next few weeks. As the secret policemen kept their usual officious watch, teams of workers stripped the cupolas of their gold leaf and copper sheets. Others strained to lower several heavy bells, and others yet removed the carvings and interior tiles. When all was ready and the site secure, the shell was blown up in a single night, leaving a ruin that took months to clear. The spoils were loaded on to fleets of horse-drawn carts (the Soviet dream of universal mechanization had yet to be realized) while an eager coterie of artists and designers collected like rapacious storks, some hoping to recycle the bell-metal for projects of their own, others to crate up and export the bronze doors and the carved statues. Despite the 1930s Great Depression, there were always cash buyers somewhere in the world.[21]

The cathedral's disappearance changed the Moscow skyline completely. But as doubters had already started to mutter, the Bolsheviks were better at removing the city's landmarks than agreeing about replacements. Fantastic plans, the more impossible the better, were always being laid. One was to build a soaring Commissariat for Heavy Industry on the site of the old trading rows (the GUM building); Ivan Leonidov's sketches for that showed that he meant to upstage the Kremlin itself.[22] Then came the Palace of Congresses, another future tallest building in the world, on the site of Ton's lost cathedral. There was the giant bank for which Golitsyn's mansion had been razed, and there were always plans for monumental factories. In every case, however, it was much easier to draw designs than to make a mad idea come true. The city, in reality, was not so much a clean slate as a rubble-pile, and the heaps of broken stone grew higher still in 1934, when the walls and gatehouse towers of Kitai-gorod were finally destroyed.[23] 'A person who thought he knew Moscow would soon find that he did not know *this* Moscow,' quipped humourists Il'f and Petrov.[24] The city never quite made sense again, and even now there are strange gaps and ugly, oddly routed streets, leaving a visitor to wonder, in footsore despair, exactly what could have been in the planners' minds.

The answer – or one answer – was that they were trying to create a modern city of concentric circles, the focal point of which would be the Kremlin, still its medieval self.[25] But here the planners' dreams gave way to the designs of a more powerful elite, for what happened in or near the fortress was never open for public debate. If Moscow's citizens had been in charge, after all, the Kremlin might have turned into a vast museum, a park, or even the base for future missions to space. It might also have been reclaimed by some kind of religious faith, and even by militant atheists. For all its visionary glory, however, this was not a revolution that remained the people's own. The Kremlin, like state power, was a resource that ultimately belonged to the very few. There had to be some editing, for the Kremlin was as much a text as any book, but in the end the new elite, Stalin's own clique, taught the old walls to speak Bolshevik Russian. In their hands, the Kremlin became Red Russia's fortress, the silhouette with five bright-lit electric stars that was, and probably remains, the world's shorthand for Soviet power.

Because of its importance as the nation's citadel, the Kremlin's architectural fate unfolded according to a set of unique rules. The Bolsheviks (at first it was Madame Trotskaya in person) began by dividing its buildings into four categories, depending on their historic or artistic value. In

1925, that initial scheme was modified to introduce the notion of utility, which freed up a good deal of space for the new government to use. The colonnade around the former monument to Alexander II (Category 3) was knocked down within weeks, and the site where Moscow's young had strolled and flirted on their pre-war summer afternoons was turned into a gasoline depot.[26] But under Trotskaya's original scheme, the oldest churches and the two monasteries had been ring-fenced on the grounds of their historical significance (Category 1), so few expected that the first significant Kremlin building to disappear entirely should have been the little Church of Konstantin and Elena in the citadel's south-eastern corner.[27] This was demolished on the Executive Commission's orders in 1928, ostensibly to enlarge the surrounding garden and make space for a new sports ground.

A year later, when there was still a lot of rubble and no sign of that sports ground, the director of the Lenin Library, a Bolshevik of long standing called Vladimir Nevsky, dared to protest about the loss of heritage, but his was an isolated voice.[28] Less voluble was a petition by the Kremlin's own recently appointed architectural director, D. P. Sukhov, who was already worried for his job.[29] He and his comrades won a minor victory in the spring of 1928, when plans to demolish the gothic-style Church of St Catherine in the Ascension Monastery were set aside, along with a scheme to melt down most of the Kremlin bells.[30] But the respite was a brief one. Just one year later, in April 1929, the news leaked out that both the Kremlin monasteries (Category 1) were doomed. No less an organ than the Party's supreme council, the Politburo, dismissed a last-minute protest, by Lunacharsky, as 'anti-communist in spirit and completely indecent in tone'.[31] As if on cue, that July the Education Commissar was relieved of his duties. The site of the two monasteries was earmarked for a military training school.

The loss this time would be serious indeed. The Chudov Monastery, founded by Metropolitan (and saint) Aleksii in the days of Mongol rule, was one of Russia's most important sites. Its oldest buildings were significant monuments; some of its icons (and the iconostasis in the monastery cathedral) were rare works of art, as were the frescoes and the carvings on the walls, and the grounds contained historic tombs, including that of Aleksii himself. In recent years, the crypt had also been used to accommodate the remains of Grand Duke Sergei Aleksandrovich, though that was not, perhaps, the best card the conservators could play. More plausibly, defenders of the buildings could at least request that they be given time to draw and photograph interiors that very few had ever seen. The country's leading conservation experts pleaded for the time to explore and to catalogue the precious space. Lenin, surely, had acknowledged what the buildings meant, for he had once approved a programme of repairs to rectify the shell damage of 1917. As architect Sukhov and his ally, the conservator-historian N. N. Pomerantsev, wrote to Mikhail Kalinin in 1929, it was also ironic, if not tragic, that 'valuable monuments to our culture which survived material hardship in the early years of the revolution' should disappear in what were meant to be enlightened times.[32]

The Ascension Monastery, the women's convent, was just as important. For centuries, this great religious house had been the burial-place of Russia's royal women. The first such lady to be buried there had been Dmitry Donskoi's widow, Evdokiya, the monastery's founder, and others included Ivan the Terrible's much-loved first wife, his scheming mother Elena Glinskaya, and the grand old princess Sofiya Palaeologa. Because the royal coffins lay in massive stone sarcophagi, the trove was important from an archaeological point of view alone, for it included grave-goods, as well as carvings, fabrics, and the science to be scraped from centuries of dust. In the summer of 1929, members of the Kremlin's restoration workshop (a body, sponsored by the Education Commissariat, that was itself heading for oblivion) raised the necessary cash, stocked up on graph paper, and prepared to survey the entire compound.[33] Most of the gold and silver from the convent had been seized in 1922, but the iconostasis in the main cathedral still remained to be surveyed. In July, experts dismantled it for safekeeping. Meanwhile, the placing and condition of the royal coffins were quickly recorded before each was lifted for last-minute storage in one of the Archangel Cathedral's crypts.[34]

The situation, at the very least, was awkward socially. Each morning, groups of men assembled by the monastery walls, perhaps holding a match to light each other's cigarettes, perhaps sharing a topical joke. The photographs survive, and they show gaunt-faced figures in dusty boots, taking their short breaks in casual shirtsleeves. All were experts, and all had Kremlin passes and police clearance, but some had come to measure and sketch the monuments and others to make sure that the dynamite to blast them was correctly laid. The trust between the two

may well have been a fragile thing. One morning, when their conservation and surveying work was far from finished, the art historians arrived
for work to find that overnight the other gang had reduced their subjects, the old walls, to rubble.

There was no possible redress for this. Instead of wasting time on
protest, the experts turned their attention to the frescoes in the Chudov
Monastery's sixteenth-century Cathedral of the Miracle of Archangel
Michael, which was still standing. The head of Kremlin conservation
had been warned that there were only weeks left to record all these, and
in early December he asked a fellow-specialist, A. I. Anisimov, to chisel
out and store some of the better examples. By now, the temperature outside had dropped. The old buildings were not heated, so conservation
workers must have cursed as they hauled their gloves on and off, blow-
ing on clumsy, painful fingers. All the same, on 17 December
1929 Anisimov still believed he had two more weeks – a short time for
so delicate a task – when he, too, arrived to find that his site had been
dynamited before dawn. For the rest of the winter, he went on picking
through the rubble, determined to rescue any viable fragments while
there was still time. Parts of this hoard are now preserved like gems in
the Kremlin's own museum.[35] Vladimir Nevsky, of the Lenin Library,
wrote to deplore the loss of two 'establishments of importance to
the architecture of Russia in the fifteenth, sixteenth and seventeenth
centuries ... which contained the work of Russian masters of the fifteenth century, amazing frescoes and ancient pieces of unimaginable
perfection.'[36] Both he and the unfortunate Anisimov were soon to end
their days in one of Stalin's camps.

No one really believed the story that the Central Executive Committee
needed the Kremlin's monastery site for a military training school. Even
in a modernizing age, few Moscow architects would touch the commission to build it, though finally the work was taken on by I. I. Rerberg, a
man now better known for designing one of Moscow's railway termin-
als.[37] The resulting complex was impractical, and it was also hard to see
what kind of military training could take place next to the Politburo's
meeting room.[38] The school was soon closed and its building converted
for use as offices, a canteen and, some years later, as a Kremlin theatre.
The fact that Stalin and his aides were content to put up with all the
noise and dust, meanwhile, suggests that what they really could not

tolerate was the sight of monastery walls, even abandoned ones, for there were always other places for a school. But as they hoped, all trace of the religious houses disappeared. In 2007, a former Kremlin resident even assured me that no such buildings had ever existed. As he repeated, shrugging at my ignorance, 'there never was a monastery in the Kremlin'.[39] The Bolsheviks, clearly, had succeeded with him.

It was far easier to make a case for some remodelling of Ton's Grand Kremlin Palace. The goal this time was to provide a better conference centre. Of course, the Palace of Soviets, on the site of the lost Cathedral of Christ the Saviour, was supposed to be about to offer this, but that skyscraper was still in its planning stages (and would ultimately never get beyond them). Meanwhile, the Communist Party needed a hall large enough to seat several thousand delegates, together with facilities like lavatories and dining-rooms, and while the Bolshoi Theatre was a stop-gap, the Grand Palace in the Kremlin was a far more promising site. A team led by an architect called I. A. Ivanov-Shits began work there in 1932, and the brief was to complete the entire job in eighteen months, in time for the Communist Party's Seventeenth Congress.[40] The burly men with barrows and ungainly piles of tools moved in again, each one requiring prior clearance – on a daily basis – from security. Rudolf Peterson, who had replaced Pavel Malkov as Kremlin commandant, later remembered the exercise as a logistical nightmare.[41]

Few onlookers could really mourn the palace halls named for the Orders of St Andrew and St Alexander. Like so much else of recent date, the Grand Palace was opulent rather than tasteful. The gold leaf and the fake marble were quickly stripped, and the two massive rooms knocked into one. The resulting titanic space, to be known as the Sverdlov Hall after one of Lenin's deceased aides, was then panelled in wood (Stalin's favourite) and fitted with raked lines of seats without much protest from conservators. More ominous, however, was the threat to nearby sites, including some of the oldest on the Kremlin hill. The fifteenth-century Faceted Palace had served as a canteen for several years, but architects now eyed the nearby Red Stair, the last survivor (albeit a copy) of the canopied lines of steps that had once linked the first-floor royal terrace to Cathedral Square. In 1934 this relic was demolished to make way for a more comfortable dining-room and toilets. Meanwhile, there was the problem of the oldest building in Moscow, the Cathedral of the Saviour in the Forest. In 1932, this much-loved house of prayer was being used to display an exhibition of communist funeral wreaths, notably those of Lenin and Sverdlov.[42] In the 1990s, the daughter of Aleksei Rykov, who had once lived nearby, told a researcher that her father believed the church's fate was sealed because it darkened the windows of the flat that Stalin's henchman, Lazar Kaganovich, inherited at the time of Rykov's fall in 1932.[43] Such trivial reasons, worthy of an emperor like Nicholas I, may well have played a part, but just as likely is the fact that Stalin's court could hardly bear to leave a church alone. This one may well have been unique, a witness to the nation's deepest past, but that weighed little in Soviet plans. The building was too close to the palace for comfort, and in an age of brilliant electric light, it smelled of candlewax, tsarism and mice.

The Saviour in the Forest came down on a spring night, possibly on 1 May 1933. Fireworks were handy things whenever real explosions needed to be masked. Although archival sources now confirm that the decision to remove the church was taken by the Politburo in September 1932, the details of the demolition job, which was almost certainly carried out by the secret police, remain obscure.[44] Publicity was stifled, so the church's loss was not noticed abroad. In 1955, two decades after it had vanished into dust, the art historian Arthur Voyce published a study of the Kremlin that included a section, with pictures, on its oldest building, which he wrongly thought to be extant.[45] Even now, photographs of the demolition remain inaccessible, as does the fate of the original carved stone. The goal, in 1933, was not to doodle in history's margins but to rewrite whole chapters at a time, erasing inconvenient pasts as if they had never happened. Even the church's foundations were lost. In 2009, when I was taken on a tour of the Kremlin's hidden chambers, my expert guide looked out across the palace yard and pursed her lips. Her verdict on the Soviet block that now stood on the old cathedral site was economical: 'A pig-sty will always be a pig-sty.'

The Kremlin's rebranding was gathering pace. By 1937, on Stalin's orders, the images of St Nicholas and the Saviour had vanished from their respective gatehouses. Only the proposal, by Stalin's close friend Abel Enukidze, to paint the brick-red outer walls light grey caused the regime to pause. That idea was abandoned, but in 1935, following recommendations by Grabar, the double-headed eagles on the towers were finally removed.[46] Their replacements, at first, were three huge metal-plated stars, each decorated with the Communist Party's hammer and sickle, but though these had been set with semi-precious stones, the metal fittings soon corroded and the stars as a whole were too heavy. In 1937, in celebration of the twentieth anniversary of the revolution, they were dismantled in their turn, to be replaced by the red stars that everybody knows today. Made of ruby-coloured glass and lit from inside by electric lamps, these substitutes, each more than ten feet across, provided just the right image. They were so solid that they outlasted the Soviet empire.[47] The Kremlin had transcended its Muscovite past. Bleaker now, and heavily guarded, it was the perfect focal point for the windswept squares and granite-fronted boulevards of Stalin's capital.

Inside, however, there were still some corners of the citadel that the reformers did not try to improve. Even Stalin did not raise a hammer to the Dormition Cathedral, though objects from its treasury continued disappearing to fund state projects.[48] As the place where every ruler had been crowned since Ivan the Terrible, it must have held a special magic, not least for Stalin himself. The Annunciation and Archangel cathedrals endured, too, though their frescoes and icons suffered badly from the damp that descended as soon as they were locked in 1918. In 1938, a group of experts from the Kremlin's Armoury Museum pronounced these buildings 'chaotic, dirty and disorderly'. It was a shock, twenty years into the new age, to find the costly chandeliers in a heap on the tile floor, while ecclesiastical treasures that should have been stored in a museum were stacked like jumble in a couple of cupboards.[49] But though the curators' concerns were genuine, they could do little to remedy the situation. Their museum had troubles of its own.

Before her husband's fall, Natalya Trotskaya had managed to preserve the Armoury Chamber as a state museum, but it had not become the public attraction she envisaged. At best, a few groups visited each month, always pre-booked and often from the higher ranks of the trade unions and government. A foreigner who visited on a tour in the 1930s was surprised to see his Russian guide looking enviously at an ancient Baedeker he was carrying in his pocket. It turned out that the Russian, a local man, had never set foot in the Kremlin before, still less read anything reliable about its past.[50] Until the war, however, when Moscow faced bombardment and potential invasion, the Armoury Museum was not entirely closed. Its main problem was to fend off government scavengers, most of whom viewed treasure as hard currency in crude bulk form.[51] First came Pomgol, the committee for relieving the famine of 1921. From 1928, it was the turn of the Finance Commissariat (Narkomfin), whose need for currency increased with every step towards industrialization and inter-war rearmament. It did not matter what an object in the great collection meant. The point was to get it abroad, and icons, pearl-encrusted robes, jewels and Fabergé eggs were all fair game. Outside Moscow, the nation's remaining monasteries were also closing one by one, and treasure from their strongrooms turned up in the Kremlin for cataloguing (and pre-export triage) almost every week. By 1929, the museum's director, Dmitry Ivanov, could stand no further strain. His health in ruins, he retired. By this time, many of his better staff had also left their posts.[52]

Ivanov's successor was a true son of the new regime. By this stage, jobs in the workers' paradise were being assigned on the basis of a candidate's social origin rather than any relevant professional experience.[53] The one employer in the land – the state – made sure that workers 'from the bench' were promoted to directorships, to boards of educational and scientific management, and, in the Kremlin's case, to curate a museum of priceless art. Sergei Monakhitin, brought to the Kremlin from the Borets armaments factory in 1929, aimed to liquidate the museum's 'patriarchal' heritage, an exercise that involved acceding to the industrializers' regular demands for gold.[54] In 1930, the year of the Sixteenth Party Congress, he also agreed to devote an exhibition to defence, arranging objects in his now-empty vitrines to illustrate steel refinement and weapons manufacture. The Marxist scheme of historical progress dictated themes for later exhibitions, which often featured stages in the development of the means of production. It turned out that there was almost nothing in the museum's collection that could show what life was like for working-class Slavs in the so-called feudal era, so models had to be made and landscapes painted to create the right sort of mood. Fakes, in other words, replaced the real treasures the museum had lost.

It was a futile, even tragic, labour. While employees packed up the real pride of the museum, now just so much silver and gold, their bosses replaced it with exhibits that had nothing to do with the site, its history, or any lived reality on earth. And their compliance did not even save them from arrest. In December 1934, Stalin's comrade, Sergei Kirov, was murdered in his Leningrad office by a killer who had managed to equip himself with a valid pass to the city's Party headquarters as well as a loaded gun. Stalin concluded that security should be tightened everywhere. His entourage, the real elite, were each assigned a full-time detail of bodyguards, and also obliged to adopt precautions that ranged from spy-devices for their cars to secret codes for almost everything.[55] A purge of Kremlin staff was inevitable, and Monakhitin's team was not exempt.[56] The Armoury Museum director himself was replaced by Kupriyan Maslov, a former Red Army commander with twelve years' experience in the security organs.[57] Other museum staff disappeared into the stronghold of Moscow's secret police, the Lubyanka, and many of the rest resigned and fled before the same fate could befall them. By 1936 the Armoury Museum was barely functioning.

For all that, the new director wanted the place to look successful, and to present a bright face to the world. In April 1936, when any Muscovite who wanted a new suit could expect to stand in a six-hour queue, Maslov decreed that his staff should be 'dressed in clean clothes', and that they should be 'neat and courteous in their relations with one another and with visitors'. He reasoned that anyone, however hungry, could force a smile, but to make sure of the grooming and attire he also fitted out a staff wardrobe, from which, at the first sign of a visitor, the more sartorially challenged of his staff could snatch something respectable. This wardrobe could have gone into an exhibition about Soviet life in its own right, for it contained the whole range of scarce but locally produced ties and shoes, hats, shirts, clean collars and even pairs of ladies' stockings.[58] By the beginning of 1939, however, there was almost no-one around to wear the stuff. The museum had only two guides left.[59]

The Seventeenth Congress of the Communist Party of the Soviet Union assembled in the reappointed Kremlin Palace in January 1934. There were almost two thousand delegates, and they came from every republic and region in the Soviet empire. For two weeks, they listened to a lot of rambling speeches and pre-scripted, tedious debates. The room was always over-hot and the speakers, who often held forth for three or four hours at a stretch, were not always audible towards the back, but the tone of the gathering was so euphoric that it was later dubbed the 'Congress of Victors'. In private, however, at least one bystander rechristened it 'the Congress of the Victor'.[60] Josef Stalin's primacy within the Party elite had been established at the end of 1929, when the state-controlled press had celebrated his fiftieth birthday (though actually it was his fifty-first[61]) by launching what was later called the 'cult of personality'. He had defeated every rival by his relentless version of politics. By the time of the meeting in 1934, Trotsky had fled, but all the others trooped up to the speakers' platform to sing Stalin's praises. They ranged from Zinoviev and Kamenev (Lenin's one-time aides) to Bukharin, Rykov and Tomsky (a trio recently accused of resistance to Stalin's more excessive economic plans), and they were all veterans of struggle, politics, and civil war. Within five years, all were dead, and over half the delegates who had cheered them on had also been arrested or shot.

One key to Stalin's seemingly uncanny power was the network of spies and thugs who reported to him alone.[62] Since Ivan III, if not before, every regime in the Kremlin had placed an unhealthy emphasis on systems of control, on locks and spy-holes, guards and hidden passageways, but Stalin's was an extreme case. The system he inherited on Lenin's death had been preoccupied with secrecy. There were ciphers and codes for almost all government work, and information about anything from social unrest to the real state of the nation's economic life was classified.[63] The value placed on all of this was made plain in 1922, when a leading Bolshevik offered a reward of a hundred million rubles for the return of a briefcase containing secret documents and an encryption code.[64] Inside the Kremlin through the civil war, the country's leaders used a system of field telephones, which was considered more secure than a conventional exchange until new secret lines could be installed in 1923.[65] But the Cheka, and its successors, the GPU and the NKVD, spied on them all, and beyond them a further, yet more inner group, Stalin's personal network, reported directly to his office on everything from the economy to local gossip and the foibles of the Kremlin commandant. Technology soon played a part – the Kremlin was riddled with ducting, passageways and secret bugs[66] – but diligent interrogation, hours of reading, and a menu of low-level crime on the state's own behalf (break-ins and blackmail, for a start[67]) formed the system's backbone. 'You could not even sneeze,' a former Kremlin aide remarked, 'without the GPU knowing it.'[68]

Although he lived in the Kremlin, Stalin's office was originally located in the Central Committee's building on nearby Old Square, where bureaucrats worked with the Party's personnel and other operational records. His move to more secure quarters was prompted by an alleged attempt on his life. In 1931, he and the Secret Department of the Central Committee took over a suite of offices in the corner of the Senate Building (now rechristened 'Kremlin Corpus No. 1'), close to the Nikolsky gates. Stalin's new sanctum, a pair of rooms, was austere, smoke-filled, and equipped with books, maps, a globe and portraits of Lenin and Kutuzov.[69] To reach it (if you had the right papers) you climbed a short flight of carpetless steps from the courtyard and crossed a guard-filled anteroom. Beyond, along an impressive stretch of corridor ('like a museum', one witness recalled[70]), there were several offices, the largest of which was a reception-room in which Stalin's private staff would be at work. Until his death in 1935, Ivan Tovstukha was the leader's right-hand man. Thereafter, the job passed to Alexander Poskrebyshev, the head of the Central Committee's Secret Department and co-ordinator of everything from Stalin's diary of appointments to classified intelligence reports.[71] No-one entered Stalin's room without speaking to Poskrebyshev, and no-one spoke to Poskrebyshev without a nod from Nikolai Vlasik, Stalin's chief bodyguard. As well as making use of secrets, Stalin exploited fully the power of awe.

His other trump card, often, was straight material largesse. The Muscovite state of the first Romanovs had operated by granting privileges (as opposed to respecting rights), and this court used a similar technique.[72] In the 1930s, the shops were empty and private trade all but extinct, so goods and services were parcelled out, rather than purchased openly, and individuals had no consumer choice. Even ordinary employees, including factory workers and labourers, received small parcels of food as well as pay each week. Party members, the elite, could expect a whole range of other benefits, graded to reflect minute variations in status. Some went on holiday to Black Sea spas, others cut open tins of caviare, but privilege of any kind was proof of civic worth, and its withdrawal was often the harbinger of disgrace and possible arrest. In the shadow of the Gulag in the 1930s, a length of quality cloth or pair of boots was more than merely scarce and precious. Its arrival was a real relief. When you unpacked your precious box, a reward for the toils of Party membership, a complimentary tin of fish was as good as a government reprieve.

The little treats were important at congress-time. It was an honour anyway for the provincials to visit Moscow, let alone the Kremlin itself, but there were other signs that proved the worth of Party men. In June 1930, for instance, each delegate to the Sixteenth Congress was issued with a set of tokens that they could exchange for goods. The list would have done justice to the seventeenth-century Muscovite court. On opening the envelope, no doubt bearing an official stamp in violet ink, each would have found that he could buy three bars of rationed soap (two of household quality, one marginally less rough), 800 grams (1¾ pounds) each of meat and cheese, a kilogram (just over 2 pounds) of salami and supplies of tinned food, sugar and cigarettes. Delegates were also to be fitted out with a rubberized raincoat each, the fabric for a suit, two sets of underwear and a pair of shoes. As a cynic noted in his private diary, the Party men who gave their 'stormy applause' to speeches about the country's 'economic achievements' would all have had in mind their private glee, just hours before, as they unpacked a precious lump of soap back in their hostel room.[73] It might have been humiliating to queue with all the rest, and even to accept the feudal-style largesse, but no-one was about to lose the parcels – sausage, rainproof coat and all – by hesitating later when they were required to vote. This was the congress that triumphantly agreed to meet the targets of the nation's economic Five Year Plan in four years.

In such a system, it was also natural that the elite should have the best. The Kremlin was more exclusive than any club. First, in the early 1920s, came the shop (unimaginatively called 'Kremlin'), located on the first floor of the former kitchen block, where merchandise could not be viewed, still less purchased, by anyone who did not have a special pass. The closed store turned out to be such a good idea that it was copied, with diminishing levels of opulence, by every public body from the secret police to larger factories and mines.[74] To protect the privacy of Kremlin shoppers (especially when the premises moved out to GUM), the windows of the elite store were masked with giant posters of the champions of the world's hungry and oppressed, Lenin and Marx.[75] Next came the private clinics, private spas, and the private canteen. Lydia Shatunovskaya, who lived above the Kremlin canteen in the 1920s, recalled that it was always busy. In the early evening, as another witness, Sergei Dmitrievsky, confirmed, it was as if Moscow's entire political class was there. The food was traditional and Russian, with home-baked bread and little pies, milk, kvass, and endless cups of tea, but the prices, as Shatunovskaya observed, were 'practically symbolic'.

While Moscow went hungry and the peasants starved, Kremlin diners lingered noisily over greasy soup and cucumbers, their conversation – in this secure place – always turning to the people at the top.[76] But hygiene here was little different from the general public norm. It is perversely gratifying to learn that almost every member of this hypocritical elite was ill with something almost all the time.[77]

Though rumours of the closed shops and the private spas built up the charisma of power, it was vital, in the workers' state, that the truth remained veiled. No-one was supposed to flaunt their wealth, and no-one could, for nothing was really secure, and the state could take everything away as quickly as it had given it. Even senior politicians and administrators had to petition the head of the Central Executive Commission, Abel Enukidze, for favours such as apartment repairs, sick leave, and the cash and permits for their holidays.[78] There were no special, ostentatious robes for Stalin's incarnation of the Kremlin court, either. 'The tablecloths are clean,' Dmitrievsky wrote, 'but the atmosphere is domestic.' He doubted that there were more than three dinner-jackets anywhere in the fortress in the 1920s, and Lunacharsky ('the dandy') was the only person who wore one regularly. The head of protocol at the Commissariat for Foreign Affairs, a man called Florinsky, once tried to make the right impression by travelling to meet a foreign visitor in a borrowed top hat. When a group of boys caught sight of him in a street near the Kremlin they started to cheer, skipping beside his car and shouting: 'The circus has come, the circus has come!'[79]

Stories of the domestic, even modest, style of life in the Kremlin are confirmed by almost every source. It was the corrupting miasma of power, rather than wealth alone, that ruined children like Vyacheslav Molotov's daughter, who began abusing alcohol in her schooldays.[80] Stalin's daughter, Svetlana Allilueva, insisted that her childhood was comfortable but not opulent. 'The apartment had two rooms for the children and I shared mine with Nanny,' she wrote. 'There was no room for pictures on the walls – they were lined with books. In addition there was a library, Nadya's [Stalin's wife's] room, and Stalin's tiny bedroom in which stood a table of telephones ... It was homely, with bourgeois furniture.'[81] Many other apartments felt more like sparse hotel-suites, and some seemed distinctly under-furnished, for the better relics from the palaces – fine chairs and sideboards, gilded mirrors and the like – had all been requisitioned and exported by the vultures from the Finance

17. Fedor Yakovlevich Alekseev, Church of the Saviour in the Forest, 1800–1810.

18. The interior of the Faceted Palace.

19. An early twentieth-century postcard of the monument to Tsar Alexander II.

20. Street scene close to the Saviour Tower and Kremlin walls, *c.* 1898.

21. S. P. Bartenev's map of the Kremlin, from *The Moscow Kremlin in Old Times and Now*, early twentieth century.

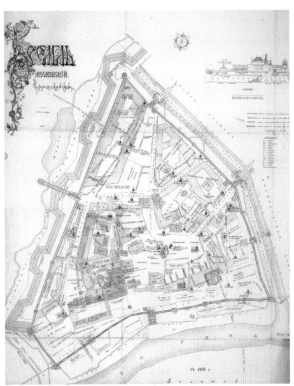

22. Henri Gervex, study for *The Coronation of Tsar Nicholas II and Tsarina Alexandra in the Church of the Assumption [Dormition] on 14th May 1896*

23. Mounted soldiers guarding the Kremlin's Nikolsky gate in the aftermath of the February 1917 revolution.

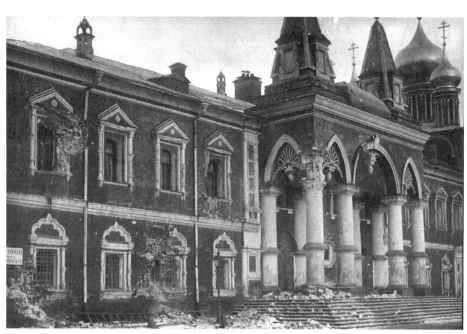

24. Shrapnel damage to the Chudov Monastery in the wake of shelling in November 1917.

25. Lenin (*third from left*) beside the Kremlin walls at the inauguration of S. T. Konenkov's commemorative bas-relief, 'Genius', 7 November 1918.

26. Alexander Gerasimov, *Joseph Stalin and Kliment Voroshilov in the Kremlin*, 1938.

27. Victory Parade in Red Square, 1945.

28. Lenin's Mausoleum on Red Square.

29. A group of Party VIPs, including Leonid Brezhnev, Nikolai Podgorny, East Germany's Walter Ulbricht, Mikhail Suslov and Mongolian leader Yumzhagin Tsedenbal, on top of the Lenin Mausoleum during a ceremonial meeting of the All-Union Winners Youth Rally, Moscow, September 1966.

30. Soviet President Mikhail Gorbachev and Russian President Boris Yeltsin at a Kremlin press conference in October 1991.

31. The exterior of the Faceted Palace, showing the reconstructed Red Stair (1992–4).

32. Russian President Vladimir Putin (*left*) and former President Boris Yeltsin on the ceremonial palace steps during the inauguration ceremony for Putin on 7 May 2000.

Commissariat.[82] 'We lived as if on an island,' Nami Mikoyan recalled. 'But it was neither exotic nor luxurious. Behind its red-brick walls, it was more like a comfortable, silent prison.'[83]

Another resident did add, however, that the service in the citadel was faultless: 'polite, discreet, modest'.[84] In this land of proletarian freedom, the servants who loaded the Kremlin's wood-burning stoves each morning were asked to wear soft slippers so that the commissars could sleep.[85] 'The comfort was apparent,' Nami Mikoyan remarked, 'in the cleanliness of the linen.'[86] There were maids and there were nurses, and any man in the circle of power could expect dancers and actresses to come and share a glass of wine after a performance. Vlasik and Poskrebyshev loved young women, Enukidze was keen on the ballet, Bonch-Bruevich held legendary parties for the artistic set, and Mikhail Kalinin, the ageing prime minister, was fond of operetta.[87] Even the most popular theatrical stars knew that they had no option if they were asked to a late dinner. There were plenty of talented women in the Siberian labour camps.

Liaisons between politicians and attractive female stars were permitted (and, in the hidden eyries of the secret police, welcomed) because they left the perpetrators open to blackmail.[88] Scandals, however, were a different affair, for Soviet leaders were expected to present a moral public face. Their most indulgent parties took place safely out of Moscow, in their dachas and at holiday resorts. Everyone knew that Enukidze liked his dancers and that secret-police chief Yagoda was dissolute, but if their private lives stayed out of sight the myth of the good Bolshevik endured. When Kalinin and a glamorous guest, the prima donna Tatiana Balch, were caught in a Moscow city traffic-jam one evening, they paid dearly for their indiscretion. A crowd formed round the marooned car, and citizens, recognizing the politician and the soft-fleshed beauty at his side, began to whistle and to throw insults, followed by stones and lumps of mud.[89] Like a naughty schoolboy, the grand old man of Russian politics faced an awkward audience with Stalin the next morning.

It was not the white sheets and the scented soap, then, but access to information and to a stock of patronage that made life in the Kremlin such a prize. To leave the fortress was to lose almost everything. Even in the 1920s, when parts of the citadel were real slums, it had proved near-impossible to move residents out.[90] From Bonch-Bruevich to the proletarian poet Demyan Bedny, the Kremlin's occupants used every guile to hold on to their flats.[91] If someone died, there was a stampede to secure their space. In 1931, in an attempt to reduce overcrowding on the hill, some were invited to move into the newly completed House on the Embankment, a luxury apartment block with views over the Moscow river, but the response was very slow. The new place might have had its own spa and closed shops, a clinic and a cinema, and it even boasted central heating and unlimited hot water in place of the Kremlin's shared old bathrooms and old-fashioned stoves, but everyone knew that the only place for an ambitious politician was inside the fort.

On the night of 8 November 1932, while her husband was lingering at a Kremlin dinner to celebrate the fifteenth anniversary of the Bolshevik revolution, Stalin's wife, Nadezhda Allilueva, retreated to her prettily furnished bedroom with its raspberry-pink rug. She was dressed for a party, but she pulled out the rose she had been wearing in her hair. She then threw off the coat that she had donned to take her final, troubled, walk around the palace. Stepping over to the dressing-table where she kept her bottles of Chanel perfume, she picked up the Walther pistol that her brother had sent her from Berlin and shot herself through the heart.[92] Stalin did not look for her when he went to bed in his own small chamber, so it was the housekeeper, Karolina Till, who found the body lying in a pool of blood the following morning. 'It was all so strange,' recalled Svetlana, who was not yet seven at the time. 'Suddenly everyone was crying and we were sent away to the dacha, to Zubalovo.'[93]

Nadezhda had succumbed to depression and strain. She could no longer tolerate the tales of peasant suffering, the deaths, the lies. Stalin did not attend her burial at the Novodevichy Monastery, but the loss struck him more deeply than he ever acknowledged. In the short term, he quit the Kremlin apartment that they had shared (he swapped with Bukharin at first, and then moved into the Senate). More generally, however, the death, which Stalin seems to have experienced as a betrayal, drove him to take extreme measures. As the official news went out that Nadezhda had died of appendicitis, his staff prepared to stifle the truth. Kremlin servants who knew the story were dismissed or arrested one by one. By the end of 1935, it was safe to assume that every cleaner and every cook who served in the citadel reported directly to the secret police. Files in the archive of Nikolai Ezhov, who later headed the Commissariat for Internal Affairs (NKVD), show that the campaign to cover up the reasons for Nadezhda's death began at once and dragged on until the eve of the coming war. Among the victims were the Kremlin commandant, Rudolf Peterson, who was held to account for the fact that the story had leaked at all, and Nadezhda's godfather, Abel Enukidze, the head of the Central Executive Commission and the man who really ran the Kremlin lives of the elite.

But Stalin's better-planned campaigns were always designed to hit more than one target. Nadezhda's death coincided with his long-running vendetta against Lenin's one-time aides, Lev Kamenev and Grigorii Zinoviev. Neither presented a viable threat to anything in 1932, but Stalin's preferred tactic was to destroy an enemy completely, not just move him aside. For that reason, the files that the police assembled from the summer of 1933, case by case, included questions that touched on Nadezhda, on Kremlin gossip, but also on the supposed crimes of Stalin's old foes. Everything was made to connect, and the first that many frightened witnesses (or defendants) would know about the overall design was when an odd, irrelevant and unexpected question came up in their second, third or later police interrogation. By that stage, most would have been too confused to dodge the bullet.

In the summer of 1933, a member of staff in the Central Executive Commission's library in the Kremlin reported that some people in her team were borrowing foreign journals. One librarian in particular, a former aristocrat with a professional interest in Persia, also appeared to be following too much gossip, to the point of noticing the cars that Party leaders drove. According to her boss, this woman, called Mukhanova, had an interest in signalling systems, and her brother was an engineer. To crown it all, she happened to be a friend of the Kamenevs, and her circle included several former Trotskyists.[94] They were all helping each other, sometimes over apartments or food, sometimes over Kremlin passes. Such things were just what the police needed to know.

The case (a web of fabrication) went no further that summer, and it could have ended, like many others, as a file in the vaults of the Lubyanka: stamped, bound and crumbling. Mukhanova, whom her employer described as 'a typical bourgeois, always ill', left her job in the Kremlin library in December 1933.[95] But the file lay waiting, and in 1935 it was reopened. By then, Sergei Kirov had been murdered, a crime that seemed to prove how devious the regime's foes could be. Though Kirov had been shot in Leningrad (and his killer was almost certainly a man he had cuckolded[96]), Stalin responded by putting the Kremlin into lockdown. The cooks and cleaners had to enter through a different gate and follow new routes on their way to work.[97] It was time, at last, to rid the place of every lurking enemy, and Stalin's men knew just how to do that. Ezhov, who ran the campaign, made frequent private visits to Stalin's Kremlin office in the Senate building all that spring, no doubt reporting on the tactics and the progress of it all.[98] By April 1935, with some prompting from his inquisitors, even the women who mopped the Kremlin floors were calmly admitting that they knew of secret caches of strychnine and hidden guns.

Several birds at once were lined up for the coming stone. As everybody knew, there were still staff in the Kremlin who had worked for the palace in the days of the last tsars. Such retainers, whose appointments owed nothing to the new regime, were no longer regarded as reliable. There were questions, too, about a large number of the rest. The police interrogators of 1935 found that many cleaners and maids had been recruited to the Kremlin in the 1920s through friends and family on the inside.[99] The right security checks might have been made, but any small circle of friends was a spy-network in the making, a web of mutual loyalty and protection, owing nothing to the Boss, Stalin. There were also far too many Kremlin passes in circulation generally (another lapse for which the Kremlin commandant, Rudolf Peterson, was soon to pay). The fortress seemed to leak gossip.[100] As Stalin read the file on his own staff, the list of reasons to get rid of the whole bunch ran on and on.

In the spring of 1935, the questioning began in earnest. An issue that came up in nearly every file was Nadezhda's death. A librarian may have heard that Stalin shot her or that she did not die in her sleep. A cleaner might have listened as a guard suggested that she killed herself, perhaps because she disagreed with her husband's politics but maybe, too, because he beat and insulted her. As they drank their tea in steamy kitchens, some may have reasoned that there must be other plots, and that Nadezhda had simply been the first to die.[101] Like most reports of NKVD interrogations, the records are replete with clues about the things that Soviet people were not supposed to be thinking or saying at the time. It was worth noting down, for instance, that a few Kremlin staff had been caught gossiping about the good life that most Europeans seemed to live. There had also been some overt talk (the truth, and therefore very dangerous) about a famine in Ukraine.[102]

Abel Enukidze, 'Uncle' Abel, was a popular figure, and he was a favourite in the circle of Stalin's own family. What emerged from the police reports on him was that he had become soft-hearted, and had offered jobs and small handouts when friends had found themselves in need. It was his doing, indeed, that so many figures from the intellectual and cosmopolitan opposition (the movement identified with Trotsky) had ended up working in the Kremlin library. Ezhov tarred Enukidze with corruption, a charge that could probably have been levelled at any officer of state with a budget to manage. Uncle or not, he lost his job in 1935, though he was left alive for two more years. Kamenev, meanwhile, could only watch in stupefaction as a cruel tale, fantastic and elaborate, was assembled around him. Mukhanova had been the first piece of the jigsaw, but in 1935 successive Kremlin hangers-on were questioned, usually over several days. A case was fabricated piece by piece, eventually forming Stalin's desired picture of a Kremlin terrorist cell with links to Kamenev, his brother, and his wife. The plotters' goal, of course, was nothing less than the murder of the Boss himself. The jigsaw was complete by the middle of 1935. It is said that Kamenev walked calmly down the Senate corridors to his final interview with Stalin. Zinoviev, however, reportedly collapsed on his way to the stifling Kremlin study and had to be carried between two of his guards.

As the Kremlin affair of 1935 gathered pace, Rudolf Peterson, the citadel's trusted commandant and holder of the Order of the Red Banner, tried to avert disaster by sending a statement to the police. As he explained, the summer of 1933 had been a time of frantic building work. His entire effort had been focused on completing the great hall of the Kremlin Palace in time for the Seventeenth Congress. Perhaps, then, he had not attended the right classes in Marxism-Leninism, and perhaps his men, working till the small hours and at weekends, had not made time to read the latest pamphlets either. Perhaps, too, he had avoided working with Finns, Estonians and Jews, but maybe he was wary of potential foreign networks and not simply an enemy of universal brotherhood. He had more trouble with tales of his drinking, and especially with reports that he had got so drunk at a party for the great hall's completion that he had danced around in it, singing and kissing the builders, but even this would not have been a problem at another time. The entire staff enjoyed a drink, and men were often drunk at work.[103] The point was that Peterson, like Enukidze, was a marked man: the

Kremlin could not be purged unless his security regime could be shown to have failed. The police found all the evidence that they required.[104] The new commandant, clearly, would have to be a ranking officer in the secret police, and he would also have to have a personal connection to Ezhov.

The 1935 Kremlin affair eventually claimed 110 people. As staff in the fortress were later told – at a closed session chaired by Ezhov himself – 'it was only thanks to Comrade Stalin that it was possible to uncover the hidden ... nest of ... scum'.[105] The library in the Kremlin was closed, and several other facilities were shut down overnight. Among those left was the private hospital, located near the Kremlin on Vozdvizhenka street. Stalin was preoccupied with his own health. He was, in fact, as fascinated by research into longevity as he was haunted by the fear of enemies. He needed doctors, but he also mistrusted them, not least because he had a team of his own working to develop undetectable poisons in a secret toxicological laboratory behind the Lubyanka.[106] While Ezhov was getting rid of Enukidze and his men, therefore, another of Stalin's aides, Karl Pauker, was sent to purge the Kremlin's medical establishment.

Pauker's team reported a series of melodramatic discoveries. In the age of Agatha Christie, the Soviet secret police could write detective fiction with the best. Some of the lapses they claimed to have uncovered at the hospital could have been merely careless: bottles of pills had been mislabelled, quantities misread. A patient had been given caffeine instead of codeine. But when it was alleged that twelve cyanide capsules had disappeared, the sleuths knew that they had a case.[107] In the hospital, as in the Kremlin itself, older staff and experts trained under the old regime came under scrutiny and were dismissed. In a series of charges that was to become standard in the years of the great purge, they were found to include former White-guardists, criminals, and foreign agents. One, unusually (the secret police were ever prudish in their use of terms), was declared to be a homosexual, a crime compounded by the discovery that he was also 'very religious' and often received visits from priests.[108] The fear and the repression followed, and medicine, like engineering, agronomy, and most forms of historical research, became a potentially lethal vocation. But so was most security work. As Stalin's aide, Pauker is said to have personally attended Zinoviev's execution. He was himself shot soon after, perhaps because he felt secure enough to sneer as he delivered his report.[109]

The Kremlin, once a much-loved landmark, became an object of dread. 'We were afraid to go near it,' Muscovites repeat as they describe its place in their affections during Stalin's rule. There were, of course, the state functions and formal banquets. Stalin is said to have made more welcome speeches to parties of shock-workers and hero-airmen in 1935 than in any other year before or after, but though the lights were bright and the food abundant, no-one warmed to the Kremlin itself.[110] The few remaining residents seem to have disliked it. In the wake of the Kremlin affair, the number of elite politicians with Kremlin apartments shrank to less than a dozen. 'It was dead,' Sergo Mikoyan (the son of Stalin's minister of foreign trade) explained. 'Just stones.' Stalin's daughter, who lived in the Kremlin for twenty-five years, claimed that she 'could not stand' it.[111] By the middle of the 1930s, the leader himself seldom spent a night there, preferring to sleep five miles away at the dacha that his architects had built for him after Nadezhda's death. Even the citadel's historic population of hooded crows was subjected to an inventive campaign of persecution by the Kremlin commandant, for Stalin could not tolerate the birds.[112] The jolliest creature in the fortress was probably Bukharin's fox, a former pet. Years after its master had been shot, Svetlana Allilueva remembered watching it playing hide and seek in the Tainitskie gardens, well out of sight of all the men in grey.[113]

The security alone must have been stifling. The bodyguards stuck to their VIPs like ticks, and also kept tabs on them for Stalin's police.[114] Whenever several members of Stalin's clique gathered at once, which happened almost every afternoon, the guards were multiplied, and on Thursdays, when the Politburo was scheduled to meet, the Kremlin as a whole was sealed. Svetlana Allilueva remembered the surreal processions that sometimes took place on the nights when her father wanted to watch a film after one of those meetings. In later life, Stalin occasionally convened the Politburo in the cinema itself, a space he had created in the former conservatory of the Grand Palace, but before 1939 there was still some semblance of collective government.[115] The official business in the Senate building would end at nine or ten in the evening, and then the whole group would move off to watch their movie, crossing the cold deserted square to the palace with young Svetlana in the lead. The gates were locked, the walls bugged, and nothing could approach the Kremlin from outside without detection, but all the same the huddled band had to be followed by an armoured car, bumping around the dark buildings at walking pace.[116]

Everything was suspect. Sergo Mikoyan remembered his father receiving a crate of wine from the Caucasus, every bottle of which had to be removed for testing. The leaders' children could not bring packets of sweets from town into their flats. No visitor could bring a parcel and no bag was left unchecked.[117] But not even Stalin could stay in the Kremlin all the time. The greatest danger threatened when the leaders had to travel. Stalin's successor, Nikita Khrushchev, remembered how the great man would order his driver to take a different route every night as he drove to and from the Kremlin. He used his own street plan of Moscow, and neither driver nor bodyguard was told the route in advance.[118] In 1949, a short-sighted woman who was careless enough to use a pair of opera-glasses to check the time by a city-centre clock accidentally caught sight of Stalin's car as it sped up to the Borovitsky gates. She was arrested and spent six years in a labour camp.[119] A Muscovite who used to live on Mokhovaya street, opposite the Kremlin, told me that his father's camera and film were seized the morning after he made the mistake of testing them by taking a single picture from the back of a room whose windows faced the Kremlin walls.[120]

And there were other secrets underground. Stalin's agents were fascinated by tunnels and hidden rooms. In 1923, during the restoration of Golitsyn's palace, the secret police combined work on their own projects with a fresh attempt to find Ivan the Terrible's lost library, searching the lower end of Okhotnyi Ryad for underground chambers and iron doors.[121] Thereafter, any city-centre work brought them down from their grisly roosts, torches and measuring-tapes in hand.[122] Always fascinated by the great leaders of Russia's past, Stalin himself took an interest, and in 1933, under Peterson's security regime, a civilian enthusiast called Stelletskii received a permit to dig inside the Kremlin. At the interview where they agreed the deal, Peterson told the explorer that his own men (all secret police) had not located any chambers during work to build the military school (he meant, of course, under the sites of the two monasteries that they had just destroyed). Obediently, Stelletskii dug on the opposite side of the fortress, carting large quantities of earth from underneath the Arsenal Tower throughout the early months of 1934.[123] His dig received some expert help from the architect Shchusev, who had found an old tunnel of his own (soon open to the elite through a private entrance near the Senate Tower) during excavations for the Lenin mausoleum.[124] There was a flicker of hope that something really new might soon be learned about the Kremlin's past, but the operation shut down for some major Party meetings in the late autumn of 1934, and then came Sergei Kirov's death.

The public would learn little more about the networks underground. The stories of a secret world under their city, however, continue to fascinate Muscovites even now. The Kremlin catacombs, they believe, are extensive enough to accommodate a large part of the nation's gold reserves, as well as a vast communications system.[125] Stalin certainly added a bomb-shelter, his bunker, which had at least two exits and very strong walls. In 1994, during the restoration of the Senate, builders found a further hidden tunnel, whose location would have allowed someone (the evidence points to the post-war secret-police chief, Lavrenty Beria) to eavesdrop on Stalin himself.[126] There are always stories about a secret metro, too. From the time of its completion, it was widely observed that the public line that started on the edge of the Alexander Gardens and ran out through the Kiev train station was unusual because it did not cross the whole city as later lines were all to do. Muscovites immediately reasoned that there had to be a hidden extension, a parallel line leading under the Kremlin. If it followed the main public route from there, like all the service tunnels that were known to exist, it could easily have reached Stalin's dacha. The most persistent story now suggests that the order to complete the connection came in the aftermath of the war, when Stalin was afraid of an atomic strike.[127] The only route really known to exist, however, is served by an antiquated underground tram, and connects the Senate building with nearby Old Square, though it may run out further under Moscow at some point.[128]

Whatever the extent of that specific line ('it is hardly a transport artery' insists a former Kremlin aide[129]), there is no doubt that Stalin's fort still sits on a maze of underground systems, far larger than the 'Pindar' network that was built for Winston Churchill under London's Downing Street. The Kremlin's director of archaeological research, Tatiana Panova, would not show me her complicated maps of groundwater and geology as we leafed through an unpublished study of the site. 'It's secret,' she insisted, flicking through to safer stuff, 'secret, secret. You can't look.' Strain as I might (for all the good it would have done to anyone), I saw nothing but coloured lines, most of which were probably out of date several geological eras ago. In 2010, I asked Mikhail Gorbachev's friend and interpreter, Pavel Palazhchenko, to help me out, at least about the mythical metro. 'Of course it exists,' he replied at once, ebulliently waving his hands. But then he lowered his voice.

> Everyone knows it exists. But if you were to find someone who had actually seen it, if you were to find someone who really knew, they would never give you any details. They would never say anything. They could not tell you that it is still part of the Kremlin's secret communications network, could they?

Before we changed the subject he grew serious. 'If you really need to know about this, I'm sure your own intelligence services can give you the facts.'

The chill that citizens had felt as they passed Stalin's Kremlin in the worst years of mass arrests and secret executions (1937–8), did not ease while the old dictator lived. By 1939, however, there was a new atmosphere in Soviet politics and with it, another change of meaning for the Kremlin. Where recently it had appeared to stand for universal brotherhood, at least to judge by the red stars, the old fort was now reinvented (yet again) as Russia's bastion. The tone of Soviet discourse shifted rightwards as Europe circled towards war, and patriotism began to take the place of proletarian unity. A famous painting of 1938 by Alexander Gerasimov, now in the Tretyakov Gallery, shows Stalin and his defence chief, Kliment Voroshilov, pacing the Kremlin's grey terraces, clearly preparing to save Moscow. At the time, no-one knew exactly whom they were about to fight, but everything pointed towards a great defensive war. In May 1941, only a month before the German invasion, Stalin himself addressed a military gathering in the Kremlin hall, effectively making himself into a war-leader but incidentally linking the old fortress to his patriotic cause.[130] Heroic themes from Russia's past would soon be resurrected for the propaganda of war-time. Setting Karl Marx aside (reverently), people now learned over again how Russia had fought and defeated Napoleon and what a horseman from the days of Dmitry Donskoi might have worn for a helmet. The Soviet film industry produced a series of historical epics, too, including the blockbusters *Alexander Nevsky* (1938) and (co-starring the Kremlin itself) *Ivan the Terrible* (1944).

The war that came, however, brought the state to near-collapse. For several months in the late summer and autumn of 1941, even the Kremlin was in real danger. Many of its illustrious occupants were evacuated (Lenin's corpse took a holiday in Siberia), and so were most of the key ministries. The fate of a mysterious cache of radium, which had been lodged for safety in an underground strongroom in the fortress in May 1941, remains unclear, but the more conventional contents of the Armoury Museum were packed off to Sverdlovsk (formerly known as Ekaterinburg, and the city where the last Romanovs met their deaths) by the tiny band of staff who had hung on.[131] At the same time, sappers working in strict secrecy laid mines under key buildings in the capital, and documents in its archive suggest that the Kremlin was included on their list.[132]

Now dubbed 'the brains of the country', the architectural complex was watched over by special troops, some of them hidden in buildings around Red Square with orders to shoot anything that looked like an enemy.[133] The Kremlin's golden cupolas were masked in black, and fake buildings were created round it to confuse attackers from the air. Even so, the fortress took several direct hits from German bombers.[134] In October 1941, when officers of the Wehrmacht could already make out the city through field-glasses, Muscovites panicked, and it took the most brutal intervention by the secret police to stop a mass flight out of town. But Stalin himself remained. In November 1941, he held the customary gala meeting for the anniversary of the 1917 revolution in the underground hall of the Mayakovsky metro station, a sensible enough precaution when the city was at risk from bombs. The next day, however, he watched the annual military parade from an open-air platform on Lenin's mausoleum, waving to the Soviet Union's troops as they marched through Red Square and straight off to the front.

It was a magnificent piece of theatre. Stalin still preferred to sleep in his heavily guarded dacha, and often worked there for parts of the day, but the Kremlin provided him with an impressive headquarters, and he was ready to exploit it. For the duration of the war, propaganda images showed the Soviet leader in his Kremlin office, receiving reports, checking maps, consulting the top generals. And records of the visits to that panelled study confirm the myth: the leader worked in it for parts of almost every day, usually seeing people from late afternoon until the early hours of the morning.[135] In August 1942, Stalin received Churchill in the Kremlin (the British prime minister declined the offer of accommodation there). The delegation that arrived included several British officials and US diplomatic staff, but a note in the record observes that all but the most senior foreign-office men were made to wait outside the inner study in an anteroom.[136] The mystique mattered, and preserved the illusion (not quite correct) that Stalin was running this war-effort on his own.

As well as reminding the Soviet people just how hard their leader worked, the Kremlin also hosted gala celebrations for Russian triumphs. The two, indeed, were meant to seem inseparable. In August 1943, Moscow reverberated to the first of a series of 120-gun salutes, this one to mark the Soviet victory at Orel. The staging of successive celebrations was minutely choreographed, each time drawing attention to the primacy of the capital, the leader, and the Kremlin. One of the most ironic of these spectacles was the solemn repatriation, from Sverdlovsk, of the Armoury Museum's treasure in February 1945. Crowns and icons that had once been awkward relics, preserved (in some cases) because they were too distinctive to sell to collectors, now returned to the fortress as the nation's patrimony. A guard of honour from the Kremlin met their train, and the crates made their entrance to the palace up the regal marble stairs.[137]

It was a glittering reminder of the glory of the Russian state, and in the years to come that state, and not its citizens, was to play the hero in Stalin's version of history. The people, and the diverse, deeply held but half-forgotten beliefs of their past, faded into the shadows as state power and state-led ideology took centre stage. On 24 June 1945, the long-awaited Soviet victory parade rolled out in drenching rain. The crowds that gathered underneath the Kremlin walls were soaked, the rows of marching men looked cold; even the planned airforce fly-past had to be cancelled. Though Stalin assumed greatest credit for the victory itself, the most conspicuous role at the ceremony that day was played by the army's hero, Marshal Georgii Zhukov. As commander-in-chief of the proceedings, he presided from the saddle of a prancing, skittish horse. He managed to stay in control of that, but to those who had learned their history before the revolution, it was a sign of fatal hubris that he chose to ride into Red Square through the citadel's Saviour Gate. The route had been so sacred once that even tsars, in piety, had dismounted and walked. That night, Stalin's grand reception speech to 2,500 military officers in the great hall of the Kremlin Palace was even heavier with depressing portents. The leader thanked the army for its efforts, to be sure, but he described the Soviet people as 'little cogs', mere components in a huge and unrelenting state machine.

If anything, the Kremlin's isolation increased in the final years of Stalin's life. 'It was not so much an administrative complex,' wrote a witness, 'as a vast and oppressive wasteland. It was forbidden to walk in its territory.'[138] The decade after the war was a bleak time for all Russians. Millions went homeless, millions slaved. There was no choice but to rebuild the factories and transport links that had been destroyed, but in their private hardship and long nights of grief, many found it difficult to remember that infrastructure and production were meant to come before the consolation of the individual. The question of lost heritage was even more awkward. Resources – labour and supplies – were so scarce that it was hard to justify the rebuilding of a palace or a stretch of wall when so many people still needed homes. But pride in the old symbols also mattered, and there was constant pressure to reconstruct the best-loved landmarks in places like Leningrad, Pskov and Novgorod. The issue became critical in Moscow as early as 1944, when it was pointed out (with official prompting) that 1947 would mark the city's eight-hundredth anniversary. A writer at the time called on his fellow-citizens to 'listen more attentively to the voice of the past . . . We must bind ourselves to the roots of our nation.'[139]

This kind of patriotic fervour soon became unwise. National history, having served its turn, was downplayed from the summer of 1944. In its place, loyal communists were supposed to rally round their ideology and leaders. Though the Party itself had instigated the talk of jubilees, its Moscow committee resolved that the celebration of the city's founding should primarily be military. One of its members even ordained that Russians needed 'more politics and less history'.[140] That left the Kremlin's role uncertain, for it was not immediately obvious what part the fortress was meant to play in the forthcoming pageantry. The answer was to treat it as a special case, the incarnation of the Soviet Russian state and spiritual home of the immortal Lenin. On that pretext, a restoration programme, costing millions, was approved in June 1945.[141] The tension must have weighed on the architects whom Stalin summoned to his Senate office, often in the dead of night, to discuss the work inside the closed and largely empty site. His interest was scrupulous, for this was almost personal. At a time of continued ethnic tension and even outright nationalist revolt inside the Soviet empire, he meant the Kremlin's Russianness to make a statement. The lines of perfect battlements that still exist today, and details in several of the churches (including the Church of the Deposition of the Robe) reflect the taste and interests of the Boss.[142]

The team that led the renovation project included several familiar names. D. P. Sukhov, who had taken part in the conservation efforts of the 1920s, was one consultant, as was I. V. Rylsky, one-time head of the State Conservation workshops. Even an aged Grabar was there, dreaming of a project to restore a small part of the fortress to its original, fifteenth-century Italian, appearance.[143] This caused a storm, and in the end a compromise – roughly corresponding to the mid-seventeenth century – was agreed. The bricks were a problem, however, for no-one made the heavy versions any more, and so, like Aristotele Fioravanti and like Boris Godunov, Stalin's restorers commissioned a factory of their own. In the midst of post-war crisis, this special unit managed to turn out one and a half million heritage building-bricks in record time.[144] Stonemasons also worked to quarry the white stone required to mend more than three hundred decorative caps on battlements and towers. To keep the construction going in the winter, someone thought of introducing outdoor stoves, which blasted the Kremlin's walls with steam to keep them warm when the mercury dropped, whatever the workers themselves may have been feeling in the freezing air.[145]

Outside the Kremlin, however, the historical elements of Moscow's 1947 jubilee were diluted with large doses of Stalinist propaganda. A monumental new statue of the city's legendary founder was fine because it echoed current views about Stalin himself, for instance, but real academic history could be dangerous. When Petr Sytin, the Moscow historian, produced a celebratory tome that included a scholarly reference to the probable Finnish origins of the name 'Moscow', a derivation that had once been mentioned by Zabelin, he found himself in trouble. Only a traitor, it was ruled, could link the Russian capital with a defeated foe.[146] Nostalgia, too, was deemed suspect, for this romantic sort of history could easily dissolve into a tale of princes and foreigners and even the church. Accordingly, all seven centuries of the pre-Soviet past were treated like a prelude to the real tale, and only events after 1917 were allowed to count as 'genuine' history. As the Moscow City Communist Party's Comrade Popov put it, the Moscow of golden domes had to give way, even in its anniversary year, to the Moscow of red stars. The floodlights for the city's jubilee lit up some ugly civic buildings, such as the new State Planning offices, but left all churches in the dark. It was proposed that children's albums of the celebration should show Red Square without St Basil's to avoid potential questions about religion.[147] The children could be pacified with the newly available luxury, ice-cream, and everyone could marvel at the fireworks.

The eight-hundredth anniversary souvenir guidebooks to the Kremlin, thin and cheaply printed in the hardship of post-war, were masterpieces of Soviet fraud. A collection of woodcuts by an artist called Matorin begins by citing Karamzin. 'The Kremlin', it announces, 'is a place of great historical memories.' But history is not the focus of the pages that follow, many of which show the smiling faces of workers in Soviet caps.[148] Another souvenir, this one a collection of photographs, begins with Lenin and Stalin, the latter in his panelled study. There is a picture of the Lenin mausoleum that contrives to make Shchusev's stark cube look like the inspiration for the (much earlier) Senate Tower behind it, and there are pictures of Communist Party meetings in the great hall. Among the few historical images, the *terema* feature because they were built 'by Russian masters in 1637' (no mention of poor John Taler), but the only other fragments of the past are military trophies. It is particularly striking that the entire book contains no image whatsoever of a Kremlin church.[149]

A chastened Petr Sytin, lost for words in his own right, could only quote Stalin. 'Moscow', he wrote, 'is the model for every capital in the world.'[150] At the heart of it, the newly painted red fortress floated like a bizarre toy above the asphalt sea with which the latest batch of city planners had surrounded it. Or maybe it was more like an unfortunate live specimen, a rhinoceros or the last dodo, imported from a distant world as an exotic freak, but now condemned to stand in lonely silence in an alien, uncomprehending land.

I I

Kremlinology

The American writer John Steinbeck had to negotiate for weeks before he was allowed to take a tour of the Kremlin. The year was 1947, and Steinbeck was in Russia with the photographer Robert Capa. Though every move they made was watched, the pair travelled extensively, visiting the post-war ruins of Stalingrad as well as Soviet Georgia and the wheat-fields of Ukraine. The short walk from their hotel to the Kremlin, however, was much harder to organize, and for once Capa had to leave his camera behind. 'We approached the long, heavily-guarded causeway,' Steinbeck wrote. 'There were soldiers at the entrance. Our names were taken, and our permission scrutinized, and then a bell rang and a military escort went with us through the gate.' It was like crossing from daylight into shadow; even their guide, a Russian hand-picked for the job, had never been inside the Kremlin in his life. The place felt barren, almost empty. 'Just two hours in this royal palace so depressed us that we couldn't shake it all day,' Steinbeck remarked. 'What must a lifetime in it have done!' As they drowned the whole experience in whisky, the pair concluded that the Kremlin was 'the most gloomy place in the world'.[1]

The party did not go to the area where Stalin's officials worked, and they seem not to have visited the cathedrals, either. Their tour began and ended with the palace and the old *terema*. It was a desultory history lesson, and there would barely have been time to shudder at Tsar Ivan's ghost before the time came to leave. Like almost every visitor before and since, the two Americans made up for that by trying to convince themselves that they had seen authentic medieval sights, but their guide – if he had been a brave one – could probably have set them straight. The palace rooms and chapels that Steinbeck and Capa saw, after all, were not 'strange, and ancient, and kept just as they were'.[2] In the decades since 1917, they had been looted, gutted and then abandoned. The purge of 1935 had driven out the last of their old-fashioned staff, and many of their recent masters were dead. Even Stalin, for years the citadel's presiding genius, was spending less and less time on the site. At night, this Kremlin's darkness could seem almost tactile.[3] Its very towers sometimes seemed to vanish into it, for there were almost no street lamps in Moscow's central zone. On moonless nights, the five red stars, repaired and serviced since the war and now the brightest lights for miles, hung in the black like strange planets.

The first signal of Stalin's death, in that darkness, was probably a low-wattage electric light, the first of many that were snapped on when the telephones began to ring. The members of the tyrant's inner circle were not at home – they had been watching at his dacha in the suburbs – but their families waited for news, and the phones would also have summoned the Kremlin commandant and the deputy who had to wake the clerks. While all these struggled to absorb what had just happened, the headlights of a black car swept up to the Saviour gates. Juddering over the cobblestones inside, they were extinguished in the courtyard of the Senate, Kremlin Corpus No. 1. The car's main occupant was Lavrenty Beria, the head of Stalin's secret police, and he had come straight from the leader's deathbed to ransack an office and empty a safe.[4] Inside it were the documents Stalin had used to lock and unlock other people's hearts, including evidence of their personal foibles as well as damning reports about the state's excessive violence. An adept in the arts of defamation and blackmail himself, the police chief wanted all of these to help secure his own claim to the vacant throne. As it turned out the bid would fail, and Beria's comrades had him shot just months later. But the Kremlin continued to be a by-word for deception, presenting an austere face to the world that belied the conspiracies and turbulence within. Though parts of the fortress were opened to the public after Stalin's death, no visitor would see beyond some bland museum-like façades. The very structures of leadership were so inscrutable that outsiders were tempted to bundle the whole government – policemen and politicians, ideologists, generals and all – into a single category: 'The Kremlin'.

In the short term, Stalin's empire was set for a new spring. His death, in March 1953, opened the way for many overdue reforms. In the Gulag (which Steinbeck did not see), tens of thousands of political prisoners were freed; elsewhere, Russia's more fortunate citizens began to test their reflexes as if awakening from a long sleep. The Kremlin, too, emerged from its deep gloom, and the first New Year of the new age, in January 1954, was celebrated in a blaze of chandeliers and tiny decorative lights. At the centre of it all was a large spruce tree, festooned and sparkling in the over-heated cavern of St George's Hall. There was music and spontaneous laughter, and the Kremlin squares saw their first snowball fight in a generation.[5] Later that year, the first escorted tours were admitted, and in July 1955 the Kremlin grounds were finally opened to the public. From a security point of view, such latitude was possible only because Stalin's ultimate heir, Nikita Khrushchev, had opted for a residence elsewhere, in equally exclusive premises on the Lenin Hills. The story persists that his wife, Nina Petrovna, refused point-blank to live in the dead tyrant's Kremlin rooms. By 1955, the last remaining Kremlin VIPs, including the Mikoyans and Molotovs, had also moved out of the fort, allowing staff to tidy up, plant shrubs on the old tennis courts, and open windows that had rusted shut.[6] But public access was the vital change. It was, some later said, 'the first step towards the liberalisation of the Soviet regime'.[7]

It was also a step closer to the Kremlin's rebirth as a tourist attraction. There had been crowds of many kinds over the centuries, there had even been foreign armies of occupation, but never before had the Kremlin seen the slack-jawed milling of excursion parties in leisure clothes. The post-war Soviet Union was a land where holidays, in the form of regimented, rather joyless groups, were virtually prescribed (not least to foster healthy productivity), and the Kremlin became a fixture on the Moscow route. The first visitors were from the capital itself: factory-workers, office-staff, proud children boasting the red necktie of the Communist Party youth organization, the Pioneers. But soon the Kremlin was attracting citizens from Ukraine and the Baltic and (in exceptional cases) the far-off republics to the east. In 1955, new staff were hired and new facilities added to cope with the crowds, including underground cloakrooms, lockers, and two rows of gruesome public toilets at the foot of the Kutafia Tower. Above all that, in the forgiving light of a Moscow summer, the gardens round the walls were planted with flowers, creating a park where visitors could stroll.[8] The red stars still lit up the night, but the real symbol of this generation's Kremlin was the scarlet Soviet flag.

It was also that flag that brought the foreigners; the brave, the scholarly, and the left-wing. Moscow was an exotic destination on the international circuit, but it was no longer sealed shut. In 1956, it hosted a major exhibition of Picasso's work, accompanied by a season of French films.[9] Russians made the acquaintance of Europe's dove of peace, and foreign guests that of Soviet hotels. According to the eminent political scientist Frederick Barghoorn, who visited from Yale in the summer of 1956, about 3,000 Soviet tourist visas were issued to Americans that year. His own trip went smoothly enough (a few years later he was snatched in a bungled spy-exchange), and he noted that he 'did not hear one word in praise of Stalin'.[10] By 1957, when 30,000 foreigners arrived in Moscow for the sixth International Festival of Youth, the Kremlin had become a fully-fledged tourist destination, complete with welcoming multi-coloured flags (the red ones came back out when the foreigners had left), new asphalt paths, and guidebooks for sale in a range of languages.[11] Russians, meanwhile, poured through the gates at every season, and by the 1960s between four and five million visitors were trooping round the Kremlin every year.[12] Their comments say a lot about the spirit of the time. 'Thank you, thank you, and thank you again to our Party and government,' a citizen gushed across the pages of the visitors' book. 'Thanks to the Communist Party of the Soviet Union for preserving this monument to Russia's past.'[13]

Nikita Khrushchev's ten-year term as leader of the Soviet Union saw a marked retreat from Stalinism. His famous speech to the Twentieth Congress of the Communist Party in 1956 attacked the late dictator directly.[14] It was the first time that a Party leader had openly discussed Stalin's tyranny, and the admission followed months of secret bargaining within the elite. Khrushchev himself knew that he had plenty to hide, as did the comrades who sat stony-faced in the best seats beside him.[15] While Stalin lived, they had all agreed to measures that they now affected to deplore, and while most accepted that reform (and the regime's very survival) depended on the repudiation of terror, the direct reference to historic crimes felt like a form of sacrilege, a blasphemy against the leader-cult that all had fervently professed. There was no question of forsaking communism itself, however. In place of Stalin's cult, the clique agreed to introduce a reverence for Lenin, and 'Leninist principles' (whatever those might mean) became their ideological touchstone. The success of their new Soviet paradise depended on illusion. In its canteens, where pilfering by staff was so rife that there was no food but thin grey soup and glasses of tooth-stripping tea, the walls were lined with posters of plump fruit and freshly glazed white bread. The cosmonaut Gagarin was a hero in a country that could not make jeans to fit.

But illusion was classic Kremlin territory. A site that had projected everything from theocratic power to steel-coated technological utopia in its eight centuries of life was bound to play a role in this new world. The question was exactly which image to choose. Khrushchev's regime was no less hostile to the Orthodox Church than Stalin's, and it was also multi-national, unable to rely exclusively on the Old Russian card. So it used the Kremlin, in the age of broadcast media, to bring a sense of dependability, even cosiness, to the rituals of Soviet life. The giant Christmas tree (or rather, New Year spruce) that went up each winter in St George's Hall helped to do that, and generations of well-behaved Moscow children were invited to admire it at the annual Kremlin party. On New Year's Eve, families across the ten time zones of the Soviet Union gathered round their radios (a television was a distant dream for most) as Moscow's own midnight approached, waiting for the first mechanical rasp from the clock on the Kremlin's Saviour Tower. It was another irony: the best this state could manage at midwinter was a festival for marking time.

A void might well have opened where the dead Stalin had been, but propagandists were quick to burnish an alternative personality cult. 'Every building and every stone in the Kremlin is a witness to the noble history of the Russian state,' a guidebook of 1956 began. 'But one of the Kremlin buildings is especially dear to our people and to all progressive people in the countries of the world. It does not speak so much about the past as about the present and about the years to come, the future of humanity as a whole.'[16] The suspense was artificial, for every Soviet citizen would have known what was coming next. In 1955, the Lenin museum-apartment opened on the third floor of the Senate building, complete with the dead leader's library of 18,000 volumes, his narrow bed, armchairs, and the kitchen pots that Krupskaya had never bothered to use.[17] Here, visitors learned, 'the great genius and leader of the world proletariat V. I. Lenin and his closest comrades organised the front during the civil war and planned the struggle against capitalist intervention'. Here, too, 'was born the great plan for Soviet electrification'.[18] There was even a picture of the father of the international proletarian revolution playing with a kitten.

The next step came in 1961, when the Kremlin acquired a dedicated department for propaganda.[19] This produced a flood of vapid platitudes, but at least people knew where they stood, which (unless they came with an official tour) was usually in a queue. Access to the Kremlin was packaged as a reward for good citizenship. For everyone else, getting into any of the best museums was fiendishly difficult.[20] Their opening hours were short, visitor numbers restricted, and the guides had instructions to deliver a litany of facts about Russian craftsmanship (the workers' contribution) rather than tempting visitors with morsels from the juicy tsarist world. 'The Kremlin is an inexhaustible source of monumental propaganda of every kind,' experts from the museums were eager to affirm. 'It is exploited for study and allows the broad mass of the people to acquaint themselves with the treasures of art and history with the aim of creating fully-developed human beings, active fighters for the better future of mankind.'[21]

On completing their Kremlin tour (main features of the hill, main landmarks, Cathedral Square, and, if you were lucky, Armoury and Diamonds), most excursions followed their guides through the exit gate down to the Alexander Gardens. The manuals for tour-leaders recommended that they visit Lenin's mausoleum at this point, although the queues for that were formidably long at any time of year.[22] To visit Lenin was to share in something greater than mere pride; it was a kind of sacrament. You did not slouch, you did not spit, and even you ground out that cigarette. Moscow's schoolchildren learned this at an early age, for someone dreamed up the idea of bringing the pick of them here, to the very presence of the corpse, when they were sworn in as young Pioneers. As they accepted their red scarf and scroll, the lucky few would glow with pride, but grinning, in the presence of Ilyich himself, was definitely not allowed.[23]

For all that, Khrushchev's thaw was genuine, and no-one warmed to it with greater glee than educated Muscovites. In the 1950s, a narrow circle of these got their first opportunity in over twenty years to take professional stock of the Kremlin. Buildings that had been assigned to the secret police since 1935 were suddenly transferred to the Ministry of Culture. The Armoury Chamber museum also expanded for a time, absorbing Marshal Voroshilov's recently vacated rooms in a wing of the Grand Palace.[24] New research staff were hired, young men with history degrees, and by 1963 there was a curator for each room for the first time in half a century.[25] They worked within an ideological frame, but they did not have to tell obvious lies. The guidebook, *Kreml' Moskvy*, had chapters on the medieval and renaissance forts by several of Moscow's most distinguished authorities, including the architectural historian V. F. Snegirev.[26] *Po Kremliu*, a volume that was published for the Festival of Youth in 1957, is still regarded as a classic. The team of authors who created it included the architect-restorer A. I. Khamtsov, and the curator of Kremlin museums, A. A. Goncharova.[27]

Stalin's shadow was not exorcized entirely. Armoury staff encountered it in an unusual way, for in the later 1950s they developed plans to hold an exhibition of the gifts the leader had received during his quarter-century in power. The collection was assembled and catalogued, and the planning went so well that tickets for a private view were printed on two separate occasions, but each time someone found a reason to delay. Eventually the exhibition was dismantled and the rooms intended for it handed back to the commandant's office, otherwise known as the ninth directorate of the KGB. By this time, as ever, the secret policemen needed extra space, but there would have been other rooms for them. In truth, while there was always scope for a museum of Muscovite tsars, and though it was vital to preserve the shrine to Lenin, no-one knew what gloss to put upon the Stalin mugs, the gilded armadilloes and the grotesque porcelain models of the Saviour Tower.[28]

Still more eccentric, as a legacy, was the rebuilding of a long-dead face. At the end of his life, Stalin had ordered that Ivan the Terrible's coffin should be opened and the bones and skull researched. The brick-built tomb gave up its secrets in April 1953, a month after Stalin's own death, but it was only in 1965 that Russia's famous 'face-finder', the forensic anthropologist M. M. Gerasimov, published his conclusions. By then, the coffins of both of Ivan's older sons had also been opened, and all three skeletons had been subjected to Gerasimov's professional attentions. As ever, his priority had been to reconstruct the faces. From Ivan's skull he shaped a thickset man – at the end of his life, this tsar had been stout, even fat – and added a sharp forehead and petulant mouth. The image was convincing, and the model had a cruel, spoiled glare. But this was no dictator for the modern world. 'The skeleton,' Gerasimov recalled,

> was partially covered with the torn pieces of a monk's garment. Over the head and masking the face were the remains of a monk's cowl and a filet on which were embroidered texts of prayers. On the breast lay a monk's apron top embroidered with the scene of the crucifixion on Golgotha.[29]

This kind of detail could cause trouble in a Kremlin where religion was all but taboo. Ivan was still a Russian hero, but monks in any guise were unwelcome. The Kremlin cathedrals, too, remained in cultural limbo. They had not been used for religious services since 1918, and by the 1950s they were badly in need of renovation and frequently closed. Any sporadic repair-schemes were liable to be undermined (sometimes literally) by other government priorities. Later, conservation was typically commissioned to coincide with jubilees such as the fiftieth anniversary of Soviet power in 1968 or the Moscow Olympic Games in 1980. It was not a recipe for consistency. Hastily completed work generally left fresh, and urgent, problems in its wake.[30] The Kremlin's most important structures hovered at the edge of ideological acceptability, the very scaffolding around them keeping the tourists at bay. The best that religion seemed able to do (apart from looking nice on a postcard) was to foster a confused Soviet pride. 'Notwithstanding their link to religious rituals,' a conference of archaeologists conceded in 1970, the preservation of the Kremlin cathedrals 'has facilitated the development of feelings of national self-consciousness and patriotism in the struggle against enemies of the fatherland, and has helped in the process of education in civic responsibility.'[31]

Within the limits of a straitened budget and distorting ideology, however, the Kremlin staff entered an age of opportunity at last. Igor Grabar died in 1960. The generation that came after him was almost entirely Soviet-educated, but culture was as valued by this younger intellectual elite as it had been by their fathers. Fresh teams of employees worked doggedly, producing careful papers, debating origins and authorship and analysing ancient paint. There were collective publishing ventures, but the high points were the formal conferences, interminable and stiflingly prestigious. Abroad, the discoveries that Soviet researchers made were often overlooked (or dismissed on the grounds of bias), but volumes in the Kremlin library are witness to the heroism of its many expert staff. They analysed fragments of sculpture, reconstructed frescoes, and traced the early shapes of the great cathedrals.[32] With tiny budgets, and often in the teeth of interference from the commandant and political elite, they pursued real scholarship.[33] They even struggled with diplomacy, and in 1979, the first joint exhibition in fifty years toured outside Russia, a show collected to display the sheer profusion of the Kremlin's cultural wealth. It included sixteenth-century reliquaries and a gilded copy of the Gospels from 1568, a copy of the Cap of Monomakh, and icons dating from the middle of the twelfth century. 'Treasures from the Kremlin' was supported, notwithstanding the Cold War, by New York's Metropolitan Museum.[34]

The post-war years were also a boom time for Soviet archaeologists, with opportunities to dig in war-damaged regions like Novgorod, Pskov and Kiev, but while academic knowledge of these places grew apace, the buried history of the Moscow Kremlin remained mysterious. It had been near-impossible to dig in Stalin's day: subterranean work was reserved for the secret police. Khrushchev was less concerned with security, but his very openness presented Moscow's specialists with a new problem. There might now be a real chance of access, and even of state funds, but no-one could agree who was to have the privilege of digging in the Kremlin first.[35]

The answer, unexpectedly, came from the underground public lavatories outside the gates. Their pit was still being excavated in the summer of 1956 when the archaeologist Mikhail Rabinovich, a man known for his expeditions to Novgorod, paid his first visit to the newly opened Kremlin. Many years later, he still remembered the horror he felt when greeted at the ticket-holders' entrance by a yawning hole in the ground. The iron bucket of a giant digger was scooping at the earth, and each enormous gulp bore off the record of six hundred years. Rabinovich wasted no time, demanding access to a telephone against the clank and rumble of the huge machines. After several calls he found the right man. The Kremlin commandant, Aleksandr Vedenin, turned out to be a cultured person with an interest in history. The digger's engines were switched off.[36]

It was a sudden, and an unexpected, debut. Rabinovich assembled a team, co-opted an eminent colleague called Nikolai Voronin, and began to dig. That year, the two men mapped the brick embankments of the old Neglinnaya, but there were greater finds to come. Although they seemed fated to work in the shadow of enormous cranes, the team would be the first to excavate the west and south-west portions of the Kremlin using modern surveying techniques. It was always a last-minute scramble, a case of glimpses snatched before another vast construction scheme began. Summer after summer, the archaeologists had to race against impatient site-managers with deadlines of their own to meet, and a good deal of the work was done in haste by inexperienced volunteers. In 1963, however, two years after the last of these expeditions, Voronin and Rabinovich published their findings, the first really new material on the Kremlin's early history to appear in print since Sytin's reports in the 1930s.[37]

The technology and time available were so limited that Rabinovich and Voronin could often do no more than confirm nineteenth-century theories. The usual ideological pressures were also there, for even at this time it did not pay to deviate from the official line. For all that, the pair were able to add important details about the Kremlin's original topography, the design and layout of early fortifications, and the thousand-year-long patterns of settlement. They also located the foundations of the tsaritsa's chambers (built for Natalya Naryshkina at the end of the seventeenth century), remnants of the old *prikazy*, and traces of Boris Godunov's palace. The Kremlin, they discovered, had the deepest of urban roots. A fort and then a trading-post, it had never been just an agricultural settlement. For a good communist, for whom the peasants always were the lowest and most boorish social tier, there was a snobbish comfort in that kind of news.

In the wake of Voronin and Rabinovich, the Kremlin's first official archaeologist, N. S. Sheliapina, was appointed in 1967. The authorities also agreed to fund an exhibition of archaeological finds, although the site they chose was an uninviting crypt under the Annunciation Cathedral. The show, which still exists today, was suspended for years when the building was closed for repair after 1979.[38] But those who missed it at the time (and still miss it now, for tickets are not easily obtained) could console themselves with the idea that it was probably a dull affair. There was certainly little enough to attract the masses in the exhibition's cheaply produced official catalogue. Fragments of bronze and shards of coloured glass were meat and drink to the professionals, but even educated members of the public might have struggled with the dim, brownish displays. If history really began with Marx and Lenin, after all, it was not clear what a person was to make of a half-rotted seventeenth-century musketeer's boot.[39] The people's history in Soviet times was simpler, firmer, brightly coloured; authentic tissue from the past was out of place.

Despite the tourists and the research teams, the Kremlin remained primarily government territory. It was a conundrum, for the old idea of a museum-reserve had not entirely disappeared. When Stalin died, no-one knew quite how his successors would decide to deal with the place. The case for letting the curators take over was strong, not least because the politicians of the 1950s still knew every recent Kremlin ghost by name. What stopped them from deserting the old place on this occasion was not so much its symbolic value as its practical utility. By 1953, the citadel was a tyrant's dream, defended by its own picked guards and furnished with enough military hardware to wage a medium-sized war.[40] Its warren of state-rooms and offices was ramshackle, but all were securely bugged, and then there were those bunkers and communications networks underground.[41] At a time when other Russians had to queue to make phone calls, the Kremlin had its own telephone and wireless system (located next to the Senate). Cutting-edge technology (because of their distinctive ring, the leaders' phones were called 'cuckoos') connected its occupants with each other if not directly with the world.[42] The network, which relied, after the Cold War ended, on communications and encryption equipment imported from Britain (and developed in laboratories at Malvern), was the pride of the political elite, whose hierarchy was partly based on levels of access to it.[43]

To leave all that untenanted would have been profligate, but Khrushchev did consider the idea. He toyed with a plan to move parts of the government away from central Moscow and up to the breezier south-west. Stalin had chosen this district for his vast post-war university complex, and there was an enclosed estate of elite housing nearby, offering every comfort in domestic terms. For a moment, it was tempting to think of moving the government there, too. Khrushchev stuck with the Kremlin in the end, but true to his peasant origins he tried to make the fortress more home-like by planting part of it with an orchard. The apple trees sounded bucolic, but the project called for hundreds of tons of quality topsoil. Khrushchev, like the Romanov tsars of old, incurred enormous costs on his regime's behalf, though in his case it was a fleet of khaki trucks, not buckets, that brought the earth up to the fort.[44]

Having settled on his headquarters, Khrushchev turned his mind to the surrounding view. Stalin's plan for Moscow had envisaged the creation of a ring of landmark towers, conceived as modern successors to the fortified monasteries that had circled the city in Muscovite times.[45] The project was delayed by the outbreak of war, and in the end, only seven skyscrapers out of the projected eight had been built (the university was one of them). Their gothic shapes, tiered and spired like hypertrophic versions of the Kremlin's own Saviour Tower, still loom out of the urban smog like evil trolls. Each one was meant to be unique: solid, massive and spacious. No expense was spared on the marble detail, the lifts, the heating, or the crystal chandeliers. They were Stalinist palaces, and in Khrushchev's eyes that made them elitist and oppressive, grotesque white elephants in a city with a housing crisis. They were too solid to demolish, but in 1955 the Communist Party officially registered its aesthetic disapproval, and Leonid Polyakov, the leading light of Moscow's civic architecture after 1945, was forced to hand back the Stalin Prize that he had won for the design of one recently completed example, the Leningradskaya Hotel.[46]

Other flagship projects were scrapped at the planning stage. The scheme for a pantheon to contain the remains of dead leaders (this was to face the Kremlin on Red Square) was dropped within months of Stalin's death. Then there was the projected Palace of Soviets, the giant that was scheduled to take the place of Ton's Cathedral of Christ the Saviour. Its architect, Boris Iofan, did some more work on the plans in 1953, but then, abruptly, they were shelved. Khrushchev had found a new use for the site, and by 1960 it had been excavated, lined and flooded to provide the city with a heated open-air swimming-pool.[47] For the next thirty years, that solved the problem of the giant hole, and it also chimed with Khrushchev's populism, his determination to house, feed and educate the socialist masses. These were the years when Muscovites expected to 'catch up and overtake America', and plenty, health and happiness beckoned to all. The people swam (as long as they turned up equipped with regulation rubber hats), and soupy water lapped and steamed in place of communism's greatest ever monument.

Khrushchev was never coy about his ambition. He was a leader who loved to dazzle on his Kremlin stage. A reception for the first female astronaut, Valentina Tereshkova, held in Ton's Grand Palace in 1962, would have been unimaginable a decade before. As a British guest recalled:

> There were dishes of cold roast fillet of beef so tender and moist that the meat dissolved like snowflakes on the tongue; sturgeon from the Volga, smoked and fresh; Pacific salmon; Kamchatka crabs; silver cups the size of a giant's thimble containing a mixture of mushrooms and sour cream or a fricassee of wild birds; and in bowls pressed into crushed ice pungent red salmon roe and caviar from the Caspian, the fat grains glittering in colours from almost yellow to darkest grey.[48]

Between the linen-covered tables milled a crowd of 'big Russians in suits' and – almost scandalously – foreigners, all craning, over the delicious food, for any glimpse of their host. The space, in fact, had started feeling just a little cramped. In 1954, a mere five years after China's communist revolution, Khrushchev had visited Beijing, where the comrades entertained him in a massive conference and banqueting hall. Not to be outdone, the Soviet leader began to dream of a palace of his own. Quickly rejecting yet another site on the Lenin Hills, he took the decision to build in the Kremlin.[49] 'Khrushchev wasn't such a dullard,' a spiteful Molotov later recalled. 'He was culturally deprived.'[50]

What Khrushchev had in mind had to be large enough for every kind of meeting, including gala congresses with vast applauding crowds. When not required for politics, it could be equipped as a theatre: a larger, better, brighter venue for Soviet opera and ballet. The idea – and the budget – grew apace. Again pursuing a personal dream, the Soviet leader appointed his own favourite architect, M. V. Posokhin, the man who had just built him a holiday retreat at Pitsunda on the Black Sea. Posokhin agreed (of course) to design, engineer and complete the entire building in time for the Party Congress of 1962. For two years, working day and night, his men drilled, dug and hammered. At one point, to bypass the need for time-consuming calculations, soldiers were asked to march heavily on the top floor, testing the structure of the balcony.[51] When Muscovites complained about the views that the building would block, Khrushchev told them to look from the other side. He backed off only when protesters started to inveigh against the demolition of parts of the Kremlin wall, dropping that aspect of the scheme but retaining – and enlarging – almost all the rest.[52] The Palace of Congresses, a stark colossus faced with glass and gleaming stone, remains the most unloved large building on the Kremlin hill, but though some have proposed that it should go (like the nearby Rossiya Hotel, which was demolished in 2006), most Russian intellectuals agree today, quite rightly, that it stands as witness to the spirit of its age.[53]

Predictably, Khrushchev's building earned the usual range of plaudits at the time. Professor Nikolai Kolli, veteran designer of underground stations, pronounced that 'the palace not only fulfils all the multiple functional requirements laid on it, but also represents a new height on the route to the formation of a socialist architecture'.[54] Without a trace of irony, Khrushchev praised the unimaginative, brutal lump as fit to grace a site 'linked with the activities of the great Lenin'. Posokhin himself liked to call it 'tactful' and 'laconic', though its 6,000-seat meeting hall and the rooftop banqueting space for another two and a half thousand could scarcely be described as minimalist.[55] The best that could be said was that Posokhin did not build above the main Kremlin roof-line, but to achieve that small degree of tact he had to drive deep into the historic soil. Egotov's nineteenth-century Armoury Museum and several older palace buildings disappeared in the process, but the most serious damage was well below ground. As conservation experts later discovered, the reckless excavation had disturbed groundwater drainage patterns under the Dormition Cathedral and some parts of the Kremlin wall. The bill for putting all that right exceeded 500 million rubles, or roughly six times the building's own original cost.[56]

'The space was formed after the removal of a few service buildings, not very important from the point of view of their architectural or artistic quality and without historical interest,' Posokhin wrote in 1974. 'Among them the only one to be preserved was a part of the Cavalry Corpus facing Communist street. On the second floor of this Lenin had his first Moscow apartment when he lived and worked here in March–April 1917.'[57] An engineer who had been involved in the construction of the new palace recently took me on a tour. He was no longer proud of it, he said, but he would make no apology. In the Leninist spirit, he still remembered the opening night, the ticket-only, all-exclusive celebration of socialism's latest monument. His mother was especially impressed by her visit to the bathrooms. These, like the dressing-rooms for dancers and the ultra-modern air-conditioning machines, were located in the basement. Unlike the lavatories outside the Kremlin gates, however, the underground facilities here were faced with marble, the doors had locks, and the paper came on real rolls, not from the grudging hands of an attendant by the door. Even the soap was free, and it was smooth, just like the stuff that delegates used to receive in Stalin's time.

It was, in part, Khrushchev's ebullience that ruined him. By 1964, the Soviet leader had been likened to a pig, a clown and a chatterbox. What he had not entirely grasped was that the post-war and post-Stalin Soviet Union yearned for quiet; the system worked best when people felt safe. In his impulsive, well-intentioned way, Khrushchev had violated several unwritten rules. The elite could not forgive him for suggesting that officials should serve for limited, fixed terms, a move that threatened countless networks and congenial private worlds. For the mass, the miners, farmers and factory engineers, his crime was that he did not cure the hardship and uncertainty of their material lives. Receptions at the Kremlin excited the criticism that he and Prime Minister Bulganin were 'drinking away the nation's wealth'. 'Khrushchev has opened the door to everyone and is treating everyone to dinner,' a Russian muttered in 1958, 'although we workers have nothing to eat.'[58]

In Stalin's time, such opposition would have been repressed before it even formed. One of the greatest testimonials to Khrushchev's term in power, ironically, was the bloodless manner in which it came to an end. In October 1964, a small group, headed by Leonid Brezhnev and his political cronies Aleksei Kosygin, Mikhail Suslov and Nikolai Podgorny, met in the Kremlin while the leader was away on holiday and engineered his involuntary but entirely comfortable retirement. By the time Khrushchev's plane touched down in Moscow, it was all over. The seventy-year-old ex-leader disappeared from public view, and other creatures from the Kremlin depths surfaced at last, effortlessly colonizing the vacated offices and bent on introducing more consensual reform.

One of the first things that they promised was 'stability of cadres', which meant jobs for the boys (and jobs for life). To create such an extensive and resilient fabric of power, they deliberately separated the two strands of Soviet politics, the interlocking tendrils of the Communist Party and the state. Since Lenin's time, the two had overlapped: the government and ministries on one hand and the 'guiding' organs of the

Party on the other, leading, shadowing, and duplicating them. Each branch of government or board of economic managers contained a Party cell, and the Party in turn had secretaries of its own to oversee each element of government. In practice, it was the Party that really called the shots, not least because it was assumed to have responsibility for strategy: as communists, its members knew the true shape of the future. Khrushchev had presumed to head both Party and State, but his successors (at first) resolved to appoint separate leaders to each. The Party leader's mantle, in this arcane system, fell on the shoulders of its General Secretary, the fifty-eight-year-old Leonid Brezhnev, a loyal bureaucrat from the Dnieper valley in Ukraine.

Of all the Soviet Union's leaders, according to the late historian Dmitry Volkogonov (who had unprecedented access to the vital files), 'Brezhnev's personality was the least complex. He was a man of one dimension, with the psychology of a middle-ranking Party functionary, vain, wary and conventional.'[59] He was also a noted womanizer (like anyone who remembers his old age, I find this difficult to credit), devoted to fine food and endless cigarettes and utterly addicted to the hunt.[60] His vanity was legendary, and in later years he enjoyed almost nothing more than giving and receiving medals and awards. In middle age, however, he was known as a political fixer, and though less flamboyant than Khrushchev, he had a reputation for shrewd management, vindictiveness, and sharp tactical skills. 'His forte', Mikhail Gorbachev believed, 'was his ability to split rivals, fanning mutual suspicion and subsequently acting as chief arbiter and peacemaker.'[61]

Talents like these were just the thing for Kremlin politics, but Brezhnev had another plan in mind. Unlike Khrushchev and Stalin, he decided to quit the fortress. Where others might have been content with a refurbishment and new name-plates, this general secretary (in a move that some have likened to Ivan the Terrible's retreat to Alexandrovskaya sloboda[62]) chose to clear out altogether, taking a picked staff with him. As a Party man, he claimed to prefer the grey Central Committee building on Old Square, Stalin's original stamping-ground. It lacked the Kremlin's charisma, but it was also free of awkward memories and tourist crowds. The second entrance, fourth floor, was its nerve-centre. No-one could visit that without prior clearance at the highest level. The staff were deferential and the atmosphere refined. Admission was strictly by list. Tuesdays were the sacred day, for that was when Brezhnev's small group decided on their week's agenda, effectively determining the business of a whole empire.

The Kremlin, then, as a contemporary later observed, became 'the external symbol of state power rather than the living heart of the country'.[63] Unexpectedly, it even developed a reputation for neutrality. With Brezhnev gone, no political body of any real significance now used it as a base. Six days a week, it was the home of the government, but that meant only relatively unimportant state officials in the Council of Ministers. Every year or so, huge congresses assembled in Khrushchev's palace, but though these were officially the sovereign organs of the land, foreign journalists were quick to dub them 'the world's biggest rubber stamp'.[64] While outsiders referred to Soviet rulers as 'The Kremlin' to save time, the magic scent of power had evaporated from the place itself, leaving a residue of museums, offices and reception-rooms under the regime of a military commandant.

On Thursdays, however, the balance changed again, for this was still the day on which the Soviet Union's supreme decision-making committee, the Politburo, convened inside the fort. The tradition – and the pompous rooms – remained unchanged till 1991. An inner circle gathered in the Senate's Walnut Room, panelled and furnished like a London club, and then the whole meeting sat down in the much larger space next door. However grinding the debates, and however somnolent the ageing members of the group became, the Kremlin setting lent a sense of history. Soon, almost nothing anywhere got done without a nod from someone in this smoke-filled room. The sheer weight of detail was self-defeating. On 1 September 1983, under Brezhnev's successor, Yury Andropov, the Politburo debated the production of chassis for self-propelled vehicles, colour television sets, methods of raising the productivity of labour, demographic research, aid to Afghanistan, and the choice of speaker for the sixty-sixth anniversary of the October revolution. Well into these toothsome discussions, a note was passed to the defence chief, Dmitry Ustinov, informing him that a Korean airliner with more than two hundred civilian passengers on board had just been shot down by Soviet planes.[65] By then, however, everyone was almost numb.

The Politburo had become the ruling caste, as influential and as ritualized as any council of boyars. But its members did not live in the Kremlin and they left as soon as their business was done. Watching the sleek black limousines as they filed out through the Kremlin's Saviour Gate on Thursday afternoons, a time-traveller from any of Russia's pasts would have recognized power. The cars left through a gate that was closed to all other traffic, and on the public streets a path was cleared for their exclusive use. But not all headed right, towards the Party building on Old Square. Some, including the hard-line Ustinov himself, were going to the Defence Ministry, whose appetite for weapons and technology was draining the entire continent of wealth. Others headed confidently left, bound for the Lubyanka.[66] By the 1960s, Soviet power relied upon the KGB, successor to Stalin's secret police, and this huge organization had its own headquarters and its own power-base. It spied on Soviet citizens, it harassed and eavesdropped on foreigners, but it also watched the Soviet Union's leaders.[67] Any embarrassing detail (the Russian word is *kompromat*) was a form of currency, and the police had plenty of customers. When Vyacheslav Kostikov, who served as Boris Yeltsin's press advisor in 1991, started to explore the office he had inherited in the Kremlin, he found that his bookcase had a false back. Behind it was a secret door leading to a room with a washbasin and a bed. Dominating the scene, however, was a massive safe, so heavy that it threatened to fall through the antique floor on to the rooms below. Double-walled, and lined with sand, the monster had once contained Brezhnev's stock of *kompromat* on colleagues in the high elite.[68]

But these divisive personal games were secret; even some of the elite did not know the extent of the spying. In public, and above all to the world, the Soviet Kremlin was united, and it was still the regime's favourite weapon for inspiring awe in outsiders. At formal receptions (the one time when he always used it), Brezhnev appeared to be serene, at home, emerging in a blaze of chandeliers to make a little speech and shake a hand. In Washington and in London, high-level delegations – and certainly those that involved a head of state – were greeted on the White House steps, or at the entrance to 10 Downing Street, but the Soviets broke all the rules. Their foreign guests were made to walk – it seemed like miles – up staircases and endless corridors around the Grand Palace. The place was confusing, 'like a series of Chinese boxes' in one victim's words, and the fierceness of the central heating felt like an assault. At last, disgruntled and hot, the visitors would be motioned to wait, standing in the belly of a cavernous, glittering hall, until a pair of double doors at the far end was flung open. The Soviet hosts then made their entrance, fresh and relaxed. All these illusions were deliberately contrived, but there was nothing fake, unfortunately, about Brezhnev's impatience with some of the guests. When the newly appointed British foreign secretary, David Owen, paid his first call, his interpreter overheard the Soviet leader asking his own foreign minister, Andrei Gromyko, whether it was really necessary to invite such an unpromising character to share a glass of tea.[69]

Brezhnev's glory was growing by the year, at least in the artificial world he had created for himself. In 1971, he decided to revert to his predecessor's ruling style by adding the title and trappings of head of state to his existing role as General Secretary. A Kremlin office went with the new position, and though Brezhnev still preferred his eyrie in Old Square, he also took over a Senate suite. This was jocularly called 'the Heights', in part because Brezhnev avoided the lower floor where Stalin had once worked.[70] The rooms were adapted to include a large office and a luxurious reception room, a smaller study for Brezhnev's own use, and, later, medical facilities and a small private canteen.[71] Further millions were devoted, at the end of Brezhnev's life, to building a marble hall in the Senate yard, designed to be invisible from Red Square and from other points inside the Kremlin grounds. Completed at the end of 1983, it was intended to host plenary meetings of the Party's Central Committee.[72]

The Kremlin, then, was still the only place where the whole Soviet leadership converged. In recognition of its importance (and because few outsiders could follow the complex structures of this government), political scientists in the capitalist world coined a new term – 'Kremlinology' – for a pursuit that soon became both urgent diplomatic task and arcane academic specialism. The Soviet leadership mattered – this was the other atomic superpower – but understanding it was no easy task. On the most desperate occasions, Kremlin-watchers were reduced to noting which stiff, unappetizing-looking man had been positioned closest to the leader at a state parade. Distinctions like this may appear absurd today, but at the time there was no other way to calibrate the hierarchy. Minute gradations said it all; the political elite of the world's first communist superpower really did spend hours deciding which of them should mount a rostrum in third place. There were the medals and bouquets, of course, but from the location of an office to the speed of its telephone connection, every Moscow-based official knew where to look for the real signs of rank and influence.[73]

The lists of Russian names and institutions were confusing – commentary had been much simpler back in Stalin's day – but the careful, usually tedious, study of who was up and who was down on Soviet state occasions had a point. Those faces, after all, belonged to people with real organizations to manage and interests to guard. There were genuine struggles for resources, a bureaucratic politics, and there were also meaningful disputes over policy. 'Brezhnev', as Gorbachev, who must have known, would later write, 'was forced to manoeuvre skilfully between different Politburo factions.'[74] By the end of his reign, the groups included a 'military-ideological' bloc of conservatives (to whom, in truth, Brezhnev inclined) and a faction, more open to reform, whose members thought the time had come to tackle the country's backwardness and economic woes. That group, ironically, was headed by the KGB's own master, Yury Andropov. 'Reform', however, had a Soviet meaning all its own. No-one was thinking of free markets. As even Gorbachev would later say, 'Our goal is to realize the full potential of socialism. Those in the West who expect us to renounce socialism will be disappointed.'[75]

There is plenty of evidence that Russians of the time approved. Not knowing any other life, many believed their political system to be more progressive, more scientific, and certainly fairer than any other.[76] When it came to the details of that fairness, however, Karl Marx himself might have been shocked. Lenin probably did work tirelessly, at least until his first disabling stroke, but in 1966 Brezhnev made it a rule that Politburo members should take ten weeks' holiday a year, and also ordered that their office hours should be restricted to nine to five each day with a compulsory break for lunch.[77] The point was to avoid excessive strain – the team was already ageing – and also to leave the general secretary with free time for Zavidovo, the hunting-lodge, just over ninety miles from Moscow, where he could hope to bag wild boar and deer. It was an open secret that the deer were caught and tethered in advance so that he could not miss.[78]

The inequalities of Soviet life were not as glaring as detractors claim. Many other economies – and certainly the United States – were scarred by greater differences between the wealthy and the very poor.[79] What made the Soviet case unusual was its hypocrisy, and with that, its obsessive, almost priest-like, secrecy. As in the past, each benefit was weighed and parcelled out; a boss lost everything if his career collapsed. In part, that was the reason why so many politicians chose to serve until they died. But graded privilege also made for a rigid structure of us and them, 'a hierarchy complex', in Dmitry Volkogonov's phrase.[80] Raisa Gorbachev, arriving in the capital from Stavropol, claimed to be shocked by the irrationality and waste. She likened the privilege system that she and her husband encountered to Peter the Great's Table of Ranks, observing that new arrivals in Moscow would get a dacha and apartment 'according to their place in the ladder of hierarchy' and not 'according to your own resources or your needs'.[81] Accommodation was only the start of it.

The system had its origins in Lenin's 'Kremlin ration', and it carried echoes of much older systems of payment in kind. But now the ranks of the privileged included a whole range of new officials and administrators, many of whom worked in the precincts of the Kremlin and Old Square. The facilities inside the fortress were inadequate to serve the swelling numbers at this modern court. The bulk of the employees' food was prepared in kitchens on Old Square, where there was also a canteen for 1,000 people. The Kremlin itself could cater for only a quarter of that, although there was a separate mess for the garrison in the arsenal. But the elite did not waste a moment in queues. Since Stalin's time, Politburo members had enjoyed the services of dedicated personal chefs (these people, always scrutinized by the police, were not allowed to tell anyone where they worked). With a precise sense of hierarchy, full members of the Politburo were serviced by three cooks and candidate members by two. Each meal was tasted by a doctor and then placed in a secure refrigerator for twenty-four hours lest any poison had been introduced.[82] If the doctor survived, presumably, the delicacies could safely be served, though Brezhnev's hunting trophies at Zavidovo bypassed the quarantine and went straight to his plate. He was sometimes known, after a really splendid meal, to waddle out to the kitchen and plant a kiss on the hot cheeks of his favourite chef.[83]

There was also a special depot near the Kremlin – Gorbachev once called it the 'feeding trough' – for the packages of gourmet food that the elite could take away.[84] The steamy canteens of the past were put to shame. By the 1970s, the Kremlin's food service employed its own meat supplier (and its own herds), as well as direct access to the foremost chefs in Moscow. Seven tons of prepared meat – roasts and joints, sausages and hams – were wrapped and sent to the collection point on Granovsky street (now known as Romanov lane) every day.[85] Elsewhere, the beautifully appointed Gastronom No. 1 (still often known affectionately by its old name: Yeliseyev's) reserved a special section in its Gorky street store for elite clients, as did the glass palace of GUM, across Red Square from the Kremlin. There was a Kremlin tailor, where Soviet leaders were fitted with the dull and scratchy suits that they were all required to wear (the fabric, after all, had to be visibly of Soviet make), a Kremlin hairdresser and dentist, and a garage for the Kremlin fleet of limousines.[86] At its most basic, all this meant that no Kremlin official's wife needed to queue, or even to make cabbage taste exciting yet again. In more creative hands, however, the system was a paradise for the corrupt. Enterprising hangers-on, most famously Brezhnev's daughter Galina, traded scarce goods on the black market, in her case feeding a passion for young men, circuses, and diamonds.[87]

The Kremlin also retained its reputation for medical care. Not far from the food depot on Granovsky street was a private clinic, staffed by the leaders' personal physicians and equipped with a room for the general secretary's exclusive use.[88] Those Kremlin doctors, famously, grew busier towards the end. By the early 1980s, the country was in the hands of very old and often very sick men. Brezhnev himself was alleged to have a dangerous addiction to sleeping pills, and in later life he also suffered from a weak heart (he had a major stroke some months before his death) as well as emphysema and several types of cancer. But he refused to step down, despite the many rumours and the jokes. 'All stand so that the leader can be carried in,' they quipped, and many talked as if he were long dead and stuffed. The head of the KGB, Andropov, seems to have encouraged the vain, weak old man to appear in public, and especially on television, to feed the general public contempt.[89] But others just colluded in the game. 'The Politburo, the Health Minister Petrovsky and his successor Chazov, and the chiefs in the Kremlin medical service were in effect carrying out an experiment to see how long a fatally sick old man could give the impression of working,' wrote Volkogonov, who had witnessed the charade.[90] By the end, people had become so used to thinking of Brezhnev as a walking corpse that his final, clinically irreversible death came as a real surprise.[91]

But die he did, at last, on 10 November 1982. The potential successors were the men who had worked with him in the highest ranks, and none was in the flower of youth. For three more years, the best way to predict the political succession at the top was to wait to see who would be put in charge of the most recent leader's funeral arrangements.[92] In Brezhnev's case that honour fell to Yury Andropov. But he was already sick – his kidneys were failing – and his infirmity prompted the new chief of the KGB, Viktor Chebrikov, to suggest a discreet modification to the Kremlin's Senate Tower. It was an escalator, designed to carry invalids the eleven feet up to the platform on the Lenin Mausoleum, and it was installed in July 1983.[93] The 'Lenin escalator' proved a boon, if not a life-saver, to almost every other member of the Politburo, and it was an essential aid to Andropov's successor, Konstantin Chernenko. This man, another victim of emphysema, in turn awarded a state prize to the designer of a pneumatic tube that blasted government papers from Old Square into the Kremlin and back in two minutes, sparing the men and women with the little carts and adding an element of farce to that old Kremlin-watchers' conundrum, 'Party–State relations'.[94]

The price of political stagnation was high. The Soviet economy became distorted and drained, haemorrhaging resources into the superpower arms race while citizens queued for basic food. From medicines and microchips to beer, the command-administrative system (as even its leaders called it) could not compete with rapid innovations in the west. A planned economy meant shortages, too, and someone who wanted a packet of nails or a pair of fashionable shoes might have to make a long pilgrimage – two or three days in a packed train – to find it. As for the major institutions of the state – the army and the KGB – these worked like mighty empires of their own, complete with food and raw material supplies, secret laboratories, and separate networks of hotels, housing blocks and hospitals. They could not win the war in Afghanistan, begun by Brezhnev and Ustinov in 1979, but their military failure did not prompt them to address deficiencies at home. As Gorbachev put it, 'On taking office as General Secretary in 1985, I was immediately faced with an avalanche of problems.'[95]

Mikhail Gorbachev was fifty-four when he became Soviet leader. There might have been other contenders, hawks from the Party old guard such as the foreign minister, Andrei Gromyko, or Moscow's Party boss, Viktor Grishin, but Gorbachev was the only candidate that the

Politburo considered with any seriousness on the night of Konstantin Chernenko's death. The consensus had shifted towards change. 'There was a thinly veiled happiness in the eyes of the assembled,' wrote Gorbachev's future aide, Anatoly Chernyaev, describing the Central Committee plenum that gathered to add its rubber stamp to the decision. 'The uncertainty is over, now it's time for Russia to have a real leader.'[96] Radio stations across the empire were dutifully playing Chopin's funeral march, but the mood in the Kremlin was optimistic, even celebratory.

This upwelling of hope was the hallmark of Gorbachev's first months in power. Though he remained a Party man, vowing to 'perfect a society of developed socialism', the new leader was keen to sweep away the barriers to creativity.[97] His initial reform programme amounted to a necessary, but very dangerous, assault on complacency and graft. He even tackled the Kremlin 'feeding trough'. Incongruous though it appeared, a man already noted for his foreign suits and slender, elegantly dressed wife set out to challenge privilege. 'We need to start with ourselves,' he told the Politburo in April 1986. 'Banquets, presents, receptions – we've been encouraging and taking part in all of this. Bosses at all levels have their own food supply centres, their wives never have to go shopping . . . This is all our own fault.'[98] Stories about Raisa Gorbachev's consumer habits ran counter to this, with rumours that she shopped at Cartier and Pierre Cardin. 'What the gullible Western public did not know,' a loyal witness, one of the Kremlin's own interpreters, wrote later, 'was that most of these stories were either planted or grossly exaggerated by the KGB.'[99]

Whatever the truth of that, it was already clear that every carefully considered step Gorbachev took was matched and stymied by determined opposition. Some of the problems were the results of years of mismanagement. Soon after that crusading 1986 Politburo speech, for instance, came the nuclear catastrophe at Chernobyl, a disaster that seemed to bring every failing of Soviet infrastructure and government into focus. But any fundamental reform was bound to upset vested interests, while the policy of *glasnost*, or openness, that Gorbachev encouraged in the wake of the nuclear accident threatened to start a witch-hunt against managers. The army and secret police were on alert at once, as were the heads of any institution whose survival depended on the status quo. The traditional working class, meanwhile, attacked their leader's policy of restructuring, or *perestroika*, for putting their wages and historic sense of class-based privilege at risk. And then there were the radical reformers, at the other extreme, who were always urging Gorbachev to do far more. In retrospect, his premiership survived for longer than the circumstances warranted. As Andrei Grachev, the Party leader's aide, would later write, 'People seldom ask how many coups d'état Gorbachev managed to avoid in six and a half years of reform.'[100]

But the Kremlin's affable new leader delighted the wider world. Whatever people thought of him at home, the level of approval he sustained elsewhere, as Chernyaev recollected, 'was like getting an honorary degree from the international community', and it earned him a Nobel Peace Prize.[101] Gorbachev's early priorities included an arms limitation treaty, negotiated in Washington, and the ending of the Soviet Union's war in Afghanistan. Even more spectacular was his encouragement of democratic change in Eastern Europe, a process that began with demonstrations on the streets and culminated in the fall of every jaded Communist regime. These triumphs were unprecedented, but it was the leader's style as much as what he promised that caught public attention. On walkabouts and public photo-calls, in Berlin, London and New York, the general secretary attracted large, adoring crowds, and journalists began to write of Gorbymania and even Gorbasm.[102] His staunch supporter Margaret Thatcher flirted with him, Ronald Reagan traded jokes with him (and also, on one occasion, his fountain pen), and even the older George Bush fell under the spell of the last and most tragic Soviet Communist leader.[103]

His was the stardom of the cheering streets, of summit meetings, foreign travel, television interviews. But though he was a man who liked to get about (itself refreshing after years of gerontocracy), Gorbachev also imbued the Kremlin with a fresh spirit of openness, even making occasional forays into its tourist areas to the amazement of the milling crowds.[104] The old place, with its Cold War connotations, was a fine set for a photo-op. Gorbachev's staff created a kind of studio there, complete with Soviet flag and rows of dummy telephones, where the leader could talk to cameramen across a gleaming desk.[105] More formally, in the staterooms of the Grand Palace, a sprightly, smiling team received official visits from Thatcher and Reagan, Helmut Kohl and François Mitterrand.[106] But all of it, from sham office to mirror-lined gallery, was theatre. As a Party man, Gorbachev preferred to work in Old Square. His main office remained there, and, as a politician, it was always his real home.[107]

Although it ultimately brought about his fall, almost everyone agrees that *glasnost* was Gorbachev's greatest achievement. Dmitry Volkogonov called it 'a unique example of the truth alone achieving what was beyond the power of a mighty state'.[108] It was a revolution where ideas acted like missiles. At first, the targets were bureaucrats, corruption, and the euphemisms that concealed decline. But then attention focused on the heroes of the past, the stern-faced men whose sculpted heads topped plinths in every square and meeting hall. Stalin was an easy target: Gorbachev himself described him as 'a criminal, devoid of any morality'.[109] But once the critics turned to Lenin and the Communist Party, the days of Soviet power were numbered. This regime had relied on lies and half-truths since the day of its foundation. History had been squeezed into a tight official frame, purged of disturbing episodes and trimmed to charm the patriotic crowds. But *glasnost* brought the true past back like an avenging ghost.[110] The archive doors were forced open, and for the first time in living memory what mattered in politics was the pressure from people on the streets, debating, questioning, and demanding their rights. In Moscow, the voices were soon pressing for multi-party elections, while in republics such as Georgia and Lithuania there were strident calls for independence. While Gorbachev continued to defend the Party and the Union, the red flag on the Kremlin's Senate dome stood for a revolution – and a state – that many wanted to cast off.

The next round in the Soviet Union's final dance was also initiated by Gorbachev. To put some energy into his country's stagnant civic life, he called for the creation of a new, elected, legislature, the Congress of People's Deputies of the USSR. The elections took place in March 1989. The outcome was preordained: large quotas of seats were reserved for the Communist Party, the Komsomol (Young Communists) and trade unions, and only one political party (Communist) had been permitted to campaign. But other points of view were represented nonetheless, for coalitions did emerge calling themselves 'platforms' or 'informal groups'. When the 2,250-strong Congress assembled in Khrushchev's Kremlin Palace in May 1989, its televised debates became a testing-ground for pluralist politics. Beyond the Soviet Union, 1989 was the year of communism's eclipse in Europe, and the fall of the Berlin Wall in November that year became an emblem of possibility and hope. The Congress of People's Deputies was an unwieldy beast by comparison, far less glamorous than the chanting crowds of East Berliners. In a spellbound Russia, however, it made an excellent platform for the emerging stars of the democratic age.

One such was Boris Yeltsin, one-time Party boss and now the Russian people's favourite tribune. He was elected to the Congress in 1989 as a representative from Moscow, just four years after he first came to the capital from the Ural city of Sverdlovsk (Ekaterinburg). Ironically, it had been Gorbachev who brought this burly man to prominence in 1985, appointing him to a Central Committee portfolio that included heavy industry, transport and planning as well as architectural affairs.[111] The two politicians seemed to work together well, for at this stage Yeltsin's energy and directness appealed to the reforming general secretary. At the end of 1985, Gorbachev promoted his protégé to the post of Moscow Party boss, replacing the long-serving conservative, Grishin. Yeltsin cultivated a populist reputation in the post, delighting Muscovites by his willingness to travel on their buses and to fight their battles with the bureaucrats. As Gorbachev recalled, 'I considered our choice for the secretary of the capital's city committee to be a success.'[112]

Inside the Kremlin, however, the real politics of *perestroika* was more discordant. In particular, Yeltsin was impatient with its slow pace, and then there was a clash of personalities. 'The Politburo was also becoming cult-ridden,' wrote Chernyaev. 'Only one member [Gorbachev] talked, while all the others listened.'[113] In September 1987, Yeltsin requested Gorbachev to release him from his posts in Moscow and the Politburo. The letter was ignored (Gorbachev was on holiday), but in October came a more open revolt. In the midst of a closed four-hour debate in the Kremlin about plans for the seventieth anniversary of the Bolshevik revolution, Yeltsin demanded to know what kind of timetable the leaders intended for more important aspects of reform. His own work had become impossible, he claimed, and he implied that conservatives in the elite were scheming to block him. Instead of responding to its substantive ideas, Gorbachev allowed his colleagues to condemn this outburst as insubordination. The confrontation marked the beginning of Yeltsin's moral ascendancy.[114] He was removed from both of his official posts, but that meant he was free to say just what he liked. His electoral campaign in 1989 was based on a platform of anti-corruption and reform. In July 1990, already a media star, he took an even more decisive step and handed in his Communist Party card. 'I was probably too liberal . . . as regards Yeltsin,' Gorbachev would later claim. 'I should have sent him as ambassador to Great Britain or maybe a former British colony.'[115]

But it was now too late for that. Yeltsin was building an independent power-base, tapping into a long-neglected ideological seam of ethnic Russian patriotism. In 1989 and 1990, nationalist demonstrations dominated the news, culminating in unilateral declarations of independence in the Baltic and armed uprisings in the Caucasus. Russians were testing their nationalist credentials as well, ambivalent about the tensions in their empire but keen to find a more coherent identity for themselves. It was in this atmosphere that Gorbachev proposed to amend the constitution, creating a new post, that of President of the USSR, with direct responsibility to the Congress of People's Deputies. The move was intended to strengthen the Union, to hold the fissile republics together by giving them a single, and distinguished, figurehead. In March 1990, without appealing to the people as a whole, the Congress elected Gorbachev to the post. The Kremlin was spruced up as the new president's official residence, and while the Politburo continued its weekly meetings on the third floor, the Senate became Gorbachev's official base. Fifteen months later, as the Soviet Union dissolved around him, the Kremlin was virtually the only territory he controlled.[116]

The world was in revolution. Spurred by the success of their neighbours in Eastern Europe, Soviet citizens pressed their demands; Lithuania's campaign for independence was particularly vocal. Even in Moscow, the crowds were taking to the streets, some calling on Gorbachev to 'Remember Romania!' and aligning him with the detested Ceauşescus, who had been executed in Bucharest in December 1989.[117] This was unfair, for it was Gorbachev who had unleashed the popular tide in Europe in the first place, but the glory of the recent past made his increasingly repressive stance appalling. Deserted by reformers almost everywhere, he had become a prisoner of the Politburo hawks, the men who would destroy it all rather than let a single Soviet republic go its own way. In January 1991, Soviet troops moved into the Lithuanian capital, Vilnius. The demonstrations there were suppressed at the cost of fourteen lives. Again thanks to Gorbachev's earlier reforms, the violence was televised, and images of Soviet tanks loomed once again across Europe. The president – and the Soviet Union – had lost the moral argument for ever.

It was not clear, however, that the bulk of Soviet citizens were ready to give up on their empire. In March 1991, Gorbachev presided over a referendum on the Union's future. The question on the ballot paper was loaded: 'Do you consider it necessary to preserve the USSR as a renewed federation of equal sovereign republics, in which the rights and freedoms of people of all nationalities will be guaranteed in full measure?'[118] Few Russians (the Baltic republics were a different case) would readily have answered 'no', but all the same, the overwhelming 'yes' vote represented a democratic victory of sorts. The states that were to form the proposed federation, however, were changing apace, and nothing doomed Gorbachev's scheme for the continued Union as decisively as the decision to create a directly elected president for each of the new republics as part of the restructuring.

First mooted in 1989 by the Kazakh leader, Nursultan Nazarbayev, the move was meant to increase regional autonomy within a reformed Soviet Union.[119] 'Perhaps, from the outside, such a collection of "presidents", who in fact had no real power, appeared somewhat ridiculous,' Yeltsin would later muse.[120] But the campaign played into his hands. The creation of elected assemblies under Gorbachev had given Yeltsin a new platform, and by 1991 he was already Speaker of the Russian parliament, a body (technically responsible to the plenary Congress of People's Deputies) that met in a building on the Moscow river called the White House. Yeltsin's frank, populist speeches there had given him the sort of profile that exasperated voters could recognize and understand. Now he could play for a direct mandate to lead them. 'Not all the members of Yeltsin's entourage displayed a peace-loving mood,' Gorbachev remembered later. 'They had worked themselves up to fever pitch.'[121] On 12 June 1991, when the votes for the Russian presidency were counted, it turned out that Yeltsin had swept the board.

The die-hards of the Soviet world stood no chance against the nationalist juggernaut. But they had never set great store by democratic methods. In the summer of 1991, while the bevy of newly elected presidents, including Yeltsin and the ingratiating Nazarbayev, were meeting with Gorbachev to discuss a new and looser future for the Union, a different set of talks, more secret, was taking place in and around Moscow. The conspiracy included senior Kremlin aides, including Gorbachev's advisor Valery Boldin, and the heads of the armed forces, the interior ministry and the KGB. George Bush took action as soon as his agents could see a pattern in the scraps of information on their wires. The United States ambassador, Jack Matlock, broke the news to Gorbachev personally: the Americans had intelligence of a conspiracy to remove him, planned for 21 June. According to Chernyaev, Gorbachev laughed. 'It's a hundred percent improbable,' he replied. 'But I appreciate George telling me about his concern.'[122]

The plot, in fact, was well advanced. They called themselves the State Committee for the State of Emergency, the GKChP, and like its title their conspiracy was clumsy. On 18 August, when Gorbachev had left for an annual holiday at Foros in the Crimea, a group of senior officials gathered in Prime Minister Valentin Pavlov's Kremlin office, armed with bottles and glasses and surrounded by a chaos of half-finished plans. Their aim was to reverse the likely fragmentation of the Union and bring back the old disciplines of Brezhnev's time. One of their first acts was to send a delegation to negotiate with Gorbachev. Later that night, when they learned of his refusal to co-operate, some clearly wished that they had never joined the plot, but by then it was too late and the only panacea was drink. There was no going back, but the way forward called for actions more decisive than these men had ever bargained for. The Kremlin once again witnessed conspiracy, but this time it took place in an atmosphere of regret, recrimination and warm government brandy.

The two main targets of the plotters were the presidents, Gorbachev (USSR) and Yeltsin (Russia). Gorbachev was placed under KGB house-arrest in the government mansion at Foros. At the same time, special troops from the crack 'Alpha' military division gathered in the woods round Yeltsin's dacha in the Moscow suburb of Arkhangel'skoe with orders for his imminent arrest. On 19 August, Muscovites woke to the sinister rumble of tanks and armoured personnel carriers. 'The coup leaders decided to shock the city with an enormous display of military hardware and personnel,' Yeltsin recalled.

I look at the tragedy of the coup plotters as the tragedy of a whole platoon of government bureaucrats whom the system had turned into cogs and stripped of any human traits . . . But it would have been far worse if that platoon of cold and robotlike Soviet bureaucrats had returned to the leadership of the country.'[123]

There were courageous moments everywhere. In Moscow itself, the crowds who confronted the plotters' tanks were gambling with their very lives. In Foros, Gorbachev, too, held out for days. When the coup leaders claimed in public that the president was ill, his entourage feared for his safety: the strain certainly told on Raisa, who later suffered a brain haemorrhage. But it was Yeltsin, breaking through the armed cordon around his home and driving straight to the Russian parliament building, the White House, who garnered the greatest credit. By the time he arrived at his office, hundreds of Muscovites had already gathered to remonstrate with the tank crews outside. The Russian president slipped by them (the Kremlin is not the only government building in Moscow with a secret entrance), but outrage – and a sense of theatre – eventually drove him back outside to join the crowd. 'I clambered onto a tank, and straightened myself up tall,' Yeltsin recalled. 'Perhaps I felt clearly at that moment that we were winning, that we couldn't lose. I had a sense of utter clarity, of complete unity with the people standing around me.'[124] He stood and read out an appeal to Russia's people and then paused briefly to talk with the men in the tank that had become his platform. It was a matter of minutes outside, but the televised images and photographs became symbolic of an entire people's victory.

The coup was the last gasp of the Soviet regime. Its leaders had launched an attack on their own people, the most overt negation of democracy, and their treachery discredited the key institutions of a failing state: the KGB, the Communist Party and the General Staff. Instead of introducing military rule, the tank crews stepped out on to pavements littered with long-stemmed red flowers. In the capital of almost every republic, popular coalitions rushed to declare their independence from the disgraced Soviet regime. Their demands were among the many things that Gorbachev was ready to rethink. From his rooms in Foros, the Soviet president resumed command of the Kremlin regiment and ordered its commandant to seal the conspirators' offices and disconnect their phones.[125] He refused to receive the plotters, too, even those who had once been his friends, resolving to create a new regime with new, untainted, men. As he put it to the reporters who were waiting when his plane landed at Moscow airport, 'I have come back from Foros to a different country, and I myself am a different man now.'[126] But that still left all the main questions moot. 'Yes, we won,' Izvestiya's correspondent commented on 23 August. 'But our victory only gives us a chance, a possibility. Will we, and will our leaders, know how to use it?'[127]

Before the last of his supporters had dispersed from the White House, Boris Yeltsin announced that he was moving into the Kremlin. For a man whose sense of destiny was so enlarged, there really was no other choice. Whatever Gorbachev was trying to defend, Yeltsin was creating a new era. In his own view – and many shared it – he was also the saviour of Russia, the sort of person who had always based his government in Moscow's citadel. At a time of tension and uncertainty, the old place seemed a perfect surrogate for consensus, the symbol of a nation that had yet to coalesce. Though no-one was yet sure what Russia was, the Russian flag – red, white and blue – was raised above the Kremlin walls on 24 August 1991.

At the time, the most positive interpretation of Yeltsin's move was that he was taking control of the fortress in the name of the common man. This president was famed for riding on the bus like everybody else, after all, and even when he was not standing bravely on a tank, he was a real Russian with the manners and the appetites to match. 'The Kremlin was the symbol of stability, duration, and determination in the political line being conducted,' Yeltsin himself explained. 'If reforms were to be my government line, that was the statement I was making to my opponents by moving into the Kremlin.'[128] But there were other ways of reading Yeltsin's ambitions. An impulsive and intolerant man, a political animal whose basic instincts were more authoritarian than democratic, Yeltsin seemed to hunger for a throne.[129] He was also eager to make his position secure. 'The country's entire defence system is hooked up to the Kremlin,' he explained. The citadel was the centre of a massive web: 'all the coded messages from all over the world are sent here, and there is a security system for the buildings developed down to the tiniest detail.'[130] As he later added, putting it in the bluntest terms, only another coup could prise a man from power once he was inside.[131]

The irony was that another leader, Mikhail Gorbachev, was still in residence. The Communist Party might have been disgraced (and Yeltsin moved against it immediately that August, seizing its assets and closing its main offices), but the people had asked Gorbachev, in the referendum in March, to redesign the Soviet Union, and the Kremlin, still in Soviet guise, remained his official headquarters. For twelve weeks at the end of 1991, there were two presidents in the Moscow fortress, which also meant two teams of presidential aides, two types of protocol, and regular collisions between rival television crews as they raced between the press-conferences of the Russian and the Soviet heads of state.

Some institutions vanished within days. Almost at once, and to a chorus of public abuse, the Communist Party's Central Committee was pitched out of its building on Old Square. The site, no longer sacrosanct, became 150,000 square metres' worth of prime city-centre real estate with a market value of 137 million rubles.[132] Crowds of protesters gathered every day, many demanding to see secret files, and at one point, on 29 August, a mob of two or three hundred threatened to storm the place. Only armed guards saved the bureaucrats inside.[133] Chernyaev was among the last to leave. He and his team had barely three hours' notice, and as the minutes slipped away the sea of faces in the street grew more and more menacing. Eventually, police appeared and led the officials to a basement. 'There our guards made phone calls for a long time,' Chernyaev wrote. The frightened group followed the policemen deeper still under the building, entering tunnels that none had ever visited before. The brightly lit *podzemka*, the underground tram, awaited. Chernyaev's team made its escape, some time later, by coming up through a vault in the Kremlin's Senate precinct.[134]

Cleared of the Party *apparat*, Old Square became the headquarters of the government of Russia. The Kremlin was reserved for presidential staff. Yeltsin's team was based in Block 14, the former theatre on the old monastery site, and his presidential office was here as well, in full view of the Senate but not quite as grand. Gorbachev still occupied the smartest rooms, but Yeltsin's aides moved into theirs with roguish triumph, hungry for the trappings and the benefits of power. The former occupants of Block 14, the stubborn henchmen of the Soviet age, were given only hours to leave, and many were obliged to abandon quantities of files, including what turned out to be the transcripts of every telephone conversation Yeltsin had made since he and Gorbachev had clashed in 1987.[135] This sort of thing was bound to sour the atmosphere, but there were also tensions inside Yeltsin's camp. In the political free-for-all that summer, two of the Russian president's closest aides, Viktor Iliushin and Gennady Burbulis, spent precious days immediately after the coup locked in dispute over a Kremlin office that had recently been renovated to the coveted 'European' standard, complete with a small annex and a private gym.[136] Yeltsin left the pair to fight: in late August, he disappeared on holiday.

His absence brought an interlude of chaos and political fudge. But in the midst of much uncertainty, some scenes that autumn could be comic. The Soviet Union's impending break-up led to a shortage of wine in the citadel, for the Kremlin cellars had been stocked with cabernet from Soviet Moldavia (soon known as Moldova, and not Soviet), and as the last supplies of that ran out no-one could bring themselves to order a foreign alternative.[137] New Kremlin staff, faced with a bank of telephones, had to call the security office to find out how they worked.[138] And the personal rivalry between Yeltsin and Gorbachev was manifest. Andrei Grachev, then Gorbachev's presidential press secretary, recalled what happened on 28 October, when Gorbachev was due to receive the Cypriot president. The Catherine Hall, where such meetings traditionally took place, had been booked in advance by Yeltsin, so Gorbachev was forced to use the studio-office that had been created in the 1980s for his television appearances. There was a piquancy, now, in the fact that the battery of photogenic telephones along the desk had never been connected to anything. Someone also noticed that one of the office doors had warped. As it swung in the draught, it creaked so loudly that the interpreters could not make out what the leaders were trying to say. A Kremlin guard had to be called to hold it shut from the outside until the session ended.[139]

The creaking and the pointless telephones were perfect metaphors for Gorbachev's presidency after August 1991. The heads of almost all the former Soviet states were still engaged in talks with him, the aim of which was to produce a new-style Union, but at the same time Yeltsin was privately canvassing the influential players with a scheme to break the whole empire apart.[140] In public, his speeches were about the things Russia could do alone. When he appeared on people's screens, it was always to the backdrop of Russia's tricolour. By contrast, Gorbachev's protocol team was regularly faced with a last-minute choice between the Russian and the Soviet banners. Left to himself, the Soviet president would always opt for the latter, and his private plane, 'The Soviet Union', boasted a scarlet tail-fin to the last.[141]

But there would soon be no Soviet land to fly over. On 1 December

1991, the people of Ukraine, Russia's most cherished close neighbour, voted overwhelmingly in favour of independence. It was the last blow to Gorbachev's plan to reconceive the Soviet Union, and it allowed Yeltsin to trump him with a treaty that he had already negotiated, in semi-secret, at the Belovezhsky Nature Reserve in Belarus.[142] This formed a patchwork of new, independent nations, who worked on their common problems together for a few more months before drifting apart. Gorbachev's purpose, his role as Union President, was dead.

There was a lot of talking in the final weeks, but at the birth of this new version of Russia, there were real things, not just ideas, to hand over. In December 1991, Yeltsin took control of an extensive nuclear weapons system: the 'button' came in the shape of a 'nuclear briefcase', made by Samsonite, containing digital codes.[143] As the clock ticked down to zero hour, however, Gorbachev also gave him several ziggurats of files. The Kremlin's hidden trove of documents included details of the Chernobyl disaster, but history played the largest role, and the records testified to many acts that were officially denied. The presidential archive contained secrets about the Afghan war, about political repression under Khrushchev, and many papers bearing Stalin's pencil marks, one of which proved to be the original draft of the Molotov-Ribbentrop Pact of 1939. Such files, like well-primed nuclear bombs, had been passing from general secretary to general secretary for half a century. Central Committee staff had always denied their existence, and even Gorbachev had not released them in the *glasnost* years. 'Take them,' he told the latest heir. 'They're yours now.'[144]

Among the very few who witnessed the two leaders' final meeting in the Kremlin's Walnut Room was Andrei Grachev. That is, he and the other closest aides waited in a nearby lobby for ten hours. 'Our only source of information', according to Grachev, 'was Zhenya, the Kremlin waiter, who was shuttling back and forth between the Walnut Room and the kitchen carrying bottles and plates.'[145] 'Our conversation was protracted and difficult,' Yeltsin later insisted, though Grachev's source reported that 'the mood seem[ed] to be good'.[146] The press did not even have Zhenya's bulletins, and state radio channels followed Soviet tradition by playing endless broadcasts of the 'Dance of the Cygnets' from *Swan Lake*. The next day, however, again in that sham television office, a solemn Gorbachev signed his last presidential statement, borrowing a pen from the man from CNN. His final address as president was dignified and he used a phrase that Russians would not often hear again. 'I make this decision,' he explained, 'based on considerations of principle.'[147]

It was all over in minutes. The cameras followed Mikhail Gorbachev inside the Senate as he closed his office door.[148] By the time the foreign journalists were ready to start filming on the streets outside, the Soviet flag had vanished from the Senate roof. The world was later treated to the spectacle of its removal by courtesy of Russian private enterprise. Though the professionals had missed it, a group of Muscovites had captured the lowering of the Kremlin's last red flag with an imported camcorder. A copy of their VHS cassette cost less than fifty US dollars, cash.[149]

I 2

Normality

Boris Yeltsin moved into Gorbachev's office as soon as the cleaners had emptied the bin. The brass plate on the former president's door was taken down that very night (Yeltsin's men would later claim that Gorbachev's staff retaliated, on their way out, by unscrewing some of the other fittings and pocketing several gold fountain pens with the official crest).[1] The red flag that had flown above the Senate roof for seven decades was gone, and many hoped that the remaining Soviet legacies would disappear as fast. Optimists had taken to describing the entire interlude of Communist rule as an aberration, an experiment; they argued that the time had come for Russia to revert to its true path. If there were doubts about what that might mean, in view of Moscow's turbulent, eclectic history, they were ignored in the euphoria of victory. As the clock on the Kremlin's Saviour Tower struck midnight at the turn of the New Year, 1992, the famous chimes were drowned out by the sound of fireworks. The champagne flowed and people sang; everyone believed they had a right, now, to what they had begun to call a normal life.[2]

What they got was hardship and uncertainty. The list of problems that the new republic faced would have challenged a far stronger and more deeply rooted regime. From environmental degradation and low productivity to the collapse of public infrastructures, the Soviet legacy was crippling enough on its own. But the new state's headlong economic reforms added further stress, precipitating high rates of mortality and record levels of crime, hyper-inflation, and shortages of everything from food to anti-cancer drugs.[3] The Russian Ministry of the Interior estimated that by 1993, 85 per cent of the new private banks had links to organized crime. So did almost half the country's businesses, which was not surprising when even an honest trader could not survive without paying for protection (colloquially known as a 'roof') and following underworld rules.[4] The official murder rate in Moscow increased eight-fold between 1989 and 1993; the true figure was probably blacker still.[5] Unsurprisingly, almost no-one was prepared to gamble on the new republic's future prosperity. The 1990s saw a massive haemorrhage of capital from Russia to safe havens such as London and New York. Since most of it was exported illegally, the figures are hard to establish, but estimates for the period 1990–95 vary between about 65 and 400 billion US dollars.[6]

In this unpromising environment the challenge Russia's leaders faced was to build a credible, resilient and dignified state. The tsars had used religious iconography and stunning public splendour to achieve this; Lenin had invoked the sacred blood of martyrs and the proletarian revolution. From Ivan the Terrible and Mikhail Romanov to Stalin, no-one had expected any newly formed regime to flourish without a convincing pedigree and some form of mission. In the 1990s, however, the new state had few options on either score. In most societies – the ones that do not doubt their own normality – shared values tend to go unspoken and are almost always fluid anyway. But post-Communist Russia faced a moral crisis. Yeltsin was keen to make sure that it remained neither Soviet nor Communist, but Russia was not European and its people were not ready to accept the triumph of the west. That left a void, a kind of vertigo, especially in a society that had lived so long in the shadow of successive all-encompassing ideas.

The republic that Boris Yeltsin had inherited could still claim to be the largest country in the world, but it was no longer a superpower, no longer the seat of a dynastic monarchy, no longer exotic or even splendid. Even its once-mighty army did not look particularly fearsome any more. Throughout Russian history, shaky and parvenu regimes had invoked versions of the past to build legitimacy in circumstances such as these, but even that was awkward for the leaders of new Russia. The state could hardly celebrate the Soviet years, and yet its leaders had been raised as communists; many had built their careers by denouncing capitalist values and systems of privilege. In his days as provincial Sverdlovsk's Party boss, Yeltsin himself had ordered the demolition of a house that had served as the final prison of Nicholas II and his family. At the time, as a communist, he had argued that the place should not become a shrine. As president, ironically, shrines were exactly what he was about to need.

If Yeltsin had consulted his old friends, the leaders of the other former republics of the old USSR, he would have heard how they made use of nationalist rhetoric, exploiting their historic sufferings to forge new nations, or at least to garner millions of votes. But Russian politicians could not take this argument too far, and not merely because theirs was the nation that had historically oppressed the rest. The other problem was that Moscow was still in charge of an empire. The population of Yeltsin's new state, which was nearly 148 million in 1991, was overwhelmingly (more than 80 per cent) Russian by ethnicity, but apart from the core 'Russian' lands, it also included the whole of oil- and gas-rich Siberia as well as formerly tribal territories on the northern slopes of the Caucasus, such as Chechnya, North Ossetia and Kabardino-Balkaria.[7] Adopting a specious label designed to incorporate these valuable minorities, Moscow dubbed its new country the 'Russian Federation', a name derived from Soviet times and intended to suggest an equal partnership between the peoples of its several regions. In reality, the Russian heartland, and the Russian nation, dominated the political landscape and continued to dictate the cultural tone. But something more was still needed: some dignity and charisma, some sense of purpose and collective pride.

The answer could have been provided by democracy itself; in many countries, after all, government gets its real splendour from the idea of consent. As the rotten Soviet empire fell apart in the autumn of 1991, there was no reason to accept that Russians were in some way doomed to perpetual tyranny, or that their future had been bound and chained by history. The chance had come to create a new state. Admittedly, the White House building in Moscow was far from regal; it looked more like an airport terminal than a palace. The parliament that sat in it, moreover, had been elected under Soviet rules, and it remained a creature of the corrupt Soviet world. But even that anachronism could have been remedied by a round of fresh elections. Unfortunately, however, Yeltsin's own ambition had centred on the only real prize he knew, Kremlin-style power, and once he had his office in the fort he left outstanding details to his aides, a group with little appetite for tedious election-fights. The crucial summer ebbed away, and in October 1991, the hacks and demagogues filed back to their accustomed seats in the White House chamber.[8]

In what became a tragedy for Russia, the leaders of its parliament turned out to be less interested in hope and freedom than in crude power-struggles of their own. In the spring of 1993, a faction finally attempted to impeach Yeltsin, aiming to take the Kremlin for itself. The attempt failed, but its main instigators continued to develop and exploit any promising-looking seams of popular discontent. On 1 May, the Communist spring festival, large crowds of opposition supporters gathered in the streets and squares near the Kremlin to demand better pensions, jobs and basic social provision. The police were unprepared, and there were violent confrontations, burning cars.[9] Similar demonstrations were to be a feature of the cityscape for five more months, sometimes accompanied by army songs, sometimes by portraits of Stalin.[10] Forlorn red flags and bitter crowds became the symbol of a thwarted, sour democracy.

The disappointment turned to crisis on 21 September 1993, when Yeltsin finally dissolved the Supreme Soviet, Russia's parliament.[11] The moment should have brought any supporters of democracy out to the streets, but most stayed quietly at home. Some later claimed to have been busy simply trying to survive. With good cause, too, they were appalled by the obstructive and self-interested politics of the White House. 'We were very tired of political meetings and U-turns, bickering and scandals,' a journalist later admitted. 'All we wanted was to get on with life.'[12] In stark contrast to 1991, when opposition to the August coup had rallied thousands of supporters of reform, the crowds who gathered to defend this incarnation of the White House included old-style communists, pensioners, and xenophobic Russian chauvinists.[13] Yeltsin surrounded the whole lot with tanks, and this time lethal shells were fired. Even Russia's official count of the White House siege speaks of 147 dead, but the casualty figures in other versions are much higher.[14] 'As I write, I can hear a familiar sort of sound through my windows, just like fireworks,' wrote the liberal journalist Otto Latsis. 'But it's not fireworks. It's the tank shells that are battering the White House. And this is not the Caucasus or the Pamirs; it's the centre of Moscow.'[15] Eight years later, when an attempt was made to call the president to account, critics confirmed that he had forbidden doctors to come to the assistance of the wounded White House defenders until his victory was sure. 'When I make a strategic decision,' Yeltsin later boasted, 'I don't punish myself with ridiculous worries over whether I might have done it differently or whether I could have found another way.'[16]

The intellectuals and journalists had feared a coup by anti-democratic communists, so Yeltsin's violence did not provoke much criticism at the time. The United States ambassador, Thomas Pickering, was not alone in declaring the defeated White House faction to have been 'fascist'.[17] 'I believe that President Yeltsin's democratic credentials are strong,' the reform-minded White House deputy Lev Ponomarev insisted. 'He has proved his commitment to democratic institutions on many occasions.'[18] But 'democratic' was an odd word to ascribe to a man who could happily state that 'someone in the country should be chief'.[19] Yeltsin's governing idea was simply to remain in power.[20] Another American diplomat, Thomas Graham, later drew a pessimistic lesson as he reflected on post-Soviet Moscow's troubled record. As he put it in 1995, 'In domestic politics, there are few committed democrats and no clans committed to democracy despite rhetoric to the contrary. Democratic procedures, including elections, are seen largely as weapons in the power-struggle.'[21]

After the coup of 1993, the chance to base the new Russia on democratic multi-party politics was lost. Anarchy and revolt seemed like more potent dangers than any excess of government. Invoking history with masterly legerdemain, Yeltsin offered Russians what they were supposed to want: firm leadership from the Kremlin. Within weeks of the anti-parliamentary putsch, he had signed the new constitution, a document that the Russian political analyst Lilia Shevtsova has described as 'not so much an agreement between society and the authorities, but a manifesto of the victorious side'.[22] Its terms were unambiguous. The president was to be head of state, head of the Security Council, and the author of foreign and defence policy. He was to have the power to nominate the prime minister and the senior figures in a range of bodies including the Central Bank, the Procuracy, and the higher courts. In addition, he (or she) could also issue decrees with the force of law. These *ukazy*, whose very name echoed old tsarist times, gave Yeltsin a near-autocratic power. The only clouds on his horizon were the elections that were to be held every four years. An extra condition was that the president should serve for no more than two consecutive four-year terms, but a helpful sub-clause permitted former holders of the post to stand for re-election after someone else had kept the office warm for just one stint.[23] The president's official residence was the Kremlin.

Moscow's red fortress was about to star, yet again, in the reinvention of the Russian state. On 6 October 1993, the guard of honour that had stood by Lenin's mausoleum since the 1920s was removed, and the ceremonial activities associated with 'Post No. 1' were eventually relocated to the nearby Tomb of the Unknown Soldier. A commission headed by the man in overall charge of Russian archives, Rudolf Pikhoia, then considered a range of emblems for the infant polity. The red stars on the Kremlin towers proved too expensive to move, but by the end of 1993 the Soviet hammer and sickle had been dropped from the Russian coat of arms in favour of the double-headed eagle.[24] The president baulked only at proscribing communism itself. Though hundreds of statues and portraits were removed from town squares and office-blocks across the land, a piece of draft legislation ordering the removal of Lenin's corpse from the mausoleum on Red Square was quietly dropped.[25]

Meanwhile, Yeltsin's immediate problem was not so much a lack of personal legitimacy, since he had been both elected and acclaimed, but the total absence of any ruling charisma for his government. The new constitution explicitly banned state ideologies. The clause was meant to outmanoeuvre unrepentant communists, but it also pointed to an absence of political ideas. Even the new republic's national anthem, Glinka's nineteenth-century 'Patriotic Song', which now replaced the rousing and familiar Soviet hymn, had no official words. The system itself was anything but charismatic. Outside the court and Yeltsin's presidential club, the institutions of government were weak and barely respected, less capable of raising taxes or controlling crime than any of their Soviet predecessors. A citizen who felt threatened was more likely to turn to private security companies or mafia groups than to the police. The Kremlin had its own life, privileged and rivalrous, but beyond it the one thing Russia did not have was an effective state.[26]

The solution, an old one, was to jazz up the idea of power by borrowing some glamour from the past. Amid the yearning for the country's lost stability and pride, Yeltsin's style began to change. In 1994, in a gesture of reconciliation that had been planned in the days of Gorbachev, Queen Elizabeth II and Prince Philip made a state visit to his capital, the first by a British monarch since the Bolshevik revolution of 1917.[27] In Her Majesty's honour, there was a full peal of the Kremlin bells, a sound Moscow had seldom heard in the previous seventy years. The president was attentive and courteous, his staff immaculate. It all went very smoothly, including the ticklish exchange of diplomatic gifts, though choosing these had been like torture for both sides. In a ceremony held in the famous indoor garden of the Grand Palace, the queen presented the Yeltsins – Boris and his wife, Naina – with a polished wooden box, each miniature compartment of which contained the seeds of a plant that grew in the gardens of Buckingham Palace. 'Oh, Borya!' the British interpreter heard Naina whispering to her husband. 'Now we can have a Buckingham Palace of our own!' 'To our regret,' Yeltsin would later confess, 'many of the seeds did not take root.'[28]

The president shared Naina's sentiment, however, and the one thing he could always cultivate was a nostalgia for the tsars. To the organizers' delight, in July 1998 he even opted to attend the ceremonial re-interment, in St Petersburg, of the bodies of the murdered Nicholas II and his family. By then, the national fever of repentance had reached such a pitch that a rival ceremony had to be organized near Moscow, for some critics insisted that the first state funeral had not been splendid enough.[29] The grandeur and the piety were all to Yeltsin's taste. 'How sad, really,' he confided to his diary after the service in St Petersburg, 'that we have lost the previous historical relics of the monarchy, that we have lost our sense of wholeness and continuity of our history. How desirable it would have been to have all of this restored in our country.'[30]

The public, meanwhile, was developing its own interpretation of that wholeness and historical continuity. Erstwhile Soviet citizens discovered a passion for titles and etiquette, and companies soon sprang up to design new coats of arms. But the longing for a strong, sound, morally acceptable collectivism, for Russia (or the Russian Federation) as it ought to be, found its most conspicuous outlet in the re-creation of old buildings, especially religious ones. The grass-roots passion for old monuments had been growing for decades by the time of the Soviet Union's collapse. Its patron saint was the veteran architect Petr Baranovsky, whose survival into the 1980s gave him the status of godfather to the heritage movement. In 1969, he had created a school for architectural conservation in a set of Moscow buildings he had fought to save, the Krutitskoe Residence (*podvor'e*), a former monastery and bishop's palace that had languished for years under the administration of the State Historical Museum.[31] But after 1991 the resurrection of lost buildings turned into a craze. Each rescued or reconstructed monument seemed like a fresh step onwards from the Soviet past, a victory for true values; it helped that ancient churches served as pools of quiet in the crude bazaar that Moscow had become. From a politician's point of view, the benefits were dazzling. The projects yielded millions in contracts. Nostalgia, meanwhile, could be made to substitute for politics, and even Yeltsin could be painted as a patron of the arts. Eventually, the Kremlin would become the centre of the most notorious restoration scheme of all, but the old fortress was not the first landmark on the investors' list. The most prominent developments of the early 1990s were sham copies, facsimiles of the buildings that equally eager crowds had reduced to rubble only sixty years before.

Free Russia's first new reconstruction was the Kazan Cathedral on the edge of Red Square. This striking building had been demolished in 1936, but Baranovsky's drawings from the 1920s had survived, and in 1991 a team led by one of his students, Oleg Zhurin, pledged to rebuild it from scratch. Baranovsky had not been able to survey the old building's foundations, but Zhurin resolved to recreate a faithful image of the original stone structure. This had in turn replaced a wooden church, funded by Prince Pozharsky in 1625, that had been dedicated as a gesture of gratitude for Moscow's deliverance from the seventeenth-century Time of Troubles. The historical resonance was explicit as Zhurin worked; he told journalists that he wanted his church to act as a symbol of Russian national peace-making after the troubles of more recent times.[32] It was a post-Communist message, but Zhurin toiled like a Bolshevik, storming to complete the project in three years.

Zhurin's new church was (and remains) eye-catching, and its success spurred others to rebuild the Iberian gates and chapel at the north-western entrance to Red Square. The mid-1990s also saw the transformation of an open space beyond the Kremlin's Alexander Gardens. Manezh Square had been cleared by Stalin to make way for the massive demonstrations that burnished his rule, but the lesson of 1991–3 was that large crowds, in a state less able than Stalin's to control them, could rapidly destroy the illusion of civil peace. The answer (conveniently from the point of view of the waiting investors) was to create clutter and diversion, a goal that Moscow's mayor, Yury Luzhkov, achieved by commissioning a water-park with streams and fountains. Since new Russia lacked serious ideas – and even heroes – of its own, the mayor's designer punctuated the space with lumpy statues of characters from Russian fairy-tales.[33] A vast underground shopping mall beneath this Disneyesque landscape drew thousands of grateful shoppers and enhanced the opportunities for profit. In 1997, when Moscow celebrated the 850th anniversary of its foundation, the theme park just outside the Kremlin walls attracted larger crowds than almost any authentic building from the past. Even the advertising logo for the jubilee event showed a fairy-tale Kremlin silhouette in place of the genuine article.[34]

The most ambitious reconstruction, however, was that of Konstantin Ton's Cathedral of Christ the Saviour. Though its demolition had been a brutal blow, Moscow's most conspicuous church had not been missed by everyone. The swimming-pool that Khrushchev commissioned on its site had proved to be extremely popular; roughly five million people used it every year, a figure that dwarfed the total number of churchgoers in Moscow, even in the early 1990s, by a factor of ten.[35] Despite its utility, however, the pool was closed in 1993. There was no public consultation, but eventually the news broke that the site had been earmarked for a monumental symbol of Russia's post-Soviet resurgence. Where the Bolsheviks had planned to raise a tower, a statement of the values of October 1917, a new regime declared that it would build as grandly in the name of whatever the new Russia was supposed to be. Seizing on the ambiguity of that, local artists and architects drafted inventive proposals, some of which recall the innovative memorial projects under construction in Berlin at the same time. One was an empty metal structure, almost scaffold-like, which was designed to mimic the exact outline of the lost cathedral (and thus also to represent its massive scale) without imposing on the city or precluding a range of different commemorative or ritual forms inside it.[36]

What Moscow's mayor had in mind, however, was a nostalgic (and profitable) homage to the nineteenth century. From 1994, the cathedral project focused on a single aim, which was to re-create – or at least to mimic – Ton's building. 'Our revolution,' Luzhkov declared, 'is only a slow return to the normal order of things.'[37] Just to make sure, he also organized a public-relations campaign to sell his idea to the Russian electorate, many of whom remained sceptical, not least about the cost. Grass-roots enthusiasm was recruited, too, by personal appeals for building funds. In 1995 and 1996, travellers on the Moscow metro were besieged by pious-looking pensioners rattling collection-boxes bearing pictures of the lost cathedral. It was no accident that 1995 and 1996 were also election years (parliamentary and presidential). At a time when the Communist Party was gathering large numbers of votes, syrupy references to Russia's rebirth and the memory of imperial Moscow, channelled through the cathedral project, served to boost the ratings of both Yeltsin and Luzhkov. The mayor was so proud of the scheme, indeed, that he made a gift of a commemorative cathedral plate to Michael Jackson when the singer visited his city in October 1996.[38]

The Cathedral of Christ the Saviour was rebuilt in a year. More accurately, the scaffolding came off the exterior in time for a grand opening ceremony during the jubilee of 1997. Thereafter, it would take more than two years to complete the work, which included the lavish interior decoration that was deemed indispensable for the future showcase of official state-sponsored Orthodoxy. To meet the self-imposed targets, Luzhkov's architects used concrete, not traditional stone, and the other modifications they specified included lifts inside the pillars (which were hollow) to permit the public to speed upwards to a viewing-platform underneath the dome. The massive building was not quite a replica, in other words, but more like a vast, expensive fake, a promise made with fingers crossed, meretricious and glib. Unlike some other kinds of fake, it was not cheap, either, and though the costs have never been disclosed, estimates range from $250 to $500 million, a large (but unacknowledged) portion of which was taken out of the federal budget at a time when Russia's provinces faced economic ruin.[39] The rest came partly from the people's small donations, but more notably from the wealthy group around Luzhkov. These worthies, the true beneficiaries of new Russia's version of normality, are commemorated with memorial plaques around the dome. The landmark indeed celebrates the spirit of its age: a gallery of oligarchs now clothes the space that Ton reserved, in his original cathedral, for the heroes of 1812.[40]

The fake cathedral glinted on the riverbank, but the Kremlin remained the most charismatic landmark in the city. It also represented Russia in a way that Luzhkov's controversial monster never really could. But the fortress had undergone a quiet change of status, the consequences of which remained unclear. In December 1990, in token of Soviet Russia's new openness to the world, the Moscow Kremlin and Red Square had been designated a World Heritage Site – one of several in what was then Soviet space – by UNESCO. The immediate benefits had been moral: inclusion meant international acknowledgement of the Kremlin's status as 'a masterpiece of human creative genius'.[41] But the plaudits and the cash came at a price. In theory, international standards of conservation now applied, and UNESCO also specified that the Russian authorities should 'observe the present configuration of the site, particularly the balance between the monuments and non-built areas'.[42] That ruled out any further concrete palaces, but it also, at least officially, barred lucrative reconstruction.[43] Finally, UNESCO took an interest (albeit remote) in issues of public access, which precluded any return to Stalin-era exclusivity. In 1992, the speaker of the Russian parliament, Ruslan Khasbulatov, revived the idea of turning the citadel into a museum-park. The proposal was dismissed as a political ruse to embarrass the incumbent Boris Yeltsin.[44]

UNESCO would soon find that its well-meaning regulations carried little weight in Russia. In 1992, Yeltsin approved the first plans for a pastiche building in the Kremlin. The work involved the removal of a shabby block of toilets and catering facilities on the corner of Cathedral Square, so there were few real tears to shed. Once the service buildings had gone, a company called Mosproekt-2 began an expensive reconstruction of the nineteenth-century incarnation of the old Red Stair.[45] In the Kremlin as in Russian politics, it was not golden Muscovy, and not the labyrinthine holiness of the Romanovs, but the confused and derivative style of nineteenth-century official nationalism that was to be the new benchmark. And the Red Stair was the first of many glitzy, profitable Kremlin jobs. Soon Yeltsin had also signed the outline plans for the restoration of the Grand Kremlin Palace, an undertaking that concluded with the resurrection of the nineteenth-century throne room.[46] By the time of Moscow's jubilee in 1997, the joke that people liked to tell was that Yeltsin and Luzhkov were competing to see whose golden cupolas, the Kremlin's or Christ the Saviour's, could be made to shine the brightest.

The man with ultimate responsibility for almost every Kremlin project at the time was a jovial character called Pavel Borodin. In 1999, the *New York Times* described him as 'the Russian that people would most love to bribe'.[47] Borodin's titles varied, but he was best known as the

Director of Presidential Affairs, a portfolio that included the upkeep and restoration of presidential real estate. In 1998, Borodin estimated the value of his empire at more than $600 billion, and it included federal dachas and apartments as well as government-owned hotels and ministerial buildings. But its crowning glory was the Moscow Kremlin. Borodin's office released no accounts ('these things are not the public's business,' a spokeswoman told *The Economist* in 1999[48]), but its spending was in the tens of millions. After the Red Stair came the Senate, the real presidential base. Under Borodin's supervision, the restoration of Yeltsin's official residence was completed, in record time, in 1994–5. The cost remains undisclosed, but millions passed through one company, Mabetex Project Engineering, which had a controlling interest in the work.[49] In terms of public benefit, the justification for such a huge outlay was shaky, for most of the Senate was off-limits to visitors and the restoration included the dismantling of its one public attraction, Lenin's apartment-museum.[50] The result, however, was spectacular, as Russian viewers could verify for themselves whenever their president appeared on television, gliding down a river of parquet or signing papers at a splendid desk.

The style was calculated to impress the Russian oligarchs who tended to drop into Yeltsin's court. As the president himself later wrote, when billionaires like Mikhail Khodorkovsky or Vladimir Potanin arrived at the Kremlin, they had to realize 'that they have come for an audience with the government and not a chat with some kind of uncle'.[51] Once the Senate renovation was complete, Borodin turned his attention to the Grand Kremlin Palace. In 1997–8, at a time when Russia faced an economic crisis and a default on its international debts, teams of builders and craftsmen laboured to restore the gutted halls, or at least to create a version that might appear to be old. Their work received a boost when several retired Kremlin staff revealed that fragments of the original interiors, carried off in secret during the 1933 demolition, still existed.[52] The treasured lumps resurfaced and were used to model replica palace rooms, albeit sometimes from cheaper materials. Finally, intricate gilt mouldings and tsarist insignia had to be copied and professionally installed. Such fine, delicate work required the skills of specialists, so craftsmen in Florence were hired for showpiece projects like the carving and the parquet floors, most of which were shipped in blocks to Moscow and assembled there.[53] But not all foreign employees were prestigious.

The basic labouring was done by workers on low pay, many of whom were brought to Moscow illegally from Central Asia and the states of the former Yugoslavia. In a land of visas and official work-permits, such 'black' labour was always vulnerable. In 1998, it was discovered that the men had gone unpaid for months at a time, while working conditions were so insanitary that scores had fallen ill and at least one had died.[54]

Foreign labour was not, however, the main story when it came to Borodin. Yeltsin's aide had an unusually sharp instinct for money. Among the anecdotes that were circulating in Moscow by 1999 was a tale from his days in Siberia. The story went that he had once refused to accept the gift of a Mercedes car, offered in gratitude by a German company whom he had sponsored for a lucrative state deal. 'I can't take bribes,' he is said to have assured the Germans, 'but of course you could always sell it to me.' When the German delegates invited him to name a price, according to the tale, he did not hesitate. 'Make it twenty kopeks,' Borodin is said to have replied, 'and I'll have two.'[55] Such brazenness usually raised laughs, not subpoenas, in Yeltsin's Moscow, but by the end of the 1990s the political atmosphere had soured. The president's second term was drawing to a close, and the constitution, to say nothing of his own ill health, barred him from standing for office again. The scandal that raged round Borodin in 1999 played to public disgust about the super-rich, but it was also part of the contest for Russia's political succession, and (appropriately) its focus was the recent renovation of the Kremlin.

The case against Borodin started to build in 1997, when the Swiss prosecutor-general and anti-mafia campaigner, Carla Del Ponte, announced an investigation into Russian money-laundering. In the spring of 1998, Russia's chief prosecutor, Yury Skuratov, who had been approached by Del Ponte for assistance, began enquiries of his own, targeting alleged corruption by people close to the tycoon Boris Berezovsky and the Yeltsin family. Potential criminal charges arose from the allegation that Borodin and Yeltsin's two daughters, Elena and Tatiana, had accepted kickbacks in the tens of millions of dollars in exchange for the award of Kremlin contracts. There were also questions to be answered by Mabetex and its Albanian-born director, Behgjet Pacolli. Del Ponte and Skuratov seemed to be making headway with their case when Yeltsin suddenly announced, in February 1999, that the chief prosecutor had been suspended, pending dismissal. In May, Russian television viewers discovered the reason – or at least the pretext – when they were given the chance to watch for themselves a grainy clip of film (aired at prime-time) that showed Skuratov disporting himself in a hotel bed in the company of two prostitutes.[56] The prosecutor's claim that he had been framed in order to block the corruption enquiry did little to help his cause.

Though deputies in Russia's Duma (the new parliament) continued to press for Yeltsin's impeachment for a range of other crimes, Skuratov's investigation had effectively been neutralized. In early August 1999, the Swiss money-laundering enquiry also hit an obstacle when Del Ponte was unexpectedly 'promoted' to the International Court in The Hague. The trail might have grown cold, but that same month, the Italian newspaper *Corriere della Sera* revealed details of credit-card slips that had been discovered in a raid on the Mabetex offices in Lugano. The company appeared to have been paying regular bills on behalf of several Kremlin luminaries, including the former head of Yeltsin's personal security team, Alexander Korzhakov, as well as Yeltsin and his two daughters.[57] Further investigations in Switzerland, assisted by an informant called Felipe Turover, cast suspicion upon other highly placed Russians, including Borodin.[58]

The storm that threatened never broke, however. The details of the rescue still remain unclear, and Russian sources contest almost all of them, but the need for some kind of cover-up was obvious enough. The scandal did not quite determine the presidential succession (too many potential candidates were implicated, after all), but Yeltsin's choice of Vladimir Putin certainly proved to be a happy one for those involved. It was under Putin that Skuratov was finally dismissed, the charges against the Yeltsin family forgotten, and, in April 2001, that Borodin was bailed from a Swiss prison for a sum, paid by the Russian government, of $2.85 million.[59] 'I am immeasurably grateful to Vladimir Vladimirovich Putin,' the alleged felon declared on his return to Moscow's Sheremetyevo airport, 'for his help, for his decency, for being a real man.'[60]

Behgjet Pacolli, of Mabetex, successfully sued Skuratov for libel in 2000. He then moved on to greater things, and in February 2011 he was elected president of Kosovo, a post he held for just two months, though he continued to serve his beloved state in high office. His company also prospered, doing especially conspicuous work in the new capital of

Kazakhstan, Astana, where its projects have included a magnificent new presidential palace for Yeltsin's old friend, Nursultan Nazarbayev.[61] As for Moscow, there is no sign of an end to the flood of development contracts. In 2007, UNESCO formally protested to the Russian government about the scale and intensity of new building around Red Square and the Kremlin. At the same meeting, it requested a report about the future management of the heritage site. The request was repeated in 2008 and 2009. In 2011, the committee was still waiting for formal replies. The Kremlin was not on the official agenda when UNESCO met in St Petersburg in 2012, but experts warned that the Russian government's persistent infringement of the citadel's historical integrity, including the construction of two entirely new buildings, could well result in its exclusion from the World Heritage List by the end of 2013.[62]

Pavel Borodin, meanwhile, has flourished in defiance of most predictions. In March 2002, a Swiss court fined him $177,000, but he refused to recognize its jurisdiction. The money was taken from the bail that Russian taxpayers had paid a year before on his behalf.[63] But the sum was trifling anyway, at least for someone in his world. In November 2006, the prosperous-looking former aide celebrated his sixtieth birthday at one of his lavish properties in the Moscow suburbs. Jennifer Lopez confounded the gossip-columnists by declining to appear, but the guests included the Speaker of the Federal Parliament, Sergei Mironov, the former defence minister, Pavel Grachev, and one-time presidential hopeful Vladimir Zhirinovsky. The cake, which was suitably vast, took the form of a cream-filled model of the Moscow Kremlin, and among the presents was a trinket-box shaped to look like the Grand Kremlin Palace.[64]

As Russia's population struggled through the miseries of restructuring, debt and international default, its leaders seemed to have nothing but fairy-stories with which to distract it. The statues that appeared in almost every Moscow square, including a particularly grotesque monument to the Russian navy, stood witness to a series of confused, escapist and often wildly inappropriate judgements about a good deal more than public art. But the age of rudderless drift was soon to end. Six months before the end of his second term, on the eve of the millennium, 31 December 1999, Boris Yeltsin announced his resignation. The news was timed so that it felt like a seasonal present from a favourite grandfather. Any potentially disturbing impact was buffered by the fact that the broadcast went out at the height of almost everybody's New Year party. Yeltsin also made it clear that he had chosen a reliable successor on the whole electorate's behalf. This person, though relatively unknown to the public, had been appointed as Prime Minister in August 1999, and he remained, as Yeltsin assured his audience, 'a strong man, fit to be president'. Vladimir Putin was to take over as caretaker head of state immediately. For the future, Yeltsin told the Russian people that he 'had confidence in their amazing wisdom'. Having brought Putin to the public's notice, the retiring president declared that he had 'no doubt about the choice that they would make' at the polls, now re-scheduled for March.[65]

At this point, Vladimir Putin was forty-eight years old. A life-long practitioner of judo, he was not only fit but sober, for which the Russian electorate, used to ailing and unsteady leaders, was certainly grateful. But he had come to Moscow from his native St Petersburg relatively recently, and was still regarded as an outsider in most of the capital's close-knit political circles. His sponsors faced an uphill task as they set out to market his political brand. The solution was an unexpected one. As a former lieutenant-colonel in the Soviet-era KGB, Putin had proved his mettle as an effective and reforming leader of its Russian successor, the FSB, and he continued to cultivate a positive image for that organization once he was president. In time his vulpine features seemed to personify all that was best – if such a notion were possible – in the ideal secret policeman.

As the euphoria of New Year's Eve wore off that January, however, Kremlin-watchers were unimpressed. Putin, wrote political analyst Lilia Shevtsova, was 'not a charismatic or a bright personality'. His qualities included 'modesty, dullness . . . and the ability to use street slang'.[66] She might have been gloomier still if she had recollected that Stalin's early rivals, such as Leon Trotsky, had once made broadly similar comments about him. In private, even Yeltsin later came to rue his choice of protégé.[67] But the president was there to stay. In March 2000, Putin took advantage of a storm of fear – the spectre of Chechen terrorism that his own security forces had worked to summon – and returned to the Kremlin with 52.94 per cent of the vote, against 29.21 per cent for his nearest rival, the Communist Party's Gennady Zyuganov.[68] Four years later, riding a wave of prosperity based on the international price of

Russia's oil and gas, he secured an even more convincing winning margin. There was an interval from 2008–12, the four-year break after two presidential terms prescribed in Yeltsin's 1993 Russian constitution, but in 2012 Putin returned to the Kremlin again, and this time he looked very much at home.

The watchwords of the new regime had been prefigured at the moment of its birth; whatever his private goals, in public, Russia's leader was to stand for anti-corruption, a sleek and steely masculinity, and an untiring fight against crime. Above all, Putin represented the stability that many tired post-Soviet Russians craved. They talked about normality as if it were a kind of right, but what they wanted was a government that looked convincing and refrained from making intrusive demands. Since the state in fact remained very weak, Putin's regime worked hardest to deliver on the looks. Instead of fear and poverty and shame, this leader seemed to promise that his people could again feel proud, infusing their beloved patriotism with a twist of xenophobia, especially towards the west.

Voters were so distracted, and so relieved, that a majority chose to ignore the tedious, depressing facts behind the fairy-tale, but the price they paid for ineffective government was high. Crime continued to rise during the Putin years,[69] and in the first decade of the twenty-first century Russia lost more citizens to terrorist attack than any other industrialized country. The only places with bleaker records were Iraq and Afghanistan.[70] Corruption among government officials reached such an extreme that by the end of 2005, ministerial posts and governorships were said to be exchanging hands for multiples of $10 million.[71] As for investment confidence, the official figures for Russian capital flight topped $40 billion in 2010, and the indications for the future offered no prospect of change.[72] But Putin really did convince large numbers that their country had returned to its essential course. Even before he took office, on 29 December 1999, his name had appeared at the foot of an online Kremlin posting about the nation's future called 'Russia at the Turn of the New Millennium'. It emphasized what was unique about the place, dismissing imported western ideas such as individual freedom of expression. 'For Russians,' Putin had written, 'a strong state is not an anomaly . . . but the source and guarantor of order, the initiator and main driving force of any change.'[73] It was that version of normality, not some imported democratic dream, that he had pledged himself to build.

The Kremlin was, of course, the only possible base for Putin's state. Personally, Russia's leader seemed more at ease in his luxurious suburban dacha, pulling pints of straw-coloured St Petersburg beer for Tony Blair or entertaining guests around a table of his own.[74] Before long, he even had a string of better palaces at his disposal, the most controversial of which, in a protected forest near the Black Sea town of Praskoveyevka, was rumoured to have cost a billion dollars to build.[75] But the Kremlin offered something beyond price. If a strong state were indeed Russia's destiny, then here was its eternal sacred heart, the nation's citadel. As Yeltsin had once put it, 'There is a strange magic to the place, the magic of the air of history. Certain defence mechanisms subconsciously kick into gear, the mechanisms of genetic memory: people realise that in spite of everything, this is the Kremlin, this is Russia, this is my country.'[76] Like so many previous Russian leaders, Putin set out to harness the aura of the red fortress. It helped that history had been his favourite subject at school.[77]

The past – or an invented version of it – became an instrument of yet another government. For glamour, the new regime invoked the romance of the tsars much as Yeltsin had done; official ceremonies and even smaller meetings were televised against the gold and crystal backdrop of the Kremlin halls. Unlike his predecessor, however, Putin also allowed his people to pretend to be good Soviets again. The Patriotic War played an ever-increasing role in public discourse, connecting present-day Russians with noble suffering, personal heroism, and world-class military glory. Its stirring music still made many hearts beat faster, as did the new national anthem, a reworked version of the war-time Soviet one, which Putin revived at the end of 2000.[78] Critics complained that a return to Stalin's tunes insulted his unnumbered victims, but their protests were to no avail. Yeltsin had sometimes looked like a foreigners' lackey, a creature of the rotten capitalist world. Putin would never play that role. His message was exactly what most Russians seemed to yearn to hear.[79] Between 2000 and 2003, repeated polls reflected ordinary Russians' belief in their country's special path, its 'unique way of life and spiritual culture', 'predestination' and, inevitably, its strong and centralized tradition of government.[80]

The exploitation of the past was systematic and sustained, but it seemed to peak around election times. In 2007, as the speculation about plans for a possible (and unconstitutional) consecutive third term for the president began to build, cinema audiences learned of a blockbuster film, *1612*, produced by Putin's great admirer, Nikita Mikhalkov. Set towards the end of the Time of Troubles, it told the story of Moscow's salvation from the invading Poles. For some reason, almost every scene in Mikhalkov's interpretation of the epic demanded the bizarre appearance of a magical unicorn, a creature that had no connection to the real Romanovs' well-documented purchases of narwhal tusk. 'It's important for me that the audience feel pride,' the director, Vladimir Khotinenko, told journalists. He did not want young people to regard the struggle against enemies as 'something that happened in ancient history but as a recent event'.[81] The film was released in Moscow on National Unity Day, 4 November, the holiday that had replaced the Soviet revolutionary festival in 2005. Its message, that the latest time of troubles had given way to a new Muscovite golden age, led critics in the liberal press to dismiss the whole thing as 'trash'.[82]

But image-makers did not take the hint. 'Do we love Moscow?' the conservative *Moskovskaya Pravda* asked in 2007. The pretext for the question was an online poll in which Russian voters had failed to place the Kremlin among the seven wonders of the modern world. The implication, couched in several pages of romantic prose, was that true patriots should speak up for the site that the poet Lermontov had called 'the altar of Russia'. 'We must learn to appreciate our connection with everything that took place and will take place in the land of our birth. The land of our fathers – in Latin, *patria* – our Motherland.'[83] To help viewers to understand the unique greatness of that national home, they were soon to be offered another historical example: tenth-century Byzantium. In 2008, a pseudo-documentary film shown on the *Rossiya* television channel praised the ancient empire's wealth, its bureaucratic structures, and its all-seeing networks of security.[84] The only flaw identified by the presenter (Putin's personal confessor, the archimandrite Tikhon Shevkunov) was the weakness of early Byzantine constitutionalism, which allegedly insisted on electing emperors for four-year terms rather than anointing them for life.[85] This proved to be too much even for Putin's office, and the reform that his successor, Dmitry Medvedev, pushed through later that year merely extended future presidential terms from four years to six.

There were a few other U-turns, not least because the internet and liberal press were giving voice to sceptics who might once have gone unheard. In 2007, a scandal erupted when a much-anticipated school textbook, *The Unknown History of Russia 1945–2006*, went so far as to excuse Stalin, describing him as 'an effective manager'. The book was withdrawn and amended.[86] But the president and his supporters continued with their vivid history lectures. Putin seemed to identify with the statist reformers of Russia's past, notably Nicholas II's prime minister, Petr Stolypin, and he enjoyed promoting their images. Yeltsin had adorned his Kremlin office with life-sized statues of Peter and Catherine the Great, but by 2005, the scale of themed redecoration had turned the Senate into a veritable pantheon. Official visitors – and television-viewers who saw the statues and portraits on screen – would never doubt which prophets of Russia's destiny were meant to be inspiring them.[87] No historical revival was more incongruous, however, than the new cult of the secret police. The 1990s had been Russia's decade of repentance. Historians had worked like archaeologists then, joining survivors and human-rights workers in a sustained effort to uncover the extent of Stalinist violence, the evidence of repression and death. The FSB had not been implicated in these atrocities, but no-one would lightly have praised its Soviet predecessors, the Cheka and NKVD.

When a new television series, *Kremlin-9*, began in 2004, it seemed innocuous enough at first. Its purpose was to tell more of the stories that had once been buried in archives. The researchers focused on the elite rather than the people, and included tales of Stalin's inner circle, war-time government, and even the decline of Brezhnev's health. The series title referred to the secret police department that had long protected the top brass. But nothing that related to the Cheka was ever quite what it seemed. The cameras took viewers on many interesting tours, but the atmosphere resembled that of a Cold War spy novel. Crime and rivalry in politics were presented as the preserve of a fictional-seeming Kremlin where life was always lived by separate rules; the people's real nightmare of mass-death and wanton cruelty was simply swept aside. And all was well, or normal, in the Kremlin of today. It was a place that Russians should again regard with pride. As the presenter, Pavel Konyshev, joked with his viewers, 'They even built the towers in the seventeenth century as if they already knew that a future Russia would be the first to send men to space.'[88]

The FSB and its forebears were about to bask in official acclaim. There was no further need to dwell on slaughter, sadism, or corruption. On the eve of the ninetieth anniversary of the Cheka's foundation, in 2008, a group of patriots proposed that the thirteenth-century prince Alexander Nevsky should become the security services' patron saint, giving their gruesome work the blessing of a paragon.[89] The Kremlin, too, was drawn into the rehabilitation of the Cheka's image. A lavish commemorative book was produced, in a scarlet-bound limited edition, to celebrate the secret policemen's ninetieth jubilee. The heads of every major state archive were listed among the contributors, and the cited documents included many that were usually inaccessible to scholars. The subject of this work was the security services' historic role as guardians of the Kremlin.[90] Everything was open now, the book implied: the Cheka and its heirs had nothing to hide. Indeed, the country's sacred heart, Moscow's Kremlin, had them to thank for its survival.

In June 2001, the Kremlin was voted Moscow's foremost tourist attraction, well ahead of the White House, Kolomenskoe, and even the Tretyakov art gallery. Although they were not very large by international standards (the Louvre has packed more than eight million people through its doors each year since 2000), its visitor numbers have remained the highest for any comparable attraction in Moscow. In 2010, they hovered at just under five thousand a day. But Sergei Khlebnikov, the Kremlin commandant, conceded that the welcome for tourists needed improvement. Plans to sell food inside the walls were duly approved. The rules about photography were also informally relaxed. The Kremlin's museum service even prepared to raise its profile (and its income) by selling branded products such as pens and T-shirts, and in December 2010 names like 'Kremlyovka' and 'Kremlin' were trademarked in advance of future vodka sales.[91] 'I am proud to think that my country has such an architectural heritage', a visitor wrote on a guest site. 'To be in Moscow and not see the Kremlin', wrote another, 'is impossible.'[92]

To visit is indeed to toy with history. 'See the palace of the Romanov tsars,' the guides near Red Square squawk through megaphones. 'See the throne of Ivan the Terrible; see the jewels of the Russian emperors, the famous crown of Monomakh.' A ticket, clearly, buys you heritage, and even possibly a glimpse of some forbidden world. Seduced by hope and promises, almost every tourist is likely to make the Kremlin a high-light of their stay in Moscow. Braving the inevitable guards, the majority enter through the Trinity Gate, walking across the dry moat (the bed of the lost Neglinnaya) from the Kutafia Tower. From there, they hasten to Cathedral Square. A short detour would have rewarded them with a view of the palace where the Stalins used to live, but the history that modern pilgrims seek is narrowly defined: like the nineteenth century's official nationalism, it is orthodox and autocratic. In pursuit of it, almost all will soon be admiring the caskets of dead Riurikids, the icon-ostasis in the Annunciation Cathedral, and the space and colour in Fioravanti's breathtaking Cathedral of the Dormition. A lucky few, armed with passports, will also tour the Grand Kremlin Palace. As they are ushered from one marble cavern to another, their guide will make sure they appreciate the effort that went into the dismantling, under Pavel Borodin, of Stalin's 1934 congress hall. On my tour, we were shown a postcard of the Soviet space, dog-eared and dimly coloured; just the thing to make the recent renovation seem as dazzling and as true as possible.

On the upper levels of the palace, beyond the lions and some heavy doors, the gold and marble give way to rich reds and deep greens, the Terem Palace of Fedor Solntsev's ambitious nineteenth-century vision. Back then, the idea was to create a fantasy of Muscovy based on exotic Russianness; today, the aim is to invoke the empire of the tsars. But now as then, the impression that the fortress is designed to make is a broadly soothing one. Whether they visit it for themselves or glimpse it on their television screens, the Kremlin reinforces Russians' unexamined pride. People see what they expect to see, and the clean-cut buildings seem to prove that yet another time of troubles has been overcome, another firebird reborn.

Reams of gold leaf must have been unrolled in the process – the Annunciation Cathedral positively blazes with the stuff – while the modern stonework of the new Red Stair is almost indistinguishable, in its sparkling newness, from the brilliant walls of the restored palace next to it. Only a few will note the many ravaged chambers that are not on view, the damage done by neglect, upheaval and cynical state vandal-ism. In the Senate, the president's library is sometimes shown to television-viewers as a show-case for efficient government, complete with Stalin's famous globe. Only the museum staff (and guests like me, thanks to their care) can climb up to the crumbling former church, high above Cathedral Square, that houses the real researchers' library, complete with crack-tiled bathroom, leaking tap and a sink stained brown by old tea leaves. The same curators are the only ones to see the bare wood and the whitewash in the padlocked palace churches. No-one else will get to hear that Russian history is difficult, contested, or fragmentary. Smooth stonework and familiar tropes create a mirror-like surface, so glassy that no awkward doubts can settle. It suits this state if citizens are contented and even half-asleep. Whatever still goes on behind the scenes, the tourist Kremlin is designed to be impressive but unchallenging; pompous, flawless, and ultimately just a little boring.

A new exhibition in the Ivan the Great bell tower brings this official line to vivid life. I was privileged to get a ticket, for visitor-numbers are ferociously restricted, and I saw it with just two other guests. The three of us were ushered into the base of the tower by a pair of guards, who quickly shut and locked the heavy door behind our backs. Armed with personal headphones, we then began our tour – our digital Kremlin experience – in the tiny, roundish ground-floor chamber. A projector here threw a succession of evocations of the medieval Kremlin over the whitewashed walls, and as the commentator spun the usual romantic line, lights also flashed on a series of fourteenth-century limestone blocks, the relics of Ivan Kalita's time, that had been stationed in convenient niches. It was the start of a fairy-tale, the first of several beautifully documented chapters that took us up, floor after floor, each time revealing yet more splendours from the seamless and organic past. The high point (literally) was our visit to the famous bells, each one a witness to the Kremlin's sumptuous, heroic history. We were encouraged to strike these to appreciate their tone (so resonant, so masculine), and then, still under the eyes of a guard, we had a chance to pause and admire the view.

The two young women who were with me (total strangers) did what many other tourists would do at this point and started taking pictures of each other. But I was keen to see everything else first, including the all-round view of Moscow. To the east, I gazed over Cathedral Square, while southwards, across the Moscow river, I could see the low-slung suburb that radiates from the spine of Great Horde Road. Luzhkov's reincarnated cathedral loomed on the Moscow riverbank, and further on I could see at least three of Stalin's massive ornate towers, including the vast complex of Moscow State University. But one direction was roped off. There was no access to the view towards the Kremlin's presidential building. Even the unprepossessing administrative Block 14, which stands on the old Chudov Monastery site, is out of bounds for everyone who does not have a special pass. Visitors to today's Kremlin are welcome to a portion-controlled helping of Russian history, but present-day politics, like any remnant of past failure or decay, are reserved for insiders. The cars that speed to Senate Square have blacked-out windows.

The cut and thrust of real politics, the compromises, corruption and deals, are hidden because everything depends on myth. Like many regimes of the past, today's Russian government continues to shelter behind iconic Kremlin walls and the Kremlin's mirror-smooth perfection. The lesson of these mighty buildings is that Russia has always been great. Its spirit shaped this fabulous fortress. Though Europe makes them fight to keep their country's place as a world power, its people show such courage and tenacity that they cannot be vanquished from outside. Their only enemy is disorder within, and to defeat it – to preserve them from their own imperfect selves – they rightly welcome strong, pure-minded rulers; just the types, in fact, for whom this citadel was built. At this point in the tale, the idea dawns that it is Russia's people, rather than their leaders, who are blamed for any history of tyranny. Nothing has changed, we might even muse, since the murky days when Riurik and his two brothers (at least according to old chronicles) were invited to rule the warring tribes round Novgorod because they could not live in peace without some outside help. As the Harvard historian Richard Pipes declared at a recent meeting of the elite Valdai club, an organization closely identified with the current leadership, the Russian people 'want a strong ruler ... Russia always needs a strong hand ... the roots for this lie deeper than is usually understood.'[93]

On the surface, today's Kremlin is like an essay on that general theme. The message it conveys is hypnotic, a repetition of the obvious and the familiar. As the obedient groups walk round, it takes a well-informed and imaginative visitor to picture the things that have vanished, such as the ghosts of ancient churches long demolished, the scorch-marks left by heavy guns, or the deep tracks, in now-buried mud, of horse-drawn carts sagging under the heavy rubble from the latest fire. The empty space where the *prikazy* used to be, or where once there were warrens for the slaves and palace rats, may yet suggest the shades of long-dead Muscovites, some wielding clubs, some armed with fists, their hearts set on plunder, justice, or the obstinate quest for a true tsar. A thoughtful visitor may picture the red flags, the crowds, the icy silence of the Stalin years. But only those who really know their history will protest, despite all the romance and gilded domes, that the state whose flag is flying here is yet another new invented thing, the choice of living individuals rather than timeless fate. Its creators are not among the milling crowds, whatever the extent of the Russian people's exasperated collusion at different historical moments. The system is not even the product of some vaguely conceived collective being called the Kremlin. Ultimate responsibility, for better or worse, rests with specific people, and they have real names.

By looking at the Kremlin over centuries of time, I have seen how successive and very different regimes have used it – and changed it – in their effort to set down firm roots in cold northern soil. The journey has been thrilling, and has led from the medieval forest to a glittering eighteenth-century court and on through Lenin's revolution to the secretive world of the black-belt president. Time after time, the fortress has witnessed the accession of new groups: new princes, new dynasties, and sometimes entirely new regimes. Few had unassailable claims to Russia's throne, but before long, each had cast itself as the bearer of some form of divine will. The message was and remains a powerful one, but it has always been crafted by real people, not handed down in tablets of stone, and the rulers' urgent purpose is always to stay in power. The Kremlin's history is a tale of survival, and it is certainly an epic, but there is nothing inevitable about any of it. Today's glorification of the Russian state, like that of previous regimes, is a deliberate and calculated choice, and real people can certainly be made to answer for it. This may not seem a cheerful conclusion, but in the end it might just be a liberating one.

A tale that started with one icon now comes to a close with two. In 2010, the Russian press reported an exciting discovery. A pair of icons – the famous images of the Saviour and St Nikola that had once hung over the Kremlin's gatehouse-towers – appeared to have survived the purge of Stalinist times. It had been thought for decades that the icons, one of which was believed to date from the early sixteenth century, had been obliterated in honour of the twentieth anniversary of the revolution in 1937. More than seven decades later, however, an Orthodox religious organization called the Foundation of St Andrew the First-Called launched a campaign to investigate the exterior brickwork in the hope of finding traces of the precious art. Backed by the Kremlin administration (including the head of state security, Evgeny Murov, as well as the Kremlin commandant and the director of the Kremlin museums), the Foundation's experts started to explore the walls, under thick protective covering, in February 2010.

In April, they announced a triumph. The story went that the workmen who had been ordered to destroy the icons in the 1930s had in fact covered them up. They had done it so skilfully that the old paint could now be restored to pristine condition. The discovery suited the government perfectly. It was a story of how pious Russians had once risked their lives – at a time of all-pervasive terror – to save Moscow's miracle-working images. In the age of Russia's national rebirth, equally pious art experts were about to make the icons live again.[94] While the relevant stretches of wall remained obscured behind their opaque sheets, the loyal press provided additional historical background. These icons, journalists reminded readers, had escaped fire and shelling in 1917. Newspapers reprinted a famous photograph that showed the features of Nikola in a penumbra of soot. And the story did not end in 1917. The images had endured both the French occupation and the fire of 1812, and almost exactly two centuries before that, they (or their predecessors) had survived the vandalism of Catholic Poles. No less a figure than Grabar had authenticated them in the 1920s. The pair were national treasures, heirlooms in a resurgent Russian state. By July 2010, the Saviour was on display, and when I visited again in 2012, a flawless St Nikola was gazing kindly from a niche not far from Stalin's former office window.

Icons, in Russian spirituality, are like mirrors. The saint is glimpsed in reverse perspective, the light is refracted; only in prayer, not in profane existence, can a person engage with the holy being beyond the painted board. It seems to me entirely fitting, then, that these recovered icons should be staring outwards from the Kremlin walls. Though they proclaim Russia's unbroken nationhood, they do not invite the crowd in the street to look beyond the surface, let alone argue. Not every Russian cares, and few have time, these days, to bow before an icon, let alone reflect about the meaning of the past. But the images, in all their factory-fresh perfection, create a certain atmosphere, adding an extra splash of colour to a message that will have been absorbed, whether consciously or not, by almost every passer-by. Experts who work in the Kremlin have assured me, somewhat awkwardly, that the icons are real, but it would scarcely matter, while the present regime rules, if both eventually turned out to be elaborate fakes. People will see what they are meant to see, and they believe because it suits them to, especially in a country where opposition is often dangerous. Less than a century ago, the grandparents of the Muscovites who are now crossing themselves beneath the rediscovered icons were burning equally prestigious ones in a fervour of the opposite belief. Whether its masters rule an effective or corrupt state, a progressive or reactionary one, whether it is a leader of the world or inward-looking and isolationist, the Kremlin is proclaimed to be as changeless as the icon-painter's gold.

Notes

INTRODUCTION

1. Walter Benjamin, 'Moscow', in *Reflections, Essays, Aphorisms, Autobiographical Writings*, ed. Peter Demetz (New York, 1978), pp. 97–100.
2. Marquis de Custine, *Empire of the Czar: A Journey Through Eternal Russia*, Foreword by Daniel J. Boorstin, Introduction by George F. Kennan (New York, 1989), pp. 412–14.
3. Mark Frankland, *The Sixth Continent: Russia and the Making of Mikhail Gorbachev* (London, 1987), p. 5.
4. Interview with K. A. (Tony) Bishop, CMG, OBE, 6 July 2006.
5. For evidence of this, it is hard to do better than the outpourings that accompanied the 1997 celebrations of Moscow's 850th jubilee. See, for example, Petr Palamarchuk, 'Moskva kak printsip', *Moskva*, 6 (June 1997), pp. 3–7.
6. On the textbooks and misuse of history, see the articles by Liudmila Rybina and Iurii Afanas'ev in *Novaia Gazeta*, 24 September 2007.
7. *The Moscovia of Antonio Possevino, SJ*, trans. Hugh F. Graham (Pittsburg, Pa., 1977), pp. 7 and 11.
8. The literature on such foreign travellers is huge. For a bibliography, see Marshall Poe, *Foreign Descriptions of Muscovy: An Analytic Bibliography of Primary and Secondary Sources* (Columbus, Ohio, 1995).
9. To name two figures from opposite political poles, I could cite the Italian socialist Antonio Gramsci, who wrote despairing comments on the feeble condition of civil society in Russia (*Prison Notebooks*, eds. G. Hoare and G. Nowell-Smith (London, 1971), p. 238), and the Polish-American historian Richard Pipes, whose classic *Russia Under the Old Regime* (New York, 1974) reads like a diatribe against this state.
10. Walter Laqueur, *The Long Road to Freedom* (London, 1989) p. 8.
11. David Satter, *It Was a Long Time Ago, and It Never Happened Anyway* (New Haven, Conn. and London, 2011), p. 228.
12. Dmitry Shlapentokh, 'Russian history and the ideology of Putin's regime through the window of contemporary movies', *Russian History*, 36 (2009), pp. 279 and 285.
13. James H. Billington, *The Icon and the Axe: An Interpretive History of Russian Culture* (New York, 1970), p. 62.

I FOUNDATION STONES

1. For a video introduction to the icon by the museum itself, see http://video.yandex.ru/users/queenksu/view/26/
2. V. Rodionov, ed., *The Tretyakov Gallery Guide*, 4th English edn (Moscow, 2006), p. 30.

3. T. N. Nikol'skaia, *Zemlia Viatichei: K istorii naseleniia basseina verkhnei i srednei Oki v IX–XIII vv* (Moscow, 1981), p. 177; see also T. D. Panova, 'Istoriia ukreplenii srednevekovoi Moskvy XII–XIV vekov', in *Materialy i issledovaniia*, vol. XV, pp. 86–93. For a discussion by one of the archaeologists involved, see M. G. Rabinovich, 'O nachal'nom periode istorii Moskvy', *Voprosy istorii*, 1 (1956), pp. 125–9.

4. Nikol'skaia, *Zemlia Viatichei*, pp. 244–7.

5. The armies were those of Mikhail Iurevich and the Rostislavovich princes Iaropolk and Mstislav. I. E. Zabelin, *Istoriia goroda Moskvy* (Moscow, 1904; repr. 2005), p. 38.

6. For an entertaining review of the possible origins of the word, see Zabelin, *Istoriia goroda Moskvy*, pp. 51–5.

7. The Viatichi paid tribute to the Khazar khaganate by the tenth century, but remained almost independent until the reign of Yury Dolgoruky in the twelfth. Nikol'skaia, *Zemlia Viatichei*, p. 12.

8. See Janet Martin, *Treasure of the Land of Darkness: The Fur Trade and its Significance for Medieval Russia* (Cambridge, 1986), pp. 5–34; the routes also fascinated Zabelin (*Istoriia goroda Moskvy*, p. 38) and they were explored by the archaeological team that prepared the ground for the Moscow metro in the 1930s. *Po trasse pervoi ocheredi Moskovskogo metropolitena imeni L. M. Kaganovicha* (Leningrad, 1936), pp. 12–13.

9. Zabelin, *Istoriia goroda Moskvy*, p. 33. The date on the coins was 862. For more on the settlement itself, which had developed into a small town by the twelfth century, see Rabinovich, 'O nachal'nom periode', pp. 126–8.

10. Al-Mukadassi, cited in Martin, *Treasure*, p. 12.

11. Omeljan Pritsak, *The Origin of Rus* (Cambridge, Mass., 1981), p. 23.

12. The debate was already raging in the eighteenth century. See Pritsak, *Origin*, pp. 3–4.

13. The evidence is reviewed in Simon Franklin and Jonathan Shepard, *The Emergence of Rus, 750–1200* (London and New York, 1996), pp. 38–9.

14. Martin, *Treasure*, p. 46.

15. Dmitri Obolensky, *The Byzantine Commonwealth* (London, 1971), pp. 181–5.

16. The tale appears in the Russian Primary Chronicle; see Timothy Ware, *The Orthodox Church* (London, 1997), p. 264.

17. For more discussion, see Franklin and Shepard, *Emergence of Rus*, pp. 160–64.

18. For the state and the Christian package, see Michael Cherniavsky, *Tsar and People: Studies in Russian Myths* (New Haven, Conn. and London, 1961), p. 33.

19. Though the Riurik legend is very old, Donald Ostrowski dates the first political prominence of the idea to the fourteenth century. See Sergei

Bogatyrev, 'Micro-periodization and dynasticism: was there a divide in the reign of Ivan the Terrible?', *Slavic Review*, 69, 2 (Summer 2010), p. 406.

20. In the eastern church at least, Rome was considered on an equal footing to the other four, which were Constantinople, Alexandria, Antioch and Jerusalem. On the patriarchate, see John Meyendorff, *Byzantium and the Rise of Russia: A Study of Byzantino-Russian Relations in the Fourteenth Century* (Cambridge, 1981), p. 30.

21. Christian Raffensperger, cited in Bogatyrev, 'Micro-periodization', p. 406.

22. The principles are described by Nancy Shields Kollmann, *Kinship and Politics: The Making of the Muscovite Political System, 1345–1547* (Stanford, Calif., 1987), p. 68.

23. The Meeting of Liubech. See Franklin and Shepard, *Emergence of Rus*, pp. 265–6.

24. Ellen S. Hurwitz, *Prince Andrej Bogoljubskij: The Man and the Myth* (Firenze, 1980), p. 50.

25. The craftsmen came from 'every land'; in practice probably modern Germany, the Baltic and the principality of Galich. See Cyril Mango, *Byzantine Architecture* (New York, 1976), pp. 332–3.

26. David B. Miller, 'Monumental building as an indicator of economic trends in northern Rus' in the late Kievan and Mongol periods, 1138–1462', *AHR*, 94 (1989), p. 367.

27. Hurwitz, *Bogoljubskij*, pp. 50–51; see also Dmitry Shvidkovsky, *Russian Architecture and the West* (New Haven, Conn. and London, 2007), p. 36; William Craft Brumfield, *A History of Russian Architecture* (Cambridge, 1997), p. 46. Very little of the original carving survived.

28. Hurwitz, *Bogoljubskij*, p. 20.

29. On Bogoliubovo, see Brumfield, *Russian Architecture*, p. 47; the Church of the Intercession on the Nerl was built to celebrate one of Andrei's victories over the Bulgars.

30. Obolensky, *Byzantine Commonwealth*, p. 355.

31. On the Vladimir Virgin, see A. I. Anisimov, *Vladimirskaia ikona Bozhiei Materi* (Prague, 1928) and the review of legends in David B. Miller, 'Legends of the icon of Our Lady of Vladimir: a study of the development of Muscovite national consciousness', *Speculum*, 43, 4 (October 1968), pp. 657–70.

32. Ware, *Orthodox Church*, p. 60.

33. Account in *PSRL*, vol. 1, ss. 460–61.

34. John Fennell, *The Crisis of Medieval Russia, 1200–1304* (London, 1983), p. 84.

35. D. G. Ostrowski, *Muscovy and the Mongols: Cross-Cultural Influences on the Steppe Frontier* (Cambridge, 1998), p. 44.

36. See Janet Martin, *Medieval Russia, 980–1584* (Cambridge, 2007), pp. 170–71.

37. On Moscow's insignificance, and the bar to Daniilovich succession, see Martin, *Medieval Russia*, p. 193.

38. G. A. Fyodorov-Davydov, *The Culture of Golden Horde Cities* (Oxford, 1984), p. 10.

39. A Fleming, William of Rubruck, passed through Batu's own capital and also Karakorum in 1253–5. His account is printed in *The Journey of William of Rubruck to the Eastern Parts of the World, 1253–55, as narrated by himself. With two accounts of the earlier journey of John of Pian de Carpine*, translated from the Latin, and edited, with an introductory notice, by W. W. Rockhill (London, 1900).

40. Batu's original Sarai was later refounded on a new site closer to contemporary Volgograd; few sources explain which of the two is being described.

41. Fyodorov-Davydov, *Golden Horde*, p. 220.

42. Fyodorov-Davydov, *Golden Horde*, p. 16, citing Ibn-Battuta and al-Omari.

43. A tradition remarked upon by Marco Polo. See Fyodorov-Davydov, *Golden Horde*, pp. 31–2.

44. For the date when Ivan became Grand Prince, see John Fennell, *The Emergence of Moscow, 1304–1359* (London, 1968), pp. 111–19. On the bell, see *PSRL*, vol. 10, s. 211.

45. Trinity chronicle, cited in Meyendorff, *Byzantium*, p. 157.

46. For the boyars, see *PSRL*, vol. 10, s. 208 (referring to the exodus of 1338).

47. N. S. Borisov, 'Moskovskie kniaz'ia i russkie mitropolity XIV veka', *Voprosy istorii*, 8 (1986), p. 35.

48. For a summary, see Martin, *Medieval Russia*, p. 189.

49. For two discussions, see *Materialy i issledovaniia*, vol. XV, and in particular pp. 44–5 (A. N. Kirpichnikov, 'Kremli Rossii i ikh izuchenie') and pp. 60–61 (V. B. Silina, 'Nazvaniia drevnerusskikh krepostnykh sooruzhenii').

50. E. I. Smirnova, *Materialy i issledovaniia*, vol. XIV, p. 34.

51. On the size of castles elsewhere in Europe, see Robert Bartlett, *The Making of Europe* (London, 1993), especially p. 66.

52. Nancy Shields Kollmann gives a figure of six families in 1371. See her table in *Kinship and Politics*, p. 76.

53. Archaeological studies of the Kremlin have added a good deal of new information to the outlines presented by Zabelin (*Istoriia goroda Moskvy*) and his successor, S. P. Bartenev, *Moskovskii kreml' v starinu i teper'*, 2 vols. (St Petersburg, 1912 and 1918). Among the pioneering works, see Rabinovich, 'O nachal'nom periode', and also I. L. Buseva-Davydova, *Khramy Moskovskogo Kremlia* (Moscow, 1997).

54. Buseva-Davydova, *Khramy*, p. 230.

55. The archaeological evidence for an older building on the same site is presented in N. S. Sheliapina, 'Arkheologicheskie issledovaniia v uspenskom sobore', *Materialy i issledovaniia*, vol. I, pp. 54–63.

56. On this, see D. Ostrowski, 'Why did the Metropolitan move from Kiev to Vladimir in the thirteenth century?', in B. Gasparov and O. Raevsky-Hughes, eds., *Christianity and the Eastern Slavs*, vol. 1 (Berkeley and Oxford, 1993).

57. For a list of Peter's political moves, see John Fennell, *A History of the Russian Church to 1448* (London, 1995), p. 135.

58. Martin, *Medieval Russia*, p. 391; Meyendorff, *Byzantium*, p. 151; Borisov, 'Moskovskie kniaz'ia', p. 34. All argue against the view that Peter was merely an ally of Moscow.

59. Meyendorff, *Byzantium*, p. 150.

60. Fennell, *Russian Church*, p. 220.

61. The source was his successor, Kiprian. Cited in G. M. Prokhorov, *Povest' o Mitiae: Rus' i Vizantiia v epokhu Kulikovskoi bitvy* (Leningrad, 1978), pp. 310–11.

62. Again, there is no firm basis for saying that he planned this long in advance. Martin, *Medieval Russia*, p. 391.

63. Peter's status was recognized in 1339. Meyendorff, *Byzantium*, p. 156.

64. For a history of this building while it was extant, see I. Snegirev, *Spas na Boru v Moskovskom Kremle* (Moscow, 1865), pp. 1–5.

65. Borisov, 'Moskovskie kniaz'ia', p. 38.

66. Zabelin, *Istoriia goroda Moskvy*, p. 3; see also Buseva-Davydova, *Khramy*, p. 15 and Miller, 'Monumental building', pp. 360–90. Miller (p. 375) suggests that Kalita's cathedral occupied no more than 226 square metres, compared with 1,183 square metres for Vladimir's equivalent.

67. V. P. Vygolov, *Arkhitektura Moskovskoi Rusi serediny XV veka* (Moscow, 1985), p. 42; there is some doubt about the date of the monastery's original foundation.

68. Though white stone anywhere in Moscow is often known as Myachkovo stone, after the village where large quantities were later quarried, the limestone for Kalita's churches and Donskoi's white walls came from the immediate region of Moscow. See S. O. Shmidt, ed., *Moskva: Entsiklopediia* (Moscow, 1997), p. 111.

69. On the 'epic project' itself, see Miller, 'Monumental building', pp. 376–9 and Sergei Bogatyrev, *The Sovereign and His Counsellors: Ritualised Consultations in Muscovite Political Culture* (Helsinki, 2000), pp. 104–5.

70. See A. A. Gorskii, *Moskva i Orda* (Moscow, 2005), p. 67.

71. For Donskoi's flight, see Gorskii, *Moskva*, p. 104.

72. Zabelin, *Istoriia goroda Moskvy*, pp. 95–6.

73. Martin, *Medieval Russia*, p. 190.

2 RENAISSANCE

1. Spiro Kostof, *A History of Architecture: Settings and Rituals* (New York, 1985), p. 5.

2. Geoffrey Parker, 'The "Military Revolution", 1560–1660 – a myth?', *JMH*, 48, 2 (June 1976), esp. pp. 203–6.

3. Nikolai Karamzin, 'Zapiski o moskovskikh dostopamiatnostiakh', cited in I. Kondrat'ev, *Sedaia starina Moskvy*, 5th edn (Moscow, 2006), p. 34. Kondrat'ev's commentary includes more prose and poetry along these lines.

4. The way the Mongols' influence on Muscovy was framed in the tale was itself the product of what one historian has recently described as the church's 'full-blown anti-Tatar ideology'. See D. G. Ostrowski, *Muscovy and the Mongols: Cross-Cultural Influences on the Steppe Frontier* (Cambridge, 1998), pp. 139–40.

5. The most famous are by N. S. Shustov (1862) and Aleksei Kivshenko (1880). For a nationalist reading of Moscow's ascendancy, see I. E. Zabelin, *Istoriia goroda Moskvy* (Moscow, 1904; repr. 2005), pp. 127–8; for an assessment of the level of tribute paid in this later period, see Michel Roublev, 'The Mongol tribute', in M. Cherniavsky, ed., *The Structure of Russian History* (New York, 1970), pp. 29–64.

6. Kostof, *History of Architecture*, p. 418.

7. P. V. Sytin, *Istoriia planirovki i zastroiki Moskvy*, vol. 1 (Moscow, 1950), p. 46.

8. Sergei Bogatyrev, *The Sovereign and His Counsellors: Ritualised Consultations in Muscovite Political Culture* (Helsinki, 2000), p. 86. The point is also made by Marshall Poe, *The Russian Moment in World History* (Princeton, 2003), p. 36.

9. For first-hand evidence, see *Travels to Tana and Persia by Josafa Barbaro and Ambrogio Contarini*, trans. W. Thomas et al. (London, 1873), pp. 165–6.

10. For a discussion, see Bogatyrev, *Sovereign*, p. 17.

11. Dmitri Obolensky, *The Byzantine Commonwealth* (London, 1971), p. 356.

12. John Fennell, *Ivan the Great of Moscow* (London, 1961), pp. 35–6.

13. S. P. Bogoiavlenskii, ed., *Gosudarstvennaia oruzheinaia palata Moskovskogo kremlia* (Moscow, 1954), p. 511.

14. Cited in Fennell, *Ivan the Great*, p. 53.

15. Fennell, *Ivan the Great*, pp. 56–60.

16. Chester S. L. Dunning, *Russia's First Civil War: The Time of Troubles and the Founding of the Romanov Dynasty* (University Park, Pa., 2001), p. 39.

17. For a crisp summary, see Ruslan Skrynnikov, *Krest' i korona* (St Petersburg, 2000), pp. 114–16.

18. Timothy Ware, *The Orthodox Church* (London, 1997), pp. 70–71.

19. *AI*, vol. 1, doc. 39, Vasily Vasilevich to Patriarch Mitrofan, pp. 71–2.

20. *AI*, vol. 1, docs. 41 and 262, pp. 83 and 492.

21. See John Fennell, *A History of the Russian Church to 1448* (London, 1995), p. 188.

22. Russell E. Martin, 'Gifts for the bride: dowries, diplomacy and marriage politics in Muscovy', *Journal of Medieval and Early Modern Studies*, 38, 1 (Winter 2008), pp. 123–6; Fennell, *Ivan the Great*, p. 158.

23. There is a huge literature on this subject. For a summary, see Janet Martin, *Medieval Russia, 980–1584* (Cambridge, 2007), pp. 295–6.

24. For Feofil, see *AI*, vol. 1, pp. 512–14.

25. See Michael Cherniavsky, 'The reception of the Council of Florence in Moscow', *Church History*, 24 (1955), p. 352.

26. *Istoriia Moskvy v shesti tomakh* (Moscow, 1952), vol. 1, p. 61.

27. V. I. Snegirev, *Aristotel' Fioravanti i perestroika moskovskogo kremlia* (Moscow, 1935), p. 66.

28. For the date of the original church, see A. A. Sukhanova, 'Podklet Blagoveshchenskogo sobora Moskovskogo Kremlia po dannym arkhitekturnykh i arkheologicheskikh issledovanii XX veka', *Materialy i issledovaniia*, vol. XVI, pp. 164–5.

29. S. P. Bartenev, *Moskovskii Kreml' v starinu i teper'*, 2 vols. (St Petersburg, 1912 and 1918), vol. 2, p. 49; Zabelin, *Istoriia goroda Moskvy*, p. 133; Snegirev, *Fioravanti*, p. 59.

30. V. P. Vygolov, *Arkhitektura Moskovskoi Rusi serediny XV veka* (Moscow, 1985), p. 96.

31. I. A. Bondarenko et al., eds., *Slovar' arkhitektorov i masterov stroitel'nogo dela Moskvy XV–serediny XVIII veka* (Moscow, 2008), pp. 619–20; Vygolov, *Arkhitektura*, pp. 9–10.

32. On the sculptures, see O. V. Iakhont, 'Osnovnye resul'taty nauchnykh issledovanii i restavratsii skul'pturnoi ikony sviatogo Georgiia-Zmeebortsa 1464 goda iz Moskovskogo Kremlia', *Materialy i issledovaniia*, vol. XII, pp. 104–19. See also Vygolov, *Arkhitektura*, p. 168. Dmitry Solunsky is better known in western Europe as Demetrios of Thessaloniki.

33. Zabelin, *Istoriia goroda Moskvy*, p. 129; Sytin, *Istoriia planirovki*, vol. 1, p. 53.

34. William Craft Brumfield, *A History of Russian Architecture* (Cambridge, 1997), p. 94.

35. Vygolov, *Arkhitektura*, p. 185.

36. Vygolov, *Arkhitektura*, p. 185.

37. The classic study of the subject is Richard Hellie, *Slavery in Russia, 1450–1725* (Chicago, 1982).

38. Dmitry Shvidkovsky, *Russian Architecture and the West* (New Haven, Conn. and London, 2007), pp. 84–5.

39. Zabelin, *Istoriia goroda Moskvy*, p. 134.

40. Zabelin, *Istoriia goroda Moskvy*, p. 134; Vygolov, *Arkhitektura*, p. 190.

41. The account is taken from Vygolov, *Arkitektura*, pp. 190–92.

42. Mario Salvadori, *Why Buildings Stand Up* (New York and London, 2002), p. 222.

43. This story, which was repeated by Sigismund Herberstein, probably originated in her own entourage. See A. A. Gorskii, *Moskva i Orda* (Moscow, 2005), p 169.

44. P. Pierling, *La Russie et le Saint Siège: Etudes Diplomatiques*, vol. 2 (Paris, 1896), p. 120.

45. Pierling, *Russie*, p. 151.

46. Pierling, *Russie*, p. 172. Ambrogio Contarini left a kinder description of Ivan. See *Travels to Tana and Persia*, p. 163.

47. See Zabelin, *Istoriia goroda Moskvy*, p. 139 and Fennell, *Ivan the Great*, p. 318.

48. An excellent account of the journey, largely based on Pierling, is given in T. D. Panova, *Velikaia kniaginia Sof'ia Paleolog* (Moscow, 2005), pp. 19–24.

49. Interpreters were so numerous that they had a residential district to themselves on the south side of the Moscow river. On the debates, see Pierling, *Russie*, p. 173 and Shvidkovsky, *Russian Architecture*, pp. 75–6.

50. For more on this elsewhere in Europe, see Kostof, *History of Architecture*, pp. 428–9.

51. For a summary of what is known (as opposed to the abundant myths) about Fioravanti, see *Dizionario Biografico Degli Italiani*, vol. 48 (Rome, 1997), pp. 95–100. There has been some debate about his name, but most agree that, in the best renaissance style, Fioravanti was christened Aristotele: Snegirev, *Fioravanti*, p. 27.

52. Shvidkovsky, *Russian Architecture*, pp. 80–82; Snegirev, *Fioravanti*, pp. 27–36.

53. Ambrogio Contarini stayed briefly in 'the house of Master Aristotele which was almost next to his Lordship's palace': *Travels to Tana and Persia*, p. 222. On the seraglio, see Snegirev, *Fioravanti*, p. 38.

54. Shvidkovsky, *Russian Architecture*, p. 82.

55. Zabelin, *Istoriia goroda Moskvy*, p. 145; on the technology, see A. N. Speransky, *Prikaz kamennykh del: Ocherki po istorii prikaza kamennykh del Moskovskogo gosudarstva* (Vologda, 1930), p. 20.

56. For more details, see Zabelin, *Istoriia goroda Moskvy*, pp. 144–7, and also I. L. Buseva-Davydova, *Khramy Moskovskogo Kremlia* (Moscow, 1997), pp. 29–30.

57. One art historian remarks that the building fused 'medieval Russian architecture with the style of an Italian palazzo'. Cyril Mango, *Byzantine Architecture* (New York, 1976), p. 338. See also Shvidkovsky, *Russian Architecture*, pp. 85–91; Brumfield, *Russian Architecture*, pp. 96–8.

58. Contarini visited too soon to see the finished work, but see, for example, Francesco da Collo, *Relazione del viaggio e dell'ambasciata in Moscovia* (1518–19, repr. Treviso, 2005), pp. 107–8. By this time Fioravanti's name has disappeared. On other Italian visitors, see Dzh. D'Amato, 'Gorod Moskva v vospriiatii ital'ianskogo chitatelia XV–XVI vekov', *Arkheograficheskii ezhegodnik* (1997), pp. 103–6.

59. Pierling, *Russie*, p. 204.

60. On Onton or Anton Fryazin, see I. A. Bondarenko, 'K voprosu o lichnosti Antona Friazina', *Materialy i issledovaniia*, vol. XV, pp. 40–43.

61. Shvidkovsky, *Russian Architecture*, pp. 92 and 99.

62. For the strongroom, which was rediscovered in the first decade of the twentieth century, see Iu. V. Brandenburg et al., *Arkhitektor Ivan Mashkov* (Moscow, 2001), p. 82, and also Bartenev, *Moskovskii Kreml'*, vol. 2, p. 71. A map, by K. K. Lopialo, appears in O. I. Podobedova, *Moskovskaia shkola zhivopisi pri Ivane IV* (Moscow, 1972), appendix.

63. The third tier and iconic cupola were added later, however. On Kalita's tower, see Zabelin, *Istoriia goroda Moskvy*, p. 316.

64. Buseva-Davydova, *Khramy*, p. 173.

65. On Ermolin's version at the Trinity-St Sergius Lavra, see Aida Nasibova, *The Faceted Chamber in the Moscow Kremlin* (Leningrad, 1981), p. 6.

66. Brumfield, *Russian Architecture*, p. 101.

67. M. V. Posokhin et al., *Pamiatniki arkhitektury Moskvy: Kreml', Kitai-gorod, Tsentral'nye ploshchadi* (Moscow, 1982), p. 36.

68. Determined efforts to explore them were made over many centuries. See I. Ia. Stelletskii, *Poiski biblioteki Ivana Groznogo* (Moscow, 1999). As I discovered, the details of the subterranean Kremlin are now state secrets.

69. Vladimir Shevchenko, *Povsednevnaia zhizn' pri prezidentakh* (Moscow, 2004), p. 20.

70. The specifications are especially detailed in Sytin's sections of the archaeological survey that took place at the time of the construction of the Moscow metro. *Po trasse pervoi ocheredi Moskovskogo metropolitena imeni L. M. Kaganovicha* (Leningrad, 1936), p. 114.

71. There is some evidence that Ivan III went in for sealed caskets, though most were probably housed in or beneath the Treasury. See G. L. Malitskii, 'K istorii oruzheinoi palaty Moskovskogo kremlia', in S. K. Bogoiavlenskii, ed., *Gosudarstvennaia oruzheinaia palata Moskovskogo kremlia* (Moscow, 1954), p. 512.

72. Stelletskii, *Poiski*, p. 184; for the second, later, excavation, see *Po trasse metropolitena*, p. 116.

73. By the 1520s, when Sigismund von Herberstein last visited Muscovy, timber for building in the city was being brought seventy miles downriver from Mozhaisk.

74. Zabelin, *Istoriia goroda Moskvy*, p. 160.

75. *Po trasse metropolitena*, p. 15.

76. Zabelin, *Istoriia goroda Moskvy*, p. 210.

77. Arthur Voyce, *The Moscow Kremlin: Its History, Architecture and Art Treasures* (London, 1955), p. 23.

78. *Po trasse metropolitena*, pp. 110–11.

79. For the European, as opposed to Byzantine, origins of Ivan's double-headed eagle, see Gustave Alef, 'The adoption of the Muscovite two-headed eagle: a discordant view', *Speculum*, 41 (1966), pp. 1–21.

80. On Italians (and Sforza in particular), see Gino Barbieri, *Milano e Mosca nella politica del Rinascimento* (Milan, 1957); on the rest, see Pierling, *Russie*, p. 211.

81. Fennell, *Ivan the Great*, pp. 117–21.

82. M. I. Mil'chik, 'Kremli Rossii, postroennye Ital'iantsami, i problema ikh dal'neishego izucheniia', *Materialy i issledovaniia*, vol. XV, pp. 509–17.

83. Pietro Annibale is known in Russian as Petrok Malyi. See Shvidkovsky, *Russian Architecture*, p. 113.

84. *Po trasse metropolitena*, p. 107.

85. *Po trasse metropolitena*, p. 107; see also Paul of Aleppo's peevish comments in *The Travels of Macarius, Patriarch of Antioch: Written by His Attendant Archdeacon, Paul of Aleppo, in Arabic*, trans. F. C. Belfour (London, 1836), vol. 2, pp. 21–2. As he also observed (p. 119), even Muscovites were not supposed to study their own Kremlin's walls too closely.

86. Posokhin, *Pamiatniki arkhitektury*, pp. 350–51 and (on foreign trade) p. 360.

87. This argument is forcibly put by Marshall Poe. See his *Russian Moment*, p. 44. On backwardness more generally, the most famous essay (to which Poe's is a partial rejoinder) is Alexander Gerschenkron's, *Economic Backwardness in Historical Perspective* (Cambridge, Mass., 1962). The star fort, or *trace Italienne*, is discussed in Parker, '"Military Revolution"', pp. 204–5.

88. Ryszard Kapuscinski, *Travels with Herodotus* (London, 2007), p. 59.

3 THE GOLDEN PALACE

1. *Travels to Tana and Persia by Josafa Barbaro and Ambrogio Contarini*, trans., W. Thomas et al. (London, 1873), p. 162.

2. Lloyd E. Berry and Robert O. Crummey, eds., *Rude and Barbarous Kingdom* (Madison, Wisc., 1968), pp. 55–6; see also Michael Flier, 'The iconology of royal ritual in sixteenth-century Muscovy', in Speros Vryonis Jr., ed., *Byzantine Studies: Essays on the Slavic World and the 11th Century* (New Rochelle, NY, 1992), p. 61.

3. The same kinds of observations were made, in the middle of the seventeenth century, by the visiting Syrian priest Paul of Aleppo. See *The Travels of Macarius, Patriarch of Antioch: Written by His Attendant Archdeacon, Paul of Aleppo, in Arabic*, trans. F. C. Belfour (London, 1836), vol. 1, pp. 342–5.

4. The most heroic explanation, and the most convincing, is Paul Bushko-vitch, 'The epiphany ceremony of the Russian court in the sixteenth and seventeenth centuries', *Russian Review*, 49, 1 (January 1990), pp. 13–14. The same article places the date of the ceremony's adoption in Moscow at

some point between 1477 and 1525. For the role of the horses and other magical aspects of the scene, see also W. F. Ryan, *The Bathhouse at Midnight: Magic in Russia* (Stroud, 1999), pp. 57 and 131–2.

5. Michael S. Flier, 'Till the End of Time: The Apocalypse in Russian historical experience before 1500', in Valerie A. Kivelson and Robert H. Greene, eds., *Orthodox Russia: Belief and Practice Under the Tsars* (University Park, Pa., 2003), pp. 127–58.

6. P. Pierling, *La Russie et le Saint Siège: Etudes Diplomatiques*, vol. 2 (Paris, 1896), p. 205.

7. She was the first cousin once removed of both Ivan III and Prince Ivan Yurevich Patrikeev. For more on the late fifteenth-century crisis, see Nancy Shields Kollmann, 'Consensus politics: the dynastic crisis of the 1490s reconsidered', *Russian Review*, 45, 3 (July 1986), pp. 235–67.

8. See Janet Martin, *Medieval Russia, 980–1584* (Cambridge, 2007), p. 247.

9. For an account, see S. P. Bartenev, *Moskovskii Kreml' v starinu i teper'*, 2 vols. (St Petersburg, 1912 and 1918), vol. 2, pp. 91–3. See also G. P. Majeska, 'The Moscow coronation of 1498 reconsidered', *JbFGO*, 26 (1978), esp. p. 356.

10. John Fennell, *Ivan the Great of Moscow* (London, 1961), pp. 339–42.

11. The story is also discussed in T. D. Panova, *Kremlevskie usypal'nitsy: Istoriia, sud'ba, taina* (Moscow, 2003), p. 58.

12. For a description of it, see Bartenev, *Moskovskii Kreml'*, vol. 2, pp. 121–8; for evidence of later weddings, see Russell E. Martin, 'Choreographing the "Tsar's Happy Occasion": tradition, change, and dynastic legitimacy in the weddings of Mikhail Romanov', *Slavic Review*, 63, 4 (Winter 2004), pp. 794–817.

13. Konstantin Mikhailov, *Unichtozhennyi Kreml'* (Moscow, 2007), p. 61.

14. Sergei Bogatyrev, 'Ivan the Terrible', in *CHR*, vol. 1, p. 243.

15. Bartenev, *Moskovskii Kreml'*, vol. 2, pp. 168–73.

16. There is no proof, of course. See Nancy Shields Kollmann, *Kinship and Politics: The Making of the Muscovite Political System* (Stanford, Calif., 1987), p. 168.

17. Isabel de Madariaga, *Ivan the Terrible: First Tsar of Russia* (New Haven, Conn. and London, 2005), p. 40. The source is not given.

18. de Madariaga, *Ivan*, pp. 40–41; Panova, *Kremlevskie usypal'nitsy*, p. 60.

19. Panova, *Kremlevskie usypal'nitsy*, p. 147.

20. Kollmann, *Kinship and Politics*, p. 170.

21. Kollmann, *Kinship and Politics*, pp. 169–74.

22. The letter is part of the famous Ivan–Kurbsky correspondence. For a discussion of its authenticity, see R. G. Skrynnikov, *Perepiska Groznogo i Kurbskogo: paradoksy Edvarda Kinana* (Leningrad, 1973) and the book that provoked it: Edward L. Keenan, *The Kurbskii-Groznyi Apocrypha* (Cambridge, Mass., 1971).

23. J. L. I. Fennell, trans. and ed., *The Correspondence between Prince A. M. Kurbsky and Tsar Ivan IV of Russia, 1564–1579* (Cambridge, 1955), letter from Ivan to Kurbsky, p. 73.

24. Bogatyrev, 'Ivan the Terrible', p. 244.

25. Sergei Bogatyrev, 'Reinventing the Russian monarchy in the 1550s: Ivan IV, the dynasty, and the church', *SEER*, 85, 2 (April 2007), p. 273.

26. R. G. Skrynnikov, *Velikii gosudar' Ioan Vasil'evich Groznyi*, 2 vols. (Smolensk, 1996), vol. 1, p. 137. Ivan III's advisors had probably used a Serbian translation of original Greek texts, and the likelihood is that Makary's men used similar materials. As Michael Angold puts the matter, it was 'much easier to absorb Byzantine influences, once Byzantium was no more'. Michael Angold, *The Fall of Constantinople to the Ottomans* (Harlow, 2012), p. 140.

27. Michael Cherniavsky, *Tsar and People: Studies in Russian Myths* (New Haven, Conn. and London, 1961), p. 45.

28. D. B. Miller, 'The coronation of Ivan IV of Moscow', *JbFGO*, 15 (1967), pp. 559–74, esp. p. 563.

29. According to the best recent scholarship, Makary further emphasized this point by withholding the ritual of anointing with holy oil from the ceremony itself. See Sergei Bogatyrev, *The Sovereign and his Counsellors: Ritualised Consultations in Muscovite Political Culture* (Helsinki, 2000), p. 164, and also his 'Reinventing the Russian Monarchy', p. 275.

30. A version of the text appears in Makarii (Arkhimandrit Veretennikov), *Zhizn' i trudy sviatitelia Makariia* (Moscow, 2002), pp. 367–9.

31. Skrynnikov, *Velikii gosudar'*, vol. 1, p. 138.

32. On the choice of date, see Flier, 'Iconology of royal ritual', p. 73.

33. See Sergei Bogatyrev, 'Micro-periodization and dynasticism: was there a divide in the reign of Ivan the Terrible?', *Slavic Review*, 69, 2 (Summer 2010), pp. 406–7.

34. The gold is referred to with special emphasis in accounts of the coronation. See *DAI*, vol. 1, pp. 41–53. On the teams who rang the Kremlin bells, see A. Olearius, *The Travels of Olearius in Seventeenth-Century Russia* (Stanford, Calif., 1967), p. 114.

35. Miller, 'Coronation of Ivan IV', p. 562.

36. The case is made by R. G. Skrynnikov, *Krest' i korona* (St Petersburg, 2000), p. 225.

37. Bogatyrev, 'Ivan the Terrible', p. 249.

38. Bartenev, *Moskovskii Kreml'*, vol. 2, p. 179. The original account of the fire, in the *Tsarstvennaia kniga*, was written thirty years or so after the fact.

39. John Stuart, *Ikons* (London, 1975), p. 102.

40. See Skrynnikov, *Krest'*, pp. 225–6.

41. *Tsarstvennaia kniga*, *PSRL*, vol. 13, s. 456; cited in Fennell, *Correspondence*, p. 81, n. 2.

42. de Madariaga, *Ivan*, pp. 61–2.

43. de Madariaga, *Ivan*, p. 63.

44. This last was the *obraznaia palata*. See S. K. Bogoiavlenskii, ed., *Gosudarst-vennaia oruzheinaia palata Moskovskogo kremlia* (Moscow, 1954), p. 514. See also O. I. Podobedova, *Moskovskaia shkola zhivopisi pri Ivane IV: raboty v Moskovskom Kremle 40x–70x godov XVI v.* (Moscow, 1972), p. 15; Stuart, *Ikons*, p. 102; on the workshops, see also I. A. Selezneva, *Zolotaia i serebrianaia palaty: kremlevskie masterskie XVII veka: organizatsiia i formy* (Moscow, 2001).

45. Podobedova, *Moskovskaia shkola*, pp. 5–8; on Ivan's throne, see Bogatyrev, *Sovereign*, p. 75.

46. For a discussion, see V. M. Sorokatyi, '"Serdtse tsarevo v rutse Bozhiei": tema nebesnogo zastupnichestva gosudariu v khudozhestvennom ubranstve Blagoveshchenskogo sobora pri Ivane IV', *Materialy i issledovaniia*, vol. XIX, pp. 67–82.

47. See also Michael S. Flier, 'The throne of Monomakh', in James Cracraft and Daniel Bruce Rowland, eds., *Architectures of Russian Identity: 1500 to the Present* (Ithaca, NY, 2003), pp. 21–33.

48. The entire cycle is decribed in an appendix to Podobedova, *Moskovskaia shkola*, using Ushakov's sketches.

49. David B. Miller, 'The Viskovatyi affair of 1553–4', *Russian History*, 8, 3 (1981), pp. 293–332.

50. de Madariaga, *Ivan*, p. 126; Heinrich von Staden, *The Land and Government of Muscovy*, trans. Thomas Esper (Stanford, Calif., 1967), p. 44.

51. Dmitry Shvidkovsky, *Russian Architecture and the West* (New Haven, Conn. and London, 2007), p. 148.

52. Sigismund von Herberstein's account, from the early sixteenth century, is vivid on this matter. See his *Description of Moscow and Muscovy*, ed. B. Picard (London, 1969), p. 60. For others see also Bartenev, *Moskovskii Kreml'*, vol. 2, p. 131.

53. Berry and Crummey, *Rude and Barbarous Kingdom*, pp. 23–7.

54. This was Jacob Ulfeldt. See Aida Nasibova, *The Faceted Chamber in the Moscow Kremlin* (Leningrad, 1981), p. 20.

55. To get my own bearings in this account, I used the plan by K. K. Lopialo reproduced in Podobedova, *Moskovskaia shkola*, appendix. See also Bartenev, *Moskovskii Kreml'*, vol. 2, pp. 70–74 and 103 (where there is another map).

56. The wall was near the Borovitsky gates. As the requirements of the tsar's stables and saddlery (and carriages) expanded in the next century, the space was eventually monopolized by the *koniushii prikaz*, the chancellery with responsibility for royal transport, mounts and caparisons. See G. L. Malitskii's essay in Bogoiavlenskii, *Gosudarstvennaia oruzheinaia palata*, p. 556.

57. This is a quibble with Daniel Rowland ('Two cultures, one throne room', in Valerie A. Kivelson and Robert H. Greene, eds., *Orthodox Russia: Belief and Practice Under the Tsars* (University Park, Pa., 2003), p. 40, note 13). Chancellor indeed called the room where he dined the 'Golden', but this word was used, confusingly, for both chambers, and it is clear that his room had a central pier.

58. For more detail, see Bartenev, *Moskovskii Kreml'*, vol. 2, pp. 137–43. The Treasury was also used for ceremonies involving foreign envoys.

59. A later visitor, Paul of Aleppo, attributed the lavish use of gold around the Kremlin almost entirely to Ivan the Terrible. See *Travels of Macarius*, vol. 2, p. 4.

60. For a discussion of exactly when the process began, taking it back to the age of Ivan III's enlarged army, see Marshall Poe, 'Muscovite personnel records, 1475–1550: new light on the early evolution of Russian bureaucracy', *JbFGO*, 45, 3 (1997), pp. 361–77.

61. For a classic account of Ivan's administrative reforms, see A. A. Zimin, *Reformy Ivana Groznogo: ocherki sotsial'no-ekonomicheskoi i politicheskoi istorii Rossii serediny XVI veka* (Moscow, 1960).

62. See Peter B. Brown, 'Muscovite government bureaus', *Russian History*, 10, 3 (1983), p. 270.

63. Another prime example from this era consisted of the Shchelkalov brothers, Andrei and Vasily, who rose to eminence entirely through court service.

64. For commentary, see Peter B. Brown, 'How Muscovy governed: seventeenth-century Russian central administration', *Russian History*, 36, 4 (2009), pp. 459–529. On the background of officials at this time, see also I. V. Rybalko, *Rossiiskaia prikaznaia biurokratiia v smutnoe vremia i nachala XVII v* (Moscow, 2011), pp. 442–5.

65. Brown, 'How Muscovy governed', p. 487.

66. von Staden, *Land and Government*, pp. 14–15.

67. Chester S. L. Dunning, *Russia's First Civil War: The Time of Troubles and the Founding of the Romanov Dynasty* (University Park, Pa., 2001), pp. 35–6.

68. Prikaz prikaznykh del. See Brown, 'Bureaus', p. 313.

69. The early term for many of these offices was *izby*, or 'chambers', but the more formal *prikaz* soon took over. For their location, see Bartenev, *Moskovskii Kreml'*, vol. 2, p. 103, and G. S. Evdokimov, 'K istorii postroek Kazennogo dvora v Moskovskom Kremle' in *Materialy i issledovania*, vol. XIX, pp. 355–76.

70. von Staden, *Land and Government*, p. 42. On *pravezh*, see also de Madariaga, *Ivan*, p. 246. There were other punishment sites in central Moscow, and as the Kremlin grew more secretive in years to come, Red Square and Nikol'skii street became the main theatres of public justice. The Kremlin ceased to be a site of official public punishment in 1685. See I. Snegirev,

Moskva: Podrobnoe istoricheskoe i arkheologicheskoe opisanie goroda (Moscow, 1875), vol. 2, p. 16.

71. Bogatyrev, *Sovereign*, p. 204.

72. For discussion, see Kollmann, 'Consensus politics', pp. 237–41.

73. See Ann Kleimola, 'The changing condition of the Muscovite elite', *Russian History*, 6, 2 (1979), pp. 210–29.

74. Sergei Bogatyrev summarizes the historical debate about marriage politics in his 'Ivan the Terrible', pp. 246–7.

75. Edward L. Keenan, 'Ivan the Terrible and his women', *Russian History*, 37, 4 (2010), pp. 350–55.

76. The questions of fecundity and female royalty are explored perceptively in Isolde Thyret, '"Blessed is the Tsaritsa's womb". The myth of miraculous birth and royal motherhood in Muscovite Russia', *Russian Review*, 53, 4 (October 1994), pp. 479–96.

77. This is the theme of Daniel Rowland's essay, 'Two cultures'.

78. For a commentary, see Arkhimandrit Makarii (Veretennikov), 'Makar'evskie sobory 1547 i 1549 godov i ikh znachenie', in *Materialy i issledovaniia*, vol. XI, pp. 5–22.

79. Daniel Rowland, 'The blessed host of the heavenly tsar', in Michael S. Flier and Daniel Rowland, eds., *Medieval Russian Culture*, vol. 2, California Slavic Studies (Berkeley, Los Angeles and London, 1994), pp. 182–99.

80. The indomitable Andrei Batalov has recently questioned whether its architects were as purely Russian as legend suggests; in his view there may have been foreign masters involved. See I. L. Buseva-Davydova, *Kul'tura i iskusstvo v epokhu peremen: Rossiia semnadtsatogo stoletiia* (Moscow, 2008), p. 89.

81. A useful discussion of the symbolic geography of the chapels is provided by Michael Flier in A. L. Batalov and L. A. Beliaev, eds., *Sakral'naia topografiia srednevekovskogo goroda* (Moscow, 1998), pp. 40–50.

82. Shvidkovsky, *Russian Architecture*, pp. 126–40; William Craft Brumfield, *A History of Russian Architecture* (Cambridge, 1997), pp. 125–9.

83. On holy fools in Ivan's reign, see Sergey A. Ivanov, *Holy Fools in Byzantium and Beyond*, trans. Simon Franklin (Oxford, 2006), esp. pp. 291–9.

84. For a thoughtful statement of the 'submission' case, see Bushkovitch, 'Epiphany ceremony', pp. 1–17.

85. Michael Flier, 'Breaking the code: the image of the tsar in the Muscovite Palm Sunday ritual', in Michael S. Flier and Daniel Rowland, eds., *Medieval Russian Culture*, vol. 2. California Slavic Studies (Berkeley, Los Angeles and London, 1994), pp. 213–42.

86. On Ivan's health, see Charles Halperin, 'Ivan IV's insanity', *Russian History*, 34 (2007), pp. 207–18, and Edward L. Keenan, 'Ivan IV and the King's Evil: *Ni maka li to budet?*', *Russian History*, 20 (1993), pp. 5–13.

87. For a discussion, see Bogatyrev, 'Micro-periodization', pp. 398–409.

88. The items were later specified by two German witnesses, Johannes Taube and Elert Kruze. See 'Poslanie Ioganna Taube i Elerta Kruze', *Russkii istoricheskii zhurnal* (Petrograd, 1922), *kniga* 8, p. 31. These two also allege that Ivan lost all his hair as a result of the stress of the 1564–5 winter.

89. Skrynnikov, *Velikii gosudar'*, vol. 1, pp. 342–4.

90. The reasons for it all are still unclear. Most historians, including Skrynnikov, see Ivan's goal to be his own freedom of action and direct arbitrary rule. For a discussion, see Dunning, *Civil War*, p. 48 and de Madariaga, *Ivan*, pp. 186–8.

91. de Madariaga, *Ivan*, p. 180.

92. On the prayers, see Skrynnikov, *Velikii gosudar'*, vol. 1, p. 330. On Ivan's view of his own divine burden, see Dunning, *Civil War*, p. 32, and Priscilla Hunt, 'Ivan IV's personal mythology of kingship', *Slavic Review*, 52, 4 (Winter 1993), pp. 769–809.

93. Sergey Ivanov discusses Ivan's contradictory behaviour in *Holy Fools*, pp. 288–9.

94. de Madariaga, *Ivan*, p. 183; Martin, *Medieval Russia*, p. 348.

95. As did von Staden; see *Land and Government*, p. 121.

96. von Staden, *Land and Government*, p. 17.

97. de Madariaga, *Ivan*, p. 231.

98. *Prince Kurbsky's History of Ivan IV*, ed. with a translation and notes by J. L. I. Fennell (Cambridge, 1965), p. 207.

99. von Staden, *Land and Government*, p. 41.

100. For a life of Filipp, see G. P. Fedotov, *Sviatoi Filipp mitropolit Moskovskii* (Paris, 1928).

101. Bogatyrev, *Sovereign*, p. 220.

102. Created in 1569 by the Treaty of Lublin.

103. Taube and Kruze, 'Poslanie Ioganna Taube i Elerta Kruze', p. 48.

104. von Staden, *Land and Government*, p. 27.

105. Taube and Kruze, 'Poslanie Ioganna Taube i Elerta Kruze', pp. 49–51.

106. G. N. Bocharov and V. P. Vygolov, *Aleksandrovskaia sloboda* (Moscow, 1970), pp. 7–8.

107. The site, Pogannoe pole, had been used for the execution of conspirators accused of Andrei Bogoliubskii's murder; a meat-market was held nearby in Ivan's time. See P. V. Sytin, *Istoriia planirovki i zastroiki Moskvy*, vol. 1 (Moscow, 1950), p. 76.

108. de Madariaga, *Ivan*, p. 258.

109. Skrynnikov, *Krest'*, pp. 297–8.

110. The *zemskii sobor* is a controversial institution, whose very name is anachronistic (the term was first coined by a nostalgic Slavophile in 1850). For more on its history, see Marshall Poe, 'The central government and its institutions', in *CHR*, vol. 1, pp. 460–62.

111. See D. Ostrowski, 'Semeon Bekhbulatovich's remarkable career as Tatar khan, Grand Prince of Rus', and monastic elder', *Russian History*, 39, 3 (2012), pp. 269–99 (a discussion also follows this article). The coronation was mentioned by Jerome Horsey, whose description of it is noted in de Madariaga, *Ivan*, p. 298.

112. Bartenev, *Moskovskii Kreml'*, vol. 2, p. 198; another Moscow residence of Ivan's was located on today's Petrovka.

113. The description of his *oprichnina* palace comes from von Staden, *Land and Government*, pp. 48–51.

114. *Po trasse pervoi ocheredi Moskovskogo metropolitena imeni L. M. Kaganovicha* (Leningrad, 1936), pp. 37–8.

115. Skrynnikov, *Velikii gosudar'*, vol. 2, p. 101.

116. von Staden, *Land and Government*, p. 29.

117. von Staden, *Land and Government*, pp. 47–9; on the English craftsmen, see Shvidkovsky, *Russian Architecture*, p. 148.

118. Hans Kobentsel' [Hans Graf Cobenzl], cited in Bogoiavlenskii, *Gosudarstvennaia oruzheinaia palata*, p. 517.

119. *The Moscovia of Antonio Possevino, SJ*, trans. Hugh F. Graham (Pittsburg, Pa., 1977), p. 11.

120. Bogatyrev, 'Reinventing the Russian Monarchy', p. 284; see also his comments on the helmet in 'Ivan the Terrible', p. 243.

121. For other grievances, see de Madariaga, *Ivan*, pp. 267–8.

122. Panova, *Kremlevskie usypal'nitsy*, p. 63.

123. Possevino, *Moscovia*, p. 12.

4 KREMLENAGRAD

1. M. V. Posokhin et al., *Pamiatniki arkhitektury Moskvy: Kreml', Kitai-gorod, Tsentral'nye ploshchadi* (Moscow, 1982), p. 50.

2. Copies were printed in successive editions of Joan (Johannes) Blaeu's *Atlas Maior* (Amsterdam, 1663–5).

3. The palaces are an exception, and seem to be in a semi-sketchy state, suggesting that the original artist had sought to represent more than the outsides of their walls.

4. Jacques Margeret, *The Russian Empire and the Grand Duchy of Moscow: A Seventeenth-century French Account*, trans. and ed. Chester S. L. Dunning (Pittsburg, Pa., 1983), p. 30.

5. Isaac Massa, *A Short History of the Peasant Wars in Moscow under the Reigns of Various Sovereigns down to the Year 1610*, trans. G. E. Orchard (Toronto, 1982), p. 95. As for Massa, two portraits, once of the merchant and his wife (1622) and one of Massa alone (1626), are in the Rijksmuseum in Amsterdam and the Art Gallery of Ontario, Toronto, respectively.

6. V. G. Vovina, 'Patriarkh Filaret (Fedor Nikitch Romanov)', *Voprosy istorii*, 7–8 (1991), pp. 55–6. Nikita's grandson (who did not survive) was given the first name Boris.

7. Chester S. L. Dunning, *Russia's First Civil War: The Time of Troubles and the Founding of the Romanov Dynasty* (University Park, Pa., 2001), p. 60.

8. For more on this, see Dunning, *Civil War*, p. 65.

9. Massa, *Peasant Wars*, p. 94.

10. Massa, *Peasant Wars*, pp. 36 and 94.

11. For summaries of Boris' personal qualities, see Dunning, *Civil War*, p. 91; S. F. Platonov, *Smutnoe vremia* (The Hague, 1965), p. 64; Ruslan Skrynnikov, *Boris Godunov* (Moscow, 1978), pp. 3–4.

12. For a discussion, see A. P. Pavlov, 'Fedor Ivanovich and Boris Godunov', in *CHR*, vol. 1, pp. 264–7.

13. In this version, I follow Dunning, *Civil War*, p. 61, but see also R. G. Skrynnikov, *Krest' i korona* (St Petersburg, 2000), p. 313, which gives a different account, featuring Bogdan Belsky as one of the four.

14. Platonov, *Smutnoe vremia*, p. 67.

15. See Platonov, *Smutnoe vremia*; Maureen Perrie, *Pretenders and Popular Modernism in Early Modern Russia* (Cambridge, 1995), pp. 12–13; Massa, *Peasant Wars*, p. 20.

16. Dunning, *Civil War*, p. 61.

17. Dunning, *Civil War*, pp. 15–16 and 55–7.

18. Platonov, *Smutnoe vremia*, p. 61; Dunning, *Civil War*, p. 55.

19. For an exposition of the economic plight of Russia's population, including the *pomeshchiki*, see Platonov, *Smutnoe vremia*, pp. 9–61, esp. pp. 35–7.

20. Dunning, *Civil War*, p. 159.

21. S. F. Platonov, *Boris Godunov* (Petrograd, 1921), pp. 50–55.

22. Vovina, 'Patriarkh Filaret', p. 56.

23. Dunning, *Civil War*, p. 62 (which again differs in emphasis from Skrynnikov).

24. Nevsky was one of the national saints canonized in 1547 by Makary's commission. For Shuisky's pedigree, see R. G. Skrynnikov, *Time of Troubles: Russia in Crisis, 1604–1618* (Gulf Breeze, Fl., 1988), p. 42.

25. Skrynnikov, *Krest'*, p. 314; on the Chudov, see S. N. Bogatyrev, ed., *Khoziaistvennye knigi Chudova monastyria 1585–86 gg.* (Moscow, 1996), p. 23, which also gives the date for Shuisky's planned coup as 14 May 1586. Ivan the Terrible's approach to Anthony Jenkinson came soon after the union of the Livonian and Lithuanian crowns in 1566.

26. Skrynnikov, *Krest'*, p. 315.

27. The measure involved suppression (temporarily) of their annual right of departure from their lord's control after the harvest on St George's Day. For more details, see Dunning, *Civil War*, p. 67, and also David Moon, *The Russian Peasantry, 1600–1913* (London and New York, 1999), pp. 66–8;

Robert O. Crummey, *The Formation of Muscovy, 1304–1613* (London and New York, 1997), p. 174.

28. Massa, *Peasant Wars*, p. 36; on the monks, see Bogatyrev, *Khoziastvennye knigi*, pp. 28 and 142.

29. Skrynnikov, *Krest'*, p. 322.

30. A. L. Batalov, *Moskovskoe kamennoe zodchestvo kontsa XVI veka: problemy khudozhestvennogo myshleniia epokhi* (Moscow, 1996), p. 257.

31. A. N. Speransky, *Ocherki po istorii prikaza kamennykh del Moskovskogo gosudarstva* (Vologda, 1930), p. 41. See also N. N. Voronin, *Ocherki po istorii russkogo zodchestva XI–XVII vv.* (Moscow and Leningrad, 1934), pp. 35–7.

32. Platonov, *Smutnoe vremia*, p. 46. As this great expert on the time observes, the tax-exempt groups could bankrupt local businesses.

33. Speransky, *Ocherki po istorii*, pp. 95–126.

34. I. A. Bondarenko et al., eds., *Slovar' arkhitektorov i masterov stroitel'nogo dela Moskvy, XV–serediny XVIII veka* (Moscow, 2007), pp. 335–7.

35. Speransky, *Ocherki po istorii*, p. 84.

36. Bondarenko, *Slovar' arkhitektorov*, p. 337; Batalov, *Kamennoe zodchestvo*, p. 81.

37. The sense of passing through successive walls is conveyed in many foreign travellers' accounts, and even in the memoirs of Frenchmen in the suite of Napoleon.

38. Speransky, *Ocherki po istorii*, pp. 8, 36–9, 80–85; Richard Hellie, *Enserfment and Military Change in Muscovy* (Chicago, and London, 1971), p. 158.

39. Platonov, *Smutnoe vremia*, p. 73.

40. In the mid-seventeenth century, a team of ninety was envisaged for the renovation of the same space. See RGADA, *fond* 396, d. 51293, ll. 3–6.

41. Aida Nasibova, *The Faceted Chamber in the Moscow Kremlin* (Leningrad, 1981), p. 16; see also I. E. Zabelin, *Domashnyi byt russkikh tsarei v XVI i XVII stoletiiakh* (Moscow, 1862, repr. 1990), vol. 1, pp. 178–84.

42. The consensus is fragile, however. Platonov (*Smutnoe vremia*, pp. 82–3) is prepared to believe that Dmitry may have survived, while Maureen Perrie, following the English witness Jerome Horsey, is among the more recent commentators to assert that Godunov had the child murdered after all. See Perrie, *Pretenders*, p. 18 and Dunning, *Civil War*, pp. 66–8.

43. Dunning, *Civil War*, pp. 64–6; Massa, *Peasant Wars*, pp. 30–31. The English travellers Jerome Horsey and Giles Fletcher both shared Massa's view about Godunov's guilt.

44. For the background, see A. L. Batalov, 'Sobor Voznesenskogo Monastyria v Moskovskom Kremle', *Pamiatniki kul'tury: Novye otkrytiia* (1983), p. 478.

45. On the importance of the Archangel Cathedral, see *Akty Rossiiskogo Gosudarstva: Arkhivy moskovskikh monastyrei i soborov XV–nachala XVII vv.* (Moscow, 1998), p. 36.

46. Batalov reconstructed the evidence from fragments, since the cathedral was destroyed in the 1920s. For plans and a description, see 'Sobor Voznesenskogo Monastyria', pp. 462–82. See also Batalov, *Kamennoe zodchestvo*, p. 257.

47. Batalov, *Kamennoe zodchestvo*, p. 78.

48. Batalov, *Kamennoe zodchestvo*, pp. 84–5.

49. Massa, *Peasant Wars*, p. 43.

50. On the throne, see Barry Shifman and Guy Walton, eds., *Gifts to the Tsars, 1500–1700: Treasures from the Kremlin* (New York, 2001), p. 76. For a discussion of the regalia, see Scott Douglas Ruby, 'The Kremlin Workshops of the Tsars and Foreign Craftsmen: *c.* 1500–1711', unpublished PhD dissertation, Courtauld Institute of Art, 2009, pp. 64–5.

51. Margeret, *Russian Empire*, p. 54.

52. Dunning, *Civil War*, pp. 94–6.

53. On the original, of 1508, see above, Chapter 2, p. 57.

54. Massa, *Peasant Wars*, p. 55.

55. M. S. Arel and S. N. Bogatyrev, 'Anglichane v Moskve vremen Borisa Godunova', *Arkheograficheskii ezhegodnik* (1997), pp. 439–55.

56. The best account of Godunov's plan is Batalov, *Kamennoe zodchestvo*, pp. 86–96.

57. Massa, *Peasant Wars*, pp. 106–7. On the model of the Sepulchre, see A. L. Batalov, 'Grob gospoden' v zamysle "sviataia sviatykh" Borisa Godunova', in A. L. Batalov and A. Lidov, eds., *Ierusalim v russkoi kul'ture* (Moscow, 1994), p. 166.

58. Massa, *Peasant Wars*, p. 44.

59. Vovina, 'Patriarkh Filaret', p. 56.

60. Dunning, *Civil War*, p. 97.

61. Massa, *Peasant Wars*, p. 50.

62. Massa, *Peasant Wars*, p. 52.

63. Massa, *Peasant Wars*, p. 57.

64. Dunning, *Civil War*, pp. 131–2.

65. For a detailed portrait, see Perrie, *Pretenders*, p. 45.

66. Dunning, *Civil War*, p. 161.

67. Massa, *Peasant Wars*, p. 81.

68. Dunning, *Civil War*, p. 195.

69. Massa, *Peasant Wars*, p. 105, and see Dunning, *Civil War*, p. 195.

70. This allegation, and many others tending to present him as a Catholic and creature of the Poles, is a motif of Skrynnikov, *Time of Troubles*, pp. 1–11.

71. On the Inquisition, and for a discussion of Dmitry's supposed Catholicism, see P. Pierling, 'Dnevnik Andreia Levitskogo', *Russkaia starina* (1900), pp. 689–706; for the informality of Dmitry's court, see Dunning, *Civil War*, pp. 202–4.

72. Margeret, *Russian Empire*, p. 86.

73. Margeret, *Russian Empire*, p. 70.

74. Dunning rejects almost all these stories (except the one where Dmitry wears Polish clothes). See his *Civil War*, pp. 210–23. For a classic diatribe against Otrepev, see also Skrynnikov, *Time of Troubles*, pp. 19–21, who does not give a source.

75. Massa, *Peasant Wars*, pp. 117–19.

76. Skrynnikov, *Time of Troubles*, pp. 3 and 26.

77. Massa, *Peasant Wars,* p. 115. On the 'Polish style', see Lindsey Hughes, *The Romanovs: Ruling Russia, 1613–1917* (London, 2008), p. 10.

78. For a contemporary's view on this, see Massa, *Peasant Wars,* p. 149.

79. On Marina's arrival, see Margeret, *Russian Empire*, p. 72 and Massa, *Peasant Wars*, pp. 128–31. More generally, see Dunning, *Civil War*, pp. 231–2.

80. Skrynnikov, *Time of Troubles*, p. 23.

81. Massa, *Peasant Wars*, p. 134.

82. On Vasily's pedigree, see Dunning, *Civil War*, p. 62.

83. Margeret (*Russian Empire*, p. 72) gives a higher, and suspiciously precise, figure for the casualties: 1,705. The truth is that the number cannot be accurately established.

84. Dunning, *Civil War*, pp. 234–5; Margeret, *Russian Empire*, p. 72; Massa, *Peasant Wars*, pp.136–8 and 144.

85. Platonov, *Smutnoe vremia*, p. 125.

86. For a list of the candidates, see Perrie, *Pretenders*, p. 177.

87. Dunning, *Civil War*, pp. 206–7.

88. On his choice of residence, see Dunning, *Civil War*, p. 246.

89. Dunning, *Civil War*, pp. 279 and 292.

90. Dunning, *Civil War*, p. 325; see also Perrie, *Pretenders*, p. 129.

91. Dunning, *Civil War*, pp. 318–19.

92. Stanislaw Zolkiewski, *Expedition to Moscow: A Memoir*, trans. M. W. Stephen (London, 1959), p. 51.

93. Its members were Fedor Mstislavskii, Ivan Vorotynskii, Vasilii Golitsyn, Ivan Romanov, Fedor Sheremetev, Andrei Trubetskoi and Boris Lykov. Skrynnikov, *Time of Troubles*, p. 93.

94. Skrynnikov, *Time of Troubles*, p. 105.

95. Zolkiewski, *Expedition to Moscow,* pp. 100–101.

96. A version that was later told to Adam Olearius. See *The Travels of Olearius in Seventeenth-Century Russia*, trans. Samuel H. Baron (Stanford, Calif., 1967), pp. 189–90.

97. Skrynnikov, *Time of Troubles*, p. 126.

98. Skrynnikov, *Time of Troubles*, p. 129, citing Conrad Bussow. For balance, it is worth noting that this is the incident that Dunning (*Civil War*, p. 418) calls a 'daring and ferocious assault by Captain Margeret's German mercenaries'.

99. Olearius, *Travels*, p. 190.

100. Skrynnikov, *Time of Troubles*, pp. 154–5.

101. Skrynnikov, *Time of Troubles*, pp. 220–21.

102. Skrynnikov, *Time of Troubles*, p. 250; S. K. Bogoiavlenskii, ed., *Gosudarstvennaia oruzheinaia palata Moskovskogo kremlia* (Moscow, 1954), p. 514.

103. Ruby, 'Kremlin Workshops', pp. 163–4.

104. Skrynnikov, *Time of Troubles*, pp. 252–3.

105. S. P. Bartenev, *Bol'shoi kremlevskii dvorets: ukazatel' k ego obozreniiu* (Moscow, 1911), p. 5; Platonov, *Smutnoe vremia*, p. 216.

106. I. Snegirev, *Moskva: Podrobnoe istoricheskoe i arkheologicheskoe opisanie goroda* (Moscow, 1875), vol. 2, p. 85.

107. Olearius, *Travels*, p. 190.

5 ETERNAL MOSCOW

1. *The Travels of Macarius, Patriarch of Antioch: Written by His Attendant Archdeacon, Paul of Aleppo, in Arabic*, trans. F. C. Belfour (London, 1836), vol. 1, pp. 353–5.

2. *Travels of Macarius*, vol. 1, p. 381.

3. *Travels of Macarius*, vol. 1, p. 389.

4. For an extended discussion of popular belief, see I. L. Buseva-Davydova, *Kul'tura i iskusstvo v epokhu peremen: Rossiia semnadtsatogo stoletiia* (Moscow, 2008), esp. pp. 24–9.

5. On continuity at elite level in the seventeenth century, see P. V. Sedov, *Zakat Moskovskogo tsarstva: tsarskii dvor kontsa XVII veka* (St Petersburg, 2006). For details of the political settlement after 1613, see also Robert O. Crummey, *Aristocrats and Servitors: The Boyar Elite in Russia, 1613–1689* (Princeton, NJ, 1983), pp. 26–7; R. G. Skrynnikov, *Time of Troubles: Russia in Crisis, 1604–1618* (Gulf Breeze, Fl., 1988), pp. 268–71.

6. See N. V. Rybalko, *Rossiiskaia prikaznaia biurokratiia v Smutnoe vremia nachala XVII v* (Moscow, 2011), which gives a figure of between 60 and 68 per cent stability for the period 1598–1613.

7. On the size of the court, see Sedov, *Zakat*, pp. 54–7. For a range of views on the pace of change, compare his conclusion (*Zakat*, p. 551) with Brenda Meehan-Waters, *Autocracy and Aristocracy: The Russian Social Elite of 1730* (New Brunswick, NJ, 1982), pp. 6–10, and Paul Bushkovitch, *Religion and Society in Russia: The Sixteenth and Seventeenth Centuries* (New York, 1992), p. 129.

8. *Travels of Macarius*, vol. 2, p. 2.

9. See S. V. Lobachev, 'Patriarch Nikon's rise to power', *SEER*, 79, 2 (April 2001), pp. 302–3. Kluchevsky discussed the issue of responsibility at length, noting that, since Muscovy was no longer a patrimony to be bequeathed in

the tsar's will, Mikhail's son, Aleksei Mikhailovich, had also to be 'elected' before he formally ascended the throne. V. O. Kluchevsky, *A History of Russia*, trans. C. J. Hogarth (London, J. M. Dent, 1913), vol. 3, pp. 80–81. That said, election – or a form of consensual proclamation – was not unprecedented, and had been used for the promotion of Boris Godunov.

10. S. F. Platonov, *Smutnoe vremia* (The Hague, 1965), p. 218.

11. Chester S. L. Dunning, *Russia's First Civil War: The Time of Troubles and the Founding of the Romanov Dynasty* (University Park, Pa., 2001), pp. 448 and 468. For the enthronement, see *DAI*, vol. 2, no. 76, pp. 185–214.

12. Isaac Massa, 1614, cited in B. Shifton and G. Walton, eds., *Gifts to the Tsars: Treasures from the Kremlin* (New York, 2001), p. 308.

13. Samuel Collins, *The Present State of Russia: A Letter to a Friend at London, by an Eminent Person residing at the Czar's Court* (London, 1671), p. 101.

14. Dunning, *Civil War*, pp. 443–5.

15. Collins, *State of Russia*, pp. 116–17.

16. For the tale that even the tsar's sceptre had disappeared, see I. Snegirev, *Moskva: Podrobnoe istoricheskoe i arkheologicheskoe opisanie goroda*, vol. 2 (Moscow, 1875), p. 12. There is some doubt, however, about this, on which see Scott Douglas Ruby, 'The Kremlin Workshops of the Tsars and Foreign Craftsmen: *c.* 1500–1711', unpublished PhD dissertation, Courtauld Institute of Art, 2009, pp. 64–5. On the gold, see S. K. Bogoiavlenskii, ed., *Gosudarstvennaia oruzheinaia palata Moskovskogo kremlia* (Moscow, 1954), p. 526.

17. Snegirev, *Moskva*, vol. 2, p. 85. The Romanovs were also attentive to their real ancestors, of course, and gave generously for the upkeep of their family shrines.

18. Russell E. Martin, 'Choreographing the "Tsar's Happy Occasion": tradition, change and dynastic legitimacy in the weddings of Tsar Mikhail Romanov', *Slavic Review*, 63, 4 (Winter 2004), pp. 794–817.

19. I. E. Zabelin, *Domashnii byt russkikh tsarei v XVI i XVII stoletiiakh* (Moscow, 1862, repr. 1990), vol. 1, p. 56.

20. Skrynnikov, *Time of Troubles*, p. 257.

21. A report, dated 1645–7, details the condition of the Kremlin walls at the beginning of Aleksei Mikhailovich's reign, confirming that the repairs dragged on for decades. See *DAI*, vol. 3, no. 3, pp. 2–5.

22. Filaret's comments on this problem are reproduced in I. E. Zabelin, *Istoriia goroda Moskvy* (Moscow, 1904; repr. 2005), pp. 181–2.

23. Bogoiavlenskii, *Gosudarstvennaia oruzheinaia palata*, p. 526.

24. Snegirev, *Moskva*, vol. 2, pp. 16–17.

25. A. N. Speransky, *Ocherki po istorii prikaza kamennykh del Moskovskogo gosudarstva* (Vologda, 1930), p. 49.

26. Even travelling priests dealt in furs when they returned home. See *Travels of Macarius*, vol. 1, p. 403.

27. This was Henry, son of Leonard, Bush. The details were discovered by Ruby, 'Kremlin Workshops', pp. 49–52.

28. For more on these foreigners, see Vladimir Chekmarev, 'Angliiskie mastera na sluzhbe u Mikhaila Fedorovicha', *Arkhitektura i stroitel'stva Moskvy*, 9 (1990), pp. 19–21; Dmitry Shvidkovsky, *Russian Architecture and the West* (New Haven, Conn. and London, 2007), pp. 152–60.

29. Buseva-Davydova, *Kul'tura i iskusstvo*, pp. 91–2.

30. On the royal family's preferences, see Collins, *State of Russia*, p. 57; Zabelin, *Domashnyi*, vol. 1, pp. 69–70.

31. E. M. Kozlitina, 'Dokumenty XVII veka po istorii Granovitoi palaty Moskovskogo Kremlia', *Materialy i issledovaniia*, vol. I, p. 99.

32. S. de Bartenev, *Le Grand Palais du Kremlin et ses neuf églises: Guide du visiteur* (Moscow, 1912), p. 11.

33. Cited in Jeremy Howard, *Christopher Galloway: Clockmaker, Architect and Engineer to Tsar Mikhail, the First Romanov* (Edinburgh, 1997), p. 19.

34. Zabelin, *Istoriia goroda Moskvy*, p. 203.

35. Zabelin, *Istoriia goroda Moskvy*, p. 206; Howard, *Galloway*, pp. 10–11.

36. Howard, *Galloway*, pp. 29–30.

37. Iu. V. Tarabarina, 'Znachenie Kremlevskikh postroek pervykh romanovykh v istorii proiskhozhdenii shatrovykh kolokolen XVII veka', www.archi.ru (2006). My thanks to Dr Alla Aronova for drawing my attention to this online item in August 2011.

38. Graf's name first appeared in Zabelin, *Istoriia goroda Moskvy*, p. 204. See also S. P. Bartenev, *Moskovskii Kreml' v starinu i teper'*, 2 vols. (St Petersburg, 1912 and 1918), vol. 1, p. 139, and Buseva-Davydova, *Kul'tura i iskusstvo*, pp. 89–91.

39. Zabelin, *Istoriia goroda Moskvy*, pp. 203–6.

40. Zabelin (*Istoriia goroda Moskvy*, p. 207) argues that we do not know what Galloway's clock looked like. Howard and others base their descriptions on the accounts of later visitors. See also Buseva-Davydova, *Kul'tura i iskusstvo*, p. 161, where Meyerberg's drawing is reproduced, and Chekmarev, 'Angliiskie mastera', p. 20, which argues that Galloway's clock survived intact until 1707. Parts of the mechanism, indeed, remain visible inside the tower to this day. For the fire, see *Travels of Macarius*, vol. 1, p. 369.

41. Zabelin, *Domashnii*, vol. 1, p. 114.

42. Collins, *State of Russia*, p. 67; Howard, *Galloway*, pp. 5 and 13.

43. P. V. Sytin, *Istoriia planirovki i zastroiki Moskvy*, vol. 1 (Moscow, 1950), p. 42.

44. Ruby, 'Kremlin Workshops', pp. 238–40; Bogoiavlenskii, *Gosudarstvennaia oruzheinaia palata*, pp. 556–7.

45. N. G. Bekeneva, *Simon Ushakov, 1626–1686* (Leningrad, 1984), esp. pp. 5–21.

46. V. G. Briusova, *Russkaia zhivopis' XVII veka* (Moscow, 1984), pp. 16–20; Buseva-Davydova, *Kul'tura i iskusstvo*, p. 91. The *d'yak* Stepan Ugotskii was in charge of the logistics. See I. Mashkov, ed., *Otchet po restavratsii bol'shago Moskovskago Uspenskago sobora* (Moscow, 1910), pp. 7–8, which reprints the original instructions.

47. Briusova, *Russkaia zhivopis'*, pp. 22–3.

48. I. L. Buseva-Davydova, 'Novye ikonograficheskie istochniki v russkoi zhivopisi XVII v', in A. L. Batalov, ed., *Iskusstvo pozdnego srednevekoviia* (Moscow, 1993), pp. 190–206.

49. Buseva-Davydova, *Kul'tura i iskusstvo*, pp. 34–5.

50. For an account, see Bogoiavlenskii, *Gosudarstvennaia oruzheinaia palata*, pp. 533–6.

51. Speransky, *Ocherki po istorii*, p. 185.

52. Richard Hellie, *The Economy and Material Culture of Russia 1600–1725* (Chicago, 1999), pp. 445–6.

53. Richard Hellie, *Enserfment and Military Change in Muscovy* (Chicago, 1971), pp. 182–3; see also M. N. Larchenko, 'K voprosu o rabote tak nazyvaemykh "pol'skikh" masterov v Oruzheinoi palate vo vtoroi polovine XVII veka', Proizvedeniia Russkogo i zarubezhnogo iskusstva XVI–nachala XVIII veka', *Materialy i issledovaniia*, vol. IV, pp. 185–92.

54. M. Poe and E. Lohr, eds., *The Military and Society in Russian History, 1350–1917* (Leiden, 2002), p. 66.

55. On the troops that lined his route in 1675, see Sedov, *Zakat*, p. 185.

56. *Travels of Macarius*, vol. 1, p. 367.

57. L. Loewenson, 'The Moscow rising of 1648', *SEER*, 27, 68 (December 1948), p. 147.

58. *The Travels of Olearius in Seventeenth-Century Russia*, trans. Samuel H. Baron (Stanford, Calif., 1967), pp. 203–4.

59. Olearius, *Travels*, p. 204; see also V. Kivelson, 'The devil stole his mind: the tsar and the 1648 Moscow uprising', *AHR*, 98, 3 (June 1993), p. 738.

60. K. V. Bazilevich, *Gorodskie vosstaniia v Moskovskom gosudarstve XVII v.* (Moscow and Leningrad, 1936), pp. 54–5.

61. Loewenson, 'Moscow rising', p. 153.

62. Loewenson, 'Moscow rising', p. 153.

63. Olearius, *Travels*, p. 209; see also Loewenson, 'Moscow rising', p. 154.

64. Olearius, *Travels*, p. 211.

65. Loewenson, 'Moscow rising', p. 155, see also Pommerening's estimate of the damage in Bazilevich, *Gorodskie*, p. 39. The highest estimate for deaths is 2,000, but all are guesses. The fire was clearly a major catastrophe in every sense. See Kivelson, 'Devil', p. 740.

66. Olearius, *Travels*, p. 212; Loewenson, 'Moscow rising', p. 155. See also Pommerening's account in Bazilevich, *Gorodskie*, p. 36.

67. Kivelson, 'Devil', p. 742.

68. For the text in an English translation, see Richard Hellie, ed. and trans., *The Muscovite Law Code (Ulozhenie) of 1649* (Irvine, Calif., 1988).

69. *Travels of Macarius*, vol. 1, p. 331.

70. I. E. Zabelin, *Materialy dlia istorii arkheologii i statistiki goroda Moskvy*, vol. 2 (Moscow, 1891), p. 2.

71. It is printed in *DAI*, vol. 3, no. 119, pp. 442–8. See also Philip Longworth, *Alexis, Tsar of all the Russias* (London, 1984), pp. 101–2.

72. Snegirev, *Moskva*, vol. 2, pp. 14–15.

73. *DAI*, vol. 4, no. 9, p. 31.

74. Samuel H. Baron, 'Nemeckaja sloboda', pp. 7–8, reprinted in his *Muscovite Russia: Collected Essays* (London, 1980).

75. Olearius, *Travels*, p. 142.

76. The reforms began in the late 1640s. See Bushkovitch, *Religion and Society*, p. 57.

77. Lobachev, 'Patriarch Nikon', p. 306, citing Johan de Rodes.

78. *Travels of Macarius*, vol. 2, p. 105; see also P. Meyendorff, *Russia, Ritual and Reform: The Liturgical Reforms of Nikon in the Seventeenth Century* (New York, 1991), p. 90.

79. *Travels of Macarius*, vol. 2, p. 171.

80. A. I. Romanenko, 'Odin iz etapov stroitel'stva patriarshikh palat', *Materialy i issledovaniia*, vol. II, p. 110. On the German architects, see *Travels of Macarius*, vol. 2, p. 224.

81. *Travels of Macarius*, vol. 2, pp. 225–6.

82. D. N. Anuchin et al., eds., *Moskva v ee proshlom i nastoiashchem*, 12 vols. (Moscow, 1909–12), vol. 2, p. 115; on serfs, see Dunning, *Civil War*, p. 473.

83. Anuchin, *Moskva v ee proshlom*, vol. 2, pp. 109–11.

84. Olearius, *Travels*, p. 265, and see Avvakum's diatribe, cited in G. Michels, *At War with the Church: Religious Dissent in Seventeenth-Century Russia* (Stanford, Calif., 1999), p. 49.

85. *Travels of Macarius*, vol. 1, p. 171.

86. *Travels of Macarius*, vol. 1, p. 410.

87. Michael Cherniavsky, 'The Old Believers and the new religion', *Slavic Review*, 25, 1 (March 1966), pp. 1–39.

88. Cited in Michels, *At War with the Church*, p. 49.

89. For a summary, see Michels, *At War with the Church*, pp. 217–29.

90. Meyendorff, *Ritual*, p. 95, citing Kluchevsky, *History*.

91. *Travels of Macarius*, vol. 1, p. 412.

92. Michael Cherniavsky, *Tsar and People: Studies in Russian Myths* (New Haven, Conn. and London, 1961), p. 63.

93. On the balance as Paul of Aleppo saw it, see *Travels of Macarius*, vol. 1, p. 316, which gives all the important cards to Aleksei.

94. *DAI*, vol. 4, no. 118, pp. 274–5.

95. Longworth, *Alexis*, pp. 127–9.

96. Zabelin, *Istoriia goroda Moskvy*, pp. 360–61; Longworth, *Alexis*, p. 168.

97. For a blow-by-blow account, see *DAI*, vol. 5, no. 102, pp. 439–510.

98. Collins, *State of Russia*, pp. 64–5.

99. Zabelin, *Domashnii*, vol. 1, p. 205. Hellie, *Economy*, pp. 590–95, contrasts the furniture in Golitsyn's palace of the 1680s with that in Tatishchev's in 1608. The latter, strikingly, had no beds and only one chair.

100. Collins, *State of Russia*, pp. 57–8.

101. Longworth, *Alexis*, p. 205.

102. Zabelin, *Domashnii*, vol. 1, p. 138; Longworth, *Alexis*, p. 134.

103. Kozlitina, 'Dokumenty', pp. 98–9.

104. Longworth, *Alexis*, p. 203.

105. Longworth, *Alexis*, p. 204.

106. For figures, see Peter B. Brown, 'How Muscovy governed: seventeenth-century Russian central administration', *Russian History*, 36, 4 (2009), pp. 488–99; on the 'new men' under Aleksei, see Marshall Poe, 'The central government and its institutions', *CHR*, vol. 1, ch. 19, esp. pp. 446–51.

107. Zabelin, *Istoriia goroda Moskvy*, p. 255; *DAI*, vol. 6, no. 50, p. 207 (relocation of *Bolshoi prikhod*, 1672).

108. The figures, given by Brenda Meehan-Waters, are 31 at the time of Aleksei's accession and 151 in 1689: *Autocracy*, p. 10. For the number living in the Kremlin, see Collins, *State of Russia*, p. 62.

109. A controversial point argued cogently by Sedov, *Zakat*, pp. 132–9.

110. Although our knowledge of this is limited, and while many elite noblemen were conservative (and relatively short of the necessary resources) when it came to collecting, there is evidence in the cases of figures such as Artamon Matveyev and Vasily Golitsyn.

111. Lindsey Hughes, *Sophia, Regent of Russia* (London and New Haven, Conn., 1990), p. 37.

112. On the education of the tsarevich, see Sedov, *Zakat*, pp. 176–8.

113. V. M. Zhivov, 'Religious reform and the emergence of the individual in seventeenth-century Russian literature', in S. Baron and Nancy Shields-Kollmann, eds., *Religion and Culture in Early Modern Russia* (DeKalb, Ill., 1997), p. 184.

114. James Cracraft, *The Petrine Revolution in Russian Architecture* (Chicago, 1988), p. 42. Buseva-Davydova's monograph on seventeenth-century art effectively disputes this notion of crisis.

115. Hughes, *Sophia*, pp. 52–88.

116. Lindsey Hughes, *Peter the Great: A Biography* (New Haven, Conn. and London, 2004), pp. 17–20.

117. For details, see Hughes, *Sophia*, p. 193.

118. *DAI*, vol. 11, no. 90, pp. 286–7; Kozlitina, 'Dokumenty', pp. 101–2. On the style, see Lindsey Hughes, 'Western European graphic material as a source for Moscow Baroque architecture', *SEER*, 55, 4 (October 1977), p. 437.

6 CLASSICAL ORDERS

1. *Dvortsovye razriady*, vol. 4 (St Petersburg, 1855), p. 911.
2. *Dvortsovye razriady*, vol. 4, pp. 920–26; *PSZ*, vol. III, pp. 220–21, no. 1536.
3. On the nuns, see I. E. Zabelin, *Materialy dlia istorii arkheologii i statistiki goroda Moskvy*, vol. 2 (Moscow, 1891), p. 8; on crime, see D. N. Anuchin et al., eds., *Moskva v ee proshlom i nastoiashchem*, 12 vols. (Moscow 1909–12), vol. 2, p. 43, citing Kotoshikhin. Traditionally (though Ivan's was an exception) royal funerals took place at night.
4. Lindsey Hughes, *Peter the Great: A Biography* (London and New Haven, Conn., 2004), pp. 202–7.
5. There had been a few European works. In 1661, for instance, an Austrian visitor to Moscow, Count Augustin Meyerberg, created two views of Aleksei Mikhailovich's Kremlin that showed the walls and towers in remarkable detail (the artist was especially impressed by the new Saviour Tower).
6. M. A. Alekseeva, *Graviura petrovskogo vremeni* (Leningrad, 1990), pp. 7–8 and 19.
7. Alekseeva, *Graviura*, pp. 23–5.
8. The chant itself had changed during Fedor Alekseyevich's reign, as polyphonic settings ('Kiev style') began to become fashionable. See P. V. Sedov, *Zakat Moskovskogo tsarstva: tsarskii dvor kontsa XVII veka* (St Petersburg, 2006), pp. 494–5.
9. For an excellent account of Peter's political activities, see Paul Bushkovitch, *Peter the Great: The Struggle for Power* (Cambridge, 2001), especially pp. 154–7.
10. Hughes, *Peter*, p. 25.
11. Lindsey Hughes, *Russia in the Age of Peter the Great* (New Haven, Conn. and London, 1998), p. 12.
12. *PSZ*, vol. III, p. 296, no. 1546 (order banning heavy carts, 19 August 1696).
13. James Cracraft, *The Petrine Revolution in Russian Architecture* (Chicago, 1988), p. 130; Dmitry Shvidkovsky, *Russian Architecture and the West* (New Haven, Conn. and London, 2007), p. 185; for a more detailed account, see A. A. Aronova, 'Azovskii triumf 1696 goda kak pervoe gosudarstvennoe torzhestvo Petra I', *Iskusstvoznanie*, 2 (2006), pp. 61–83. One of the earliest official references to Red Square, referring only to the space between the Saviour Gate and St Basil's (the current square did not exist), was an *ukaz*

of 1658; popular use of the name may well date from the completion of the Saviour Tower three decades earlier.

14. Samuel Collins, *The Present State of Russia: A Letter to a Friend at London, by an Eminent Person residing at the Czar's Court* (London, 1671), p. 33.

15. J. G. Korb, *Diary of an Austrian Secretary of a Legation: at the Court of Czar Peter the Great*, trans. and ed. by the Count MacDonnell, 2 vols. (London, repr. 1968), vol. 2, p. 145.

16. Korb, *Diary*, vol. 1, pp. 255–6; on tobacco (and other merriment) see also Horace W. Dewey and Kira B. Stevens, 'Muscovites at play: recreation in pre-Petrine Russia', *Canadian-American Slavic Studies*, 13, 1–2 (1979), p. 192.

17. On the meaning of Peter's court, see Ernest A. Zitser, *The Transfigured Kingdom* (Ithaca, NY and London, 2004). Similar remarks, with special reference to the patriarchate, are made by V. M. Zhivov. See his 'Church reforms in the reign of Peter the Great', in A. G. Cross, ed., *Russia in the Reign of Peter the Great: Old and New Perspectives* (Cambridge, 1998), p. 67.

18. For the wedding, see Hughes, *Peter*, pp. 109–11 and also her 'Playing games: the alternative history of Peter the Great', *School of Slavonic Studies Occasional Papers*, no. 41 (London, 2000), p. 10.

19. Korb, *Diary*, vol. 1, p. 157.

20. Korb, *Diary*, vol. 1, pp. 159–60; see also Hughes, *Peter*, p. 53.

21. Johann Korb, 'A Compendious Description of the Perilous Revolt of the Strelitz of Muscovy' (reprinted as part of his *Diary*, vol. 2), p. 85.

22. Korb, 'Compendious Description', p. 81.

23. I. Snegirev, *Moskva: Podrobnoe istoricheskoe i arkheologicheskoe opisanie goroda*, vol. 2 (Moscow, 1875), p. 18.

24. RGADA, 1184/1/195, 256–7; *PSZ*, vol. III, p. 680, nos. 1735 and 1736.

25. *PSZ*, vol. IV, p. 182, no. 1887; on the visual aids, see also Lindsey Hughes, 'Russian culture in the eighteenth century', in *CHR*, vol. 2, p. 67.

26. An illustrated commentary on the Old Believer attitude appears in Michael Cherniavsky, 'The Old Believers and the new religion', *Slavic Review*, 25, 1 (March 1966), pp. 1–39. See also Michael Cherniavsky, *Tsar and People: Studies in Russian Myths* (New Haven, Conn. and London, 1961), p. 76.

27. Hughes, 'Russian culture', p. 77.

28. Korb, *Diary*, vol. 1, pp. 179–80.

29. On religious transformation, see Zhivov, 'Church reforms', passim.

30. Hughes, *Russia in the Age of Peter*, pp. 208–9.

31. Cracraft, *Petrine Revolution*, p. 128.

32. *PSZ*, vol. IV, p. 177 (no. 1879) and p. 192 (no. 1909).

33. Korb, *Diary*, vol. 2, p. 150.

34. I. E. Zabelin, *Domashnii byt russkikh tsarei v XVI i XVII stoletiiakh* (Moscow, 1862, repr. 1990), vol. 1, p. 70; S. de Bartenev, *Le Grand Palais du Kremlin et ses neuf églises* (Moscow, 1912), p. 15; I. A. Bondarenko et al.,

eds., *Slovar' arkhitektorov i masterov stroitel'nogo dela Moskvy XV–serediny XVIII veka* (Moscow, 2008), p. 577.

35. Cracraft, *Petrine Revolution*, p. 122; Snegirev, *Moskva*, vol. 2, pp. 16–17.

36. Alekseeva, *Graviura*, p. 33.

37. Bondarenko, *Slovar' arkhitektorov*, p. 332.

38. Cited by Maria di Salvo, in Simon Dixon, ed., *Personality and Place in Russian Culture: Essays in Memory of Lindsey Hughes* (London, 2010), p. 96.

39. See Cherniavsky, *Tsar and People*, pp. 76–7; Richard S. Wortman, *Scenarios of Power: Myth and Ceremony in Russian Monarchy* (Princeton, NJ, 1995), vol. 1, p. 48.

40. Hughes, *Peter*, p. 60.

41. Hughes, *Peter*, p. 63.

42. A. Aronova, 'Petropavlovskaia krepost': istoricheskii mif i gradostroitel'naia real'nost", *Iskusstvoznanie*, 2 (2001), pp. 370–80, which corrects the more widely accepted version in Hughes, *Peter*, pp. 66–8.

43. The Dutch engineer-designer was assisted by one of Peter's own artillery officers. See N. A. Skvortsov, *Arkheologiia i topografiia Moskvy: kurs lektsii* (Moscow, 1913), p. 100.

44. S. P. Bartenev, *Moskovskii kreml' v starinu i teper'*, 2 vols. (St Petersburg, 1912 and 1918), vol. 1, p. 69.

45. Albert J. Schmidt, *The Architecture and Planning of Classical Moscow* (Philadelphia, Pa., 1989), pp. 18–19; Cracraft, *Petrine Revolution*, p. 122; M. P. Fabricius, *Kreml' v Moskve: ocherki i kartiny proshlogo i nastoiashchego* (Moscow, 1883), p. 142.

46. Alekseeva, *Graviura*, pp. 117–21.

47. I. E. Zabelin, *Istoriia goroda Moskvy* (Moscow, 1904; repr. 2005), p. 172; Bartenev, *Moskovskii kreml'*, vol. 1, p. 70.

48. Zabelin, *Istoriia goroda Moskvy*, p. 168.

49. *Istoriia Moskvy v shesti tomakh* (Moscow, 1952), vol. 2, p. 337; Anuchin, *Moskva v ee proshlom*, vol. 4, p. 9.

50. For evidence, see Zabelin, *Domashnii*, vol. 1, p. 125; Korb, *Diary*, vol. 1, p. 254.

51. Bartenev, *Moskovskii kreml'*, vol. 1, p. 70.

52. Bartenev, *Grand Palais*, p. 14.

53. Zabelin, *Domashnii*, vol. 1, pp. 125–6.

54. Zabelin, *Materialy dlia istorii*, vol. 2, pp. 6–7.

55. Hughes, *Russia in the Age of Peter*, p. 338.

56. See Catherine the Great's playful remarks on the subject in her letter to Voltaire of 15/26 March 1767, reprinted in W. F. Reddaway, ed., *Documents of Catherine the Great* (Cambridge, 1931), p. 15.

57. Zhivov, 'Church reforms', p. 74; Lindsey Hughes, 'Seeing the sights in eighteenth-century Russia: the Moscow Kremlin', in R. Bartlett and G. Lehmann-Carli, eds., *Eighteenth-century Russia: Society, Culture, Economy:*

Papers from the IV International Conference of the Study Group on Eighteenth-century Russia (Berlin and London, 2007), p. 316.

58. V. S. Dediukhina et al., eds., *Sokhranenie pamiatnikov tserkovnoi stariny v Rossii XVIII–nachala XXv. Sbornik dokumentov* (Moscow, 1997), pp. 18–19, referring to *ukazy* of December 1720 and February 1722.

59. M. K. Pavlovich, 'Reorganizatsiia Kremlevskikh sokrovishchnits i masterskikh pri Petre I', *Materialy i issledovaniia*, vol. XIII, p. 139; Richard Hellie, *The Economy and Material Culture of Russia 1600–1725* (Chicago, 1999), p. 571.

60. See *Petr Velikii v Moskve: Kalatog vystavki* (Moscow, 1998), pp. 114–15.

61. Dediukhina, *Sokhranenie*, p. 18.

62. On Romodanovsky, see Bartenev, *Moskovskii kreml'*, vol. 2, pp. 206–7; see also I. Ia. Stelletskii, *Poiski biblioteki Ivana Groznogo* (Moscow, 1999), pp. 273–4.

63. The same impression was reported by a visitor of 1711. Hughes, 'Seeing the sights', p. 318.

64. On the gardens, see Korb, *Diary*, vol. 1, p. 288, and Zabelin, *Domashnii*, vol. 1, pp. 103–7.

65. F. Bekhteev, cited in A. I. Mikhailov, *Bazhenov* (Moscow, 1951), p. 99.

66. Bushkovitch, *Peter*, pp. 385–6.

67. N. A. Ogarkova, *Tseremonii, prazdnichestva, muzyka russkogo dvora* (St Petersburg, 2004), pp. 11–14.

68. S. A. Amelekhina, 'Koronatsiia Ekateriny I. 1724', in *Petr Velikii i Moskva*, p. 169.

69. Zabelin, *Domashnii*, vol. 1, p. 120; see also Amelekhina, 'Koronatsiia', p. 170.

70. Amelekhina, 'Koronatsiia', p. 170.

71. E. V. Anisimov, *Five Empresses: Court Life in Eighteenth-century Russia*, trans. Kathleen Carroll (Westport, Ua., 2004), p. 31.

72. Richard S. Wortman, *Scenarios of Power: Myth and Ceremony in Russian Monarchy*, 1-vol. edn (Princeton, NJ and Oxford, 2006), p. 37.

73. For the procession, see Amelekhina, 'Koronatsiia', p. 171; for Dmitry of Uglich, see above, pp. 119–27.

74. Pungent comments on the inconvenience appear in Catherine the Great's letters. See, for example, her comments to Nikita Panin in *SIRIO*, vol. 10, pp. 276–7. For prejudice against Moscow by other courtiers, see *SIRIO*, vol. 23, pp. 11–12. On the role of the Guards, see Anisimov, *Five Empresses*, p. 8, citing Campredon.

75. On this reform, enacted by Peter III, see Cherniavsky, *Tsar and People*, p. 125. For its impact on cities, see, for example, Schmidt, *Architecture and Planning*, p. 5.

76. Cited in John T. Alexander, 'Catherine II, bubonic plague, and the problem of industry in Moscow', *AHR*, 79, 3 (June 1974), p. 640.

77. A. Pypin, ed., *Sochineniia Ekateriny II* (St Petersburg, 1907), vol. 12, pp. 169–70.

78. A. S. Shchenkov, ed., *Pamiatniki arkhitektury v dorevoliutsionnoi Rossii* (Moscow, 2002), p. 17; Luba Golburt, 'Derzhavin's ruins and the birth of historical elegy', *Slavic Review*, 65, 4 (Winter 2006), pp. 670–93.

79. On Russian ideas of the picturesque, see Christopher Ely, *This Meager Nature: Landscape and National Identity in Imperial Russia* (DeKalb, Ill., 2002).

80. Cracraft, *Petrine Revolution*, pp. 40–41, 150–51.

81. For a discussion, see Schmidt, *Architecture and Planning*, p. 8.

82. Shchenkov, *Pamiatniki*, vol. 1, p. 18 (citing a Senate report of 1770).

83. Bartenev, *Grand Palais*, p. 49; on Napoleon, see below, pp. 211–15.

84. Cited from her Reflections, in Pypin, *Ekateriny II*, vol. 12, p. 642. See also Simon Dixon, *Catherine the Great* (London, 2009), p. 10.

85. Shvidkovsky, *Russian Architecture*, pp. 229–31.

86. Peter II (b. 1715) was the son of Peter the Great's murdered heir, Aleksei Petrovich. In 1730, after barely two years on the throne, he died of smallpox. Unlike almost all Peter the Great's other imperial successors, he was buried in the Kremlin.

87. Snegirev, *Moskva*, vol. 2, p. 88.

88. I. M. Snegirev, *Spas na Boru v Moskovskom Kremle* (Moscow, 1865), p. 7.

89. Mikhailov, *Bazhenov*, p. 49.

90. For an account, see Dixon, *Catherine*, pp. 4–22.

91. Catherine's instructions were reprinted and their consequences deplored in I. Mashkov, ed., *Otchet po restavratsii bol'shogo Moskovskago Uspenskago sobora* (Moscow, 1910), pp. 5–7.

92. For her disappointment with the place, see *SIRIO*, vol. 23, p. 22 (letter to Grimm of 29 April 1775).

93. Fabricius, *Kreml'*, pp. 156–7.

94. Mikhailov, *Bazhenov*, p. 102.

95. *PSZ*, vol. XVIII, p. 696, no. 13142 (1 July 1768).

96. Mikhailov, *Bazhenov*, p. 98.

97. For a discussion of Bazhenov's plans, with diagrams, see Mikhailov, *Bazhenov*, pp. 70–81.

98. Mikhailov, *Bazhenov*, pp. 77–80; William Craft Brumfield, *A History of Russian Architecture* (Cambridge, 1997), p. 323.

99. Mikhailov, *Bazhenov*, p. 80.

100. Alexander, 'Catherine II', p. 661.

101. Cited in Reddaway, ed., *Documents*, p. 135 (letter of 6/17 October 1771).

102. Fabricius, *Kreml'*, pp. 158–60.

103. Mikhailov, *Bazhenov*, p. 84.

104. Cited in Mikhailov, *Bazhenov*, pp. 86–7.

105. A. I. Vlasiuk et al., *Kazakov* (Moscow, 1957), pp. 13–15; Shvidkovsky, *Russian Architecture*, pp. 248–9.

106. Mikhailov, *Bazhenov*, p. 182.

107. Brumfield, *Russian Architecture*, pp. 328–9; Schmidt, *Architecture and Planning*, p. 64; Vlasiuk, *Kazakov*, pp. 31–2.

108. Hughes, 'Russian culture', p. 68.

7 FIREBIRD

1. Cited in B. Meehan-Waters, *Autocracy and Aristocracy: The Russian Service Elite of 1730* (New Brunswick, NJ, 1982), p. 100.

2. The planners' efforts to 'improve' Moscow by opening up squares and more elegant streets are discussed in P. V. Sytin, *Istoriia planirovki i zastroiki Moskvy*, vol. 2 (Moscow, 1954), pp. 390–93, and also Albert J. Schmidt, *The Architecture and Planning of Classical Moscow* (Philadelphia, Pa., 1989). See also A. S. Shchenkov, ed., *Pamiatniki arkhitektury v dorevoliutsionnoi Rossii* (Moscow, 2002), pp. 231–44.

3. P. V. Sytin, *Istoriia planirovki i zastroiki Moskvy*, vol. 3 (Moscow, 1972), p. 15. On the wooden theatre, see ibid., vol. 2, p. 392.

4. M. V. Posokhin et al., *Pamiatniki arkhitektury Moskvy: Kreml', Kitai-gorod, Tsentral'nye ploshchadi* (Moscow, 1982), vol. 1, pp. 371–3; *Vedomosti* was founded by Peter the Great at the beginning of the eighteenth century.

5. Population figures from Sytin, *Istoriia planirovki*, vol. 3, pp. 13–18. For a survey of Moscow's elite life, see Alexander M. Martin, *Romantics, Reformers, Reactionaries: Russian Conservative Thought and Politics in the Reign of Alexander I* (DeKalb, Ill., 1997), pp. 58–9.

6. Sytin, *Istoriia planirovki*, vol. 3, pp. 13–18.

7. Among the earliest of abolitionists was the foreign-educated radical Alexander Radishchev (1749–1802). Catherine the Great herself famously considered the issue of serfdom, but her intellectual interest in its abolition was never translated into policy.

8. Sytin, *Istoriia planirovki*, vol. 3, pp. 13–18.

9. The nobility was expanding in this period, but still constituted less than 1 per cent of the population of the empire as a whole. See Dominic Lieven, 'The elites', in *CHR*, vol. 2, p. 230.

10. For commentary, see Shchenkov, *Pamiatniki*, pp. 30–40.

11. For a reflection on Moscow, see Sytin, *Istoriia planirovki*, vol. 3, p. 16. On Batiushkov and landscape, see A. Tosi, *Waiting for Pushkin: Russian Fiction in the Age of Alexander I, 1801–1825* (New York and Amsterdam, 2006), esp. pp. 60–61.

12. For more discussion of Russian perceptions of the landscape at this point, see Christopher D. Ely, *This Meager Nature: Landscape and Identity in Imperial Russia* (DeKalb, Ill., 2002), p. 50.

13. Ely, *Meager Nature*, pp. 50 and 64.

14. Cited in T. Slavina, *Konstantin Ton* (Leningrad, 1989), p. 157.

15. Sytin, *Istoriia planirovki*, vol. 2, p. 386.

16. These were noted by the Comte de Ségur as he approached the Kremlin with Napoleon in 1812. See his *History of the Expedition to Russia Undertaken by the Emperor Napoleon in the Year 1812*, 2 vols. (London, 1826), vol. 2, p. 4.

17. William Craft Brumfield, *A History of Russian Architecture* (Cambridge, 1997), p. 339; the other palace used was Kazakov's Petrovskii dvorets.

18. Cited in I. E. Zabelin, *Istoriia goroda Moskvy* (Moscow, 1904; repr. 2005), p. 281.

19. Zabelin, *Istoriia goroda Moskvy*, p. 281.

20. Lindsey Hughes, *The Romanovs: Ruling Russia, 1613–1917* (London, 2009), p. 134.

21. Schmidt, *Architecture and Planning*, p. 51.

22. Sytin, *Istoriia planirovki*, vol. 3, p. 10.

23. For a discussion of Francophobia in the years before 1812, see Martin, *Romantics*, pp. 58–142.

24. *Istoriia Moskvy v shesti tomakh* (Moscow, 1952), vol. 3, p. 46.

25. Hughes, *Romanovs*, pp. 143–4.

26. Richard S. Wortman, *Scenarios of Power: Myth and Ceremony in Russian Monarchy* (Princeton, NJ and Oxford, 2006), p. 95. The room, in Petersburg's Michael Castle, was still closed to visitors in the late 1990s.

27. Wortman, *Scenarios*, p. 99.

28. Wortman, *Scenarios*, p. 103; see also S. M. Liubetskii, *Starina Moskvy i russkogo naroda* (repr. Moscow, 2004), pp. 99–100.

29. *Istoriia Moskvy v shesti tomakh*, vol. 3, p. 47.

30. Martin, *Romantics*, p. 58.

31. For a thoughtful introduction, see A. M. Martin, 'Russia and the legacy of 1812', in *CHR*, vol. 2, esp. p. 148.

32. For an overview of political thought in the period, see Nicholas V. Riasanovsky and Mark D. Steinberg, *A History of Russia*, 7th edn (New York and Oxford, 2005), vol. 1, pp. 323–8.

33. Shchenkov, *Pamiatniki*, p. 43.

34. *Istoriia Moskvy v shesti tomakh*, vol. 3, p. 25.

35. RGADA, 197/1/39, 25; on Olenin's interventions in 1806–7, see Irina Bogatskaia's essay in Cynthia Hyla Whittaker, ed., *Visualizing Russia: Fedor Solntsev and Crafting a National Past* (Leiden and Boston, Mass., 2010), pp. 63–4.

36. S. P. Bartenev, *Moskovskii kreml' v starinu i teper'*, 2 vols. (St Petersburg, 1912 and 1918), vol. 1, p. 82; on Valuev, see *Materialy i issledovaniia*, vol. XVI, pp. 208–18.

37. Sytin, *Istoriia planirovki*, vol. 2, pp. 385–6.

38. The tower was the Gerbovaia bashnia. Among the other buildings demolished were the Trinity *podvor'e* and part of the Poteshnyi dvorets. See S. de Bartenev, *Le Grand Palais du Kremlin et ses neuf églises* (Moscow, 1912), p.19; Bartenev, *Moskovskii kreml'*, vol. 1, pp. 81–4; Shchenkov, *Pamiatniki*, p. 44.

39. F. F. Vigel', cited in Sytin, *Istoriia planirovki*, vol. 2, p. 386. The main fountain used to play where the Krasnaia Presnia metro station now stands. On the clearance and its effects, see also Posokhin, *Pamiatniki arkhitektury Moskvy*, pp. 146–8.

40. Adam Zamoyski, *1812: Napoleon's Fatal March on Moscow* (London, 2005), pp. 78–84.

41. Cited in Daria Olivier, *The Burning of Moscow 1812* (London, 1966), p. 33.

42. Ségur, *Expedition to Russia*, vol. 1, p. 214. Ségur believed the Russians had set the Smolensk fire.

43. General Armand de Caulaincourt, Duke of Vicenza, *With Napoleon in Russia*, from the Original Memoirs as edited by Jean Hanoteau; abridged with an introduction by George Libaire (Mineola, NY, 2005), p. 77.

44. Zamoyski, *1812*, pp. 220–21.

45. S. V. Bakhrushin, *Moskva v 1812* (Moscow, 1913), p. 13, citing M. A. Volkova.

46. Bakhrushin, *Moskva*, p. 33.

47. N. Dubrovin, *Otechestvennaia voina v pis'makh sovremennikov 1812–1815 gg.* (1882; repr. Moscow, 2006), p. 123.

48. Dubrovin, *Otechestvennaia voina v pis'makh*, p. 122 (doc. 119).

49. Bakhrushin, *Moskva*, p. 12.

50. Ségur, *Expedition to Russia*, vol. 1, pp. 330–33; Zamoyski, *1812*, p. 288.

51. Ségur, *Expedition to Russia*, vol. 2, p. 127.

52. Dubrovin, *Otechestvennaia voina v pis'makh*, p. 133.

53. M. P. Fabricius, *Kreml' v Moskve: ocherki i kartiny proshlogo i nastoiashchago* (Moscow, 1883), p. 172; Konstantin Mikhailov, *Unichtozhennyi Kreml'* (Moscow, 2007), p. 95.

54. Olivier, *Burning of Moscow*, p. 23.

55. Cited in Caulaincourt, *Napoleon in Russia*, p. 127.

56. Georges Lecointe de Laveau, *Moscou, avant et après l'incendie* (Paris, 1814), p. 111.

57. Ségur, *Expedition to Russia*, vol. 2, pp. 3–4, 27.

58. Ségur, *Expedition to Russia*, vol. 2, p. 34.

59. Ségur, *Expedition to Russia*, vol. 2, p. 37; Caulaincourt, *Napoleon in Russia*, p. 112 (on the clocks).

60. Cited in Kathleen Berton Murrell, *Moscow: An Architectural History* (London, 1977), p. 151.

61. Ségur, *Expedition to Russia*, vol. 2, pp. 40–42.

62. Ségur, *Expedition to Russia*, vol. 2, p. 40.

63. Olivier, *Burning of Moscow*, pp. 61–5; Ségur, *Expedition to Russia*, vol. 2, pp. 45–6.

64. One famous (though fictional) prisoner, whose story and encounters reflect later Russian perceptions of these events, was Pierre Bezuhov in Tolstoy's *War and Peace*.

65. Martin, 'Legacy of 1812', p. 148.

66. Dubrovin, *Otechestvennaia voina v pis'makh*, p. 252; Lecointe, *Moscou*, p. 116; Ségur, *Expedition to Russia*, vol. 2, p. 50.

67. Murrell, *Moscow*, p. 152.

68. Fabricius, *Kreml'*, p. 180.

69. Ségur, *Expedition to Russia*, vol. 2, p. 85.

70. Dubrovin, *Otechestvennaia voina v pis'makh*, pp. 169–70.

71. Bakhrushin, *Moskva*, p. 27; Murrell, *Moscow*, p. 153.

72. Ségur, *Expedition to Russia*, vol. 2, p. 119; Fabricius, *Kreml'*, p. 184; Lecointe, *Moscou*, p. 135.

73. Ségur, *Expedition to Russia*, vol. 2, p. 119.

74. Ségur, *Expedition to Russia*, vol. 2, p. 122.

75. Sytin, *Istoriia planirovki*, vol. 3, p. 30.

76. Sytin, *Istoriia planirovki*, vol. 3, p. 25.

77. Sytin, *Istoriia planirovki*, vol. 3, p. 115.

78. Bakhrushin, *Moskva*, p. 36.

79. The figures testifying to this appear in Sytin, *Istoriia planirovki*, vol. 3, p. 34.

80. Martin, *Romantics*, p. 142; P.-P. de Ségur, *Defeat: Napoleon's Russian Campaign*, trans. J. David (New York, 2008), p. 92; translator's note.

81. For details, see Rostopchin's letter of 27 October 1812 to Viazmitinov and Balashov, reprinted in *Russkii arkhiv*, 3, 1 (1881), p. 222.

82. Martin, *Romantics*, p. 136.

83. Dubrovin, *Otechestvennaia voina v pis'makh*, p. 253.

84. Dubrovin, *Otechestvennaia voina v pis'makh*, pp. 314–17, citing Avgustin's letter of 12 November 1812.

85. L. Tolstoy, *War and Peace*, trans. Rosemary Edmonds (London, 1982), p. 1314.

86. Population figures from Sytin, *Istoriia planirovki*, vol. 3, p. 33; on planning, see Albert J. Schmidt, 'The restoration of Moscow after 1812', *Slavic Review*, 40 (Spring 1981), pp. 37–48.

87. Fabricius, *Kreml'*, p. 186.

88. Schmidt, *Architecture and Planning*, p. 153; Sytin, *Istoriia planirovki*, vol. 3, pp. 125–6.

89. Sytin, *Istoriia planirovki*, vol. 3, p. 64.

90. Marquis de Custine, *Empire of the Czar: A Journey Through Eternal Russia*, repr. with an intro. by George F. Kennan (New York, 1989), p. 405.

91. Slavina, *Ton*, p. 93.

92. Sytin, *Istoriia planirovki*, vol. 3, p. 175.

93. Shchenkov, *Pamiatniki*, p. 62, citing RGIA, 471/1/292.

94. On gothic reconstructions, see Dmitry Shvidkovsky, *Russian Architecture and the West* (New Haven, Conn. and London, 2007), p. 326, and for the Catherine Church, see also Mikhailov, *Unichtozhennyi*, p. 177. For the Filaret Tower, see Shchenkov, *Pamiatniki*, p. 65.

95. Cited in Zabelin, *Istoriia goroda Moskvy*, p. 217.

96. The red paint was applied in 1827. See N. A. Skvortsov, *Arkheologiia i topografiia Moskvy: kurs lektsii* (Moscow, 1913), p. 103. The walls, but not the towers, were also lime-washed several times between 1818 and 1849.

97. Bove's painting is reproduced in G. I. Vedernikova, ed., *Oblik staroi Moskvy* (Moscow, 1997), p. 79. The lime-trees were his own idea, and formed part of his landscaped garden project. Other contemporary images are reproduced in the same volume, and also, among others, in E. Ducamp, ed., *Imperial Moscow: The Moscow Kremlin in Watercolour* (Paris, 1994).

98. Martin, 'Legacy of 1812', p. 150.

99. On memorial plans, see Sytin, *Istoriia planirovki*, vol. 3, p. 165.

100. Quarenghi's entry, for instance, was almost entirely based on the Pantheon, complete with portico and open dome. See E. Kirichenko, *Khram Khrista Spasitelia v Moskve* (Moscow, 1992), p. 19.

101. Sytin, *Istoriia planirovki*, vol. 3, p. 166; Martin, 'Legacy of 1812', p. 149. It was moved to its current site, near the Lobnoe mesto, in 1825.

102. On this, see Richard Wortman's essay in Whittaker, ed., *Visualizing Russia*, pp. 22–3. The helmet had, in fact, been fashioned in the seventeenth century for Mikhail Romanov.

103. Vitberg's cathedral is explored in detail in Kirichenko, *Khram Khrista*, pp. 28–37.

104. Custine, *Empire of the Czar*, pp. 136–7.

105. Custine, *Empire of the Czar*, p. 157.

106. R. Taruskin, *Defining Russia Musically* (Princeton, NJ, 1997), p. 26.

107. Custine, *Empire of the Czar*, pp. 165 and 171.

108. Snegirev's diaries give a vivid, if stuffy, picture of this social circle. See *Dnevnik Ivana Mikhailovicha Snegireva, vol 1, 1822–1852* (Moscow, 1904).

109. Custine, *Empire of the Czar*, pp. 392–5, 410.

110. Custine, *Empire of the Czar*, p. 184.

111. Custine, *Empire of the Czar*, p. 426.

112. Mikhail Bykovsky's lecture of 1834, cited in Shvidkovsky, *Russian Architecture*, p. 326.

113. Cited in Bartenev, *Grand Palais*, pp. 20–22.

114. Biographical notes from Slavina, *Ton*, p. 205.

115. Brumfield, *Russian Architecture*, p 398; Shvidkovsky, *Russian Architecture*, p. 328.

116. On the style, see Slavina, *Ton*, p. 102.

117. RGADA, 1239/22/27, especially l. 35; on the railwaymen, see ibid., l. 11.

118. The bundles of these, including accounts as well as detailed daily reports, are in RGADA, 1239/22/dd. 3–69.

119. Bartenev, *Grand Palais*, p. 25.

120. Richard Southwell Bourke, 6th Earl of Mayo, *St Petersburg and Moscow: A Visit to the Court of the Czar*, cited in Lawrence Kelly, ed., *Moscow: A Traveller's Companion* (London, 1983), p. 128.

121. Slavina, *Ton*, pp. 166–7; Bartenev, *Grand Palais*, p. 25.

122. Bartenev, *Grand Palais*, p. 26.

123. Bartenev, *Grand Palais*, p. 26.

124. I. Snegirev, *Moskva: Podrobnoe istoricheskoe i arkheologicheskoe opisanie goroda*, vol. 2 (Moscow, 1875), pp. 23–5; for drawings, see N. D. Izvekov, *Tserkov vo imia Rozhdestva Sv. Ioanna Predtechi v Moskovskom Kremle* (Moscow, 1913).

125. See Snegirev, *Dnevnik*, vol. 1, p. 65; Zabelin, *Istoriia goroda Moskvy*, p. 64.

126. Zabelin, *Istoriia goroda Moskvy*, pp. 64–5.

127. Zabelin, *Istoriia goroda Moskvy*, pp. 66–7.

128. Custine, *Empire of the Czar*, p. 429.

8 NOSTALGIA

1. For a bracing commentary from a different angle, see Richard Taruskin's remarks in his *Defining Russia Musically* (Princeton, NJ, 1997), p. 46.

2. A. G. Mazour, 'Modern Russian historiography', *JMH*, 9, 2 (June 1937), pp. 169–202.

3. For a brief overview and context, see Geoffrey Hosking, *Russia and the Russians: A History from Rus to the Russian Federation* (London, 2001), pp. 344–52.

4. One turning-point was Europe's revolutionary year of 1848. See I. Snegirev, *Dnevnik Ivana Mikhailovicha Snegireva, vol. 1, 1822–1852* (Moscow, 1904), p. 406.

5. The most famous expert in this field, Vladimir Dal (1801–72) was later one of Lenin's favourite authors.

6. S. Romaniuk, *Moskva: Vokrug Kremlia i Kitai-goroda. Putevoditel'* (Moscow, 2008), p. 52; on others, see, for example, the diaries of Ivan Snegirev, who frequently thanks his patrons for saving manuscripts by buying them.

7. The gallery's own guidebook supplies the basic facts. See V. Rodionov, ed., *The Tretyakov Gallery*, 4th edn (St Petersburg, 2006), pp. 4–10.

8. This theme has been explored extensively by Richard Wortman. See, for example, 'Moscow and St Petersburg: The problem of a political center in tsarist Russia, 1881–1914', in S. Wilentz, ed., *Rites of Power: Symbolism, Ritual and Politics Since the Middle Ages* (Philadelphia, Pa., 1985), pp. 260–62.

9. *The Letters of Tsar Nicholas and Empress Marie. Being the confidential correspondence between Nicholas II, last of the Tsars, and his mother, Dowager Empress Mariya Fedorovna*, ed. Edward J. Bing (London, 1937), pp. 143–4 (letter dated 5 April 1900).

10. This egg, one of the very few to have remained in Russia without interruption, is kept in the Kremlin museums.

11. Both quotations from Richard S. Wortman, *Scenarios of Power: Myth and Ceremony in Russian Monarchy*, 2 vols. (Princeton, NJ, 1995), vol. 1, p. 352.

12. The other two major national events of the era were the bicentenary of the Battle of Poltava in 1909 and the centenary of the national sacrifice at Borodino in 1912.

13. Richard Wortman also gives an excellent account of this. See his '"Invisible Threads": the historical imagery of the Romanov tercentenary', *Russian History*, 16, 2–4 (1989), pp. 389–408.

14. Imp. Mosk. arkheologicheskii inst., *Vystavka drevne-russkogo iskusstva ustroennaia v 1913 godu v oznamenovanie chestovaniia 300-letiia tsarstvovaniia Doma Romanovykh* (Moscow, 1913), p. 13.

15. See, for example, I. E. Zabelin, *Dnevniki i zapisnye knizhki* (repr. Moscow, 2001), p. 215.

16. See *Istoriia Moskvy s drevneishikh vremen do nashikh dnei*, vol. 3 (Moscow, 2000), pp. 17–21; S. O. Shmidt, ed., *Moskva: Entsiklopediia* (Moscow, 1997), p. 28.

17. For an insider's view of this colourful world, see V. A. Giliarovskii, *Moskva i Moskvichi* (Moscow, 1968).

18. Oleg Tarasov, *Icon and Devotion: Sacred Spaces in Imperial Russia* (London, 2002), pp. 30, 244.

19. The Museum of the History of Moscow has a fine collection, and photographs of some of them are reproduced in G. I. Vedernikova, *Oblik Staroi Moskvy: XVII–nachala XX veka* (Moscow, 1997), esp. pp. 200–225.

20. On Argamakov and his era, see M. K. Pavlovich, 'Proekt muzeefikatsii serediny XVIII veka: oruzheinaia palata i A. M. Argamakov', *Materialy i issledovaniia*, vol. XVI, pp. 202–7.

21. There is a discussion of the ewer, complete with photograph, in S. Orlenko, 'O rukomoinom pribore v posol'skom obychae XVI–XVII vekov', *Materialy i issledovaniia*, vol. XX, pp. 81–97.

22. He reorganized the Armoury staff in 1805. See A. P. Petukhova, 'P. S. Valuev i oruzheinaia palata', *Materialy i issledovaniia*, vol. XVI, pp. 210–11.

23. On Olenin, see V. Faibisovich, *Aleksei Nikolaevich Olenin: Opyt nauchnoi biografii* (St Petersburg, 2006).

24. Comments on this are offered separately by I. A. Rodimtseva and A. P. Petukhova in *Materialy i issledovaniia*, vol. XIV, pp. 7 and 14.

25. Petukhova, 'Valuev', p. 213.

26. A. P. Petukhova, 'Muzei v kremle kak gosudarstvennoe uchrezhdenie', *Materialy i issledovaniia*, vol. XIV, pp. 13–15.

27. Petukhova, 'Valuev', p. 216, citing the report by I. P. Polivanov.

28. See F. G. Solntsev, 'Moia zhizn'', *Russkaia starina*, 5 (1876).

29. Solntsev, 'Moia zhizn'', p. 634.

30. See Anne Odom, 'The politics of porcelain', in *At the Tsar's Table: Russian Imperial Porcelain from the Raymond F. Piper Collection* (Patrick and Beatrice Haggerty Museum of Art, Marquette University, 2001). See also G. V. Aksenova, *Russkii stil': Genii Fedora Solntseva* (Moscow, 2009), esp. pp. 37–8.

31. Wendy Salmond and Cynthia Hyla Whittaker, 'Fedor Solntsev and crafting the image of a Russian national past: the context', in Cynthia Hyla Whittaker, ed., *Visualizing Russia: Fedor Solntsev and Crafting the Image of a Russian National Past* (Leiden and Boston, 2010), p. 13.

32. A. S. Shchenkov, ed., *Pamiatniki arkhitektury v dorevoliutsionnoi Rossii*, vol. 1 (Moscow, 2002), p. 89.

33. Shchenkov, *Pamiatniki*, pp. 105–6; Wendy Salmond, *Russia Imagined, 1825–1925: The Art and Impact of Fedor Solntsev*, catalogue for an exhibition at the New York Public Library (New York, 2006); see also Aida Nasibova, *The Faceted Chamber in the Moscow Kremlin* (Leningrad, 1981), p. 13.

34. Essays on that theme by J. Robert Wright and Lauren M. O'Connell respectively are included in Whittaker, ed., *Visualizing Russia*.

35. For commentary, see Rosamund Bartlett, 'Russian culture: 1801–1917', in *CHR*, vol. 2, p. 98.

36. Although only 600 copies were produced, and fewer still survive, the entire collection can be seen by consulting the New York Public Library's online digital gallery.

37. *Materialy i issledovaniia*, vol. XIV, pp. 7–8 and 31–3; V. K. Trutovskii, *Oruzheinaia palata* (Moscow, 1914), p. 8.

38. Trutovskii, *Oruzheinaia palata*, p. 8.

39. For the cramped space, see E. I. Smirnova, 'Oruzheinaia palata. 19 vek', *Materialy i issledovaniia*, vol. XIV, p. 40; on the conditions and complaints of Armoury staff in 1861, see RGADA 1605/1/5957.

40. For an incidence of this in 1874, see Zabelin, *Dnevniki*, p. 111.

41. Trutovskii, *Oruzheinaia palata*, p. 11.

42. Visitor numbers for the period to the 1990s are discussed by L. I. Donetskaia and L. I. Kondrashova, 'Iz istorii prosvetitel'skoi deiatel'nosti v Moskovskom Kremle', *Materialy i issledovaniia*, vol. XIV, pp. 299–309; the nineteenth century is covered on p. 300.

43. The relevant report is RGADA 1605/1/5962.

44. Lindsey Hughes, *The Romanovs: Ruling Russia, 1613–1917* (London and New York, 2009), p. 183.

45. Trutovskii, *Oruzheinaia palata*, pp. 13–14. On the English silver, see Natalya Abramova and Irina Zagarodnaya, *Britannia and Muscovy: English Silver at the Court of the Tsars* (London, 2006).

46. The hardship felt by Kremlin staff in 1861 is set out in RGADA 1605/1/5957, which clearly shows that Moscow's palace personnel received smaller cuts from the overall imperial cake than St Petersburg's.

47. Hughes, *Romanovs*, p. 183.

48. M. Zakharov, *Putevoditel' po Moskve i ukazatel' eia dostoprimechatel'nosti* (Moscow, 1856), p. 15. Similar sentiments were ubiquitous in later nineteenth-century guides. See, for example, I. Kondrat'ev, *Sedaia starina Moskvy* (1893, repr. Moscow, 2006), p. 3.

49. Ivan Snegirev, *Dnevnik Ivana Mikhailovicha Snegireva*, vol. 2 (Moscow, 1905), p. 63.

50. Cited in J. Blum, *Lord and Peasant in Russia from the Ninth to the Nineteenth Century* (Princeton, NJ, 1971), p. 570.

51. For commentary, see Larisa Zakharova, 'The reign of Alexander II: a watershed?', in *CHR*, vol. 2, esp. p. 610.

52. It appeared in this guise at the coronation of Nicholas I, for example, and also later in the century. See Aksenova, *Russkii stil'*, pp. 19 and 31 (engravings from 1826 and 1851).

53. Zabelin, *Dnevniki*, pp. 91–2; Nasibova, *Faceted Chamber*, pp. 12–13.

54. *Opisanie sviashchennogo koronovaniia ikh imperatorskikh velichestv Gosudaria imperatora Aleksandra Tret'ego i Gosudaryni imperatritsy Marii Fedorovny vseia Rossii* (St Petersburg, 1883), especially pp. 43–6.

55. On the opening, see E. Kirichenko, *Khram Khrista Spasitelia v Moskve* (Moscow, 1992), pp. 140–45. See also Kathleen Berton Murrell, *Moscow: An Architectural History* (London, 1977), p. 170, which takes the usual view about the cathedral's disproportionate size, and T. Slavina, *Konstantin Ton* (Leningrad, 1989), pp. 112–15, which is more sympathetic (at least to Ton).

56. Kirichenko, *Khram*, p. 152.

57. I. E. Zabelin, *Istoriia goroda Moskvy* (Moscow, 1904; repr. 2005), pp. 259–6.

58. For an idea of these (from the leading architect himself), see N. V. Sultanov, *Pamiatnik imperatoru Aleksandru II v Kremle* (St Petersburg, 1898).

59. Konstantin Mikhailov, *Unichtozhennyi Kreml'* (Moscow, 2007), p. 203.

60. *Putevoditel' po Moskve* (Moscow, 1918), p. 10.

61. For the scarf, made by the Daniilov factory, see Vedernikova, *Oblik*, p. 223. As for the gilded youth, see RGADA 1239/24/2990, a 1914 register of fines and reprimands to Kremlin staff, which includes details of fines issued to Kremlin guards for allowing couples to smoke near the monument.

62. 'Steny Kremlya: Chto oni takoe, i chto oni mogli by byt',' *Russkii arkhiv*, 3 (1893), pp. 365–73.

63. Apollinari Vasnetsov published a collection of imaginary views of medieval Moscow in 1914, still available as his album *Drevniaia Moskva*. See also Shmidt, *Entsiklopediia*, pp. 158–9. Much of the brothers' work is still on show at the museum-reserve at Abramtsevo, near Moscow.

64. *Pravoslavnye sviatyni Moskovskogo Kremlia v istorii i kul'ture Rossii* (Moscow, 2006), p. 368.

65. GARF 130/2/160, 17.

66. *Pravoslavnye sviatyni*, p. 373.

67. On the Synod choir, which was sometimes joined by the great star Konstantin Rozov, see Kirichenko, *Khram*, pp. 190–93. The disappointed commentator was Tolstoy's widow, Sofiya. See *The Diaries of Sofia Tolstaya*, trans. Cathy Porter (London, 1985), p. 690 (entry for 12 March 1911).

68. On their resentment of the term, expressed in 1917, see RGADA 1239/24/3297, 1–3. The Russian word is *lakei*.

69. RGADA 1239/24/2893 (on the resident population in 1914) and 1239/24/2985, 90 on arrests.

70. Diary entry from Tolstaya, *Diaries*, p. 841; Tolstoy's account appears in Louise and Aylmer Maude's translation of *Anna Karenina* for The World's Classics (repr. Oxford, 1983), part 5, chapters 1–6, and this quotation is on p. 445.

71. RGADA 1239/3/19277 gives details of this process in 1857 and RGADA 1239/24/2986 discusses the same preparations for a state visit in 1914. On this occasion, the Kremlin administration was required to find accommodation for just over 2,000 military personnel alone.

72. Tolstaya, *Diaries*, p. 14 (29 Jan. 1862).

73. Snegirev, *Dnevnik*, vol. 1, p. 297.

74. Snegirev, *Dnevnik*, vol. 1, p. 302.

75. See Zabelin, *Dnevniki*, pp. 7–23.

76. Snegirev, *Dnevnik*, vol. 2, p. 35.

77. Zabelin, *Dnevniki*, p. 47.

78. Zabelin, *Dnevniki*, pp. 239 and 245.

79. For Sergei Aleksandrovich's anti-Semitism, see Richard S. Wortman, *Scenarios of Power: Myth and Ceremony in Russian Monarchy* (Princeton, NJ and Oxford, 2006), pp. 311–12.

80. Cited in Wortman, *Scenarios*, p. 364.

81. Zabelin, *Dnevniki*, p. 214.

82. Konstantin Bykovskii, cited in William Craft Brumfield, *A History of Russian Architecture* (Cambridge, 1997), p. 423.

83. A record of its publications was edited in 1915 by V. K. Trutovskii as *Spisok izdanii Imperatorskogo Moskovskogo Obshchestva po 50 let ego deiatel'nosti*. See also Shchenkov, *Pamiatniki*, p. 249.

84. For an account, see I. Mashkov, ed., *Otchet po restavratsii Bol'shogo Moskovskago Uspenkago Sobora* (Moscow, 1910), pp. 6–23. For the developing

criticism, which was led by I. E. Grabar, see the first report of the Commission for the Preservation of Historic and Artistic Treasures, reprinted in V. N. Kuchin, ed., *Iz istorii stroitel'stva sovetskoi kul'tury 1917–1918. Dokumenty i vospominaniia* (Moscow, 1964), pp. 149–53.

85. On the mosaics, and also other problems with the interior restoration, see B. Iu. Brandenburg et al., *Arkhitektor Ivan Mashkov* (Moscow, 2001), pp. 81–4. On the church's attitude to the building more generally, see RGADA 1239/24/3082.

86. Zabelin, *Dnevniki*, pp. 91–2.

87. See Zabelin, *Dnevniki*, pp. 17–18.

88. On the Kremlin trove, see T. D. Panova, 'Arkheologicheskoe izuchenie territorii Moskovskogo kremlia v kontse XVIII–XX veke', *Materialy i issledovaniia*, vol. XIV, esp. pp. 351–2.

89. Zabelin, *Dnevniki*, p. 112.

90. For a Soviet-era account, see V. M. Raushenbakh, 'Rossiia v 1861–1917g' in *Mezhdunarodnyi sovet muzeev: Konferentsiia komitet muzeev arkheologii i istorii* (Moscow and Leningrad, 1970), pp. 3–11.

91. These finds were lovingly explored in Zabelin, *Istoriia goroda Moskvy*, pp. 82–3.

92. Zabelin, *Dnevniki*, p. 91.

93. Panova, 'Arkheologicheskoe', p. 350.

94. N. P. Likhachev, *Biblioteka i arkhiv moskovskikh gosudarei v XVI stoletii* (St Petersburg, 1894), p. 4.

95. Zabelin, *Istoriia goroda Moskvy*, pp. 82–3.

96. Panova, 'Arkheologicheskoe', pp. 352–3.

97. N. A. Skvortsov, *Arkheologiia i topografiia Moskvy: Kurs lektsii* (Moscow, 1913), p. 80; Zabelin, *Istoriia goroda Moskvy*, p. 65.

98. Likhachev, *Biblioteka*, p. 1.

99. S. P. Bartenev, *Moskovskii kreml' v starinu i teper'*, 2 vols. (St Petersburg, 1912 and 1918), vol. 2, pp. 202–6; Likhachev, *Biblioteka*, p. 5.

100. Bartenev, *Moskovskii kreml'*, vol. 2, pp. 204–5.

101. Likhachev, *Biblioteka*, pp. 2–5.

102. For some examples, see Likhachev, op. cit. and also A. I. Sobolevskii, 'Eshche raz o kremlevskom tainike i tsarskoi biblioteke', *Arkheologicheskie izvestiia i zametki*, no. 12 (1894), pp. 400–403; idem (1894), pp. 33–44; see also S. O. Shmidt, ed., *Biblioteka Ivana Groznogo. Rekonstruktsiia i bibliograficheskoe opisanie* (Moscow, 1982).

103. Panova, 'Arkheologicheskoe', p. 353.

104. The Moscow Duma was set up under a statute of 1870. By 1905 it had 160 deputies and met in splendid premises on Voskresenskaia Square. See *Istoriia Moskvy s drevneishikh vremen*, vol. 3, pp. 27–8.

105. Two reprints appeared in 2005 alone. The book is also available in at least three versions as a PDF.

106. *Moskovskii kreml' v starinu i teper'*. The volumes appeared between 1912 and 1918. They were reprinted in 2011.

107. A list of residents appears in RGADA 1239/24/2985.

108. Built in 1900; see *Istoriia Moskvy s drevneishikh vremen*, vol. 3, p. 21.

109. Palace staff uniforms are debated in RGADA 1239/24/2894 and 2901.

110. Mikhailov, *Unichtozhennyi*, pp. 275–81.

111. Zabelin, *Dnevniki*, pp. 213–15.

112. *Letters of Nicholas and Marie*, p. 188.

113. *Letters of Nicholas and Marie*, pp. 188 and 203.

114. *Istoriia Moskvy s drevneishchikh vremen*, vol. 3, pp. 97–100.

115. The best examples are printed in Vasnetsov, *Drevniaia Moskva*.

116. See Wortman, *Scenarios*, pp. 334–43.

117. The phrase 'ideal Christian state' occurs on the first page of text in Nicholas II's coronation album. *Sviashchennoe koronovanie . . . Nikolaia Aleksandrovicha*, vol. 1, p. 1.

118. I. Tokmakov, *Istoricheskoe opisanie vsekh koronatsii rossiiskikh tsarei, imperatorov i imperatrits* (Moscow, 1896). The picture of Riurik is on p. vii; there are equally beguiling ones of St Vladimir of Kiev and Moscow's Vasily II.

119. *Sviashchennoe koronovanie . . . Nikolaia Aleksandrovicha*, vol. 1, p. 245.

120. *Letters of Nicholas and Marie*, pp. 115–16.

121. *The Times*, 10 May 1896, p. 3.

122. *The Graphic*, Saturday 6 June 1896. More recent casualty estimates would suggest between 1,000 and (at most) 2,000 fatalities.

123. Illus; *Sviashchennoe koronovanie . . . Nikolaia Aleksandrovicha*, vol. 1, pp. 176, 284–5.

9 ACROPOLIS

1. For the Paris event, see Jennifer Homans, *Apollo's Angels: A History of Ballet* (London, 2010), pp. 317–18 and Modris Eksteins, *Rites of Spring* (London, 1989), pp. 10–16.

2. For contrasting views of the ballet's significance, see Richard Taruskin, *Defining Russia Musically* (Princeton, NJ, 1997), pp. 49 and 378 and Homans, *Apollo's Angels*, p. 312.

3. Critics' comments from A. V. Krusanov, *Russkii avangard, 1907–1932: istoricheskii obzor v trekh tomakh* (Moscow, 1996), vol. 1, pt 2, pp. 196–8; see also *The Knave of Diamonds in the Russian Avant Garde*, trans. Kenneth MacInnes (St Petersburg, 2004). For the artists, see Aristarkh Lentulov, *Katalog vystavki* (Moscow, 1968) and http://www.foto-a.narod.ru/collection/polonchuk/ropot/ropot_dok_3.htm (accessed 23 Jan. 2013) for a facsimile of the 1914 exhibition catalogue.

4. Cited from Norbert Lynton, *Tatlin's Tower: Monument to Revolution* (New Haven, Conn. and London, 2009), p. 46. Malevich's views on art can also be found in his *The Non-Objective World*, ed. Howard Dearstyne (Mineola, NY, 2003), and see also Charlotte Douglas, *Kazimir Malevich* (London, 1994).

5. Richard Stites, *Revolutionary Dreams* (Oxford, 1991), p. 170.

6. *Istoriia Moskvy s drevneishikh vremen do nashikh dnei v trekh tomakh*, vol. 3 (Moscow, 2000), p. 33.

7. Evgenii Tret'iakov, 'Otkrytie metro', *Moskva*, 9 (September 2007), p. 137.

8. *Istoriia Moskvy s drevneishikh vremen*, vol. 3, pp. 21–2 and 27.

9. Cited in Karl Schlögel, *Moscow* (London, 2005), p. 18.

10. Timothy J. Colton, *Moscow: Governing the Socialist Metropolis* (Cambridge, Mass., 1995), pp. 56–7.

11. *Istoriia Moskvy s drevneishikh vremen*, vol. 3, p. 23.

12. *Istoriia Moskvy s drevneishikh vremen*, vol. 3, p. 108. See also J. N. Westwood, *Endurance and Endeavour: Russian History 1812–1992*, 4th edn (Oxford, 1993), pp. 210–11.

13. V. N. Kuchin, ed., *Iz istorii stroitel'stva sovetskoi kul'tury 1917–1918. Dokumenty i vospominaniia* (Moscow, 1964), p. 332.

14. RGADA 1239/24/3012, 99–105.

15. RGADA 1239/24/3012, 20 and 28.

16. Westwood, *Endurance*, p. 212. On the legendary courage of Russian troops, see C. Merridale, *Ivan's War* (London, 2005), pp. 11–12.

17. RGADA 1239/24/3012, 106.

18. The most vivid account is still O. Figes, *A People's Tragedy* (London, 1996), pp. 307–44.

19. The Russian calendar makes the events of this year more than usually difficult to follow. Nicholas abdicated on 15 March according to the new (and current) calendar, but in Russia at the time the date was calculated differently, and lagged twelve days behind the European norm.

20. Allan Monkhouse, *Moscow, 1911–1933* (London, 1933), pp. 59–61.

21. Eduard M. Dune, *Notes of a Red Guard* (Urbana, Ill. and Chicago, 1993), pp. 32–4.

22. Dune, *Red Guard*, p. 35.

23. RGADA 1239/24/3230, 2.

24. RGADA 1239/24/3230, 5.

25. RGADA 1239/24/3297, 1–3.

26. RGADA 1239/24/3297, 31.

27. Near Trubnaia Square. For an account, see V. S. Kundius' memoir in Kuchin, *Iz istorii*, pp. 298–9.

28. See I. E. Grabar, *Pis'ma, 1917–1941* (Moscow, 1977), p. 15. See also V. P. Lapshin, *Khudozhestvennaia zhizn' Moskvy i Petrograda v 1917 godu*

(Moscow, 1983), p. 232. On the notion of an acropolis, see also Elena Gagarina, writing in *Materialy i issledovaniia*, vol. XV, p. 200; Konstantin Mikhailov, *Unichtozhennyi Kreml'* (Moscow, 2007), p. 38.

29. A. S. Shchenkov, ed., *Pamiatniki arkhitektury v Sovetskom Soiuze* (Moscow, 2004), pp. 14–15.

30. Lapshin, *Khudozhestvennaia zhizn'*, pp. 84–5.

31. For a short biography, see http://www.kreml.ru/ru/history/ReferenceData/guidance-museum/Trutovskiy (accessed 6 June 2012).

32. RGADA 1239/24/3272, 1–2.

33. A. Resis, ed., *Molotov Remembers: Conversations with Felix Chuev* (Chicago, 1993), p. 98.

34. For the view of a conservative Moscow historian, see Terence Emmons, trans. and ed., *Time of Troubles: The Diary of Iurii Vladimirovich Got'e* (London, 1988), pp. 72–3.

35. Monkhouse, *Moscow*, p. 67.

36. John Reed, *Ten Days That Shook the World* (Harmondsworth, 1966), p. 226.

37. Lapshin, *Khudozhestvennaia zhizn'*, p. 228.

38. Episkop Nestor Kamchatskii, 'Rasstrel' Moskovskogo Kremlia', repr. *Moskovskii zhurnal*, 4 (1992), p. 24.

39. A. N. Kashevarov, *Pravoslavnaia rossiiskaia tserkov' i sovetskoe gosudarstvo, 1917–1922* (Moscow, 2005), p. 87.

40. See *Novaia zhizn'*, 3 November 1917. This translation cited from Reed, *Ten Days*, pp. 220–21.

41. Emmons, *Got'e*, p. 80.

42. Monkhouse, *Moscow*, p. 68.

43. Lapshin, *Khudozhestvennaia zhizn'*, p. 234.

44. Reed, *Ten Days*, pp. 227–30.

45. A. Abramov, *U Kremlevskoi steny* (Moscow, 1981), p. 34; Kashevarov, *Pravoslavnaia rossiiskaia*, p. 90.

46. Abramov, *Kremlevskoi steny*, p. 52.

47. Lapshin, *Khudozhestvennaia zhizn'*, p. 226.

48. Episkop Nestor, 'Rasstrel', pp. 27–9.

49. Lapshin, *Khudozhestvennaia zhizn'*, p. 228.

50. Lapshin, *Khudozhestvennaia zhizn'*, p. 231; for Malevich, see Shchenkov, *Pamiatniki . . . v Sovetskom Soiuze*, p. 49.

51. S. V. Mironenko, ed., *Moskovskii kreml' tsitadel' Rossii* (Moscow, 2008), p. 218.

52. P. D. Malkov, *Zapiski komendanta kremlia* (Moscow, 1968), p. 118.

53. Grabar, *Pis'ma*, pp. 22–3.

54. Joel A. Bartsch and the curators of the Moscow Kremlin museums, eds., *Kremlin Gold: 1000 Years of Russian Jewels and Gems* (New York, 2000), p. 62.

55. Decree on the Kremlin monuments, 5 January 1918, reprinted in Kuchin, *Iz istorii*, p. 55; see also Mironenko, *Moskovskii kreml'*, p. 185.

56. Decree of April 1918 in Kuchin, *Iz istorii*, p. 69.

57. Testimony of V. C. Kundius in Kuchin, *Iz istorii*, pp. 301–2.

58. Shchenkov, *Pamiatniki ... v Sovetskom Soiuze*, p. 49; Emmons, *Got'e*, p. 91.

59. Emmons, *Got'e*, p. 102.

60. Kuchin, *Iz istorii*, p. 63; Shchenkov, *Pamiatniki ... v Sovetskom Soiuze*, p. 49.

61. Kuchin, *Iz istorii*, p. 65.

62. On the commission, see Oranovsky, 'Kreml' akropol'', in Kuchin, *Iz istorii*, pp. 317–56.

63. Shchenkov, *Pamiatniki ... v Sovetskom Soiuze*, p. 17.

64. Mironenko, *Moskovskii kreml'*, p. 218.

65. Oranovsky's testimony in Kuchin, *Iz istorii*, p. 322.

66. The letter is reproduced in Kuchin, *Iz istorii*, p. 264.

67. Emmons, *Got'e*, p. 121.

68. Kuchin, *Iz istorii*, p. 157.

69. V. D. Bonch-Bruevich, *Vospominaniia o Lenine* (Moscow, 1965), p. 210. See also Malkov, *Zapiski*, p. 116.

70. Mironenko, *Moskovskii kreml'*, p. 185.

71. *Istoriia Moskvy s drevneishikh vremen*, vol. 3, pp. 122–3.

72. Robert Service, *Lenin: A Biography* (London, 2000), p. 343.

73. Bonch-Bruevich, *Vospominaniia*, p.197.

74. Mironenko, *Moskovskii kreml'*, p. 194.

75. Bonch-Bruevich, *Vospominaniia*, pp. 200–205.

76. Kuchin, *Iz istorii*, p. 80.

77. Malkov, *Zapiski*, p. 117.

78. Malkov, *Zapiski*, p. 116.

79. Malkov, *Zapiski*, p. 113.

80. Bonch-Bruevich, *Vospominaniia*, p. 211.

81. Service, *Lenin*, p. 345.

82. On the lift, see GARF R-130/2/199, 17; for the plumbing, see Aleksandr Kolesnichenko, 'Mesto propiski: Moskva', *Argumenty i fakty*, 17 June 2009.

83. Interview, Moscow, September 2008; see also S. O. Shmidt, ed., *Moskva: Entsiklopediia* (Moscow, 1997), p. 401.

84. Resis, *Molotov Remembers*, p. 98.

85. Shchenkov, *Pamiatniki ... v Sovetskom Soiuze*, pp. 20 and 57.

86. Leon Trotsky, *My Life* (Harmondsworth, 1984), p. 368.

87. G. Bordiugov (compiler), 'Kak zhili v kremle v 1920 godu: Materialy kremlevskoi komissii TsK RKP(b)', in V. A. Kozlov, ed., *Neizvestnaia Rossiia* (Moscow, 1992), vol. 2, p. 267. The material cited here gives a figure of 1,112, which other sources confirm.

88. Mironenko, *Moskvoskii kreml'*, p. 210. Roughly half of the total were civilians, the rest were soldiers or members of the security forces. See Bordiugov, 'Kak zhili v kremle', p. 267.

89. Trotsky, *My Life*, p. 366.

90. Trotsky, *My Life*, pp. 366–7.

91. GARF R-130/2/160, 203.

92. GARF R-130/2/199, 204; see also Mironenko, *Moskovskii kreml'*, p. 210.

93. GARF R-130/2/199, 203.

94. Malkov, *Zapiski*, p. 120.

95. GARF R-130/2/162.

96. Ia. N. Shchapov, ed., *Russkaia pravoslavnaia tserkov' i kommunisticheskoe gosudarstvo, 1917–1941* (Moscow, 1996), p. 39.

97. GARF R-130/2/160, 7.

98. GARF R-130/2/160, 17.

99. Cited by T. A. Tutova in *Materialy i issledovaniia*, vol. XX, p. 305. For the whole incident, see her 'Trotskaia protiv Stalina. Piat' pisem k Leninu ob Oruzhenoi palate', *Materialy i issledovaniia*, vol. XX, pp. 298–322.

100. Mironenko, *Moskovskii kreml'*, p. 285.

101. Dune, *Red Guard*, p. 86.

102. *Istoriia Moskvy s drevneishikh vremen*, vol. 3, pp. 134–5.

103. Trotsky, *My Life*, pp. 366–7. See also Dune, *Red Guard*, p. 86.

104. Bordiugov, 'Kak zhili v kremle', pp. 265 and 270.

105. Tamara Kondratieva, *Gouverner et nourrir: du pouvoir en Russie, XVIe–XXe siècles* (Paris, 2002), p. 174.

106. Service, *Lenin*, p. 368.

107. Cited in D. Volkogonov, *The Rise and Fall of the Soviet Empire: Political Leaders from Lenin to Gorbachev* (London, 1998), p. 63.

108. Malkov, *Zapiski*, pp. 159–60.

109. On the garage, see *Argumenty i fakty*, 23 March 2011 ('Shef v Kreml'! Istorii iz zhizni garazha osobogo naznacheniia'); Malkov, *Zapiski*, p. 109; Mironenko, *Moskovskii kreml'*, p. 210; on the Delaunay-Belleville, see also Sean McMeekin, *History's Greatest Heist* (New Haven, Conn., 2008), p. 39. The tsar had owned a fleet of his favourite marque, so there were a few replacements at Lenin's disposal.

110. *Istoriia Moskvy s drevneishikh vremen*, vol. 3, p. 127.

111. Kondratieva, *Gouverner et nourrir*, p. 101; Bonch-Bruevich, *Vospominaniia*, p. 225.

112. For a discussion, see C. Merridale, *Night of Stone* (London, 2000), p. 129.

113. Kuchin, *Iz istorii*, pp. 25–6. See also A. Mikhailov, 'Programma monumental'noi propagandy', *Iskusstvo*, 4 (1968), pp. 31–4 and idem, 5 (1968), pp. 39–42.

114. Malkov, *Zapiski*, pp. 218–19.

115. By July 1918. See the report of the State Control Commission in Kuchin, *Iz istorii*, p. 105.

116. Mikhailov, 'Programma monumentalnoi', *Iskusstvo*, 4, p. 34; see also Kuchin, *Iz istorii*, pp. 32–7 for resolutions reflecting Lenin's impatience.

117. On Gerasimov, see Stites, *Revolutionary Dreams*, p. 50.

118. Kuchin, *Iz istorii*, p. 45.

119. Abramov, *Kremlevskoi steny*, p. 45. See also Stites, *Revolutionary Dreams*, p. 87.

120. There was also a request to open the reserve in Holy Week. See GARF R-130/2/161, 1.

121. Kuchin, *Iz istorii*, pp. 353–4.

122. GARF R-130/2/157, 3–4.

123. N. A. Krivova, *Vlast' i tserkov' v 1922–1925 gg.* (Moscow, 1997), p. 15; Shchenkov, *Pamiatniki . . . v Sovetskom Soiuze*, p. 10.

124. Shchapov, *Russkaia pravoslavnaia tserkov'*, p. 36, resolution of 17 March 1918.

125. Shchapov, *Russkaia pravoslavnaia tserkov'*, p. 36.

126. GARF R-130/2/160, 2; see also Shchapov, *Russkaia pravoslavnaia tserkov'*, pp. 40–41; on the cult of the saints in general, see S. A. Smith, 'Bones of contention: Bolsheviks and the struggle against relics, 1918–1930', *Past and Present*, 204 (August 2009), pp. 155–94.

127. Kuchin, *Iz istorii*, pp. 37–45, citing SNK resolution of 17 July 1918.

128. Kuchin, *Iz istorii*, pp. 45–6 and 164 ff. on the chaos in the artistic world.

129. *Istoriia Moskvy v shesti tomakh* (Moscow, 1953) vol. 6, p. 186 describes the bas-relief on 1 May 1919, when it was also decorated with palm-fronds and pictures of Karl Marx.

130. Shchenkov, *Pamiatniki . . . v Sovetskom Soiuze*, p. 8.

131. Krivova, *Vlast' i tserkov'*, p. 30.

132. Krivova, *Vlast' i tserkov'*, p. 30.

133. Cited in Richard Pipes, *The Unknown Lenin* (New Haven, Conn., 1996), pp. 152–5.

134. Krivova, *Vlast' i tserkov'*, p. 50.

135. McMeekin, *Greatest Heist*, p. 83.

136. McMeekin, *Greatest Heist*, p. 84.

137. The figure was well over 1,000. See McMeekin, *Greatest Heist*, p. 83.

138. Shchenkov, *Pamiatniki . . . v Sovetskom Soiuze*, p. 23.

139. Mikhailov, *Unichtozhennyi*, p. 114.

140. Grabar's declaration of 26 July 1922 (*Pis'ma*, p. 65) refers to this.

141. Grabar, *Pis'ma*, p. 179.

142. Shchenkov, *Pamiatniki . . . v Sovetskom Soiuze*, p. 21.

143. E. Kirichenko, *Khram Khrista Spasitelia v Moskve* (Moscow, 1992), p. 228.

144. The deliberations of the delightfully named Immortalization Commission can be followed in Y. M. Lopukhin, *Bolezn', smert' i bal'zamirovanie V. I. Lenina* (Moscow, 1997).

10 RED FORTRESS

1. Walter Benjamin, 'Moscow', in *Reflections, Essays, Aphorisms, Autobiographical Writings*, ed. Peter Demetz (New York, 1978), pp. 101 and 126.

2. *Istoriia Moskvy s drevneishikh vremen do nashikh dnei v trekh tomakh*, vol. 3 (Moscow, 2000), pp. 148 (on unemployment) and 151 (on the workers' meetings).

3. For a discussion and illustrations, see Catherine Cooke, *Russian Avant-garde: Theories of Art, Architecture and the City* (London, 1995).

4. A point made by Dmitry Shvidkovsky, *Russian Architecture and the West* (New Haven, Conn. and London, 2007), p. 364.

5. On Baranovsky's labours, see Iu. A. Bychkov et al., eds., *Petr Baranovskii: trudy, vospominaniia sovremennikov* (Moscow, 1996).

6. A. S. Shchenkov, ed., *Pamiatniki arkhitektury v Sovetskom Soiuze* (Moscow, 2004), p. 145.

7. S. Dmitrievsky, *Sovetskie portrety* (Berlin, 1932), p. 59.

8. E. Kirichenko, *Khram Khrista Spasitelia v Moskve* (Moscow, 1992), p. 221.

9. Kirichenko, *Khram*, p. 221, citing Grabar's article in *Stroitel'stvo Moskvy*, 7 (1925).

10. V. Kozlov, 'Pervye snosy', *Arkhitektura i stroitel'stvo Moskvy*, 8 (August 1990), pp. 27–8.

11. Shchenkov, *Pamiatniki*, pp. 35–6.

12. Cited in Shchenkov, *Pamiatniki*, p. 42.

13. On the uses of the Kazan Cathedral, see Shchenkov, *Pamiatniki*, p. 166.

14. Shchenkov, *Pamiatniki*, p. 36; see also Timothy J. Colton, *Moscow: Governing the Socialist Metropolis* (Cambridge, Mass., 1995), p. 277; Cooke, *Russian Avant-garde*, p. 202.

15. Shchenkov, *Pamiatniki*, p. 83.

16. Cited in Kirichenko, *Khram*, pp. 224–5.

17. V. Kozlov, 'Tragediia monastyrei: god 1929-i', *Moskovskii zhurnal*, 1 (1991), p. 34; see also Kirichenko, *Khram*, p. 225.

18. Kirichenko, *Khram*, p. 225. The plan was to use the same themes for exhibitions in the Kremlin's Armoury Museum. See I. Ia. Kachalova, 'Istoriia otdela pamiatnikov kremlia,' *Materialy i issledovaniia*, vol. XIV, p. 184.

19. Richard Stites, *Revolutionary Dreams* (Oxford, 1991), pp. 109–12.

20. Kirichenko, *Khram*, p. 246.

21. V. A. Kozlov, ed., *Neizvestnaia Rossiia*, vol. 2 (Moscow, 1992), pp. 337–48, and Kirichenko, *Khram*, p. 251.

22. Cooke, *Russian Avant-garde*, pp. 202–6.

23. There are numerous histories of this. For a summary, see Shchenkov, *Pamiatniki*, pp. 35–6.

24. Shchenkov, *Pamiatniki*, p. 43.

25. Shvidkovsky, *Russian Architecture*, p. 369; for an illustration from the 1940s, see Shchenkov, *Pamiatniki*, p. 210.

26. S. V. Mironenko, ed., *Moskovskii kreml': tsitadel' Rossii* (Moscow, 2008), p. 239.

27. Mironenko, *Moskovskii kreml'*, pp. 294–5.

28. Mironenko, *Moskovskii kreml'*, p. 295.

29. Kachalova, 'Istoriia', p. 183.

30. Kozlov, 'Tragediia monastyrei', p. 38.

31. Mironenko, *Moskovskii kreml'*, p. 296.

32. Kachalova, 'Istoriia', p. 183.

33. Kozlov, 'Tragediia monastyrei', p. 39.

34. See T. D. Panova, *Kremlevskie usypal'nitsy* (Moscow, 2003), pp. 198–202.

35. Some of the stones feature in the diorama that was opened in 2009 in the Ivan the Great bell tower, for instance, although the tale of how they got there is not part of the commentary.

36. Kozlov, 'Tragediia monastyrei', p. 39.

37. *Pravoslavnye sviatyni Moskovskogo Kremlia v istorii i kul'ture Rossii* (Moscow, 2006), p. 308; Rerberg had earlier designed the Kievskii railway station.

38. A point protesters did make at the time. See *Pravoslavnye sviatyni*, p. 308.

39. The respondent was interviewed in Moscow in September 2007.

40. Mironenko, *Moskovskii kreml'*, p. 297.

41. RGASPI 671/1/103, 163.

42. Kachalova, 'Istoriia', p. 184.

43. Colton, *Moscow*, p. 268.

44. On the decision, see Mironenko, *Moskovskii kreml'*, p. 300. The proposer was Abel Enukidze. For this specific use of fireworks, see *Stolitsa*, 3 (1991), pp. 38–9.

45. A. Voyce, *The Moscow Kremlin: Its History, Architecture, and Art Treasures* (London, 1955), p. 67.

46. Mironenko, *Moskovskii kreml'*, p. 300.

47. Mironenko, *Moskovskii kreml'*, p. 302.

48. T. V. Tolstaia, 'Muzei "Uspenskii sobor" Moskovskogo kremlia. Stranitsy istorii', *Materialy i issledovaniia*, vol. XIV, p. 209.

49. Kachalova, 'Istoriia', p. 186, citing the Kremlin archive.

50. Lidiya Shatunovskaya, *Zhizn' v Kremle* (New York, 1982), p. 25.

51. See *Materialy i issledovaniia*, vol. XIV, pp. 105–10.

52. T. A. Tutova, 'Direktor oruzheinoi palaty D. D. Ivanov i bor'ba za sokhranenie muzeinikh tsennostei v 1922–1929 godakh', *Materialy i issledovaniia*, vol. XIV, pp. 106–9.

53. The practice was called *vydvizhenie*, 'promotion', and it makes today's affirmative action look anaemic.

54. M. K. Pavlovich, 'Oruzheinaia palata Moskovskogo Kremlia v 1930-e gody', *Materialy i issledovaniia*, vol. XIV, pp. 113–15.

55. M. Dokuchaev, *Moskva. Kreml'. Okhrana.* (Moscow, 1995), p. 49.

56. The so-called Kremlin affair. See below, pp. 321–5.

57. Pavlovich, 'Oruzheinaia palata', p. 116.

58. Pavlovich, 'Oruzheinaia palata', p. 117.

59. Kachalova, 'Istoriia', p. 186.

60. I. I. Shits, cited in I. V. Pavlova, *Stalinizm: Stanovlenie mekhanizma vlasti* (Novosibirsk, 1993), p. 77.

61. Stalin's date of birth was only one of many secrets that he kept by promoting a lie. See Robert Service, *Stalin: A Biography* (London, 2004), pp. 13–14.

62. For a thorough exposition, see Pavlova, *Stalinizm,* esp. pp. 90–138.

63. Pavlova, *Stalinizm*, p. 87.

64. Pavlova, *Stalinizm*, p. 90.

65. Mironenko, *Moskovskii kreml'*, p. 248; for later telephone systems, see Kolesnichenko's article on the subject in *Argumenty i fakty*, 16 February 2011.

66. For Molotov's own comment on the bugging, see A. Resis, ed., *Molotov Remembers: Conversations with Felix Chuev* (Chicago, 1993), p. 224. For the Kremlin systems more generally, see also Mironenko, *Moskovskii kreml'*, esp. pp. 232–48, Tamara Kondratieva, *Gouverner et nourrir: du pouvoir en Russie, XVIe–XXe siècles* (Paris, 2002), p. 173 (citing Presidential library staff), and Dokuchaev, *Moskva.*, p. 64.

67. See Dmitrievsky, *Sovetskie portrety*, pp. 159–63, for a menu of police techniques.

68. Boris Bazhanov, cited in Colton, *Moscow,* p. 162.

69. B. S. Ilizarov, *Tainaia zhizn' Stalina* (Moscow, 2002), pp. 152–3, testimony of aviator Yakovlev from 1939.

70. Ibid., p. 152.

71. Details from Mironenko, *Moskovskii kreml'*, pp. 378–82; see also Pavel Sudoplatov (who called on Stalin in sinister circumstances), *Spetsoperatsii: Lubianka i kreml' 1930–1950 gody* (Moscow, 1997), p. 102. On Poskrebyshev and Stalin's inner 'kitchen', see also Pavlova, *Stalinizm*, p. 137.

72. The argument is elaborated at far greater length in Kondratieva, *Gouverner et nourrir.*

73. Pavlova, *Stalinizm*, p. 74.

74. On the facilities more generally, see, for example, Shatunovskaya, *Zhizn' v Kremle*, pp. 42–4 and Pavlova, *Stalinizm*, pp. 51–2.

75. Mironenko, *Moskovskii kreml'*, p. 210. On the later relocation of the Kremlin shop to GUM, see idem, p. 239.

76. Dmitrievsky, *Sovetskie portrety*, pp. 23–4.

77. Shatunovskaya, *Zhizn' v Kremle*, p. 41; Dmitrievsky, *Sovetskie portrety*, pp. 27–8. On conversation, see Dmitrievsky, *Sovetskie portrety*, pp. 24–5.

78. Concrete examples appear in Enukidze's files. See RGASPI 667/1/ 1–59. See also Dmitrievsky, *Sovetskie portrety*, p. 30.

79. Dmitrievsky, *Sovetskie portrety*, pp. 24 and 73.

80. Testimony of Mikoyan. On children more generally, see L. Vasileva, *Deti kremlia* (Moscow, 1996).

81. Resis, *Molotov Remembers*, p. 210; R. Richardson, *The Long Shadow. Inside Stalin's Family* (London, 1994), p. 119.

82. Dmitrievsky, *Sovetskie portrety*, p. 25.

83. Cited in Kondratieva, *Gouverner et nourrir*, p. 183.

84. Klemenko, cited in Kondratieva, *Gouverner et nourrir*, p. 173.

85. Shatunovskaya, *Zhizn' v Kremle*, p. 42.

86. Kondratieva, *Gouverner et nourrir*, p. 183.

87. The evidence is littered across memoirs of the time. See, for instance, Resis, *Molotov Remembers*, pp. 222–5.

88. For the use of women in this way, see Dmitrievsky, *Sovetskie portrety*, p. 163.

89. Dmitrievsky, *Sovetskie portrety*, pp. 39–40.

90. Mironenko, *Moskovskii kreml'*, p. 248.

91. On Bedny, for instance, see RGASPI 667/1/18.

92. On the room, see Richardson, *Long Shadow*, p. 122. On the suicide, see, for instance, Simon Sebag Montefiore, *Stalin: The Court of the Red Tsar* (London, 2004), pp. 1–21.

93. Richardson, *Long Shadow*, p. 123.

94. Sokolova's original deposition against Mukhanova is in RGASPI 671/1/103, 3–19.

95. RGASPI 671/1/103, 24.

96. On the Kirov murder, see S. Deviatov et al., 'Gibel' Kirova. Fakty i versii', *Rodina*, 3 (2005), pp. 57–63. This summarizes the findings of the joint Russian Federal Security and Ministry of Defence enquiry into the murder, carried out in 2004.

97. RGASPI 671/1/107, 85–6.

98. *Istoricheskii arkhiv*, 3 (1995), pp. 156–7 shows Ezhov making his first visits.

99. For an example, see RGASPI 671/1/106, 107.

100. Such details were collected by some guards, for instance. See RGASPI 671/1/103, 76.

101. All these rumours appear in the Kremlin affair files. For examples, see RGASPI 671/1/107, 74–86.

102. RGASPI 671/1/106, 85.

103. For Peterson's statement, see RGASPI 671/1/103, 163.

104. RGASPI 671/1/103, 157.

105. RGASPI 671/1/105, 105–6.

106. Ilizarov, *Tainaia zhizn'*, p. 118; Sudoplatov, *Spetsoperatsii*, pp. 440–41.

107. RGASPI 671/1/23, 1.

108. RGASPI 671/1/23, 7.

109. Ilizarov, *Tainaia zhizn'*, p. 92.

110. On 1935, see R. Medvedev and Zh. Medvedev, *The Unknown Stalin* (London, 2003), p. 271. On the parties, see Stalin's engagements in RGASPI 558/11/1479.

111. Svetlana Allilueva, *Twenty Letters to a Friend* (London, 1967), p. 10.

112. Dokuchaev, *Moskva*, p. 115.

113. Allilueva, *Twenty Letters*, p. 87.

114. Allilueva, *Twenty Letters*, p. 135; see also Dokuchaev, *Moskva*, p. 49.

115. Edward Crankshaw, ed., *Khrushchev Remembers* (London, 1971), p. 297.

116. More on the cinema appears in G. Mar'iamov, *Kremlevskii tsenzor: Stalin smotrit kino* (Moscow, 1992).

117. For more detail, see Mironenko, *Moskovskii kreml'*, p. 243.

118. Crankshaw, *Khrushchev Remembers*, pp. 298–9.

119. Colton, *Moscow*, p. 323.

120. The respondent was interviewed in Moscow in September 2010.

121. For the search, see Dmitrievsky, *Sovetskie portrety*, p. 59, and Mironenko, *Moskovskii kreml'*, p. 98.

122. Dmitrievsky, *Sovetskie portrety*, p. 60.

123. For the digging and the discoveries elsewhere, see *Po trasse pervoi ocheredi Moskovskogo metropolitena imeni L. M. Kaganovicha* (Leningrad, 1936).

124. Stelletskii's obsessive notes and diary are printed in I. Ia. Stelletskii, *Poiski biblioteka Ivana Groznogo* (Moscow, 1999), pp. 272–316; on Shchusev, see Mironenko, *Moskovskii kreml'*, pp. 48–50.

125. Mironenko, *Moskovskii kreml'*, p. 116.

126. A film of this discovery was shown as part of the *Kremlin-9* television series in 2004.

127. See Colton, *Moscow*, p. 324.

128. V. Shevchenko, *Povsednevnaia zhizn' pri prezidentakh* (Moscow, 2004), pp. 194–5.

129. Ibid., p. 195.

130. On the Kremlin gathering, see Medvedev and Medvedev, *Unknown Stalin*, p. 218.

131. Mironenko, *Moskovskii kreml'*, p. 306; E. I. Smirnova, 'Oruzheinaia palata v 1941–1945 godakh', *Materialy i issledovaniia*, vol. XIV, p. 127.

132. Smirnova, 'Oruzheinaia palata', p. 124.

133. Interview in Moscow, September 2010.

134. Dokuchaev, *Moskva*, pp. 105–6; Smirnova, 'Oruzheinaia palata', pp. 124–6.

135. *Istoricheskii arkhiv*, 5–6 (1995); *Istoricheskii arkhiv*, 2, 3 and 4 (1996).

136. *Istoricheskii arkhiv*, 4 (1996), p. 33.
137. Smirnova, 'Oruzheinaia palata', p. 127.
138. Iu. Korolev, *Kremlevskii sovetnik: XX vek glazami ochevidtsev* (Moscow, 1995), p. 12.
139. I. Shmelev, cited in *Moskovskii zhurnal*, 9 (1992), pp. 2–3.
140. *Istoriia Moskvy s drevneishikh vremen*, vol. 3, p. 256.
141. Mironenko, *Moskovskii kreml'*, p. 356.
142. L. A. Petrov, 'Restavratsionnye raboty v Moskovskom kremle', *Arkhitektura i stroitel'stvo Moskvy*, 10 (1995).
143. Shchenkov, *Pamiatniki*, p. 403.
144. Shchenkov, *Pamiatniki*, p. 401; I. A. Rodimtseva, *Ocherki istorii Moskovskogo Kremlia* (Moscow, 1997), p. 122.
145. Shchenkov, *Pamiatniki*, p. 403.
146. *Istoriia Moskvy s drevneishikh vremen*, vol. 3, p. 256.
147. *Istoriia Moskvy s drevneishikh vremen*, vol. 3, p. 256.
148. *Moskovskii Kreml'* (Moscow, 1947).
149. *Kreml' i Krasnaia ploshchad'. Al'bom* (Moscow, 1947).
150. P. V. Sytin, *Istoriia planirovki i zastroiki Moskvy*, vol. 1 (Moscow, 1950), p. 7.

11 KREMLINOLOGY

1. John Steinbeck, *A Russian Journal* (London, 1949; repr. 1994), pp. 212–13.
2. Steinbeck, *Journal*, p. 212.
3. A. Adzhubei, *Te desiat' let* (Moscow, 1989), p. 118.
4. The story appears in Svetlana Allilueva, *Twenty Letters to a Friend* (London, 1967), pp. 16–18.
5. M. K. Pavlovich, 'Oruzheinaia palata v seredine 1940-x – nachale 1980-x godov (k istorii ekspozitsii)', *Materialy i issledovaniia*, vol. XIV, pp. 132–3; see also *Istoriia Moskvy s drevneishikh vremen do nashikh dnei v trekh tomakh*, vol. 3 (Moscow, 2000), p. 270, which describes the other tree in the Tainitskie gardens.
6. On Mrs Khrushchev, see Larissa Vasileva, *Kremlin Wives*, trans. Cathy Porter (New York, 1994), pp. 200–202; on the rest, see Timothy J. Colton, *Moscow: Governing the Socialist Metropolis* (Cambridge, Mass., 1995), p. 364.
7. V. Shevchenko, *Povsednevnaia zhizn' pri prezidentakh* (Moscow, 2004), p. 43, citing Ehrenburg.
8. Pavlovich, 'Oruzheinaia palata', p. 132.
9. A. S. Shchenkov, ed., *Pamiatniki arkhitetury v Sovetskom Soiuze* (Moscow, 2004), p. 218.
10. Frederick C. Barghoorn, 'The partial reopening of Russia', *Slavic Review*, 16, 2 (April 1957), pp. 146 and 158.
11. *Istoriia Moskvy s drevneishikh vremen*, vol. 3, p. 274.

12. L. I. Donetskaia and L. I. Kondrashova, 'Iz istorii prosvetitel'skoi deiatel'nosti v Moskovskom kremle', *Materialy i issledovaniia*, vol. XIV, p. 304.

13. *Kreml' Moskvy* (Moscow, 1957), p. 30.

14. The full text is available online. See www.marxists.org/archive/khrushchev/1956/02/24.htm.

15. For an account see Dmitry Volkogonov, *The Rise and Fall of the Soviet Empire: Political Leaders from Lenin to Gorbachev*, trans. Harold Shukman (London, 1998), pp. 141 and 201–7.

16. *Kreml' Moskvy*, p. 5.

17. Shevchenko, *Povsednevnaia*, p. 31; interview with Iu. V. Firsov, Moscow, September 2009.

18. *Kreml' Moskvy*, p. 4.

19. Donetskaia and Kondrashova, 'Iz istorii prosvetitel'skoi', p. 304.

20. Interview with Firsov, Moscow, 2009.

21. *Mezhdunarodnyi Sovet Muzeev: Konferentsiia komiteta muzeev arkheologii i istorii, 9–18 sentiabr' 1970* (Leningrad and Moscow, 1970), p. 12.

22. *Mezhdunarodnyi Sovet Muzeev*, guide for tour-leaders, p. 13.

23. I base these observations on the testimonies of friends and colleagues in Moscow who either earned the privilege described or sniggered (later) at the few who had. As to questions of demeanour, I can draw on my own repeated experience.

24. Donetskaia and Kondrashova, 'Iz istorii prosvetitel'skoi', p. 304; Ol'ga Sosnina and Nikolai Ssorin-Chaikov, eds., *Dari vozhdiam: Katalog vystavki* (Moscow, 2006), p. 302.

25. N. S. Vladimirskaia, 'Etapy stanovleniia nauchnoi deiatel'nosti muzeia', *Materialy i issledovaniia*, vol. XIV, p. 283.

26. It was issued by the publishing house Moskovskii Rabochii in 1957.

27. It, too, was published by Moskovskii Rabochii, and went through several editions after 1957.

28. For the objects, see the catalogue, edited by Sosnina and Ssorin-Chaikov, *Dari vozhdiam*, passim.

29. M. M. Gerasimov, *The Face-Finder* (London, 1971), p. 187. See also M. M. Gerasimov's account for his peers, 'Dokumental'nyi portret Ivana Groznogo', in *Kratkie soobshcheniia instituta Akademii Nauk SSSR*, 100 (1965), pp. 139–42.

30. I. A. Rodimtseva, *Iz glubiny vekov: ocherki istorii Moskovskogo Kremlia* (Moscow, 1997), p. 124, describes some of the work. For more detail, and a criticism of the projects of this period, see V. V. Vladimirskaia, 'Restavratsiia pamiatnikov arkhitektury moskovskogo kremlia. XX vek', *Materialy i issledovaniia*, vol. XIV, pp. 331–3.

31. *Mezhdunarodnyi Sovet Muzeev*, p. 1.

32. *Mezhdunarodnyi Sovet Muzeev*, pp. 8–10. See also I. L. Buseva-Davydova, *Khramy Moskovskogo Kremlia* (Moscow, 1997), p. 15.

33. The first volume of the Kremlin staffs' occasional series of research papers, *Materialy i issledovaniia*, appeared in 1973. It had no single theme, but included essays on the history of the Kremlin museums, on conservation, and on individual treasures.

34. The catalogue, with colour illustrations, was *Treasures from the Kremlin: An Exhibition from the State Museums of the Moscow Kremlin* (New York, 1979). The show took five years to arrange.

35. M. G. Rabinovich, *Zapiski sovetskogo intellektuala* (Moscow, 2005), p. 241.

36. Rabinovich, *Zapiski*, pp. 297–8.

37. N. N. Voronin and M. G. Rabinovich, 'Arkheologicheskie raboty v Moskovskom Kremle', *Sovetskaia arkheologiia*, 1 (1963), pp. 252–72. Sytin, of course, had worked with the metro-digging teams.

38. T. D. Avdusina, 'Vystavka "arkheologiia moskovskogo kremlia"', *Materialy i issledovaniia*, vol. XIV, p. 271.

39. N. S. Vladimirskaia (Sheliapina), ed., *Arkheologicheskaia vystavka muzeev kremlia: katalog* (Moscow, 1983), passim.

40. For the garrison, see A. Korzhakov, *Boris El'tsin: ot rassveta do zakata* (Moscow, 1997), p. 39.

41. Shevchenko, *Povsednevnaia*, p. 193.

42. On the telephone system of the 1960s, see J. Patrick Lewis, 'Communications output in the USSR: a study of the Soviet telephone systems', *Soviet Studies*, 28, 3 (July 1976), pp. 406–17.

43. The story of the British angle was related to me by K. A. (Tony) Bishop, CMG, OBE, official interpreter on the British side; for the graded telephone systems, see Korzhakov, *Boris El'tsin*, p. 129.

44. S. V. Mironenko, ed., *Moskovskii kreml': tsitadel' Rossii* (Moscow, 2008), p. 51.

45. C. Cooke, 'Manhattan in Moscow', *Domus*, 840 (September 2001), p. 95.

46. V. A. Vinogradov, ed., *Moskva 850 let*, vol. 2 (Moscow, 1997), p. 140; Colton, *Moscow*, p. 371.

47. Colton, *Moscow*, p. 366. I remember the swimming pool from my own student days, an open-air giant that was heated right through the coldest Moscow winters.

48. Mark Frankland, *Child of My Time* (London, 1999), pp. 31–3.

49. Konstantin Mikhailov, *Unichtozhennyi Kreml'* (Moscow, 2007), p. 264.

50. A. Resis, ed., *Molotov Remembers: Conversations with Felix Chuev* (Chicago, 1993), p. 187.

51. Interview with engineer P., September 2009.

52. Mikhailov, *Unichtozhennyi*, p. 251.

53. V. V. Vladimirskaia, 'Restavratsiia', *Materialy i issledovaniia*, vol. XIV, p. 330; Mikhailov, *Unichtozhennyi*, p. 250.

54. M. V. Posokhin et al., *Kremlevskii dvorets s"ezdov* (Moscow, 1974), p. 8.

55. For the dimensions, see ibid., pp. 50–60.

56. Mikhailov, *Unichtozhennyi*, p. 44.

57. Posokhin, *Kremlevskii*, p. 22.

58. V. A. Kozlov, S. Fitzpatrick and S. Mironenko, *Sedition* (New Haven, Conn., 2011), pp. 113 and 136.

59. Volkogonov, *Rise and Fall*, p. 264.

60. On the women, see Vasileva, *Wives*, p. 208. The same source also deals with stories of the hunting and the food.

61. Mikhail Gorbachev, *Memoirs* (London, 1995), pp. 143–4.

62. A. S. Gratchev, *La Chute du Kremlin* (Paris, 1994), p. 26.

63. Gratchev, *La Chute*, p. 28.

64. J. N. Westwood, *Endurance and Endeavour: Russian History 1812–1992*, 4th edn (Oxford, 1993), p. 427.

65. Volkogonov, *Rise and Fall*, p. 362.

66. Gratchev, *La Chute*, p. 61.

67. See Volkogonov, *Rise and Fall*, p. 330.

68. V. Kostikov, *Roman s prezidentom: zapiski press-sekretaria* (Moscow, 1997), p. 39.

69. The story was another memory related to me in 2006 by the interpreter K. A. (Tony) Bishop, CMG, OBE.

70. The name was also a pun on the 'commanding heights' of the economy.

71. Mironenko, *Moskovskii kreml'*, pp. 383–4.

72. Mironenko, *Moskovskii kreml'*, pp. 48–50; Volkogonov, *Rise and Fall*, p. 380. On the poor state of Cathedral Square at this time, see V. V. Vladimirskaia, 'Restavratsiia', p. 333.

73. See, for example, Iu. Korolev, *Kremlevskii sovetnik: XX vek glazami ochevidtsev* (Moscow, 1995).

74. Gorbachev, *Memoirs*, p. 101.

75. Anatoly S. Chernyaev, *My Six Years with Gorbachev*, trans. and ed. by Robert D. English and Elizabeth Tucker (University Park, Pa., 2000), p. 52.

76. For an excellent study of the post-war mentality, see Donald J. Raleigh, *Soviet Baby Boomers: An Oral History of Russia's Cold War Generation* (New York, 2011).

77. Volkogonov, *Rise and Fall*, p. 307.

78. Vasileva, *Wives*, pp. 206–7.

79. Mervyn Matthews, *Privilege in the Soviet Union* (London, 1978), pp. 36–40.

80. Volkogonov, *Rise and Fall*, p. 500.

81. B. D. Moroz, ed., *Raisa: vospominaniia, dnevniki, interv'iu, stat'i, pis'ma, telegrammy* (Moscow, 2000), p. 49. The issue clearly rankled with the Gorbachevs. See Gorbachev, *Memoirs*, pp. 137–8.

82. Shevchenko, *Povsednevnaia*, pp. 122–4; interview with S. Mikoyan, Moscow, September 2007.

83. Shevchenko, *Povsednevnaia*, p. 125.

84. Chernyaev, *Six Years*, p. 28.

85. Colton, *Moscow*, p. 524.

86. Shevchenko, *Povsednevnaia*, p. 135; Matthews, *Privilege*, pp. 38–42.

87. The scandal, which had been the talk of Moscow's kitchens for some years, was finally reported in *Moskovskaia Pravda*, 10–16 September 1986.

88. Shevchenko, *Povsednevnaia*, p. 135.

89. Volkogonov, *Rise and Fall*, p. 330.

90. Volkogonov, *Rise and Fall*, p. 308.

91. Gorbachev, *Memoirs*, p. 174.

92. Volkogonov, *Rise and Fall*, p 329.

93. Volkogonov, *Rise and Fall*, p. 372.

94. Volkogonov, *Rise and Fall*, p. 403; Shevchenko, *Povsednevnaia*, p. 195.

95. Gorbachev, *Memoirs*, p. 219.

96. Chernyaev, *Six Years*, p. 19.

97. Gorbachev, *Memoirs*, p. 222.

98. Chernyaev, *Six Years*, p. 64.

99. Igor Korchilov, *Translating History* (New York, 1997), p. 59.

100. A. Grachev, *Final Days: The Inside Story of the Collapse of the Soviet Union*, trans. Margo Milne (Boulder, Colo., 1995), p. xi; see also Rodric Braithwaite, *Across the Moscow River: The World Turned Upside Down* (London, 2002), p. 54.

101. Chernyaev, *Six Years*, p. 202.

102. Korchilov, *Translating History*, p. 123.

103. Chernyaev, *Six Years*, p. 234.

104. Chernyaev, *Six Years*, p. 165.

105. Gratchev, *La Chute*, p. 56.

106. Chernyaev, *Six Years*, pp. 147–8.

107. Shevchenko, *Povsednevnaia*, p. 38.

108. Volkogonov, *Rise and Fall*, p. 506.

109. Chernyaev, *Six Years*, p. 159.

110. As David Remnick put it, 'When history was no longer an instrument of the Party, the Party was doomed to failure.' *Lenin's Tomb: The Last Days of the Soviet Empire* (London, 1994), p. 7.

111. Volkogonov, *Rise and Fall*, p. 499.

112. Gorbachev, *Memoirs*, p. 236.

113. Chernyaev, *Six Years*, p. 131.

114. Volkogonov, *Rise and Fall*, p. 506.

115. Cited in interview with Jonathan Steele, *Guardian*, 16 August 2011: www.guardian.co.uk/world/2011/aug/16/gorbachev-guardian-interview (accessed 15 May 2012).

116. Shevchenko, *Povsednevnaia*, pp. 39–40; Volkogonov, *Rise and Fall*, p. 524.

117. Braithwaite, *Moscow River*, pp. 190–91.

118. The translation is from Braithwaite, *Moscow River*, p. 177.

119. Gorbachev, *Memoirs*, p. 413.

120. Boris El'tsin, *Zapiski Prezidenta* (Moscow, 1994), p. 54.

121. Gorbachev, *Memoirs*, p. 766.

122. Chernyaev, *Six Years*, p. 352.

123. Boris Yeltsin, *The View from the Kremlin*, trans. Catherine A. Fitzpatrick (London, 1994), p. 56.

124. Yeltsin, *View*, pp. 68–9.

125. Chernyaev, *Six Years*, p. 378.

126. Gorbachev, *Memoirs*, p. 826.

127. *Izvestiia*, 23 August 1991, p. 1. A few days later, on 27 August, the same paper demanded 'normality' in the name of its readers.

128. Yeltsin, *View*, p. 124.

129. A point made in so many words by Gorbachev. See his *On My Country and the World* (New York, 1999), p. 151.

130. Yeltsin, *View*, p. 123.

131. El'tsin, *Zapiski Prezidenta*, p. 162.

132. *Izvestiia*, 27 August 1991.

133. Shevchenko, *Povsednevnaia*, p. 40.

134. Chernyaev, *Six Years*, p. 380.

135. Volkogonov, *Rise and Fall*, p. 513.

136. Korzhakov, *Boris El'tsin*, p. 119.

137. Kostikov, *Roman s prezidentom*, p. 131.

138. Kostikov, *Roman s prezidentom*, p. 37.

139. Grachev, *Final Days*, pp. 56–9.

140. Korzhakov, *Boris El'tsin*, p. 119; Gorbachev, *On My Country*, p. 148.

141. Grachev, *Final Days*, pp. 56–9.

142. Gorbachev, *On My Country*, p. 148; Yeltsin, *View*, pp. 111–15.

143. On the briefcase itself, which is one of three, see Shevchenko, *Povsednevnaia*, pp. 59–60.

144. El'tsin, *Zapiski Prezidenta*, pp. 160–61.

145. Grachev, *Final Days*, p. 181.

146. Yeltsin, *View*, p. 121.

147. Cited in Gorbachev, *On My Country*, p. 157.

148. The photograph was printed all over the world. See *Izvestiia*, 26 December 1991.

149. Grachev, *Final Days*, p. 191. Grachev later moved to Paris, so the figure he actually quoted was 200 French francs.

12 NORMALITY

1. A. Grachev, *Final Days: The Inside Story of the Collapse of the Soviet Union*, trans. Margo Milne (Boulder, Colo., 1995), p. 194; V. Shevchenko, *Povsednevnaia zhizn' pri prezidentakh* (Moscow, 2004), p. 42; Boris Yeltsin,

The View from the Kremlin, trans. Catherine A. Fitzpatrick (London, 1994), p. 12.

2. *Izvestiia*, 2 January 1992.

3. The shortages and high prices had begun before Yeltsin took power. See Otto Latsis, *Izvestiia*, 2 January 1992. On foreign aid, and the reasons for it, see 'IMF Approves Stand-by Credit for Russia', IMF Press release for 11 April 1995, available at https://www.imf.org/external/np/sec/pr/1995/pr9521.htm (accessed 26 Aug. 2011).

4. Paul Klebnikov, *Godfather of the Kremlin: Boris Berezovsky and the Looting of Russia* (New York and London, 2000), p. 33.

5. Klebnikov, *Godfather*, p. 36. The collapse of the Russian population was the subject of several international colloquia in the mid-1990s. For an analysis, see N. G. Bennett et al., 'Demographic implications of the Russian mortality crisis', *World Development*, 26 (1998), pp. 1921–37.

6. On the Bank of New York scandal in particular, see 'Russia misled IMF on loan', *Washington Post*, 1 July 1999.

7. For detailed statistics, see Richard Sakwa, *Russian Politics and Society*, 4th edn (Abingdon and New York 2008), pp. 36–8.

8. Again, these matters are outlined in Sakwa, *Russian Politics*, p. 30.

9. See Otto Latsis and also Sergei Taranov, both writing in *Izvestiia*, 4 May 1993.

10. The old Communist Party paper, *Pravda*, was a so-called 'red-brown' in its own right, as witness its reportage of the 1 May demonstrations.

11. Viacheslav Kostikov, *Roman s Prezidentom: zapiski press-sekretaria* (Moscow, 1997), p. 173, citing the editor of *Argumenty i fakty*, Vladislav Starkov. For an account of the events themselves, see Sakwa, *Russian Politics*, p. 52.

12. Vladimir Snegirev, writing in *Rossiiskaia gazeta*, 3 October 2003.

13. For the composition of these crowds, and their motives, see Michael Urban, 'The politics of identity in Russia's postcommunist transition: the nation against itself', *Slavic Review*, 53, 3 (Autumn 1994), p. 734. The liberal press referred to them as 'hoorah-patriots'. See *Izvestiia*, 21 September 1993, pp. 1 and 4.

14. The highest counts are in the low thousands. The figure of 147 is cited in Sakwa, *Russian Politics*, p. 52, and is on the low side, as even the Procurator's office gave a total amounting to 249 (148 inside the White House and 101 on the streets).

15. *Izvestiia*, 5 October 1993, p. 1.

16. Yeltsin, *View*, p. 241; on the issue of medical services, see David Satter, *Darkness at Dawn: The Rise of the Russian Criminal State* (New Haven, Conn. and London, 2003), p. 61. An entirely different view of events, from the red-brown perspective, was presented in *Pravda*, 25 September 1993 ('Rossiia protiv diktatura').

17. Cited by Robert Conquest, *Washington Post*, 10 October 1993.

18. *Washington Post*, 16 October 1993.

19. Cited by Lilia Shevtsova, in A. Brown and L. Shevtsova, eds., *Gorbachev, Yeltsin, Putin: Political Leadership in Russia's Transition* (Washington, DC, 2001), p. 69.

20. As Vasily Pribylovsky put it, 'The idea of power was the ideology that he supported.' See David Satter, *It Was a Long Time Ago, And It Never Happened Anyway* (New Haven, Conn. and London, 2011), p. 158.

21. Cited in Andrew Jack, *Inside Putin's Russia* (London, 2004), p. 227.

22. Brown and Shevtsova, *Gorbachev, Yeltsin, Putin*, p. 76.

23. The Russian constitution is available online at www.constitution.ru.

24. The decisions are reviewed in Shevchenko, *Povsednevnaia*, pp. 52–62.

25. The proposal's sponsor was Yury Luzhkov. See Kostikov, *Roman s Prezidentom*, p. 263.

26. For a discussion, see Brian D. Taylor, *State Building in Putin's Russia* (Cambridge, 2011), esp. pp. 294–8. See also Edward Lucas, *The New Cold War: How the Kremlin Menaces both Russia and the West* (London, 2008), p. 43.

27. On Gorbachev and John Major, see Rodric Braithwaite, *Across the Moscow River: The World Turned Upside Down* (London, 2002), p. 217.

28. Boris Yeltsin, *Midnight Diaries* (London, 2000), p. 160; I am grateful to K. A. (Tony) Bishop, CMG, OBE, for the other side of the story, related to me in July 2006.

29. The BBC reported this in detail. See http://news.bbc.co.uk/1/hi/world/europe/133725.stm (accessed 31 Jan. 2013).

30. Yeltsin, *Midnight Diaries*, p. 304.

31. Iu. A. Bychkov et al., eds., *Petr Baranovskii: Trudy, vospominaniia sovremennikov* (Moscow, 1996), p. 142.

32. Ruslan Armeev, 'Kazanskii sobor vozrozhden!', *Moskovskii zhurnal*, 1 (1994), p. 2.

33. For an analysis of the fairy-tale element in Moscow's reconstruction at this time, see Benjamin Forest and Juliet Johnson, 'Unravelling the threads of history: Soviet-era monuments and post-Soviet national identity in Moscow', *Annals of the Association of American Geographers*, 92, 3 (September 2002), pp. 524–47.

34. L. G. Georg'ian, ed., *Podgotovka k prazdnovaniiu 850-letiia osnovaniia Moskvy: sbornik statei opublikovannykh v gazetakh Moskvy i podmoskov'ia v 1995–1997 gg.* (Friazino, 1997), p. 53.

35. Dmitri Sidorov, 'National monumentalization and the politics of scale: the resurrection of the Cathedral of Christ the Savior in Moscow', *Annals of the Association of American Geographers*, 90, 3 (September 2000), p. 561.

36. Sidorov, 'National monumentalization', p. 561.

37. Y. Luzhkov, *My deti tvoi, Moskva* (Moscow, 1996), p. 193.

38. Aleksandr Korzhakov, *Boris El'tsin: ot rassveta do zakata. Posleslovie* (Moscow, 2004), p. 456.

39. Zoe Knox, 'The symphonic ideal: the Moscow patriarchate's post-Soviet leadership', *Europe-Asia Studies*, 55, 4 (June 2003), p. 586.

40. Sidorov, 'National monumentalization', p. 565.

41. This is the first criterion for the selection of cultural sites, and was specifically mentioned in the Kremlin's case. For a full list, see http://whc.unesco.org.en/criteria/.

42. The resolution by UNESCO was taken at its 14th session in December 1990.

43. The contrast with nearby Kolomna, whose Kremlin walls have been rebuilt in finest pastiche, is striking.

44. Konstantin Mikhailov, *Unichtozhennyi Kreml'* (Moscow, 2007), p. 245.

45. www.nkj.ru/archive/articles/13604 (*Nauka i zhizn'*, 4 (2008), the recollections of A. Grashchenkov, a former member of the Kremlin museum team, accessed 25 Aug. 2011).

46. Mikhailov, *Unichtozhennyi*, p. 244.

47. *New York Times*, 16 September 1999.

48. *The Economist*, 16 September 1999.

49. *New York Times*, 27 August 1999.

50. A fact bemoaned by its former director in conversation in Moscow in September 2007.

51. Yeltsin, *Midnight Diaries*, p. 96.

52. Shevchenko, *Povsednevnaia*, p. 38.

53. The companies involved included Martolini and Maioli, based in the historic artisan quarter of Florence.

54. *Nezavisimaia gazeta*, 17 November 1998.

55. The story is repeated in the *New York Times* profile of Borodin, 1 July 2001.

56. There is a good account of this in David Satter, *Darkness at Dawn*, pp. 57–9.

57. *Corriere della Sera*, 25 August 1999.

58. *New York Times*, 8 September 1999. Turover's reliability as a witness was later challenged. *Moscow Times*, 6 March 2001.

59. *New York Times*, 13 April 2001.

60. *Moscow Times*, 16 April 2001.

61. For more, see its website, www.mabetex.eu, where visitors can explore its promise that 'we build the future'.

62. Grigorii Smolitskii, 'Moskovskii kreml' mogut iskliuchit' iz spiska Iunesco', *Izvestiia*, 10 August 2012, available at http://izvestia.ru/news/532590.

63. *Moscow Times*, 18 March 2002.

64. *Ekspress gazeta online*, 3 November 2006, available at http://www.eg.ru/daily/sports/8410 (accessed 25 Aug. 2011).

65. For the full text, in English translation, see http://news.bbc.co.uk/1/hi/world/monitoring/584845.stm.

66. Shevtsova in Brown and Shevtsova, *Gorbachev, Yeltsin, Putin*, p. 93.

67. Lilia Shevtsova, writing in Lilia Shevtsova and Andrew Wood, *Change and Decay: Russia's Dilemma and the West's Response* (Washington, DC, 2011), p. 42.

68. There are many accounts of the bombings, allegedly staged by the FSB, that precipitated the second Chechen war. For a recent summary, see Satter, *Long Time Ago*, p. 301.

69. For officially derived figures, see Hans-Henning Schroder, 'What kind of political regime does Russia have?', in Stephen White, ed., *Politics and the Ruling Group in Putin's Russia* (Basingstoke, 2008), p. 20.

70. Taylor, *State Building*, p. 293.

71. Anders Aslund, 'The hunt for Russia's riches', *Foreign Policy*, 152 (Jan–Feb 2006), p. 47.

72. Figures cited by Lilia Shevtsova in Shevtsova and Wood, *Change and Decay*, p. 102.

73. http://valdaiclub.com/politics/37000.html, cited by Clifford Gaddy and Fiona Hill, 'Putin and the Uses of History', Valdai Discussion Club, 10 January 2012, p. 4.

74. As witnessed by the late British interpreter, K. A. (Tony) Bishop, interviewed in July 2006.

75. For reportage in English, see Andrew Osborn's article in the *Daily Telegraph*, 14 February 2011, available at http://www.telegraph.co.uk/news/worldnews/europe/russia/8323981/Vladimir-Putin-has-600-million-Italianate-palace.html.

76. Yeltsin, *View*, pp. 210–11.

77. Gaddy and Hill, 'Putin and the Uses of History', p. 2.

78. For commentary, see Satter, *Long Time Ago*, p. 188.

79. A point made by Arkady Ostrovsky, 'Enigma variations', *The Economist*, 29 November 2008, pp. 3–18. See also Satter, *Long Time Ago*, pp. 212–15.

80. Lilia Shevtsova, *Putin's Russia* (Washington, DC, 2003), pp. 169–70.

81. http://www.heraldscotland.com/kremlin-funded-blockbuster-casts-putin-in-a-tsar-role-1.829539 (accessed 15 Jan. 2013).

82. *Nezavisimaia gazeta*, 26 October 2007 ('Russkii tresh').

83. 'Liubim li my Moskvu?', *Moskovskaia pravda*, 30 August 2007.

84. *Gibel' imperii: Vizantiiskii urok* (a book based on the film was also published by Eksmo in 2008). I am grateful to Sergei Ivanov for introducing me to this material at a lecture in London in 2009.

85. 'Uroki istorii: rabota s natsional'noi ideei', *Nezavisimaia gazeta*, 30 December 2008.

86. On the proposed textbook, by Aleksandr Filippov, see *Novaia gazeta*, 24 September 2007, 'Poslednii pisk istorii gosudarstva rossiiskogo', and the critical remarks by Iurii Afanas'ev ('Eta kniga – sledka s sovest'iu'). On its fate, see also Satter, *Long Time Ago*, p. 212.

87. The statues were described to me by K. A. Bishop. On Putin's devotion to Petr Stolypin, and also on the prominent displays of historical figures that Valdai Club members observed in the Kremlin of 2005, see Gaddy and Hill, 'Putin and the Uses of History', pp. 1–2.

88. The episode, *Neizvestnyi kreml'*, was broadcast in 2004.

89. 'Aleksandra Nevskogo predlagaiut v pokroviteli FSB', http://news.bbc. co.uk/go/pr/fr/-/hi/russia/newsid_7629000/7629205.stm (accessed 26 Sept. 2008).

90. The book, whose general editor was Sergei Mironenko, was entitled *The Moscow Kremlin: Russia's Citadel (Moskovskii kreml': tsitadel' Rossii)*.

91. marker.ru/news/3124 (accessed 2 Sept. 2011).

92. These and other comments can be accessed on autotravel.ru/otklik. php/3490.

93. http://valdaiclub.com/history/a162860813.html (accessed 31 Jan. 2013).

94. 'Na bashniakh Kremlia obnaruzheny ikony', *Izvestiia*, 12 May 2010.

Acknowledgements

I could not have written this book without the generous support of the Leverhulme Trust, whose Major Research Fellowship released me from my teaching duties and also supported a good deal of travel and research. Such funding, graciously awarded and administered with the lightest touch, is both a life-line and a real inspiration. I am indebted to the Trustees, and also to the friends who supported my application, especially Emma Rothschild, Stephen A. Smith and the late Tony Judt. At an early stage in the work, also thanks to Tony Judt, I was a visiting Fellow at New York University's Remarque Institute, a stimulating experience for which I should also like to thank Jair Kessler and Katherine E. Fleming.

In the course of the research itself, I received expert help, advice and consolation from so many people that it is impossible to name them all. I owe a particular debt to Elena Gagarina and her staff in the Kremlin Museum Reserve and Library. Andrei Batalov, the director of the Kremlin's historic buildings, was generous with his time and knowledge, and I also thank Tatiana Panova, the director of Kremlin archaeology. On many visits to Moscow, I was welcomed by the enthusiastic staff of its State Historical Library and by the staffs of several of the major state archives, including the State Archive of the Russian Federation and the Archive of Ancient Acts. I am also indebted to the State (Lenin) Library of the Russian Federation, the State Historical Archive, the State Archive of the Economy and the Shchusev Museum of Architecture. Moscow colleagues and friends were generous as always, and I should especially like to thank Sergo Mikoyan, Stepan Mikoyan, Pavel Palazhchenko, Vsevolod Pimenov and Sergei Romaniuk.

I had to read so many rare books and collections in the past few years that the staff of Oxford's Bodleian Library, and especially those in the

Upper Reserve and the Taylorian Slavonic Library, will probably have noticed a welcome drop in their daily workload since this manuscript was finished. It was a privilege to read in such company, and I should also like to thank the staffs of the British Library, the Library of the School of Slavonic Studies at University College London, the London Library, and the Cambridge University Library. In addition, I am indebted to the staff of the New York Public Library (and especially its much-loved Slavic and Baltic Division), notably Edward Kasinec. The staff of the Hillwood Museum and Library in Washington welcomed me in 2007, and I should particularly like to thank Scott Ruby, who not only introduced me to the collection but also shared some of his unpublished findings.

The project took me well outside my accustomed research areas – that was a large part of the initial attraction – but it also left me more than usually indebted to readers with a special expertise in its individual fields. I am grateful for the kindness of Alla Aronova, Sergei Bogatyrev, Anna Pikington, Donald Rayfield and Jonathan Shepard, each of whom read parts of the draft and offered detailed and extremely generous comments. None, of course, bears any responsibility for my mistakes. Nor do the many others who talked me through individual aspects of the book, in which connection I should like to thank Brigid Allen, Jill Bennett, Kathleen Berton Murrell, Sir Rodric Braithwaite, Clementine Cecil, Robert Dale, Simon Dixon, Vladimir Faekov, Baron Hennessy of Nympsfield, Jeremy Hicks, Valerie Holman, Geoffrey Hosking, Baron Hurd of Westwell, Ira Katznelson, Igor Korchilov, Vladimir Kozlov, Sue Levene, Kate Lowe, Sir Rodrick Lyne, Isabel de Madariaga, Anne McIntyre, Philip Merridale, Nicola Miller, Serena Moore, Sergei Orlenko, Tina Pepler, W. F. Ryan, Andreas Schonle, Simon Sebag Montefiore, Jon Smele, Nikolai Ssorin-Chaikov, Elena Stroganova, Katherin Townsend, Tamar de Vries Winter and Richard Wortman. The members of the Early Slavists online discussion forum provided numerous new leads, and I am also indebted to the late Tony Bishop, who never got to see what I made of his delightful notes. In a different vein, and somewhat later in the process, Octavia Lamb provided expert assistance in tracking down many of the illustrations and Charlotte Ridings helped prepare the final text.

Just as it is usual to thank everyone who was involved (and the thanks are very real), so it is customary to absolve them all of any responsibility for the book itself. In the case of my greatest debts, however, such absolution can only ever be technical, for a few people have worked so hard on my behalf that the book would simply not exist without them. Two talented editors, Sara Bershtel at Metropolitan and Simon Winder at Penguin, put their prodigious energies to work, bombarding me with questions while somehow adding fresh coherence and fluency to the text. They would never have seen a manuscript at all, however, had it not been for Peter Robinson, who generously allowed me to redefine his duties as literary agent to include unhealthy quantities of reading along with his unfailing support, intellectual as well as practical and moral. I thank them all, and hope the published book will reflect each of their very different kinds of creativity. Meanwhile, and always, I am most grateful of all to Frank Payne. It was never going to be easy to make this journey, but he not only stayed the entire distance but managed to fall in love with Moscow in the process. May there be many Moscows to come.

Suggestions for Further Reading

This book has covered nine hundred years in the history of the Russian state, and a bibliography that attempted to catalogue every source would present a formidable and probably impenetrable challenge to the reader. I have given full references in the endnotes, but here I offer a more general guide to further reading, restricting myself mainly to materials that are available in English.

GENERAL

The brave company of authors who have written on the whole sweep of Russian history is small but distinguished. Among the best general books are Geoffrey Hosking's *Russia and the Russians: A History from Rus to the Russian Federation* (London, 2001) and James A. Billington's *The Icon and the Axe: An Interpretive History of Russian Culture* (New York, 1966). In preparing this book, I also consulted W. Bruce Lincoln's *Between Heaven and Hell: The Story of a Thousand Years of Artistic Life in Russia* (New York, 1998), Nicholas Riasanovsky's *Russian Identities: A Historical Survey* (Oxford, 2005) and Mark D. Steinberg and Nicholas Riasanovsky's two-volume *A History of Russia*, 7th edn (New York and Oxford, 2005). Michael Cherniavsky's *Tsar and People: Studies in Russian Myths* (New York, 1969) was an inspiration, as was the much older *The Russian Idea* (London, 1947) by Nikolai Berdyaev. For an equally ambitious work that was written, refreshingly, by an expert in the medieval and early modern Russian world, see Marshall Poe, *The Russian Moment in World History* (Princeton, NJ, 2003). Readers with a taste for controversy will also enjoy Richard Pipes' classic *Russia Under the Old Regime* (London and New York, 1974), which proposes the idea of the patrimonial state. By contrast, a brilliant collective endeavour, the *Cambridge History of Russia* (multiple volumes, 2006–8), presents very recent research in accessible form. Many of the individual essays are cited elsewhere in this survey.

The general histories of the Kremlin are more disappointing. The most serious one in English is Arthur Voyce's *The Moscow Kremlin: Its History, Architecture and Art Treasures* (London, 1955). For more sumptuous illustrations (but fewer words), see David Douglas Duncan, *Great Treasures of the Kremlin* (New York, 1967). By contrast, Laurence Kelly's collection of excerpts, *Moscow: A Traveller's Companion* (London, 1983) includes a section on the Kremlin that provides glimpses of the fortress and the myths that have surrounded it. For the architecture of Moscow in general, see also Kathleen Berton Murrell's *Moscow: An Architectural History* (London, 1977).

William Craft Brumfield's *History of Russian Architecture* (Cambridge, 1993) is the best general introduction to its subject, while Dmitry Shvidkovsky's *Russian Architecture and the West* (New Haven, Conn. and London, 2007) contains much valuable new material in a stunningly beautiful volume. There are several general histories of Russian art (the classic English-language work, in three volumes, is George Hamilton's *Art and Architecture of Russia* (Harmondsworth, 1954)), but one of the most accessible is Tamara Talbot Rice, *A Concise History of Russian Art* (New York, 1963). Icons are discussed in illuminating ways by John Stuart, *Ikons* (London, 1975) and Oleg Tarasov, *Icon and Devotion: Sacred Spaces in Imperial Russia*, trans. Robin Milner-Gulland (London, 2002). As for the Orthodox Church itself, Timothy Ware, *The Orthodox Church* (London, 1997) provides the best general introduction.

MEDIEVAL RUSSIA

Among the best introductions to the story of Rus is Simon Franklin and Jonathan Shepard, *The Emergence of Rus 750–1200* (London and New York, 1996). The early chapters of Janet Martin's wonderful *Medieval Russia, 980–1584* (Cambridge, 2007) also cover early Rus. The Byzantine connection is beautifully presented in Dmitri Obolensky, *The Byzantine Commonwealth* (London, 1971) and John Meyendorff,

Byzantium and the Rise of Russia: A Study of Byzantino-Russian Relations in the Fourteenth Century (Cambridge, 1981). Omeljan Pritsak, *The Origin of Rus* (Cambridge, Mass., 1981) deals with important controversies about the traders from the north. On Bogoliubsky, see Ellen S. Hurwitz, *Prince Andrej Bogoljubskij: The Man and the Myth* (Firenze, 1980).

A traditional survey of early Muscovy is provided by John Fennell's two volumes: *The Crisis of Medieval Russia, 1200–1304* (London, 1983) and *The Emergence of Moscow, 1304–1359* (London, 1968). A bracing antidote can be found in D. G. Ostrowski, *Muscovy and the Mongols: Cross-Cultural Influences on the Steppe Frontier* (Cambridge, 1998), which delivers a refreshing view of the lasting role of Mongol culture. Further grist to that mill appears in G. A. Fyodorov-Davydov, *The Culture of Golden Horde Cities* (Oxford, 1984), C. J. Halperin, *Russia and the Golden Horde: The Mongol Impact on Russian History* (London, 1987), and even Michel Roublev, 'The Mongol tribute', in M. Cherniavsky, ed., *The Structure of Russian History* (New York, 1970), pp. 29–64. For the role of trade, as well as a discussion of the region's international networks, see Janet Martin, *Treasure of the Land of Darkness: The Fur Trade and its Significance for Medieval Russia* (Cambridge, 1986).

For an introduction to the sacred architecture of the Orthodox world, see Cyril Mango, *Byzantine Architecture* (New York, 1976). The impact of Mongol conquest on building in the Moscow region is traced in David B. Miller, 'Monumental building as an indicator of economic trends in Northern Rus' in the late Kievan and Mongol periods, 1138–1462', *American Historical Review*, 94 (1989), pp. 360–90, and the same author has written on the most famous of Russian icons in 'Legends of the icon of Our Lady of Vladimir: a study of the development of Muscovite national consciousness', *Speculum*, 43, 4 (October 1968), pp. 657–70. The artistic connections between Byzantine and early Russian art are explored in Robin Cormack's useful introduction, *Byzantine Art* (Oxford, 2000).

RENAISSANCE

The only biography of Ivan III in English is John Fennell, *Ivan the Great of Moscow* (London, 1961), and the period of his reign has not attracted large numbers of English-speaking specialists. For an overview of the era as a whole, see Robert O. Crummey, *The Formation of Muscovy, 1304–1613* (London and New York, 1987). For different aspects of the evolution of Ivan's court, see Gustave Alef, 'The adoption of the Muscovite two-headed eagle: a discordant view', *Speculum*, 41 (1966), pp. 1–21, and G. P. Majeska, 'The Moscow coronation of 1498 reconsidered', *Jahrbücher für Geschichte Osteuropas*, 26 (1978), pp. 353–61.

Ivan the Terrible has drawn a larger press, including Isabel de Madariaga's biography, *Ivan the Terrible: First Tsar of Russia* (New Haven, Conn. and London, 2005). Today, the most thoughtful writing on Ivan the Terrible and his era is the work of Sergei Bogatyrev, and an introduction to it might be his chapter, 'Ivan the Terrible', in Maureen Perrie, ed., *The Cambridge History of Russia, Vol. 1: From Early Rus' to 1689*. On the coronation, see also D. B. Miller, 'The coronation of Ivan IV of Moscow', *Jahrbücher für Geschichte Osteuropas*, 15 (1967), pp. 559–74. Ivan's peevish correspondence with his former courtier Andrei Kurbsky was translated by J. L. I. Fennell as *The Correspondence between Prince A. M. Kurbsky and Tsar Ivan IV of Russia, 1564–1579* (Cambridge, 1955), but see also Edward L. Keenan, *The Kurbskii-Groznyi Apocrypha* (Cambridge, Mass., 1971) for the suggestion that the whole thing might be a fraud. On Ivan's health, see Charles Halperin, 'Ivan IV's insanity', *Russian History*, 34 (2007), pp. 207–18 and Edward L. Keenan, 'Ivan IV and the King's Evil: *Ni maka li to budet?*', *Russian History*, 20 (1993), pp. 5–13; for his image and later reputation, see Maureen Perrie, *The Image of Ivan the Terrible in Russian Folklore* (Cambridge, 1987).

The structure of the Muscovite elite is discussed in Gustave Alef, *Rulers and Nobles in Fifteenth-Century Moscow* (London, 1983), Nancy Shields Kollmann, *Kinship and Politics: The Making of the Muscovite Political System* (Stanford, Calif., 1987) and also Ann Kleimola, 'The changing condition of the Muscovite elite', *Russian History*, 6, 2 (1979), pp. 210–29. The whole issue of slavery, which played such a role in large state projects at this time, is explored in Richard Hellie, *Slavery in Russia, 1450–1725* (Chicago, 1982), and a related but more technical issue of court language in Marshall Poe, 'What did Russians mean when they called themselves "Slaves of the Tsar"?', *Slavic Review* 57, 3 (1998), pp. 585–608. For the structure of Ivan's new bureaucracy, see Peter B. Brown, 'Muscovite government bureaus', *Russian History*, 10, 3 (1983). Art, religion and court ideology are discussed in two articles by Daniel Rowland: 'Moscow – the third Rome or the new Israel?', *Russian Review*, 55 (1996), pp. 591–614, and 'Two cultures, one throne room', in Valerie A. Kivelson and Robert H. Greene, eds., *Orthodox Russia* (University Park, Pa., 2003), pp. 33–57. Michael Flier's essay in the same volume ('Till the end of time: the apocalypse in Russian historical experience before 1500') provides an insight into the mentality of the times, and also see his essay on the Palm Sunday ritual: 'Breaking the code: the image of the tsar in the Muscovite Palm Sunday ritual', in Michael S. Flier and Daniel Rowland, eds., *Medieval Russian Culture*, vol. 2, California Slavic Studies (Berkeley, Los Angeles and London, 1994), pp. 213–42.

For European travellers' tales, see W. Thomas et al., trans., *Travels to Tana and Persia by Josafa Barbaro and Ambrogio Contarini* (London, 1873), which relates Contarini's experience of Ivan III's Moscow. The impressions of Jenkinson and others are collected in Lloyd E. Berry and Robert O. Crummey, eds., *Rude and Barbarous Kingdom: Russia in Accounts of Sixteenth-Century English Voyagers* (Madison, Wisc., 1968). Staden's vivid memoir of Ivan the Terrible's Muscovy is available in English as Heinrich von Staden, *The Land and Government of Muscovy*, trans. Thomas Esper (Stanford, Calif., 1967), and Possevino has been translated by Hugh F. Graham as *The Moscovia of Antonio Possevino, SJ* (Pittsburg, Pa., 1977).

TIME OF TROUBLES

Among the English sources, I learned most from Chester S. L. Dunning, *Russia's First Civil War: The Time of Troubles and the Founding of the Romanov Dynasty* (University Park, Pa., 2001), a thoughtful as well as thought-provoking study of early modern Russia. Maureen Perrie's *Pretenders and Popular Modernism in Early Modern Russia* (Cambridge, 1995) was also illuminating, and the chapter on Boris Godunov's career in volume 1 of the *Cambridge History of Russia* that she edited and translated (A. P. Pavlov, 'Fedor Ivanovich and Boris Godunov', pp. 264–85) is insightful.

The most respected Russian historian of the Troubles is S. F. Platonov, whose authoritative but dated *Time of Troubles* has been translated by John T. Alexander (Lawrence, Kans., 1985). Two biographies of Boris Godunov, one by Platonov (Gulf Breeze, Fl., 1973) and one by Ruslan Skrynnikov (Gulf Breeze, Fl., 1982) are accessible in English, as is Skrynnikov's vivid *Time of Troubles: Russia in Crisis, 1604–1618* (Gulf Breeze, Fl., 1988).

The travellers whose witness illustrated my account deserve a chapter of their own. The most colourful are Jacques Margeret, *The Russian Empire and the Grand Duchy of Moscow: A Seventeenth-century French Account*, trans. and ed. Chester S. L. Dunning (Pittsburg, Pa., 1983); Isaac Massa, *A Short History of the Peasant Wars in Moscow under the Reigns of Various Sovereigns down to the Year 1610*, trans. G. E. Orchard (Toronto, 1982); Stanislaw Zolkiewski, *Expedition to Moscow: A Memoir*, trans. M. W. Stephen (London, 1959) and *The Travels of Olearius in Seventeenth-Century Russia*, trans. Samuel H. Baron (Stanford, Calif., 1967).

Readers with an interest in maps may pursue it through Valerie Kivelson's *Cartographies of Tsardom: The Land and its Meanings in Seventeenth-Century Russia* (Ithaca, NY, 2006). The economic background to the Troubles is one subject of Richard Hellie, *Enserfment and Military Change in Muscovy* (Chicago and London, 1971) and similar problems are also explored in Marshall Poe and Eric Lohr, eds., *The Military and Society in Russian History, 1350–1917* (Leiden, 2002).

ROMANOV MUSCOVY

I can think of no more entertaining introduction than Paul of Aleppo's notes, the full version of which is available in English as *The Travels of Macarius, Patriarch of Antioch: Written by His Attendant Archdeacon, Paul of Aleppo, in Arabic*, trans. F. C. Belfour, 2 vols. (London, 1836). The history of the period, however, is covered more soberly in Paul Dukes, *The Making of Russian Absolutism, 1613–1801* (London, 1982) and Robert O. Crummey, *Aristocrats and Servitors: The Boyar Elite in Russia, 1613–1689* (Princeton, NJ, 1983). Religion, which played such a prominent role at the Romanov court, is explained by Paul Bushkovitch, *Religion and Society in Russia: The Sixteenth and Seventeenth Centuries* (New York, 1992), while P. Meyendorff, *Russia, Ritual and Reform: The Liturgical Reforms of Nikon in the Seventeenth Century* (New York, 1991) and G. Michels, *At War with the Church: Religious*

Dissent in Seventeenth-Century Russia (Stanford, Calif., 1999) both deal with the Great Schism. For blood-curdling detail of the results, see Michael Cherniavsky, 'The Old Believers and the New Religion', *Slavic Review*, 25, 1 (March 1966), pp. 1–39.

The Romanovs are the subject of Lindsey Hughes' book of the same title (London, 2008), and Philip Longworth has a biography of Aleksei Mikhailovich, *Alexis, Tsar of all the Russias* (London, 1984). The impressions of Aleksei's doctor, Samuel Collins, were published as *The Present State of Russia: A Letter to a Friend at London, by an Eminent Person residing at the Czar's Court* (London, 1671). Aleksei's law code can be consulted in Richard Hellie, ed. and trans., *The Muscovite Law Code (*Ulozhenie*) of 1649* (Irvine, Calif., 1988), and serfdom's effects on the peasants, then and later, are discussed in David Moon, *The Russian Peasantry, 1600–1930* (London and New York, 1999) as well as Jerome Blum's older, magnificent, *Lord and Peasant in Russia from the Ninth to the Nineteenth Centuries* (Princeton, NJ, 1961). At the time of writing, one of the most illuminating eye-witness accounts of the Muscovite court, written at the Swedish court by the defector Grigory Kotoshikhin, was being translated into English in its entirety for the first time; the publication will add considerably to the general appreciation of this arcane world among English-speaking readers.

EIGHTEENTH CENTURY

Lindsey Hughes' biography of Sofiya, *Sophia, Regent of Russia* (London and New Haven, Conn., 1990) remains the best available in English, and her biographies of Peter (*Peter the Great: A Biography* (New Haven, Conn. and London, 2004)) and the more comprehensive *Russia in the Age of Peter the Great* (New Haven, Conn. and London, 1998) are models of scholarship and clear writing. For even more, see Robert K. Massie's award-winner, *Peter the Great* (London, 1980 and reissued several times). Catherine has also attracted many biographers, the most recent of whom include Isabel de Madariaga (*Russia in the Age of Catherine the Great* (London, 1981)) and Simon Dixon (*Catherine the Great* (London, 2009)). The rulers after Peter's death are the subjects of E. V. Anisimov, *Five Empresses: Court Life in Eighteenth-century Russia*, trans. Kathleen Carroll (Westport, Va., 2004).

Among the most illuminating pieces of new scholarship on this era, Ernest A. Zitser's, *The Transfigured Kingdom* (Ithaca, NY and London, 2004) stands out for its approach to Peter's raucous court. A more traditional work, which covers the development of court ceremony and Russian sovereignty since Peter's time, is Richard Wortman's magnificent *Scenarios of Power: Myth and Ceremony in Russian Monarchy*, most widely available now in a single volume edition (Princeton, NJ and Oxford, 2006). For politics at the beginning of Peter's reign, see Paul Bushkovitch, *Peter the Great: The Struggle for Power* (Cambridge, 2001).

The sudden change in architectural style is the subject of James Cracraft, *The Petrine Revolution in Russian Architecture* (Chicago, Ill., 1988) and Albert J. Schmidt, *The Architecture and Planning of Classical Moscow* (Philadelphia, Pa., 1989). Cracraft's later volumes include *The Petrine Revolution in Russian Imagery* (Chicago, Ill., 1997), which continues many of the discussions begun in his work on buildings. Catherine's passions are among the subjects discussed in Dmitry Shvidkovsky's work on Charles Cameron, *The Empress and the Architect: British Architecture and Gardens at the Court of Catherine the Great* (New Haven, Conn. and London, 1996). For a more general survey, see Lindsey Hughes, 'Russian culture in the eighteenth century', in Dominic Lieven, ed., *The Cambridge History of Russia, Vol. 2, Imperial Russia 1689–1917* (Cambridge, 2008), pp. 67–91.

NINETEENTH CENTURY

The nineteenth century began with the Napoleonic Wars and ended on the eve of revolution, so the potential literature is vast. An introduction to the war of 1812 is Adam Zamoyski's *1812: Napoleon's Fatal March on Moscow* (London, 2005), which draws on many Russian sources. Daria Olivier, *The Burning of Moscow 1812* (London, 1966), is a more specific account of Moscow's suffering. Among the memoirs available in English (it would take a whole book to list those in French or Russian), the best is probably Comte P.-P. de Ségur, *History of the Expedition to Russia Undertaken by the Emperor Napoleon in the Year 1812*, 2 vols. (London, 1826) or the abridged *New York Times* edition, *Defeat: Napoleon's Russian Campaign*, trans. J. David (New York, 2008).

Another first-hand source is General Armand de Caulaincourt, Duke of Vicenza, *With Napoleon in Russia,* from the Original Memoirs as edited by Jean Hanoteau; abridged with an introduction by George Libaire (Mineola, NY, 2005).

The conservative intellectual atmosphere in Moscow is reviewed in Alexander M. Martin, *Romantics, Reformers, Reactionaries: Russian Conservative Thought and Politics in the Reign of Alexander I* (DeKalb, Ill., 1997). Martin's essay in the *Cambridge History of Russia* ('Russia and the legacy of 1812', vol. 2, pp. 145–61) is another excellent starting-point for the culture of the period, as is Rosamund Bartlett, 'Russian culture: 1801–1917' in the same volume, pp. 92–115. On romanticism, and especially its view of landscape, see Christopher D. Ely, *This Meager Nature: Landscape and Identity in Imperial Russia* (DeKalb, Ill., 2002). The mid-century romantic nationalist movement is the subject of Cynthia Hyla Whittaker, ed., *Visualizing Russia: Fedor Solntsev and Crafting a National Past* (Leiden and Boston, Mass., 2010), and was also featured in a major exhibition at the New York Public Library, *Russia Imagined*, from March–June 2007 (catalogue by Wendy Salmond (New York, 2006)). The best introduction to the music of the era is Richard Taruskin's *Defining Russia Musically* (Princeton, NJ, 1997).

Slavophilism is treated brilliantly in the classic study by Andrzej Walicki, *The Slavophile Controversy: History of a Conservative Utopia in Nineteenth-Century Russian Thought* (Oxford, 1975), while the origins of Russian history as a discipline may be explored in Anatole G. Mazour, 'Modern Russian historiography', *Journal of Modern History*, 9, 2 (June 1937), pp. 169–202, and subsequent individual studies such as A. G. Cross, *N. M. Karamzin: A Study of His Literary Career* (London, 1971).

The court of Nicholas I would not be complete without an introduction from the marquis de Custine: *Empire of the Czar: A Journey Through Eternal Russia*, reprinted with an introduction by George F. Kennan (New York, 1989). For a biography of Nicholas himself, see W. Bruce Lincoln, *Nicholas I: Emperor and Autocrat of All the Russias* (London, 1978), and for Alexander II, W. E. Mosse, *Alexander II and the Modernisation of Russia* (London, 1958). Moving into the tenser world of the later nineteenth century, Anna Geifman's *Russia Under the Last Tsar: Opposition and Subversion, 1894–1917* (Oxford, 1999) provides a good introduction to dissident politics. For 1905, see Sidney Harcave, *First Blood: The Russian Revolution of 1905* (London and New York, 1964), while John Klier, *Imperial Russia's Jewish Question, 1855–1881* (Cambridge, 1995) and S. Hoffmann and E. Mendelsohn, *The Revolution of 1905 and Russia's Jews* (Philadelphia, Pa., 2008) deal with official (and unofficial) anti-Semitism. For biographies of Nicholas II, start with D. C. B. Lieven, *Nicholas II: Emperor of All the Russias* (London, 1993) or Marc Ferro, *Nicholas II: Last of the Tsars* (New York, 1993). The literature is voluminous.

REVOLUTION

Utopia is a wonderful subject, and Russia's version has attracted wonderful historians. For an introduction, see Richard Stites, *Revolutionary Dreams* (Oxford, 1989), which covers the range of utopian thinking. Semen Kanatchikov's memoir, translated and edited by Reginald Zelnik (*A Radical Worker in Tsarist Russia: The Autobiography of Semen Ivanovich Kanatchikov* (Stanford, Calif., 1986)) provides a grass-roots testimony, as does Eduard M. Dune's *Notes of a Red Guard*, ed. and trans. S. A. Smith and Diane Koenker (Urbana, Ill. and Chicago, 1993). Avant-garde painting is the subject of John E. Bowlt, ed., *Russian Art of the Avant-Garde: Theory and Criticism 1902–1934* (New York, 1976 and 1988), while the Knave of Diamonds is covered in an introduction called *The Knave of Diamonds in the Russian Avant-Garde* (St Petersburg, 2004). Malevich is the subject of an extensive literature, but his own views are reflected in *The Non-Objective World*, ed. Howard Dearstyne (Mineola, NY, 2003). For critical biography, see Charlotte Douglas, *Kazimir Malevich* (London, 1994) and A. S. Shatskikh, *Black Square: Malevich and the Origins of Suprematism* (New Haven, Conn., 2012).

The atmosphere in Moscow in the early twentieth century is beautifully captured in Karl Schlögel's *Moscow* (London, 2005), and this is also the point to introduce Timothy J. Colton, *Moscow: Governing the Socialist Metropolis* (Cambridge, Mass., 1995), which is strongest on the Soviet period and especially the first half of the twentieth century. For architecture, see Catherine Cooke, *Russian Avant-Garde: Theories of Art, Architecture and the City* (London, 1995).

A full bibliography of writing on the revolution itself would require another volume, for which I have to thank *The Russian Revolution and Civil War, 1917–1921: An Annotated Bibliography*, compiled and edited by Jonathan D. Smele (London, 2003). The best account of the February revolution in Petrograd is Orlando Figes, *A People's Tragedy* (London, 1996); Moscow's revolution was the subject of Diane Koenker's *Moscow Workers and the 1917 Revolution* (Princeton, NJ, 1981). For a (jaundiced) alternative view, that of one of Moscow's conservative intellectuals, see Terence Emmons, trans. and ed., *Time of Troubles: The Diary of Iurii Vladimirovich Got'e* (London, 1988), while John Reed, *Ten Days That Shook the World* (Harmondsworth, 1966) is unfailingly positive about Lenin and his revolution.

On the man himself, Robert Service, *Lenin: A Biography* (London, 2000) is unlikely to be bettered in the near future, while Leon Trotsky's memoir, *My Life* (London, 1984) provides an account of the Bolsheviks in the Kremlin as well as outside it. For Soviet leaders more generally, Dmitry Volkogonov's *The Rise and Fall of the Soviet Empire: Political Leaders from Lenin to Gorbachev* (London, 1998) marked a watershed in that its author had access to archive materials no-one had seen before (and even to some that ordinary mortals would not see again).

The Bolshevik campaign against the church has been the subject of a number of recent studies. For focus on the saints themselves, see Robert H. Greene, *Bodies Like Bright Stars: Saints and Relics in Orthodox Russia* (DeKalb, Ill., 2010) and S. A. Smith, 'Bones of contention: Bolsheviks and the struggle against relics, 1918–1930', *Past and Present*, 204 (August 2009), pp. 155–94. Sean McMeekin, *History's Greatest Heist* (New Haven, Conn., 2008) discusses the seizure of assets generally, including those of the church and of wealthy individuals (and the tsarist state). For one of several eye-witness accounts of the famine that was the pretext for some of this, see C. E. Bechhofer, *Through Starving Russia, being the record of a journey to Moscow and the Volga provinces, in August and September 1921* (London, 1921).

SOVIET RUSSIA

The story of the Kremlin's partial destruction in the late 1920s has not been told in any detail in an English-language source. The best introductions to this era, then, are those that deal more generally with Stalin and Stalinism. On the man himself, start with Simon Sebag Montefiore,

Young Stalin (London, 2007) before graduating to the mature dictator in the company of Donald Rayfield's *Stalin and His Hangmen: An Authoritative Portrait of a Tyrant and Those Who Served Him* (London, 2005) or Robert Service's *Stalin: A Biography* (London, 2004). Oleg Khlevniuk's *Master of the House: Stalin and his Inner Circle* (New Haven, Conn., 2009) extends the story further with the aid of new archival material. Rosamund Richardson, *The Long Shadow. Inside Stalin's Family* (London, 1994) provides a unique account of family life in the Kremlin, and complements the memoir of Stalin's daughter Svetlana Allilueva herself: *Twenty Letters to a Friend* (London, 1967). Larissa Vasileva's best-selling *Kremlin Wives*, trans. Cathy Porter (New York, 1994) gives another alternative view of the leadership, albeit an informal one.

The politics of the era have attracted saturation coverage, especially since the recent declassification of many Soviet archives. Among the more intriguing accounts of high politics are J. Arch Getty and Oleg Naumov, *The Road to Terror: Stalin and the Self-Destruction of the Bolsheviks* (New Haven, Conn., 1999) and *Stalinist Terror: New Perspectives*, ed. J. Arch Getty and Roberta Manning (Cambridge, 1993). For further essays, see S. Fitzpatrick, *Stalinism: New Directions* (London, 2000) and David L. Hoffmann, *Stalinism: The Essential Readings* (Oxford, 2003). A classic account, still worth reading today, is Roy Medvedev's *Let History Judge: The Origins and Consequences of Stalinism*, revised, edited and translated by George Shriver (London, 1995). For Stalinist society, start with Sheila Fitzpatrick's brilliant *Everyday Stalinism: Ordinary Life in Extraordinary Times* (Oxford, 1999) and see also Stephen Kotkin, *Magnetic Mountain: Stalinism as a Civilization* (London, 1995). Post-war Soviet politics are the subject of Yoram Gorlitzki and Oleg Khlevniuk's *Cold Peace: Stalin and the Soviet Ruling Circle, 1945–1953* (Oxford, 2004).

John Steinbeck's 1949 memoir, *A Russian Journal* (with Robert Capa's pictures) was reprinted in 1994, while Mark Frankland's memoir, *Child of My Time* (London, 1999), which covers a later period, is even more revealing. For an excellent study of the post-war mentality, see Donald J. Raleigh, *Soviet Baby Boomers: An Oral History of Russia's Cold War Generation* (New York, 2011) which traces the post-war generation to the present. On Khrushchev, see William Taubman, *Khrushchev: The Man and His Era* (London, 2003), and also Sergei N.

Khrushchev's *Nikita Khrushchev and the Creation of a Superpower* (University Park, Pa., 2000).

By the 1960s, Soviet leaders were beginning to write memoirs for themselves, most notably *Khrushchev Remembers*, intro., Edward Crankshaw, trans. and ed., Strobe Talbott (Boston, Mass., 1970) and *Khrushchev Remembers: The Last Testament*, intro., Edward Crankshaw, trans. and ed., Strobe Talbott (London, 1974). For Gorbachev, see his best-selling *Perestroika: New Thinking for Our Country and the World* (London, 1987) and also his *Memoirs* (London, 1995).

One of the best accounts of the Soviet Union's dramatic end is David Remnick's *Lenin's Tomb: The Last Days of the Soviet Empire* (London, 1994). For insiders' accounts, see also A. Grachev, *Final Days: The Inside Story of the Collapse of the Soviet Union*, trans. Margo Milne (Boulder, Colo., 1995) and Rodric Braithwaite, *Across the Moscow River: The World Turned Upside Down* (London, 2002).

DEMOCRATIC RUSSIA

Boris Yeltsin wrote (or at least signed) a lot of memoirs, most of which have been translated into English. In chronological order, the most significant are *Against the Grain: An Autobiography*, trans. Michael Glenny (London, 1991), *The View from the Kremlin*, trans. Catherine A. Fitzpatrick (London, 1994) and *Midnight Diaries*, trans. Catherine A. Fitzpatrick (London, 2000).

For more balanced analysis, a good place to start would be A. Brown and L. Shevtsova, eds., *Gorbachev, Yeltsin, Putin: Political Leadership in Russia's Transition* (Washington, DC, 2001), while Richard Sakwa's textbook, *Russian Politics and Society*, 4th edn (Abingdon and New York, 2008) provides basic context. Among discussions of the dilemmas of Yeltsin's Russia, two articles by Michael Urban deal with issues raised in Chapter 12. For more, see his 'The politics of identity in Russia's Postcommunist transition: the nation against itself', *Slavic Review*, 53, 3 (Autumn 1994), pp. 733–65, and 'Remythologising the Russian state', *Europe-Asia Studies*, 50, 6 (September 1998), pp. 969–92. For a concise discussion of organized crime, see Joseph L. Albini et al., 'Russian organized crime: its history, structure and function', *Journal of Contemporary Criminal Justice*, 11, 4 (December 1995), pp. 213–43. Another readable account, this time with a biographical focus, is Paul Klebnikov, *Godfather of the Kremlin: Boris Berezovsky and the Looting of Russia* (New York and London, 2000).

Putin's regime is already the subject of numerous readable studies, including David Satter, *Darkness at Dawn: The Rise of the Russian Criminal State* (New Haven, Conn. and London, 2003), Andrew Jack, *Inside Putin's Russia* (London, 2004) and Edward Lucas, *The New Cold War: How the Kremlin Menaces both Russia and the West* (London, 2008). For a selection of academic views, see Stephen White, ed., *Politics and the Ruling Group in Putin's Russia* (Basingstoke, 2008). Brian D. Taylor, *State Building in Putin's Russia* (Cambridge, 2011) is a particularly perceptive study of the weak new Russian state, and its problems are also reviewed in Lilia Shevtsova and Andrew Wood, *Change and Decay: Russia's Dilemma and the West's Response* (Washington, DC, 2011).

On the abuse of history by the current Russian regime, see David Satter, *It Was a Long Time Ago, And It Never Happened Anyway* (New Haven, Conn. and London, 2011). Architecture is a more specialized topic, but I was inspired by Benjamin Forest and Juliet Johnson, 'Unravelling the threads of history: Soviet-era monuments and post-Soviet national identity in Moscow', *Annals of the Association of American Geographers*, 92, 3 (September 2002), pp. 524–47, and Dmitri Sidorov, 'National monumentalization and the politics of scale: the resurrection of the Cathedral of Christ the Savior in Moscow', *Annals of the Association of American Geographers*, 90, 3 (September 2000). On the destruction of Moscow's historic buildings, see Edmund Harris, ed., *Moscow Heritage at Crisis Point*, 2nd edn (Moscow, 2009).

Index

Illustrations are indicated by page reference in *italics*. Notes are referred to by an *n* after the page number and followed by the note number, eg. 167*n*8

military reform 177; building projects 177–8; builds arsenal in the Kremlin 178; military campaigns 179–81; re-fortifies Kremlin 180; moves court to St Petersburg 181; signs Peace of Nystad with Sweden 181; creates Senate 182; abolishes the Orthodox patriarchate 183; and record keeping 183–4; reform of the alphabet 184; disinherits Aleksei Petrovich 185; crowns his wife Catherine I 186–8; European influences on court 187; introduces European architectural practices 189–90; coffin desecrated by Bolsheviks 297; funeral 168–9

Peter III, Tsar 191

Peter, Metropolitan of Kiev and all Russia (the 'Wonder-Worker) 12, 19, 32–3, 48, 230

Peter Petrovich (infant son of Peter the Great) 185

Peter-Paul Cathedral, St Petersburg 169

St Petersburg 2, 3, 185, 188, 199; choice of site 180; transfer of Peter the Great's court to 168–9, 181; 1917 revolution 269; Winter Palace 190; under Catherine the Great 192; Kazan Cathedral 222; Church of the Saviour on Spilled Blood 244; changes name to Petrograd 269; storming of the Winter Palace 274; desecration of Tsar's tombs 297; re-interment of Romanov family, 1998 376 see also Leningrad; Petrograd

Peterson, Rudolf 310, 321, 322, 323

Petrograd 269, 271, 273, 274, 297; re-named Leningrad 303 see also St Petersburg

Petrovna-Solovaya, Praskovya 99

Petrovsky, Boris 355

Petrovsky Palace 213

Philip, Duke of Edinburgh 375

Picart, Pieter 170

Picasso, Pablo 265, 337

Pickering, Thomas 374

Pikhoia, Rudolf 375

Pimen, archbishop of Novgorod 94

Pipes, Richard 393

Piscator, Johannes 148

plague: (1570) 97; (Moscow, 1654) 154–5; (Moscow, 1771) 195

Platon, Metropolitan of Moscow 197, 225

Plekhanov, Georgy 235

Pleshcheyev, Levonty 151, 152

Podgorny, Nikolai 348

Pogodin, Mikhail 252

Pokrovsky Convent 99

Poland 39, 94, 119; Polish influence on court of False Dmitry 122–5; ambition for Russian throne 128–30; Polish troops occupy and loot the Kremlin 130–33; Treaty of Eternal Peace 167; as source of radical ideas 250; represented in film 1612 388

Poland-Lithuania 107, 111, 120

Politburo 307, 309, 311, 325, 357; Thursday meetings in Kremlin 350; working conditions relaxed under Brezhnev 353

Polotsky, Simon 164

Polovtsy (tribe) 20, 25

Polyakov, Leonid 345

Polytechnical Exhibition, 1872 252

Pomerantsev, N. N. 308

pomeshchiki 106